BLACK'S
NEW TESTAMENT COMMENTARIES

General Editor: Morna D. Hooker

THE GOSPEL ACCORDING
TO ST JOHN

BLACK'S
NEW TESTAMENT COMMENTARIES

THE GOSPEL ACCORDING TO SAINT JOHN

ANDREW T. LINCOLN

PORTLAND PROFESSOR OF NEW TESTAMENT
UNIVERSITY OF GLOUCESTERSHIRE

LONDON • NEW YORK

BLACK'S NEW TESTAMENT COMMENTARY
THE GOSPEL ACCORDING TO SAINT JOHN

First published 2005, Continuum, London
Copyright © 2005 Andrew Lincoln

Printed in the United States of America

Reprinted March 2006 by Hendrickson Publishers, Inc.

Published in the USA by
Hendrickson Publishers, Inc.
P.O. Box 3473
Peabody, MA 01961-3473

www.hendrickson.com

Hendrickson Publishers ISBN 1-56563-401-2 (hardcover)

US Library of Congress Cataloging-in-Publication Data
Lincoln, Andrew T.
    [Commentary on the Gospel according to St. John]
    The Gospel according to Saint John / Andrew T. Lincoln,
        p. cm.—(Black's New Testament commentaries ; 4)
    Originally published: A commentary on the Gospel according to
St. John. London : Continuum, 2005.
    Includes bibliographical references and indexes.
    ISBN 1-56563-401-2 (alk. paper)
    1. Bible. N.T. John—Commentaries. I. Title. II. Series.
    BS2615.53.L56 2005
    226.5′077—dc22

                                            2005025970

Published in the UK by
Continuum
The Tower Building
11 York Road
London, SE1 7NX

www.continuumbooks.com

British Library Cataloguing-in-Publication Data
A catalogue record for this book is available from the British Library.

Continuum ISBN 0-8264-7139-0 (paperback)
Continuum ISBN 0-8264-7943-X (hardcover)

Typeset by Fakenham Photosetting Limited, Fakenham, Norfolk

The mosaic fretwork on the cover comes from the Galla Placidia Mausoleum in
Ravenna and is used courtesy of ITALCARDS, Bolongna, Italy.

CONTENTS

PREFACE

From time to time writers of biblical commentaries are put on the spot by being asked, 'Why another commentary? Don't we have more than enough?' One can attempt to offer a more theological answer, suggesting that canonical texts, because of their testimony to the particular subject matter that they purport to convey, have a richness and value that cannot be exhausted by any one interpreter and so there is always the possibility of further insight from another close study. When such a reply does not have the desired effect, this writer has also given a more pragmatic response and appealed to the needs of a well-established and respected series. While there are, of course, excellent large one-, two- and three-volume commentaries on John's Gospel, Black's New Testament Commentaries have endeavoured to provide more moderately sized commentaries that are accessible to serious students yet reliable and up to date in their scholarship. In the Black series this commentary is a successor to that written by J. N. Sanders and B. A. Mastin and first published in 1968. The bulk of that commentary was in fact produced by Sanders during the late 1950s and Mastin then performed the valuable task of editing and completing Sanders' work after the latter's untimely death. There is much still to be learned from their commentary, but the more than four decades that have elapsed since most of it was written have seen major changes in scholarly approaches to the New Testament and in Johannine studies. More recent approaches have included those associated with a newer literary criticism with its interest in narrative and readers, social-scientific, rhetorical and cultural criticisms, feminist readings, readings from various social and political locations, renewed quests for the historical Jesus and a concern for the theological interpretation of the New Testament as Scripture. More specifically within Johannine scholarship, different theories about the Fourth Gospel's relationship to the Synoptics, about a signs source on which the Gospel draws, about a community behind the Gospel, about expulsion from the synagogue and about the depiction of 'the Jews' have waxed and waned in popularity. There has been much of value in the resulting mass of secondary literature and this commentary has attempted to distil and pass on some of its insights. At the same time this secondary literature also provides a salutary reminder of the inevitable cultural conditionedness of biblical interpretation and the passing nature of its various methods and theories. The best tests of their validity remain how well they explain the evidence within the text and how much light they shed on the message of that text. There is no escaping, however, the fact that judgements on these matters are strongly influenced by the concerns that readers bring to the text.

This commentary's concerns centre on the literary, historical and theological dimensions of the text, although its writer remains acutely conscious that the brevity of the discussions is not able to do any of these justice. In line with the aims and scope of this series, and particularly its commentaries on longer narrative texts, the commentary proper does not attempt to interact explicitly with the major commentators or other scholarly contributors to the interpretation of John's Gospel. Despite the temptation to name names at various points, this self-denying ordinance has been strictly observed, since anything other than a relatively full engagement with other scholars risks the appearance of arbitrariness. As should be apparent, not least from the select bibliography supplied at the end, the commentary does, however, build on interaction with a great deal of this secondary literature, and others who are familiar with it will no doubt be able to recognize its great indebtedness to the views of predecessors and to attach particular names to the various positions discussed. The purpose of avoiding explicit interaction with other inter-preters is not simply to keep the commentary within reasonable bounds but also to keep the focus on the conversation with the text. In the process, it is hoped that the commentary's part in the conversation has provided some fresh insights and will be a stimulus to its readers' further engagement with the message of this both enthralling and enigmatic, both provocative and profound Gospel.

Again, in line with the rest of the series, the translation provided is the commentator's own. It deliberately errs on the side of literalness rather than elegant or idiomatic English style in order to indicate as far as possible both some of the interpretative options allowed by the Greek text and the foundations for the interpretations of the text adopted in the commentary. The translation does, however, attempt to employ inclusive language for humans, wherever such use is considered not to be too distortive of the original or simply too cumbersome stylistically.

Finally, I am grateful to Professor Morna Hooker, the General Editor, for her astute observations on the original draft, which have ensured that the final version has greater clarity at various points.

Andrew T. Lincoln
Cheltenham, December 2004

ABBREVIATIONS

The text of the Greek New Testament, on which the translation offered in the commentary is based, is that of B. Aland, K. Aland, J. Karavidopolous, C. M. Martini and B. M. Metzger (eds), *The Greek New Testament* (London: United Bible Societies, 1993). The symbols and abbreviations used in the commentary's text-critical notes are explained in the Introduction to the United Bible Societies' text.

The abbreviations for ancient texts and for journals and periodicals are those set out in *The SBL Handbook of Style* (Peabody, Mass.: Hendrickson, 1999).

In discussion of the relation of John's Gospel to the Synoptic Gospels, the abbreviation 'par.' is used in the case of one parallel to the text of Mark in the other Synoptics and 'parr.' where there are parallels in both Matthew and Luke.

INTRODUCTION

THE APPROACH OF THE COMMENTARY

The primary goal is to explore and elucidate the significance of the Fourth Gospel in its canonical form. While there will be a recognition that some of the awkwardnesses in the narrative reflect the history of its writing, and a later section of the Introduction will explore stages in the composition of the Gospel, the focus of the commentary will be on the final product. As a result of this decision, chapter 21, for example, which is considered by many to have been added after an original conclusion at the end of chapter 20, will be treated as an integral part of the narrative, because, whenever this section was actually written, there is no evidence that the Gospel ever circulated without it. On the other hand, there is considerable evidence that the account of Jesus' dealings with a woman seized in the act of adultery in 7.53—8.11, although often included within the narrative, but also within parentheses, in English versions of the Bible, did not circulate as part of the earliest written Gospel. It is therefore not treated as an integral aspect of the Gospel's narrative but is assessed independently at the end of the commentary in the Appendix, where the issues surrounding its origins, interpretation and canonicity are discussed more fully.

In pursuing our primary goal, and as noted in the Preface, the commentary will concentrate on the literary, historical and theological dimensions of the text. These dimensions are related to what are sometimes described as the world in or of the text, the world behind the text, and the world in front of the text. By definition, a commentary makes the text as it has come to us the centre of its attention, and so what will concern us most is the way the Fourth Gospel communicates its message about Jesus through this particular narrative. At the same time, however, the commentary endeavours to keep in view the historical and social factors that are important features in any adequate explanation of this text as a communication between its final author and readers in a particular first-century CE context. The content of this Gospel and its appeal to its readers to believe its message make the theological dimension arguably the most important aspect of interpretation. Because of the nature and scope of the series of which this commentary is a part, exploration of this dimension takes place primarily through highlighting and explicating the narrative's major theological themes but cannot extend to critical theological appropriation of the text's message.

Some features of each of the three main dimensions will be surveyed in the sections that follow. Within the commentary itself, discussion of individual pericopes and their verses raise points relevant for all three dimensions. Matters of narrative sequence and plot are therefore treated at the start of major sections and suggestions about the structure of individual passages are provided before their detailed treatment. A discussion of the relationship of a passage to the Synoptic Gospels and, if appropriate, of its historicity may be found either before or after such passages. The purpose of the comparisons with the Synoptics is twofold. They explore John's dependence or independence in relation to the other canonical Gospels and at the same time they serve to highlight the distinctiveness of this Gospel's own story of Jesus. A commentary on the Fourth Gospel is not, of course, a study of the historical Jesus. Nevertheless, the story told by the fourth evangelist raises questions about its relation to what is likely to have been the case in the life of the earthly Jesus. Conclusions about this, as will be seen, are tied up with decisions about the relationship between this Gospel and the Synoptics and about the amount of authentic historical tradition conveyed by the Synoptics. It would be impossible to analyse the reliability of traditions in all the cases where this Gospel has material that overlaps with the Synoptics, but in significant cases, where it contains incidents that are unique to its story rather than merely distinctive elaborations on earlier traditions, some attempt has been made to discuss likely historicity. A summary of the theological thrust and, again where appropriate, the likely social function of a passage is provided after the commentary on it.

Within the individual sections of commentary, eclectic use is made of methods appropriate to each of the different dimensions of the text, while attempting not to fall into the trap of confusing their distinctive concerns. This accounts, for example, for the shifts in terminology that will be found. Sometimes talk will be of the narrator or the implied author and sometimes of the evangelist, depending on whether the literary or the historical aspect of a given passage is in view in the comments. For those not familiar with this terminology, narrative criticism of the Gospels focuses attention on the present form of the text as a story. For these purposes it is interested not so much in the historical entities of the real author or the real readers but in what it calls the 'implied author' and the 'implied readers'. These latter categories refer to the author and the readers whose profiles can be reconstructed from the clues provided by the narrative itself, whatever it is thought can be known from other sources about the actual historical author or first readers. The implied author can sometimes take on a specific voice within the narrative, that of the narrator – the one who is actually relating the story. One further and connected terminological explanation should be given. The designation 'John' is sometimes used as shorthand for the fourth evangelist or for the Fourth Gospel. This should not be thought to entail any historical conclusion about the actual author of this Gospel but simply reflects as a matter of convenience the attribution and title of the Gospel in early tradition. The Gospel itself does not name its author as John but does in fact have another important character of that name. Although significantly the Fourth Gospel, unlike the Synoptics, does not call this character 'the Baptist', the commentary will refer to him as John the Baptist in order to avoid confusion.

Whole books have been devoted to the introductory issues that surround the Fourth Gospel and entire monographs have been written about most of the individual introductory topics. This Introduction can only select some of the more important topics and summarize the writer's perspective on them. At the end of each section, it will therefore point to one or two significant, helpful or alternative treatments of the topic in English.

Further Reading

For two recent accessible treatments of introductory and interpretative issues, see R. E. Brown, *An Introduction to the Gospel of John*, ed. F. J. Moloney (New York: Doubleday, 2003) and R. Edwards, *Discovering John* (London: SPCK, 2003). On a literary approach to John and for explanation of key terms in narrative criticism, see R. A. Culpepper, *Anatomy of the Fourth Gospel: A Study in Literary Design* (Philadelphia: Fortress, 1983). For an attempt at critical theological appropriation of some aspects of John's message, see A. T. Lincoln, *Truth on Trial* (Peabody, Mass.: Hendrickson, 2000), 354–497.

NARRATIVE OUTLINE, SHAPE AND PLOT

The outline that follows indicates what appear to be the main structural divisions of the narrative and suggests further sections and subsections and their content. The main value of such an outline is as an initial map offered by a more experienced reader to enable other readers to negotiate what may be the relatively unfamiliar terrain of a narrative's content and sequence. Provided that it makes no strong claims to having been the design in the original author's mind and that the need for its modification or expansion, as readers make their own discoveries, is acknowledged, then the attempt to produce one may have a provisional and limited usefulness. This outline has two further functions. It displays the divisions

and their headings that will be employed within the commentary and it
serves as a reference point for the more detailed ensuing discussion of the
shape of the narrative.

In discussing the shape of this Gospel's story, attention can only be drawn to some of the more salient features in the arrangement of its sequence and thematic presentation. In the final form of the Fourth Gospel's narrative a prologue (1.1–18) and an epilogue (21.1–25) surround the main story, which itself has two main parts. The first of these (1.19—12.50) deals with Jesus' public career, the second (13.1—20.31) with his departure from this world. The second part itself has two clear subsections. 13.1—17.26, in which the departure is interpreted by Jesus for 'his own', the disciples, and then 18.1—20.31, in which the departure takes place as the story line culminates in the passion and resurrection. The two main parts should not, of course, be thought of as sealed off from each other. Not only are there themes that run throughout, but also the action of the last part of Jesus' public mission in particular prepares for his departure.

The prologue provides an extended introduction to the main character, Jesus, in which the implied author's point of view is made clear. The identity of the central figure is disclosed as that of the divine Logos through whom all things came into being (1.1–3, 14), and the implied reader is given clues about the significance of this figure's mission. It involves his glory (1.14), it contrasts with Moses and the law (1.17), and it entails making God known (1.18). There is also a preview of the outcome of this mission in 1.11–12 which announces a divided response with some, however, through their acceptance of the Logos, being enabled to become children of God.

The public career of Jesus as the incarnate Logos is presented through his deeds and words. Jesus' deeds are predominantly depicted as signs, and there are seven of these, which run through section B on the outline (cf. 2.1–11; 4.46–54; 5.1–18; 6.1–15; 6.16–21; 9.1–41; 11.1–53). Some (e.g. Dodd 1953: 289; Moloney 1998: 23; Brown 2003: 299) have been so impressed by this feature that they have called this section of the Gospel 'the Book of Signs'. Despite the apparent elasticity of the term 'signs' later in 20.30–1, where it may stand for the ministry as a whole, this title is not precise enough to describe the public mission, since it makes the specific signs more dominant than they in fact are and does not do enough justice to the speech material. Nevertheless, the explicit association of signs with the theme of glory (cf. 2.11; 11.4), which pervades the narrative discourse, should be noted, since this provides a major element of continuity with the second half of the Gospel's story. This has been indicated on the outline by the parenthetical subheadings for sections B and C – Signs of Glory and Departure as Glory.

The words through which Jesus makes God known are mainly found in the form of extended discourses. These do not necessarily involve a complete monologue from Jesus, and, where there is extended speech material on the lips of Jesus that is interrupted more than usual by debate or questions, 'dispute' may sometimes be a more accurate categorization than discourse. Given this and granted that there must be some uncertainty, as the discourses are far less clearly demarcated than the signs, it can be argued that there are seven major discourses in the public ministry as well as seven signs (cf. 3.1–21; 4.1–26; 5.19–47; 6.22–59; 7.14–36; 8.12–59; 10.1–21, with the fourth, fifth and sixth of these passages having more of the character of disputes).

There is no consistent pattern of relationship between the discourses and the signs as they are interwoven in the narrative, although clearly the fourth sign and the fourth discourse are related, as the feeding of the five thousand prepares for the discourse on the bread of life. Similarly the sixth discourse and the sixth sign are linked through the 'I am the light of the world' saying, which is found not only in the sign passage about the blind man receiving his sight in 9.5 but also in the preceding discourse material in 8.12. In relation to the action in general the discourses can often continue a dialogue occasioned by a specific situation in Jesus' mission and in so doing leave behind the occasion which prompted them. Persons involved in conversation with Jesus can disappear from the scene while Jesus' discourse continues. This appears to happen, for example, with Nicodemus in 3.1–21 and with 'the Jews' in 5.19–47.

The public career of Jesus has a clear beginning and a clear end (1.19–51 and 12.36b–50). Its initial opening treats John the Baptist and the gathering of disciples around Jesus. The narrative discourse here is almost exclusively concerned with John the Baptist as providing witness or testimony to Jesus. This highlights a motif which will be highly significant, and since the force of testimony is juridical, it is closely associated with such other major themes as judgement and truth. The narrator's very first words about the public ministry in 1.19 are 'This is the testimony given by John' and previously in the prologue John the Baptist had already been introduced as a witness (1.7, 8, 15). The narrative will also end with this motif in its twofold reference in the epilogue to the testimony of the Beloved Disciple in 21.24, thereby forming an *inclusio* – an element found at the beginning and the end of a unit, here the entire story, and tying it together. In regard to activity within history, the Fourth Gospel begins with the witness of John the Baptist and concludes with the witness of the Beloved Disciple.

Returning to the account of Jesus' public mission, it can be seen from the outline that both the beginning and the summary ending are linked to larger opening and closing units. After disciples begin to collect around Jesus, there is then a depiction of the start of his mission proper, introduced and concluded by a sign in Cana (2.1—4.54). Similarly, the summary of the mission in 12.36b–50 is the final element of a section which describes Jesus' move towards his hour of death and glory (11.1—12.50). The From Cana to Cana section introduces further themes that will characterize Jesus' mission and the conflict it will produce. In particular, the first major deed – changing water into wine (2.1–11) – both rounds off the initial response of the disciples to Jesus and anticipates what is to be the significance of Jesus' mission, as the water of the Jewish rites of purification gives way to the wine and joy of the new life that Jesus provides. The next episode, in the temple in Jerusalem (2.13–22), also sets the tone for what is to follow, as it shows Jesus from the start of his mission confronting the Jewish authorities at the heart of their religious system, and it is made clear by the dialogue that follows and the narrator's comments that the resurrected Christ is in fact to be the new locus of God's presence, fulfilling what to this point has been represented by the temple. From these first two major activities of Jesus it immediately becomes clear that the relation of Jesus to the symbols and institutions of Judaism will be dominant issues in his public mission. The discourse with Nicodemus emphasizes the need for God to be at work through the Spirit if people are to accept Jesus' message, speaks of that message in terms of Jesus' witness, and introduces both the notion of Jesus' death as the lifting up of the Son of Man and the concept of judgement with its twofold outcome of either life or condemnation. Jesus' encounter with the Samaritan woman presents him as the source of eternal life, the agent and embodiment of true worship of God, and the one who can employ the divine self-identification of 'I Am', a formulation that will have an important role in the next section of the narrative. The ready acceptance of Jesus' mission by Samaritans also contrasts with the far more divided reception of his message in that next section.

Jesus' testimony about himself in controversy with 'the Jews' is at the heart of the narrative of his public mission (5.1—10.42). This takes place primarily in the environs of the temple in Jerusalem but also in a synagogue setting in Capernaum. This part of the mission is marked by hostility and conflict and much of it takes the form of interrogations or mini-trial scenes (5.19–47; 7.14–36; 8.12–58; 10.22–39). In these scenes the issue is the truth of Jesus' witness about himself – as the Son who is one with the Father, as 'I Am', as the source of light and life – and he is accused of being in breach of the law, of leading the people astray as a false prophet, and of blasphemy. In the process the witness of the accused himself becomes accusatory and in fact he claims to be the ultimate judge. The intensity of the hostility this provokes on the part of the Jewish authorities is indicated by their decision to kill him (5.18; 7.1, 25), their attempts to arrest him (7.32, 44, 45; 10.39) and their moves to carry out the death sentence by stoning him (8.59; 10.31). In this central section not only is there the threat of death from Jesus' opponents, but he himself already makes clear that his death will be necessary if there is to be a judgement producing life rather than condemnation. In the discourse in 6.22–59 the bread Jesus will give for the life of the world is his flesh. In the dispute of 8.22–59 he claims that people will die in their sins 'unless you believe that I Am' and that they will know him as 'I Am' when they have lifted up the Son of Man. In 10.1–21 Jesus announces that, as the good shepherd, he will lay down his life for the benefit of the sheep. As part of the portrayal of hostilities resulting from Jesus' mission, an extended passage is devoted to the depiction of the recipient of one of Jesus' signs – the man born blind, who, in coming to belief in Jesus, undergoes his own interrogation by the authorities and is cast out of the synagogue by them.

One other feature of this section should be mentioned. Throughout its narrative Jesus' activities are set against the backdrop of Jewish feasts.

Already the temple incident had had as its temporal setting 'the Passover of the Jews' (2.13). Now the mention of such feasts becomes more frequent and it becomes clear that Jesus is to be seen as fulfilling what these festivals signified (cf. 5.1; 6.4; 7.1–13, 14, 37; 10.22). This is particularly highlighted in relation to the Feast of Tabernacles, whose elements of prayer for rain and the illumination of the Court of Women are taken up in Jesus' provision of water and light (7.37–9; 8.12; 9.5) and to the Feast of Dedication, where the dedication or sanctification of the altar is taken up in Jesus' claim to be the one whom God has sanctified (10.36).

The hostility directed towards Jesus by the religious authorities leads into the final phase of his public mission – the move towards his hour of death and glory (11.1—12.50). In particular, it is the last sign in that mission – the raising of Lazarus – that precipitates Jesus' death. This extended episode (11.1–53) is the midpoint and pivot of John's story as a whole. Ironically, Jesus' embodiment of his claim to be the resurrection and the life results in the Sanhedrin's verdict that he should be put to death. Mary's anointing then anticipates the burial preparation for Jesus, Jesus enters Jerusalem for the final time at the festival of Passover (12.12, 20), and the coming of some Greeks to see Jesus signals that his hour has now come, an hour in which his death will also be his lifting up and his glory (12.20–36a). After this, 12.36b–50 forms the appropriate conclusion to the public ministry, summarizing the response first to Jesus' signs and glory and then to his words, which will serve as final judge.

There is no further public teaching or activity of Jesus in Jerusalem, but the action does not move immediately to Jesus' arrest and passion. Instead these are preceded by a lengthy section in which Jesus bids farewell to his disciples, so that the second main part of the narrative consists of Jesus' farewell, passion and resurrection (13.1—20.31). It has been entitled by some 'The Book of Glory' (e.g. Moloney 1998: 24; Brown 2003: 299). Although this captures the sense in which the death and exaltation are the particular moment of Jesus' glorification, it does not sufficiently recognize that the signs themselves are signs of glory and that for the Fourth Gospel the whole of Jesus' life is a manifestation of his glory (1.14). It is somewhat more accurate, therefore, to sum up this part as Jesus' Departure as Glory. Indeed the farewell episode (13.1—17.26) speaks immediately of Jesus' departure (13.1) and its discourse uses this language of going away throughout. There is also no mistaking that this departure from the world is to be interpreted in terms of glory, which is the perspective set out at the beginning of the discourse (13.31–2) and in the prayer at the end of the section (17.1, 4, 5, 22, 24). All the aspects of the farewell section – the footwashing, the prediction of betrayal, the two-part discourse, and the prayer of Jesus – are meant to prepare the disciples for what is about to happen, in regard not only to Jesus' destiny but also to their own future in the world after Jesus' mission is completed.

In going away to his Father, Jesus will also prepare a place for his disciples, return to remain with them, and send them the Paraclete or Advocate, the latter connotation being important for the narrative's juridical motif. His followers are to be witnesses to Jesus' cause and, in carrying out this role, will face hostility from the world in the form of persecution and exclusion from the synagogue, but they will also experience Jesus' gifts of joy and peace as they remain in a relationship with him characterized by faith and love.

The events for which Jesus has been preparing his disciples unfold quickly in the passion account (18.1—19.42). In line with his prior knowledge of these events, Jesus is portrayed as in sovereign control in the midst of what happens. After manifesting his divine identity by means of an 'I Am' saying, he gives himself over to the Roman and Jewish forces who have come to seize him. Since Jesus has been on trial before the Jewish authorities throughout the major part of his mission and the Sanhedrin have already reached their verdict, what follows is simply an interrogation of Jesus by Annas, at which Jesus declines to repeat or elaborate on teaching he has already given openly. At the same time Peter is also undergoing a more informal interrogation in the courtyard of the high priest's residence, but, in contrast to Jesus' boldness, he denies three times being a follower of Jesus.

Via Caiaphas, Jesus is passed from Annas to Pilate, and an extensive depiction of his trial before the Roman prefect then becomes the centre-piece of this Gospel's passion account (18.28—19.16a), preceded by the accounts of his arrest and interrogation and followed by those of his crucifixion and burial. The Roman trial both places Jesus' mission in a wider setting, that of empire, and underscores themes that have appeared earlier. Under interrogation for claims of being King of the Jews and Son of God, Jesus sums up his whole mission in terms of witness to the truth. The accused is the central figure and the ultimate judge, while his would-be judges – Pilate and 'the Jews' – are shown to be those on trial here. Pilate proves himself culpable, because despite his threefold avowal of Jesus' innocence, he allows Jesus to be crucified. The Jewish leaders are exposed by their choice of Barabbas, a known bandit and insurrectionary, instead of Jesus, and by their confession of sole allegiance to Caesar.

Even after Jesus has been handed over to be crucified, he is portrayed as in control of events. He carries his own cross, on which the inscription pronounces him to be King of the Jews. While soldiers cast lots for his clothes, he continues to care for his own from the cross by uniting his mother and the Beloved Disciple. Through the terminology of 'completion' in relation to Scripture and to Jesus' cry from the cross, his death is shown to be the fulfilment of God's will and of his own mission. After it is clear that he is dead, his body is pierced with a spear and blood and water flow out, indicating that this death is the source of life, a verdict to which the Beloved Disciple gives testimony. Jesus' body is given a hasty but proper burial and is prepared with an amount of spices fit for a king.

The Resurrection account (20.1–31) begins with Mary Magdalene's discovery of the empty tomb and is followed by the Beloved Disciple seeing and believing on entering the tomb. Mary Magdalene then meets but does not at first recognize Jesus. When she does, she is commissioned to announce to the disciples that Jesus is ascending. At an appearance to the disciples later on the same day, the risen Jesus authorizes and empowers them for mission. At a further appearance to them, Thomas, absent previously and still unbelieving, now utters the climactic confession, 'My Lord and my God' (20.28). The narrative comes to an initial conclusion with a statement of why it has been written, emphasizing the need, if its readers are to obtain life, for belief in Jesus as the Christ and the sort of Christ who is Son of God.

The epilogue (21.1–25) opens with the risen Jesus appearing to his disciples in Galilee, enabling them to make an extraordinary catch of fish, symbolic of the success of their mission when directed by Jesus. The episode leads into a dialogue between Peter and Jesus, accompanied by comments from the narrator, which ties up some loose ends from the main narrative about the relationships between Jesus and Peter and between Peter and the Beloved Disciple. Peter is rehabilitated after his threefold denial through a threefold avowal of love for Jesus and a threefold commissioning to feed Jesus' sheep, and is told that he will die a martyr's death. There has been a rumour that Jesus said that the Beloved Disciple would not die before his final coming. This rumour is scotched and the epilogue concludes with the narrator making clear that the Beloved Disciple will bear faithful witness through his involvement in the writing of the Gospel. In these ways the epilogue bridges the gap between the time of the earlier story and the time of its implied readers.

In attempting to gain an overall perspective on the narrative, with which more detailed study can then be in interplay, it is helpful to consider its plot. The three most basic categories for plot analysis are commission, complication and resolution. In the main plot of this narrative Jesus has been given a commission by God. Indeed he repeatedly describes God as 'the Father who sent me' and speaks of the task or work God has given him to do (cf. e.g. 4.34; 9.4; 17.4). The nature of the commission is described in a variety of ways, some of which are explicitly formulated as mission statements ('I have come to . . .'). Among the more prominent descriptions are making God or God's name known (cf. 1.18; 17.6, 26), being glorified and bringing glory to God (cf. e.g. 13.31–2; 17.4), bringing life (cf. e.g. 3.16; 10.10; 17.2), bearing witness to the truth (cf. e.g. 3.32–3; 8.14; 18.36) and judging (cf. e.g. 5.22, 27; 8.15, 16; 9.39). The complication or element of conflict in the plot is provided by the resistance to Jesus' mission on the part of a number of opponents, who include the chief priests and Pharisees, 'the Jews' in the sense of unbelieving Jews who reject Jesus' witness, 'the world' in its negative sense of humanity hostile to God, the devil or ruler of this world, Judas, and Pilate. The opposition's rejection of Jesus' mission takes the form of interrogations, accusations, charges, attempts to arrest him and to stone him, the Sanhedrin's verdict that he must die, his final arrest, interrogation by Annas, trial before Pilate, judgement and crucifixion. Despite the apparent success of the opposition in ending Jesus' mission, this ironically turns out to be the resolution of the plot, the goal or 'the hour' to which it has all the time been moving. Jesus' cry from the cross – 'It is completed' or 'It is finished' (19.30) – indicates that the culmination of his mission lies in his death (cf. also the anticipation of this in 17.4). The resolution includes not only the accomplishment of the commission but the judgement and overcoming of the opposition. Jesus' hour with its suffering and death is to be seen as involving both the judgement of this world (12.31) and the conquering of the world (16.33).

The pattern of this plot is of crucial significance for the message conveyed by the narrative. The varying descriptions of Jesus' commission are not simply disparate but form a network of motifs that are linked thematically, especially by their dominant juridical associations. Jesus is sent as God's uniquely authorized agent in a process of divine judgement that is taking place. Within that process he is both witness and judge. The issue at stake is the truth about God's identity or name and about God's glory, the divine reputation and honour, both of which are inseparable from Jesus' identity and glory. The outcome of the process is either eternal life or condemnation, and the verdict depends not only on the divine action in Jesus but on the human response to Jesus. The resolution of the plot in Jesus' death entails a radical reversal of ordinary categories of judgement. Against all appearances, it means that God is most truly known in the weakness and suffering of Jesus' death as a victim and that the divine glory and honour is most fully displayed in the humiliation and shame of the crucified Messiah. What is more, the death of Jesus is the focus for God's judgement of the world. To appreciate the interrelation of juridical motifs in John's narrative, it must be remembered that in the world of thought of the Jewish Scriptures, which this Gospel to a large extent inhabits, divine judgement was not primarily a negative concept. For God to act as judge was for God to establish justice and to restore conditions of well-being. To call on God as judge frequently involved asking God to be faithful to the covenant and to rescue Israel from its plight. So for God to enact justice was also for God to save. To say, therefore, that in this narrative God's judgement is carried out in Jesus' death is to make a primarily salvific point. Through Jesus' death God deals with the world's plight and restores conditions of well-being through establishing the positive verdict of life, symbolized in the blood and water that flow from Jesus' side.

Finally, this analysis of the plot, concentrating on the commission of the central character and seeing the resolution in his death, raises two further issues about the shape and content of the narrative. Does it not make the resurrection accounts superfluous (a criticism of this Gospel by, among others, Bultmann 1955: 56)? And does it not neglect the substantial amount of attention devoted in the narrative to followers of Jesus? It could be said in response to both questions that this sort of analysis inevitably deals with the protagonist and the main story line that centres around him and with a commission that he consciously carries out. But this still does not entirely meet the objection about the resurrection, because this narrative is distinctive in making not only God but also Jesus himself the agent of his resurrection (cf. esp. 10.17–18). What needs to be added, therefore, is that in this narrative the notion of Jesus' death as glory or as exaltation presupposes his resurrection. The climax of the story as a whole is not the death as such or the resurrection as such but the exaltation of the crucified Jesus in a resurrected body. Jesus has claimed in his mission to be the embodiment of resurrection and life (cf. 11.25) and through his death has rendered the verdict of life, and now the claim and the verdict are confirmed and substantiated in the resurrection accounts. In those accounts the risen Jesus tells Mary Magdalene to pass on the message that he is ascending (20.17), so that both death and resurrection are integral stages in his exaltation and return to the Father who sent and commissioned him. As the incarnate Logos, in whom was life, Jesus does not abandon the body but ascends to the Father with a body marked by death yet transformed by life (20.20).

The role of Jesus' followers is important for the plot, because the process of divine judgement reaches its decisive stage in Jesus' death and resurrection yet continues to be worked out through the mission of these followers in the world. What this will entail is previewed within Jesus' public mission through the lengthy account of the man born blind, his interrogation, increasingly bold witness and eventual expulsion from the synagogue (9.1–41). It is particularly in the Farewell section (13.1—17.26) that disciples are prepared for their future mission, as they are given a fuller understanding of Jesus and his death and told that, like Jesus, they are to be witnesses, a role for which they have been qualified by having accompanied Jesus from the beginning and in which they will have the help of the witness of the Spirit as Advocate (15.26–7). Critical for their role in the midst of persecution and trial is that they be a community of love and unity in a sustaining relationship with Jesus. For this subsidiary story line about the disciples the resurrection accounts are again by no means superfluous. It is not until after the resurrection that they are actually commissioned and empowered with the Spirit to engage in a mission involving a declaration of judgement. This declaration reflects the divine verdict and is one of either the forgiveness or retention of sins, depending on the response to their witness (20.21–3). The epilogue takes the story line about the continuation of Jesus' mission through his followers, and especially through the important roles of Peter and the Beloved Disciple, up into the time of the readers. The shape and sequence of the narrative remain significant in this secondary story line. The most extensive material on the disciples' continuation of Jesus' cause in the world (13.1—17.26) comes before their post-resurrection mission and in fact before the passion narrative. This enables believing readers to see Jesus' witness under interrogation, trial, suffering and death as a paradigm for what they have just been told about the witness of his followers. What is more, the juxtaposition of Peter's failure and Jesus' steadfastness under interrogation (18.12–21) reinforces the starkly contrasting choices which confront them in their continuation of the Gospel's story. Before the epilogue concludes, however, Peter's rehabilitation will provide the encouragement that failure is not necessarily the last word.

Further Reading

For a survey of the overall narrative, see D. M. Smith, *The Theology of the Gospel of John* (Cambridge: Cambridge University Press, 1995), 20–48, and for discussion of an outline, see R. E. Brown, *An Introduction to the Gospel of John*, ed. F. J. Moloney (New York: Doubleday, 2003), 298–316. For various approaches to structure and plot, see R. A. Culpepper, *Anatomy of the Fourth Gospel* (Philadelphia: Fortress, 1983), 77–98; F. F. Segovia, 'The Journey(s) of the Word of God: A Reading of the Plot of the Fourth Gospel', *Semeia* 53 (1991), 23–54; M. W. G. Stibbe, *John's Gospel* (London: Routledge, 1994); R. A. Culpepper, 'The Plot of John's Story of Jesus', *Interpretation* 49 (1995), 347–58.

GENRE

After exploring the sequence and shape of the narrative and its story lines, there is still the question – what sort of narrative is John's story of Jesus? The Fourth Gospel describes itself in two ways. There is a reference to 'this book' (20.30), but this leaves a similar question – what sort of book? There is also a reference to its story as a witness to Jesus' significance (21.24). But witness or testimony is not itself a genre; it can be given in a variety of literary forms. The term 'Gospel' is also not particularly helpful in determining genre. In its early Christian usage it denoted the proclamation of good news, but it only became attached to written accounts of Jesus' life or teachings later, during the second century. The canonical

Gospels with their accounts of the mission of Jesus, written in Greek, are most likely to have been thought of by their first readers as sharing the broad characteristics of the *bios* or Life, that is, as belonging to the literary genre of ancient biography. The conventions for an ancient biography should not be confused with those for a modern one. The genre of *bios* was a flexible one and operated within a continuum that stretched from ancient history writing on the one side through to the encomium on the other. Ancient Lives also often shared features with other sorts of writing such as moral philosophy or the romance or novel.

To be sure, the canonical Gospels have features that make them distinctive within ancient biography. In their accounts of Jesus they have been influenced by accounts of the history of Israel and of its leaders and prophets within the Jewish Scriptures and the writings of the second temple period. These, of course, see Israel's God at work in history, but they also, especially in the later of these writings, already show the influence of Hellenistic historiography. In addition to their concern with God's purposes in history, the Gospel writers also attribute an ultimate significance to Jesus and pay particular attention to his death, and the purpose of their accounts is to persuade their readers to believe in Jesus as Messiah and Son of God. Yet these are differences in content rather than form. In any case, ancient biographers were interested in the impact of their subjects and their significance for ethical and philosophical issues, they could give the greatest amount of space to what they considered the subject's most important period, they wrote their Lives for many different purposes, and in the process they employed a variety of rhetorical techniques to persuade their readers.

Just as the Gospels of Matthew and Luke follow that of Mark, in presenting the message about Jesus in the form of an ancient biography, so also, despite its distinctive features, does the Fourth Gospel. The question of genre is important because it indicates the shared general expectations of author and readers about a particular work. In particular, questions of historicity loom large in the study of the Gospels, not least John's Gospel. In these matters it is vital that present-day readers do not impose modern expectations about biographical or historical writing. It has become clear that the Fourth Gospel tells a well-crafted, deliberately patterned and thematically coherent story about Jesus. But what is its relation to the actual events of Jesus' life and to what he taught? Modern categories have often forced polarized answers – either the whole story is historical in its detail (and therefore complex harmoniza-tions with the Synoptics also need to be sought) or it is an imaginative, even if theologically profound, creation (and therefore of little worth for gaining historical knowledge of Jesus). Examination of some of the features of ancient biography helps to reshape modern assumptions and to indicate the general range of expectations about historicity within which John's Life of Jesus would have been expected to fall.

We have noted that ancient biography had links with ancient histori-ography, but the latter was itself a variegated phenomenon, ranging from those writings conforming somewhat more closely to present notions of historical investigation to far more popular accounts dealing in anecdote and aiming to entertain. But even historians, such as Thucydides and Tacitus, who claimed to have investigated their subject matter closely and to have sought out oral or, where available, written sources, would compose the discourses that take up a large amount of space in their histories in accord with what they thought would fit the character of the speaker and the occasion. Similarly, in relating events such historians would mix more factual reporting with accounts of incidents that might or could have happened. What was important to them was that this elabor-ated material be plausible and illustrate the general truths they wanted to draw out about their subject.

In ancient biography there was even less of a distinction between what we would call 'factual' and 'fictional' elements. While some biographies stayed closer to the conventions of historiography, some did not, and a sustained correspondence with history was not one of the distinguishing features of ancient biography. Plutarch in his *Lives* is an example of a biographer who adhered somewhat more closely to the conventions of ancient historiography, but even with him the various *Lives* can differ considerably in their concern with history. In his biographies, as in ancient history writing, invention or free composition was a central feature. He frequently rewrote sources, changing and elaborating emphases and adding anecdotes, as part of a creative and retrospective exposition of what he perceived to be the significance of his subject's life. What mattered was the plausibility of the portrait and to achieve this Plutarch was willing 'to help the truth along'. For Plutarch, as a biographer with a historical bent, what counted as historical truth was not, then, what could be authenticated by evidence but what was agreed in prevailing convention to be adequately plausible.

Whereas Lives of politicians and military leaders, such as those produced by Plutarch, naturally tended to stay closer to history writing, Lives of philoso-phers and religious leaders or holy men were more idealized and often used by adherents of a philosophy or a religious tradition to influence beliefs or to serve as propaganda against competitors. In such biographies the writers' overall convictions are even more in play in their portraits of their subjects. From early on writers such as Xenophon and Aristoxenus used legendary traditions, invented characteristic traits, and fabricated anecdotes, which they employed in a mix with more authentic material, in producing portraits of philosophers that functioned as claim and counter-claim between rival philo-sophical schools. Accounts of events and discourses became the vehicle for the biographers' ideals taking graphic form within a historically framed narrative, thereby creating verisimilitude.

The point of this sketch of the genre of ancient biography should be clear. It is a category mistake to judge the Fourth Gospel's Life of Jesus by the canons even of ancient historiography, let alone those of modern biographical or historical study. Instead, what we know of this genre should lead us to expect, as ancient readers would also have done, a narrative which contained a substratum of core events from the tradition with substantial correspondence to what happened in the past but which was now shaped by an interpretive superstructure with varying amounts of embellishment, including some legendary or what we would call 'fictive' elements. Most ancient hearers or readers of John's story would not have been concerned to sift critically this mixture of material but would have been satisfied if the resultant portrait was plausible and in continuity with what they knew from elsewhere.

Present-day readers, however, are not so easily satisfied. While recognizing that John's story should be treated on its own terms and that the idea of an objective account of what happened in the past is illusory, they are still likely to want to explore as far as possible how much of that story belongs to the historical substratum and how much to the embellishment of the interpretive superstructure. The attempt to do so will necessarily be carried out primarily in relation to particular passages, but two other general areas bear on such exploration. The first is authorship. How close is the relationship of the story's author to the events his narrative depicts? The second is this Gospel's relation to the Synoptic Gospels. How does this ancient biography compare with those three other accounts of the life of Jesus? And is it in some way dependent on them or does its portrayal provide a largely independent source?

Further Reading:

On ancient biography, see A. Momigliano, *The Development of Greek Biography* (Cambridge, Mass.: Harvard University Press, 1971); C. B. R. Pelling, 'Truth and Fiction in Pluarch's *Lives*', in D. A. Russell (ed.), *Antonine Literature* (Oxford: Clarendon, 1990), 19–52. On the Gospels as ancient biography, see R. A. Burridge, *What Are the Gospels? A Comparison with Graeco-Roman Biography* (Cambridge: Cambridge University Press, 1992) and on the Fourth Gospel in particular, ibid. 220–39.

DATE AND AUTHORSHIP

A fragment containing 18.31–3, 37–8 constitutes the earliest evidence of the existence of the Gospel. This is p[52], part of an Egyptian papyrus now kept in the John Rylands Library in Manchester, and dated by scholars to the early part of the second century CE. The clearest early references to various parts of the Fourth Gospel are found in fragments of an apocryphal gospel contained in Egerton Papyrus 2. This was discovered in Egypt, is now kept in the British Museum, and is dated from palaeographical evidence to the middle of the second century. In addition, Justin Martyr, writing *c.* 155 CE, clearly draws on Jesus' discussion with Nicodemus in 3.1–5 (cf. *1 Apol.* 61.4–5). The evidence suggests that, wherever the Gospel was written, it is likely to have been known in Egypt as early as the beginning of the second century. But what is the earliest it is likely to have been written? Here internal evidence from the narrative has to come into play, particularly the references to expulsion from the synagogue in 9.22; 12.42; 16.2. Even if these refer to the decision of a local synagogue, this is not likely to have occurred much earlier than 80 CE (see the discussion under Setting). If the Fourth Gospel shows knowledge not only of Synoptic tradition but also, on some occasions, of material that is thought to be the editorial work of the Synoptic evangelists (see the discussion under Relation to the Synoptic Gospels), then this also suggests an earliest date of around 85 CE. The best guess of most scholars, then, is that the Gospel in its final form was completed and began to be circulated at some time between 90 and 110 CE.

For many, the more important question is about the identity of its author. But here also a definite answer is hard to come by. The traditional answer, reflected in the title of the Gospel, is that the author was John and that this John was one of Jesus' twelve disciples and therefore an eyewitness of the events he narrates. If this were true, it would obviously have a significant bearing on the assessment of how much authentic historical tradition is included in this Gospel's life of Jesus. But the title 'The Gospel according to John' is first found as a superscription on p^{66} and p^{72}, manuscripts dating from the late second and early third century respectively. The Gospel itself, like the other canonical Gospels, is anonymous. At the end of the epilogue, in 21.24–5, the narrator for the first time refers to himself in the first person singular. On the most likely reading of these verses, this 'I' can also be designated as 'we', as he aligns himself with other believers who endorse 'his testimony', that is, the testimony of the Beloved Disciple (cf. vv. 20–3) who has written or caused to be written the material in the book as a whole. It appears that the writer of the epilogue, not just its final two verses, is to be distinguished from the Beloved Disciple but that the bulk of the Gospel is in some sense being attributed to the Beloved Disciple. In the rest of the narrative 'the disciple whom Jesus loved' is never given another name. The evidence adduced for the Gospel being known by the middle of the second century – Egerton Papyrus 2 and Justin Martyr – does not name the author of the Gospel, so why by the end of the second century had it come to be attributed to John?

The clearest indication of this tradition is found in Irenaeus, who, writing *c.* 180 CE., states in *Haer.* 3.1.1 (quoted in Eusebius, *Hist. eccl.*

5.8.4) that 'John, the disciple of the Lord, who leaned on his breast, also published the Gospel while living at Ephesus in Asia.' It would appear that Irenaeus claimed to have received this tradition from Polycarp, because he also related how, as a boy, he had heard the aged Polycarp, who died in 155 CE, recount his meeting with 'John and with the others who had seen the Lord, how he remembered their words, and what were the things concerning the Lord which he had heard from them' (cf. Eusebius, *Hist. eccl.* 5.20.4–8). Irenaeus assumed this John was the apostle John. But it is quite possible that his memory or his childhood understanding have confused him, because elsewhere Irenaeus also says that Papias was 'a hearer of John and companion of Polycarp' (*Haer.* 5.33.4). Yet, as Eusebius notes, Papias (*c.* 125–50 CE), according to his own testimony, was not a hearer of John the apostle but of John the Elder, who was living in Papias' day – 'If, then, anyone came who had been a follower of the elders, I enquired into the sayings of the elders – what Andrew, or what Peter ... or John, or Matthew, or any other of the disciples of the Lord said – and the things which Aristion and the Elder John, the disciples of the Lord, were saying' (*Hist. eccl.* 3.39.3–4, 33). Is it this presbyter named John who was referred to by Polycarp, and is this the same person who is designated as 'the elder' in 2 John 1 and 3 John 1?

Other considerations make it difficult to place any confidence in Irenaeus' assertion about authorship. Neither Polycarp nor Papias say anything about a Gospel associated with John. Polycarp's letters do not mention John and neither Ignatius' letter to the Ephesians nor other early Christian literature associated with Ephesus gives any indication of knowing about a ministry of John there. It is also clear that Irenaeus was concerned that the major authoritative writings in use in the churches could be traced to apostles and their circle, because this was a way of refuting heretical claims (cf. *Haer.* 3.11.2). In the case of this Gospel he would have a chain of legitimating tradition reaching back from his own time through Polycarp to John the apostle. But the links in the chain are stretched to breaking point. Irenaeus has to go back to his own childhood memories about Polycarp, and, while Polycarp did live to an old age, he would have had to go back to his own childhood to have had contact with any of the remaining first disciples of Jesus, and, as has been noted, Polycarp, as the crucial link, unfortunately fails to mention John as the writer of a Gospel.

It is not surprising that the scholarly consensus has not been impressed by this tradition about Johannine authorship and that two of the twentieth century's major Roman Catholic commentators on the Fourth Gospel started their work with the inclination to give the tradition the benefit of the doubt but ended it with a clear change of mind (cf. Brown 1966: pp. lxxxvii–cii with Brown 1979: 31–4 and Schnackenburg 1980: 100–4 with Schnackenburg 1982: 381–7). Hengel (1989) has put forward a learned but speculative hypothesis (proposed earlier and more briefly by Streeter 1924: 430–61), which he believes to account for the patristic evidence. He holds that the Gospel's author was John the Elder, who, through the figure of the Beloved Disciple, wanted to point in his narrative to John, the son of Zebedee, as the ideal disciple. Strangely, this view selects as reliable some of the details in the late second-century tradition and weaves them together in a proposal which requires the rejection of this tradition's main contention, namely, that the author of the Gospel was John, the son of Zebedee, and which substitutes for it an author the tradition never suggests and about whom nothing else is known.

If the tradition will not bear the weight of critical scrutiny, what, then, about the internal evidence of the narrative? Does it provide any clues as to the identity of the Beloved Disciple? A large number of candidates have been suggested. Those worth mentioning here include John, the son of Zebedee, Lazarus, Thomas and Nathanael. Particularly if the patristic tradition is allowed to be influential, a case can be made for John the apostle by a process of elimination among the twelve disciples. The Synoptic Gospels single out Peter, James and John as a favoured group within the twelve. Peter has a prominent role alongside the Beloved Disciple within the Fourth Gospel; James, according to Acts 12.2, suffered an early martyrdom; and so, of the three, that leaves only John who could be the disciple in an intimate relation with Jesus. But the initial assumption that the Beloved Disciple has to be one of the twelve, and then one of the twelve's inner group of three, is by no means a necessary one. The twelve play only a minor role in this narrative, being mentioned only in 6.70–1 and 20.24, and none of the Synoptic incidents in which the inner three are said to have participated is recounted in this Gospel. The sons of Zebedee (literally, 'those of Zebedee') are mentioned in only one incident – the fishing trip in the epilogue (cf. 21.2) – and the Beloved Disciple is mentioned in the same incident but not in any way that would lead readers to think he was one of these sons. Finally, if the apostle John was the Beloved Disciple, it is difficult to imagine that it would be thought necessary for someone else to endorse the truth of his witness, as is done in 21.24. A number of scholars (including Sanders and Mastin 1968: 29–32; Stibbe 1992: 77–82) contend that the best case can be made for Lazarus as the Beloved Disciple. After all, it is explicitly said that Jesus loved him (11.3, 5), the Beloved Disciple is first mentioned in the narrative after the raising of Lazarus (13.23), he would have been in a position to take Jesus' mother to his own home at Bethany (19.27), it would be uniquely appropriate if he were the one to recognize the significance of the placing of Jesus' grave-clothes in the tomb (20.6–8) and, since he had already died once, it would make sense that he would be the object of the rumour that he would not die again (21.23). On the other hand, a real person appears to lie behind the figure of the Beloved

Disciple, and yet a strong case can be made that Lazarus is part of the author's creative embellishment of tradition (see commentary on 11.1– 53). Though he is said to be loved by Jesus, Lazarus is nowhere actually called a disciple, so would he merit the description 'the disciple whom Jesus loved'? In addition, if, as many hold, the anonymous other disciple of 18.15 is to be identified with the Beloved Disciple, then it makes little sense that in the Lazarus story the chief priests are out to kill Lazarus, while in the later incident this other disciple has privileged access because he is known to the chief priests.

Charlesworth (1995: 115–26, 225–87), while providing an almost exhaustive account of scholarly suggestions about the identity of the Beloved Disciple, attempts to make his own case for Thomas. This includes as one of its main arguments that, in order to have known about the wound in Jesus' side, Thomas must have been the Beloved Disciple who is said to have witnessed it in 19.35. But this reading of the narrative is an extremely literal one that ignores the obvious inference that when the other disciples were shown Jesus' hands and side (20.20) and later told Thomas they had seen the Lord, they also told him what they had seen. It also means having to labour to overthrow the scholarly consensus that 20.8 – 'he saw and believed' – refers to the Beloved Disciple believing in Jesus' resurrection, and adopting instead the unsatisfactory view that he merely believed Mary's words about the body having been taken out of the tomb. Occasionally Nathanael has been proposed as the Beloved Disciple (see Catchpole 2000: 162–72 for recent advocacy of this). Nathanael is mentioned at the very beginning and end of the narrative (1.43–51; 21.2) and is not a disciple known to the Synoptics. His confession about Jesus in 1.49 forms the climax to the responses of the first disciples to Jesus, matches that in the purpose statement of the Gospel (20.31) and shows him to have greater insight than Peter, as will be the case in the later comparisons of the Beloved Disciple and Peter. In addition, Jesus sees in him an Israelite in whom there is no deceit (1.47), a representative of the new Israel, making him a candidate for Jesus' special affection and choice as successor, and he is promised that he will see greater things (1.50) and the Beloved Disciple is to be the one who sees the blood and water flowing from the crucified Jesus and sees the empty tomb. Of course, if Nathanael is meant to be the Beloved Disciple, this would rule out the view of many that the other disciple of 1.37–40 constitutes the first anonymous appearance of the Beloved Disciple in the narrative. More importantly, it does not explain why, having named this disciple at the outset, the evangelist then chooses not to make any explicit link between him and the Beloved Disciple and to hide this identification in the rest of the narrative.

There is a major problem with all these attempts to find clues to the identity of the Beloved Disciple within the narrative. They appear to hold that the scholarly task is not completed until the mystery and anonymity of this figure are unveiled. Yet this does not take seriously precisely the fact that he remains anonymous throughout the narrative. His identity would have been known to those within the evangelist's circle, yet the evangelist deliberately chooses not to identify him to those who do not possess this knowledge. If later readers were meant to discover his identity, the evangelist would have provided far clearer clues. Some scholars have held that this is what the writer intends in supplying the names of some of those who go out in the boat in 21.2. It is to indicate that, when the Beloved Disciple features in the incident, he is one of these – either Thomas, Nathanael or one of the sons of Zebedee. But if this is the writer's intention, he fails completely to achieve it. There is nothing to link the Beloved Disciple with one of these and the most obvious reading of the passage is that his anonymity is retained and that he is one of the 'two others of his disciples' who are also listed as part of the group.

It should not be surprising that, recognizing the problems with identifying the Beloved Disciple and noting some of the ways in which this figure is portrayed in the narrative, some scholars have concluded he is a purely symbolic character. For some, 'the disciple whom Jesus loved' is representative of all disciples whom Jesus loves, particularly those in the community from which the Gospel emerged (cf. e.g. Casey 1996: 160–4). For others (e.g. Bultmann 1971: 484–5), he represents Gentile Christianity, while Peter represents Jewish Christianity. While, as will be noted shortly, there are clear symbolic elements in the Beloved Disciple's role, this view has difficulty in explaining two aspects of his depiction in the epilogue. Whoever wrote chapter 21 appears to treat the Beloved Disciple as an actual person. He depicts the community as being concerned about the death of this figure and about rumours that he was not supposed to die before the parousia (21.20–3) and attributes a role in the writing of the Gospel to him (21.24). Both references make best sense if the Beloved Disciple was someone who had a leading role in the community that lies behind the Gospel and whose death was a cause of concern and contributed to the felt need to have in written form the distinctive interpretation of Jesus' life that he had been the major influence in shaping.

For this reason the dominant scholarly view is that the Beloved Disciple was a founding figure and teacher in a particular group of Christians. His identity is irrecoverable and he may or may not have been a minor follower of Jesus during his Jerusalem ministry, but he has now been idealized and given a role at significant points in the narrative about Jesus in order to emphasize and legitimate its perspective. Whoever he was and whatever his relationship to the earthly Jesus, in the narrative he functions as the ideally perceptive disciple and therefore the witness to Jesus par excellence. At the last supper he alone knows by whom Jesus will be betrayed (13.13–27), at the crucifixion the mother of Jesus is entrusted to his care as Jesus' successor (19.26–7), in all probability it is he who witnesses to the life-giving significance of Jesus' death (19.34–5), and at the empty tomb he sees and believes on the basis of the grave-clothes before Peter or any of the other disciples believe Jesus has been raised (20.3–10). There is no corroborative evidence from the Synoptics for a disciple doing any of these things and indeed these incidents appear to have been added to the substratum for the evangelist's narrative found in the Synoptic tradition. What is more, it is striking that in none of these episodes does the Beloved Disciple's insight affect other characters or the action in the plot as a whole. Only in the epilogue, in 21.7, is his privileged knowledge passed on to another character, when Peter is shown to be dependent on the insight and word of the Beloved Disciple for his recognition of the risen Jesus. This observation is worth underlining from the first episode in which this character is introduced as the disciple whom Jesus loved. Peter asks him to discover the identity of Jesus' betrayer (13.24). Although he learns this from Jesus' subsequent action, he does not in fact tell Peter or, of course, do anything to prevent Judas from carrying out the betrayal. To add to the strangeness, the narrator's own comments in 13.28 about Jesus' words to Judas ignore the Beloved Disciple's role – 'Now no one at the table knew why he said this to him.' This conveys the impression that the Beloved Disciple is at the same time both inside and outside the story line. He possesses the privileged knowledge of the narrator and the implied readers rather than really participating in the story line. Such features strongly suggest that the Beloved Disciple's role in the narrative constitutes a literary device. He enables the narrator's retrospective knowledge to be communicated to the readers within the story line while giving it the authority of a character who was apparently present at the time. Something similar holds for his role in 19.35. Here the reference to his witness is parenthetical. The narrative flows smoothly without it, so that 'these things' that are said to be the fulfilment of Scripture in 19.36 are a reference to the events of 19.31–4. The Beloved Disciple is again not a real participant in the action. His seeing and testifying is not for the benefit of other characters but for the readers – 'so that you also may believe'. As a literary device, his role once more allows the narrator to draw the implied readers into the story line, inviting them to share the perspective of this witness that Jesus' death was life-giving.

How, then, is the Beloved Disciple's witnessing to be understood? Is he an eyewitness of events? Or is this too part of the literary device? It is the epilogue that attributes not just the immediately preceding account but, as most hold, the Gospel as a whole to the witness or testimony of the Beloved Disciple (21.24). Discussion of what this witness entails needs to do justice to two main features of the narrative. On the one hand, in the prologue and then throughout the rest of the narrative the language of seeing and witnessing functions predominantly as part of an overarching metaphor of God's trial or judgement of the world. It serves primarily as a functional equivalent of believing and confessing. From this perspective there would be no reason simply to assume that the reference to testimony in 21.24 is a reference to the Beloved Disciple's literal eyewitnessing which vouches for the historical accuracy of the preceding account. One would be more likely to assume that this witness is like that attributed at the beginning of the narrative to John the Baptist, whose evaluative testimony is to the significance of Jesus' identity as the divine light and to his pre-existence as the Logos. The narrator would now be claiming the Beloved Disciple's witness as the authority for the distinctive confessional perspective on Jesus' identity that has shaped the entire narrative. At the same time, however, there are also suggestions towards the end of the narrative that, in the case of the Beloved Disciple, literal eyewitnessing is involved. In 19.35, where he sees and testifies that blood and water came from Jesus' side, and in 20.8, where he sees and believes at the empty tomb, this disciple is depicted as an eyewitness of significant events. These earlier references make it possible for readers to take the final mention of his witness in 21.24 to include not only a confessional perspective but also an eyewitness role, which might extend either from 13.23, where he is explicitly introduced, or, if he were to be also identified with the unnamed disciple in 1.35–40, for the whole of Jesus' mission. Closer reflection, however, shows that it is extremely difficult to take this reading at its face value. It has already been observed that when the Beloved Disciple himself appears in the narrative, his knowledge fails to be a significant factor in the action. In addition, there is no way in which the narrator for some of the episodes (e.g. the encounter between Jesus and the Samaritan woman in the absence of the disciples in 4.17–26, the events befalling the blind man in the absence of Jesus in 9.8–34, or Jesus' trial before Pilate in 18.28—19.16) can be thought to be the Beloved Disciple as eyewitness. Any eyewitness element within the testimony attributed to the Beloved Disciple is best seen, therefore, as part of the literary device constituted by his role in the narrative. It helps both to give an impression of verisimilitude and to legitimate the narrator's perspective on the significance of the person of Jesus.

This stance on the role of the Beloved Disciple does not, of course, entail that no eyewitness material at all informs the traditions that have been incorporated into the Fourth Gospel. The reference to the witness of the disciples in 15.27 indicates that their having been with Jesus 'from the beginning' qualifies them for this task. They are depicted as providing a clear link to the mission of Jesus, much of which they will have actually seen. Rather, what is being discussed is the role the Beloved Disciple is made to play in the final form of the Gospel, and the claim is that that final form, even allowing for elements of reflection, cannot be held to represent the historical record of his eyewitnessing. The Gospel's original readers would not have had any difficulty in recognizing eyewitness elements in a narrative as a literary device. Within contemporary Jewish literature there were first person eyewitness reports on the part of the patriarchs in the narratives that surround the visions in apocalypses such as *1 Enoch* or *The Apocalypse of Abraham* and the testamentary material in *The Testaments of the Twelve Patriarchs*. In Graeco-Roman historiography also what many ancient historians claimed to do, and what some actually did, was to include material that was originally oral, based on their own eyewitnessing or reports of others' eyewitnessing. But such claims became sufficiently widespread that they were found to be necessary as part of the rhetorical arsenal of those who wanted to be able to legitimate the accounts they produced in order to persuade their audiences (cf. Byrskog 2002: 199–223). What appeared to be a signal of factuality often turned out to function quite differently. Informed readers would be aware that the convention of having eyewitness elements in a narrative frequently served as a way of lending that narrative verisimilitude and of authenticating its writer's later perspective.

To designate a character as 'the disciple whom Jesus loved' is certainly an effective means of guaranteeing the credibility and reliability of his witness. His intimacy with Jesus is reinforced by the depiction of him lying in the lap of Jesus (13.23), the same position Jesus is said to occupy in relation to the Father and on the basis of which he is able to make God known (1.18). The Beloved Disciple's witness is the human instrument for making Jesus known. Indeed, he acts as the link between the completion of Jesus' mission and the present situation of the readers. As the witness in 19.35, the Beloved Disciple testifies to the pronouncement of God's positive verdict of life through the death of Jesus. The function of his witness here is the same as that of his witness in the Gospel as a whole (cf. 20.31); it is in order that the readers might believe. Despite his death, that witness continues into the time of those who must bear their own testimony to Jesus as it now takes on a new written form (21.24).

Obviously known to the final writer and his Christian community, this influential teacher remains anonymous in the narrative. This is in line with what is known about the composition of much of the literature in the Jewish Scriptures and the function of anonymity there. Authors and editors remained anonymous because they were concerned not with themselves but with attributing the content of their work to the authoritative source of their community's traditions – whether Moses, Solomon, David or Isaiah. This Gospel's narrative, which appears to end at 20.31, was anonymous in the interest of pointing to Jesus as the authoritative source of its traditions. When the final version's epilogue attributes authorship to the Beloved Disciple, this is still to an anonymous figure and it is in the interest of pointing to the authoritative tradition's transmission through an authoritative mediator. Just as the implied author's views about Jesus have been attributed to Jesus in his earthly mission, so the implied author's insights, especially about the events surrounding Jesus' death and resurrection, have been attributed to the Beloved Disciple as the ideal witness. Any known identity of this originating witness has been effaced in favour of the tradition that he authenticates. His anonymity has a further function. For later readers, the lack of a specific name to distinguish his identity sharply from theirs encourages identification with this unnamed character. It invites them to share in his perceptive witness and therefore also the implied author's point of view.

The discussion below on the composition of the Gospel and its relation to other Johannine literature will have more to say about the evangelist and the final editor whose work is attributed to the Beloved Disciple. But from what has already been said about this disciple's function in the narrative, it should be clear that it is highly unlikely that the writer of this Gospel had direct or immediate access to the events which his narrative recounts or that talk of the Beloved Disciple's eyewitnessing should be taken straightforwardly as actually guaranteeing the historical reliablity of the narrative.

Further Reading

On the traditions about John, see R. A. Culpepper, *John, the Son of Zebedee: The Life of a Legend* (Minneapolis: Fortress, 2000). On scholarly attempts to identify the Beloved Disciple, see J. H. Charlesworth, *The Beloved Disciple* (Valley Forge, Pa.: Trinity Press International, 1995), 127–224. For discussion of the role of the Beloved Disciple, see R. J. Bauckham, 'The Beloved Disciple as Ideal Author', *JSNT* 49 (1993), 21–44 and A. T. Lincoln, 'The Beloved Disciple as Eyewitness and the Fourth Gospel as Witness', *JSNT* 85 (2002), 3–26.

RELATION TO THE SYNOPTIC GOSPELS

The issue of John's relation to the Synoptic Gospels is a complex and intriguing one, about which there is no scholarly consensus. All that can be done in this Introduction is to survey the topic and the main types of explanation and to indicate, with a brief justification, the stance that will be taken in the Commentary. The common designations – the Synoptic Gospels and the Fourth Gospel – already reflect the perception that, because of the major similarities in the order and wording of their narratives, the first three canonical Gospels belong together in a way that distinguishes them from the fourth. This perception is not simply the result of modern critical studies. The well-known assertion of Clement of Alexandria, 'that John, last of all, conscious that the outward facts had been set forth in the Gospels, was urged on by his disciples, and divinely moved by the Spirit, composed a spiritual Gospel' (Eusebius, *Hist. eccl.* 6.14.7), was an early attempt to explain the obvious differences.

Any comparison of John and the Synoptics needs to do justice to both the similarities and the differences. We start, then, with some of those most frequently observed. Among the major similarities are the following. The Fourth Gospel, like the Synoptics, presents its message in the form of a narrative life of Jesus. Indeed its structural outline has similarities with that of Mark, with the preaching of John the Baptist near the beginning (1.19–36; cf. Mark 1.4–8) followed by a movement into Galilee (1.43; 4.3; cf. Mark 1.14–15). Near the centre of the public mission of Jesus there is the feeding of the five thousand (6.1–15; cf. Mark 6.34–44) followed by walking on the water (6.16–21; cf. Mark 6.45–52), which is in turn followed by a confession from Peter (6.68–9; cf. Mark 8.29–31). There is then a departure for Jerusalem (7.10–14; cf. Mark 10.1, 32) with an anointing (12.1–8; cf. Mark 14.3–9) and an entry into Jerusalem (12.12–15; cf. Mark 11.1–11), where John has reversed the order, followed by a last supper (13.1–30; cf. Mark 14.17–26). The basic outline of the ensuing passion story is also similar – an arrest leading to a Jewish trial (Mark) or an interrogation (John), which is sandwiched with the scene of Peter's threefold denial, and then a Roman trial, followed by crucifixion, burial and resurrection. Within this overall outline there are episodes closely related to those in the Synoptics, such as the incident in the temple (2.13–17; cf. Mark 11.15–17 parr.), though the chronology here is significantly different, and the healing of an official's son at Capernaum (4.46b–54; cf. Matt. 8.5–13; Luke 7.1–10). There are also sayings closely related to those in the Synoptics, such as that about losing one's life (12.25; cf. Mark 8.35 parr.) and that about receiving one whom Jesus sends being the same as receiving him and the one who sent him (13.20; cf. Matt. 10.40; Mark 9.37).

The greatest differences are to be found in the Fourth Gospel's portrayal of Jesus, where, unlike the Synoptics, he is presented as the Logos, as pre-existent and one with God, and where there is an explicit and full development of his sonship in relation to the Father. Part of this distinctive portrayal lies in Jesus' use of the divine self-identification, 'I Am', and the emphasis on the divine glory being revealed throughout Jesus' mission but especially in his death. Some of this distinctive depiction is conveyed through Jesus' own teaching. Here it is striking that whereas the chief content of Jesus' teaching in the Synoptics is about the kingdom of God, in John it is about himself. The statistics drive this point home. The term 'kingdom' is found on Jesus' lips 47 times in Matthew, 18 times in Mark, 37 times in Luke and only 5 times in John, while the pronoun 'I' is found on his lips 17 times in Matthew, 9 times in Mark, 10 times in Luke, but 118 times in John. The style of the teaching is also significantly different. In the Synoptics this is characterized by pithy sayings, epigrams or parables, while in John it is characterized by long and involved discourses and disputes. Indeed the style and language of Jesus in the Fourth Gospel is closer to that of the evangelist and of the Johannine epistles than to the Synoptics. In regard to Jesus' deeds, the exorcisms, characteristic of the Synoptics, have disappeared in John and instead there are fewer and more remarkable 'signs'. Specific Synoptic episodes are missing, so that, for example, there is no account of Jesus' baptism, temptation, transfiguration, agony in Gethsemane, institution of the last supper, Sanhedrin trial, or cry of dereliction from the cross (as found in Mark and Matthew). Instead there are episodes unique to John, such as the wedding at Cana, the encounters and conversations with Nicodemus and the Samaritan woman, the raising of Lazarus, and the washing of the disciples' feet. Finally, some of the geographical and chronological differences should be mentioned. While in the Synoptics the focus for Jesus' mission is Galilee, followed by one climactic visit to Jerusalem, in John the focus is Judaea with movements back and forth between Galilee and Jerusalem. The resurrection appearances also have different settings. In Matthew it is Galilee (and this setting is also predicted in Mark) and in Luke it is Jerusalem, while John has appearances in both Jerusalem and Galilee. In the Synoptics Jesus' public mission appears to last for approximately one year, while in John it is for approximately three years. Whereas the temple incident constitutes Jesus' last public act in the Synoptics, in John it is found at the beginning as his second public act. The Synoptics have the last meal and crucifixion at the same time as the feast of Passover, while John has them one day earlier at the time of the preparation for Passover when the lambs were slaughtered.

How, then, are these sorts of continuities and discontinuities between John and the Synoptics to be explained? While not averse to attempts at some harmonization, the earliest interpreters of John generally held that the distinctive portrayals of Jesus represented by his Gospel and the Synoptic Gospels could not ultimately be harmonized and that, knowing the other Gospels, John chose to exercise a spiritual freedom in supplementing them, particularly in order to draw out the divinity of Jesus (cf. Wiles 1960: 13–21). With some slight variations, this became the dominant view of the relationship even among critical scholars of the nineteenth and early twentieth centuries. The twentieth century was, however, to see a remarkable shift in the scholarly consensus. In the English-speaking world this was brought about primarily through the brief work of P. Gardner-Smith, *St. John and the Synoptic Gospels* (1938), which was followed up by the more rigorous and comprehensive study of C. H. Dodd, *Historical Tradition in the Fourth Gospel* (1963). Both argued that the agreements between John and the Synoptics were better explained in terms of common oral tradition, which may have had points of convergence at a pre-Synoptic stage, rather than literary dependence, and that the divergences were so great as to confirm John's independence and lack of knowledge of the written Synoptic Gospels. This view was accepted by some influential German scholars, such as E. Haenchen (his earlier acceptance is also reflected in his later commentary, 1984), and at the same time R. Bultmann developed in his commentary, first published in 1941, a hypothesis about the composition of the Fourth Gospel that had no need for the notion of dependence on the Synoptics. Bultmann held that the Fourth Gospel was dependent instead on a distinctive signs source, containing the miracles later taken up in the Gospel, a revelation discourse, and a passion narrative parallel to but not derived from the Synoptics, and that these had been adapted to express the evangelist's own theology. So, whether by emphasizing John's use of independent oral tradition or his use of his own sources, particularly the signs source, a new consensus emerged which held that John was not dependent on the Synoptics. This consensus was reflected in nearly all the major commentaries of the second half of the twentieth century, and in the English-speaking world the work of R. E. Brown in his commentary (1966, 1970) and other later studies (1979, 1994, 2003) was particularly influential in promoting such a view. Bultmann's hypothesis of a signs source also had its advocates in the English-speaking world, where this source has also been called a Signs Gospel. In particular, R. T. Fortna, in *The Gospel of Signs* (1970) and *The Fourth Gospel and its Predecessor* (1988), attempted to set it on a firmer critical footing and saw the crucial stage of the Gospel's composition as involving the combination of the Signs Gospel with a passion narrative, and U. C. von Wahlde (1989) also produced his own somewhat different reconstruction of this signs source.

Among the major commentators on John, however, there was a notable exception to the prevailing view. C. K. Barrett (1st edn 1955, 2nd edn 1978) held out for the explanation that John knew and used the Synoptics. He has now been joined in this stance by a sizeable number of scholars, so that since the last decade of the twentieth century there can no longer be said to be a consensus on the matter. This resurgence of the older view in a variety of forms has been spearheaded by the work of F. Neirynck (1977, 1982, 1991) and his associates (cf. Sabbe 1991, 1992, 1994, 1995), who have also been joined by others (cf. Denaux (ed.) 1992). There are two main prongs to their attack on the earlier consensus. The first is to show that there are clear signs of John's dependence on the Synoptics in the resurrection narratives, the passion narratives and then elsewhere in the Gospel, which cannot be satisfactorily explained by other means. The second is to undermine the hypothesis of a signs source, which in any case has had only limited acceptance among Johannine scholars, due in part to the variety of its reconstructions. The major problem with this hypothesis, however, has always been with establishing convincing criteria for isolating the source material from the Gospel as we now have it. Linguistic and stylistic criteria are particularly difficult to apply, since what can be seen as typically Johannine features are to be found distributed throughout the Gospel. This point was underlined in the thorough summary and critique of the signs source theory by G. van Belle (1994). In the absence of any new scholarly consensus, there have also been attempts to show that John was in fact a source for Luke's Gospel and even that John's Gospel or an earlier version of it may have been the first Gospel.

This historical sketch has indicated that a key issue is whether one looks to literary relationships or to use of oral traditions. This is also an important area of debate for the Synoptic problem itself. In treating the question of the relation of the Fourth Gospel to the other three canonical Gospels, it is sometimes assumed that, while this question remains open, the nature of the relationship among the Synoptics themselves is a relatively settled issue. Since they have so much material in common, the Synoptics must have a primarily literary relationship, whether the preferred view is that Matthew and Luke independently employed as sources Mark and Q (the two-document hypothesis) or that Mark was used by Matthew and then Luke used Mark and Matthew (the Farrer–Goulder hypothesis) or that Matthew was written first, then Luke was produced and then Mark produced a shorter version, employing the other two (the Griesbach hypothesis). Recently, however, there has been renewed emphasis on oral tradition, with a number of scholars claiming that the dominant theories have given too much attention to literary sources and suggesting that many of the similarities and differences among the Synoptics are better explained by aspects of oral tradition and its transmission. On this view, attention switches from editorial alteration of written documents to the stability of core sayings and incidents and the variation and flexibility entailed in their various oral performances. While this recent emphasis provides a healthy reminder that the Gospels were produced in a predominantly oral culture in which the vast majority of people were illiterate, it should not be used to create a polarization between oral and literary categories. The Synoptic Gospels were written versions of what may have been in large part prior oral performances and most of their recipients experienced them as they were then read aloud in a further oral performance. There is also no reason to think that once versions were written down and circulated, the process of oral transmission of parts of the tradition or of the longer versions suddenly ceased. At the same time, it remains obvious that, whatever our best guesses about how the oral traditions developed, our only access to such traditions is through the written documents, and in the case of the Synoptics these written documents both bear the marks of the arrangement and distinctive thought and purposes of the individual evangelists and clearly have some literary relationship. Exploration of the latter relationship should not, however, be carried out in a rigid way that ignores the oral culture. So, if, for example, as appears highly likely, Matthew and Luke are dependent in a literary fashion on Mark, it cannot be ruled out that they may on occasion have reworked Mark in the light of their knowledge of oral traditions of some of the same material found in their source. Of course, the longer the period after the writing down of the source, here Mark, the more likely it is that that written version with its precise wording and stability will come to dominate over less precise, more fluid oral versions of material in the memory of individuals or groups.

This digression into the debate about Synoptic relationships has a number of purposes. First, the emphasis on the oral culture surrounding the written Gospels should remind us that the original recipients of John would have heard it read. When, therefore, the commentary talks of 'readers' of the Gospel, this should be understood, in the case of the original readers, as involving primarily the hearing of its message. Second, when it comes to exploring John's relationship to the Synoptics, it should not necessarily be assumed that the only form of dependence is the sort of strictly literary one in which a writer has the written sources before him as he writes or that, if this kind of close copying of material cannot be proved throughout the bulk of the narrative, then the only alternative is to view the Fourth Gospel as working with independent traditions about the life of Jesus. Third, it should be allowed in principle that there could be a mixture of dependence on other documents and use of independent oral traditions. Fourth, it is also necessary, when thinking about dependence, at least to allow for a mixture of forms of knowledge of other documents. The writer(s) of the Fourth Gospel may, for example, have known earlier Gospels both through having heard them performed orally several times and through having a copy that was available for consultation when necessary. In fact, from all we know about ancient scribal practice, writing desks were not in use until later and it would not have been possible to have a number of other documents spread out before one to consult as one composed. With the aid of an assistant, a scribe could have one other scroll held open before him for consultation or for reading out to him as he wrote but he could also draw on earlier or present reflection in which particular stories, phrases or emphases were remembered from previous readings or oral performances of texts and developed into fresh interpretations. Other Gospels would have been readily accessible to the fourth evangelist in this way. It is clear that, soon after they were written, the Gospels would have become widely available via the social network of early Christians by means of copying and oral performance (cf. e.g. Alexander 1998; Thompson 1998). To claim that the view that John employed the Synoptics is an anachronistic imposition by modern scholars, who imagine him as having had Mark, Matthew and Luke spread out before him on his desk and picking from each a phrase here or a theme there, and to dismiss this view on such grounds, is to engage in caricature.

The preceding discussion has laid the foundation and set the parameters for the explanation of the stance taken in this commentary. Not every scholar can be an expert on all matters. Hence the dominance of the notion of a consensus in the earlier sketch of scholarship. Those who write more generally on John's Gospel, even those who produce commentaries, usually have to rely substantially on the work of those who have done detailed studies of particular aspects, and so to a certain extent have to presuppose the soundness of experts' studies on such a matter as the relation of John to the Synoptics. When, as now, there is no consensus among the experts on this matter, it is even more incumbent on a commentator to take responsibility for his or her own views and to provide some justification for them. When this writer started work on the commentary, he had been most influenced by those who saw John as independent of the Synoptics, but, as a result of keeping comparison with the Synoptics in view throughout, he has become persuaded that the Fourth Gospel provides evidence that its writer and editor not only knew Mark, to which it is most substantially indebted, but also knew and used both Matthew and Luke. Two major criteria need to be met if dependence of one document on an earlier source is to be established. First, there have to be signs in the later document of knowledge of similar content, sequence, vocabulary or style from the earlier one. Second, there has to be a satisfactory explanation of the differences in the later document, plausible reasons why the earlier material has been adapted to take the form it now has. While there are some instances of similarities with Synoptic material, where an equally strong case for John's use of Synoptic-like independent tradition might be made, this commentary argues that in the majority of instances, on the basis of the above criteria, the much stronger case is that John knows the Synoptic Gospels themselves. The case becomes even stronger when not simply isolated pericopes are compared, as is frequently done, but when whole units of material or whole motifs are also taken into account, as will be indicated below.

Before then, some further clarifications need to be made. (i) The Synoptics are obviously not the only source material for the fresh interpretation in John. There is material that is unique to him which can be attributed either to his own creativity or to his use of traditions quite distinct from those found in the Synoptics or to a combination of both. (ii) A general stance that John knows the Synoptics themselves does not of course rule out the possibility that on some occasions he may also have used independent oral traditions which had at some point influenced the

Synoptics or been influenced by them. This would have to be established as the better explanation in an individual case. (iii) This is different from a general appeal to the use of independent oral tradition. While, as has been acknowledged, there may well have been multiple versions of sayings of Jesus and of stories about him in the oral tradition and these would not have ceased to circulate immediately the written Gospels were produced, to appeal constantly to such unknown or speculatively reconstructed versions as John's independent sources becomes unconvincing. This is especially the case when these sources are said to be 'very similar to Mark' or 'close to the version found in Luke' and when there is another, simpler explanatory option that works with the known rather than the unknown, namely, that John knew Mark or Luke. (iv) This option does not hold that John has worked with those accounts in the same way that Matthew and Luke worked with Mark, incorporating and making modifications to whole blocks of verbatim material. Instead he has treated such sources far more independently and creatively, a treatment that, as has been noted, would fall well within the scope of what might be expected of the writer of an ancient biography. The creative freedom of the Johannine tradition is evident and usually accepted when it comes to the discourses placed in the mouth of Jesus, where frequently on the basis of a saying to be found in the Synoptic tradition, which has been reworked into John's own idiom, an extensive monologue or dialogue is built up. Why should it be thought that the evangelist would exercise less freedom and independence when it comes to dealing with narrative material?

Readers will have to judge the plausibility of this commentary's general stance on John and the Synoptics in the light of its brief comparisons with the Synoptics in the discussions of individual pericopes. There is only space in this section of the Introduction for developing a few specific examples. The first comes from the passion narrative. One of the distinctive features of Mark's style is the literary device of intercalation, sometimes called the 'Markan sandwich'. In a given passage the beginning of one event is narrated, then the whole of a second event is narrated, and finally the narration of the first event is completed (cf. e.g. Mark 3.20–35; 5.21–43; 6.7–30; 11.12–21; 14.1–11). The point of the device is not simply stylistic but also theological. The two events are seen to be mutually interpretive and help to emphasize particular Markan concerns. Just such an intercalation is also found in Mark 14.53–72, which narrates a scene with Peter in the courtyard of the high priest's residence, warming himself at the fire, before moving to an account of Jesus' trial before the Sanhedrin, and then returning to the scene with Peter, in which he denies Jesus three times. This produces an effective ironic contrast, in which Jesus gives faithful testimony, although this will lead to his death, while Peter fails to confess his relation to Jesus in order to avoid arrest. This does not represent the inevitable way of relating these episodes, as is made clear by the fact that, although Matt. 26.57–75 follows Mark's arrangement, Luke 22.56–71 does not but has all of Peter's denials precede Jesus' giving of faithful testimony. The significance becomes obvious when we turn to John 18.15–27. John replaces Mark's Sanhedrin trial, having taken up its issues and verdict in 10.22–39 and 11.47–53, with an interrogation before Annas, retaining only the mention of Jesus being struck by a guard (cf. John 18.22 with Mark 16.65). But, more importantly, he does keep Mark's distinctive intercalation at this point, even following Mark's repetition of the mention of Peter warming himself. He not only keeps it but also intensifies it by having one of Peter's denials before Jesus' witness under interrogation and then returning to the other two after it. His main point is similar to Mark's – the contrasting models for witness of Peter and Jesus.

Lest this clear example of John's dependence on a characteristic Markan feature be thought to occur only in the passion narrative, it is worth considering John 6. The fact that the feeding of the five thousand is followed by the walking on the water in both John 6.1–21 and Mark 6.32–52 is often explained, because of the differences between the two accounts, as an instance of common dependence on the oral tradition. Yet John's differences from Mark in the narration of these two incidents can all be accounted for plausibly in terms of John's particular literary and theological concerns (see the commentary), and, once the whole block of material from Mark 6.32—8.33 is taken into account, the oral tradition explanation becomes less likely than the one that John knew well this section of Mark. The idea of following the feeding with a discourse on bread is not unique to John. It needs to be remembered that in Mark 8.1–10 there is a second feeding – of the four thousand – and this is followed by a discourse on bread in 8.14–21. That discourse with its questions addressed to the disciples underlines that they have not understood the significance of the feedings (cf. also Mark 6.52). More precisely, they have failed to understand the revelation that has taken place in the breaking of the bread. John's discourse develops this theme Christologically in terms of Jesus being the bread given for the life of the world. It includes a demand from 'the Jews' for a sign, despite the fact that Jesus has just performed one in the feeding (6.30). Similarly, Mark has the Pharisees ask for a sign immediately after the feeding of the four thousand (Mark 8.11–13). Shortly after the bread discourse Mark has Peter's confession (Mark 8.29) and John has the equivalent confession of Peter shortly after the bread of life material (6.68–9). When in Mark Peter takes offence at Jesus' subsequent teaching about the necessity of his suffering, he is rebuked as Jesus calls him Satan and contrasts the thinking determined by the divine realm and the thinking that is confined to human categories (Mark 8.31–3). Jesus' reply in John also links a disciple with Satan or the devil, but John makes this Judas rather than Peter. Peter's response to the prediction of Jesus' suffering in Mark has its equivalent in John in those disciples who take offence at the necessity of believing that the Son of man's flesh is to be given for the world's life, and in this context John's equivalent to the contrast between divine and human ways of thinking is the contrast between Spirit and flesh, where the latter term indicates the response to the revelation in Jesus that remains on the merely human level (6.60–3). By far the most reasonable explanation of this sequence and its content throughout John 6 is that the evangelist is familiar with Mark's editorial arrangement in the similar sequence and content to be found in Mark 6.32–52 and 8.1–33.

John's knowledge of Matthew and Luke's editorial activity can also be shown. Here we can only provide one instance where knowledge of Matthew is indicated. In John 4.46–54 the healing of the official's son invites comparison with the similar healing at a distance of the centurion's servant or son in Matt. 8.5–13 and Luke 7.1–10. The major differences in John result from his characteristic concerns. As elsewhere where there are Synoptic parallels to the Johannine miracles, John intensifies the miraculous. Here he has Jesus heal not just from a distance within Capernaum but from the neighbouring town of Cana (4.46–7, 50a). His story is also moulded to deal with a theme treated elsewhere – the difference between believing on the basis of signs and believing simply on the basis of Jesus' word (4.48, 50b). None of the details of John's version appear to be more primitive than those in Matthew or Luke or to require positing an oral tradition earlier than the material Matthew and Luke have in common. And in fact John's closest agreements with their accounts is not with the material Matthew and Luke have in common but in the places where they diverge. At the beginning it is only Luke 7.2 and John 4.47 that have the sick person on the point of death and at the end it is only Matt. 8.13 and John 4.52–3 that stress the synchronicity between the hour of Jesus' word of healing and the hour the healing occurs. But there is a further significant detail in John's story that confirms dependence on Matthew. In John 8.52 the report is given that 'the fever left him'. This is the first time fever has been mentioned in the story and it is not mentioned in either of Matthew's or Luke's versions of the story. In fact, with only one exception, sick people in the Gospels are never reported as having fever. That exception is Peter's mother-in-law (Mark 1.31 parr.), of whom it is also reported that 'the fever left her'. And Matthew alone places that statement immediately after his account of the healing of the centurion's servant (Matt. 8.14–15). John, then, almost certainly has to be familiar with Matthew's editorial arrangement.

The examples given so far have dealt primarily with events. But John also derives particular sayings of Jesus from the Synoptics. Many of the sayings prefaced by the double Amen formulation provide instances of this phenomenon. Sometimes the Synoptic sayings have been heavily coloured by the Johannine idiom and sometimes they have been left relatively untouched before they are placed on the lips of John's Jesus. The first such saying, in 1.51, is an example of the former approach – 'You will see heaven opened and the angels of God ascending and descending on the Son of Man.' The Synoptic text that has the three elements of the heavens being opened or shaken, seeing the Son of Man, and angels accompanying him is Mark 13.25–7. It has been reworked in the light of John's more realized eschatology and his use of Gen. 28.12 to refer to the present mission of Jesus. Similarly, the sayings in 3.3, 5 about not seeing or entering the kingdom of God unless one is born from above or born of water and the Spirit are Johannine reformulations of the single Amen saying in Luke 18.17 and Matt. 18.3. The saying about the necessity of eating the Son of Man's flesh and drinking his blood in 6.53 is a reformulation of the commands to eat and drink found only in the eucharistic words of Matt. 26.26–8. Jesus' assertion that he is the door in 10.7 is John's Christological interpretation of Matt. 7.13–14 and Luke 13.24. The sayings of 13.16, 20 are derived more straightforwardly from those in Matt. 10.24, 40 respectively, while 13.21, 36b are taken almost verbatim from the single Amen sayings in Mark 14.18 and Matt. 26.34 respectively. Later, in the farewell discourse, 16.20, 23 involve reworkings of Luke 6.21, 25 and Luke 11.9–10 respectively. Other double Amen sayings could be mentioned in this regard but these suffice to show that in some cases they have come from Mark, in others from Matthew and in still others from Luke, and in these examples there are no obvious indicators that John knew the sayings from some other source. Other examples of John's knowledge of and yet creative freedom with Jesus' teaching in the Synoptics could be given, but in one place a whole monologue appears to have been built up from such a base. The prayer of Jesus in 17.1–26 takes up the so-called 'Lord's Prayer' (Matt. 6.9–15; Luke 11.1–4), is closest to the Matthean version, adapts its clauses into the Johannine idiom and weaves them into its own distinctive portrait of Jesus (see the commentary on this passage).

Finally, John's creativity with his Synoptic sources can be seen not only in the way he has handled particular events or sayings but also in the way he has employed them to develop his own larger themes. Of these the relationship of Jesus as Son to God as Father is particularly dominant. In the Synoptics such a relationship comes to expression in the saying found in Matt. 11.27 and Luke 10.22 – 'All things have been handed over to me by my Father; and no one knows the Son except the Father, and no one knows the Father except the Son and anyone to whom the Son chooses to reveal him.' Various aspects of this saying are taken up in the Fourth Gospel – the handing over of all things to the Son (3.35; 5.22; 17.2), the Son's knowledge of the Father (7.25; 8.55; 17.25), the mutual knowledge of Father and Son (10.14–15), and the knowledge of the Father by chosen others through the Son's revelation of him (8.19; 14.7, 9; 15.15b–16a; 17.6, 26). But it is not just that there are specific references that reflect this saying. The evangelist has allowed its concepts to shape decisively and in a variety of ways much of the rest of his presentation of Jesus in the narrative. That presentation is based on the conviction that Jesus is the Son who has unique knowledge of his Father and has been given full authorization by him and therefore is in the position of being able to reveal God as Father in such a way that others can share in knowing God.

As noted earlier, another prominent way of shaping the narrative is through the cluster of juridical metaphors which, together with actual interrogations and trials, constitute the judgement or trial motif. In concluding this section, attention will be drawn briefly to a few instances of the creative use of the Synoptics in developing this motif (see Lincoln 2000: 307–26 for a more extensive discussion). The judgement motif in the Fourth Gospel, with its conviction that God's sovereign claim on the world is being established in Jesus, is a Johannine replaying of the Synoptic notion of God's kingdom or rule being inaugurated by Jesus. John presents Jesus as on trial before 'the Jews' throughout his public mission. In doing so, he takes up elements from the Synoptic account of the trial of Jesus before the Sanhedrin, which he distinctively omits from his own passion narrative, and shows clear knowledge of Mark and Luke. The accusation of false witnesses in Mark 14.58 that Jesus threatened to destroy the temple and build another in three days is turned into an assertion of Jesus himself in 2.19. The question and answer about Jesus as Messiah and Son of God and the issue of blasphemy found in Mark 14.61–4 are treated towards the end of the public mission in the trial scene with 'the Jews' in 10.22–39, and the role of the high priest in securing the agreement of the Sanhedrin to put Jesus to death in Mark 14.63–4 is taken up in 11.47–53 in the account of Caiaphas' decision, at a meeting of the Sanhedrin, that Jesus is to die. As in Luke 22.67–71, in 10.22–39 John separates out the two issues of whether Jesus is Messiah and whether he is Son of God, and the opening of his dialogue in 10.24–5 – ' "if you are indeed the Christ, tell us plainly." Jesus answered them, "I told you, and you do not believe" ' – corresponds most closely to Luke 22.67–8 – ' "If you are the Christ, tell us." He replied, "If I tell you, you will not believe." ' John's story about the healing of a paralysed man on the sabbath in 5.1–18 leads into a trial scene, with the Jewish religious leaders interrogating Jesus about his identity in 5.19–47. For the healing story John has combined elements from Mark 2.1–12 about the healing of a paralysed man and Mark 3.1–6 about a healing on the sabbath, and Jesus' command to the man in 5.8 corresponds in wording to the command in Mark 2.9, 11. John, therefore, appears to know the controversy stories of Mark 2.1—3.6 but transforms such Synoptic controversies about the law, purity and table fellowship with sinners into extended interrogation scenes where what is at issue is Jesus' witness to his relationship as Son to God as his Father.

In the farewell discourse the evangelist has combined material from two farewell settings in Mark – Mark 13.1–37, where Jesus talks of a future coming of the Son of Man, and Mark 14.17–31, where he speaks of the Son of Man's going – and has reinterpreted Jesus' departure and return from his own distinctive perspective. It is here that he also deals with the continuation of the judgement process after Jesus' departure, as both the Spirit of truth as Advocate and the disciples continue Jesus' witness in a context where the disciples will be hated and face death (15.18—16.4a). All these elements have been developed from Mark 13.9–13 in particular, where the disciples are told that because of their allegiance to Jesus they will find themselves handed over to councils, beaten in synagogues and standing before governors and kings to bear witness to them. When they are brought to trial, however, they are not to be concerned about what to say, but to utter whatever is given to them at the time, because it will not be they who speak but the Holy Spirit. This will also be a period when they experience betrayal and death through the opposition of other family members and 'will be hated by all because of my name'. The judgement or trial motif receives further elaboration in John's passion narrative, primarily through the evangelist providing a much more extensive version of the Roman trial account in Mark 15.1–15 and making this the centrepiece of the passion narrative. All the changes to Mark's account can be explained by John's knowledge of the Matthean and Lukan versions and by his own stylistic and theological concerns. Illustrative of the latter is the way in which the exchange about kingship from Mark 15.2 is reworked to make kingship subordinate to Jesus' role in God's process of judgement – 'Pilate therefore said to him, "So, then, you are a king?" Jesus replied, "You say that I am a king. For this I was born and for this I came into the world, to bear witness to the truth. Everyone who is of the truth listens to my voice." '(18.37).

What should be clear from the preceding discussion is that the fourth evangelist handles his source material from the Synoptics with a creative and imaginative freedom in order to promote his own theological and persuasive ends. He is so thoroughly familiar with these earlier versions of the story of Jesus that, in reflecting on them in his own setting and in the light of the issues with which it confronts him, he is able to weave parts of them into his fresh attempt to set the story in a cosmic context and to penetrate the implications of its protagonist's unique relationship with God. In many ways to adopt this perspective is to return to what ancient interpreters meant by calling John a 'spiritual Gospel' in relation to the Synoptics. The evangelist supplements the other Gospels not so much by providing additional historical information about Jesus but by enhancing their portrayal of him through a further narrative that makes more explicit the significance of his oneness with God.

Further reading

For an account of twentieth-century research on this topic, see D. M. Smith, *John among the Gospels* (Minneapolis: Fortress, 1992). For the view that John is independent of the Synoptics, see C. H. Dodd, *Historical Tradition in the Fourth Gospel* (Cambridge: Cambridge University Press, 1963). For a variety of essays espousing John's dependence on the Synoptics, see A. Denaux (ed.), *John and the Synoptics* (Louvain: Louvain University Press, 1992).

HISTORICITY AND TRUTH

So far it has been argued that the Fourth Gospel is a carefully crafted narrative whose story line is carried along by means of major themes and that it belongs to the genre of ancient biography, in which there was a wide range of mixes of more reliable and more legendary elements. In regard to the mix found in the Fourth Gospel, it has also been argued that it is highly unlikely that its traditions stem from an eyewitness author, such as John, the son of Zebedee. In addition, the previous section has claimed that in those cases where the material in the Fourth Gospel overlaps with that in the Synoptics, the most likely explanation is that this is because the fourth evangelist knew and adapted for his own purposes parts of the Synoptic Gospels and that in doing so he exercised considerable creative freedom. This too has a bearing on the matter of John's historicity. One of the attractions, for some, of the opposing view that John has independently used oral traditions that were also employed by the Synoptics is that this makes the Gospel more likely to contain its own reliable historical sources (cf. esp. Dodd 1963). But if John has used the Synoptics, this obviously means that he can no longer be treated as an independent witness to the material that they have in common.

But what then of the materials that are unique to John? How should they be evaluated in terms of their likely historicity? Certainly there should be no initial prejudice, based on the conviction that only the Synoptics have any value for reconstructing the life of the historical Jesus, against such materials, which need to be assessed on a case-by-case basis. They can only be discussed briefly here and the commentary will provide somewhat fuller treatments of most of them in the appropriate places. It should also be remembered that conclusions about such matters will, of course, nearly always be in terms of greater or lesser probability. It should also be expected that, if ancient readers were both disinclined and frequently unable to disentangle the factual and the legendary, the paucity of evidence and sources and the lapse of so much time will make it a lot more difficult than is sometimes assumed for present-day readers to distinguish these elements clearly, and so sometimes a conclusion may need to be that the evidence is inconclusive. Frequently, even the most positive conclusion that can be reached is that a particular episode or saying goes back to the earliest layer of tradition and in that form may also therefore have some degree of probability for the setting of Jesus' mission, as best we can reconstruct the latter's contours.

The discourses or dialogues of Jesus for the most part contain material that is unique to this Gospel. Sometimes they may be built up from or include a reformulated Synoptic saying. Sometimes some piece of otherwise unknown oral tradition may lie behind Johannine sayings. It is not implausible, for example, that 5.19–20 is based on an earlier proverb about an apprentice son, as some have argued, or that the sayings about sowing, reaping and the harvest in 4.35–7 or about a grain of wheat in 12.24 have a traditional background, since Jesus is known from the Synoptics to have used such agricultural analogies in his teaching. But the bulk of the words unique to Jesus in this Gospel consist of major assertions about his own identity and mission, assertions in which he claims to have a unique relationship with God, to be aware of his pre-existence, to have the Father dwelling in him, to embody life or light or truth and to give his flesh as life for the world. Again the seeds for some of these assertions may be implicit in the Synoptic tradition, but, with the notable isolated exception of the saying found in Matt. 11.27 and Luke 10.22, there is nothing in the Synoptics to compare with this teaching that makes the identity of Jesus its explicit focus. If the profound Christological claims of the Fourth Gospel really corresponded to the words of the historical Jesus, it is quite implausible that none of the Synoptic evangelists would have picked them up. Instead these are the developed post-resurrection convictions about Jesus which have become contentious in the evangelist's own time and setting and have been read back into the teaching of Jesus and the disputes of his day. This conclusion is decisive for the judgement that the material in 5.18–47; 6.25–65; 8.12–59; 10.1-18, 22–39; 13.31—17.26 is secondary and makes it unlikely that the content of the conversations with Niocodemus (3.1–21) and the Samaritan woman (4.7–30) have any claim to be reliable historical tradition.

In terms of historicity, then, can a distinction perhaps be made in the material unique to John between the presentation of Jesus' identity in the speech material and the events in the story line with their geographical and chronological framework? The Synoptics give the impression that Jesus' mission lasted for a year, while John has it spread over a three-year period. Is not John's information more reliable at this point? The issue, however, is not quite as straightforward as this. Mark (followed by Matthew and Luke) actually shows no interest in the length of Jesus' ministry but, in composing what has been called his 'passion narrative with an extended introduction', has clustered together parables, conflict stories and miracles that may have happened over a much longer period in order to make them lead into the one visit to Jerusalem that he is interested in, namely Jesus' last one. He and his sources may well have assumed that, like other observant Jews, Jesus made other festival pilgrimages to Jerusalem, but he has no particular interest in these. The Q saying in which Jesus addresses Jerusalem and says, 'How often have I desired to gather your children together as a hen gathers her brood under her wings, and you were not willing' (Luke 13.34–5 and Matt. 23.37–8), strongly suggests that Jesus took his message to Jerusalem on more than just this one occasion. So it is highly probable that Jesus' mission lasted longer than a year, but this does not necessarily mean that John's account is therefore an accurate one. Since the first of Jesus' four visits to Jerusalem in the Fourth Gospel is to initiate the cleansing of the temple incident, which the Synoptics place far more plausibly toward the end of Jesus' mission as the catalyst for his arrest and death, this does not inspire confidence. And John does have a particular interest in the festivals, because he wishes to show that Jesus fulfils what they symbolize, and so it suits his purposes to have Jesus attend some of these in Jerusalem. The number of visits to festivals and the temple in John also produces its own problem for the plot. The hostile reception each time results in various unsuccessful attempts to kill, arrest or stone Jesus and in his unexplained escapes (cf. 5.18; 7.32, 45–6; 8.59; 10.31, 39), which appear rather contrived. Certainly the evangelist has a particular interest in Jesus' contacts with Jerusalem and he or his tradition have enough accurate topographical knowledge of the city to supply convincing settings for what may well be Johannine versions of Synoptic miracles in 5.1–18 and 9.1–12 (see the commentary on these passages). But, beyond the entirely plausible assumption that Jesus' mission lasted longer than a year, it is by no means clear that the chronological framework of the Fourth Gospel's narrative reflects more than literary and theological concerns at work.

Within the public mission of Jesus the first and the last signs – the turning of water into wine and the raising of Lazarus – are unique to the Fourth Gospel. Here it needs to be said that a negative historical evaluation on either or both of these incidents should not be dismissed as the result of bias against the miraculous. It is not inconsistent, for example, to believe in the resurrection of Jesus or to find it probable that he was able to heal miraculously and still to hold on literary and historical grounds that a particular account of some other miracle is unlikely to be reliable. In the case of turning water into wine, as the commentary shows in some detail, problems arise from the strangely allusive recounting of the actual miracle and the way in which the reactions of those involved are not reported and only the disciples, who were not involved and whose understanding of the occurrence is not explained, are said to have believed. In addition, almost all the key ingredients that make this story a sign belong to specifically Johannine stylistic structures, literary motifs and theological themes. These include the mention of Jesus' address to and relationship with his mother, the pattern of request, rebuff and then response on Jesus' own terms, the motifs of the hour and of the ignorance of the origin of Jesus' gift, the theme of the fulfilment/replacement of the significance of Jewish religious observances, and the symbolism of the wine as the abundance Jesus provides for living and of the wedding at which Jesus is the true bridegroom. If one were to remove most of these, there would be very little indeed left of any underlying incident. More basically, the story's essential content depends on a belief about Jesus that arose only after the resurrection, namely, that he was a divine being who was able to transform one of the four elements. This accounts also for the closest parallels to and likely influences on the story coming from the traditions about Dionysus. This legendary story enables John to begin the mission of Jesus with the bold claim that the abundant life offered by this Jewish Messiah who is one with God not only surpasses the provision of the law but also the claims made on behalf of rival gods.

Some different factors have to be taken into account in assessing the story of the raising of Lazarus. This story is crucial to the Fourth Gospel's plot, because it, and not the temple incident, as in the Synoptics, precipitates the actions of the authorities leading to Jesus' death. It is far less historically plausible in this pivotal role than Jesus' symbolic action in the temple designed to disrupt the sacrificial system. The core action in the episode, the raising of a dead person, does, however, have attestation from the Synoptic tradition. The raising of Jairus' daughter and the son of the widow of Nain are found in Mark 5.21–43 parr. and Luke 7.11–17 respectively, and the Q saying (Luke 7.22; Matt. 11.5), in the report of Jesus' ministry to be relayed to the imprisoned John the Baptist, mentions that 'the dead are raised'. Evidently reports about Jesus' power to raise the dead circulated from a very early stage. But the present form of John's story, with its particular figures and their characterization, its other literary features and its clearly Johannine theological themes in the dialogue, appears to be a skilful composition on the part of the evangelist, in which the named characters Martha, Mary and Lazarus have been taken over from Luke's Gospel (Luke 10.38–42; 16.19–31). John's narrative could well be a very extensive literary elaboration based on the general tradition that Jesus raised the dead or on one particular tradition of the raising of a dead man, which he has set in Bethany and associated with a family said to be close to Jesus, and whose miraculous character he has heightened by having the dead man already in the tomb for four days.

While the change in the Fourth Gospel's portrayal of John the Baptist from the Synoptic prophet of coming judgement to this Gospel's witness to its high Christology is clearly a secondary feature, its presentation of the early part of Jesus' mission as, unlike the Synoptics, having Jesus and John the Baptist operating at the same time and Jesus also baptizing (3.22–36) is another matter. This feature of the account has been deemed historically accurate by a significant number of scholars. They suggest that Mark, followed by Matthew and Luke, has good literary and theological reasons for its clear sequence in which John the Baptist's mission is completed before that of Jesus begins. They then argue that, if the historical Jesus was baptized by John and held him in high regard, it would make sense that initially he would have spent some time with John and under his influence practised similar baptismal rites. One problem here is with the term 'similar'. Proponents of this view do not agree on what was entailed in Jesus' baptizing activity, with some considering that Jesus' baptism merely continued the significance of John's, others supposing that it had its own distinctive significance, and some holding that it was a temporary phenomenon (which is a conjecture, since the Fourth Gospel tells us no such thing) and others that it continued throughout Jesus' mission. Those who hold that it simply continued the significance of John's baptism also argue that the evangelist or his tradition would not have created an incident which suggests Jesus simply continued John the Baptist's baptism and its significance, because this would have been an embarrassment, as in the case of Jesus' baptism by John, where it is agreed that the latter is almost certain to be historical since it would not have been invented. But this argument appears to backfire. Given that the fourth evangelist had already gone to such lengths to show John's subordinate role and had suppressed Jesus' baptism by John in the process, it becomes extremely difficult to imagine that he would now include such a tradition if he understood it to involve Jesus simply carrying on John's baptism. If it is held, as other scholars do, that, for Jesus, baptizing constituted a sign that those baptized had accepted his new message about the kingdom of God, had entered into its reality and had become his disciples, then his baptism takes on a significance akin to the later Christian rite and it becomes almost incredible that the Synoptics and the Fourth Gospel elsewhere fail even to hint that this was part of people's response to Jesus' message. If the origins of Christian baptism lay in a practice initiated by Jesus himself, which had a different meaning from John's baptism, it is extremely hard to see why there is no indication of this important link between the church and its founder in other early Christian writings. There are in fact no strong reasons to doubt that the Synoptics, which are substantially reliable in their other information about John the Baptist's mission, are right that that mission concluded with his arrest and imprisonment before that of Jesus began. At the same time, given John's pervasive rewriting of the Baptist tradition in order to establish Jesus' superiority, it is not hard to see why he would also have wanted to show that baptizing with water, which had become a major feature of Christian initiation, is not to be thought of as the earlier exclusive prerogative of John but that Jesus and/or his followers had also engaged in this activity, which went back to the same period as John the Baptist's activity (see the discussion of 4.2 in the commentary). This enables the two baptisms to be juxtaposed within the narrative and a clear answer to be given from the mouth of John himself about which of the two is to be endorsed. The contemporaneity of the two missions also provides the appropriate setting for John's announcement, 'He must increase, but I must decrease.' The evidence about the early part of Jesus' career is meagre, but the above considerations should give pause to any confidence that the Fourth Gospel provides accurate information at this point and indicate that at best this account contains material of uncertain historical value.

If we move from the beginning of the Gospel to the end, what can be said about the material unique to John in the passion narrative? Does this have a greater claim to historical reliability? On such matters as the washing of the disciples' feet, the involvement of the Romans in Jesus' arrest and the interrogation before Annas, readers should consult the appropriate places in the commentary. Here we can only discuss briefly the major difference between John and the Synoptics on the date of the last supper and the death of Jesus. Despite the attempts of some to harmonize the two or to suggest reckoning according to different calendars, the most straightforward interpretation of their narratives is that Mark (followed by Matthew and Luke) presents Jesus' last meal with his disciples as a Passover meal and has Jesus die later on the same day, 15 Nisan, whereas John has the meal and the death on the preceding day, 14 Nisan, the day of preparation for the Passover. Mark 14.12–16 makes it clear that the preparations for the meal take place the preceding day, 'when the Passover lamb is sacrificed', and that the preparations are for the Passover meal. In Mark 14.17–25 the meal itself is set in the evening, at the beginning of the next day, when the Passover meal was supposed to be eaten, and, although the term 'Passover' is not now used (but cf. Luke 22.15), what is described is completely compatible with what readers have been led to expect. Mark's interest is, of course, in Jesus' words about his death and betrayal and in the interpretation he gives to the bread and the wine. A Passover celebration would have included interpretation of the various elements in the meal – the meat of the Passover offering, the unleavened bread and the bitter herbs. Jesus gives a new interpretation of the bread and adds to this an interpretation of the wine that would have accompanied the meal. The Hallel psalms (Pss 113–18) were supposed to be sung at Passover and Mark's account mentions the singing of one of these at the end of the meal. John's account is quite different. There is nothing in the account of the last meal to suggest that it is a Passover meal and there are no words of interpretation of bread and wine. Instead the chronological setting for the meal is 'before the festival of Passover' (13.1) and there is an indication in the account of this meal that the

Passover meal is still future (13.29). After Jesus is arrested later on the same day and eventually put on trial before Pilate, there are two further time references in regard to Passover. In 18.28 those who take Jesus to Pilate are said not to enter the praetorium because they did not want to become ritually impure but to be able to eat the Passover. Again the Passover meal remains a future event. The precise dating becomes clear in 19.14 – 'now it was the day of preparation for the Passover'. The dating is repeated in the crucifixion account in 19.31, where its significance for the interpretation of Jesus' death also becomes apparent, because, after the report that the soldiers did not break Jesus' legs (19.33), it is then stated in 19.36 that 'these things happened in order that the scripture might be fulfilled, "None of his bones will be broken." ' This takes up texts about the Passover lamb (Exod. 12.46; Num. 9.12) and the righteous sufferer (Ps. 34.20). Jesus' death is to be seen as that of the true Passover lamb (cf. also 1.29, 36) and it takes place on the day of preparation, the time of the slaughter of the Passover lambs. Thereby it fulfils and replaces the significance of the death of the Passover sacrificial victims.

In theory, both accounts might be wrong, but, given that there is no reason to doubt that Jesus died around the time of Passover and assuming that one of the two earliest conflicting traditions is likely to be right, again a significant number of scholars hold that here it is John, and not Mark, who has the accurate dating. The arguments are, however, fairly evenly balanced. Those who prefer John's dating have three main arguments. The first is that the nature and amount of activities that Mark's account places on the day of Passover tell against it; the schedule is too packed and its activities would not have been permitted on this special feast day. The second is that, since the Christian Lord's Supper was seen in terms of the Passover, Mark or his tradition thought that the last supper should also be depicted as a Passover meal. The third argument claims that the theological interpretation in John's account – the synchronicity between Jesus' death and the slaughter of the Passover lambs – is not explained but works only through subtle allusion and therefore it does not appear that John has created the chronology on the basis of a prior theological conviction. None of these arguments is especially compelling. Presenting Jesus' arrest, trial and crucifixion within a twelve-hour period is a problem, but it is a problem for John as much as for Mark. The problem is simply shifted to one day earlier, and most of the activities that were usually not permitted on the day of Passover would also not have been permitted on the eve of a festival. But in any case the regulations appealed to are taken from the later Mishnah and may not have been in force earlier, and there were plenty of instances in which exceptional circumstances were allowed to override laws. As regards the second argument, if John's dating were right, Mark or his tradition would be erasing the clear symbolism of Jesus as the Passover lamb in order to create a link between Passover and the celebration of the Christian eucharist, which was not at all necessary, since the eucharist was not tied to the annual Passover but observed far more frequently. The motivation for such a change would appear to require a far more convincing explanation. In addition, the tables can be turned at this point and it can be claimed about Mark what the third argument suggests about John. In Mark 14.17–25 the evangelist can simply assume the various elements of the Passover meal. If Mark was changing an earlier tradition or creating a new one, he would have made sure all the Passover aspects of the meal were more explicit. The third argument is the weakest. John does give very clear clues in order to alert his readers to the significance he is attaching to Jesus' death. His Jewish readers would not need any explanation that the day of preparation was the day of the slaughter of the lambs. But then John alone has added to his account of the crucifixion the report that the soldiers did not break Jesus' legs and an accompanying Scripture text to draw out the point he is making. Add to this that his account alone has the strange mention of hyssop (19.29), which recalls the hyssop used to sprinkle the blood of the Passover lamb on the doors of the Israelites' houses (Exod. 12.22), and it can be seen that he provides a variety of pointers to the meaning he wants to convey. What is more, this particular motif of Jesus' death as that of the true Passover lamb fits one of John's other major theological concerns, namely, to show Jesus as the fulfilment and replacement of the symbolism of the Jewish festivals. To say, as some do, that there are solid grounds for preferring John's dating is to make an entirely misleading claim. If anything, the previous observations about the way John's theological concerns have shaped his account outweigh anything that can be demonstrated about Mark's concerns and tilt the balance of probabilities in favour of the historicity of Mark's dating. And if, as we have argued, John knew and used Mark, then that too supports the view that John's dating is a modification, similar to others, introduced into the narrative for theological rather than historical purposes.

Enough examples have now been discussed to indicate that very little of the material unique to John can be said with any confidence to provide additional reliable historical information about the life of Jesus. The implication of such a conclusion is that, as regards historicity, for the most part the assessment of John's Gospel is dependent on the assessment of the Synoptic accounts that this Gospel has taken up, modified and embellished for its own purposes. If, as appears highly likely, the core of those Synoptic traditions of deeds and sayings, which have been creatively incorporated into the Fourth Gospel, provides reliable historical reminiscence about the mission of Jesus, then this Gospel's own retelling of the story has the same foundations. We are now in a position to appreciate more fully the force of the earlier discussion about genre. The Fourth Gospel, like many other ancient biographies, is a narrative which contains a substratum of core events from the tradition with substantial claims to reliability, but one which is now shaped by an interpretive superstructure which contains a considerable amount of embellishment, including some legendary or fictive elements. More specifically, the Fourth Gospel's interpretive superstructure is determined by the evangelist's theological convictions arising from his post-resurrection faith and its development in particular circumstances. He allows his interpretive framework to pervade his life of Jesus far more extensively than do the Synoptic evangelists, who, of course, also shape their biographies according to their distinctive theological concerns.

In several places the Fourth Gospel reflects awareness of this narrative strategy. It indicates that the significance being attached to events is a result of the disciples' later remembrance in the light of their post-resurrection belief and accompanying fresh understanding of their Scriptures (cf. 2.17, 22; 12.16; 13.7). Frequently the moulding of the story of Jesus by the concerns of a later perspective is such that the two are collapsed together and Jesus, in the setting of his mission and in debate with his opponents, expresses the convictions of the evangelist and his community in their debates with opponents. One striking instance of this compression of the two perspectives is the account of the giving of sight to the man born blind (9.1–41), where the repercussions of the healing miracle very soon begin to reflect the repercussions of belief in Jesus in the later situation. This is clearly signalled in the central scene, in which the parents of the man born blind are said to fear 'the Jews', because the latter had already agreed that anyone who confessed Jesus to be the Messiah should be put out of the synagogue (9.22). All the aspects of this description are anachronistic in respect to Jesus' earthly mission and pertain to the situation faced by later Johannine Jewish Christians. This sort of phenomenon has led to the Gospel being described as a 'two-level drama' (Martyn 1979: 60). Some have claimed that recent study has undermined the notion of the narrative working at two levels. It has done nothing of the sort. It has simply raised some questions about particular ways in which this insight has been developed by certain scholars. The narrative's clear merging of perspectives is attributed by the Gospel itself to the guidance of the Spirit. In the physical absence of Jesus, the Advocate continues his teaching role, enabling Jesus' followers to remember constructively his words and deeds in a way that makes the past contemporary and helps to form their future (cf. 14.26). The function of the Spirit is to witness to the significance of Jesus and its implications and thereby, as the Spirit of truth, lead believers into all the truth (15.26; 16.13). The evangelist's contemporizing interpretive narrative is part of this truth. And since the Spirit also takes what belongs to Jesus and declares it to his followers (16.14–15), from the point of view of the Gospel it is indeed Jesus who speaks in its narrative, not so much the earthly Jesus but the exalted Jesus who speaks through the Spirit to his followers' present needs. In the Gospel's epilogue the evangelist's interpretive embellishment of the tradition is attributed to the witness of the Beloved Disciple and the final writer and his community endorse that testimony as true (21.24).

How are such truth claims to be related to the conclusions reached about the Gospel's historicity? The two matters are related but should not be confused, as has frequently been the case. It needs to be underlined that a claim to truth is specific to whatever genre is under discussion. There is the truth of a poem, of a historical monograph, of a scientific treatise, of a novel, or, in the case of the Fourth Gospel, of an ancient biography, since that is the form its witness takes. As has been discussed earlier, to judge the integrity or truth of such a biography on the basis of either ancient or modern historiography is simply to misunderstand the literary tradition of which it is a part and to make a category mistake. The question of the Fourth Gospel's truth is rather this: does it, through its mixture of tradition and creative interpretation, reliably draw out the significance of the life which it narrates? Such a question in fact coheres with this Gospel's own notion of truth, which, in its most general sense, stands for the reality of God's revelation in Christ. But, as has been noted earlier, the concept takes on a distinctive force through its association with the judgement or trial motif and its Scriptural presuppositions. As part of the latter, truth is frequently paired with righteous judgement or justice (cf. e.g. Isa. 42.3; 45.19; 48.1; 59.14). For God to judge justly is for God to determine, declare and demonstrate the truth. In the context of a trial, then, truth will stand for the whole process of judging, culminating in the verdict, and its specific content will be dependent on the particular issue at stake. According to 20.31, the issue in this Gospel is whether a particular Jew, Jesus of Nazareth, is the Messiah, the Son of God, and, from the rest of the narrative discourse it can be added, therefore one with God. The discourse's depiction of the relation between Jesus and God also justifies putting the issue the other way around. As it concerns God, it is whether God is the God who is now known in the crucified Jesus and whether through him God has effected a judgement that means life for the world. Truth is the affirmative judgement on these interrelated issues and can even be said to be embodied in Jesus. The notion of truth, then, is far more comprehensive than matters of historicity, and the use of ancient biography as the vehicle for witnessing to this truth means that it was not confused with the factual accuracy of its narrative.

Once this is clear, the overlap between this truth and history can also be stressed. As with other ancient biographers, it is important for the fourth evangelist that his subject actually existed; in this case it is essential, given his claim that this was the Word who became flesh (1.14). It is also important that the broad contours of the life narrated cohere with what he and his readers would know from elsewhere about the subject – that, for example, he was a Jewish teacher who attracted disciples, performed miracles, said things about God and God's relation to Israel and the world that provoked controversy and led to hostility towards him on the part of the religious authorities, was arrested, put on trial, crucified by the Romans and then raised from the dead. With this foundation of basic features from the historical tradition in place, the evangelist employs the other conventions of ancient biographies, such as embellishment and invention, to devote his narrative to drawing out the all-important truth of this particular life. When the final writer and his community confirm the truth of this witness, they do so, among other reasons, because they trust the perspective of the Beloved Disciple, because they find it plausible and in line with whatever they already know about the traditions of Jesus' life and death, and because this interpretation of the significance of that life and death provides a persuasive explanation of and vision for their experience of life in the world as a particular group of Christian believers. Later Christian readers gave a further, similar endorsement to the Fourth Gospel's truth claims as they acknowledged its canonical status.

Late-modern readers bring a distinctive set of concerns about history to their engagement with this Gospel. They are heirs of the Enlightenment preoccupation with what actually happened in the past and its accompanying series of quests for the historical Jesus. At the same time they share the more recent recognition that all historical 'facts' already involve interpretation and its accompanying perception that the writing of history is also the writing of narrative containing inevitable elements of fictionalization. It is inevitable and valid that such readers will continue to pursue historical criticism in a chastened fashion, as our earlier discussion has attempted to do with its talk of core historical traditions, material of dubious historical quality and legendary elements. The probable results of that criticism in regard to how much historical tradition and how much fiction-like embellishment this Gospel contains need not, however, provide any obstacle to a potential recognition of its truth. Indeed, as we have seen, in regard to the truth of the narrative in its own terms, the attempt to disentangle precisely how much of the detail is historically reliable and how much is fictive misses the point. Such attempts need to be pursued as rigorously as possible and will always be contested but they will not provide the determinative criteria of truth by which this Gospel is to be judged.

Further reading

For a very different, maximalist assessment of John's historicity, based on the Gospel's author being the disciple John, the son of Zebedee, see C. L. Blomberg, *The Historical Reliability of John's Gospel* (Leicester: Inter-Varsity Press, 2001). For a critical minimalist assessment, see M. Casey, *Is John's*

Gospel True? (London: Routledge, 1996). For a fuller discussion of truth and its appropriation in relation to the Fourth Gospel, see A. T. Lincoln, *Truth on Trial* (Peabody, Mass.: Hendrickson, 2000), esp. 354–454.

COMPOSITION OF THE GOSPEL AND RELATION TO OTHER JOHANNINE LITERATURE

The commentary attempts to make sense of the final form of the Gospel. Only in relation to the most obvious signs of editing, such as hymn-like material behind the prologue or the gloss in 4.2 or the second part of the farewell discourse in 15.1—16.31 or the epilogue in 21.1–25, does it refer to the history of the Gospel's composition. Yet, as these examples indicate, there are a number of awkward features of the narrative which provoke questions about how it was composed and what design or process lay behind it. But detecting signs of editorial work is one thing; reconstructing the process of composition with any precision is another. Even the attempt to sketch what might be its main stages involves inevitable guesswork.

Yet there is evidence that points to such a process. Much of this consists of perplexing or apparently faulty connections, which scholars call aporias. It might be claimed that some of these difficulties are in the eye of the beholder or can be plausibly explained without going behind the present narrative. But the latter type of explanations often stretch credibility too far and most of the following examples do require some hypothesis that takes into account the history of the text's composition. Within the prologue, for example, 1.15 ('This was he of whom I said ...') is a strange introduction to a statement by John the Baptist, when there is no report of him saying anything earlier, and when the statement will be repeated later in 1.30. The healing of the official's son is called Jesus' second sign in 4.54, yet, after turning water into wine, Jesus had done other signs before this one (cf. 2.23). The transition between chapters 5 and 6 is extremely awkward geographically. The setting for chapter 5 is Jerusalem and then without any indication of Jesus leaving Jerusalem, 6.1 states that after this Jesus went to the other side of the Sea of Galilee. In 7.1–13 there is a discussion between Jesus and his brothers in which they urge him to go to Judaea and the upcoming festival in Jerusalem so that he can perform his miracles publicly. Again, however, Jesus had already been doing signs in Jerusalem (2.23–5; 3.2) and 5.1–18 reported another such miracle. Similarly, there is a discussion between Jesus and 'the Jews' in 7.19–24, in which Jesus attributes their hostility towards him to the 'one work' he has performed, namely, the healing on the sabbath. But this is reported back in 5.1–18 and, according to 6.1—7.1, Jesus had been involved in a range of activities in Galilee since then. The debate in

7.19–24 with Jesus' mention of the opposition's trying to kill him (7.19, cf. 5.18) looks as though it ought to follow on from the healing in chapter 5. At the beginning of the Lazarus story, his sister, Mary, is introduced in 11.2 as if her anointing of Jesus' feet in 12.1–8 had already taken place. After Jesus is said to have gone into hiding in 12.36b, he immediately makes a public proclamation in 12.44–50. Notoriously, 'Rise, let us go from here' in 14.31 brings Jesus' farewell discourse to an end, but that discourse then continues for two chapters, as though the words had not been uttered, and Jesus also offers an extended prayer in chapter 17 before 14.31 finds its natural continuation in 18.1. Similarly, the narrative appears to come to its conclusion with the statement of purpose in 20.30–1 but it then continues in chapter 21 with a further conclusion in 21.24–5.

Other awkward features could be mentioned, but why do they appear in what is otherwise such a carefully crafted piece of writing? Some have attempted to explain them by claiming that the original Gospel accidentally became disordered and then an editor attempted not very successfully to piece it together. A number of those who take this route then attempt their own elaborate rearrangements of the order, which usually also run into their own set of problems of coherence. Bultmann's outstanding commentary (1971) provides the classic example of this approach. Like a number of other proponents of this approach, however, he fails to explain the practicalities of displacement and rearrangement of an original written either on a papyrus scroll or in a codex. A better, and less speculative, explanation of the phenomena we have listed is that which posits a number of stages of composition and revision. The suggestion made here involves three main stages. The briefest way of outlining this approach and showing how it deals with the aporias is to set out the content of the first version that results from its analysis and then to indicate the revisions that must have been made in order to have produced the version we now have in 1.1—20.31. The addition of chapter 21 at a third stage will then be treated.

The first version of the Gospel would have begun with the material on John the Baptist and the gathering of disciples and then narrated Jesus' mission in Galilee and Samaria, with the two Cana miracles framing this Galilean period. This was followed by the conversation between Jesus and his brothers about going public and taking his mission to Judaea and Jerusalem. The narrative then moved to a period of mission in Jerusalem, in which two miracles – the healings of the paralytic and of the man born blind – frame various encounters between Jesus and the religious authorities. The material in our present chapter 10 followed, with vv. 40–2 providing an *inclusio* with the initial John the Baptist account and concluding the first half of this version. The second half then began with the entry into Jerusalem and the temple incident. The account of the latter in 2.13–22 in any case contains indications that it belongs to this later context with its notion that Jesus' zeal will consume him, its use of the false witness statement from Mark's Sanhedrin trial, and the talk of the disciples remembering Scripture, which elsewhere is found only in the account of the entry into Jerusalem. After this came the decision of Caiaphas and the Sanhedrin to put Jesus to death. An anointing story followed, then the Johannine version of Jesus' Gethsemane prayer and a summary of his mission, as found in our present 12.36b–43. The narrative then moved to Jesus' last meal with the disciples and his farewell speech up to our present 14.31. Next came the passion narrative proper with accounts of the arrest, interrogation, Roman trial, crucifixion, burial and resurrection, and this first version ended with the present 20.30–1. Most of this material was substantially in its present Johannine form. As has been observed, Johannine style and thought is so pervasive as to make it virtually impossible to find earlier layers of tradition by stripping it away. For this reason also it makes good sense to see the subsequent revisions and rearrangements being made by the same person who composed the earlier version.

The second main stage of composition involved this sort of reworking. The first version had begun with the wording of 1.6 – 'there was a man sent from God, whose name was John' (cf. the introduction of the Samson and Samuel stories in Judg. 13.2; 1 Sam 1.1). Its place is now taken by the prologue, with its exalted poetic style and its treatment of the Logos who became flesh. But instead of simply displacing the original opening, the revision incorporates part of this within the prologue (1.6–8, 15) along with the writer's own comments on the hymnic material. He also decides that he will introduce the theme of Jesus as the new temple much earlier and moves the temple incident so that it now follows on from the first sign of turning water into wine. This is part of a major new literary strategy in which the public mission will be structured around a number of journeys to Jerusalem for the major festivals. It means also that the material about Jesus' signs and the encounter with Nicodemus can be introduced here, with the latter providing an appropriate counterpoint to the encounter with the Samaritan woman. The evangelist has developed material on the feeding of the five thousand connected with an extensive midrashic interpretation of Jesus as the bread of life. This he inserts into the Jerusalem period of the first version, placing it after Jesus' extended defence of his healing of the paralytic, because this concludes with a reference to Scripture witnessing to and Moses writing about Jesus, and the bread of life discourse provides a showcase example of how they do so. The discussion between Jesus and his brothers that had led into the Jerusalem period of the earlier version is moved so that it comes after the new Galilean episode of chapter 6 and introduces instead another visit to Jerusalem for a festival. Since the temple incident has been switched to near the beginning of Jesus' mission, this leaves a gap in the plot. Its function is replaced by the Lazarus story, which is now inserted before the entry into Jerusalem and made the major factor provoking Jesus' arrest and death. The story has to be integrated into the surrounding material from the first version. This is accomplished by making the Sanhedrin decision the immediate aftermath of raising Lazarus and by associating the anointing story with the Bethany family. The effects of the Lazarus story are also made to spill over into the account of the entry into Jerusalem. As a result of these changes, the first half of the second version now ends with the material in chapter 12, where a summary of Jesus' mission on his own lips is added at the end. There is far less scope for change with the second half of the first version. The sequence is fixed, but within that sequence new material can be added, and so the further teaching on discipleship in the form of the discourse in chapters 15 and 16 and of Jesus' prayer in chapter 17 is inserted after the ending of the original discourse.

Like the first version, the second version ended with the statement of purpose in 20.30–1. It is unlikely that the epilogue of chapter 21 was part of the second stage of revision. Despite its continuities with the second version, this chapter also introduces some major tensions and discontinuities (see the commentary for details). Among the discontinuities are some differences of style and these suggest not just a later addition but also a different hand. So, while the first version and its revisions can be substantially attributed to the same writer, the evangelist, chapter 21 would be the work of a final editor. It is in this chapter, of course, that authorship of the Gospel as a whole is attributed by the final editor to the Beloved Disciple, and it may be that the literary device of the Beloved Disciple, based on a revered teacher in the community who has now died, was introduced and integrated into the earlier part of the narrative at this late stage. In regard to the Beloved Disciple materials in the Gospel, there are two main possibilities. One is that the evangelist responsible for the first and second versions was someone other than the Beloved Disciple but had been influenced by this teacher and had already begun to employ him as the idealized Beloved Disciple in the interpretation of the passion and resurrection accounts. This process would then have been continued by the final editor, who also attributes the authority for the whole tradition lying behind the narrative to the Beloved Disciple. The second possibility is that it was this revered teacher, the Beloved Disciple himself, who was responsible for the composition of 1.1—20.31. His work was completely anonymous and the final editor, who composed chapter 21 and attributed the Gospel to the Beloved Disciple, was the one who also added the earlier references to the Beloved Disciple as part of his further editing of the whole narrative for broad circulation. These additions to the earlier narrative, which make the Beloved Disciple the ideal witness and author, would then have served to bolster this teacher's authoritative interpretation of the life of Jesus in the bulk of the Gospel.

The details of this hypothesis would need further justification, but if its broad features are anywhere near right, it would mean that thematic considerations related to changing circumstances were most influential in the evangelist's revision of his work. The minor anomalies in details of chronology and geography introduced by the revisions, if they were noticed at all, were obviously of far less importance than the theological points that needed to be made through the addition of fresh material and the new structuring of Jesus' public mission. The final editor's work was limited to additions, primarily chapter 21, minor glosses and possibly material about the Beloved Disciple. He clearly did not see fit to do any radical revisions that might have eliminated the anomalies produced by the second version. In favour of this reconstruction is that it accounts for the main aporias without becoming over-complicated. It also fits with the conclusions arrived at independently and on other grounds about the Gospel's relationship to the Synoptics and historicity. The suggested use of the Synoptics holds for both main versions, and, interestingly, the structure of the first version looks very much like the framework of Mark's narrative. The reshaping of the public mission around journeys to Jerusalem was dictated by literary and theological reasons rather than by the evangelist at a very late stage being in receipt of traditions with additional historical information. The emphases of the new material supplied in the second version also fit with the most likely view of the developments in the evangelist's community that are reflected in the narrative as a whole. There is an insistence on the reality of Jesus' flesh and on his suffering in the flesh (in the prologue and in chapter 6); there is an indication of worsening relationships between Jewish Christians and the synagogue (especially in 15.18—16.4a); there is a heightening of the theme that Jesus now fulfils and replaces the institutions and symbols of Judaism (through the moving of the temple incident and the restructuring of the public mission); and there is an underlining of the need for unity (in chapter 17). The section on Setting below will take the discussion of these developments further. It remains only to suggest approximate dates for the various versions of the Gospel. Since the first version already reflects the issue of the break with the synagogue through expulsion, it would appear to have been written in the mid-80s and the revised version would have followed in the early 90s with the addition of the epilogue before circulation towards the end of that decade.

What materials the evangelist and his community had before the composition of the first version and before their acquaintance with the Synoptics has to be the subject of even more speculation. We are probably safe in assuming at least the following. They were heirs of oral traditions about the basic Christian gospel message of the saving significance of the death and resurrection of Jesus, including some knowledge of the Pauline version of this message. They would also have been familiar with the same sort of traditions about the life and teaching of Jesus that lie behind Mark and are represented in the Q source. They had already begun to reflect on both types of tradition in the light of their own circumstances and of their own knowledge of the Jewish Scriptures, finding fresh links and interpretations. Finally, the distinctive style of the Johannine discourses would have already begun to emerge, so that pronouncements in the name of Jesus, expressed in their own idiom and offering insight into their own setting, would have been features of their own assemblies. Both inspired utterances and more extensive homilies using this mode of direct address from Jesus would have been attributed to the working of the Spirit in prophets and teachers, among them the evangelist in particular.

In relation to the composition of the Gospel, interpreting the traditions about Jesus for present circumstances, through knowledge of the Synoptics and in the light of the Scriptures, has been seen to be the work of at least two and possibly three people – the Beloved Disciple and the evangelist, who may or may not have been the same person, and the final editor. It was common for an influential teacher to have followers who continued his mode of teaching. It is usually held that the deutero-Pauline letters were produced by followers of Paul who continued his method of communicating the message to his churches after his death. It is likely that from such a group associated with the Beloved Disciple came not only those involved in the composition of the Gospel but also those who produced the other Johannine literature in the New Testament – the three Johannine letters and possibly Revelation. Traditionally, since the time of Irenaeus (e.g. *Haer.* 3.11.1; 4.20.11), the Gospel, the epistles and Revelation were all thought to be by one author, the apostle John. Only Revelation claims to be written by a John (1.1, 4, 9; 22.8), and 2 and 3 John are by an unnamed elder, but once the tradition that the Gospel was written by John, the son of Zebedee, was in place, and given the similarities among the writings, it appeared a natural move to identify the evangelist, the elder and the seer as the same person, the apostle John.

Defenders of the common authorship of all five documents (whether by the apostle or by the elder) can still be found, but this is very much a minority view in recent scholarship, which prefers to explain similarities and differences by positing that the writings come from the group of teachers associated with the original Beloved Disciple, sometimes loosely called a 'Johannine school', or from a common church context in Asia Minor. The Gospel's closest links are with the epistles. Whatever the order in which these letters were written, there are no strong reasons for doubting that they were both composed by the same person, the elder of 2 John 1 and 3 John 1. There are, however, stronger reasons for doubting that this person was also the evangelist. On the one hand, as has been observed earlier, the style and language of the Johannine Jesus are closer to those of these epistles than they are to the Jesus of the Synoptics. The clear similarities between the Gospel and the epistles include use of the same major themes of light, life, death, testimony, truth, love, abiding, and an ethical dualism, in which the world is seen as the sphere of unbelief and as hating believers. On the other hand, there are also subtle differences of style, with more grammatical obscurity observable in the epistles, and different uses of shared themes, so that some concepts associated with Jesus in the Gospel are associated with God in the epistles and, in contrast to the Gospel, the Spirit is not designated as the Paraclete in the epistles, whereas Jesus is (though Jesus as Paraclete is also an implication of John 14.16). In contrast to the dominant realized eschatology of the Gospel, the eschatology of the epistles is future-oriented and includes an expectation of Jesus' imminent return (1 John 2.28; 3.2–3). Terms such as 'glory' and 'seek', which occur frequently in the Gospel, are absent from the epistles; key terms in the epistles, such as 'antichrist', 'anointing' and 'fellowship', are not found in the Gospel. It is particularly striking that the epistles contain no citations from or mention of Scripture and only one reference to a scriptural character – Cain (1 John 3.12). There are also no hints of the conflict between Jewish Christians and the synagogue and instead conflict is within the church. In the first two epistles there is talk of those who, from the point of view of the writer, have seceded from the churches because they have a defective understanding of Jesus that denies his humanity has importance for salvation (1 John 2.18–23; 4.2–3; 2 John 7) and a defective notion of ethics in which they boast of fellowship with God while continuing to sin and denying such sin (1 John 1.6, 8, 10; 2.4–6; 3.6–8). These two errors could well have been related, so that if Jesus' life in the flesh was unimportant, what they themselves did in the flesh also would not matter. In the brief and enigmatic third epistle the conflict is between the elder and a certain Diotrephes. A plausible explanation of the references is that, in a situation where church structures had been informal, Diotrephes, seeing the need for authoritative leaders in order to combat false teaching, had earned the disapproval of the elder by arrogating too much authority to himself.

Though some hold that the epistles (or at least 1 John) precede the Gospel and some that their relationship is one of building on common Johannine tradition, most scholars consider that the situation they address is one that derives from different understandings of the thought contained in the Gospel, especially the implications of its portrayal of Jesus, and that they were written later. What is deemed false teaching appears to be incipiently docetic, moving towards the view that Christ only appeared to be human. The Gospel's depiction of a Jesus who has come from above and who at times has divine rather than ordinary human characteristics could have given rise to this tendency when taken up by those, perhaps Gentile Christians, who did not share the original presuppositions of the Gospel's writer. It is also possible that the second version of the Gospel was being completed at roughly the same time as the issues reflected in 1 and 2 John were emerging, since it appears in places to have their situation in view, and that the final redaction of the Gospel coincides with the emergence of the issues reflected in 3 John, since in chapter 21 it too has an eye on matters of ecclesiastical authority. In any case, the epistles originated from a leader within the same group of churches with which the evangelist and the final editor of the Gospel were also associated. The Gospel's relation to Revelation is a far more disputed matter. Critics of the view of common authorship can be found from early on, such as Dionysius and Eusebius in the third and fourth centuries. The author of Revelation does not refer to himself as an apostle and appears to distance himself from the apostles, who are seen as figures of the past, part of the church's foundation (21.14). Nor, for that matter, does he designate himself 'the elder'. Instead, the seer thinks of himself as a prophet (1.3; 22.6, 7, 9, 10, 19). Clear differences in style and content have been enough to convince most that the 'John' of Revelation is not the writer of the Gospel. The quality of his Greek usage is much inferior and the way he employs the Jewish Scriptures diverges markedly from that of the Gospel. Although he is steeped in the Scriptures, his use of them is always by means of allusion with no actual citations. Some words characteristic of one document do not appear in the other, so that, for example, 'truth' and 'joy', which are common in the Gospel, are absent from Revelation and, conversely, 'endurance' and 'wisdom', which are found in Revelation, are absent from John. The obvious major difference of content is in the area of eschatology. While there are a few elements of future expectation in the Gospel, for the most part traditional Jewish and early Christian hopes have been extensively reinterpreted in terms of a 'realized' eschatology. It is difficult to imagine that the same person who had engaged in this reshaping of the tradition would also write an extended work so pervasively focused on future expectation and with so much use of the conventions of Jewish apocalyptic writings. In principle, it is certainly not impossible for one author to employ two quite different genres, here ancient biography and apocalypse, but it would be extremely strange that it is precisely the apocalyptic material to be found in the Synoptics' lives of Jesus that this author had chosen to omit or to reinterpret radically in his ancient biography.

Although common authorship is highly unlikely, there are, nevertheless, some striking similarities between the Gospel and Revelation, despite their different genres. They do have major themes in common, such as witness and martyrdom, salvation through judgement, life, death, the notion of conquering in a spiritual sense, invitations to those who are thirsty to drink of the water of life. Revelation has an ethical dualism, similar to that found in John, in which the world's political powers are hostile to believers and negative references are made to the synagogue

(2.9; 3.9). It too can picture Jesus as both shepherd and lamb (7.17) and call him the Logos (19.13). It has direct addresses of the risen Christ to the churches and in places these sound very similar to the way Jesus speaks in the Gospel, particularly his 'I Am' sayings (1.17–18; 2.23; 22.13, 16) and his talk of receiving authority from the Father (2.28). The only places in the New Testament where Zech. 12.10 is applied to the crucifixion of Jesus are John 19.37 (through citation) and Rev. 1.7 (allusively) and both writers exhibit a fondness for the number seven in the way they arrange material.

What might account for such similarities? Revelation is clearly linked to the seven churches in Asia Minor. If the Gospel and epistles also came from the Ephesus area, one could then claim that all these writings had a common church context. The problem is that the tradition about Ephesus as the place of origin of the Gospel and letters is late second century and there is nothing in those documents themselves to support this claim (see further under Setting below). In order to do justice to the similarities and to keep the association between Revelation and the other Johannine literature, some have suggested that Revelation represents an earlier product of the Beloved Disciple that was revised and circulated at a later date by one of his followers and that other followers were responsible for the Gospel and its final editing and for the epistles. This suggestion does not specify to what situation the original version of Revelation was addressed and in what ways it was revised for a later situation, and its speculation is not compelling. Given that there is so little sound external evidence available, one should probably be content with the more reasonable but also more general conclusion that the similar features of the Gospel and Revelation stem from extended contact at some point between the itinerant prophet who composed the latter and the Johannine churches and their teachers. On this view the seer and prophet of Revelation has a rather more distant relationship to the Beloved Disciple, the evangelist, the final editor, and the elder than they have to each other.

Further Reading

For discussion of issues of composition, see J. Ashton, *Understanding the Fourth Gospel* (Oxford: Clarendon, 1991), esp. 76–101, 160–204. For a major and influential treatment of the relation of the Gospel to the Johannine epistles, see R. E. Brown, *The Epistles of John* (New York: Doubleday, 1982), 14–35, 69–115. For opposing views on the relationship between the Gospel and Revelation, see E. S. Fiorenza, 'The Quest for the Johannine School: The Apocalypse and the Fourth Gospel', *NTS* 23 (1977), 402–27 and S. S. Smalley, *Thunder and Love: John's Revelation and John's Community* (Milton Keynes: Nelson Word, 1994).

THE GOSPEL'S PERSPECTIVE ON CHRISTOLOGY AND THE RELATION TO JUDAISM

Clearly this is not the place for anything like a comprehensive discussion of the theology of the Fourth Gospel. Limitations of space mean that it is necessary to be highly selective and to focus on two topics that have been to the forefront of recent interpretation of the Gospel and of both positive and negative evaluations of its theological contribution, namely, its presentation of Jesus and its stance towards Judaism. Here the attempt will be made to set out briefly the Gospel's own perspective on these matters. The following two sections of the Introduction will explore the setting that produced such emphases and highlight the questions they raise.

Christology

As would be expected from an ancient biography, the Fourth Gospel's focus is on its subject, Jesus of Nazareth. What would not necessarily be expected from an ancient biography, but what immediately becomes clear, is that its subject is so closely related to the God of Israel that the focus on Jesus of Nazareth also becomes a focus on this God. What are reflected in the narrative's actions and symbols are convictions not only about Jesus but about God, so that Christology and theology are intimately interwoven.

Whatever the tensions between the Gospel's genre of ancient biography and its distinctive view of its subject, it is important to appreciate that the two are held together. The evangelist takes for granted that he is interpreting the life of a fully human figure. In doing so, as will be seen, he emphasizes Jesus' divine qualities, so much so that these overshadow his subject's human traits. One scholar in particular has argued that the resulting portrait of Jesus takes 'the form of a naïve docetism' in which 'John changes the Galilean teacher into the God who goes about on earth' (Käsemann 1968: 26, 27). Though overstated, this depiction has a point. Certainly the emphasis on Jesus' sovereign knowledge and control over his own mission means that he sometimes appears to act without normal human sympathies and limitations. Yet, even in the Lazarus story, where Jesus shows a strange form of love by waiting for Lazarus to die in order to be able to demonstrate his glory (11.5–6) and where he prays, not because he needs to but for the sake of the crowd (11.41–2), he can also be portrayed at his most human as he weeps and becomes angry (11.33, 35, 38). Jesus' humanity is not stressed elsewhere, however, because this would have been common ground in the disputes that the narrative reflects. What was challenged was the nature of Jesus' relationship to God and so inevitably this is the aspect of Jesus' mission that the evangelist's portrait underlines. The aspects of Jesus' humanity that do become explicit are somewhat more than the minimally necessary costume of a heavenly visitor to earth, but the resulting presentation as a whole, when divorced from its original context, has the potential for producing a view of Jesus that significantly undervalues his full humanity. For this reason it is crucial to underscore that the evangelist's choice of the genre of biography and his dependence on the Synoptic traditions indicate that the unquestionably human life of the Jew, Jesus of Nazareth, is the indispensable presupposition for his elaborately developed portrait.

Some of the dynamics of the Gospel's dominant interest in the relationship between Jesus and God emerge from one of the major categories employed for Jesus' mission, that of agency. Again and again Jesus describes himself as sent by God or the Father or speaks of God as the one who sent him. The verbs πέμπειν (25 times) and ἀποστέλλειν (17 times) are used interchangeably in such contexts. Drawing on Jewish and Graeco-Roman conventions about messengers or envoys, this language conveyed notions of commissioning and of authorized representation. Agents had behind them the full authority of those who sent them, whose message they were to communicate and whose interests they were to promote, so much so that the somewhat later rabbinic literature can speak of a person's agent as the equivalent of that person (cf. *m. Ber.* 5.5; *b. Naz.* 12b). In this way, to honour or to dishonour the one sent was also to honour or dishonour the sender. Jesus, then, is viewed as God's authorized agent, who fully and reliably represents the intentions and cause of the one who has sent him (cf. 4.34; 7.28–9; 8.29), who in his own person is the human equivalent of the divine sender (10.36; 12.45; 17.3), and who, having carried out his commission, returns to his sender (cf. 7.33; 16.5). People's response to Jesus as the sent one is therefore also their response to God as his sender (cf. 5.23–4, 38; 12.44; 13.20). The use of the sending language gives Jesus' claims and deeds divine legitimation; they are not simply made or performed on his own initiative (cf. 5.30; 7.16; 8.16; 12.49). At the same time it makes clear that all that happens in the mission of Jesus points to the person and purposes of its divine originator (cf. 5.36; 12.45).

Other aspects of the narrative draw out the implications of the unique relationship in which Jesus as the sent one fully represents God as his sender. Its prologue establishes the identity of the one who is sent. His relationship with God is so intimate that he can be regarded as the Logos, which, in the light of Jewish Wisdom literature, means that he is God's self-expression, God's immanent presence within the creation, which now takes human form (1.1–4, 14). As the Logos, he is also the light, who illuminates the world with the true knowledge of God, but whose coming into the world produces a crisis or judgement, with either positive or negative consequences (1.4–13; cf. also 3.18–21). What is at stake in Jesus' mission is his glory or reputation, which is like that which an only son derives from his father (1.14), and, since only God can reveal God, the sent one who makes the sender known is himself 'only God' (1.18).

In what follows two key roles for Jesus in the mission on which he is sent are those of witness and judge. In the climactic trial before Pilate Jesus himself underlines his mission as witness – 'For this I was born, and for this I came into the world, to bear witness to the truth' (18.37). The truth to which Jesus testifies is primarily the truth about God and God's disclosure in Jesus' own mission. In witnessing to God, therefore, Jesus also bears witness about himself, and in testifying about himself, he bears witness to God. This testimony to the truth takes place through his deeds and words, the signs and discourses, and supremely in his death.

The witness of Jesus' 'works', which include his signs, points both to himself and to his representation of the Father who sent him (cf. 5.36; 10.25). In the LXX the term 'sign' was particularly employed of divine actions through Moses at the time of the exodus that attested to Moses as the divine agent, judged the Egyptians and their gods, and brought about the liberation of Israel (cf. e.g. Exod. 4.1–9, 28–31; 7.1–7; 10.1–2; 12.12–13). In the prophetic writings signs also attested to the prophets as God's agents, confirmed their message, and frequently also served as a vehicle for conveying that message (cf. e.g. Isa. 20.1–4; Ezek. 4.1–4; 12.8–16). Jesus' signs also attest his divine agency. Their nature, however, underlines the unique status of this agent as the giver of life in abundance, who, in overturning dearth, disease and death, exercises the divine prerogative, particularly that of the bestowal of life, and anticipates the positive outcome of the process of judgement in the experience of eternal life. In regard to his works, such as healing on the sabbath, the Son's witness is the Father's witness and vice versa, because the Son does only what he sees the Father doing (5.19).

The witness of Jesus' words is also formulated in terms of his relationship to God and his sending by God. As the fully authorized agent, he speaks the words of the God who has sent him (cf. 3.33–4). Like all human witnesses, Jesus speaks of what he has seen and heard, but there is a striking difference, because what Jesus has seen and heard and what becomes the content of his witness are heavenly things (3.11–12). The portrayal of Jesus as both human and divine affects the way this witness is presented. As a human witness Jesus accedes, at least formally, to the legal demands that there should be more than one witness in his case (cf. 5.31; 8.17). But even when Jesus lists more than one witness or talks of the Father as the second witness, these are not the sort of witnesses the law or his accusers had in view and only serve to highlight that ultimately

Jesus is testifying about himself and his relation to God. Despite the law, such testimony is to be deemed to be true because of Jesus' unique identity (8.14). Because of his divine origin and destiny his witness is self-authenticating. In the nature of the case only God could confirm such testimony and from the evangelist's perspective Jesus is one with God. At the same time the complete dependence of the Son as agent on the Father as authorizer enables their witness to be depicted as a collaborative one – 'I Am the one who witnesses about myself and the Father who sent me witnesses about me' (8.18).

Jesus also represents the one who has sent him in his role as judge. The nature of Jesus' witness as self-authenticating entails that it is also the criterion of judgement and that as witness he is also judge. Indeed in the trial scene of chapter 8 Jesus' testifying and his judging are intimately connected (8.13–18), and, after pronouncing the judgement that his interrogators will die in their sins unless they believe, he claims that his negative judgement has the backing of the one who sent him (8.21, 26). Again, however, it should be emphasized that the primary goal of the process of judgement is not condemnation. Its overall purpose is the reversal of alienation and death and the establishment of well-being and life. Jesus' mission statement – 'I have come that they may have life and have it in abundance' (10.10) – is in complete harmony with the preceding mission statement about judging – 'I came into this world for judgement, so that those who do not see might see and those who see might become blind' (9.39), because the goal of the judging is the positive verdict of life. Only where there is wilful refusal to receive this life and its light is there the secondary outcome of a judgement of death and blindness (cf. also 12.47b–8). In regard to the relationship between Jesus and God, a similar pattern is at work in judging as in witnessing. Because in his judging Jesus is doing the will of the one who sent him (cf. 5.30; 12.48–9), responsibility for judging can be attributed to either Jesus or God or both. Jesus can say that the Father judges no one but has given all judgement to the Son or the Son of Man (5.22, 27) but then state that God is the ultimate judge (8.50) and he himself judges no one (8.15). Immediately the latter statement is qualified by the dynamics of the sending relationship – 'even if I do judge ... I am not alone, but it is I and the Father who sent me' (8.16). Jesus' role as God's authorized agent produces a collaborative unity within the work of judgement.

Jesus as the sent one represents and points to God as the sender not only in the course of his mission but in its completion in his death and resurrection. Again this can be seen in regard to the particular roles of witness and judge. That Jesus' passion and death are of a piece with his witness, and indeed form its culmination, is signalled from the start, where the first words of Jesus explicitly designated as testimony include the assertion that the Son of Man must be lifted up (3.14). This is then made clear by the major mission statement about his having come to testify to the truth (18.37) being placed in the context of the trial whose outcome Jesus already knows will be the sentence of death. That context is also one of a dialogue about power and kingship and of a struggle for power between Pilate and the Jewish religious authorities. The mission statement subordinates the issue of royal power to that of truth, makes clear that Jesus' witness eschews the use of this-worldly force and, along with the crucifixion account, indicates that the apparent weakness of death is essential to his mission. As a witness to the truth, Jesus gives his life for that truth, and his suffering and death become the paradigm for his witnessing followers. The dynamics of agency entail that the divine sender is so passionately committed to the mission of the one who has been sent that the latter's witness in death means that the former can be identified as 'the crucified God'.

Jesus' crucifixion is also the death of the judge. By the time of the trial before Pilate Jesus' activity as judge has been so clearly depicted that here it can be established primarily by irony that the accused whose mission is to witness to the truth is also the judge. He holds centre stage between Pilate and 'the Jews', whose words and actions expose both to judgement. He is mocked as King of the Jews, with all the associations of that messianic title with just judgement, and in all probability, as part of the mockery, seated on the judge's bench. The one sent to pronounce the verdict of life or death on others is himself then sentenced to death. His death on the cross is the point at which his mission of judging is completed and the divine verdict is rendered. From the evangelist's perspective, the world's judgement of Jesus is in reality his judgement of the world and its ruler (cf. 12.31; 16.11, 33). In the death of the judge who is judged the negative verdict of death is absorbed and from Jesus' side flow blood and water, the symbol of the positive verdict of life (19.34). In this process the one who has sent Jesus is revealed through his representative to be not an aloof sovereign judge but a judge who in love for the world is prepared to undergo the sentence of death in order to secure for that world restoration of its well-being and life.

The story line about the divine agent concludes, however, not with his death but with his resurrection. Since both sender and sent one are sources and bestowers of life, this Gospel can speak distinctively of Jesus as active in his own resurrection. The resurrection confirms the witness of the one who has promised not only to lay down his life but also to take it up again (10.17–18; cf. also 2.19) and who has claimed to be the embodiment of resurrection and life (11.25). In terms of the mission of judging, Jesus has claimed that the two aspects of divine judgement – the giving of life and condemnation – have been delegated to him and that he has the authority both in the present and future to pronounce the verdict of life (cf. 5.19–29). The future aspect will involve the bodily resurrection of the dead and so his own resurrection is both a vindication of his mission and an anticipation of that future judgement. He embodies ahead of time the positive verdict of life in the overall process of divine judgement. In this way both his death and his resurrection are essential to the completion of Jesus' mission and the establishing of his identity. In the ascent of the crucified Jesus in a resurrection body to the Father (20.17), the sent one returns to his sender in a form which bears the marks of the judgement's sentence of death as well as displaying its verdict of life (20.20).

The various titles given to Jesus express further aspects of his identity as the divine agent. This Gospel, along with the rest of early Christianity, holds Jesus to be the Messiah, the anointed one of Jewish expectation, but whereas in the Synoptics this designation is rarely used of Jesus in his lifetime, here Messianic titles are employed from the beginning of his mission. John the Baptist denies that he is himself the Messiah and points instead to Jesus as the one coming after him (1.20, 27, 30; 3.28), while Andrew announces Jesus as Messiah (1.41) and Nathanael sees him as Son of God and King of Israel (1.49). The Samaritan woman expresses the messianic expectation – 'I know that the Messiah is coming' – and the 'I Am' of Jesus' response has 'the Messiah' as its implied predicate (4.25–6). The signs Jesus performs are the signs of the messianic age, so that many believe and rightly ask, 'When the Messiah comes, will he do more signs than this man has done?' (7.31), and Jesus himself, when asked to state clearly whether he is the Messiah, says that he has already done so and that his works testify to who he is (10.24–5). When the Galilean crowds want to make Jesus king, he distances himself from them (6.15). By the time of his entry into Jerusalem, however, Jesus is willing to accept the Jerusalem crowd's greeting of him as King of Israel, because he can make clear the nature of his kingship by immediately seating himself on a donkey (12.13–15). A similar reinterpretation of this messianic category takes place in Jesus' dialogue with Pilate, when he makes clear that his kingship does not have its origin in this world and subordinates his role as king to that as witness to the truth (18.36–7). For the evangelist, confessing Jesus to be the anointed divine agent was basic to a correct evaluation of him, but it needed to be understood in the light of the nature of Jesus' mission as a whole and by itself it did not go far enough. For Jews to hold that a particular figure was the Messiah may have been controversial, but in itself it would not have been the cause of excommunication from the synagogue, despite the wording of 9.22. R. Akiba believed Simon bar Kochba was Messiah at the time of the second Jewish revolt (132–5 CE) and other Jews accepted other messianic claimants without running the risk of expulsion. It was what they believed about the nature of this Messiah that produced conflict for Johannine Christians and so in particular the evangelist wants to persuade his readers to echo

Martha's faith and to believe that Jesus was not only the Messiah but also the sort of Messiah who was Son of God (11.27; 20.31).

What is involved in confessing Jesus as Son of God is seen not just in the evangelist's uses of this title but, because Sonship is such a dominant category, also in the whole range of ways in which Jesus' relation to God as Father is depicted. In the Jewish Scriptures 'son of God' could be applied to specific individuals in a limited way – to the king (cf. 2 Sam. 7.14; Ps. 2.7) and to the righteous man (cf. Wis. 2.10–20; 5.5). The Qumran writings indicate that the expected royal Messiah could also be linked with the notion of God's son (cf. 1QSa (1Q28b) 2.11–12; 4Q174 (4QFlor) 1.10–12). In the broader Graeco-Roman world legendary heroes, rulers and even famous philosophers could be called sons of God. Among early Christians it was on the basis of the resurrection that the term began to be employed of Jesus (cf. Rom. 1.3; Acts 13.3), but for the Fourth Gospel, as its most pervasive Christological title, it had come to stand for all that was unique about Jesus' relation to God (cf. also 1 John 4.15; 5.5).

'Son of God' or simply 'Son' are used interchangeably in this Gospel, and the terminology of Son and Father has already occurred frequently in connection with our discussion of the use of 'sending' language for the relation between Jesus and God. The use of the family metaphor in this context intensifies the notion of Jesus as authorized representative by adding the dimension of personal intimacy. The sent one as Son is in a uniquely close relation of special trust and favour to the sender as Father; he is loved by the Father (cf. e.g. 3.35; 5.20; 15.9; 17.24). Jesus is not just any commissioned agent but comes from and will return to the presence of the Father in heaven (cf. 6.38–9; 8.42; 10.36; 14.12; 16.10). The earthly mission of Jesus is an extension into history of a pre-existent relationship and in it the Son exercises the Father's prerogatives of giving life and judging (5.21–2). What is more, the Father remains present with the Son during this mission (8.29; 16.32) and their relationship is so close that it can be spoken of in terms of mutual indwelling (10.38; 14.10–11; 17.21). The Father and the Son are completely one in the work of salvation (10.30), though the Son retains an element of subordination (14.28; cf. also 10.29). However, the language of dependency of the Son on the Father – 'the Son can do nothing on his own' – stresses not so much the subordination of the former to the latter as the total alignment of the wills and activities of the two (cf. 5.19, 30; 8.28; 12.49–50).

The Fourth Gospel maintains a consistent distinction between Jesus as 'Son' and believers as 'children' of God (cf. 1.12; 11.52; cf. also 1 John 3.1–2, 10; 5.2). The uniqueness of Jesus' Sonship is underlined by the use of the term μονογενής – he is the only Son of God (1.14; 3.16, 18). This uniqueness prompts reflections on Jesus' own divinity, as will be discussed below, but it is worth noting here that, on the most probable reading of the text of 1.18, the one who is the only Son of 1.14 can also be called 'only God', using the same adjective, μονογενής, and depicted as in the most intimate possible relationship to the Father – always in the Father's lap.

Jesus not only is presented as the Son, but also, as in the Synoptics, speaks of himself as the Son of Man. In the Synoptics this self-designation is found in three main contexts – in references to Jesus' present ministry, in references to the necessity of suffering and death, and in references to future glory and a role as judge at the parousia. In the Fourth Gospel such traditions have been reshaped to serve the evangelist's distinctive emphases. The judging activity of the Son of Man is now both present and future (cf. 5.27–9; 9.35, 39). The Son of Man designation is closely linked to the Gospel's cosmic framework involving heaven and earth and therefore to notions of ascent and descent. As the ladder on which the angels ascend and descend, he forms a bridge between heaven and earth (1.51). He himself originates in the heavenly realm, with God, descends into the earthly realm, and will ascend after the completion of his mission (cf. 3.13; 6.62). These two references clearly imply the pre-existence of the Son of Man, a notion absent from the Synoptic sayings. In the Fourth Gospel Jesus' suffering and glory are telescoped together. Where that happens in the double meaning of the 'lifting up' sayings (3.14; 8.28; 12.34), it is not surprising that it is of the Son of Man that such a lifting up in crucifixion and exaltation is predicated. The other major aspect of the reshaping of the tradition is that Son of Man language tends to become assimilated to the more dominant Son of God or Son terminology. So, for example, within the same passages belief in the Son of Man brings life (3.15; 6.27) but also belief in the Son brings life (3.16; 6.40), and in 5.25–7 Son of God, Son and Son of Man stand parallel and without any significant difference in their meaning or function. In this way Son of Man can also take on some of the connotations of this Gospel's distinctive Son of God Christology.

The distinctiveness of this presentation of Jesus as the divine agent who is also the divine Son lies primarily in the elevated claims it makes about what these roles mean for Jesus' own divine status. Two of the most striking aspects of the depiction of Jesus' relation to God are found in the way he is linked to the divine glory and in the way he employs the formula of God's own self-identification. In the Jewish Scriptures glory (LXX δόξα) has connotations of the splendour or radiance of the divine presence and also of the honour and reputation of the divine name. The Fourth Gospel's prologue indicates that this divine glory was present in Jesus for those with eyes to see it ('we saw his glory' – 1.14). Glory sums up the life of the incarnate Logos and, as noted in the discussion of the Gospel's structure, this can be seen in the shaping of the narrative about him. In his public mission the signs in particular manifest Jesus' glory (cf. 2.11; 11.4, 40) and towards its end there is the announcement that the hour has come for the Son of Man to be glorified (12.23). During the mission Jesus asserts that it is the Father who seeks his glory and indeed glorifies him (8.50, 54) and the reason the divine prerogative of judging is delegated to Jesus is that all may honour the Son. So bound together is the honour of Jesus with that of God, such that 'anyone who does not honour the Son does not honour the Father' (5.22–3). The second half of the main narrative then depicts Jesus in the hour of his glory and makes clear that his departure from the world in death by crucifixion, which in normal evaluation would be seen as the greatest humiliation and shame, is in fact to be regarded as the supreme moment of that glory (cf. 13.31–2; 17.1). A standard objection from other Jews to Jewish Christian claims about Jesus was to point to the absence of evidence of the divine glory that should have accompanied the Messiah and the bringing in of the messianic age and to hold such claims to be completely undermined by the fate Jesus had actually met, the ignominy of death on a Roman cross. A typical Christian response, based on the Synoptic tradition, might be to explain that the Messiah came first in humiliation and had to suffer and that only after the suffering could there be vindication and glory, partly through the resurrection and exaltation but fully at the parousia when he would come again in glory. In fact his followers had been given a preview of that future glory on one particular occasion when Jesus was transfigured before them. The Fourth Gospel's response is rather different and tackles the premises of the objection. It claims that a proper evaluation of Jesus would have recognized the divine glory all the way through his mission and far from considering the cruci-fixion as the point of deepest shame would have perceived in it the fullest revelation of God's glory. The problem lies not in Jesus' mission but in the opponents' judgement, which has become so influenced by merely human conceptions of honour and glory that it fails to use the right criteria and therefore fails to see the glory when it is before their eyes (cf. 5.44; 7.18, 24; 12.43). In line with this perspective, there is, of course, no account of the transfiguration. In a mission suffused with glory, the transfiguration would simply not stand out sufficiently. There is also no account of the anguish of Jesus in Gethsemane. In the Johannine equivalent the one hint of suffering – 'Now is my soul troubled' – is immediately turned into a recognition of its glory: ' "for this reason I have come to this hour. Father, glorify your name." Then a voice came from heaven, "I have glorified it, and I will glorify it again" ' (12.27–8), underlining again that not only Jesus' but God's reputation is at stake in Jesus' mission. In accomplishing Jesus' glory, God secures God's own honour (cf. also 13.31–2). It is no surprise to learn from Jesus' prayer that the glory revealed in his mission on earth is the same glory he enjoyed with his Father before the world was made and will enjoy again with him after his departure (17.4–5, 24).

Jesus does not lay aside his divine glory in coming to earth and dying; rather his incarnation and death become vehicles for its expression.

The other remarkable aspect of this Gospel's perspective on Jesus' identity is found in its placement of 'I Am' pronouncements on Jesus' lips. These are the sayings which involve the emphatic Greek construction ἐγώ εἰμι. Normally only the verb would be required to express 'I am . . .' so that, literally, the force of the emphatic formulation is 'I myself am . . .' In some of the uses, however, it soon becomes clear that something other than mere emphasis on the speaker is being conveyed. There are in fact three types of use of the formulation. The most straightforward are the references in which 'I am' is accompanied by a predicate (6.35, 51; 8.12, 18; 10.7, 9, 11, 14; 11.25; 14.6; 15.1, 5). These include claims on the part of Jesus to embody the significance of major Jewish symbols or expectations, such as the bread of life, the light of the world, the resurrection and life, the good shepherd and the true vine. More puzzling initially are the references in which 'I am' has no predicate and appears to be used in an absolute sense (8.24, 28, 58; 13.19). Here Jesus' audience is meant to believe or know that 'I Am' or is simply told 'Before Abraham came to be, I Am.' The clue to their force is provided by the way in which the Septuagint has translated the divine self-identifications in Deut. 32.39; Isa. 41.4; 43.10, 25; 45.18–19; 46.4; 51.12; 52.6 with the use of ἐγώ εἰμι. Of particular interest is the fact that the Isaiah references occur in the context of divine lawsuits with Israel and the nations, in which God's claim to be the only God, who is sovereign over history and acts to save God's people, is at stake and Israel is called to be a witness to the reality of this claim, to testify that I Am. The divine self-identification functions as the equivalent of the divine name. There can be no doubt that this LXX usage lies behind the references in the Fourth Gospel. It is not only the 'I Am' formulation itself but also the language of believing and knowing that I Am which has been drawn from this source (cf. Isa. 43.10 LXX). So, just as God in the Jewish Scriptures identifies Godself by this self-predication, now Jesus utters the same self-predication, indicating that Jesus and God are to be seen as sharing the same identity. It is not surprising that the response of Jesus' audience to the utterance of 8.58 is to attempt to stone him for blasphemy.

Once this implication of the absolute sayings has been observed, it colours the force of the sayings with predicates. Jesus can claim to be the light of the world or the truth or the life only because of the unique relationship with God conveyed by the introductory 'I Am'. Knowledge of the LXX background is also decisive for the interpretation of a third group of 'I Am' sayings – those with an implied predicate and therefore a double meaning (cf. 4.26; 6.20; 18.5–6). In response to the Samaritan woman's assertion of the expectation of the Messiah, Jesus responds, 'I Am, the one who is speaking to you.' This could be taken simply as an acknowledgement that he is this Messiah, but knowledge of the LXX rendering of Isa. 45.19 and 52.6, where God proclaims 'I Am the one who speaks', indicates that more is going on and that Jesus is including but transcending the messianic title in his announcement. He is the sort of Messiah who is one with God. The other two references involve playing with the possible ordinary meaning of 'I am he' or 'It is I' and the more profound connotations of the formulation. In the case of both the walking on the water and the arrest by soldiers further clues are provided in the context that show the incidents are to be taken as theophanies, appearances of the divine with the typical accompanying phenomena – the command not to be afraid and the response of falling prostrate on the ground. The way in which the divine self-predication functions as an equivalent to the divine name in the Jewish Scriptures suggests that, when Jesus claims to have been given God's name and to have made it known in his mission (cf. esp. 17.6, 11, 12, 26), these remarkable 'I Am' sayings may be particularly in view.

Does the Fourth Gospel go further still in its presentation and actually call Jesus God? The answer is in the affirmative. The very first verse of the prologue describes the Logos, who is to become incarnate, as God, employing θεός without the article (see the commentary) and on the most likely reading of its final verse holds that the one who has made God known is himself 'only God' (1.18). Significantly, during Jesus' mission the man born blind is depicted as paying homage to or worshipping him (the Greek verb προσκυνεῖν can have a spectrum of meanings), a response, which in the context of his preceding confession and of the Gospel as a whole, suggests an action which might normally be expected to be directed solely to God. But the portrayal of Jesus as God is made even more explicit in Thomas' confession, which is at the same time an acclamation of worship – 'My Lord and my God!' (20.28). Readers might well be expected to set such an acclamation over against imperial claims, such as those made about Domitian in terms of *dominus et deus noster*, 'our Lord and our God' (Suetonius, *Dom.* 13.2). But if Jesus is a rival to other would-be gods, he is not a rival to the God of Israel. The title Lord (κύριος) is a designation for this God in the LXX, and its combination with God (θεός) in acclamation of the risen Jesus, conveys this Gospel's high evaluation of Jesus as the divine agent. The words of Jesus' prayer summarize the evangelist's perspective on what this entails – 'Now this is eternal life, that they should know you, the only true God, and Jesus Christ whom you have sent' (17.3). Although Jesus as God's uniquely authorized agent is clearly depicted as one with God, this is not seen as detracting from the monotheism that holds the God of Israel to be the only true God. How then is knowledge of Jesus as well as of God necessary for life? How does Jesus share the divine glory and identify himself by means of God's self-identification, and how is he worshipped and designated as God without becoming a second god? Since in the words of the prayer there remains only one true God, Jesus, as the incarnate Logos and in his relationship of Son to the Father, must somehow be intrinsic to this one God's identity. As the prayer's petition goes on to indicate, he always has shared in the glory and identity of the one God from before the foundation of the world (17.5). The notion of the divinity of Jesus, in the sense of his full inclusion in the identity of the one God of Israel, is not, then, a later invention of or development within patristic debate but is already part of the witness of the Fourth Gospel. Within that witness its force is also a practical one. It drives home the conviction that the mission of Jesus is no take-it-or-leave-it affair; it does not even involve a decision merely about the message of a prophet or the identity of the Messiah. That mission is of critical import, involving issues of life and death, because, if Jesus is God in God's self-revelation in the world, one's judgement about Jesus is at the same time a judgement about God. Given this evaluation of Jesus' identity, it is not surprising that this Gospel includes on the lips of Jesus the claim to exclusive access to God that is so disturbing to modern sensibilities – 'No one comes to the Father except by me' (14.6).

Relation to Judaism

Equally disturbing to modern sensibilities are this Gospel's frequent use of the term 'the Jews' in a negative or hostile sense and the fierce polemic between Jesus and his opponents that sometimes accompanies such use. Indeed, some interpreters allege that these two disturbing features are inextricably connected and that the Gospel's claims about Jesus' divinity are un-Jewish and necessarily lead to a perspective on Judaism that is anti-Jewish. Is this Gospel, which is so profoundly influenced by the Jewish Scriptures and developments within second temple Judaism, at the same time antagonistic to Judaism, and, if so, in what ways?

The use of the term 'the Jews' (οἱ 'Ιουδαῖοι) is certainly a prominent feature of the Fourth Gospel, where, if the three references to the term in the singular are also included, it is found 72 times in comparison with five times in Matthew, six times in Mark and five times in Luke. However, some popular misconceptions about this usage need to be dispelled. First, by no means all the references have negative connotations. The usage is varied. Sometimes the reference is primarily to Jewish feasts and institutions, so that, for example, there is talk of the purification rites, the festival, the Passover or the burial customs 'of the Jews' (cf. 2.6, 13; 5.1; 19.40). 'Jews do not have dealings with Samaritans' (4.9) is a straightforward description and, while some of the other references of this sort can have a distancing effect, they are certainly not in themselves negative. In other places there is a divided response among 'the Jews', with some having at least what appears to be an initially positive reaction to Jesus (cf. e.g. 8.31; 10.19–21; 11.45; 12.9). In 4.9 Jesus himself is designated as a Jew and in the passion narrative is portrayed as 'the King of the Jews'. Even more positively, in 4.22 salvation can be said to be from 'the Jews'. At the very most, only just over half the references have in view those Jews who have an unbelieving or hostile attitude to Jesus. This includes a spectrum of responses from, at one end, 'the Jews' who ask for a sign and then misunderstand Jesus' response after the temple incident (2.18, 20) to, at the other, those who are seeking to kill him (e.g. 5.19) or who demand his death at the Roman trial (e.g. 19.14–15). Second, it is not the case that all the negative references have the religious authorities in view. This may be true of the majority of such references, but a significant number refer to the crowds or general populace, who in some cases are explicitly distinguished from the authorities (cf. e.g. 6.41, 52; 7.35; 8.22; 11.45–7). Third, although a number of scholars espouse this view, 'the Jews' should not be replaced in translation by 'the Judaeans'. This is wrong on two major counts. It does not fit the data in the Gospel, where in 6.41, 52 the term refers to the Galilean crowds, and it is not the way the expression οἱ 'Ιουδαῖοι was used at the time. Although in its earlier usage the term primarily applied to Judaeans, from the mid-second century BCE it was used to denote a broader national, religious and political grouping by no means any longer limited to those who lived or had parents who lived in Judaea. Indeed, Diaspora Jews were also generally known as οἱ 'Ιουδαῖοι and had no problems in accepting this designation for themselves.

So the sense of the term is the broad one of the Jewish people as distinct from other ethnic groupings but it can then have a variety of specfic referents. As the designation of a group of characters in the narrative, like the depiction of nearly all the characters, it frequently serves a representative function. The response of 'the Jews' indicates different types of belief and unbelief. A hostile and unbelieving response is primarily associated with 'the Jews' as the Jewish religious authorities, but similarly negative responses can also come from 'the Jews' as members of the more general Jewish population. But, as indicated above, among 'the Jews' can also be found a somewhat different response, primarily from members of the general populace, though also from some leaders, in which there is greater openness to Jesus' mission, positive assessments are made when there is a division of opinion, and a hovering between belief and unbelief appears to be taking place. Among this group are Nicodemus (cf. 3.1–10; 7.52; 19.39), the authorities who believe but will not confess their belief (cf. 12.42–3), the crowds in Galilee who have acclaimed Jesus as prophet-king and followed him because of the feeding miracle but then take offence at his teaching (cf. 6.14–15, 41, 52), and those of the Jerusalem crowds who are designated as 'the Jews who believed in him'

(8.31) but whose belief turns out to be inadequate so that they become simply 'the Jews' (8.48) who eventually attempt to stone Jesus. Also among this group are 'the Jews' in the Lazarus story, who sympathize with the two sisters in their loss and some of whom then believe on the basis of the raising of Lazarus (cf. 11.19, 33, 36, 45). Whether these more positive responses will ultimately prove to be adequate remains, however, to be determined. In this Gospel's narrative, belief on the grounds of seeing signs is an appropriate first stage but, in order for it to be deemed properly authentic, has to progress from seeing the sign to full comprehension of what it signifies. The judgement of Jesus about the first Jews to believe because of the signs – that he would not entrust himself to them, because he knew all people (2.24–5) – hangs programmatically over Nicodemus and all those subsequently said to believe in Jesus after seeing a sign. The divided response among 'the Jews' in the narrative functions as a call to readers to believe Jesus' claims and to have the sort of faith that is able to see through the signs to what they signify about Jesus' identity as the life-giver.

It is significant that in the farewell section 'the Jews' are mentioned only once (13.33) and that the unbelieving and hostile response is now said to come from 'the world' (cf. e.g. 14.17, 23; 15.18–19; 16.8; 17.14–16). But the synagogue's hostile response to the disciples is part of the world's hatred of them, and so the effect of this shift of terminology for the narrative as a whole is to highlight that 'the Jews' who are depicted negatively are representatives of the unbelieving world as a whole. In its more negative usage the term 'the Jews' retains its ethnic sense but its referent now transcends merely ethnic categories. There is a strangeness about this usage that makes clear that the term cannot refer to all Jews but only to those who are representatives of the unbelieving world, as three of many possible examples indicate. In 9.22 the parents of the man born blind, who are of course ethnically Jewish, are said to fear 'the Jews'. In 13.33 Jesus, a Jew, says to his disciples, themselves Jews, 'as I said to the Jews, so now I say to you. . .' Then in 18.35 Pilate, the Roman governor, asks the ironic question, 'I am not a Jew, am I?', to which the answer he expects is a negative one but the answer the implied reader is supposed to supply is in the affirmative. In his response to Jesus Pilate proves himself to be a Jew in the special negative sense of this narrative's discourse, namely one who belongs to the world that does not believe in Jesus. This phenomenon is the reflection of intra-Jewish conflict. Instead of calling unbelieving Jews 'this generation', as the Synoptics do, the evangelist has read back into the mission of Jesus the attitudes and actions of those Jews in his locale who either have initially responded favourably to Jewish Christian claims about Jesus and then failed to maintain their adherence when this was tested, or have rejected such claims, put those who held them out of the synagogue, and even killed some of them (cf. 9.22; 12.42; 16.2). The synagogue authorities clearly held that those they excommunicated were in some sense no longer true Jews and it is a reasonable inference that in the light of this conflict the evangelist concedes the disputed name and employs it in his negative references to mean unbelieving as opposed to believing Jews.

The fierceness of this conflict's polemic is also reflected in the Gospel. In particular, in chapter 8, Jesus accuses his opponents of trying to kill him and on this basis asserts, 'You are of your father, the devil, and you want to do your father's desires. He was a murderer from the beginning . . .' (8.44). As the commentary on this verse points out, such rhetoric needs to be heard in its first-century context, where calling others 'children of Satan' was a commonplace in disputes, where this and other such terminology functioned as ways of labelling one's opponents as opponents, and where the polemic on the lips of Jesus would not have sounded any different to Jewish ears than some of the fierce indictments made of Israel in its own Scriptures. It is clearly not addressed to all ethnic Jews. Despite the horrendous misuse of this passage in the Gospel's later reception, in the Gospel itself it has nothing to do with anti-Semitism. In fact, in this particular context it appears to be addressed to those Jews who have believed in Jesus but have not continued in their belief in a way the evangelist finds satisfactory (cf. 8.31–2). By remaining in the synagogue instead of identifying with those who made the full Johannine confession, they have, from the evangelist's perspective, sided with the opposition and can be accused of sharing its stance towards Jesus. Loose characterizations of the language of John 8 as the polemic of hatred and as inducing violence miss the point. In its original context it is the language of reproach in the face of violence, intending to convey in strong terms that those who act violently toward the message of Jesus and his followers or who side with those who do so are doing evil and their behaviour reflects that of the diabolical agency, who, within the Jewish world-view, was considered 'a murderer from the beginning'.

The opposition between Jesus' followers and 'the Jews', when that term is used negatively for the representatives of the world, has to do with two different systems of values, one determined by belief in Jesus and one ultimately determined by unbelief, and ethnic Jews are of course found on both sides of this divide. For the Fourth Gospel, however, this divided state of affairs is meant to be temporary and the note of condemnation of those who do not believe functions as a warning against choosing to exclude oneself from the God of Israel's loving and life-giving purposes for an alienated and hostile world (cf. 3.16). In the meantime, despite the unbelief of the majority of Jews, God's purposes for Israel are not thwarted but are continued through the Jewish Messiah and his followers. The Logos' own people as a whole did not accept him (1.11) but those who did receive him are born into God's new family, which is no longer defined solely in terms of ethnic descent (1.12–13; cf. also 3.3–7) and Jesus' disciples can now be designated as 'his own people' (13.1). The positive term for an ethnic Jew whose identity is defined by allegiance to Jesus is not so much 'Jew' but 'Israelite', so that Nathanael can be called 'truly an Israelite in whom there is no deceit' (1.47) and can respond by confessing that Jesus is the King of Israel (1.49). This same title is used to acclaim Jesus as he enters Jerusalem later (12.13). It also raises questions about how it is related to the title 'the King of the Jews', which predominates in the passion narrative. Clearly the traditions about the charge against Jesus and the inscription on the cross have been determinative in regard to the latter title. Yet at the same time this designation for Jesus is developed extensively in his presentation as king in the trial before Pilate, where the blatant irony dictates that readers are meant to see the designation as in fact a statement of the true state of affairs. The irony is underscored in the crucifixion scene when the narrator also points out that the inscription 'Jesus of Nazareth, the King of the Jews' was in three languages – Aramaic, the vernacular; Latin, the language of the Roman government; and Greek, the language of trade and commerce – indicating the universality of this king's reign (19.20). In this way God's purposes for Israel in the world are fulfilled. Salvation is indeed 'of the Jews' and in such a way that the king of the Jews is also the Saviour of the world (cf. 4.22, 42). Jesus' Jewish followers are sent into the world as witnesses to this salvation (15.27; 17.17; 20.21–3), as they point to God's verdict, revealed in Jesus' death, that life is available to all, both Jews and Gentiles equally, through believing that Jesus is the Jewish Messiah, the Son of God (cf. 20.31).

At the heart of the clash between Jesus and those Jews who are presented in a negative light is the interpretation of the Mosaic law. This is reflected clearly in the account of the giving of sight to the man born blind, where his interrogators tell him, 'You are his disciple, but we are disciples of Moses' (9.28). The reason for their preferred allegiance to Moses is that 'we know that God has spoken to Moses, but as for this man, we do not know where he comes from' (9.29). Their point of certainty, and therefore their criterion for judgement, is the law as the divine revelation to Moses. On this basis, elsewhere in the Gospel such opponents hold Jesus to be a lawbreaker or sinner in four major respects. His healing constitutes work on the sabbath (cf. 5.16; 7.23; 9.16, 20). He blasphemes, particularly in the way he talks of God as his Father, making himself equal to God (cf. 5.17–18; 8.58–9; 10.30–9; 19.7). In terms of Deut. 13.1–5 and 18.21–2, the signs he performs and the claims he makes show him to be a false prophet who is leading the people astray and therefore an enemy of the nation (cf. 7.12b; 11.47–50). When put under interrogation on such charges, he can only witness to himself, which is an infringement of the law about the necessity of two or three witnesses (cf. 8.13, 17; cf. also 5.31). For these reasons the opposition sees Jesus as deserving the law's sentence of death (cf. esp. Lev. 24.16; Deut. 13.10; 18.20). From the evangelist's perspective, however, this is to judge on the basis of appearances or of merely human standards (cf. 7.24; 8.15), since Jesus' words are now the criterion of divine judgement and require a radically new stance towards Torah. This perspective is apparent from the beginning of the Gospel. In the prologue not only is the grace and truth previously associated with the glory of Yahweh in the covenant with Moses (cf. Exod. 34.6) now associated with the glory of the incarnate Logos (1.14), but a contrast can also be made between the two – 'the law was given through Moses; grace and truth came into being through Jesus Christ' (1.17). This is not a denial that before the coming of the Logos the law was previously an expression of Yahweh's grace and truth. It is rather an assertion on the part of believers in Jesus that now they have seen the fullness of grace and truth in the Logos' glory, these qualities need no longer be sought in the law. The contrast with Moses continues into the following verse. The statement that no one has seen God at any time also serves as a denial of any claims that might be made for Moses. Since God is inaccessible, only God can make God known. This makes Jesus superior to Moses as the mediator of divine revelation. He is 'only God', always in the most intimate relationship possible with God, and this qualifies him to make God known. Knowledge of God through Jesus, therefore, becomes the criterion by which previous knowledge of God through the Mosaic law is to be judged and not vice versa.

This theme is developed in a variety of ways. There is little attempt to show that the law has been misinterpreted on its own terms. In two places there are arguments that point to an ambiguity in the law that can be exploited for Jesus' cause (cf. 7.19–24; 10.33–8). In the first Jesus points out that in order that the law about circumcision not be broken, another law, the sabbath law, does have to be broken and then argues from the lesser to the greater to justify healing a whole body on the sabbath. In the second Jesus appeals to the law in its broadest sense (Ps. 82.6) to point out that it can call those addressed by God 'gods' and then again to argue from the lesser to the greater for the appropriateness of calling himself, as the one who embodies God's address to humans, 'God's Son'. But the dominant way of presenting the clash between Jesus and the law is not to dispute that the law is being rightly interpreted but to see Jesus as an exception to the law because he is above the law. So in 5.17 Jesus simply admits that he is working on the sabbath, but appeals to the notion that God never ceases creative activity and so claims to be in unity with God in this. And here when the blasphemy issue surfaces (cf. 5.18–30), the law about making oneself equal to God is not debated. This would hold for other humans. But Jesus' point is that he is different. In his case it is not a question of making himself equal to God; this equality in judging and giving life has been bestowed on him by God. Similarly, later there is acknowledgement of the law about the need for two or three witnesses, but Jesus is seen to be an exception because of who he claims to be in relationship with God (8.14). Because of this overall perspective on Jesus and the law the discourse can also sometimes put a distance between the two. Jesus, the Jew, talks not about 'our law' or 'the law' but 'your law' (8.17; 10.34) or speaks of Moses giving 'you' the law and circumcision (7.19, 22) or of 'their law' (15.25). The discourse clearly subordinates the law to Jesus. Moses is to be seen as having written about Jesus, so that those who refuse to believe Jesus can be indicted for in fact not believing Moses. Moses, whom they are employing to accuse Jesus, will therefore turn out to be the one who accuses them (5.45–7). In 12.48–50 Jesus' summary of his mission recalls what is said of the prophet like Moses. Because he is the prophet like Moses, his word, which is the Father's commandment of eternal life, will serve as the ultimate criterion of judgement. Previously the Mosaic law was seen as giving life and as the standard of judgement, but now it is the witness of Jesus.

Once Jesus' unique identity is recognized, then the law in its various aspects can be perceived to be fulfilled by him, but his unique identity also means that he fulfils the law by transcending it. One major way in which this is developed has often been called the Fourth Gospel's 'replacement motif', whereby, in fulfilling the significance of Torah, its symbols and institutions, Jesus can also be said to replace them. Some scholars, sensitive to the dangers of a Christian supersessionism which holds Jewish religious practices to have no continuing validity, dispute that one should talk of replacement in this connection. But Johannine thought and contemporary Christian theology should not simply be collapsed into one another. It seems clear that, for the evangelist, Jesus' fulfilment of Torah not only entails continuity with what it signified but also discontinuity. The law, its symbols and institutions remain crucial for interpreting what has taken place in Jesus. In that sense they cannot be replaced. But in terms of present Christian experience and practice their fulfilment means that they have been surpassed and are no longer appropriate. For followers of Jesus who had been barred from the synagogue and therefore from the practices of Judaism, the fulfilment motif must at the same time have been a replacement motif, through which the benefits of their belief in Jesus could be seen as more than compensating for the loss of access to those institutions that could now be recognized as pointing forward to his significance. In the first sign (2.1–11), the water turned into wine is not just any water that was available but water to be employed for the Jewish rites of purification. Jesus replaces this with the abundant wine of the messianic age. A similar point is made in the very next episode, where the holy place and its practices established by the law, that is, the temple and sacrifices, are shown to give way to the action and presence of Jesus. Indeed, his crucified and risen body is the new indestructible temple, the new dwelling place of God (2.19–21). Jesus' conversation with the Samaritan woman about worship makes the implications explicit (4.21–4). In announcing that the time has come when God is to be worshipped in the Spirit and truth that he makes available, Jesus also asserts that the inauguration of this eschatological period means that worship is no longer appropriate either at Mt Gerizim or in Jerusalem. As the new locus of God's presence, Jesus replaces previous worship arrangements, even those legislated by the law.

As noted earlier, the public mission of Jesus is structured around journeys to Jerusalem for major festivals. Jesus is presented as the fulfilment of the significance of a number of these feasts. The feeding of the five thousand and the discourse about bread is set at the time of Passover (6.4). As the true bread from heaven, Jesus fulfils what was signified not only by the manna of the exodus but also by the unleavened bread of Passover, and Jesus' flesh and blood are now the food and drink of the true Passover meal (6.51–8). What is more, this Gospel's chronology of the passion places Jesus' death at the same time as the slaughter of the Passover lambs (19.14, 31) and his crucified body is compared to that of the Passover lamb through the citation from Exod. 12.46 (19.36), recalling John the Baptist's earlier witness to Jesus as the lamb of God (1.29, 36). Two major elements of the Feast of Tabernacles, the setting for chapters 7 and 8, were the prayer for rain with its water rites and the illumination of the Court of Women. Jesus fulfils their symbolism as he claims to be the source of living water (7.37–9) and the true light (8.12). The setting for the dispute in 10.22–39 is the Feast of Dedication, celebrating the dedication of the temple altar at the time of the Maccabees, and here Jesus claims that he is the one who has been consecrated by the Father (10.36). For Jewish believers who have been cut off from the celebration of the law's festivals, what Jesus signifies now fulfils the meaning of these festivals and takes their place.

What is true of the symbolism of the festivals also holds for the symbols and terminology associated with the law itself. Previously it was Torah that was considered to be God's word, the embodiment of divine wisdom and revelation, and held to have pre-existed with God; now these claims are made for Jesus (1.1, 2, 14; 17.5). Torah was the source of light and life; now this is said of Jesus (e.g. 9.5; 11.25; 14.6). Grace and truth, previously linked with the law given through Moses, now come into being through Jesus Christ, so that grace is in place of grace (1.14, 16, 17). In the new order the language of obedience to the law – 'doing the will of God', 'doing the works of God', 'keeping the word', and 'keeping the commandments' – assumes a new meaning and refers to believing in Jesus and carrying out his word (cf. e.g. 6.28, 29, 40; 8.51; 14.21, 23; 15.10).

The relation between Jesus and the law is such a major issue because the identity of two groups within Judaism is at stake. Those depicted as 'the Jews' in its negative sense define their identity in terms of the law ('we are disciples of Moses' – 9.28) and see this as necessitating the rejection of Jesus and his claims. The Jewish Jesus and his Jewish followers, however, see no necessary incompatibility between believing Moses and believing in Jesus. A true disciple of Moses would be a disciple of Jesus, because Moses wrote about Jesus (cf. 5.45–7). Those whose identity is determined by their allegiance to Jesus interpret the law in the light of who he is and thereby possess its hermeneutical key. At the same time the Fourth Gospel reflects the reality that 'the Jews' have made their view of the law the criterion for condemning Jesus (cf. 19.7 – 'We have a law, and according to that law he ought to die, because he has made himself the Son of God') and for determining who can remain in the synagogue and be held to have authentic Jewish identity (cf. 9.22). The evangelist, in his discourse about the law, represents those Jews who, when forced to make a choice between Jesus and this use of the law, chose Jesus because they believed he transcended the law and were able to see in him its fulfilment and replacement. This stance towards the law treats it not as an independent criterion of judgement but as part of Scripture's witness to Jesus as the Christ, the Son of God.

In distinction from the distancing that can take place when the law is under discussion, the Fourth Gospel does not refer to the Scriptures as the Scriptures 'of the Jews' or as 'your Scriptures'. Nevertheless, there is still an indictment of the opposition's misuse of Scripture. In 5.39–40 Jesus acknowledges that his opponents search the Scriptures, but what is wrong with the search is that 'you think that in them you have eternal life'. This accusation *is* similar to the perspective on the law. Just as the law in itself is not to be seen as the sufficient criterion for judging, so the Scriptures in themselves are not to be seen as sufficient for experiencing eternal life. It is only as the Scriptures are seen as a witness to Jesus as the one who gives life that they play their proper part in the positive outworking of God's judgement. The ensuing bread of life discourse (6.25–59) functions as a model for how such a perspective works, as the evangelist makes a commentary on a scriptural text (6.31) serve as a commentary on Jesus' own saying (6.27). Both the form and the content of the passage show Jesus as the giver of life who is the key to the understanding of Scripture.

The wrong sort of searching of Scripture on the part of the opposition to Jesus is illustrated in the discussion of whether the Messiah or a prophet is to come from Galilee (7.42, 52). Some of the crowd assert that the Messiah does not come from Galilee and that Scripture states the Messiah is descended from David and comes from Bethlehem. The former claim ignores the promises about David's royal descendant bringing light to the people of Galilee in Isa. 9.1–7. The latter point is not disputed. But readers are in all probability expected to know of the Synoptic traditions that Jesus was in fact born in Bethlehem and, more importantly, to understand that to focus on Jesus' geographical origins is to employ the wrong categories because the narrative has constantly made clear that the answer to the question about where Jesus is from is that he is from God, from above or from heaven. Later, when Nicodemus suggests that 'our law' does not judge people without first hearing them, the religious authorities, who despise the crowd as not knowing the law, are depicted as saying, 'Investigate and you will see that no prophet is to arise from Galilee' (7.52). The authorities engage in a searching of Scripture that excludes the possibility of their listening to Jesus and in the process show themselves in fact to be more ignorant than the despised crowd, because Scripture does talk of a prophet from Galilee (cf. 2 Kgs 14.25).

The evangelist's own use of Scripture as one of the major witnesses to Jesus involves both the citation of particular passages that find their fulfilment in Jesus' mission and the use of scriptural symbols that have their referent in Jesus. There are far fewer actual citations of Scripture than in each of the Synoptic Gospels. Nevertheless, the early Christian practice of employing such proof-texts for showing that what happened in Jesus' mission was according to the divine will is maintained. So, for example, Jesus' action in the temple fulfils the words of Ps. 69.9 (2.17), the entry into Jerusalem had been written about in Zech. 9.9 (12.15), and Judas' betrayal is in fulfilment of Ps. 41.9 (13.18). Particularly in the passion narrative scriptural texts that have not been used in the Synoptic passion accounts are employed. The casting of lots for Jesus' seamless garment is prepared for by Ps. 22.18 (19.24), in saying 'I thirst' Jesus brings Ps. 69.21 to fulfilment (19.28), and when, after his death, his legs are not broken but instead his side is pierced, this is seen as in line with two Scriptures – Exod. 12.46/Ps. 34.20 and Zech. 12.10 (19.36–7). From this perspective the Jewish Scriptures function basically as prophecy, pointing forward to key moments in Jesus' mission and at the same time legitimating Christian claims that that mission was a carrying-out of the previously revealed will of God. What the Fourth Gospel lacks in the quantity of its citations, it makes up for in its overall indebtedness to the Jewish Scriptures for its typology, symbols, allusions and patterns of thought. A few examples will have to suffice. Jesus' saying about the angels ascending and descending on the Son of Man alludes to Gen. 28.12 and Jacob's dream at Bethel (1.51), and the lifting up of the serpent in the wilderness from Num. 21.8–9 is seen as a type of the lifting up of the Son of Man (3.14), just as the manna in the wilderness in Exod. 16 provides the type for Jesus as the true bread from heaven (6.31–3). The symbol of the lamb of God for Jesus (1.29, 36) appears to allude to more than one place in Scripture. The Passover lamb of Exod. 12, which does not take away sin, is merged with the reference to the servant as a lamb in Isa. 53, where the context is the bearing of sins. A similar phenomenon occurs when the words 'Out of his belly shall flow rivers of living water' are introduced as a scriptural citation (7.38). There is no one source for this quotation. Rather it appears to bring together terminology and allusions from a number of sources – the water from the rock struck by Moses in Exod. 17.6 and Ps. 78.16, 20, the water of the coming time of salvation in Isa. 43.20 and 44.3, and the water flowing from the temple in Ezek. 47.1–12 and Zech. 14.7–8. The clustering together of a number of scriptural notions is seen again in the extended figures of speech about the shepherd and the vine (10.1–18; 15.1–17). There Synoptic tradition and a variety of associations of the imagery of shepherd and sheep and of the vine from the Jewish Scriptures are given a Christological interpretation. Sometimes longer passages of Scripture are taken up and reworked in the light of what is believed to have taken place in Jesus. Gen. 1 is employed in this way in the first verses of the prologue, Exod. 16 and 17 are taken up in chapters 6 and 7, and, in particular, Isa. 40—55 with God's lawsuits against both Israel and the nations is reworked in this Gospel's trial motif and provides a major source for its language about witness and glory and its use of the 'I Am' formulation. In addition, particular figures can be called upon from within the overall scriptural witness, so that, just as Moses can be said to have written about Jesus (5.46), so Abraham is portrayed as having rejoiced to see Jesus' day (8.56) and Isaiah as having seen Jesus' glory (12.41). These varied uses of Scripture reflect the conviction expressed by Philip early in the narrative – 'We have found the one about whom Moses in the law and the prophets wrote, Jesus, son of Joseph, from Nazareth' (1.45).

While the law, in the sense of the Mosaic regulations that govern Israel's life, is no longer determinative for Jesus' followers because of its fulfilment in him, the law, in the sense of Scripture as a whole, though also fulfilled in Jesus, is by no means seen as a past phenomenon but retains its authority as God's revelation and as the essential vehicle for understanding and articulating the new revelation embodied in Jesus. For true insight into Jesus' mission it is necessary to recall and believe both Scripture and Jesus' word (2.22). At the same time Scripture is also subordinate to Christ as its hermeneutical key (cf. 5.39). His words, and not the words of Scripture in themselves, provide the ultimate criterion of eschatological judgement (cf. 12.48). His words, and not the words of Scripture in themselves, provide the means of life (cf. 6.63).

Within the context of the Fourth Gospel, it is hard to see that the high claims for Jesus in themselves produce a corresponding anti-Judaism. What they produce is a division within Judaism. The claims about Jesus and the claims about the law are initially part of an intra-Jewish debate. From the evangelist's perspective, any distancing or supersessionist stance towards the law and any negative use of the term 'the Jews' have become necessary only because those Jews in the majority have defined the law and Jewish identity in such a way as to exclude the claim that Jesus is Son of God and exclude those ethnic Jews who believe it. Once that competing definition has been allowed to become the determinative definition of religious Judaism, then the Gospel can be seen as anti-Jewish in the sense that it continues to dispute the majority view. In so doing, it refuses, however, to abandon the Jewish Scriptures or the notion that to be a true descendant of Abraham, a true Israelite and a true disciple of Moses entails belief in Jesus. Indeed, there is an important sense in which the Gospel's 'high' Christology, far from undermining the Jewish roots of the faith of those who believe in Jesus, reinforces them. It holds that the human flesh taken on by the Logos is Jewish flesh, the human face in which God is now decisively disclosed is a Jewish face. Jesus is the Saviour of all the world but because *Jesus* is Saviour, salvation is of the Jews. In the light of God's disclosure in Jesus, the symbols of Jewish history are reinterpreted but it is *Jewish* symbols that receive this treatment. The judgement that takes place and that produces a division within Israel means that it is Jewish believers who originally constitute the believing community, and it is into this community that Gentile believers then enter on the basis of the same faith. The Fourth Gospel could not be clearer that there is a continuing dispute between this community and those Jews who remain in unbelief, a dispute, which, because it is not just about Jesus' Messiahship but about the identity of God, affects all the basic aspects of their common tradition. It could also not be clearer that, in the midst of this dispute, the understanding of Jesus' significance, of their own identity and of their witness in the world on the part of both Jewish and Gentile believers remains dependent on the relationship to Judaism in all its complexity and contentiousness.

Further Reading

For a succinct treatment of John's theology, see D. M. Smith, *The Theology of the Gospel of John* (Cambridge: Cambridge University Press, 1995). For fuller discussions of or alternative approaches to the two aspects sketched above, see P. N. Anderson, *The Christology of the Fourth Gospel* (Tübingen: Mohr, 1996); J. Ashton, *Understanding the Fourth Gospel* (Oxford: Clarendon, 1991), 121–373; R. Bieringer *et al.* (eds), *Anti-Judaism and the Fourth Gospel* (Assen: Royal van Gorcum, 2001); R. Bultmann, *Theology of the New Testament*, vol. 2 (London: SCM Press, 1955), 33–69; M. Casey, *Is John's Gospel True?* (London: Routledge, 1996), 30–62, 111–39; E. Käsemann, *The Testament of Jesus* (London: SCM Press, 1968); A. T. Lincoln, *Truth on Trial* (Peabody, Mass.: Hendrickson, 2000), 193–207, 231–42, 397–417; M. J. J. Menken, *Old Testament Quotations in the Fourth Gospel* (Kampen: Kok Pharos, 1996); S. Pancaro, *The Law in the Fourth Gospel* (Leiden: Brill, 1975); M. M. Thompson, *The God of the Gospel of John* (Grand Rapids: Eerdmans, 2001).

SETTING AND PURPOSES

If the shape and plotting of John's narrative take the form indicated earlier and if its Christology and perspective on Judaism have the emphases just identified, what construal of the Fourth Gospel's setting and purposes might best account for these and other major characteristics?

It should be clear from the earlier discussions that, in terms of its broad intellectual and cultural setting, the Fourth Gospel sits squarely within the religious thought-world of the Judaism of the late first century CE. This was a Judaism that defined itself in terms of its interpretation and practice of Torah and Scripture as these had been developed during the second temple period, and that had interacted in a variety of ways with the social codes of its Mediterranean world and with the political, economic and cultural aspects of its dominant Graeco-Roman environment. It is not surprising, therefore, that some parallels can be found between the Gospel's conceptual framework and that of strands of Judaism which were either more resistant or more accommodating to the surrounding culture. The Fourth Gospel's modified dualism, its use of the symbolism of light and darkness, its talk of the Spirit and of the truth – to take a few examples – have features in common with the Qumran writings, although no direct influence of the latter on the former can be clearly established. Similarly, the Fourth Gospel's use of Hellenistic Jewish Wisdom traditions, particularly in the prologue and in some of Jesus' discourses, has elements in common with the use made of the same traditions by Philo of Alexandria. Both, for example, link the Logos with Wisdom, see knowledge of God as being made available through the Logos, and develop some of the same biblical imagery, such as Jacob's ladder, the manna and the brazen serpent, but again no direct dependence of the Fourth Gospel on Philo can be demonstrated. While the thought reflected in the Gnostic writings of the second century may also have had antecedents in the dualistic terminology, the light and darkness imagery, the notion of Wisdom as a descending revealer and the emphasis on knowledge in these forms of Judaism, the once-popular attempt to interpret John's Gospel as influenced by or responding to Gnosticism has now rightly been abandoned, although the presence of these elements in the Gospel may account for its heavy use by later Christian Gnostic teachers, such as Heracleon. Within this Jewish thought-world, the fourth evangelist is also obviously the heir of early Christian teaching, particularly, as has been seen, in the development of this in the Synoptic traditions and probably in the Synoptics themselves. He is also likely to have been familiar with elements of the Pauline development of the gospel, some of which, as a number of scholars hold, may have been in any case mediated through Mark's Gospel.

Critical in the distinctive development of the Fourth Gospel's message about Jesus was the conflict within the local Jewish community between those whose views are represented by the evangelist and those who opposed them. The conflict escalated to the point where the religious authorities took the drastic step of expelling the former group from the synagogue and this is reflected in three references within the narrative which are clearly anachronistic for the time of the earthly Jesus' mission (9.22; 12.42; 16.2). Within the New Testament only the Fourth Gospel depicts Christians as being made ἀποσυνάγωγος or being put out of the synagogue. The similar language of being excluded and having one's name cast out as evil in Luke 6.22 could reflect the same formal punishment but might be a reference to no more than informal social ostracism and verbal abuse. The fierce antagonism that produced excommunication is reflected in 16.2, which adds that those responsible for the expulsion will also kill some of those expelled and will do so out of zeal for God, presumably the same motivation that lay behind the expulsion (cf. also Matt. 23.34; Luke 21.16).

There is external evidence for Jewish Christians being excommunicated from the synagogue in a Jewish source whose tradition may date to around the same time as the composition of the Gospel, but the nature of this evidence and its relation to the Gospel's references are disputed. The source is *b. Ber.* 28b–29a, which states that the twelfth of the synagogue's Eighteen Benedictions, the *birkat ha-minim*, was reformulated by Samuel the Small at the instigation of Gamaliel II at Jamnia during the penultimate decade of the first century. The reformulated wording is 'For the apostates let there be no hope and let the arrogant government be speedily opposed in our days. Let the Nazarenes and the Minim be destroyed in a moment and let them be blotted out of the Book of Life and not be inscribed with the righteous. Blessed art thou, O Lord, who humblest the proud!' The second sentence appears to have been added to an older benediction, which called for the overthrow of Israel's enemies, in order now specifically to associate the Nazarenes (Christians) and the Minim (heretics) with such enemies. Martyn (1979) held that this twelfth benediction lay behind the Johannine references to excommunication and functioned in a way that would filter out Christians, who would not want to utter a curse on themselves when required to lead the congregation in a recitation of the benediction. It is doubtful, however, that the *birkat ha-minim* can be so directly related to the Fourth Gospel. The tradition and its connection with Jamnia is found in a relatively late strand within rabbinic literature. Whatever its relation to Jamnia, it can nevertheless be dated to the first part of the second century because of the evidence for its use provided by Justin (*Dial.* 16, 96), who refers to Jews cursing Christians in the synagogue. That the benediction is called *birkat ha-minim* suggests that originally Nazarenes (*notsrim*) did not appear in the reformulation. That term would not in any case have been needed in order to exclude Jewish Christians, since this group would have been the prime candidate for the category of Minim or heretics. *Notsrim* is likely to have been added later, possibly after the Bar Kochba revolt of 135 CE, not as a reference to the Jewish Christian sect of the Nazoreans but in order to broaden the curse to include the Nazarenes, all followers of Jesus of Nazareth. The Fourth Gospel does not, of course, mention cursing in the synagogue prayers, and so this mechanism may not have been the means of expulsion experienced by Johannine Jewish Christians. In fact, the Fourth Gospel appears to reflect the impact of a more formal and drastic decision. In drawing attention to the twelfth benediction, Martyn illuminated aspects of the experience of expulsion but moved too far beyond the available evidence in making the benediction's formulation at Jamnia the precise cause of the expulsion of Johannine Jewish Christians. It is safer to see the excommunication referred to in John as a local and more radical manifestation of the same post-70 CE move among the Tannaitic rabbis to close ranks, ensure unity and reinforce Jewish identity that produced various forms of informal and formal ostracism of dissidents, including the formulation of the twelfth benediction, which later rabbinic writings then associated with Jamnia.

More important than being able to pinpoint a date or a connection with Jamnia is an attempt to understand the causes and consequences of the expulsion behind the Fourth Gospel. Clearly it was their views about Jesus that got these Jewish Christians into trouble. According to 9.22, 'the Jews had already decided that if anyone confessed him as the Christ, that person would be expelled from the synagogue'. As already noted, the acclamation of someone as Messiah would not in itself have been enough to warrant such a punishment. In the case of Jesus, the confession would have been more difficult to tolerate because it was being made about someone who was perceived to have been a lawbreaker and to have died a shameful death. But what caused the greatest offence was the view that this Messiah was Son of God and the nature of the relationship to God that these Jewish Christians read into this title. The synagogue authorities took their view to mean that Jesus had made himself, and his followers were making him, Son of God (19.7), equal with God (5.18), or God (10.33) and therefore to be a threat to the primary axiom of Judaism as expressed in the Shema – 'Hear, O Israel: the Lord our God is one Lord' (Deut. 6.4). The Christology of the Fourth Gospel was honed in the midst of this dispute. The belief that Jesus was the Son of God who was one with God led to the expulsion from the synagogue of those who held it, and the circumstances surrounding the expulsion contributed to the way this belief was shaped and expressed in response to the objections that had been encountered and to the experiences that followed. The evangelist does indeed hold that Jesus was Son of God, equal with God, and God, but is at pains to make clear that Jesus does not arrogate this status to himself; it is granted him by God so that this is who he really was. Jesus does not somehow replace God. The Son is equal to the Father but is not the Father. But this does not mean that Jesus is a second god. The Fourth Gospel stresses the oneness of the Son with the Father (10.33; 17.22) so that the Son is to be seen as sharing in the identity of the one God of Israel (17.3). The evangelist would have claimed that this was not a breach of monotheism but instead a variation within it which already had a precedent within Jewish Wisdom traditions. Here the prologue is important in making the Logos the key category for interpreting the mission and status of Jesus as the Son. The Logos category comes from within the Wisdom theology of Judaism, where it was not seen as threatening monotheism because it stood for the one God of Israel in this God's immanence within the world. Used of Jesus, it indicates from the start of the narrative that the divine sonship of Jesus does not make him a second god but is to be seen in terms of the immanence in history of the one God.

The experience resulting from expulsion and also contributing to the shaping of the Gospel's Christology would have been a traumatic one. Excommunication from the synagogue was a continuation of earlier Jewish disciplinary measures against apostasy and blasphemy. The Deuteronomic laws had put perpetrators of such offences under a curse leading to destruction and called for these evils to be purged from the midst of the people by the putting to death of those who practised them (cf. Deut. 13; 17.1–13; 28.15–68). During the second temple period, however, exclusion from the community became a substitute for the death penalty, though it was still seen as a covenantal curse and associated with death. When, as 16.2 suggests, some Johannine Christians were killed at the hands of the authorities, this would have been seen as an act of religious zeal that simply extended what was already entailed by excommunication. Most, however, would have experienced the latter not only as being cut off from the synagogue's meetings, observances and festivals but also as a more general social ostracism and shaming. They discovered that the cost of their confession of Jesus was a profound religious and social dislocation. At stake in believing Jesus to be Son of God were not only their previous notions about God but also their roots in a tradition, their sense of identity, their social relationships and their honour. It is not surprising that, for those deprived of Jewish observances and festivals, the Gospel narrative treats Jesus as the fulfilment and replacement of the significance of Torah and its feasts, that, for those who were under a ban that was a substitute for death, it makes the experience of life the chief benefit of belief in Jesus, and that, for those who had experienced social shaming, it tells the story of Jesus and his followers to a large extent in terms of glory or honour.

One further factor arising from this setting should be mentioned. Some who had initially professed faith in Jesus as the Messiah appear to have been unwilling to accept the consequences of making the full public confession of Jesus as Son of God and stayed within the synagogue. Those who had experienced expulsion felt betrayed by these secret believers and attributed to them fear and complicity in the hostile actions of the authorities. This group is represented in the narrative by, among others, Nicodemus, who comes to Jesus by night, and Joseph of Arimathea, 'a secret disciple for fear of the Jews'. While these figures are treated more sympathetically, some of the harshest language in the Gospel is reserved for those Jews who had believed in Jesus but failed to continue in his word (cf. 8.31–59). In one place those who believed but who did not confess their faith for fear that the Pharisees would put them out of the synagogue are said to value human reputation or honour more highly than the honour or glory that God bestows (12.42–3).

It is not easy to say how much time elapsed between the experiences associated with the expulsion from the synagogue and the composition of the bulk of the Gospel. Enough time must have passed for Jewish Christians to have become a separate community with an identity differentiated from that of the synagogue and, as is suggested by the Gospel's universal perspective on salvation, for Gentiles to have joined them. Equally clearly, not enough time had elapsed for the scars from such experiences to have disappeared and for the trauma to be viewed now as a matter of the distant past. The extent and nature of the Gospel's depiction of the confrontation between Jesus and 'the Jews' are such that the issues still appear to be vital ones.

But the Gospel also gives indication that the new community of Christians had been in existence long enough for a new crisis to be brewing. The first two Johannine epistles reflect the results of that crisis and report a split within the new community. From the point of view of their writer, one faction had seceded from the rest (1 John 2.19) and a major accusation levelled against it is its deficient assessment of Jesus. Those who eventually seceded may have been able to confess that Jesus was Son of God but were not able to make the equally important confession that he had come in the flesh, in full humanity (cf. 1 John 4.2–3; 2 John 7). On the most likely construal of their views, they underplayed the reality or redemptive significance of Jesus' human life and death and this was linked with claims to their own superior spiritual status, which gave them an immunity to sin. In any case, the writer not only reports their breaking of fellowship but deems them to have departed from traditional and essential Christological beliefs. A number of scholars suggest plausibly that this defective Christology may not be unrelated to the presentation of Jesus in the bulk of the Gospel. In the dispute with the synagogue authorities, there was no issue about Jesus' humanity. This was assumed by both sides. What had had to be emphasized was Jesus' divinity and so his pre-existence, glory, divine powers and sovereign control and knowledge dominate the narrative. The trouble was that the next generation of community members, and particularly some of its Gentile converts, may not have shared the original presuppositions about Jesus' humanity and the reality of his suffering and death and therefore took its high Christology in what became an unacceptable direction. What are in all probability some of the latest stages of the Gospel's composition reflect awareness of this danger and of the impending internal crisis. That Jesus' glory was that of the Logos who became flesh is underscored in the prologue (1.14) and that the reality of his suffering and death in the flesh was essential to his salvific mission is made plain in the bread of life discourse (6.25–59). Jesus' unity with the Father is shown to entail the need for unity between believers (17.1–26), and in a setting where ecclesial structures were in danger of being fragmented by those who appealed to their own new spiritual insights, the epilogue indicates the importance of Peter's pastoral leadership of the wider church and the authority of the tradition represented by the Beloved Disciple (21.15–25).

Given that these sort of crises in its setting are reflected in and have helped to shape the Fourth Gospel's narrative, what might be said about the purposes for which it was written? Clearly 20.30–1 should come into play at this point, since these verses sum up the persuasive aim of the narrative's presentation of Jesus and, in so doing, directly address the readers. The commentary on them and the textual note set out the reasons for opting for the present subjunctive of the verb 'to believe' and for translating the purpose clause as 'in order that you may continue to believe that Jesus is the Christ, the Son of God ...' The witness of this book to the life, death and resurrection of Jesus is meant to produce continuance in belief. The shape of the argument, whereby implied readers are expected to share the point of view set out in the prologue if they are to appreciate the ironies of the unfolding story and then to be confirmed in this perspective by the time the narrative reaches its conclusion, also suggests that its primary purpose is to reinforce the faith of those who are already Christian believers. The account of Jesus' public mission is not formulated as if the intent were to make a case about Jesus to unbelievers. In particular, Jesus' discourses and disputes with opponents presuppose some knowledge on the part of believing readers about the issues faced in their own time about Jesus' identity. Those issues are being replayed in the time of Jesus so that such readers can be confirmed in the appropriate beliefs about his identity. In addition, implied readers are expected to identify in particular with the role of Jesus' followers in the narrative and a large portion of that narrative (chapters 13—17) is devoted to addressing explicitly the concerns of such followers. Quite different rhetorical strategies would be required if the aim were to persuade readers to come to initial belief.

The importance of having the right sort of faith in Jesus should be evident from the Christological issues at the heart of the crises that have been sketched above. The summary statement of purpose reflects the evangelist's conviction that the authentic belief that leads to life is belief in Jesus as the sort of Messiah who is Son of God, with all the connotations of a unique relationship to God that the latter designation bears in this Gospel. The 'you' of 20.31 who need to be strengthened in such belief can be seen as embracing a wide variety of implied readers. Clues from the text suggest that they would all have been expected to have a basic knowledge of the story of Jesus but then that there were differing levels of understanding. Some needed to have basic Hebrew or Aramaic terms explained and Jewish customs pointed out, others would be expected to have a good knowledge of the Jewish Scriptures and appreciate the use made of them, and others might be expected to be aware of Synoptic versions of the events recounted. The intended readership would have included those whom the evangelist represents – the Jewish Christians who have come through the experience of expulsion from the synagogue and may still have questions about whether the cost was worthwhile, and these and Gentile Christians who are facing new issues about Jesus' identity within their community. The narrative's sympathetic portrait of some 'secret believers', such as Nicodemus and Joseph of Arimathea, suggests that it may still hope to win over even some of those who had professed initial belief but had remained in the synagogue. But while the narrative was shaped by the setting of the Christians the evangelist represents, its writing down and circulation indicates it was intended for a much wider audience. The convictions about Jesus to which the evangelist had come were seen as essential for all believers if they were to bear effective witness. They would not have had the same experiences but could be expected to face analogous conflicts within their own particular setting in the Graeco-Roman world if they made, as they should, the same confession about Jesus as the Christ, the Son of God. Some would need to make this confession in the face of rival claims for Dionysus (see comments on 2.1–11) or for Domitian (see comments on 20.28) and readers of the epilogue are expected to be aware of Peter's martyr death during the persecution under Nero (cf. 21.18–19). To all those who found their confession about the identity of Jesus in dispute and who suffered the consequences, this Gospel's interpretation of his mission was meant to provide reassurance about that confession and about its being the means of experiencing the life and well-being of the age to come in the midst of present conflicts and trials.

Although it has been possible to reconstruct with a relatively high degree of probability features of the setting that lies behind the Gospel, it is impossible to say with any precision in which location Jewish Christians were excommunicated from the synagogue, whether, as some suggest, the evangelist and his community had moved from Palestine to a new setting at some point, or even where the Gospel was finally produced. In regard to the last, Ephesus, Antioch, Alexandria and the region of northern Transjordan have all been suggested. The long-standing view that the Gospel originated in Ephesus drew most of its justification from traditions associating John the apostle with that city (cf. Irenaeus, *Haer.* 3.1.1) and from positing a close relation between the Gospel and Revelation.

Once doubts are cast on the identification of this apostle with the Beloved Disciple and on the Gospel having the same author as Revelation, any strong reasons for linking the Gospel to this particular city are also undermined. The most likely place of origin remains an urban centre outside Palestine and one in which there was a sizeable Jewish population, and on this basis Ephesus remains one of the possible and more plausible candidates. But, as has been noted, wherever it emerged, the Gospel was written with a wide circulation in view. Important as the setting and purposes that originally shaped the Gospel are for its interpretation, its message nevertheless transcends the circumstances of its production. The cosmic aspect of the narrative, in which God addresses the world through a process of judgement, lent itself to the universalization of the scope of this message. The message still reflected the contingency of contested claims about Jesus but was not thereby robbed of the right to be treated, as it was when received into the New Testament canon, as authoritative or normative.

Further Reading

J. Ashton, *Understanding the Fourth Gospel* (Oxford: Clarendon, 1991), 166–98; R. A. Culpepper, *Anatomy of the Fourth Gospel* (Philadelphia: Fortress, 1983), 205–27; M. Davies, *Rhetoric and Reference in the Fourth Gospel* (Sheffield: JSOT Press, 1992), 349–75; G. D. Fee, 'On the Text and Meaning of Jn 20, 30-31', in F. van Segbroeck (ed.), *The Four Gospels 1992: Festschrift Franz Neirynck* (Louvain: Louvain University Press, 1992), 193–205; A. T. Lincoln, *Truth on Trial* (Peabody, Mass.: Hendrickson, 2000), 171–82; 266–301; J. L. Martyn, *History and Theology in the Fourth Gospel*, 2nd edn (Nashville: Abingdon, 1979).

IMPACT

For the earliest Christians the good news was that the God of Israel had raised Jesus of Nazareth from the dead. The Gospels can be seen as expanded narrative identifications of this crucified and risen Jesus in the form of ancient biographies. If the Synoptic Gospels ground their post-resurrection identification more firmly in the traditions about the human life of Jesus, the Fourth Gospel more freely allows Christian convictions to colour its narrative identification. As it takes its place alongside the Synoptics in the New Testament canon, from a later perspective it can be seen to probe, in particular, what is Christian about Jesus the Jew, because Jesus' unique relationship to God is the crux and scandal of Christian faith. For this Gospel that relationship is the dividing line between unbelieving Jews and Jewish and Gentile Christian believers. For the patristic period it set the boundaries of orthodoxy. For contemporary Christians it remains the particular and distinctive source of their religious identity in their conversations with each other and in their witness to others.

For those who are more comfortable with the so-called historical Jesus, a human Jesus reconstructed primarily from traditions behind the Synoptics, and who can be viewed as an insightful Jewish prophetic figure and teacher of his day, the identification of Jesus in the Fourth Gospel, in particular, is likely to be disturbing and alienating. Yet, as we have observed, this Gospel's narrative presents the experience of disturbance and alienation as surrounding Jesus from the start and as central factors in the production of its portrait of Jesus in the first place. Those represented by the evangelist found the traditions of the mission, death and resurrection of Jesus to be deeply disturbing, not capable of being accommodated comfortably within the conventional categories of the time for classifying religious figures, and compelling a stretching and transformation of those categories that incurred alienation and traumatic social consequences.

It is little wonder that the Fourth Gospel interprets Jesus' life as evoking a crisis for humanity, demanding radical decision-making, and that it sets this life in the context of the enacting of God's judgement within the world. Its reflection on the significance of Jesus in dramatic narrative form is rightly viewed as constituting, along with the letters of Paul, one of the most profound pieces of early Christian theologizing. It presses hard the implications of Christian truth claims and from within its own particular setting and formulations at the end of the first century grapples with some of the most difficult questions for Christian theology, questions that will not go away. What does it mean to claim that Jesus is the revelation of God and that now God is to be known decisively through Jesus? If God was uniquely at work in this human being, what does that say about the significance of his life and death? How does one coherently hold and articulate that this particular Jew could be fully human and yet fully one with God? In what sense was he one with God in his suffering crucifixion and what does that indicate both about God and about suffering and death? Does belief in Jesus as the incarnation of God break the bounds of Jewish monotheism? If Jesus is the definitive fulfilment of Torah and all the major religious symbols of Judaism, are they thereby replaced by Jesus or do they have continuing validity? What is the status of a Judaism that rejects such Christian claims for Jesus? Can it be said that Jews and Christians still worship the same God, and if so, in what sense? If, with the Spirit, the divine Son now reveals the identity of the one trinitarian God, what is the relation of this God to the God of Israel?

On all such matters John's Gospel presents us with Christianity's 'scandal of particularity' in one of its starkest forms. Christians continue to wrestle with this Gospel's own answers and implications. It would be hard to conceive of an allegiance to Jesus which did not hold that in him God was incarnate as still Christian belief in any meaningful sense. But do some of the other implications the fourth evangelist draws from this conviction necessarily follow? In a time of greater awareness of other major world religions and increased sensitivity to Judaism in the light of the consequences of Christian anti-Judaism and the Shoah, what is to be made of this Gospel's seemingly exclusive claims for the unique disclosure of God in Jesus? Its formulations cannot simply be repeated in what are quite different circumstances, but there can be no evading their logic and rigour if any participation in and reflection on dialogue with Judaism in particular, but also with other religions and world-views, are to be honest and to remain in touch with the roots of Christian belief in Jesus. In all these ways John's Gospel continues to confront its readers with the question of how to assess the uniqueness of Jesus' life and with the implications that follow from that assessment for their own ultimate commitments in life. In sum, if, as the Fourth Gospel claims, the life of Jesus shows us God, what does that say about God and what does it say about us? Readers, then, have to be prepared not only to bring their own probing questions to the Gospel but to find themselves and their values radically questioned by the one to whom it bears witness as the criterion of truth and judgement. But, as the Gospel's statement of purpose makes clear, the goal of its unsettling perspective is to invite trust in its subject. That is clearly more than an intellectual response. It is one in which faith seeks understanding and in which a commitment to Jesus as the revelation of God entails a willingness to participate in his continuing story within a community that is meant to be characterized by love and unity. To assent to the witness of this Gospel about Jesus as true (cf. 21.24b) is thus also to risk a way of life and acts of service that eschew coercion and genuinely have the interests of the other in view.

TRANSLATION AND COMMENTARY

A. THE PROLOGUE   1.1–18

(1) In the beginning was the Word, and the Word was at God's side, and what God was, the Word was. (2) This one was in the beginning at God's side. (3) All things came into being through him, and not one thing that has come into being came into being without him.[1] (4) In him was life, and the life was the light of humans; (5) and the light shines in the darkness, and the darkness did not overcome it.

(6) There was a man sent from God, whose name was John; (7) he came for the sake of witness, in order that he might testify about the light, so that all might believe through him. (8) He was not himself the light, but came in order that he might testify about the light. (9) The true light that enlightens every person was coming into the world. (10) He was in the world, and the world came into being through him, and the world did not know him. (11) He came to what was his own, and his own people did not receive him. (12) But to whoever received him, he gave authority to become children of God, that is, to those who believed in his name, (13) who were born neither of bloods nor of the will of the flesh nor of the will of the male but of God.

(14) And the Word became flesh and dwelt among us, and we saw his glory, glory as of an only son of a father, full of grace and truth. (15) John testifies about him and cried out, saying, 'This was he of whom I said, "He who comes after me has become

---

[1] The earliest manuscripts contain no punctuation. There is a division, however, among some other manuscripts over where the sentences should be punctuated. The major alternative would provide the translation 'and without him not one thing came into being. What has come into being in him was life ...' This has the stronger support, but there are very good grounds for preferring the punctuation reflected in the translation above. The repetition in depicting the Word's relation to creation corresponds to the preceding repetition in depicting the Word's relation to God, and 'in him was life' corresponds to the narrative's later claims about the relation between Jesus and life.

**ahead of me, because he was before me." ' (16) For from his
fullness we have all received, grace instead of grace; (17) for the
law was given through Moses; grace and truth came into being
through Jesus Christ. (18) No one has at any time seen God;
the only God[2], who rests in the Father's lap, he has made him
known.**

The Fourth Gospel's account of the significance of Jesus of Nazareth will,
in dependence on Mark's Gospel, take the form of an account of Jesus'
life, a version of the ancient biography. Its prologue makes unmistakably
clear that this ancient biography is about a unique subject. Whereas Mark
begins with the baptism of Jesus, and Matthew and Luke probe his origins
further in their birth narratives, John's account signals that the beginning
of its subject's life is to be linked to the beginning of the world and
beyond that to the life of the Creator. Not only does this give its subject
cosmic significance, it also takes up immediately what will be of primary
importance in the rest of its story – the issue of Jesus' identity in relation
to that of God.

There is a rhythmic, poetic character to much of this prologue in the
Greek. It is broken up by prose passages, particularly those that refer to
John the Baptist, but its repetitive style and use of parallelism cause it to
stand out from the rest of the Gospel. In its present form it is not a hymn,
but several scholars have argued, with some plausibility, that it has taken up
and adapted for its own purposes hymnic material, or perhaps an exalted
prose piece, celebrating Christ as Logos, that this original composition
was influenced by the variegated Jewish Wisdom tradition, and that it
would have been familiar to and used in the evangelist's community. Most
of those who take this view would include vv. 1–5, 10–12ab, 14 and 16
as part of the original material. This would constitute a traditional piece
about the Logos in creation, the Logos in the world, and the community's believing response to the Logos. The other verses would then
consist in the evangelist's relating of the content of the hymnic material
to the figure with whom Mark's Gospel starts its story about Jesus – John
the Baptist – and then also making some interpretative and polemical
comments. Other scholars have claimed, instead, that the evangelist could
just as easily have composed the whole of the prologue himself as a unity
and that its poetic character can be accounted for on the premiss that it
was modelled on and reflects the style of a Wisdom poem, such as that
in Proverbs 8. However, the several key words that do not recur in the
body of the Gospel (particularly the use of 'Word' as a title, 'grace' and

---

[2] Following p[66] ℵ* B C* L, p[75] also reads θεός but adds the definite article. Other
manuscripts read 'the only Son' or 'the only one'. The former could well be the result
of later assimilation to 3.16, 18, while the latter is poorly attested.

'fullness'), the references to John the Baptist that appear to be insertions into an already structured piece (especially v. 15), and the way in which vv. 12c–13 read like editorial expansion on the preceding lines in v. 12ab are among the factors that suggest the greater plausibility of the former view. But in the nature of the case there must remain uncertainty about any source for the prologue and its extent, and in the end a decision on this matter does not decisively affect the more important concern of discovering the significance of its present form for the message of the Gospel.

In its present form the prologue falls into four parts – (1) vv. 1–5 – the Word in relation to God and creation; (2) vv. 6–8 – the witness of John the Baptist to the Word as light; (3) vv. 9–13 – the Word in the world and the two types of response; (4) vv. 14–18 – the community's confession about the Word.

1. The Word in Relation to God and Creation   1.1–5

The poetic character of these verses is evident in their step or staircase parallelism, whereby a term prominent in one line is taken up in the next. In this way 'Word' in v. 1a is employed again in v. 1b, and the same phenomenon occurs with 'God' in v. 1b and v. 1c, with 'came into being' in v. 3a and v. 3b, with 'life' in v. 4a and v. 4b, with 'light' in v. 4b and v. 5a, and with 'darkness' in v. 5a and v. 5b.

1 This first part of the prologue invites comparison with the beginning of the Jewish Scriptures, the first verses of Genesis. The very first phrase, **In the beginning**, is the same in the Fourth Gospel as in the LXX version of Gen. 1.1. But whereas in Genesis the reference is to the beginning of creation, in this Gospel it is to the absolute beginning in the sphere of God, and the creation is not mentioned until v. 3. The parallel with Genesis continues with the themes of word, creation, light and darkness. In Genesis, it should be remembered, each stage of creation is depicted as a result of God's word. Here in v. 3 the creation is also seen as the coming into being of all things through the Word. In Genesis God's word first creates light, and here the prologue describes the Word in relation to the world of humanity in terms of light (vv. 4b, 5, 7–9). In addition, in both Genesis and the Fourth Gospel the motifs of light and darkness appear in opposition to one another. In Genesis God speaks and there is light where darkness had previously prevailed; God then separates the light from the darkness, and there is night and day. In this prologue the contrast between light and darkness is also dominant, and it will recur in the ensuing narrative as part of its modified dualism.

In the sphere that lies beyond created space and time the Word was already in existence – **In the beginning was the Word**. What would have been the force of this key term, the Word (ὁ λόγος), for the evangelist's readers? Its general use to indicate an instance of a person's self-expression in verbal activity should remain determinative even when we are forced, as here, to see the term employed analogously or metaphorically in relation to the divine. In other words, the basic force of 'the Word' is God's self-expression. Yet there may well have been further connotations deriving from a variety of usages with which the evangelist and his readers would have been familiar. Some have seen a possible influence from Stoic usage, in which the Logos stood for the rational principle guiding and directing all things. But in Stoicism this principle alone was regarded as divine, so that there would have been no precedent for the notions of both God and the Logos existing together. Philo, in his attempt to mediate between Jewish tradition and Hellenistic thought, did, however, have the Logos as an intermediary between Creator and creatures (cf. e.g. *Her.* 2–5; *Quaes. Gen.* 2.62), and identified the Logos with the figure of Wisdom in the Jewish Scriptures (cf. e.g. *Fug.* 97, 108–9; *Somn.* 2.242, 245). Yet, as in Stoicism, so also in Philo the Logos was conceived not only as a divine principle but also as the reasoning faculty within humans. In this way it represented thought coming to expression both in God and in humanity (cf. e.g. *Her.* 119, 233–4; *Mos.* 2.127–9). Although it may appear that, in using this concept to bridge the gulf between God and humanity, Philo's formulations sometimes blur the distinction between Creator and creature, he was convinced the gulf remained ultimately unbridgeable (cf. *Somn.* 1.61–72, 241; *Post. Caini* 16–20) and that his speculation did not in the least compromise his monotheism. But there is no clear evidence that John knew Philo's writings from the first half of the first century CE. It is more likely that his thought or his earlier source for the prologue runs parallel to that of Philo and that both have independently developed Wisdom categories in terms of the Logos. Another possible first-century usage is sometimes posited as a major influence on the prologue. In the Aramaic targums the term *memra*, 'word', is often employed with reference to God and it is argued that it functions in a similar way to 'Logos' here. But only in a very few places does it stand for God's revelatory activity, and most frequently it is used as a way of avoiding the divine name and does not function in terms of personification or a figure that can be distinguished in some way from God. In addition, all the targumic evidence comes from later than the first century and there can be no certainty about how early or widespread may have been any usage of the term other than as a circumlocution for the divine name.

The origins of the prologue's use of 'the Word' are in all probability to be found within earlier Jewish thought about both Wisdom and the Word of God. The creative function of God's word in Genesis 1 has already been noted, but Ps. 33.6 has the same notion – 'By the word of the Lord the heavens were made', as does Wis. 9.1 – 'O God of my ancestors and Lord of mercy, who have made all things by your word'. Then there are passages where the word of God exercises independent functions that are almost personal. Two of the most striking are Isa. 55.11 – 'So shall my word be that goes out from my mouth; it shall not return to me empty, but it shall accomplish that which I purpose, and succeed in the thing for which I sent it' – and Wis. 18.15–16 – 'Your all-powerful word leaped from heaven, from the royal throne, into the midst of the land that was doomed, a stern warrior carrying the sharp sword of your authentic command, and stood and filled all things with death, and touched heaven while standing on the earth.' God's Word here has been personified dramatically but has not become some independent personal agent. It is rather a way of talking about God in God's approach to humanity. Wis. 9.1–2 puts God's Word and God's Wisdom in a parallel formulation – 'who have made all things by your word, and by your wisdom have formed humanity', and Wisdom could be personified in a similar way to the Word. Wisdom existed at the beginning before the creation of the world (Prov. 8.22–6) and was at God's side and instrumental in creation (Prov. 8.27–31). She was with God and can be sent from heaven (Wis. 9.9–10) and is associated with life (Prov. 8.35). There are also notable resemblances between what can be said of Wisdom and what is said of the Word later in John's prologue. Wisdom finds no reception among humans (*1 Enoch* 42.2; cf. John 1.11) and can be told to make her dwelling or to pitch her tent – 'My Creator chose the place for my tent. He said, "Make your dwelling in Jacob"' (Sir. 24.8; cf. John 1.14). Again such talk involves a personification of a divine function, a way of speaking of God's immanence in the creation, God's active engagement in the world and with Israel, without compromising God's transcendence.

Adding to the likelihood that it is Jewish thought about Wisdom and the Word of God that has been most influential in the prologue's use of 'the Word' is the fact that such thought had already begun to associate both Wisdom (cf. Sir. 24.23–4) and God's Word (cf. Isa. 2.3) with Torah and also talked of Torah in terms of light (cf. Ps. 119.105; Prov. 6.23) and life (cf. Ps. 119.93; Prov. 4.4, 13). From this perspective the prologue's later identification of the Word with Jesus can be seen as one more strand in this Gospel's response to Judaism in terms of the replacement by Jesus of Torah and its attributes and institutions (cf. also v. 17).

The particular choice of 'the Word' rather than 'Wisdom' in the prologue may be due to two main factors. Since the incarnation of the Word in Jesus is in view, the masculine noun ὁ λόγος is likely to have been seen as more appropriate than the feminine ἡ σοφία and its association with the figure of Lady Wisdom. Already in early Christian thought the Word had become an important concept. Paul used it for the gospel, the message about Jesus (cf. e.g. 1 Thess. 2.13; 1 Cor. 1.18; 2 Cor. 4.2;

Gal. 6.6), and he also appears to identify the message about Christ with Christ himself, so that he can talk of preaching Christ and not just the message about Christ (cf. e.g. 1 Cor. 1.23; 15.12; 2 Cor. 1.19; 4.5). Given early Christian belief in the pre-existence of Christ, it was only a short move from Christ understood as the word preached to the prologue's conception of Christ as the pre-existent Word who became incarnate.

In the prologue, then, the Word is pre-existent. It does not come into being. Unlike those texts that speak of Wisdom being created (e.g. Sir. 1.4; 24.9), the Word simply was in the beginning and it **was at God's side**. Literally, the Greek reads 'towards God', but in koiné Greek the preposition πρός with the accusative, 'towards,' can be equivalent to the preposition παρά with the dative, 'with, near, beside', and the latter is also employed of Wisdom's relation to God (Prov. 8.30 LXX). Later in the prologue this relation will be depicted in even more intimate terms (cf. v. 18). Just as in the Jewish Scriptures Wisdom can be placed at God's side without this figure being seen as a threat to monotheism, so from the Fourth Gospel's perspective envisaging the Word as in God's presence would not have been thought as transgressing the bounds of Jewish monotheism but as a vivid way of talking about God's self-communication. Indeed, **what God was, the Word was**. In the Greek of v. 1c there is no definite article with 'God', as there was in v. 1b. This can be explained by saying that 'God' is the predicate and frequently predicate nouns that precede the verb, as here, are without an article, so 'the Word was God' is an acceptable and straightforward translation. But this grammatical observation is not quite as clear-cut as it may appear, since there are also frequent occasions when statements of identity do have the article with the predicate. What is more, Philo (*Somn.* 1.227–30) has a commentary on Gen. 31.13 LXX which shows that the distinction between talk of 'God' with or without an article could be of major significance in a context similar to that of the prologue. He writes, 'the holy word in the present instance has indicated him who is truly God by means of the article, saying "I am the God", while it omits the article when mentioning him who is improperly so called, saying "Who appeared to thee in the place", not "of the God", but simply "of God" (Gen. 31.13). Here it gives the title of "God" to his chief Word.' This is one of the passages where Philo shows he can happily call the Logos God without infringing his monotheism, and it is precisely the absence of the article that is important for his formulation. In order to preserve this distinction between the use of 'God' with and without an article in the prologue, some prefer a translation such as 'the Word was divine'. But if this were what is meant, there is an adjective (θεῖος) that would have made it clear. For this reason, 'what God was, the Word was' (cf. also NEB, REB) may well be a better mediating translation that preserves the oddness of the Greek without saying too little or too much.

Even though the framework of the prologue remains within the creational monotheism of the Jewish Scriptures, theological questions are still raised by its first verse. It confronts its readers with the paradox that the Word is to be identified with God and yet is distinct from God, the paradox that will be formulated in the rest of the narrative in terms of Jesus as Son being one with the Father and yet distinct from the Father. Even if it is true, as some insist, that the prologue is speaking of the Word and not of Jesus at this point and that only at v. 14 does it move from personification language in the Jewish tradition to the Word's incarnation in an actual person, it appears quite artificial to hold the two entirely apart. Anyone, except a first-time reader, knows that the Word is to be identified as Jesus, and this becomes clear as early as vv. 9–12, and so inevitably the person of Jesus is associated with the personification of the Word. This is reinforced later in the narrative when Jesus is portrayed as thinking of himself as pre-existent and sharing a relation with God before the foundation of the world (cf. e.g. 17.5). If the pre-existence of the Torah for Jews was a way of expressing its supreme religious import-ance for them, does the same apply to the pre-existence of the Word who is to be identified with Jesus? Is it a metaphor or a mythological way of expressing Jesus' ultimate significance for those who believe in him? Or, once the historical person of Jesus is associated with the Word, is the prologue's talk of this Word any longer simply a personification and does it not require something like the later Christian modification within monotheism? The questions John 1.1 provokes in the light of the rest of the prologue are those which later credal and doctrinal formula-tions attempted to answer and contemporary Christology continues to explore. Often scholars attempt to distance their exegesis of the prologue as much as possible from later Christian confessions. In fact, it might well be claimed that most of the Christological affirmations of an ecumenical confession, such as the Nicene Creed, are already implicit in the prologue read within the Gospel as a whole.

2–3 In a summary and clarification of what has preceded, **This one** underlines that it is the divine Word who was the subject of the first two clauses of v. 1. There then follows an emphatic statement about the role of the Word in creation – **all things came into being through him, and not one thing that has come into being came into being without him**. Some argue that γίνεσθαι can mean 'to come to pass' or 'to happen' and see a similarity with 1QS 11.11, which speaks of all things coming to pass by God's design. But in the context of the preceding allusion to Gen. 1.1 it is more natural to see a reference to the role of the Word in creation rather than to the Word's providential control of history. The assertion is in line with other early Christian statements about Christ's role in creation (cf. 1 Cor. 8.5–6; Col. 1.15–17; Heb. 1.2). The emphasis that every single thing in the cosmos owes its existence to the mediation of the Logos not only reinforces the point that the pre-existent Logos is on the side of the Creator rather than the creature but also makes clear that when the Logos becomes incarnate and comes to his own, he comes into a sphere of existence that already truly belongs to him and is not simply alien territory.

4–5 The Word is now associated with life and light, two terms that will be characteristic of this Gospel's discourse, with 'life' (ζωή) occurring 37 times and 'light' (φῶς) 22 times. **In him was life**, God's energizing and life-giving power, sustaining created existence in relation to its Creator, and **the life was the light of humans**, displaying and communicating true knowledge of God to humanity. In Judaism, as has been noted, Torah brings life (cf. also Deut. 30.15–20; Sir. 17.11), as does Wisdom (cf. Prov. 8.35), while Torah is also light (cf. Ps. 119.105) and Wisdom is 'a reflection of eternal light' (Wis. 7.26). Both life and light are linked with Torah in Bar. 4.1–2. The contrast which follows between light and darkness is one that would also have been familiar from Jewish tradition, whether in the creation narrative of Gen. 1.3–5, in apocalyptic writings (cf. e.g. *1 Enoch* 89.8) or, in more developed form, in the Qumran literature (cf. e.g. 1QM with its war between the sons of light and the sons of darkness). In the more developed form of the contrast, light and darkness came to represent the two sides of a modified dualism in which God, on the side of light, is ultimately in control and will triumph in the end. The Fourth Gospel, in which 'darkness' (σκοτία) occurs eight times, shares this perspective. In the opposition between light and darkness, **the light shines in the darkness, and the darkness did not overcome it**. The verb in the second clause (καταλαμβάνω) can mean 'to grasp, comprehend, understand' as well as 'to master, overcome'. The latter is its force in the one other usage in this Gospel, which has a similar context – 'Walk while you have the light, lest the darkness overcome you' (12.35). Darkness represents the world in its alienation from the true source of life and remains as part of the narrative world of the Gospel. There can be no peaceful coexistence between such darkness and the light, but the darkness is not able to prevail or to extinguish the light of the Word.

2. The Witness of John the Baptist to the Word as Light   1.6–8

If the first five verses have focused attention primarily on realities beyond the created world of time and space, vv. 6–8 move explicitly into the realm of human history. With the transition in thought goes a transition of style – from the more poetic to the prose style typical of the opening of a narrative (cf. e.g. 1 Sam. 1.1 LXX). If the Gospel as we now have it went through a number of stages of composition, as many plausibly hold, then it could be that v. 6 was at one time the opening of the narrative before the prologue in its present form displaced it. In any case, as in the Synoptic tradition, John the Baptist is the figure whose mission serves as the introduction to that of Jesus. The difference is that in the Fourth Gospel his sole function is to act as a witness to Jesus. In this commentary John is frequently referred to as John the Baptist in order to avoid any confusion with the 'John' whose name has traditionally been associated with the Gospel's authorship. But the Gospel itself, unlike the Synoptics, does not give this first human witness the title of 'the Baptist'. The significance of this will be discussed later in the comments on the ending of chapter 3.

6–7 There was a man sent from God makes clear the origin of the Baptist's mission. Just as Jesus will frequently talk of having been sent by the Father, so the narrator makes clear that John's mission has the same divine origin. And just as Jesus will assert that he came to bear witness (cf. 18.37), so also the narrator can say that John came to do the same – **he came for the sake of witness, in order that he might testify about the light**. Nevertheless, the latter's mission of witness is immediately subordinated to that of Jesus. His witness is to the Word as light, whereas Jesus is the Word incarnate and is the light. John's witness is so that all might believe through him, whereas Jesus' witness is so that all might believe in him. The terminology of 'witness' and 'to testify' is found frequently throughout this Gospel. The noun (μαρτυρία) occurs 14 times in comparison with four times in the three Synoptics together, while the verb (μαρτυρεῖν) is found 33 times in comparison with twice in the three Synoptics. Together with such concepts as judgement, truth and life, this language forms part of a larger motif, that of a trial or lawsuit, which shapes much of the narrative. John's witness serves the same purpose – **so that all might believe through him** – as the Gospel itself – 'so that you may believe' (20.31). The language of belief is also characteristic of this Gospel, in which the verb 'to believe' occurs 98 times in comparison with 136 times in the rest of the New Testament. To believe through John is to receive his witness as true, and throughout the Gospel believing truly in Jesus is not simply to give assent to information about him but entails a person's total allegiance to and wholehearted trust in him. The formulation of the scope of John's witness as for all is also significant. The Baptist's mission is no longer seen as one that is simply within Israel but is now given a more universal audience.

8 This verse contains an ellipsis in its second clause, in which a main verb – 'came' – needs to be supplied – **but came in order that he might**

testify. The denial that John was the light and the repetition of his role as witness about the light suggests a polemical purpose, as if the narrator wishes to stress Jesus' superiority to John in the face of rather different claims. What are likely to be in view are the beliefs of those followers of John the Baptist who remained in rivalry with the Christian movement during its early development, some of whom considered the Baptist to be the Messiah (cf. Acts 19.1–7; Ps.–Clementine, *Recognitions* 1.54.60).

3. The Word in the World and the Two Types of Response   1.9–13

9 This section returns to the Word in relation to the world. In comparison with John, whose task was to point to the light, the Word is **the true light**, the genuine source of illumination, universal in its scope, enlightening every person. There is also another implicit comparison with the Torah, since in Jewish writings the law was said to be given to Israel in order to enlighten all people (cf. *T. Levi* 14.4 – 'the light of the law which was granted to you for the enlightenment of every man'; cf. also Wis. 18.4). An ambiguity surrounds the second half of this verse, in which the participle 'coming' could be taken with 'person' or with 'the true light' as part of a periphrastic imperfect construction. The former yields the translation 'enlightening every person who was coming into the world', while the latter is represented in our own translation – **The true light that enlightens every person was coming into the world**. Although 'all who come into the world' is an expression found in later rabbinic writings as the equivalent of 'every person', it would appear awkward to have both 'every person' and part of its equivalent together. Given the context, in which in the next verse the light is said to be in the world, a prior reference to its coming into the world makes more sense here. In addition, Jesus will later declare, 'I have come as light into the world' (12.46). The Word, then, has a transcendent power of illumination that is indispensable for all people. How far humans have allowed themselves to be illumined and guided by this divine light of life is not yet in view.

10 When the prologue now begins to deal with what in practice has been the human response to the light, the assessment of the response of humanity as a whole is not a positive one. All people may indeed be dependent on the light, just as they live only through the creative Word of God, but the world that ought to have recognized the light, by which alone it survives, does not do so. **He was in the world** is not a reference to the presence of the Light/Word in Israel's previous history, as is argued by some, but anticipates the presence of the incarnate Word. The broader meaning may have been in view in an earlier form of the material, but, as the prologue now stands, the prior reference to John in vv. 6–8 and the continuation of the thought in v. 12 make clear that the mission of the incarnate Logos is already the focus, although the incarnation will not be explicitly mentioned until v. 14. The massive irony is that **the world came into being through him, and the world did not know him**. The term 'world' (κόσμος) is another characteristically Johannine term and occurs 80 times in the Gospel. It is employed with two different nuances in this verse. In the first two instances the reference is to the created world, the world that constitutes humanity's environment and that includes humanity itself. In the third instance – **the world did not know him** – the reference is to the world of humanity that by its response reveals its devastating plight of having become alienated from and hostile to the Light/Word that sustains it. It is this second negative connotation of 'world' that will become dominant in the Fourth Gospel.

11 The sphere of the Word's mission now becomes more specific. **He came to what was his own, and his own people did not receive him**. Here there are two uses of the phrase 'his own'; the first is a neuter plural, signifying his own possession, property or domain, while the second is a masculine plural, signifying his own people. The encounter between the Word and the world is in this way given a particular context in history. The Word comes to Israel, the nation that thought of both its land and itself as God's possession (cf. e.g. Exod. 6.8; 19.5; Lev. 14.34; 20.26; Deut. 4.20–1; 9.26, 29), and it is the people of Israel who incomprehensibly fail to receive the Word. This provides a preview of the perspective of the narrative, in which 'the Jews' will become the prime historical representative of 'the world' in its negative sense. It also provides a preview of the first part of the narrative, where in 1.19—12.50 Jesus' mission to Israel provokes a divided response, but a predominantly hostile one from the nation's leaders.

12–13 But to whoever received him, he gave authority to become children of God, that is, to those who believed in his name. This summary of the positive response previews the second part of the narrative, where in 13.1—17.26 Jesus is portrayed with those who did receive him, a new group that can be called 'his own' (13.1). Here the Word authorizes the constitution of a new people of God, putting people in the position of being able to become God's children. While there is a later discussion of who can validly claim to have God as their Father (cf. 8.41–7), this designation for God's people occurs only once more in the Gospel (cf. 11.52; cf. also the diminutive form 'little children' in 13.33), though it is found more frequently in the Johannine epistles (cf. 1 John 3.1, 2, 10; 5.2). Becoming a child of God occurs through believing in the name of the Word, which, as the ensuing narrative will show, is the same as the name of Jesus (cf. 2.23) or the name of the only Son of God (cf. 3.18). As in the Jewish Scriptures, 'name' indicates more than just the verbal designation of a person. It signifies all that a person represents. To believe in Jesus' name is, therefore, to entrust oneself to who he is and what he stands for. A further explanation in antithetical form is then given of what it means to be a child of God. It distinguishes this notion from ethnic definitions of the people of God by making clear that it has nothing to do with ordinary human birth. This point is made three times to ensure that it is grasped. What is entailed is not **of bloods**, a reference to the ancient theory of conception, whereby a male's sperm was viewed as derived from his blood and as mixing with the blood of a female in procreation. It is not **of the will of the flesh**, that is, it is not a birth initiated by sexual desire. Nor is it **of the will of the male**, that is, in terms of the patriarchal outlook on family life, this birth cannot be traced back to the husband's decision to produce children. Instead, a child of God can only be produced by God – he or she is born **of God**. This claim about divine origin will be made again in a different form in 3.3–8, which talks of a person's need to be born from above, to be born of water and the Spirit. For the Fourth Gospel, just as *the* Son is from above not from below, so those who believe in him, the children of God, have the same origin, from God or from above. Some, including a much later textual tradition that has the relative pronoun and the verb in the singular, have attempted to see in the threefold denial of physical birth in v. 13 an allusion to Christ's virgin birth. But this is extremely unlikely. Unless the notion of a virgin birth were read in from Matthew's and Luke's birth narratives, it would not occur to a reader to find it here. If anything, the implication of the verse would work in the reverse direction. The stress on a non-physical birth is being made in regard to humans whose actual births have nothing abnormal about them. The attribution of a divine origin to the Son may well also have been thought not to have any necessary implications for the nature of his physical birth (cf. also 1.45, where Jesus is straightforwardly described as 'son of Joseph').

4. The Community's Confession about the Word   1.14–18

14 With this section of the prologue a change of perspective is introduced. In vv. 14 and 16 there is a switch to the first person plural, as the narrator places himself and those whom he represents among those who have believed and have become children of God, and as this community of believers makes its confession about the Word.

The content of its confession begins with the astounding claim that **the Word became flesh and dwelt among us**. This would be astounding both for those from the Jewish tradition and for those familiar with Graeco-Roman thought. For the latter it would have seemed like a merging of ultimately incompatible opposites, since the Logos was the rational and spiritual principle primarily to be experienced through the overcoming of physical and material existence. For the former it would appear to have breached the clear distinction between the Creator and the creature. Wisdom might have her children, wise men and women who followed her ways, but this formulation goes far beyond any personification of the divine wisdom to claim that this Wisdom has become incarnate in a particular human. The divine Word might come through particular individuals but here the claim, implicit until now in the prologue, is made explicit that the Word actually became this one person, Jesus of Nazareth. 'Flesh' (σάρξ) does not have here the negative ethical force it frequently, but by no means always, has in the Pauline writings. It simply refers to the createdness of human existence in comparison with that of God, and therefore to its finitude, weakness and transience. So the believing community's confession is that in Jesus God's self-expression entered fully into human physical life, God's self-communication became embodied. The basis of the Christian doctrine of the incarnation can be found in a number of other places and forms in the New Testament, but this Gospel's prologue provides its clearest and most explicit expression. It leaves no room for docetism, the notion that Jesus only appeared to be human or simply took on the outward appearance of a human. It is significant that this sort of Christological issue is at stake in the Johannine epistles, where the key test becomes the confession that 'Jesus Christ has come in the flesh' (1 John 4.2; 2 John 7).

In becoming flesh, the Word **dwelt among us**. It is sometimes pointed out that the Greek verb (σκηνόω) has as its cognate noun σκηνή, which means tent or tabernacle, and so could have the force of 'pitched his tent' or 'tabernacled'. Etymological derivation is not a reliable guide to meaning, but it is not needed here for similar connotations to come into play. They come once an informed reader considers the Jewish background for the notion of a divine dwelling among humans. In the Jewish Scriptures it is the tabernacle and the temple that provide the special locations for such a dwelling. There is further encouragement to hear such connotations, because, as we have seen, in Sir. 24.8–11 Wisdom, as God's immanent presence, could be said to take up its dwelling both in the tabernacle and in Zion, and because the nature of that presence as glory – the Shekinah – will also be taken up in the rest of the confession about the Word. Here then the specific place of the divine dwelling and presence among humans is seen to be in Jesus rather than in tabernacle or temple, a fulfilment-and-replacement theme that will be developed in the rest of the narrative (cf. e.g. 1.51; 2.19–21; 4.21–6).

In the light of this discussion it is not surprising that the next clause is **and we saw his glory**, where the 'seeing' is the perception of faith, the appropriate evaluation of the significance of what has taken place in Jesus and of who he really is. Faith finds in Jesus the glory of the divine presence. 'Glory' (δόξα) when associated with God in the LXX can refer to the radiancy and splendour of God's presence in its visible manifestation but also to God's reputation or honour. Its mention here introduces another significant motif for the Gospel as a whole. The noun 'glory' occurs 19 times, while the verb 'to glorify' is to be found 23 times. The Johannine confession, 'we saw his glory', sums up much of the force of what was at stake in the community's controversy with Judaism over the status of Jesus. In the light of Jewish expectations about the Messiah and of the ignominious fate of Jesus, it would have been natural to ask, in the face of messianic claims for Jesus, where the divine glory was that should have accompanied him. The early Christian response that is evident from the Synoptic Gospels was that the Messiah had to suffer first and only then would there be vindication and glory, partly through the resurrection and exaltation to God's right hand, but fully at the parousia, when he would come again in glory. But the Fourth Gospel's response is that, for those with the eyes of faith, there was glory all the way through Jesus' life. It was there in the signs and it was there above all in what appeared to be the moment of greatest humiliation – the crucifixion. Since 'glory' also has the force of 'honour', such a perspective can also be seen to be an important part of a response to the social issues that confronted Johannine Christians in a culture where honour and shame were pivotal values and where both their allegiance to an apparently disgraced leader and the shaming of many of their number through expulsion from the synagogue would have ensured their experience of the consequences of such values.

At this point in the prologue, however, the glory attributed to Jesus is described in two further ways. It is **glory as of an only son of a father**. There are no definite articles in the Greek clause, indicating that it is best taken in terms of a human comparison rather than as a direct reference to Jesus as the only Son in relation to the Father. The latter will, of course, come to the fore as John's characteristic Christological formulation, but at this point is only anticipated by the human analogy. In human families in Mediterranean culture honour or glory was particularly tied to lineage. People were ascribed honour through their origin and were dependent on the reputation of their fathers. In this way an only son would have an incomparably privileged status in the family. In the light of what has been said earlier in the prologue about the children of God, this comparison ensures that Jesus' status and glory in relation to God are viewed as unique. The second elaboration on Jesus' glory depicts it as **full of grace and truth**. The terms 'grace' and 'truth' in combination are almost certainly meant to recall the frequent paired expression in the Jewish Scriptures, 'steadfast love and faithfulness', which was employed of God's loyalty to the covenant with Israel and revealed in a vision of God's glory. This part of the prologue recalls in particular the narrative of Exod. 33.12—34.9, where Moses asks to see God's glory and in the end 'The Lord passed before him and proclaimed, "The Lord, the Lord, a God merciful and gracious, slow to anger and abounding in steadfast love and faithfulness"' (Exod. 34.6). Although the LXX translation does not use the term χάρις at this point, John's Greek phrase is a valid translation of the Hebrew one, and so 'full of grace and truth' is to be seen as the prologue's equivalent of 'abounding in steadfast love and faithfulness', which in the Exodus passage is part of the explanation of Yahweh's name. So the community's confession is that the mercy and dependability, uniquely characteristic of God (cf. also Ps. 86.15) and previously associated with the covenant with Israel, have now been displayed in the incarnate Word and that the Word's grace and truth are the evidence of his glory.

The considerable space already devoted to v. 14 suggests something of its importance for the theology of John's Gospel. But one further issue should be noted in the light of its juxtaposition of 'flesh' and 'glory' in its depiction of the Word. It has been held with some plausibility that the fact that the humanity of Jesus became an issue among Johannine Christians (cf. 1 and 2 John) is evidence that the Christology in the body of the Gospel's narrative that emphasizes Jesus' divine glory was capable of being interpreted in a proto-docetic fashion. It is pertinent to ask, therefore, whether, in the narrative that follows, the 'flesh' or humanity of Jesus is kept in balance with his divine 'glory' or whether one overshadows the other. The perspective taken in this commentary is that, because of the issues being addressed by the Gospel, the emphasis of its story is clearly on Jesus' divine glory and this inevitably predominates. This emphasis was originally made on the assumption that the Jesus of Nazareth to whom such glory is attributed was a fully human person. Nevertheless, by the time the Gospel reached its final form, it had become clear that such an assumption needed to be spelled out explicitly for some readers, and this part of the prologue is one of the places that enables the full Johannine belief about the nature of Jesus as the divine Word incarnate to come to expression.

15 Although the most natural continuation of v. 14 would be the thought of v. 16, the flow is interrupted by a further statement about the witness of John. This contains a pronouncement from the Baptist that is found in a very similar formulation in 1.30. In both cases it is introduced as a statement that John has already made. Here the introductory words are **This was he of whom I said**, which seems particularly strange at this stage, when, of course, there has been no prior account of John's words. It may well provide another indication that the prologue was composed after the body of the Gospel and that the saying as a whole was adapted from 1.30 and re-employed here. The saying that is involved plays on the notion of being 'before'- **He who comes after me has become ahead of me, because he was before me** – that is, 'he who comes after me is before me in rank, because he was before me in time'. It is a witness to the Baptist's subordinate status through being at the same time a witness to Jesus' pre-existence. Later the narrative will make a similar point about Abraham's relation to Jesus on the basis of the latter's pre-existence – 'Before Abraham was, I Am' (8.58). Clearly this sort of insight into Jesus' significance goes far beyond anything attributed to John the Baptist in the Synoptics. It is an instance of a phenomenon to be found throughout the Fourth Gospel, namely, the beliefs of the narrator and those he represents being read back into the story of Jesus, including here into the Baptist's introductory role.

16–17 As we have seen, v. 16 refers back to the last part of v. 14 and takes up the phrase 'full of grace and truth'. The believing community sees itself as the beneficiary of the abundance of glory displayed in Jesus – **from his fullness we have all received, grace instead of grace**. There has been much dispute over the translation and force of the last phrase. Some translate it as 'grace upon grace' and see it as referring to an abundance of grace and thereby elaborating on the 'fullness' of the first part of the verse. The problem with this is that the preposition used here, ἀντί, never has this sense, which is normally conveyed by ἐπί. It has been claimed that a parallel expression is found in Philo, *Post*. 145, where it clearly refers to abundance of grace. In fact, however, the Philo reference refers not to an accumulation of graces but a substitution in which one kind replaces another. It seems best, then, to attempt to interpret the more difficult 'grace instead of grace'. It could still be taken as referring to an abundance of grace which is always being renewed as one kind replaces another. But it seems likely that it is primarily meant to point forward to v. 17, which begins with the connective 'for', and that it is claiming that the grace found in Jesus and his glory replaces that associated with the Mosaic covenant. The next verse does not, of course, speak of grace in association with the Mosaic covenant, but the whole of vv. 14–18 through its reworking of themes in Exod. 33—4 assumes that original association.

The reference back to v. 14c continues in v. 17 with its language of grace and truth, but now this becomes part of an antithetically structured parallelism – **the law was given through Moses, grace and truth came into being through Jesus Christ**. The language of 'coming into being' certainly makes this a strong claim. It obviously raises the question of whether it is meant to entail a denial of the association we have already noted between grace and truth and the Mosaic covenant. Its force is that the fullness of grace and truth that has now been displayed in Jesus is such as to consign to relative insignificance the previous manifestation of these qualities in regard to the law. It is probably best to recognize, however, that the narrator is here not so much interested in the previous existence of these qualities as in stressing that they are now embodied in Jesus and that, since the new reality replaces the old, it is no longer relevant to claim them for the old. Such an assertion clearly anticipates the perspective on the controversy with Judaism that shapes the rest of the narrative.

18 The statement that **No one has at any time seen God** continues the contrast of the previous verse, denying any claims that might be made for Moses. It has in view again Exod. 33.12—34.9 as proof of Moses' failure actually to see God, since no human could see God and live (cf. Exod. 33.20). The stress is on God's hiddenness and inaccessibility. Only God can make God accessible; only God can reveal God. But this is where Jesus as the Word is held to be superior to Moses. He is **the only God** (μονογενὴς θεός), who has not only therefore seen the Father but is always **in the Father's lap**, in intimate relationship to God. Some translations adopt the reading 'the only Son', but, though easier, this may have been the result of scribal assimilation to 3.16, 18. The reading preferred here is not only the more difficult reading but has the stronger external support and yet is also in line with the use of 'God' without an article for the Word earlier in v. 1c. The unique relationship of the divine Word to God the Father qualifies him to be the one who **has made him** [God] **known**. The end of the prologue, therefore, brings us back to its beginning; the Word as divine is God's self-expression, the form in which God makes Godself known.

The prologue as a whole gives its narrator's point of view on the one who will be the central character in his narrative. Jesus is to be seen in eternal cosmic perspective as the divine Word who became incarnate. In this way it becomes clear that the narrative about Jesus that follows is also a story about God, about God's unique self-expression in this narrative's protagonist. The prologue at the same time indicates the protagonist's primary task – making God known (v. 18) – and suggests in advance the outline of the plot (vv. 11–12). It sheds light too on the nature of the divided response that will ensue. This will involve a dispute about the claims of Jesus in relation to those made about Moses and the law. Grace and truth come through Jesus, no longer through Torah (v. 17). Jesus, not Torah, is to be seen as the incarnation of God's Word, as the embodiment of Wisdom, and Jesus as the Word, not Torah, mediates life and light. In introducing Jesus and his mission, the prologue also establishes some of the major themes that will be repeated throughout the story – life, light and darkness, witness, truth, belief and unbelief, the world, and glory. By such means readers are being equipped from the start to be able to share the narrator's guiding perspective as they follow the rest of the story and therefore to be in a position to appreciate as fully as possible the import of the nuances and ironies in its discourse and unfolding plot. The emphases within the prologue's assessment of Jesus already suggest that this story is aware of a different assessment – one that, from its vantage point of adherence to Moses and the law, denies the qualities of divinity and glory to Jesus, holding that such claims about him amount to blasphemy and seeing in his career only shame and disgrace.

In the prologue the impersonal, though personified, Word is now identified with the person of Jesus of Nazareth. Through such an introduction to the main figure in the narrative the prologue set the agenda for all future thinking about Christ. How does one retain belief in the one God and yet make room for this person who is the incarnate Word? How does one speak appropriately of this Word who is what God was and can even be called the only God, and yet can be said to be with God and therefore in some sense distinct from God? How does one maintain the full humanity of the Word as flesh while portraying his life as one that exhibited the divine glory?

The prologue's profound theological implications emerge from a radical reshaping of Israel's story. Israel's God, its Scriptures and its symbols are now reconfigured around the one who is the subject of the Gospel's own story. Genesis 1, Torah, Moses, Exodus 33 and 34, Wisdom, God's Word, glory, the identity of the people of God, covenantal grace and truth, all help to interpret the distinctive significance of Jesus, but in the process all are themselves reinterpreted in the light of what is believed to be the decisive revelation that has taken place in him. Yet the prologue is not simply an effective presentation of Jesus' identity within the framework of Jewish thought. As its last part makes explicit, it is a confession on the part of the narrator and the community of believers he represents. They claim to have seen God's glory made accessible now in Jesus in a way quite different from what was possible for Moses and Israel at Sinai, and their witness is not only to the new and ultimate significance of Jesus but also to his transforming power in the grace they have experienced through him.

B. JESUS' PUBLIC MISSION (SIGNS OF GLORY) 1.19—12.50

1. Beginnings: John the Baptist's Testimony; the Response of Jesus' Disciples 1.19–51

(i) John the Baptist's testimony *1.19–34*

(19) And this is the testimony of John, when the Jews sent priests and Levites from Jerusalem in order to ask him, 'Who are you?'

(20) He confessed and did not deny, but confessed, 'I am not the Christ.' (21) And they asked him, 'What then are you? Are you Elijah?[1] And he said, 'I am not.' 'Are you the prophet?' And he answered, 'No.' (22) So they said to him, 'Who are you? Let us give an answer to those who sent us. What do you say about yourself?' (23) He said, 'I am the voice of one crying in the wilderness, "Make the way of the Lord straight"', as Isaiah the prophet said. (24) They had been sent by the Pharisees. (25) And they asked him, saying, 'Why then are you baptizing if you are neither the Christ nor Elijah nor the prophet?'(26) John answered them, saying, 'I baptize in water; among you stands one whom you do not know, (27) the one who is coming after me, the strap of whose sandal I am not worthy to untie.' (28) These things took place in Bethany on the other side of the Jordan, where John was baptizing.

(29) The next day he saw Jesus coming towards him, and said, 'Look, the lamb of God that takes away the sin of the world. (30) This is he about whom I said, "After me comes a man who has become ahead of me, because he was before me." (31) I myself did not know him, but I came baptizing in water for this reason, that he might be revealed to Israel.'(32) And John testified, saying, 'I saw the Spirit descending from heaven like a dove, and it remained on him. (33) I myself did not know him, but the one who sent me to baptize in water said to me, "He on whom you see the Spirit descending and remaining, this is he who baptizes in the holy Spirit." (34) I myself have seen and have testified that this is the Son of God.'[2]

The narrator now sets his account squarely within the arena of human history – during John's mission of baptizing – and on earthly terrain – Bethany (cf. v. 28). The dominance of the characterization of John the Baptist as witness can be seen from the *inclusio* which frames this passage. It begins with the narrator describing the testimony (μαρτυρία) given by John (v. 19) and ends with John himself talking about his activity of witnessing (μεμαρτύρηκα – v. 34). The passage falls into two parts – vv. 19–28 and vv. 29–34, the latter set on the following day. In the first,

[1] The punctuation of this question is in doubt. The translation follows that found in p75 C⋆ Ψ. The major alternative variants would lead to the translation "What then? Are you Elijah?'

[2] Some manuscripts (including p5vid ℵ⋆) have 'the chosen one of God', but external attestation is stronger for 'the Son of God' and includes p66,75 ℵc A B C. The decision here is difficult, since the former variant could be held to be the more difficult reading and it may be easier to account for a scribal change from 'elect one' to 'Son' than vice versa.

John's testimony is primarily about his own identity and mission and only secondarily about Jesus, while in the second it is directly about Jesus and his identity and mission.

19 And this is the testimony of John, when the Jews sent priests and Levites from Jerusalem in order to ask him, 'Who are you?' John's testimony is provoked by interrogation. He is bombarded with questions about his identity in these verses. This depiction of John's mission anticipates one of the major forms the depiction of Jesus' mission will also take, as the narrative is carried forward through interrogations and mini-trial scenes. As will be the case throughout most of the narrative, the interrogators are the Jewish religious authorities. Priests and Levites have been sent from Jerusalem by 'the Jews' or the Pharisees (cf. 1.24).

20–1 The terminology of confession and denial used about John is closely associated with that of witness and has clear forensic overtones. Confession will be used in conjunction with the threat of being excommunicated from the synagogue (cf. 9.22 and 12.42), while denial is used of Peter under interrogation (cf. 13.38; 18.25, 27). In regard to himself John confesses and does not deny that he is neither the Messiah nor Elijah nor the prophet. This demonstrates beyond doubt his subordination to the one who will be the chief witness. But more is at stake. The strong emphasis of the formulation – **he confessed and did not deny, but confessed** – and the triple negative content of the confession about his identity cry out for further explanation. This phenomenon corresponds with the strictly superfluous negative statement of 1.8 – 'he himself was not the light' – and with the later repetition of the denial of Messiahship (cf. 3.28), the assertion by John that he must decrease while Jesus must increase (cf. 3.30), and the declaration that John performed no signs (cf. 10.41). From the perspective of the Fourth Gospel, and in contrast to the Synoptic tradition, John is not to be thought of as Elijah (cf. Matt. 11.14; 17.12; Mark 9.13; cf. also Luke 1.17) or even as the prophet (cf. Luke 1.76). His role is strictly limited to that of a witness to Jesus. This begins to make sense in the light of the narrative's later depiction of the concerns of John's disciples about the success of Jesus' ministry (cf. 3.26) and on the basis of such evidence about the continuing activity of John's followers as Acts 18.24—19.7 and Justin, *Trypho* 80, with its reference to the baptists. The later Pseudo-Clementine *Recognitions* 1.54, 60 also posit a continuing movement of followers of the Baptist who made high claims for their leader. It appears highly likely that at some stage Johannine Christians came into dispute with such a group and that in this way John's testimony has secondary apologetic force in relation to this dispute. The narrative stresses that there is to be no doubt about the Baptist's secondary status in comparison with Jesus.

22–3 John's interrogators are not content with his denials. They want to be able to take back a clearer report **to those who sent us**. It is significant that in terms of the structure of the narrative's plot not only are both John (cf. 1.6, 33) and Jesus (cf. e.g. 3.17, 34) depicted as sent or commissioned by God, but the opponents of their missions can also be said to be sent. Here the commissioning opposition has already been identified as 'the Jews' (1.19; cf. also 1.24). When John does identify himself positively, it becomes clear that he has a highly significant but nonetheless limited role as a preparatory witness. He quotes words from Isa. 40.3 to this effect – **I am the voice of one crying in the wilderness, 'make the way of the Lord straight'**. Whereas in the Synoptic narratives this Scripture is part of the narrators' comments on the mission of John, here it constitutes John's self-identification and adds the authority of Scripture to his witness.

24–5 There is dispute over how to construe the syntax of v. 24. Some (e.g. REB, NIV) understand it to mean that those who were sent were 'from the Pharisees' in the sense of belonging to the Pharisees. **They had been sent by the Pharisees** appears preferable, however, since, although priests and Levites could be Pharisees, employing 'the Pharisees' as an equivalent to 'the Jews' (cf. 1.19) for speaking of the religious authorities is characteristic of the Gospel's usage elsewhere (cf. e.g. 3.1; 7.32, 35; 9.13–18). The delegation's follow-up question now reverts to John's denial of being the Messiah, Elijah or the prophet and demands to know why then he is baptizing.

26–7 John's response, **I baptize in water**, has an implied contrast that is not made explicit until v. 33. Again this activity is preparatory, for **among you stands one whom you do not know, the one who is coming after me, the strap of whose sandal I am not worthy to untie**. The at present unrecognized successor to John will be so superior in status that he, John, is not worthy even to carry out toward him the sort of duty a slave might be expected to perform. The wording of John's statement has its roots in the Synoptic tradition (cf. Mark 1.7–8 parr.). This Gospel adds the notion of Jesus being at present unknown and, in placing 'I baptize in water' at the beginning of the saying, follows the Matthean and Lukan order over against Mark.

28 At this point the narrator's geographical note specifies the location for John's baptizing activity as **in Bethany on the other side of the Jordan**. The Synoptic Gospels place John's baptizing in the Judaean desert not far from Jerusalem, since the crowds are able to go out from Jerusalem to be baptized by him. The Fourth Gospel appears to assume a similar location, although it is not entirely clear where the narrator understands Bethany to be. Later Bethany will be mentioned in connection with the home of Lazarus, Mary and Martha and will be said to be some two miles from Jerusalem (cf. 11.1, 18; 12.1), yet it does not appear to be the same Bethany, since Jesus is said to be in the place on the other side of the Jordan where John had done his baptizing (cf. 10.40) when he receives the news of Lazarus' illness and declares, 'let us go to Judaea again' (11.7). It may well be, then, that here the Fourth Gospel refers to a trans-Jordanian town known as Bethany, of which there no longer remains any trace.

John's more direct testimony to Jesus in vv. 29–34 makes three major claims about him – he is the lamb of God (v. 29), he possesses the Spirit (vv. 32–3) and he is the Son of God or God's chosen one (v. 34).

29 Look, the lamb of God that takes away the sin of the world. This Gospel's use of Scripture and its imagery is frequently hard to pin down. It often draws from a cluster of sources rather than a single identifiable one. This may well be the case here in the identification of Jesus with the lamb of God that takes away the sin of the world, which appears to combine the imagery from Deutero-Isaiah (Isa. 53.4–12) of the servant-witness who bears the sin of many and is led as a lamb to the slaughter with that of the Passover lamb, which did not, of course, deal with sin (Exod. 12.1–11). The latter colours the depiction of Jesus' death, which, in this narrative, occurs at the same time as the slaughter of the Passover lambs (cf. 19.14, 31) and is seen as that of an unblemished Passover lamb (19.36, citing Exod. 12.46). The cause of the world's hostility to its Creator's purposes, manifesting itself in its refusal to acknowledge the Logos (cf. 1.10), is sin. If Jesus' mission of saving the world (3.17) and of giving life to it (6.35, 51) is to be accomplished, then the world's sin has to be dealt with, and one of the ways in which this Gospel's narrative portrays Jesus is as the sacrificial victim, whose death removes the primary obstacle to the world's reception of the divine gift of life.

30–1 John now repeats the saying about Jesus' priority of rank because of his priority through pre-existence. Since the original utterance is not recorded in the narrative, **This is he about whom I said** functions at this point as a prompt to the reader to recall the prologue's earlier version of the saying (1.15). In the Synoptics John's baptism has the goal of producing repentance in view of the coming judgement, but here John makes clear that his baptizing with water had as its primary purpose the revealing to Israel of the one who was previously unknown (cf. also 1.26). The one whom the narrative depicts as the Revealer must himself first be revealed, and it is John's baptismal activity that is the initial catalyst for this revelation to God's own people, Israel.

32–3 In contrast with the accounts in Matthew and Mark, this narrative does not actually relate Jesus' baptism. That Jesus was baptized by John is suppressed (again to avoid any suggestion that Jesus could be considered subordinate to John in some sense), and only if readers were familiar with this event through other accounts would they find here an allusion to it through John's testimony. In that testimony John claims that he too did not know Jesus until the means of recognizing the baptizer with the Holy Spirit – a means communicated to him by God – was confirmed, and he **saw the Spirit descending from heaven like a dove, and it remained on him**. The verb μένειν, 'to remain', which can be used elsewhere in the narrative of the permanence of the relationship between the Father and Jesus and of the relationship between Jesus and the disciples, is employed here for the permanence of the Spirit's relationship to Jesus. This qualifies Jesus to be the one **who baptizes in the holy Spirit**, a function he performs for his followers after the resurrection (cf. 20.22). It is significant that Isaiah's messianic prophecy about the one who will judge with equity and not by appearances speaks of the Spirit of the Lord resting upon him (Isa. 11.2–5).

34 But John's testimony to Jesus is more than that he is the Christ; it is that **this is the Son of God**, a key title in this Gospel, standing for everything unique in Jesus' relationship to God and for the oneness between the Father and the Son (cf. 10.30). In the Synoptic tradition, at Jesus' baptism a voice from heaven had declared Jesus to be the beloved Son, but in this narrative this declaration has become part of John the Baptist's testimony. As has been noted, however, the reading 'Son of God' is disputed. It has the stronger manuscript support, but it is possible, as a number of scholars hold, that the variant ὁ ἐκλεκτὸς τοῦ θεοῦ – 'God's elect or chosen one' – should be accepted. If the latter reading is preferred, it takes up the allusion to Isa. 42.1, present in the Synoptic accounts of the baptism, but in distinctive fashion keeps in view the LXX wording (ὁ ἐκλεκτός μου) that underlines the elect status of the servant. The two perfect tenses – **I myself have seen and have testified** – emphasize the continuing present significance of John's witness as a testimony that remains on record for the readers. The ordinary language associated with the stance of an eyewitness is now used instead to speak of the insight of belief that leads to confession. In his seeing and testifying John initiates this narrative's sequence of faithful witnessing that will continue with the seeing and testifying of Jesus and the community (cf. 3.11), of Jesus himself (cf. 3.32), and of the Beloved Disciple (cf. 19.35).

The major contrasts with the Synoptic depiction of John the Baptist have been pointed out in the commentary on individual verses. The most obvious interpretation of these is that the evangelist knows of such traditions but, in the interest of his concern to make John clearly subordinate to Jesus, has chosen to go his own way. Even Synoptic evaluations of John as Elijah or the prophet are here denied by John himself and any account of John baptizing Jesus is suppressed, so that John can emerge simply as a witness, albeit a completely reliable one, to the exalted status and identity of Jesus. His testimony is to the overwhelming superiority of Jesus in comparison with himself, to the pre-existence of Jesus, to the soteriological significance of his death, to his possession of and ability to bestow the Spirit, and to his divine sonship or uniquely chosen status. These are convictions of the evangelist and his community that have been in dispute and John's character becomes the effective narrative means of presenting their distinctive point of view.

(ii) The response of Jesus' first followers   *1.35–51*

(35) The next day again John was standing with two of his disciples, (36) and, when he watched Jesus walking by, he said, 'Look, the lamb of God!' (37) And the two disciples heard what he said and followed Jesus. (38) When Jesus turned and saw them following, he said to them, 'What are you looking for?' They said to him, 'Rabbi' (which, when translated, means Teacher), 'where are you staying?' (39) He said to them, 'Come and see.' So they went and saw where he was staying, and they stayed with him that day. It was about the tenth hour. (40) Andrew, Simon Peter's brother, was one of the two who heard what John had said and followed Jesus. (41) He first found his own brother Simon and said to him, 'We have found the Messiah' (which is translated Christ). (42) He then brought him to Jesus. When Jesus saw him, he said, 'You are Simon, son of John. You will be called Cephas' (which is translated Peter).

(43) The next day Jesus decided to leave for Galilee, and he found Philip. Jesus said to him, 'Follow me.' (44) Now Philip was from Bethsaida, the city of Andrew and Peter. (45) Philip found Nathanael and said to him, 'We have found the one about whom Moses in the law and the prophets wrote, Jesus, son of Joseph, from Nazareth.' (46) Nathanael said to him, 'Can anything good come from Nazareth?' Philip said to him, 'Come and see.' (47) Jesus saw Nathanael coming toward him and said of him, 'Look, truly an Israelite in whom there is no deceit.' (48) Nathanael said to him, 'Where did you get to know me?' Jesus answered and said to him, 'Before Philip called you, I saw you under the fig tree.' (49) Nathanael answered him, 'Rabbi, you are the Son of God, you are the King of Israel.' (50) Jesus answered and said to him, 'Do you believe because I said to you that I saw you under the fig tree? You will see greater things than these.' (51) And he said to him, 'Truly, truly, I say to you, you will see heaven opened

and the angels of God ascending and descending on the Son of Man.'

John's testimony has pointed to the superiority of Jesus. Now the logic of such a testimony for any who had followed John is indicated. They need to cease being disciples of the Baptist and to become followers of Jesus. Just such an account introduces the first of the two similarly structured sequences describing the response of some of Jesus' earliest followers. The first sequence is depicted in vv. 35–42 and the second in vv. 43–51. Both begin with a chronological marker – 'the next day' (vv. 35, 43). In the first passage two disciples follow Jesus, who says, 'Come and see.' Andrew then finds his brother Simon and tells him, 'We have found the Messiah.' Jesus identifies Simon and promises he will be known as Peter. In the second passage Jesus finds Philip and tells him to follow. Philip in turn finds Nathanael and tells him, 'We have found the one about whom Moses and the prophets wrote.' He invites him to 'Come and see.' Jesus identifies Nathanael as an Israelite in whom there is no deceit and promises that he will see greater things.

The accounts of the beginnings of discipleship for these characters, with their invitations to come and to see Jesus, are particularly important in engaging the intended readers, whatever their own stage of discipleship or belief. This appears to be confirmed by the fact that three basic translation notes are found in the first episode. Rabbi, Messiah and Cephas in vv. 38, 41, 42 are explained, presumably, by the final editor, who was aware that the Gospel's audience would include Gentile readers with only minimal acquaintance with Jewish names. Why does the phenomenon occur here in particular? If the editor had been consistent, should not Messiah have been explained at 1.20? And why does not such basic translation occur in the same way at later points in the narrative? The most likely explanation is that this section provides the first major opportunity for readers to identify with characters in the narrative, who, like them, are would-be followers of Jesus. Aware of this, the final editor wanted to make the episode as user-friendly as possible and hence provided help for those unfamiliar with Jewish terminology.

35–7 The phrase **the next day**, which was previously employed in v. 29 and will be repeated in v. 43, simply serves as a loose temporal marker. Attempts to find symbolic or theological significance in the number of days or their sequence in this section of the Gospel fail to convince because the evangelist has not left enough clear clues in the text to prompt readers to look for some additional level of meaning. John the Baptist repeats his identification of Jesus as **the lamb of God** (cf. 1.29). This time, however, **two of his disciples** are specified as his audience and they act on the implications of John's testimony by following Jesus.

38–9 Despite their having taken the initiative, the two former disciples of John need prompting and encouragement from Jesus. This takes the form of a question – **What are you looking for?** – which is general in nature and attempts to elicit a response about their motivation in following him. For readers who are familar with the later narrative, however, the formulation takes on deeper significance, since the verb used (ζητεῖν) is characteristic of the evangelist's vocabulary and will be employed to speak of people's attitude to Jesus and their deepest commitments. Jesus himself is the object of people's seeking in 6.24, 26; 7.11, 34, 36; 8.21; 11.56; 13.33 and 20.15. On the positive side, the verb is also used of seeking God's will (5.30) and God's glory (5.44; 7.18). On the negative side, it will be employed of those seeking to arrest Jesus (7.30; 10.39; 18.4, 7, 8) or to kill him (5.18; 7.1, 19, 20, 25; 8.37, 40; 11.8). At this stage the two disciples address Jesus as Rabbi and thereby appear to signal their intention of attaching themselves to Jesus as their teacher in the conventional way in which some Jews would select particular rabbis to be their instructors. The full force of Jesus' question is deflected, however, by their posing a seemingly mundane counter-question – **where are you staying?** Again, however, deeper dimensions are hinted at by the terminology employed. To stay or remain (μενεῖν) is one of the evangelist's distinctive verbs, and is used in particular for the relationship between Jesus and his followers, in which they are to remain in him, his words or his love, while he remains in them (cf. 6.56; 8.31; 15.4, 5, 7, 9–10). Jesus' invitation in response – **Come and see** – continues to evoke another level of meaning, because later in this Gospel's discourse both 'to come' to Jesus and 'to see' him are synonyms for 'to believe' in him (cf. e.g. 5.40; 6.35–7, 40, 44–5, 62, 65; 9.37–8; 12.45; 14.6–7, 9). In this light Jesus' words can be viewed as also constituting an invitation to believing discipleship, an invitation that will be extended by other witnesses, most immediately by Philip in 1.46 but also by the Samaritan woman in 4.29. At the literal level, which is primary at this point in the narrative, the first two disciples accept Jesus' invitation – **they went and saw where he was staying, and they stayed with him that day**.

40–2 One of the two disciples is now named – **Andrew, Simon Peter's brother**. The fact that he is designated as brother of Simon Peter suggests clearly that the latter was expected to be the more familiar name to readers of the Gospel and that they are assumed to know about him from the tradition or from their knowledge of the Synoptic Gospels. Nevertheless, Andrew is given not only the initial mention but also the more prominent role in this episode. In contrast with the Synoptic call stories, where Simon and Andrew are called by Jesus from their fishing at the same time, Andrew is credited with recognizing and testifying to Jesus as Messiah and then on the basis of this knowledge finding his brother and bringing him to Jesus. Andrew will also feature more prominently in the later narrative than he does in the Synoptic accounts. He is mentioned in conjunction with Philip in 1.44 and, together with the latter, is given a minor role, not depicted in the Synoptics, in the feeding of the five thousand and the coming of the Greeks to Jesus (cf. 6.8; 12.22).

That only one of John's two former disciples is named has given rise to much discussion about the likely identity of the other. This would scarcely be a matter of particular interest were it not for the attribution in 21.24 of the writing of this Gospel to the anonymous Beloved Disciple and his witness. Some have interpreted that verse to be claiming that the Beloved Disciple was an actual eyewitness of everything that is narrated in the Gospel, and, since this disciple is not explicitly mentioned until 13.23, the presence of an unnamed person as one of Jesus' first two disciples would allow that this could have been the Beloved Disciple, who was therefore present to witness and later recall both John the Baptist's ministry and the whole of Jesus' public ministry. If one were persuaded on other grounds of this particular interpretation of 21.24 and its implications for authorship, there is nothing to prevent one seeing the unnamed disciple as the Beloved Disciple. That this was the intention of the evangelist is another matter altogether. The mere presence of an unnamed disciple should not lead one to make this identification, as the reference in 21.2 to two unnamed disciples, of which only one could be the Beloved Disciple, ought to make clear. If the evangelist had intended this to be a first reference, however allusive, to the Gospel's author, one would expect some signal. Instead, this other disciple is not given any description or even further specific mention in the entire episode.

Andrew's testimony about Jesus is remarkable. The first utterance of an individual disciple of Jesus in this narrative is **We have found the Messiah**. In the Synoptics it is not until much later in the ministry of Jesus that his own disciples, represented by Simon himself, are able to come to the recognition of Jesus as Messiah, and even then this is immediately shown to be a flawed understanding that has not taken the necessity of Jesus' suffering and death into account (cf. Mark 8.29–33; Matt. 16.15–23; Luke 9.20–2). Here, however, Jesus' Messiahship is a basic conviction about his identity which can be taken for granted by his followers from the start. What they will have to grapple with later is the unique sense in which this Messiah can be said to have come from and be going to God. This difference of emphasis from the Synoptics reflects the history of Johannine Christians, in which it was not the confession of Jesus as Messiah that had proved problematic in relation to the synagogue. Contemporaries could be identified as Messiah by Jews without this being thought heterodox, as the example of Rabbi Akiba's belief that Simon bar Kochbah was the Messiah indicates. What proved critical for Johannine Christians in regard to their remaining within the synagogue was the status and identity they attributed to Jesus as Messiah in his relation to God.

Andrew and his testimony are the means of his brother's introduction to discipleship – **He then brought him to Jesus.** The impression is given that this takes place in the same location, somewhere near Jerusalem. But Simon has not been said to be a disciple of John the Baptist and therefore has no particular reason for being nearby rather than back in Galilee. This Gospel's formulation of Jesus' response to Simon again moves to an earlier point that in the Synoptics is found later, that is, the promise of change of name – **You are Simon, son of John. You will be called Cephas.** Mark 3.16 and Luke 6.14 refer to this in passing in their listing of the twelve, while Matt. 16.17–18 makes it a major feature of the account of Simon's confession at Caesarea Philippi. The change of name to Cephas (Aramaic) or Peter (Greek), with its meaning of 'rock', signals the leadership role Simon will have in the church. Here that significance is not explicitly developed and the name change functions more as a way of underlining Jesus' foreknowledge of Simon's later role.

43–4 The next day Jesus decided to leave for Galilee. This geographical note underlines another difference from the Synoptics in the account of the gathering of Jesus' very first disciples (see the discussion below). Whereas in the Synoptics Jesus calls Peter and Andrew in Galilee (cf. Mark 1.16), here they have followed him in the Jerusalem area. Only after this does Jesus make his way to Galilee, and now he himself takes the initiative in recruiting disciples – **he found Philip** – and issues the call, **Follow me.** Philip is said to be from **Bethsaida, the city of Andrew and Peter.** Despite having followed Jesus while he was near Bethany, Andrew and Peter are in fact linked with one of the towns around the Lake of Galilee. The Synoptics again make a somewhat different connection, associating the pair primarily with Capernaum, where they are said to have a house (cf. Mark 1.29).

45–6 Philip found Nathanael. The beginnings of discipleship continue to be spoken of in terms of looking for, finding and being found. Philip carries on the process begun by Jesus as he finds Nathanael, a figure who is not known in the Synoptic tradition and who, despite his prominent and climactic role in this early episode, will only be mentioned briefly again in John's narrative in the epilogue (cf. 21.2). Philip's testimony is **We have found the one about whom Moses in the law and the prophets wrote, Jesus, son of Joseph, from Nazareth.** Jesus is again identified in terms of Jewish expectations. Andrew had spoken of him as Messiah. Philip sees him as the one predicted in the Scriptures – both by Moses in the law and by the prophets. The evangelist builds on the early Christian view that the Jewish Scriptures point to Jesus – Luke 24.27 also formulates this conviction in terms of Moses and the prophets – and indeed they will be one of the witnesses enlisted on his behalf (cf. 5.39). Later

119

the narrative will adduce particular scriptural texts that Jesus fulfils, but here, more generally, passages about the prophet like Moses from the law and Messianic passages from the prophets may well be in view. Moses will again be said to have written about Jesus in 5.46 and Isaiah the prophet to have spoken of him in 12.39–41. Jesus is also identified in human terms as the son of Joseph (cf. also 6.42) and from Nazareth. The challenge with which the Gospel will present its readers is whether, with Nathanael in v. 49, they will also believe that ultimately Jesus is the Son of God and from heaven. At this point Philip's witness meets resistance, as Nathanael asks, **Can anything good come from Nazareth?** In the light of the formulation about Moses and the prophets, the question reflects the fact that Nazareth does not figure in any scriptural prophecies (cf. also 6.41–2). From the perspective of the evangelist's prologue, to which the reader is already party, the question is highly ironic. That which comes from Nazareth is in reality the incarnation of the Logos who was what God was and through whom all things came into being! The question is not given an answer but instead Nathanael receives the same invitation from Philip that Jesus had extended to the first two disciples – **Come and see**.

47–8 Just as Philip, who was found by Jesus, can at the same time say he has found Jesus, so Nathanael, who accepts the invitation to see Jesus, can also be said to have been seen by Jesus. Jesus had in fact seen Nathanael before Philip called him and on seeing him again now makes the remarkable identification – **Look, truly an Israelite in whom there is no deceit**. It was Jacob, whose name meant supplanter or deceiver (cf. Gen. 25.26; 27.35–6), who was first given the name Israel after wrestling with God (cf. Gen. 32.28; cf. also 35.10). Nathanael surpasses the original Israel in being without guile or deceit. His response to Jesus can therefore be viewed as paradigmatic for those who would be faithful Israelites and as what is meant to happen when Jesus is revealed to Israel (cf. 1.31). Despite questions about Scripture not speaking of Nazareth as the place of the Messiah's origin, he is able to perceive Jesus' true identity. This is the only time the term 'Israelite' is employed in the Gospel and it has none of the more dubious connotations that will be attached to the term 'Jew'.

In response to Nathanael's surprise that Jesus should know about him, he is told, **Before Philip called you, I saw you under the fig tree**. This is in line with the narrator's portrayal of Jesus as possessing special knowledge and indicates that his seeing of people is the sort of perception that knows them through and through (cf. 2.24–5). In regard to his followers in particular, Jesus shows himself to be the good shepherd who knows his own (10.14). Whether any significance is to be attached to Nathanael's location under the fig tree and what that significance might be is debated among the commentators. In 1 Kgs 4.25, Mic. 4.4 and Zech. 3.10 the imagery of people being under their vines and fig trees stands for security within the land, but this connotation does not appear to have any particular relevance here. There are later traditions about rabbis studying or teaching under fig trees (cf. *Midr. R.* on Eccl. 5.11) and this can be linked with Philip's initial witness to Nathanael about the law. Yet it is doubtful whether readers would have been expected to catch such an allusion. The most obvious symbolic force of the fig tree itself is that it stands for Israel (cf. Jer. 8.13; Hos. 9.10; Mic. 7.1; also Mark 11.12–14). To associate Nathanael with this symbol would therefore reinforce his identification as 'truly an Israelite'. If the mention of the fig tree does have any particular significance, this may well be the most likely. The main point of the reference, however, is the part it plays in demonstrating Jesus' unique knowledge and in the comparison in v. 50 with the greater powers he will later display.

49–50 As a result of his encounter with this extraordinary teacher, Nathanael, the true Israelite, is able to recognize Israel's true king and to confess, **Rabbi, you are the Son of God, you are the King of Israel**. At this stage in the story line the designation 'Son of God' may well be simply synonymous with that of 'King of Israel' (cf. also 12.13) as a messianic title. As Ps. 2.7 indicates, God's anointed king could also be thought of as God's son. The rest of the narrative will set out the evangelist's conviction that Jesus as Messiah is Son of God in the unique sense of being totally at one with God the Father. It will also make clear that even the title of King of Israel needs to be understood in the right way and is not simply to be accommodated to popular expectations. Jesus withdraws when the people want to make him king (6.15) and he explains to Pilate that his kingship does not have its origin in this world and is not exercised by force but by means of his witness to the truth (18.36–7). The remarkable nature of Nathanael's believing confession, which is in line with the Gospel's statement of purpose (cf. 20.31), is highlighted by a comparison with the Synoptic tradition. Luke does not use 'Son of God' as a title addressed to Jesus by his followers; neither does Mark, though he has the title on human lips for the first time when the centurion witnesses Jesus' death (Mark 15.39). Matthew also employs it in the centurion's confession (Matt. 27.54) but is willing to use it earlier in the disciples' recognition of Jesus after he has walked on the water and in Peter's confession at Caesarea Philippi (Matt. 14.33; 16.16). John's Gospel, however, has Jesus recognized by his followers as Son of God from the outset of his ministry and then develops this category as the key to understanding Jesus' true identity.

Jesus responds to Nathanael's confession of faith with a promise. If he has come to believe on the basis of Jesus' demonstration of his superhuman knowledge, then he **will see greater things than these**, which will also no doubt deepen his faith (cf. 2.11). The 'greater things' are predominantly the signs Jesus will perform, the first of which, the turning of water into wine, will be recounted almost immediately.

51 Jesus' final words are introduced by a solemn formula that will occur a further 24 times in this Gospel – **Truly, truly, I say to you**. The first two words translate the repetition in the Greek text –Ἀμήν, ἀμήν – and underscore the truth and authority of what follows. The Greek term is a transliteration of Hebrew, in which the 'Amen' was a formulaic expression, frequently used liturgically, that confirmed and strengthened a preceding statement. It could sometimes be doubled for special emphasis (cf. Num. 5.22; Neh. 8.6; Pss 41.14; 72.19). The Synoptics have Jesus employ the single Amen in a striking position – before the assertion that is to be stressed. This occurs 31 times in Matthew, 13 times in Mark and six in Luke. Only John uses the double Amen formula, and in his narrative this usage depicts Jesus as giving his word of honour and, in contexts where he is portrayed as the chief witness in God's lawsuit, this is the equivalent to his swearing an oath to the truth of his testimony. Frequently, though by no means always, the formula signals the Johannine adaptation of a saying of Jesus which is deeply embedded in early Christian tradition and has a Synoptic version. In this case **you will see heaven opened and the angels of God ascending and descending on the Son of Man** has most in common with Synoptic sayings about seeing the future coming of the Son of Man, when the heavens will be shaken and he will be accompanied by angels (cf. Mark 13.25–7; 14.62; Matt. 16.27–8; 24.29–31). In line with the more realized eschatology of the Fourth Gospel, this material has now been adapted to refer to Jesus' earthly mission. Its formulation has also been decisively influenced by the account of Jacob's dream in Gen. 28.12, in which 'the angels of God were ascending and descending on' a ladder connecting earth and heaven. The angels no longer accompany the Son of Man at his final coming, as in the Synoptics, but are to be seen as ascending and descending upon him. As has been noted, the Jacob story has already been invoked in the conversation with Nathanael. Now it is made clear that this true Israelite will see something greater than Jacob saw. He will see not simply a ladder but a person, the Son of Man, as the connection between earth and heaven. For Jacob the place of his dream became Bethel, the house of God, and the gate of heaven (Gen. 28.17, 19). For the evangelist Jesus now embodies God's address on earth, fulfilling all that was previously represented by such locations as Bethel, the tabernacle or the temple (cf. also 1.14; 2.19–21; 4.21–4).

This verse contains the first reference in the Gospel to the Son of Man. As in the Synoptics, it is a phrase found on Jesus' own lips and an allusive self-reference with echoes of the 'one like a son of man' in Dan. 7.13. In the Synoptics it is found in three contexts: references to a future coming of this figure in glory, predictions of his suffering and death, and talk of his present authority. As will be seen, in John's perspective the glory of the Son of Man does not await the end of history but is related particularly to his death as his hour of glory (cf. 12.23; 13.31–2), and suffering and glory are collapsed into one in the threefold predictions of the lifting up of the Son of Man (3.14; 8.28; 12.34). Characteristic of John's presentation also is the notion of the Son of Man as the link between heaven and earth found here and later in 3.13 and 6.62, along with references in which the Son of Man is synonymous with the title 'Son' or 'Son of God' (cf. esp. 5.25–7).

This saying about the Son of Man is not, however, addressed solely to Nathanael. The singular 'you' of v. 50 becomes a plural 'you' in v. 51, signalling a broader audience that includes the readers of this narrative. They too are promised that in what will follow in the bulk of the narrative about the mission of Jesus, culminating in his death as exaltation, they will see greater things in which the Son of Man is disclosed as the bridge between heaven and earth, replacing Jacob's ladder and serving as the very gate to heaven.

It is worth highlighting the differences between the account of the gathering of the first disciples around Jesus in the first part of this passage and that in the Synoptics. Again the evangelist appears to know those traditions and the characters involved but to have his own purpose in retelling the story in a quite different way. In the Synoptics, after John the Baptist has been arrested, Jesus himself takes the initiative in calling disciples. He issues a summons to discipleship to Simon and Andrew together while they are engaged in their fishing business and they leave this occupation in order to accompany Jesus (cf. Mark 1.16–20; Matt. 4.18–22; cf. also Luke 5.1–11). John's account is distinctive in just about every respect. (i) John the Baptist is still on the scene and Jesus' first disciples originated with John. (ii) As a result of the Baptist's testimony with its identification of Jesus, two of the Baptist's disciples take the initiative and begin to follow Jesus. (iii) Andrew is not at first accompanied by his brother, Simon, but is with another, unnamed disciple. (iv) Only later, and as a consequence of holding Jesus to be the Messiah, does Andrew bring his brother to Jesus. (v) In this way Jesus is recognized by disciples as the Christ from the very start of his ministry. (vi) John's Gospel introduces from the start of Jesus' relation to Simon the notion of a change of name, which is mentioned only later by the Synoptics. (vii) The Fourth Gospel's account gives no indication that the first disciples were fishermen, although the writer of the epilogue, with its post-resurrection fishing expedition, appears to assume that readers will have such knowledge from the Synoptic tradition. (viii) The overall effect of these differences is that while in the Synoptics discipleship is depicted as an unmediated response to the bare call of Jesus and entails the leaving behind of one's everyday employment, in this Gospel, for these first followers, discipleship is on the basis of a prior identification of Jesus as Lamb of God or as Messiah and entails leaving behind a previous religious commitment – to John the Baptist and his mission. Telling the story of the gathering of the disciples in this way and highlighting the necessity of a break with John fits with all that has previously been said about the Baptist and his identity and status vis-à-vis Jesus and with the polemical dimension that surrounds this depiction because of continuing rivalry between early Christians and followers of the Baptist.

This passage as a whole moves to a climax with Jesus' interaction with Nathanael. Surprisingly, Simon Peter, the foremost discile in the Synoptic tradition, is passed over swiftly in order to highlight the otherwise unattested Nathanael. Simon Peter remains silent, making no confession about Jesus, and instead the same sort of confession he makes in Matt. 16.16 is here placed in the mouth of Nathanael. In concluding with Jesus' promises made in response, particularly about the Son of Man, the passage offers its readers a further Christological perspective by which to interpret the account of the ministry that will follow. With its language of seeking, coming, seeing, finding, following, and staying or remaining this episode as a whole invites readers to respond in discipleship with Jesus' first followers and to discover that to do so is inseparable from having the right view of Jesus' identity. Andrew in the first scene identifies Jesus as the Christ, while Nathanael in the second scene confesses Jesus to be Son of God. Together, already at the outset of the narrative these first followers have come to the recognition to which the readers of the whole Gospel are invited to come by the end, namely, 'that Jesus is the Christ, the Son of God' (20.31). As readers follow the rest of the story with its 'greater things', their understanding of the initial testimonies will be deepened and they will be confirmed in their belief that the protagonist is indeed the unique link between earth and heaven. What is more, they will also be shown that the cross, where the Son of man is lifted up, far from undermining such a conviction, is the place in which those two realms most truly meet.

2. The Opening of Jesus' Mission: From Cana to Cana 2.1—4.54

A new section of the narrative begins here with the miracle at Cana. The return to Cana, with its reminder of the first miracle and the account of a second sign (cf. 4.46, 54) mean that 4.46–54 forms an *inclusio* with 2.1–11 and marks the close of the section. The section has seven major scenes and the material it contains focuses on the revelation taking place through Jesus, whether by means of the recounting of the two Cana signs and the action in the Jerusalem temple, the discourses with Nicodemus and the Samaritan woman, or the further testimony of John the Baptist or the comments of the narrator. The concentration is particularly on Jesus' self-disclosure through his word (cf. e.g. 2.19–21; 3.11, 12, 29, 32–4; 4.26, 29, 41–2). The opening and closing signs do not detract from this perspective. In the first Jesus' Jewish mother believes in the effectiveness of Jesus' word (2.5) and in the second a possibly Gentile official believes in Jesus' word (4.50). The response to Jesus in this section is predominantly positive, even if there are questions raised about the perceptiveness involved in the acceptance of his signs on the part of both Jerusalemites and Galileans (cf. 2.23–5; 4.43–5).

(i) Water into wine at Cana   *2.1–12*

(1) On the third day there was a wedding at Cana in Galilee, and the mother of Jesus was there. (2) Jesus and his disciples had also been invited to the wedding. (3) When the wine ran out, the mother of Jesus said to him, 'They have no wine.' (4) Jesus said to her, 'What concern is that to me and to you, woman? My hour has not yet come.' (5) His mother said to the servants, 'Do whatever he tells you.' (6) Now six stone water jars for the purification rites of the Jews were standing there, each holding from eighty to one hundred and twenty litres. (7) Jesus said to them, 'Fill the jars with water.' And they filled them to the brim. (8) He said to them, 'Now draw some out and take it to the master of the banquet.' So they took it. (9) When the master of the banquet tasted the water that had become wine and did not know where it had come from, though the servants who had drawn the water knew, the master of the banquet called the bridegroom (10) and said to him, 'Everyone serves the good wine first and the inferior when people become drunk. You have kept the good wine until now.' (11) Jesus did this, the first of the signs, in Cana of Galilee and revealed his glory, and his disciples believed in him. (12) After this he went down to Capernaum with his mother, brothers and his disciples, and they stayed there a few days.

The first of the 'greater things' that shows Jesus' heaven-sent role is now narrated. This inaugural scene of Jesus' mission sets its stamp on the readers' construal of Jesus' character and identity. The portrayal of the extraordinary deed of turning water into wine associates him both with the plenty of the messianic age and with divine beneficence. The account takes the basic form of a miracle story, a form found frequently in the Synoptic Gospels. So vv. 1–2 provide the initial setting, vv. 3–4 depict the situation of need, vv. 5–8 set out Jesus' miraculous intervention in response, vv. 9–10 serve as confirmation of the miracle, and v. 11 gives the narrator's concluding comment on the incident. The four pieces of conversation – between Jesus and his mother (vv. 3–4), his mother and the servants (v. 5), Jesus and the servants (vv. 7–8) and the steward and the bridegroom (vv. 9–10) – are elaborations within this structure. As the final verse in this section, v. 12 functions as a transition statement before the next major event in Jerusalem.

1–2 The temporal reference – **on the third day** – has, somewhat surprisingly, received much discussion. There have already been three references to 'the next day' (1.29, 35, 43), which would indicate four days to this point. This reference is taken by some to continue the sequence and produce a week, in which the miracle to be related would occur on the last day. This week has then been compared to the week of creation or to the week running up to the celebration of the giving of the law in later Jewish traditions about the feast of Pentecost. But it is by no means clear that there are any clues in the text strong enough to suggest that the reader is expected to interpret the sequence of days in this way. It is more likely that this temporal marker simply forms a loose connection between the Cana story and the promise to Nathanael, which it can be seen as fulfilling. Some have seen in its language of 'on the third day' an allusion to the resurrection, but 2.19,20 talk of 'in three days', the phrase, 'on the third day', in connection with the resurrection does not occur in John, and there is nothing in the account of the event at Cana that points specifically to the resurrection. If there is an allusion here, it is more likely that it is to the use of 'on the third day' in Exod. 19.11 (cf. 19.16), when God appears in glory to give the law. Here in John on the third day Jesus manifests his glory which surpasses that associated with the law (see on v. 6).

The narrator supplies the setting for Jesus' inaugural deed – **a wedding at Cana in Galilee**. The modern Khirbet Qana, at which archeological excavations are taking place, is thought to be the most likely site of ancient Cana and is some nine miles north of Nazareth. It is noteworthy that the first and last signs in which Jesus reveals himself are in the midst of key events in the human life cycle – here a wedding and, in the Lazarus episode, a death in the family. The most significant persons for the narrator's account of this first sign are introduced in order of their appearance. The bridegroom, the bride and the other guests do not receive a mention here because the focus will be on Jesus' deed and the wedding simply provides the necessary stage for its occurrence and the interpretation of its significance. The master of the banquet and the bridegroom will have a minor role later in vv. 9–10 in confirming that a miracle has taken place. **The mother of Jesus was there.** Strikingly, in this Gospel (cf. also 19.25–7) she is not given her personal name of Mary, known from the Synoptics and presumably familiar to Christian readers from the tradition. Attention is concentrated on her familial relationship to Jesus, which enables her to have an important intermediary function in involving her son in dealing with an embarrassing situation of need (cf. vv. 3–5). **Jesus and his disciples had also been invited to the wedding.** The mention of the disciples here prepares for the narrator's comment about their belief in v. 11, since they do not appear again in the story itself. The response of the other characters to Jesus after his deed is not of interest to the narrator. What counts is the effect of the sign on his disciples.

3–4 The situation of need to which Jesus eventually responds – **the wine ran out** – might appear to modern readers to be a trivial one and therefore Jesus' use of miraculous powers to be somewhat frivolous. Weddings, however, were not simply private family affairs but could often involve a whole village and in Jewish custom the wedding feast lasted for a week with guests coming and going during that time and the groom being responsible for ensuring there was sufficient wine for the whole period, often through organizing donations ahead of time from close relatives and friends. To run out of wine was not simply a social embarrassment but entailed a serious loss of family honour, suggested a lack of cooperative friends and had dire implications for the web of reciprocal obligations in which a person was involved.

When Jesus' mother apprises him of the situation, he rebuffs her. The question **What concern is that to me and to you . . . ?** can denote either a peaceable or hostile response depending on the context. Jesus' question here clearly expresses a refusal to become involved and a rejection of his mother's implied request that he should do so. There is an interesting parallel to this question in 1 Kgs 17.8–24 LXX, where the widow of Zarephath uses precisely the same words to Elijah. The dialogue is surrounded by two miracles. In the first Elijah replenishes the meal and oil that have run out and in the second restores the widow's son to life. Elijah's words, 'Your son lives', are also the same as Jesus uses to the official in 4.50. It could well be that the formulation of the first two Johannine signs draws on the Elijah traditions and is designed to show Jesus as a greater prophet than Elijah in his miraculous powers. Addressing one's mother as **woman** would not have been usual. It need not, however, express a harsh attitude, as is clear from Jesus' use of the same address to the Samaritan woman (4.21), his mother again at the cross (19.26), and Mary Magdalene at the empty tomb (20.15). Yet, employed by a son to a mother, it does suggest distancing.

My hour has not yet come supplies the reason for such distancing. This is the first mention of a theme that will be pervasive in the narrative. Its plot moves towards Jesus' future hour, which is depicted as an hour of glory and has at its heart his crucifixion and exaltation (cf. 7.30; 8.20; 12.27–8; 13.1; 16.32; 17.1). The hour is also an eschatological hour in that the exaltation of Jesus inaugurates the benefits of the life of the age to come and its resurrection (cf. 4.21; 5.28). There is a further twist to this theme in that John's Gospel frequently collapses two temporal perspectives, that of the post-exaltation period and that of Jesus' earthly mission, so that the hour can already be anticipated in the offers of life and other benefits of the new order that Jesus makes (cf. 'the hour is coming, and now is' in 4.23; 5.25). The force of this first reference to his hour is that Jesus is working according to a schedule and agenda not determined by humans but by God, not instigated by his earthly mother but by his heavenly Father. A similar pattern will be at work later in 7.1–10, as Jesus responds to his brothers' suggestion that he go and show his works publicly at the feast in Jerusalem. Jesus rebuffs them, saying that his time has not yet come, but then goes to the Feast of Tabernacles anyway. The pattern can also be seen with the second and seventh signs. Both the official and the two sisters, Mary and Martha, do not have their request granted immediately but instead receive different forms of rebuff (cf. 4.48; 11.4–6) before Jesus eventually acts. The characterization of Jesus is clear. It is not that he is indifferent to human need. He listens and responds, but he does so on his own terms. His initial refusal to do anything also heightens the tension by prolonging the crisis.

But a further question is raised by this verse. If 'My hour has not yet come' is the reason for not acting, does this mean that when Jesus does act, his hour *has* come and within a very short lapse of time? The hour as a whole remains future, awaiting the end of Jesus' mission, but, as has been noted in other references to the hour, it can be anticipated at points in Jesus' ministry. Since the hour is an hour of glory and the narrator will explicitly state that in this sign Jesus revealed his glory (v. 11), the turning of water into wine should be seen as one of those proleptic eschatological moments.

5 The narrator does not move straight to the miracle but builds suspense again through depicting the response of Jesus' mother. This response comes as a surprise. Jesus' words should have had the effect of discouraging her, but instead she is expectant and tells the servants, **Do whatever he tells you**. With her leaving of the initiative to Jesus and her trust in the efficacy of her son's words, she serves as a model for believing readers.

6 Now six stone water jars for the purification rites of the Jews were standing there. A family would normally possess only one such jar, so others may have been brought in for the occasion. But such an observation concentrates attention on the surface level of the narrative. The number and size of the jars remain unusual and the symbolic nature of what will occur is signalled by the mention of Jewish purification rites. The number six may well then represent the imperfection or insufficiency of the old order of Judaism. The objection that Jesus does not add a seventh jar that contains the wine is insubstantial. Six can represent imperfection without seven as perfection having to be explicitly mentioned, and the evangelist's fondness for seven as representing completion is in any case established by his reporting of seven signs in the ministry and his shaping of narrative episodes into seven scenes. Jesus will transform that which represents the old order into that which symbolizes the new. The note that each jar held **from eighty to one hundred and twenty litres** underlines the abundance of the provision of wine Jesus will make.

7–8 The process which produces the supply of wine is depicted briefly, but precisely when and how the transformation occurs are not narrated. Jesus' response is to give an order that appears to have nothing to do with the need that has been pointed out. The command to the servants – **Fill the jars with water** – suggests that the jars stood empty. The servants' compliance with the command has been prepared for by the instructions they have received from Jesus' mother. That they fill the jars **to the brim** again suggests the abundance of the supply that will follow. They are then instructed to take a sample to **the master of the banquet**, the head servant who was in charge of the arrangements for the festivities (cf. the only other extant use of the Greek term in Heliodorus, *Aeth.* 7.27.7). To tone down the miracle by suggesting, as some commentators have done, that only the water that was drawn out became wine is to miss its point, which lies precisely in the extravagance of Jesus' provision.

9–10 Only through the reaction of the master of the banquet upon tasting the sample is it made clear that **the water . . . had become wine**. Unlike the servants, he does not know from where (πόθεν) the wine has come. This foreshadows what will be said about people's ignorance of the origins of various aspects of the new order, including Jesus himself, its inaugurator (cf. e.g. 3.8; 4.11; 7.27–8; 8.14; 9.29–30; 19.9) and is another of the signals that the wine symbolizes that new order. In the Jewish Scriptures wine in abundance signifies the salvation of the end time – 'The time is surely coming, says the Lord, when . . . the mountains shall drip sweet wine, and all the hills shall flow with it. I will restore the fortunes of my people Israel, . . . they shall plant vineyards and drink their wine' (Amos 9.13–14; cf. also Isa. 25.6; Jer. 31.12; Joel 3.18). *2 Bar.* 29.5 and *1 Enoch* 10.19 continue this tradition in their depictions of the messianic age. In addition, wine stands for life and joy (cf. Ps. 104.15; Eccl. 10.19; Sir. 31.27–8; 40.20). In inaugurating the new order, Jesus provides life that is to be enjoyed.

The comment of the master of the banquet – **Everyone serves the good wine first and the inferior when people become drunk. You**

have kept the good wine until now – functions on a number of levels. It confirms indirectly that a miracle has taken place, though its speaker does not know that this is what he has witnessed. It indicates that Jesus' supply has not only saved the bridegroom's honour but also enhances it. His hospitality surpasses the norm, even if the guests might not be in the best condition to appreciate it. There is also an irony in the master of the banquet attributing the supply of good wine to the bridegroom, when in reality it has come from Jesus, who will shortly be depicted as the true bridegroom (3.29). Jesus is a guest at a wedding, in which the bridegroom fails in a crucial aspect of his role. He fulfils the role of the bridegroom and does so in a way that exceeds all its usual expectations. In addition, the reversal of what is alleged to be the usual practice at such feasts also has symbolic force by underscoring the time sequence in the order of salvation. The best comes last; the good wine of the new age has been saved 'until now'. The 'now' is at a wedding banquet and in the Jewish Scriptures this serves as another image of the end time, when God, the bridegroom, rejoices in his bride, Israel (cf. Isa. 62.4–5). Elsewhere in the New Testament Rev. 19.7, 9 presents Jesus as the bridegroom at the eschatological wedding banquet.

11 Jesus' miraculous act is described as **the first of the signs**. The term translated as 'first' (ἀρχή) can also mean beginning (cf. 1.1–2) or foundation. This opening miraculous deed will set the pattern for the rest. In the LXX σημεῖον, sign, was used of visible phenomena, not necessarily miraculous, that conveyed further knowledge or meaning. It is associated with Moses in Exod. 4.1–17, where three miraculous signs are meant to confirm to the people his call from God and to produce belief. One of these is the turning of water into blood. Later the plagues are described as signs, designed to pass judgement on Pharaoh and to show that Yahweh is the one true God (Exod. 7.3; 10.2). Deut. 13.1–5, however, establishes that the display of signs and wonders are not sufficient in themselves to authenticate a prophet; the prophet's teaching must also be in line with God's commandments. In the Synoptics Jesus, of course, performs miracles but they are not designated as signs. Instead, when asked for a sign, he states that none will be granted (Mark 8.11–12), except the sign of Jonah (Matt. 12.39; 16.4; Luke 11.29–30). In Graeco-Roman writings 'sign' had a broad variety of connotations, but in religious contexts most frequently referred to portents or omens and in discussions of forensic rhetoric referred to the sort of argument or evidence that did not in itself constitute proof but, as part of a cumulative case, could be convincing. In John the signs testify to who Jesus is, just as Moses' signs had testified to his status as God's messenger. But they are not unambiguous and indeed the opposition to Jesus believe that, like the false prophet of Deut. 13, he is deceiving or leading the people astray (cf. 7.12, 47). As in the

Synoptics, when asked, Jesus does not submit to the demand for some unambiguous proof on which people might base their belief (cf. 4.48; 6.30). Nevertheless, he performs signs which, for those with eyes to see, serve to establish and confirm his identity. Given the forensic themes in this Gospel, it may well be that its audience would have also associated 'signs' with their rhetorical function and considered them not as proofs but as part of the cumulative witness of the narrative to Jesus' identity. After all, Jesus' works are said to testify to who he is (cf. 5.36; 10.25) and the evangelist's statement of purpose confirms that the signs have been written down as part of the Gospel's overall testimony in order that the readers might continue to believe that Jesus is the Christ, the Son of God (cf. 20.30–1; 21.24).

In this opening sign Jesus **revealed his glory, and his disciples believed in him**. Glory has been mentioned earlier in the prologue, where it is that of the incarnate Logos and full of grace and truth, replacing the grace and truth associated with the law and Moses (1.14, 16, 17). The reality of the incarnation is underlined by the sheer materiality of this action in the midst of normal human life, while at the same time the divine glory of the Logos is disclosed precisely in and through his enabling water to become wine. Again, such glory surpasses that associated with the law, as the wine of the end time replaces the water used for the law's purification rites. This perspective is reinforced, if, as noted above, 'on the third day' may be seen as an allusion to the glory manifested in the giving of the law in Exod. 19.16. Jesus' glory both awaits its full demonstration and confirmation in the future hour of death and exaltation and is disclosed in anticipation in his earthly mission. The last sign in that mission, the raising of Lazarus, is also explicitly connected to the revelation of this glory (cf. 11.4, 40) and the *inclusio* thereby provided suggests that this is the perspective from which to view all the signs.

The narrator gives no explanation of how the disciples knew about the miracle when the master of the banquet did not. Nevertheless, they are said to have believed and their response to this sign raises the question of the relation between signs and belief, which will surface again in the narrative, most immediately in 2.23–5. Here the disciples have been shown to have already a considerable measure of belief in Jesus (cf. 1.35–51) and so presumably the sign strengthens and confirms them in that belief. More generally, the evangelist will be concerned neither to advocate a faith that is merely dependent on signs nor to devalue such signs. Instead the self-disclosure of Jesus through the signs is seen as creating the conditions which can initiate or reinforce the response of faith (cf. e.g. 10.37–8; 11.15; 20.31).

12 This transitional verse describes a move to Capernaum after the wedding and a limited stay there on the part of Jesus, his family members and the disciples. His **brothers** have not been mentioned as being at the wedding, but, as these were family affairs, it is highly likely that the narrator intends it to be understood that they were also there. They will reappear in 7.1–10. Capernaum was at the north-western corner of the Sea of Galilee and features in the Synoptics as a centre of Jesus' Galilean activity. In John it has less emphasis, being mentioned in 4.46b and then providing the setting for Jesus' discourse on the bread of life in 6.17, 24, 59. The narrator's comment at this point that Jesus and his entourage remain there only **a few days** directs readers' attention away from this location and prepares them for his next move – to Jerusalem (v. 13).

While the form of this miracle story is familiar from the Synoptic tradition, the miracle itself is unique to John's Gospel. The most likely scriptural influence on the shaping of this account is provided by the Elijah stories in 1 Kings 17, and the conceptual and linguistic parallels between them and the first two signs in John have already been noted (see comments on v. 4). The parabolic sayings in the Synoptics about the bridegroom and new wine (Mark 2.18–22 parr.) also feature in discussions of the origins of the Cana miracle. The Lukan version of this cluster is particularly interesting. In response to the criticism that his disciples eat and drink, Jesus says, 'Can you make the wedding guests fast while the bridegroom is with them?' (Luke 5.34). The sayings about new wine requiring fresh wineskins then include the critical observation that those who drink old wine are not able to appreciate the new – 'And no one after drinking old wine desires new wine, but says "The old is good"' (Luke 5.39). Certainly the account of the miracle reflects these themes. Disciples and wedding guests drink freely in the presence of the true bridegroom, who supplies wine in abundance, and here it is the new that is most definitely the good wine. Whether the Lukan sayings in themselves would provide a sufficient basis for the construction of the miracle story is another matter.

The closest parallels to the actual miracle and its significance are in fact found in the Dionysus legends, despite the too easy dismissal of such parallels by some commentators. Dionysus was the Greek god of fertility and new life and was known as Bacchus in the Roman world. In the myths of his origins he is depicted as the divine son of Zeus and of a mortal mother, Semele. Among his titles were the Saviour, the Fruit Bringer and the Abundance of Life. He was particularly famed as the god of wine, who had given this gift to mortals. During the spring festival the drinking of wine was the most prominent feature of his cult and it represented the fullness of life and the presence of the god. In the second century BCE Pausanias (*Descr.* 2.26) reports a miracle involving wine occurring among Dionysus' adherents – 'three pots are brought into the building by the priests and set down empty in the presence of the citizens and of any strangers who may chance to be in the country. The doors of the building are sealed by the priests themselves and by any others who may be so inclined. On the morrow they are allowed to examine the seals, and on going into the building they find the pots filled with wine.' The basic points of contact with John's story are obvious, although here there is no water in the pots that is transformed into the wine. Elsewhere, however, there are stories of Dionysus in which such a transformation does occur. Rivers taste of wine (Lucian, *Ver. hist.* 1.7) and fountains and springs produce wine on the days that celebrate the appearance of the god (Pliny, *Nat.* 2.231, 31.13; Diodorus Siculus, *Hist.* 3.66.2). Particularly striking is the story in Achilleus Tatius (*Leuc. Clit.* 2.2.1–6) of how wine came to the people of Tyre. Dionysus visits a hospitable herdsman who can only offer him the same drink 'as that of the oxen, since vines did not yet exist'. They drink a toast and the drink becomes wine. 'The herdsman, drinking of it, danced for joy, and said to the god: "Where did you get this purple water, my friend?"' Dionysus then takes him to a vine and says, 'Here is your water . . . this is its source.' Since worship of Dionysus was widespread in the Graeco-Roman world and stories about him well known, particularly in Asia Minor and Ephesus, at the very least John's readers would have picked up on the implied comparison and contrast. But if that is the case, then it is equally likely that the account was composed with these parallels in view. The Dionysian stories were also known in Palestine and may have already penetrated the retelling of Israel's history. Haggadic legends include miraculous supplies of wine in the stories of the patriarchs and depict the water which comes from the rock struck by Moses as tasting of new wine (cf. *Mek. Exod.* 18.9). Philo had already depicted both Melchizedek (cf. *Leg. Alleg.* 3.82) and the Logos (cf. *De Som.* 2. 249) in Dionysiac terms. There is a further dimension to the parallels. Rulers were depicted as emulating Dionysus and his role as the provider of life was attributed to them. They include Alexander the Great and Roman emperors such as Trajan, Hadrian and Commodus, with an inscription about the last proclaiming him as the 'new Dionysus'. Martial (*Epig.* 8.26) even describes Domitian as surpassing Bacchus. In this light the evangelist begins his account of Jesus' deeds with a story of a prodigious supply of wine that sets this Jewish Messiah who is believed to be God over against any other gods and rulers who are held to be the givers of life in abundance.

Whether there is any actual incident in the life of Jesus that gave rise to this story is extremely hard to know. Some hold that it is likely that the evangelist himself considered he was retelling a miracle story from his tradition that had a basis in the ministry of Jesus, since for him a 'sign' is not merely symbolic but a concrete deed that points to the glory of Jesus and the significance of his mission. How present-day readers deal with the historicity of so-called nature miracles would then be another matter, and negative evaluations need not be thought to be dependent on a world-view that rules out the miraculous altogether. But the evangelist is also capable of creating history-like material that points to the significance of Jesus and his mission (see, for example, the later discussion of the conversations of Jesus with Nicodemus and with the Samaritan woman or the Lazarus story or the blood and water flowing from Jesus' side). In this case, in particular, there are strong reasons to think that this story may have been the result of such a process. All the other signs have some parallel in the miracle stories of the Synoptic tradition, but this first one is unique and its recounting of the actual miracle is more allusive than in any of the other sign narratives. There is a further peculiarity about the way it is told. Of all the characters actually participating in the event only the servants, who had drawn off the sample taken to the master of the banquet, are said to have known its origin and none of them, including Jesus' mother, are depicted as then having a response to its miraculous element. Only the disciples, who have not been involved in what happened and whose understanding of it is not explained, are said to have believed in Jesus as a result. The rarity of the term used for the master of the banquet has already been noted but his function also raises historical difficulties. His final comment suggests a familiarity with the bridegroom that seems more appropriate to a friend or fellow-guest than to a servant. This is a family occasion in a small Galilean peasant town, while, even allowing for Hellenization of Galilee, a master of the banquet is more at home in the Graeco-Roman urban setting of a symposium, where he would usually be chosen from among the guests. But more important than this apparent importation into the story is the observation that nearly all its features only take their force as part of a sign because they are elements within specifically Johannine stylistic structures, literary motifs and theological themes. Jesus' relation to his mother, the pattern of request, rebuff and then response on Jesus' own terms, the motifs of the hour and of the ignorance of the origin of Jesus' gift, the theme of fulfilment/replacement of Jewish observances, the spectacular nature of the miracle (the other signs all have features showing Jesus as surpassing the miraculous activities depicted in the Synoptics), the symbolism of the wine as the abundance Jesus provides for living and of the wedding at which Jesus is the true bridegroom (cf. 3.29 and the betrothal-type scene which follows in 4.1–42) – all these key ingredients of the meaning of the account derive from the evangelist's distinct perspective which fashions the Gospel as a whole. If one were to add to this list influences from the Dionysus tradition, in which pots are filled with wine and water becomes wine, then it would become almost impossible to isolate within the present account any core historical tradition for this event set in Cana. In fact, the essential content of the whole story depends on a view of Jesus that arose only after the resurrection, namely, that he was a divine being.

But preoccupation with matters of facticity, however understandable on the part of the modern reader, may well lead to missing the point of this story, which lies precisely in its extraordinariness and extravagance. Ancient readers of the Gospel, with knowledge of God's activities in the history of Israel and of the reports about the deeds of other gods, are not likely to have found it offensive or incredible but to have seen it as part of the overall claim being made in the narrative about Jesus' divine power. After all, this Gospel does attempt to persuade its readers that Jesus has divine status and is indeed the divine Logos incarnate. The evangelist, then, chooses to tell the story of an inaugural deed which will provide the paradigm for the other signs. Messianic titles have already been applied to Jesus by his first followers, but Jesus is to be seen as surpassing ordinary messianic expectations and as the sort of Messiah who is himself divine. The depiction of him as turning water into wine at a wedding banquet, thereby ensuring that the wine does not run out and, what is more, that the best is saved until last, makes clear that through his mission Jesus is offering the gift of the life of the new age. His bestowing of the conditions for human flourishing surpasses, explicitly, the provision of the law and, implicitly, the claims of rival gods, especially Dionysus, and imperial rulers. Wine, grain and oil were the three staples of human existence and an appropriate quantity of wine enabled life to be celebrated with joy. It is no accident that the first sign and the last 'I Am' saying with a predicate – 'I am the true vine' (15.1) – emphasize this theme. The sheer quantity in Jesus' provision of wine will be replicated later in the provision of bread and fish for five thousand and its significance is spelled out in the mission statement of 10.10 – 'I have come that they may have life and have it in abundance' (cf. also 1.16). The prologue has already stated that the created world came into being through the Logos and that in the Logos was life. This sign now shows the incarnate Logos exercising his power over the created elements by transforming water into wine and by dispensing the life he embodies. In composing this first sign, the evangelist stakes out the bold claim the overall narrative makes about Jesus. The other signs, which have Synoptic equivalents, will provide corroborating evidence of his life-giving powers. There is a further dimension to its paradigmatic function. It suggests already that the nature of Jesus' power and of his bestowal of life will also be very different from what would traditionally have been expected of a messianic figure or of other gods and rulers. Jesus' statement that his hour has not yet come and the narrator's comment that this sign revealed Jesus' glory anticipate the fuller development of the notion that the supreme hour of Jesus' glory will paradoxically entail his crucifixion, and his mother's only other appearance in the narrative will be at that point. From the evangelist's perspective, Jesus' divine power and glory displayed in this sign is most truly seen in the apparent powerlessness and shame of the cross, and the supply of abundant life, indicated by the extravagant quantity of wine, has been made available for humans only by the incarnate Logos' absorption of death. The fulfilment of the promised vision of the marriage of heaven and earth through the Son of Man (cf. 1.51) is given its first instalment in the story of the sign performed at a wedding in Cana, but this story also points ahead to the crucial final instalment, to the hour when this Son of Man will be lifted up (cf. 3.14; 8.28; 12.32–3).

(ii) Jesus and the temple   2.13–22

(13) The Passover of the Jews was near, and Jesus went up to Jerusalem. (14) He found in the temple those selling cattle, sheep and doves and money changers seated there. (15) Having made a whip[1] out of cords, he drove them all out of the temple, both sheep and cattle, and poured out the money changers' coins and overturned their tables, (16) and said to those selling doves, 'Take these out of here; do not make my Father's house a house of trade.' (17) His disciples remembered that it was written, 'Zeal for your house will consume me.' (18) The Jews then responded and said to him, 'What sign can you show us for doing these things?' (19) Jesus answered them, 'Destroy this temple, and in three days I will raise it up.' (20) The Jews then said, 'This temple has been in construction forty-six years, and are you going to raise it up in three days?' (21) But he was speaking about the temple of his body. (22) When, therefore, he was raised from the dead, his disciples remembered that he had said this, and they believed the scripture and the word that Jesus had spoken.

In its context in the narrative this passage follows on from the incident of Jesus' turning of water into wine, which adumbrated the theme of his fulfilment of the old order within Judaism. Up until this point Jesus has been depicted in Galilee, but now the same theme is played out in a dramatic new way as, at the time of the major Jewish festival, Passover, Jesus goes to Jerusalem and to the heart of Jewish religious life – the temple. There, at the beginning of his public mission and through a symbolic act in the tradition of the prophets, he provokes a confrontation with the religious authorities. Since Jerusalem and the temple were regarded as God's own possession in a special way, Jesus' activity there can also be seen as a graphic illustration of the prologue's formulation about the Logos coming to 'what was his own' (1.11a).

After its depiction of the setting in v. 13, this account falls into two parts. The first (vv. 14–17) treats Jesus' actions and accompanying words in the temple incident itself, while the second (vv. 18–22) relates the

---

[1] Some manuscripts read ὡς φραγέλλιον, 'like a whip' or 'a sort of whip'. Despite the early date of two of the witnesses – p[66] and p[75] – this appears to be a clear scribal attempt to soften the portrayal of Jesus' action.

dialogue between Jesus and 'the Jews' that the incident provokes. Both parts conclude with a reference to the disciples' remembering (cf. vv. 17, 22).

13 By describing the approaching festival as the **Passover of the Jews**, the narrator is not simply adding an explanation for Gentile readers; it is likely that he is also putting distance between himself and Jewish religious festivals. Throughout the controversy with 'the Jews' in Jesus' public mission, the narrator will offer reminders that the action takes place against the backdrop of particular festivals (cf. also 5.1; 6.4; 7.2; 10.22; 11.55), and on a number of occasions will portray Jesus' words and deeds as the fulfilment of the significance traditionally attached to the festival concerned.

14–15 In comparison with the Synoptic tradition about the temple incident (cf. Mark 11.15–17; Matt. 21.12–13; Luke 19.45–6), John's account is more detailed. It adds to the selling of doves that of cattle and sheep, has Jesus actually tip out the coins collected by the money changers, and describes the means by which they are all driven out – an improvised whip made out of cords. John's addition of animals as large as cows has produced some questions about its verisimilitude. Jewish sources fail to mention such animals in the temple precincts and their excrement would have caused problems of pollution of the sacred site. There is a possible ambiguity in the formulation, **he drove them all out of the temple, both sheep and cattle**. Does the reference to sheep and cattle qualify the 'all', so that it is the sheep and cattle which are driven out? Or does the 'all' refer back to those previously mentioned in v. 14, so that the force is 'he drove them all out, the sheep and cattle as well'? The latter is the more likely construal, particularly in the light of the Synoptic tradition, which clearly has the human sellers and buyers being driven out. The presence in the temple precincts of animals and birds to be bought for sacrifice was a necessity if the Torah's requirements for sacrifice were to be obeyed. The money changers had to be there too, if the money in the possession of pilgrims was to be changed into the coinage acceptable to the temple, not only for the purchase of sacrifices but also for the payment of the half-shekel temple tax levied on all Jews. This had to be paid in the coinage of Tyre that did not have on it the image of the emperor. It is unlikely, then, that Jesus' activity is being depicted as a 'cleansing of the temple' from commercial abuse. Rather, this disruption of one of the most significant feasts of the year is seen as a symbolic action that temporarily brings to a halt the sacrificial system understood to be ordained by God in the law. Within the context of John's narrative as a whole it also anticipates the end of temple sacrifices through the death of Jesus as the true Passover lamb (cf. 1.29; 19.36; also 18.34).

16 The words with which Jesus accompanies his action are distinctive to this account. Whereas the Synoptic tradition has Jesus quote Scripture, in a combination of Isa. 56.7 and Jer. 7.11, to reprimand his audience for turning God's house, which should be a house of prayer for all nations, into a den of robbers, John's **do not make my Father's house a house of trade** contains instead an allusion to Zech. 14.20–1. This passage looks forward to the day of the Lord and to God's presence in a renewed Jerusalem. At that time all nations will keep the Feast of Tabernacles and the final words of the prophecy are 'there shall no longer be traders in the house of the Lord of hosts on that day'. The trading previously associated with the sacrificial system will not be necessary, because in the end-time worship of Yahweh as king all aspects of life will have become sacred. Indeed, 'every cooking pot in Jerusalem and Judah shall be sacred to the Lord of hosts'. The saying of John's Jesus underlines the significance of his action. It constitutes a prophetic gesture pointing to the end of the present temple order and its sacrifices in the expectation of their replacement by the new arrangements appropriate for God's eschatological presence in Jerusalem. It is not that the traders Jesus drives out were doing anything wrong but rather that, in the new order Jesus has come to bring, their presence will not be needed at all. The dialogue that follows in vv. 18–21 spells out how this new order finds its fulfilment in the person and mission of Jesus.

17 First, however, Jesus' action in the temple is linked to his death through the Scripture his disciples are said to have remembered. It is not made clear here at what point the disciples remembered Ps. 69.9. The verse could be read as indicating that they remembered these words at the time of the incident. It seems more likely, however, that readers are meant to understand the remembering as a post-resurrection phenomenon, as is made explicit when the disciples' remembering is discussed again in v. 22. In fact, the early church frequently employed Ps. 69 in its explanation of Jesus' suffering and death as a fulfilment of Scripture. This Gospel will take up v. 4 of the psalm in 15.25 and v. 21 in 19.28–9 (cf. also Mark 15.36; Matt. 27.34, 48; Luke 23.36). Acts 1.20 uses v. 25 in connection with the fate of Judas, while Paul takes over vv. 22–3 to speak of the rejection of Christ by the majority within Israel in Rom. 11.9–10, and v. 9b to confirm the attitude he ascribes to Christ in Rom. 15.3. In the citation here the evangelist has changed the past tense of the psalm verse to a future – **Zeal for your house will consume me.** It functions, then, not simply as a comment on the burning intensity of Jesus' zeal but to make the point that his zealous activity in the temple would be what would consume Jesus in the sense of leading to his destruction in death. There appears, then, to be a strong reminiscence of the Synoptic tradition's depiction of the temple incident as the catalyst that brought about his crucifixion. In the context of John's account the association of Jesus' temple action with his death also prepares the way for the link between the temple and his resurrection in vv. 20–2.

18 In line with the narrative's dominant portrayal of the opposition to Jesus, those who respond to his action are simply designated 'the Jews'. Their question – **What sign can you show us for doing these things?** – indicates that, having failed to recognize the sign that Jesus' prophetic act could be seen as constituting, they now demand an authorization for Jesus' action that would take the form of some convincing miraculous deed. Whereas for the evangelist a 'sign' is revelatory of the presence and glory of God in Jesus' actions, for the opposition a 'sign' is a warrant whereby Jesus has to justify himself. The opposition's question reflects this Gospel's combination of two pieces of Synoptic tradition. In the first there is also a question, posed by the chief priests, elders and scribes shortly after the temple incident, asking by what authority Jesus has acted in the way he has (cf. Mark 11.27–33; Matt. 21.23–7; Luke 20.1–8). There Jesus replied with a question of his own about the authority by which John had baptized. Here, the formulation of the Jewish religious leaders' question in terms of a sign takes up their demand from a second piece of Synoptic tradition. Jesus' response to the request for a sign in Mark 8.11–12 is 'no sign will be given to this generation', while the other Gospels qualify this with 'except the sign of the prophet Jonah' (cf. Matt. 12.38–40; 16.1–4; Luke 11.16, 29–32). Matthew's version spells out that the sign of Jonah is an allusion to the resurrection, since just as Jonah was in the belly of the great fish three days, so Jesus will be in the earth three days. The allusion to the resurrection and the mention of three days also occur in Jesus' quite differently formulated response here in John.

19 Destroy this temple, and in three days I will raise it up. Jesus' response continues the evangelist's creative reworking of Synoptic material. There, of course, Jesus predicts the destruction of the temple (Mark 13.2; Matt. 24.2; Luke 21.6), but more significant, because of the closeness of the wording, is the accusation about a saying of Jesus at his Sanhedrin trial, although it is said to be brought by false witnesses – 'We heard him say, "I will destroy this temple that is made with hands, and in three days I will build another, not made with hands"' (cf. also Matt. 26.61). This is repeated in the mockery of the passers-by at the crucifixion – 'Aha! You who would destroy the temple and build it in three days ...' (Mark 15.29; Matt. 27.40). John's version of such a saying has some slight differences. While Mark and Matthew use καταλύω for 'to destroy', it simply employs λύω, and whereas they have οἰκοδομέω for 'to build, rebuild', it has ἐγείρω, 'to raise up', which can be used of a building but more readily evokes the following interpretation in terms of the resurrection. This version also has the first verb in the imperative rather than as a prediction or threat in the first person singular. The imperative can have the force of a concession – 'if you destroy', that is, 'if the temple is destroyed by someone', and this change is again in line with the following explanation that the temple is Jesus' body. Jesus could scarcely predict that he would destroy his own body. In the light of this fuller perspective on the saying, an ironical force of the imperative also becomes possible. Jesus might then be taken as saying, 'Go ahead and destroy this body, and in three days I will raise it up.' However, the opposition's intent to kill Jesus does not become explicit in John's narrative until 5.18.

20–1 But in any case Jesus' reply is lost on his opponents. **This temple has been in construction forty-six years, and are you going to raise it up in three days?** is the first instance in the narrative of what will become the familiar misunderstanding motif. 'The Jews' take Jesus in a literal fashion and remain on a merely earthly plane, as they respond in terms of the impossibility of rebuilding the temple in three days when it had taken forty-six years to construct. This formulation raises questions about the evangelist's perspective. The building of Herod's temple began in 19 BCE and was not completed until 63 CE (cf. Josephus, *Ant.* 15.380). Does the formulation suggest that the building had been completed, and, if so, is the evangelist, writing a significant time after the completion, allowing this knowledge to colour the way the question is worded? In fact, the grammar is not strained if the verb is taken as meaning that the construction is still going on at the time. Precisely the same tense of the verb is employed in Ezra 5.16 LXX to indicate that the temple had been under construction but not yet completed. The verisimilitude of the narrative at this point is also furthered by the mention of forty-six years, since this would bring the dating of the incident to around 27 CE, which is plausible for an account that sets the incident at the beginning of an approximately three-year public mission on the part of Jesus. There is a further implication arising from the evangelist's temporal perspective. Writing for readers at a time when he and they knew not only that the temple had been completed but also that shortly afterwards it had been destroyed, there would be additional ironies to this exchange.

In order that readers should not become victims of Jesus' metaphor along with the opposition, the narrator intervenes on this occasion to point out the misunderstanding – **But he was speaking about the temple of his body.** The force of this explanation, which readers need to understand if they are to share the privileged perspective of the evangelist, is that, for believers in Jesus, the Jerusalem temple now gives way to the temple constituted by the body of Jesus, and, in the light of the discussion of the preceding verses, this new temple is ultimately indestructible. God's presence, which previously had its special focus on earth in the Jerusalem temple, is now supremely manifested in the crucified and risen body of Jesus. The interpretation of Jesus' temple saying in Mark, with its addition of 'without hands' in relation to the new temple, in all probability has in view the part in the new order played by the Christian community, in line with the use of temple imagery for this community in 1 Cor. 3.16–17; 2 Cor. 6.16; Eph. 2.20–2; 1 Pet. 2.4–5. For John, however, the reference of the new temple is Christological rather than ecclesiological.

22 The narrator further explains that the first followers of Jesus came to this insight when they remembered his saying after the resurrection. It was not until this stage that **they believed the scripture and the word that Jesus had spoken**. The scripture in view is presumably Ps. 69.9, which they are said to have remembered in v. 17, and the word of Jesus is the saying in v. 19. It is significant that for the narrator Scripture and Jesus' word can be spoken of in the same breath as the object of belief. And what this verse makes clear is that both were interpreted in the light of the resurrection. With regard to the Scripture, it is not just that a proof-text, whose detail fits later Christian belief, can be found, but that in the light of his resurrection Jesus can now be seen as the speaker of the psalm, as the righteous one, whose zeal for God's cause leads to his suffering but later vindication. With regard to Jesus' word, a post-resurrection perspective enables the tradition of the saying that climaxes the temple incident to be seen as decisively prefiguring what was to be embodied in Jesus' death and resurrection. The narrator's comments only make explicit what is implicit in much of the narrative, namely, that its telling of Jesus' story combines two levels – that of traditions about Jesus' earthly mission and the post-Easter faith and experience of the evangelist and his community. Readers will be told later that it is the Spirit who enables the creative merging of the two perspectives, because it is the function of the Paraclete to bring to a remembrance, which is full of understanding, all that Jesus had said (cf. 14.26; 16.14).

A number of historical questions are raised by the Fourth Gospel's account. The most obvious, assuming a core of historicity to the tradition and given the contrast between the placement of the incident here and that in the Synoptics, where it occurs at the end of Jesus' mission, is – when is it likely to have happened? It appears inherently unlikely that an unusual event of this sort would have taken place twice, and in any case the two versions describe basically the same elements – the driving out of those who sold doves, the overturning of the tables of the money changers, and a saying of Jesus referring in some way to the temple as God's house. There are a minority of scholars who favour John's chronology. The two major arguments for such a view are (i) that in the Synoptic tradition itself, when asked about his authority for his action, Jesus replies with the question whether the baptism of John was from heaven or from humans, and this would fit better with the beginning of his mission closer to John's baptizing activity; and (ii) that the Synoptics have in any case put too much into the one short last week of Jesus' life for their accounts to be plausible. Neither argument is particularly compelling. To read Jesus' question about John in the Synoptic tradition as a question about a figure whose activity is now in the past presents no problems whatsoever, and in any case the Fourth Gospel's chronology of the temple incident is too early to make good sense of Jesus' question, since its narrative will later tell of John's baptizing activity still going on alongside Jesus' mission (cf. 3.22—4.2). Furthermore, contrary to popular impression, the Synoptic tradition does not in fact give a precise chronology for the week before the Passover. The only incidents to be precisely dated are those that occur after the plotting of the authorities two days before the Passover (cf. Mark 14.1; Matt. 26.1–2). It is only John's account that puts the entry into Jerusalem five days before Passover (12.1, 12)! Even if the tradition does compress into a shorter period events from the last part of the mission which may have been spread out over a longer period, this does not in itself entail that it has the chronology of the temple incident completely wrong and that it really happened right at the beginning. An overt attack on the temple arrangements for sacrifice is far more readily understandable historically as part of the culmination of Jesus' public mission and as the event that sealed the decision to have him arrested.

In fact, in their reconstruction of the history of composition of the Fourth Gospel a number of scholars plausibly suggest that at an earlier stage the temple incident was associated with the triumphal entry into Jerusalem in chapter 12 but was removed to make room for the Lazarus story, which in this narrative provides the chief motive for Jesus' arrest. In any case, as it now stands in the final version of the Gospel, the account still retains clear links with the passion narrative. Verse 17 has an implicit reference to Jesus' death and its citation of Ps. 69 is from a psalm extensively quarried by the early church for scriptural witness to the passion. Jesus' saying in v. 19 is a version of a saying which has an important role in Mark and Matthew in their accounts of the Sanhedrin trial and the crucifixion. It appears, then, that, as with a number of other features of the Fourth Gospel, theological rather than historical concerns have shaped the narrative's presentation and in this case determined the place of the temple incident in the plot. Placing the temple incident at the beginning helps to structure the whole narrative of Jesus' public mission in terms of a major confrontation between his claims and the views of official Judaism.

The original significance of such an incident in the ministry of the historical Jesus is still hotly debated. Some defend the traditional notion of the 'cleansing' of the temple and see Jesus as attacking some specific halakhic infringement or priestly abuses. Others insist that everything he expels was necessary for temple worship as legislated in Torah, so that his action was aimed at the temple cult as such, most likely in the expectation of its imminent end in the consummation of God's rule and possibly its replacement by a new temple given by God from heaven. Certainly none of the extant accounts gives any clear hints of priestly abuse. The corruption suggested by the Synoptic interpretation of the incident, through Jesus' accusation about turning the temple into a den of robbers, is of a different kind. The citation from Jer. 7.11 comes from a chapter containing a bitter attack on those who, instead of acting justly, have been oppressing the alien, the orphan and the widow, have broken the commandments and have gone after other gods. They then have the effrontery to think that their worship in the temple provides some guarantee against judgement and the temple's destruction. So the temple was not the place where their thievery or robbery was taking place but the den to which those who in their daily lives were ignoring the will of God were retreating as a safe hide-out. Similarly, in the Synoptic tradition, the robbery is not so much what is actually taking place in the temple; it is the injustices in the life of Israel that both the people and the religious aristocracy were using the temple system to legitimate.

John's interpretation has most in common with the view that the historical Jesus temporarily disrupted trade by a symbolic action that was an attack on the divinely ordained sacrificial system in anticipation of the coming new order. At the bedrock of the tradition the incident appears to have been accompanied by a saying of Jesus that spoke of the temple as God's house (cf. also *Gos. Thom.* 71). If the original incident was eschatologically motivated, then John's version of the saying, with its allusive use rather than direct quotation of Scripture, might even have some claims to being authentic, although Zech. 14 will later also serve as a source for John's distinctive light and water imagery. Certainly the other saying of Jesus in v. 19 is John's reformulation of wording about the destruction and rebuilding of the temple that goes back to Jesus in some form. There appears to have been both some embarrassment about this saying on the part of the early church and yet the need to preserve it and deal with it. So Mark and Matthew, as we have seen, attribute it to false witnesses yet allow it an ironic positive force, while Luke omits the saying from both his trial and the crucifixion accounts but handles it by having false witnesses attribute it to Stephen in Acts 6.14 – 'we have heard him say that this Jesus of Nazareth will destroy this place'.

The evangelist has, however, thoroughly reworked the traditions, including the Synoptic tradition, with which he was familiar. In setting his interpretation of the temple incident at the beginning of Jesus' public mission he wants his readers to understand from the outset the significance of what has happened in Jesus. His coming has brought radical

implications for the central symbols and institutions of Judaism, anticipating the end of the sacrificial system and, even further, the replacement
of the temple itself through his indestructible crucified and risen body.
Jesus himself is to be seen as the new locus of God's presence, the new
place of worship. Jesus' fulfilment and replacement of the significance of
Jewish holy spaces is a prominent motif in this narrative. The Shekinah
glory of the tabernacle is now to be found in the incarnate Logos (1.14);
as Son of Man Jesus is the new Bethel, the house of God (1.51); as the
new place of worship he replaces the holy mount and temple of both the
Samaritans and the Jews (4.21–4); and at the Feast of Dedication Jesus
himself rather than the temple altar is to be seen as consecrated (10.36).
In this way the Fourth Gospel's Christological emphasis opens up a
perspective that frees people from particular holy spaces while at the same
time allowing them to see all space as holy because of Christ. The vision
of the time of the new temple in Zech. 14.20–1, taken up in v. 16, which
does away with traditional distinctions between sacred and secular, is held
to have become a reality in Christ.

(iii) Reaction to Jesus in Jerusalem   *2.23–5*

**(23) While he was in Jerusalem during the Passover festival, many
believed in his name, because they saw the signs that he was
doing. (24) But Jesus for his part would not trust himself to them
because he knew all people, (25) and had no need for anyone to
testify about people; for he himself knew what was in people.**[1]

This transitional passage provides a summary of the response to Jesus'
time in Jerusalem at the Passover feast and serves as an introduction to
the discourse with Nicodemus that follows.

23 The response to Jesus' initial visit to Jerusalem appears to be positive
– **many believed in his name**, and believing in Jesus' name is, for
the evangelist, the proper response to Jesus' mission (cf. 1.13; 3.18). It
is certainly more appropriate than the misunderstanding of 'the Jews'
that has just been recounted, but it will become increasingly clear that
this response still falls short of what is required. The first hint is given
immediately, as the narrator tells of the cause of this belief. It was **because
they saw the signs that he was doing**. In itself, this description need
not raise suspicions. After all, the disciples have believed in Jesus on the
basis of the first of his signs (2.11), Jesus himself can exhort people to

---

[1] On both occasions in this verse where the term 'people' has been used in the translation, the Greek has a form of the singular of ἄνθρωπος, 'human being', with the
definite article.

believe the works he has done (10.38), and the purpose of the signs written down in the Gospel is to produce belief (20.30–1). It is only what follows which reveals that Jesus finds this response on the basis of the signs inadequate and that therefore there is a type of belief which remains at the level of being impressed by the signs and fails to see through the signs to what they signify – the glory of Jesus in his oneness with God (cf. also 4.48; 7.3–5). This faith does not grasp the significance of Jesus' person and commit itself to the implications of that significance. The mention of signs in Jerusalem (cf. also 3.2) points to a lacuna in the narrative. The only act explicitly labelled as a sign has been performed in Cana rather than in Jerusalem. It may well be that readers are meant to understand Jesus' prophetic action in the temple as a sign, but this would still not account for the plural term 'signs'. The plural encourages readers to treat the statement as a thematic one which has in view the sort of response to the signs in Jesus' mission as a whole that the evangelist deems inadequate.

24–5 Its inadequacy is made explicit through Jesus' distancing of himself from those who have responded in this way. Though they trusted in his name, he **would not trust himself to them** (the same verb – πιστεύω – is employed in both cases). In stating the reason for this stance, the narrator provides one of a number of 'inside views' of Jesus that underline his omniscience – **because he knew all people**. In this case, as the elaboration makes plain, Jesus' omniscience includes knowing what goes on inside a person, and therefore being able to discern whether their outward profession comes from an authentic or inauthentic faith. A similar inside view of Jesus' sovereign knowledge of people will be given in 6.64 – 'For Jesus knew from the first who were the ones who did not believe, and who was the one who would betray him.' In this respect Jesus **had no need for anyone to testify about people**; he perceives directly and immediately the depth and validity of people's commitment. He is himself the true witness not only about God but also about humanity. He is the true judge of people and embodies his own later exhortation about judging with right judgement and not by appearances (cf. 7.24).

The singling out of a type of faith – a signs faith – that is unsatisfactory and insufficient may well reflect the experience of the evangelist and his community in their disappointment with those who initially showed evidence of belief but who failed to follow through when it came to the test and when persecution and expulsion from the synagogue loomed as the consequences of faith in Jesus. The Nicodemus episode will elaborate on this point of view in its portrayal of this Jewish religious leader as a representative of just such a deficient signs faith (3.2).

(1) Now there was one of the Pharisees named Nicodemus, a leader of the Jews. (2) This man came to Jesus at night and said to him, 'Rabbi, we know that you are a teacher who has come from God; for no one is able to do the signs that you are doing unless God is with him.' (3) Jesus answered him, 'Truly, truly I say to you, without being born from above, a person cannot see the kingdom of God.' (4) Nicodemus said to him, 'How can a person be born after growing old? Is it possible for someone to enter the mother's womb a second time and be born?' (5) Jesus answered, 'Truly, truly I say to you, without being born of water and the Spirit, a person cannot enter the kingdom of God. (6) What is born of the flesh is flesh, and what is born of the Spirit is spirit. (7) Do not be astonished that I said to you, "You[1] must be born from above." (8) The wind blows where it wills, and you hear its sound, but you do not know where it comes from or where it is going; so it is for everyone who is born of the Spirit.' (9) Nicodemus replied to him, 'How can these things be?' (10) Jesus responded, 'Are you a teacher of Israel and do not know these things? (11) Truly, truly I say to you, we speak of what we know and we testify to what we have seen, but you[2] do not receive our witness. (12) If I have spoken to you of earthly things and you do not believe, how can you believe if I speak to you of heavenly things? (13) No one has ascended into heaven except the one who descended from heaven, the Son of Man.[3] (14) And just as Moses lifted up the serpent in the wilderness, so the Son of Man must be lifted up, (15) so that everyone who believes in him may have eternal life.

(16) 'For God so loved the world that he gave the only Son in order that everyone who believes in him may not perish but have eternal life. (17) For God did not send the Son into the world in order to condemn the world but in order that the world might be saved through him. (18) The one who believes in him is not condemned; but the one who does not believe is condemned already because that person has not believed in the name of the only Son of God. (19) This is the judgement, that the light has

---

[1] This second occurrence of 'you' in the verse is in the plural in Greek.

[2] Again the second occurrence of 'you' in the verse is plural, this time translating the second person plural form of the verb.

[3] There is a variant reading, in which 'who is in heaven' is added after 'Son of Man'. It is widely distributed but does not have as strong or as early manuscript support as the shorter reading and appears to have been added in conformity with the thought expressed in 1.18.

come into the world and people loved the darkness rather than the light, because their deeds were evil. (20) For all who do evil hate the light and do not come to the light lest their deeds are exposed; (21) but those who do the truth come to the light so that their deeds might be clearly seen as having been accomplished in God.'[4]

This episode provides readers with the first extended discourse on the part of Jesus. It begins as a dialogue, but then Jesus' conversation partner disappears from view and from v. 13 the exchange is replaced by a series of assertions that employ third person formulations. This phenomenon also raises the notorious problem of whether the passage in fact also contains the comments of the narrator, and if so, where Jesus' words end and the narrator's reflections begin. The issue becomes apparent in comparing English translations, which are not consistent in their placing of the final quotation marks (NRSV, REB, NJB and NIV have Jesus' discourse run through until 3.21, but RSV and NAB complete it at 3.15). The same phenomenon will be seen at the end of this chapter, where it is not immediately apparent whether vv. 31–6 are a continuation of John the Baptist's words or the commentary of the narrator. In regard to the earlier passage, some hold that the narrator's words begin at v. 13 where the first and second person language ceases. It is true that until this point in the narrative Jesus' discourse has been clearly marked by its first person language and that third person language about him has been confined to the narrator's prologue or to other characters. But soon Jesus speaking of himself in the third person as the Son or the Son of Man in relation to God or the Father will be a clear feature within the framework of a first person discourse (cf. e.g. 5.19–30). The style does not, therefore, decisively rule out seeing the whole of vv. 13–21 as also belonging to Jesus' discourse. A mediating view recognizes that the content of vv. 13–15, with its mention of ascent to and descent from heaven and of the lifting up of the Son of Man, follows on directly from the mention of heavenly things in v. 12, and that the other two usages of the distinctive 'lifting up' terminology in v. 14 are on the lips of Jesus himself (cf. 8.28; 12.32). The content of vv. 16–21, however, has no such clear links with what has preceded but takes up the more general topic of God's purposes for the world and does so primarily in terms of this Gospel's characteristic theme of judgement. This would make the end of v. 15 the most likely point for the conclusion of Jesus' own discourse arising out of the conversation with Nicodemus.

There is, however, a sense in which any decision on this issue is immaterial. The discussion simply reveals that in this Gospel not only do

---

[4] In the Greek text of vv. 20–1 the formulations are in the third person masculine singular.

Jesus, John the Baptist and the narrator represent the point of view of the implied author, but also that, in doing so, their language coincides. The difference between the language of the Johannine Jesus and that of the Synoptic Jesus, on the one hand, and the similarity between the language of the Johannine Jesus and that of the Johannine epistles, on the other, confirm that, when Jesus speaks in this Gospel's narrative, he speaks the characteristic language of the evangelist and his community. The evangelist may well, then, not have been particularly concerned to provide clear demarcations between the words of Jesus and those of the narrator. As will be seen, he is at much greater pains to make clear that both Jesus and Nicodemus are representative figures, with the former in solidarity with the post-resurrection perspective of the believing community and the latter standing for sympathetic Jews within the synagogue. The stance to be taken here will be that, although vv. 16–21 originated as the evangelist's reflections, this is only a matter of degree, since the material is so largely attributed to Jesus, whatever the elements of tradition lying behind it. In the final form of the Gospel there are no markers to indicate that the narrator is now commenting and so it is best to read vv. 16–21 as part of Jesus' discourse, which has now moved clearly from dialogue to monologue.

It may well be that the discussion with Nicodemus has been developed out of Synoptic material. The sequence in Luke 18.15–30 is particularly significant. There Jesus' saying, 'Truly, I say to you, whoever does not receive the kingdom of God like a child shall not enter it' (18.17), which has its equivalent here in v. 3, is immediately followed by the episode in which someone, whom Luke alone (18.18) calls a 'ruler' (cf. v. 1), comes to Jesus and addresses him as a teacher (cf. v. 2), asking a question about inheriting 'eternal life', the term that becomes John's preferred equivalent to 'the kingdom of God' (cf. v. 15). Jesus eventually says of the man, 'How hard it is for those who have riches to enter the kingdom of God!' (18.24) and goes on to make clear that to enter the kingdom (18.17, 24–5), to be saved (18.26) or to have eternal life (18.18, 30) is an impossibility for humans and has to be made possible by God (18.27). This last topic is reworked in the Nicodemus episode in terms of the necessity of birth from above and of the contrast between the flesh and the Spirit.

The passage falls into two halves – vv. 1–10 and vv. 11–21. The second half itself can be subdivided into two sections – vv. 11–15 and vv. 16–21. After the introduction of Nicodemus, it is his confession about Jesus in v. 2 that sets the agenda. 'We know . . .' makes this view of Jesus representative of that of some Jews, including leading ones, who are sympathetic to Jesus' cause. But the remainder of the first half exposes the inadequacy of such a perspective, culminating in Jesus' ironic question in v. 10. Verse 11 marks a shift in focus, as Jesus now also speaks in the first person plural, with his 'we know . . .' providing a counterpart to that of Nicodemus.

Jesus is also, then, a representative of a larger group, the evangelist and his community, and their witness or confession is set out in vv. 11–21 over against that which was found to be inadequate (cf. also the plural language of witness in 1 John 1.2–3). This perspective develops what it really means to believe that Jesus is from God. It insists that he is the one who descended from and ascended to heaven, the Son of Man who was lifted up, and then makes clear that he is the unique Son, whose special relationship with God has as its purpose to bring about the judgement of either life or condemnation.

1–2 Nicodemus is described as a Pharisee and as a ruler or **leader of the Jews**. The context of his return to the narrative later in 7.50–2 suggests that he derived the latter status from being a member of the ruling council or Sanhedrin. Here in v. 10 he will also be designated as a teacher, that is, a teacher of the law. The note that he comes to Jesus **at night** suggests that, although he is attracted to Jesus, he does not wish this to be known openly and his attempt to understand Jesus has as its context the potential disapproval of other members of the Sanhedrin. This teacher is prepared to recognize Jesus as also a teacher, as is underscored both by his address, **Rabbi**, and by his acknowledgement – **we know that you are a teacher who has come from God**. Getting right in what sense Jesus has come from God is a crucial issue in this Gospel. Its perspective is that Jesus has come from God as God's unique agent, as the Son sent by the Father, as the incarnate Logos. It becomes clear that Nicodemus does not intend this interpretation. His affirmation of Jesus is based on the signs Jesus has been performing, and the preceding pericope (2.23–5) has already alerted readers to the fact that such a signs faith may prove deficient. It leads Nicodemus to see Jesus as 'from God' in the sense that **God is with him**, that he has the divine approval. But the same thing had been said about others, including Moses (Exod. 3.12) and Jeremiah (Jer. 1.19). Nicodemus' acknowledgement of Jesus, therefore, is one that fits Jesus into his own traditional categories.

3–4 Jesus does not reply directly to Nicodemus' statement. Instead his answer is intended to disturb traditional categories and to show the necessity of a radically different perspective. It is introduced by the double Amen formulation (see the comment on 1.51). A number of sayings that employ this introduction are sayings that have their roots in the Synoptic tradition but have now been reworked in distinctive fashion. That this may be the case here is signalled by the kingdom of God terminology, which is so rare in the Fourth Gospel. The correspondence with Luke 18.17 has already been pointed out above. The same saying is preserved in another form in Matt. 18.3 – 'Truly, I say to you, unless you change and become like children, you will never enter the kingdom of heaven.' John's version of the Synoptic saying is **Truly, truly I say to you, without being born from above, a person cannot see the kingdom of God** (cf. also v. 5, which retains the language of 'entering' the kingdom of God). The prologue has already spoken of the necessity of being born of God in order to become children of God (1.12–13). Now the notion of changing and becoming like children, taken from the tradition, lends itself in this perspective to being formulated in terms of being born from above (ἄνωθεν). To be born from above is to be born from God. Jesus himself is 'from above' (3.31; 8.23). The belief that has genuine insight, that is able to *see* – to see past the signs to the divine reality, the rule of God, to which they point – has to be given from above, to have the same origin as Jesus himself.

But the same term, ἄνωθεν, can also be understood simply as 'again' and this is how Nicodemus takes it, as he plays the role of the straight man, who asks the dumb questions. He remains on the earthly, literal plane, asking about a second physical birth, and through his crass misunderstanding serves as the foil for Jesus' further teaching.

5–6 Jesus' second attempt to enlighten Nicodemus varies the terminology from seeing the kingdom of God to entering it and from being born from above to being **born of water and the Spirit**. The one previous mention of the Spirit (1.31–3) had been in the context of John's testimony, where his own baptizing with water was seen as preliminary and subordinate to Jesus' baptizing with the Spirit. Here, however, water and the Spirit are intimately associated as the source of the believer's birth. The best explanation is that the two terms are functional equivalents, with water serving as a symbol of the Spirit. Water has this function in both the Jewish Scriptures (e.g. Ezek. 36.25–7 – 'I will sprinkle clean water upon you . . . a new heart I will give you and a new spirit I will put within you . . . I will put my spirit within you') and the Qumran literature (e.g. 1QS 4.19–21 – 'He will cleanse him of all wicked deeds by means of a holy spirit; like purifying waters he will sprinkle upon him the spirit of truth'). The Fourth Gospel itself makes clear precisely this same connection in 7.38–9 – ' "Out of his belly shall flow rivers of living water." Now this he said about the Spirit'. So, instead of spatial imagery – from above – being employed of the believer's birth, this second saying has a reference to the Spirit, who is from above in the sense of being 'of God' and who was traditionally associated with the life of the future kingdom and of the age to come. It should not be surprising that entry into the kingdom requires an experience of the power that sustains its life. In a Christian context there may well be a secondary connotation for water as a reference to baptism, and immediately following there will be references to Jesus baptizing in water (cf. 3.22, 26; 4.1–2). Yet it is noticeable that in the exchange with Nicodemus water drops out of the discussion in favour of a concentration on the role of the Spirit. So the emphasis is not so much on the initiatory rite as on the Spirit, whose activity in giving birth to believers is presumably to be associated with Jesus' agency as the baptizer of people with the Spirit.

The necessity of the Spirit's work is underlined by the contrast between flesh and Spirit. 'Flesh' is ordinary human existence in its weakness and transience, and the prologue has already contrasted being born of 'the will of the flesh' with being born 'of God' (1.13). It should be clear that flesh and Spirit are not two parts of a person. What is in view is the birth or origin of the whole person, who either remains part of the merely human order or is transformed by the Spirit that mediates the divine order. The flesh, humanity left in its own state, is powerless to see or enter the divine realm (cf. also 6.63).

7–8 For this reason Nicodemus should not be astonished at the necessity of a birth from above. The repetition of Jesus' saying is not a verbatim one. Originally he had spoken of this with a third person formulation, but now the saying is taken as having addressed Nicodemus directly – **I said to you, 'You must be born from above.'** Since the second 'you' is plural, Nicodemus represents all Jews who echo his sympathetic appraisal of Jesus without under-standing its radical implications and, by extension, all who remain on the level that knows only a fleshly birth. The necessity of a different sort of birth should not be astonishing, but there is an element of mystery about such a birth from above through the Spirit, and this is elaborated by means of the analogy with the wind. The analogy is sparked by a wordplay, since the Greek term πνεῦμα can mean both spirit and wind. Like the wind, the Spirit is mysteriously experienced – **you do not know where it comes from or where it is going**. In the same way, in the case of those who are born of the Spirit their whence and whither, their origin and destiny, remain hidden to those who are restricted to a merely human perspective. There is a parallel to how the narrative depicts Jesus himself. Where he has come from and where he is going have to be revealed, since they cannot be perceived by those who remain on the level of the flesh.

9–10 Nicodemus' final question – **How can these things be?** – makes clear that his perception remains that of the flesh, which sees only impos-sibilities rather than divine possibilities. The inadequacy of his perspective is underlined as Jesus turns the tables on its original affirmation – 'we know that you are a teacher . . .' – with the question **Are you a teacher of Israel and do not know these things?** This teacher of the law simply does not have access to the knowledge from above, the knowledge which the narrator and implied readers share.

11 That Jesus represents the perspective of the evangelist and his community becomes evident in the first person plural formulation that follows – **we speak of what we know and we testify to what we have seen**. Jesus is the chief witness in the narrative's pervasive trial motif and his testimony is at the centre of the process of judgement, but his followers with the aid of the Spirit (15.26–7) and, in particular, the narrator in the persona of the Beloved Disciple (21.24), continue in solidarity with his witness. In contrast to Nicodemus' supposed knowledge (v. 2) but actual ignorance (v. 10), they speak of what they know. And in contrast to his inability to see (cf. v. 3), they witness to what they have seen. The introductory double Amen functions here as a solemn oath underlining the truth of Jesus' testimony on behalf of the believing community. This first explicit mention of witness on the part of Jesus is not made under hostile interrogation, but its setting is still one of a clash of commitments, as the following assertion makes plain – **but you do not receive our witness**. The 'you' is plural, indicating that Nicodemus and those Jews he represents, though on one level sympathetic to Jesus, are ultimately opposed, because they do not accept his true testimony.

12 Jesus claims that so far he has spoken to Nicodemus of **earthly things**, and that, since he has failed to believe, there is no point in going on to speak of **heavenly things**. Readers might well ask whether the topic of Jesus' conversation in vv. 3–8 was not already heavenly realities. It is likely, however, that 'earthly things' is a reference to Jesus' attempt to move from the earthly level of physical birth and the blowing of the wind to the heavenly. Since such an attempt failed to evoke faith, it would be useless to try to speak directly of heavenly things without analogy to the earthly.

13 In fact, however, Jesus is uniquely qualified to speak of heavenly realities, of what belongs to the realm above, since **No one has ascended into heaven except the one who descended from heaven, the Son of Man**. Over against any notions of ascents through visionary experiences in order to achieve heavenly knowledge, particularly some current notions that associated such mystical ascent with Moses, the Son of Man alone has the credentials for revealing true knowledge of heavenly realities. In this narrative the title 'Son of Man', which, as in the Synoptics, is characteristically reserved for the lips of Jesus himself, is given a distinctive twist by its frequent association with the narrative's descent–ascent schema and its heaven-and-earth framework. Because only the Son of Man has descended from heaven – in the incarnation – and has ascended to heaven – in the exaltation – he can bear true witness to what he has seen of the heavenly realm and its realities (cf. also the implications of 1.18). The verb employed for the motion of ascending is in the perfect tense, implying that the exaltation has already taken place. Clearly this does not fit at this point in the story of the earthly Jesus and underlines that the community's later Christological witness is being given by Jesus himself. It now becomes apparent how Jesus' words serve to make clear the true sense in which he is 'from God' in contrast to Nicodemus' insufficient confession. He is from God, because he is a heavenly being, the descending and ascending Son of Man. While no person who remains on the fleshly level, like Nicodemus, can make this confession about Jesus, the believing community, the 'we' Jesus represents, can bear such a witness because, having been born from above, its members have first been enabled to receive Jesus' witness about heavenly things.

14–15 The distinctive manner and purpose of Jesus' exaltation to heaven is explained through the notion that **the Son of Man must be lifted up**. Being lifted up bears the grim double entendre of exaltation through crucifixion. The Greek verb ὑψόω has no reference to crucifixion in ordinary usage, but the narrator's comment after its use in 12.33 makes clear that it includes this meaning for him. Perhaps the major catalyst in producing the double meaning originally was Aramaic, where the verb אזדקף does have both connotations – to crucify and to exalt. Isa. 52.13 LXX may also have played a part, with its reference to the servant who will be lifted up and glorified, a judgement of the servant after his death. The use of 'to be lifted up' here in 3.14, in 8.28 and in 12.32–4 can be seen as this narrative's equivalent to the threefold passion prediction about the Son of Man in Mark 8.31, 9.31 and 10.33. But the double meaning of 'to lift up' is exploited in the Fourth Gospel because it encapsulates the point of view that the Son of Man's suffering and humiliation is his glory. Instead of the Synoptic pattern of suffering followed by glory, the lifting up of the Son of Man collapses suffering and glory, crucifixion and exaltation into one. This lifting up is compared to the incident in which **Moses lifted up the serpent in the wilderness** on a standard. In Num. 21.8 it was said of the serpent that 'everyone who is bitten shall look at it and shall live'. Now, according to v. 15, everyone who believes in the lifted-up Son of Man may have eternal life, the life of the age to come that can be experienced already in the present. Wis. 16.6–7 had already interpreted the serpent in the wilderness as 'a symbol of deliverance to remind them of your law's demands' and observed that 'the one who turned toward it was saved, not by the thing that was beheld, but by you, the Saviour of all'. Here in John God's power to save is not mediated through the law but attributed to the crucified Son of Man.

16 The way in which this verse speaks of God's purposes through Jesus has been justly celebrated. The formulation – **God so loved the world that he gave the only Son** – brings emotional power to material that in all probability originated as the evangelist's reflections. Some argue that the term 'world' here simply has neutral connotations – the created human world. But the characteristic use of 'the world' (ὁ κόσμος) elsewhere in the narrative is with negative overtones – the world in its alienation from and hostility to its creator's purposes. It makes better sense in a soteriological context to see the latter notion as in view. God loves that which has become hostile to God. The force is not, then, that the world is so vast that it takes a great deal of love to embrace it, but rather that the world has become so alienated from God that it takes an exceedingly great kind of love to love it at all. The greatness of the divine love is not simply an inspiring theological concept but is demonstrated in its gift, that of the only Son. The gift has in view the whole of the Son's mission and therefore also the giving up of his life through crucifixion, the cruellest form of public execution. The amazing nature of such a gift is highlighted through recalling what this narrative says of the Father's intimate relation to the Son. Jesus can speak to the Father of 'your love for me before the foundation of the world' (17.24) and later in chapter 3 the narrator claims that 'the Father loves the Son and has given all things into his hands' (3.35). In this light, one might have expected here the thought that 'God so loved the Son that he gave him the world.' Instead, the startling force of this verse's formulation is that 'God so loved the world, this alienated and undeserving world, that of his love he gave the only Son to die in order that such a world might live.' Left to themselves, those in the world deserve to **perish**, but the result of the divine gift of the Son is the further gift of eternal life. The use of 'to perish' or 'to suffer destruction' (cf. also 10.28; 17.12) is one of a number of ways that the narrative depicts the plight of the world as one of death, to which the corresponding solution is the divine verdict of eternal life made possible through the mission of Jesus.

This verse, then, continues the community's witness, in contrast to Nicodemus' deficient confession, to the relationship between Jesus and God. Not only is Jesus 'from God' in the sense that he is the descending and ascending Son of Man who provides the link between heaven and earth, but he is also 'from God' in that he is the unique (μονογενής) Son whom God gave to the hostile world as the supreme demonstration of the divine love.

17 Given that the state of the world is depicted in terms of perishing, what is needed is a divine rescue mission – **For God did not send the Son into the world in order to condemn the world but in order that the world might be saved through him.** Here the rescue mission or salvation begins to be described in the categories of the process of judgement. This is no contradiction in terms. In the Jewish Scriptures Yahweh's judgement involved acting to establish justice and to restore conditions of well-being and life in place of exploitation and death. The covenantal lawsuits in Isaiah designate God as both Judge and Saviour and have a number of passages where salvation and righteous judgement stand in parallel. For God to judge righteously is for God to save, and for God to save is for God to judge righteously. In terms of the community's true witness to him, Jesus can be said to be 'from God', in the sense that, as the Son, he has been sent into the world as God's fully authorized agent and representative in the divine lawsuit with the world. The terms κρίνω, 'to judge', and κρίσις, 'judgement', can have either the more neutral connotation of putting on trial or the more negative connotation of condemning and punishing, depending on the context. In this instance the latter connotation is in view. The purpose of the Son's mission in putting the hostile world on trial is not the negative one of condemnation, however much the world might deserve it, but rather the positive one of salvific judgement. After all, the reason for the Son being sent was that God loved the world (cf. v. 16).

18 The response of belief in Jesus enables a person to experience the positive verdict in the trial rather than the negative one of condemnation – **The one who believes in him is not condemned**. But if there is a positive realized eschatology of judgement, there is also a negative one. Despite the primary intention of the Son's mission being to produce salvation with its eternal life, for those who do not believe in the unique Son of God their negative response produces a negative verdict ahead of time in the lawsuit – **the one who does not believe is condemned already**. For the narrator, people's response to Jesus constitutes their judgement; their judgement on him is at the same time a judgement on themselves.

19–21 In terms of the cosmic framework of the divine lawsuit with the world, Jesus' mission is seen as the focal point of the struggle between light and darkness and the whole process of judgement is provoked by Jesus as the light coming into the darkness of the world – **the light has come into the world and people loved the darkness rather than the light, because their deeds were evil**. If above and below, heaven and earth, provide the spatial co-ordinates for the lawsuit, light and darkness, determinative categories from the prologue (1.4–9), symbolize the moral and spiritual distinction that colours the spatial contrast and characterizes the relationship between the two parties. The coming of the light makes apparent people's ultimate allegiance, whether they love darkness or light, and in doing so puts their whole lives – not merely their words but also their deeds – under scrutiny. On the negative side, those who do evil **do not come to the light lest their deeds are exposed**. The verb ἐλέγχω can mean 'to expose' or 'to convict'. The latter, juridical connotation is clearly to the fore later in 8.46 and 16.8. Here the light and darkness imagery make 'to expose' an obvious connotation. But the context is one in which the light judges the darkness and so the notion of the conviction of the guilt of evil deeds can hardly be absent. On the positive side, those who are willing to come to the light are described as **those who do the truth** and the judgement of the light reveals that their deeds have **been accomplished in God**. This unusual expression reflects an underlying issue in the narrative, namely, that people's response to Jesus is indicative of their relation to God. The trial constituted by Jesus' mission exposes whether one's deeds are in conformity to its true judgement, and thus those who do the truth are revealed to be on the side of God rather than the world, which is opposed to the divine verdict.

The language of darkness and light in these final verses prompts readers to think back to the initial description of Nicodemus as coming to Jesus at night (v. 2). Does this suggest in addition to the note of secrecy that, despite his move toward the light, he is thought of as remaining in the darkness? The ensuing dialogue certainly gives this impression. Yet he will also make two further appearances in the narrative which indicate that a final evaluation may need to be more ambivalent. In 7.50–2 he is willing to attract the derision of other Pharisees by appealing for due process under law, yet he is not portrayed as having faith but as 'one of them', that is one of the group of Pharisees who are seeking Jesus' arrest. Then in 19.38–42 Nicodemus is reintroduced as having come to Jesus at night and is linked with Joseph of Arimathea, who is characterized as 'a secret disciple of Jesus for fear of the Jews', in the activity of burying Jesus' body. On the one hand, he engages in a courageous act, yet, on the other, the exaggerated quantity of burial ointments that he brings can be seen as a final, poignant example of his sympathetic but ultimately fleshly appreciation of Jesus. It is not clear whether he is viewed as having distanced himself entirely from the group the narrator describes in 12.42–3 – 'many, even of the authorities, believed in him, but because of the Pharisees they would not confess it lest they be put out of the synagogue; for they loved human glory more than the glory of God'.

Jesus' witness on behalf of the believing community in vv. 11–21, then, is made in the face of those who, from the narrator's perspective, were by no means hostile but were unable to make an adequate confession about Jesus when put to the test. Viewed in the light of that setting, the criterion for the divine judgement is precisely the issue that brought about the expulsion of the community that did bear authentic witness, namely, belief in 'the name of the only Son of God' (v. 18). Yet now that community's judges are to be seen as the ones who have themselves been put on trial and have in fact condemned themselves by their failure to believe.

This first section of extended teaching brings together a number of significant themes. Jesus' encounter with Nicodemus is the occasion for contrasting inadequate signs faith with authentic faith. It is the occasion not only for Jesus confronting the sympathetic views of a Jewish religious leader but also for the believing community confronting those not overtly hostile within the synagogue. Authentic faith, with its knowledge of heavenly realities and its present enjoyment of eternal life, is held to come from a person's having been born from above, born of the Spirit, and therefore being a child of God. Authentic faith is also faith in Jesus as the only Son of God, the one who is from God because he is from above, the descended and ascended Son of Man. His ascent through the lifting up on the cross is confessed as the supreme demonstration of the divine love for a hostile world. The judgement that takes place in Jesus' mission shapes a realized eschatology, in which salvation and the life of the age to come can be experienced already or in which, in the absence of a believing response, condemnation takes place already. The framework for these notions with their Christological focus is the narrative's modified dualism of light and darkness, which provides the cosmic setting for its pervasive motif of a lawsuit between God and the world, to which the themes of witness and judgement so clearly point. In the case of each aspect of the passage highlighted in this summary, not just the jarring wordplay on being 'lifted up', its repetition and development in the rest of the narrative enable it to become more sharply delineated and its relation to the Gospel as a whole to become increasingly apparent.

(v) John the Baptist's final testimony　　　　　　　　　　*3.22–36*

(22) After this Jesus went with his disciples into the Judaean countryside and spent some time there with them and baptized. (23) John also was baptizing at Aenon near Salim, because there was plenty of water there, and people were coming and were being baptized; (24) for John had not yet been thrown into prison. (25) Now a dispute arose between some of John's disciples and a Jew[1] about purification. (26) They came to John and said to him, 'Rabbi, the one who was with you across the Jordan, to whom you testified, look he is baptizing and all are coming to him.' (27) John answered and said, 'A person cannot receive anything unless it is given to that person from heaven. (28) You yourselves can testify to me[2] that I

---

[1] The manuscript evidence is divided evenly between the singular and plural Greek terms for 'Jew'. Since elsewhere in the Gospel the plural predominates, it is more likely that the singular was altered to conform to the more typical usage. Some scholars have found both readings to be so awkward in this context that they have opted to emend the text and conjectured that the original read 'Jesus' here.

[2] The dative 'to me' is not in two early witnesses (p75 א). It makes no difference to the overall sense and may for that reason have been omitted. The evidence in support of its inclusion is very strong.

said, "I am not the Christ but I have been sent ahead of him." (29) The one who has the bride is the bridegroom. The friend of the bridegroom who stands and listens to him is overjoyed at the bridegroom's voice. This joy of mine has therefore been made complete. (30) He must increase, but I must decrease.

(31) 'The one who comes from above is above all; the one who is from the earth belongs to the earth and speaks as one from the earth. The one who comes from heaven is above all.[3] (32) He testifies to what he has seen and heard, but no one accepts his witness. (33) Whoever accepts his witness has attested that God is true. (34) For the one whom God has sent speaks the words of God, since he gives the Spirit without measure. (35) The Father loves the Son, and has given all things into his hands. (36) Whoever believes in the Son has eternal life; whoever disobeys the Son will not see life, but the wrath of God remains on that person.'

John will be referred to again in 5.33–6 and 10.40–1, but this passage incorporates his last actual appearance in the narrative. The first witness to the Logos (cf. 1.6–8) has already testified in 1.15, 19–34 and now gives his final testimony. How far that testimony extends is, however, a matter of some debate. The issue is similar to that already discussed in relation to 3.1–21. Like vv. 16–21, vv. 31–6 clearly derive from the evangelist's reflections. Indeed, they pick up a number of themes from vv. 11–21 and a number of scholars have therefore suggested that they belong more appropriately as a continuation of those verses and have been displaced in transmission. There is, however, no textual evidence for this very plausible theory and the final compiler of the Gospel appears to have consciously placed them or left them at this point after the testimony attributed to John the Baptist. Most commentators and translations deal with this by having John's discourse finish at v. 30 and then treating vv. 31–6 as further commentary from the narrator (but cf. NJB, NIV). But it has already been noted that it is notoriously difficult to distinguish sharply between the language and theological convictions of the evangelist and those of the significant characters such as Jesus or John, who are the vehicles of such convictions in the narrative. Since, in the Gospel's present shape, there is no demarcation indicating another voice in these final verses

---

[3] Some manuscripts omit 'is above all' and so read 'the one who comes from heaven testifies to what he has seen and heard'. The weight of the external evidence is evenly balanced. The omission could have been made because the language was thought to be repetitious or the words could have been added under the influence of the first part of the verse. The sort of repetition entailed by the longer reading is by no means alien to the evangelist's style and here would produce an *inclusio* for the thought of v. 31. For this reason the longer reading has been retained as the basis of the translation.

of the chapter, they are best read as part of John the Baptist's testimony, whatever their origin or place in some earlier stage of composition. That they contain developed Christian views about Jesus is no obstacle to such a reading, because all the previous testimony of John does so and is far removed from what is likely to have been the perspective of the historical figure.

This interpretation gives a structure to the last part of the chapter that is parallel to that of the first part. 2.23–5 had served as an introduction to the dialogue between Jesus and Nicodemus in 3.1–15, which then becomes a monologue by Jesus in 3.16–21. Now 3.22–4 function as an introduction to the dialogue between John's disciples and their teacher in 3.25–30, which becomes a monologue by John in 3.31–6.

22–4 These verses, in placing the activities of Jesus and John alongside each other, provide the setting which will lead to the dialogue introducing John's testimony. Jesus moves with his disciples from Jerusalem, where the conversation with Nicodemus has been set, **into the Judaean countryside** and there he **baptized**. For those familiar with the Synoptic tradition, this description of Jesus' activity would strike a surprising note, since nowhere in the Synoptics is Jesus said to have baptized. For the historical issues raised by such a statement and its later qualification in 4.2, see the discussion below after the comments on this pericope. John's similar activity is next introduced. He **also was baptizing at Aenon near Salim, because there was plenty of water there.** John's baptizing in Bethany on the other side of the Jordan was mentioned earlier in 1.25–8. Now he has moved north, leaving Jesus baptizing in the general area of the lower Jordan valley where he had previously been. The two most likely original sites of Salim are both in Samaria – either near ancient Bethshan or Scythopolis in northern Samaria on the west side of the Jordan, or just to the east of Shechem, an area in which there were many springs. The apparently superfluous note – **for John had not yet been thrown into prison** – is best seen as underscoring, for those familiar with the Synoptic tradition where Jesus is portrayed as only beginning his own ministry after John's imprisonment (cf. Mark 1.14; Matt. 4.12; Luke 3.20), that the present story has to be set in an earlier period in which the two figures were operating concurrently.

25–6 The logic of these verses is not readily apparent. John's baptizing is the catalyst for a **dispute . . . between some of John's disciples and a Jew about purification.** As a result the disciples go to their teacher with a statement, and implied query, about what they have heard about the success of Jesus' baptizing – **Rabbi, the one who was with you across the Jordan, to whom you testified, look he is baptizing and all are coming to him.** Readers are left with a number of gaps to attempt to fill. Why a dispute about purification? Purification rites included ritual washings and so John's baptizing would presumably have been perceived as falling under this rubric. Other Jews might well have questioned how John's baptism related to the washings required by the law, especially since John's baptism was in all probability an immersion administered only once in contrast to repeated washings. The whole question of what any baptism on the part of Jesus would have signified in comparison with that of the Baptist is fraught with difficulties. But, in order to make sense of this passage with its immediate bringing of Jesus into the picture, readers would need to assume that Jesus' baptism had been part of the discussion of purification because apparently his baptism was associated with different, presumably less stringent, teaching about the moral holiness meant to accompany the external cleansing. In the view of John's disciples this might well underlie the greater popularity of Jesus' baptism, to which they point as they look for some response to this situation by their teacher. In doing so, they recall John's earlier testimony to Jesus.

This episode can be seen as the Fourth Gospel's version of the material in Matt. 11.2–19 and Luke 7.18–35. It corresponds particularly to the Lukan version, which opens with John's disciples reporting to him the popularity of Jesus' ministry. There John's response is to send disciples to Jesus asking him whether he is the one to come. Here, typical of the evangelist's perspective on the Baptist, John himself will tell them that Jesus is that one.

27–8 The scene has now been set for John's response to be one that continues his role of bearing witness to Jesus. His witness begins with a general statement – **A person cannot receive anything unless it is given to that person from heaven.** The force of this appears to be that, whatever their roles and comparative success, these have been granted to both John and Jesus by God and are to be seen as part of God's unfolding will. John's disciples are then made to be witnesses (**You yourselves can testify**) to his own previous witness – **I am not the Christ but I have been sent ahead of him.** Interestingly, the formulation of this relationship between John and his followers anticipates the pattern for the relation that will be set out in regard to Jesus and his followers. Just as John is the first witness, whose disciples bear witness to his witness, so Jesus will be the chief witness, whose disciples also bear witness to his witness. Here John refers back to his witness, first, that he was not the Messiah (cf. 1.20) and, secondly, that he had been sent ahead of the Messiah (cf. 1.23 with John's citation from Isaiah about making straight the way of the Lord and 1.26 with his statement about the one coming after him). In this way John's witness in his last appearance is shown to be consistent with that of his first appearance, and the declarations that follow in vv. 29–30 only elaborate what his testimony has already made clear.

29–30 John indicates his relation to Jesus by employing the analogy of the relation of the friend of the bridegroom to the bridegroom. Naturally, at a wedding the bridegroom is the focus of attention because he is **The one who has the bride**. The bridegroom's friend had an important but ancillary role in making sure that the arrangements went smoothly. It may well be that the talk of standing and listening for **the bridegroom's voice** has reference to the last task of the bridegroom's friend – leading the bridegroom to the bride and then standing watch outside the bridal chamber until the bridegroom announced the consummation of the marriage. The main point, however, is that the satisfaction of the bridegroom's friend lies in sharing the joy of the bridegroom. For informed readers the imagery would recall the Jewish Scriptures in which Yahweh was pictured as the bridegroom with Israel as his bride (cf. Isa. 62.5; Jer. 2.2; Hos. 2.14–20). For the early Christians Jesus took on the role of the bridegroom in relation to the people of God as his bride (cf. Mark 2.19–20; Eph. 5.25–7; Rev. 19.7; 21.9–10) and this verse both reminds readers that Jesus has already taken on the role of the bridegroom at the wedding in Cana and prepares for Jesus being portrayed in the same role in the following chapter with its betrothal type-scene. But, as the bridegroom's friend, John's role has been brought to a conclusion and his joy completed as the bridegroom's voice is heard and people respond to Jesus' word. The importance of listening to Jesus' voice will be reinforced in 5.25; 10.1, 3, 4, 16, 27 and 18.37. Just as on the wedding day the bridgroom takes centre stage and the bridgroom's friend fades into the background, so, according to John's testimony, **He must increase, but I must decrease.** The two verbs are used elsewhere of the waxing and waning of the sun or the moon. Here John accepts that, according to the divine purpose, his role as the one who is only a witness to the light must recede, since his task has been completed, and instead the one who is himself the light must now shine for all to see. Appropriately, he makes no further actual appearance in the narrative after his testimony in this section.

31–2 In the evangelist's reflections, which pick up earlier themes from this chapter but, in their present position, can now be read as a continuation of John's testimony, John elaborates on the superiority of the one to whom he is deferring. **The one who comes from above**, or, in the repetition of the statement, **from heaven**, is said to be **above all**. He is superior not only to John but to all human beings, who, by contrast, are described as **from the earth**, that is, determined by the merely human sphere in their allegiance and speech. The contrasting statement has its earlier parallels in 3.6 – 'what is born of the flesh is flesh' – and 3.11, which contrasts earthly and heavenly things. The 'from above' language of 3.3, 7 is now applied to Jesus, who has already been described as the Son of Man who descended from heaven in 3.13. In the earlier context

Jesus has also claimed to be able to speak of heavenly things and testify to what he has seen precisely because of his own heavenly origin and yet can accuse those addressed of not having accepted his witness (cf. 3.11–13). Now in the recapitulation of these ideas, it is said that Jesus **testifies to what he has seen and heard, but no one accepts his witness**. If John has functioned as the first witness, in his final testimony he now reinforces the notion that Jesus is the chief witness in the process of God's judgement of the world and that his heavenly origin qualifies him for this role. Unlike those whose words are limited to the earthly sphere, he is able to speak words of witness about the sphere above. How the statement that no one receives his witness is related to the immediately preceding description of the response to his baptizing, where it is said that 'all are coming to him', is not clear. The statement appears to be a retrospective evaluation of the response to Jesus' mission as a whole. In this light it has in view the world as a whole and 'the Jews' in general as the representatives of the world, as in 1.10–11, where 'the world did not know him' and 'his own people did not accept him'.

33–4 Just as in the prologue, where these statements are followed in 1.12 by 'but to all who received him . . .', so here the general failure to receive Jesus' testimony is followed by the assertion that **Whoever accepts his witness has attested that God is true.** The verb translated as 'has attested' means more literally 'has set one's seal' and entails certifying one's approval. It may well have had juridical connotations, since it was often employed of setting one's seal on a legal document and thereby ratifying it as a witness. What might have been expected here was a statement to the effect that to receive Jesus' testimony is to certify as a witness that his claims are true. Instead the formulation again underscores that a decision about Jesus is in fact a decision about God. What is at stake in this Gospel's narrative is not just the truth of claims about Jesus but ultimately the truth of conflicting claims about God. Is God the God who is known in Jesus? As 1 John 5.10 will put it, those who do not believe in the testimony concerning God's Son make God a liar.

The connection between Jesus' testimony and God's truth is now made explicit – **For the one whom God has sent** (cf. the language of sending the Son in 3.17) **speaks the words of God, since he gives the Spirit without measure.** The giver of the Spirit could be either Jesus or God in this formulation. But God is the more immediate antecedent and Jesus, who is here the focus of attention, is more likely than believers to be the implied recipient of the gift of the Spirit. Jesus' words of witness in the overall trial fully represent God. The prophets were given the Spirit by measure, but Jesus has been given the Spirit without measure so that he speaks God's words continuously. The mention of the Spirit picks up on the earlier reference in the discussion with Nicodemus in 3.5–8 but more particularly recalls John the Baptist's previous witness in 1.32–3 about Jesus' permanent endowment with the Spirit. Jesus is the fully authorized agent of God and the one on whom the Spirit remains, and so his words are God's words. This depiction, which is not surprising in the light of the prologue's portrayal of Jesus as the divine Logos, will be reinforced as the narrative progresses. Jesus' words are Spirit-endowed (6.63) and are not simply his own but words from God (cf. e.g. 7.17; 8.26, 47; 12.49–50; 14.10, 24; 17.8).

35–6 The Father loves the Son. This is the first time that the intimate relationship between the Father and the Son is formulated in terms of the Father's love for the Son, but this will become a prominent theme (cf. 5.20; 10.17; 15.9–10; 17.23–4, 26). In the Father's love for the Son he **has given** not just the Spirit but **all things into his hands** and the 'all things' include authority to judge (cf. 5.22, 27). As in 3.18–21, Jesus is the fully authorized agent in the judgement, and again both positive and negative outcomes of the judgement are delineated. Belief in the Son results in the positive verdict of **eternal life** (cf. 3.16). On the negative side, the wrong response to Jesus is described this time not as unbelief but as disobedience, corresponding to the emphasis in 3.19–20 on people's evil deeds, while the consequence is formulated not simply as people's condemnation but as the punishment of **the wrath of God** remaining on them. The combination of the notions of God's wrath and remaining, using the same Greek words as here, is found in Wis. 16.5 LXX – 'your wrath did not remain till the end'. This is the only time the term 'wrath' occurs in the Fourth Gospel and the formulation has echoes of the Synoptic tradition's depiction of the Baptist's message about fleeing from the wrath to come (Matt. 3.7; Luke 3.7). In this variation on the narrative's negative realized eschatology, the wrath, which could be expected at the end-time judgement, is seen as precipitated by Jesus' mission and as remaining in effect.

As has been noted, the reference in this passage to Jesus baptizing is unique in the Gospels and raises questions about its likely historicity. Since the recent consensus among scholars has been that at this point the Fourth Gospel may well preserve an authentic tradition about an early period in which the missions of John the Baptist and Jesus overlapped and Jesus for a while took up John's practice of baptizing, it is worth considering in a little more detail. The claims that can be presented in favour of authenticity include the following. We should be suspicious of the Synoptic presentation, because Mark (and Matthew and Luke in following him) has good reason for his schema of having Jesus' ministry commence after John's imprisonment. John's mission as the forerunner is thereby tied up neatly before the work of his successor begins. The notion of the earthly Jesus baptizing fits very awkwardly within the Fourth Gospel's own perspective and therefore is unlikely to have been created by the evangelist. After all, this story has had John testify that, while he baptizes with water, the coming one will baptize with the Holy Spirit (1.31–3), something that does not take place until after the ministry and after Jesus' glorification (cf. 7.39; 19.30; 20.22). A Jesus who baptizes with water and not the Spirit appears out of place. What is more, Jesus baptizing in this way would be embarrassing, since it suggests he simply continues the work of John. In the case of Jesus' baptism by John, which had similar embarrassing connotations of John being Jesus' superior, it is almost certain that this could not have been an invention on the part of the Gospel writers. Here too, then, it can be argued that the evangelist would not have created an incident in which Jesus baptized, especially since whoever wrote 4.2, whether the evangelist himself or a final redactor, later recognized the embarrassment and attempted to modify the tradition by having not Jesus but his disciples do the baptizing. It is also claimed by some that the note in 3.24 that John had not yet been imprisoned is the evangelist's deliberate indicator for those familiar with the Synoptics that he is here correcting their chronology and that the material recorded in 1.19—4.43 took place before the Galilean ministry of the Synoptics began. More generally, it is proposed that, if the historical Jesus was baptized by John and held him in high regard, it would make sense that initially he would have spent some time with John and under his influence practised similar baptismal rites before developing the distinctive emphases of his own mission.

But the matter is not nearly as straightforward as these arguments might appear to suggest. It is one thing to find historically plausible some overlap between John's mission and that of Jesus, but another to include baptizing activity on the part of Jesus in such an overlap. This scenario of a temporary baptizing ministry in any case involves conjecture. There is no indication in the text that the practice was simply an initial one and that at some later point Jesus and/or his disciples ceased to baptize. If it was a short-lived phenomenon, then presumably Jesus' baptizing, like John's, would have been simply a baptism of repentance, inviting people to save themselves from the judgement shortly to be exercised by the coming one. If so, then despite his baptism, and the distinctive experience attributed to him at that point by the Gospel writers, Jesus would certainly not yet have seen himself as the coming one, for whom John was preparing the way, nor even as having any role that differentiated him from John. This is by no means implausible. But if the evangelist had a tradition which was understood to mean that Jesus simply continued John's baptism and its significance, how probable is it that he would not have seen its negative implications for Jesus' status? Given that he has already gone to such lengths to show John's subordinate role and has entirely suppressed Jesus' baptism by John in the process, it becomes extremely difficult to imagine that he would now include such a tradition. If it is replied that he was constrained to do so, because it was such a strong tradition, then this would apply even more to Jesus' own baptism, as the Synoptic evidence indicates, yet the evangelist felt no such constraint in relation to that tradition. More seriously, there is no evidence that during John's lifetime, anyone other than John performed this baptism. His disciples are not said to have baptized. The exercise of the rite is specifically focused on John himself, hence the title of the Baptist, which he has in all our sources, including Josephus, *Ant.* 18.5.2, except the Fourth Gospel. Why would Jesus be the only disciple of John carrying out John's baptism?

It is not surprising that some scholars who hold that Jesus baptized suggest that the significance of his act must have been different from that of John's. They presume that, in Jesus' case, his baptizing constituted a sign that those baptized had accepted his new message about the kingdom of God, had entered into its reality and had become his disciples. But then his baptism takes on a significance akin to the later Christian rite and it becomes almost incredible that the Synoptics and the Fourth Gospel elsewhere fail even to hint that this was part of people's response to Jesus' message. If the origins of Christian baptism lay in a practice initiated by Jesus himself, which had a different meaning from John's baptism, there would have been no reason at all for early Christians to have suppressed this and every reason for them to have indicated the continuity between the church and its founder.

There is a further problem with the arguments for historicity outlined above. The view that Jesus' baptizing with water causes difficulties for the evangelist's own overall perspective on Jesus as baptizer with the Spirit and therefore is likely to be traditional is also not as strong as might be thought. Despite the schema in which the Spirit is only given after glorification, there are instances in the ministry where Jesus already assumes the Spirit is a present gift. He requires Nicodemus to be born from above or of the Spirit. He offers the Samaritan woman the gift of living water which represents the Spirit and tells her the hour for worship in Spirit and in truth is now here. Are these occasions to be considered historical tradition because they fit awkwardly with the overall schema? Are they not, as in the case of expulsion from the synagogue for belief in Jesus during his ministry (cf. 9.22; 12.42), more likely to be retrojections from the post-Easter period?

Advocates of the historicity of the tradition of Jesus' baptizing activity frequently ask what reason the evangelist or an earlier tradition would have had for creating this material. But answers are not hard to suggest. Elsewhere John retrojects aspects of later Christian belief and experience back into the life of Jesus. The placing of baptism back into Jesus' ministry has at least two possible settings. The presentation of John in this first part of the Gospel is pervaded by obvious signs of apologetic. The emphatic transformation of John's role into that of a witness has already betrayed hints of the later confrontation between Johannine Christians and the Baptist sectarians who continued to champion the cause of their founder rather than to accept Christian claims about Jesus. John has already been made to deny that he is the Christ, Elijah or the prophet and to utter Christian convictions about Jesus. What is more, he has already been divested of his historical title of 'the Baptist', presumably because this would sound like an exclusive claim, and having Jesus and/or his disciples also baptizing continues this tendency. Baptizing with water, which had become a major feature of Christian initiation, is not to be seen as the earlier exclusive prerogative of John; Jesus and his early followers had also engaged in this activity. It is not difficult to imagine that, in exchanges with Christians, followers of the Baptist would point out that, in comparison with their own tradition, Christian baptism lacked adequate historical credentials. The response by Johannine Christians might well have been to claim that the practice of Christians was not simply a later development but had its antecedent in the mission of their own founder and went back to the same period as John the Baptist's activity. And the comparative merits of the two baptisms can be treated in the narrative and a clear answer given from the mouth of John himself about which of the two is to be endorsed. An alternative scenario is to see such debate not as direct confrontation with continuing adherents of the Baptist's cause but as part of the dispute with the synagogue that also shapes the narrative. This would account for the apparently strange role of a Jew in initiating the discussion in v. 25. Other Jews at the time of the evangelist would have been aware of the existence of those who followed the Baptist and been capable of using this to attempt to discredit Christian claims and practice. The later contradiction in 4.2 of the emphasis on Jesus baptizing causes difficulty for both sides of the argument about historicity. For those who take Jesus' practice of the rite to be a retrojection, this verse can still be interpreted as the narrator or final redactor revising the earlier claim, once he has seen that it might have the unwanted negative implication that Jesus' activity merely continued John's. Whoever made the revision presumably had no awareness of a tradition of Jesus' baptizing in which it had a significance clearly different from John's; otherwise he would not have needed to insert his gloss. As it stands, the parenthetical comment in 4.2 still maintains the claim that Christian baptism went back to the same time as John's baptism, but through its distinction between Jesus and his disciples Jesus himself is shielded from being viewed simply as taking up John's practice.

Where, as here in the examination of the early part of Jesus' career, the evidence is so meagre, it would be presumptuous to come down firmly on one side or other of the argument about historicity. The discussion may have some value, however, if it has indicated that even in this case, which is frequently held to be one of the few places where Johannine material has a greater claim to authenticity than the Synoptics, such a claim is not particularly persuasive and can involve no more than possibility. Both sides in the debate inevitably have to resort to historical conjectures, but it may well be that, after a review of the arguments, slightly fewer difficulties will be found with the possibility that the discussion of Jesus baptizing is the result of the evangelist's creativity.

The inconclusiveness of the historicity discussion should also serve as a reminder that, for the evangelist, the material we have been considering is not of interest in its own right but only as it serves as a platform on which John can provide his final testimony. In the context of a comparison between John's and Jesus' baptizing activity and just before Jesus' mission extends into Samaritan territory, in that testimony John sums up his role in relation to that of Jesus and makes clear what is entailed in the superiority of the latter's identity and mission. In being made to state that his own task and joy are complete now that Jesus has appeared on the scene and that the bridegroom and not the bridegroom's friend is the significant figure, John has an unmistakable message for any later followers of his who are promoting his continuing significance or his superiority to the one he baptized. Openness to the voice of the bridegroom himself is what now counts, since Jesus as the witness, who comes from the heavenly rather than the earthly realm and has been given the Spirit unstintingly, speaks the words of God and executes everything to do with God's judgement. As he moves off the stage, the one who had earlier pointed to Jesus as the lamb of God who dealt with the sin of the world now announces the seriousness of having the right response to Jesus as the source of eternal life.

(vi) Jesus and the Samaritan woman   *4.1–42*

(1) Now when Jesus[1] knew that the Pharisees had heard that Jesus was making and baptizing more disciples than John – (2) although Jesus himself was not baptizing but rather his disciples – (3) he left Judaea and went again to Galilee. (4) He had to go through Samaria. (5) So he came to the Samaritan city called Sychar, near the land which Jacob had given to his son, Joseph. (6) Now Jacob's well was there. So Jesus, tired from his journey, was simply sitting at the well. It was about the sixth hour.

[1] The manuscript evidence is fairly evenly divided between 'Jesus' (א D Θ) and 'Lord' (p66,75 A B C) as the subject. It appears more likely that a scribe would have found the two mentions of Jesus in this sentence awkward and replaced the first with 'Lord' than that an original 'Lord' would have been changed to 'Jesus' with the resultant infelicity of style.

(7) A Samaritan woman came to draw water. Jesus said to her, 'Give me a drink,' (8) for his disciples had gone into the city to buy food. (9) The Samaritan woman said to him, 'How is it that you, a Jew, ask a drink of me, a Samaritan woman?' (For Jews do not have dealings with Samaritans.[2]) (10) Jesus answered and said to her, 'If you knew the gift of God and who is saying to you, "Give me a drink," you would have asked him and he would have given you living water.' (11) The woman said to him, 'Sir, you have no bucket and the well is deep; so from where do you get the living water? (12) Are you greater than our father Jacob, who gave us the well and drank from it himself together with his sons and his cattle?' (13) Jesus answered and said to her, 'Everyone who drinks from this water will thirst again; (14) but whoever drinks from the water which I shall give will never thirst; rather the water which I shall give that person will become within him or her a spring of water gushing up to eternal life.' (15) The woman said to him, 'Sir, give me this water, so that I might not thirst nor keep coming to this place to draw water.'

(16) He said to her, 'Go and call your husband and come back here.' (17) The woman answered and said to him, 'I do not have a husband.' Jesus said to her, 'You have rightly said, "I do not have a husband"; (18) for you have had five husbands and the one you now have is not your husband; what you have said is true.' (19) The woman said to him, 'Sir, I see that you are a prophet. (20) Our ancestors worshipped on this mountain, and you say that in Jerusalem is the place where one must worship.' (21) Jesus said to her, 'Believe me, woman, the hour is coming when you will worship the Father neither on this mountain nor in Jerusalem. (22) You worship what you do not know; we worship what we know, because salvation is from the Jews. (23) But the hour is coming, and now is, when true worshippers will worship the Father in Spirit and in truth, for the Father seeks such people as this as his worshippers. (24) God is Spirit, and those who worship

---

[2] There are both translation and textual issues surrounding the sentence in parentheses. It is suggested by some that its verb συγχράομαι means 'to use vessels together with'. Although it can mean 'to make use of', its more specific reference to vessels remains doubtful, and the more general force of 'to have dealings with' is also attested. The last option is preferred in this context. But is the sentence part of the original? It is omitted in ℵ*D it[a,b,d,e], for example. Its presence in the majority of the early manuscripts would be in line with other narratorial asides in the Gospel for the sake of later Gentile readers who might be ignorant of Jewish names and customs. The omission could then be explained as a correction on the part of a scribe who considered its generality inaccurate.

him must worship in Spirit and in truth.' (25) The woman said to him, 'I know[3] that the Messiah is coming, who is called Christ. When he comes, he will announce all things to us.' (26) Jesus said to her, 'I am, the one who is speaking to you.'

(27) At this point his disciples came, and they were amazed that he was speaking with a woman, but no one said, 'What are you seeking for?' or 'Why are you speaking with her?' (28) So the woman left her water jar, and went into the city and said to the people, (29) 'Come and see a man who told me everything I ever did. This is not the Christ, is it?' (30) They left the city and came to him.

(31) Meanwhile the disciples were urging him, 'Rabbi, eat.' (32) But he said to them, 'I have food to eat that you do not know about.' (33) So the disciples were saying to one another, 'No one has brought him something to eat, have they?' (34) Jesus said to them, 'My food is to do the will of him who sent me and to complete his work. (35) Do you not say, "There are four months yet and then the harvest comes"? Look, I tell you, lift up your eyes and observe the fields, because they are white for harvest already. (36) The harvester receives wages and gathers in the crop for eternal life, so that the sower and the harvester may rejoice together. (37) For here the saying is true, "One is the sower and another is the harvester." (38) I have sent you to harvest that for which you have not laboured. Others have laboured, and you have entered into the result of their labour.'

(39) Many of the Samaritans from that city believed in him because of the word of the woman who testified, 'He told me everything I ever did.' (40) So when the Samaritans came to him, they asked him to remain with them; and he remained there two days. (41) And many more believed because of his word. (42) They said to the woman, 'We no longer believe because of what you said, for we ourselves have heard and know that this is truly the Saviour of the world.'

The passage falls into five sections. Verses 1–6 set up the story that follows by discussing Jesus' change of location and his arrival at a well near Sychar. Verses 7–26 contain the dialogue between Jesus and the Samaritan woman at the well. In vv. 27–30 there is a transition as the disciples arrive and the woman departs. There is then a dialogue between Jesus and the

---

[3] Some texts have 'we know' at this point, but the earliest of these are corrected texts, p[66c] ℵ[c], and their originals and other early and important witnesses have the singular formulation. The alterations are the result of copyists adapting the singular to the plural in the light of the plural both in Jesus' preceding assertion in v. 22b and in the woman's following statement here in v. 25.

disciples in vv. 31–8. Finally the episode concludes with the encounter between Jesus and the Samaritans from Sychar in vv. 39–42.

As the story develops, readers are caught up in attempting to understand the dialogue and its shifts and in negotiating the different levels on which it works. Particularly important are the initial expectations that would be set up for readers by an encounter between a man and a woman at a well. Indeed, a major element in the account's literary structuring is the way it builds on but subverts the betrothal type-scene. The scene is found in a number of places in the Jewish Scriptures – Gen. 24.1–67, where Abraham's servant, Eliezer, obtains Rebekah for Isaac; Gen. 29.1–14, where Jacob encounters Rachel; and Exod. 2.15–22, where Moses gains Zipporah as his wife. The standard features of this type-scene are that a potential bridegroom or his representative travels to a foreign land, he encounters a woman at a well, there is a dialogue about water, in which water is asked for or offered, the woman hurries home to report the stranger's arrival, and the bridegroom is then invited to the future father-in-law's home, where a betrothal is arranged at a meal. In the two Genesis stories the male stranger also reveals his identity.

As will be seen more fully in the comments, this account of Jesus, who has travelled to Samaria and finds himself at a well with a woman, deliberately recalls the conventions of the betrothal type-scene for its readers. This framework is reinforced by other factors. At the wedding in Cana Jesus had taken over the responsibility of the bridegroom in supplying wine, and immediately before this present story John the Baptist has spoken of his relationship to Jesus in terms of the way the bridegroom's friend relates to the bridegroom (3.29). This imagery is dependent on the frequent depictions in the Jewish Scriptures of the covenant relationship between God and Israel in betrothal and marital terms, where Yahweh is husband or bridegroom and the people are wife or bride (cf. e.g. Isa. 54.1, 5–6; 62.4–5; Jer. 2.2–3, 32; Ezek. 16; 23; Hos. 2.2–23). Now Jesus, as the uniquely authorized representative of God, is the bridegroom, but who then is the bride, the newly constituted people of God? There will be a surprise, because, through this episode, readers will meet her not as represented by righteous Israelites but as represented in the person of the Samaritan woman. The two aspects of scriptural background – the betrothal type-scene and the relationship between God and God's covenant people – provide the clues for how this story moves between the literal and the symbolic and give coherence to its content. The move from the discussion of the woman's marital history to discussion of worship, for example, makes sense, because in the Jewish Scriptures the idolatry of the people of God and their failure to remain faithful in their worship of Yahweh are frequently depicted in terms of broken marriage and sexual promiscuity.

1–4 Jesus' presence in Samaria is prepared for by intimating why he left Judaea, where he was located in 3.22: **the Pharisees had heard that**

Jesus was making and baptizing more disciples than John. The inference to be drawn here is that the Pharisees saw the large numbers of Jesus' followers as a threat (cf. their interrogation of John the Baptist in 1.24–7). A further inference is that Jesus **left Judaea and went again to Galilee** because of the resulting potential for increased tension and conflict. So Jesus leaves on the journey that will take him through Samaria because of the opposition of the Pharisees. In the betrothal scene of Exod. 2 Moses had come to Midian because of the hostility of Pharaoh.

But there is also a comment pointing out that **Jesus himself was not baptizing but rather his disciples**. This appears to contradict the earlier narrative in 3.22, 26 where the focus is on Jesus as the one baptizing. Some hold that, since the Greek term for 'although' in this clause does not occur elsewhere in the New Testament and the insertion of the clause here is awkward, it may well be that the gloss has been made not by the narrator but by a later editor in an attempt either to bring the passage into line with the Synoptics, in which, of course, Jesus does not perform such an initiation rite, or to avoid the implication that Jesus was simply imitating the Baptist. On the former view, however, the gloss would introduce its own, though lesser, difficulty, because in the Synoptics the disciples do not baptize either. It is not impossible that the clause is a narratorial gloss, which is meant also to apply retrospectively to the earlier verses and to indicate that there too mention of Jesus baptizing was actually shorthand for the disciples baptizing. But if this is the narrator's comment, why did he not make the matter clear in 3.22 and save himself contradiction? The most likely answer is that he realized the possible negative implications of the earlier material only after this more explicit and direct comparison between Jesus' baptizing activity and John's in 4.1. As has been noted in the discussion of the historicity of 3.22, 26, he has been at pains to make clear Jesus' superiority to John and so now distances Jesus himself from an activity that might suggest he was merely continuing John's function. If the gloss is in fact that of the final editor, this last observation also provides its most probable motivation.

Since there is no geographical necessity for someone travelling from Judaea to Galilee to take the shorter route through Samaria, **He had to go through Samaria** is best taken as referring to the constraints of Jesus' mission. He is under divine necessity as the Father's envoy in seeking worshippers from Samaria (cf. v. 23).

5–6 The Samaritan city called Sychar is immediately associated by the narrator with the patriarch Jacob. It is described as **near the land which Jacob had given to his son, Joseph** and it is said that **Jacob's well was there**. These Jacob traditions had developed from Gen. 48.22 and Josh. 24.32 and were linked with Shechem, the old Samaritan city, which was destroyed in *c.* 108 BCE and replaced on the same site by Sychar.

The account places Jesus at Jacob's well at **about the sixth hour**. There is some debate about the system used for reckoning time in this Gospel, but most hold that the sixth hour would have been noon. The betrothal scene between Jacob and Rachel at the well also has the meeting in broad daylight (cf. Gen. 29.7). This incident with Jacob will be recalled again in v. 12. These initial references to Jacob and his well provide the clues that a new betrothal scene is about to take place.

7–9 The only other major element missing is now supplied. **A Samaritan woman came to draw water. Jesus said to her, 'Give me a drink.'** The conversation between Jesus and the woman has similarities to that between Eliezer and Rebekah in Gen. 24, where Eliezer asks to drink from the woman's jar. Now Jesus asks for a drink and the woman's jar will be mentioned later in v. 28. Readers are being led, then, to interpret the narrative on the usual level of an encounter between a man and a woman with a physical betrothal in view. They are further encouraged in this by the narrator then emphasizing that Jesus and the woman are alone – **for his disciples had gone into the city to buy food** – a comment that also anticipates the later dialogue about food after the disciples have returned (vv. 27, 31–4). The woman's response to Jesus' request expresses her surprise at Jesus' twofold breach of custom. In the only passage in the Gospel where Jesus is explicitly called a Jew, she says, **How is it that you, a Jew, ask a drink of me, a Samaritan woman?** First, Jesus as a male Jew is talking with a woman in a public place, and second, this particular woman is from Samaria, whose inhabitants were regularly despised by Jews, who held contact with them through eating or drinking to be defiling. For Gentile readers unaware of the shocking nature of this encounter and its request, the narrator adds an explanatory comment – **For Jews do not have dealings with Samaritans.**

Though the comment is rather too general, it does reflect the ambiguous relation of Samaritans to first-century Palestinian Judaism. A number of references in the Gospels view them as neither fully Jewish nor fully Gentile, as straddling the borders between the Jewish and Gentile worlds (cf. e.g. Matt. 10.5–6). The origins of the Samaritans and the timing of their increased divergence from elements of mainstream Judaism are shrouded in obscurity because of the sparsity of the sources and their predominantly polemical nature. There is a high probability, however, that they were descendants from a number of the northern tribes of Israel, mainly Ephraim and Manasseh, who in the first century CE lived in Samaria along with other ethnic groups. In the period of the Hasmonaean rulers, relations between Jews and Samaritans deteriorated badly, culminating in John Hyrcanus destroying the Samaritan sanctuary on Mt Gerizim in 128 BCE and then the town of Shechem some twenty years later. Thereafter, not surprisingly, relations between Jews and

Samaritans in general remained hostile and strained, though on some occasions and in particular circumstances more tolerant attitudes on both sides were possible.

10–12 Jesus counters the woman's question with an enigmatic reference to his identity, which, if it were recognized, would produce a reversal in who was asking whom for water: **If you knew the gift of God and who is saying to you, 'Give me a drink,' you would have asked him and he would have given you living water.** Readers know that Jesus, as the gift of God, brings the accompanying gift of eternal life (cf. 3.16), but, as yet, the woman is not in a position to realize this, and the various levels on which the symbols of water and living water work mean that the typical Johannine devices of misunderstanding and irony are able to be brought into play.

At the ordinary human level water and living water signify that which is in the well and which is necessary for survival – fresh running water. But at this level the giving and receiving of water also carried sexual overtones and represented the exchange of fluids necessary for the procreation of life. The betrothal framework with its conversation between a man and a woman at a well about water means that this possibility should not be ignored. Again, the Jewish Scriptures indicate clearly how such terminology was a well-known euphemism for sexual relations. In warning against promiscuity and adultery, Prov. 5.15–18 exhorts, 'Draw water from your own cistern, flowing water from your own well. Should your springs be scattered abroad, streams of water in the streets? Let them be for yourself alone, and not for sharing with strangers. Let your fountain be blessed, and rejoice in the wife of your youth.' Drinking water from a cistern or well refers to sexual intercourse, with springs specifically having in view semen, and wells and fountains the vagina and its emissions. The LXX of Prov. 9.17–18 spells out what is meant by 'stolen water is sweet' by adding, 'Turn away; do not linger in the area; do not let your eye gaze at her. Step across another man's water, and pass by another's river. Abstain from someone else's water, and do not drink from another's fountain.' Not surprisingly, the imagery is also there in the Song of Solomon 4.12, 15, where the woman described as 'my sister, my bride' is said to be 'a fountain sealed . . . a garden fountain, a well of living water, and flowing streams from Lebanon'. Both human connotations for water were capable of being taken up and employed at the divine level. It should be remembered that in both Jewish and Samaritan writings water and well imagery was employed in connection with God's self-disclosure in the law (cf. e.g. CD 6.2–5; Philo, *Ebr.* 112–13; *Memar Marqah* 6.3), so that in this passage a comparison between what is offered in the Mosaic law and what is provided by Jesus may well be in play, as it is more clearly elsewhere in the narrative. In addition, the divine revelation which brings life is depicted in terms of Wisdom's offer of water (cf. e.g. Sir. 15.3; 24.21, 30–3), and, as already noted in the dialogue with Nicodemus, water serves as a symbol of the Spirit (cf. e.g. Ezek. 36.25–7). The sexual imagery associated with the receptacles for water was used of the relation between Yahweh and Israel in, for example, Jer. 2.13 (cf. also 17.13) – 'they have forsaken me, the fountain of living water, and dug out cisterns for themselves, cracked cisterns that can hold no water'. Both types of imagery will enable readers to interpret the encounter between Jesus and the woman as a symbolic betrothal consummated through the divine life mediated by the Spirit.

The woman's responses to the mention of 'living water' remain on the merely human level. The question **from where do you get the living water?** is ironic because readers know that this language – 'from where' (πόθεν) – is used frequently about Jesus and his gifts and in such contexts is associated with ignorance about their origins (cf. e.g. 2.9; 3.8; 6.5; 9.29), which are in fact from above or from God. The irony continues with the further question, **Are you greater than our father Jacob . . .?** This evokes a comparison with Jacob not only in terms of his patriarchal status but also in terms of his vigour in opening up a well of water on his own. It may also have in view the miraculous powers attributed to Jacob and his well in the tradition. The question expects an answer in the negative, while readers know the answer is clearly a positive one. They have already been told in 1.51 that Jesus is the fulfilment of Bethel, the house of God, for which Jacob erected an altar. His identity and his giving will far exceed those of Jacob.

13–15 Jesus' answer focuses on the gift of water in a further attempt to clarify its significance: **Everyone who drinks from this water will thirst again**. Even the legendary abundance of Jacob's gift of ordinary water could not assuage thirst permanently. The water of which Jesus speaks will do so – **whoever drinks from the water which I shall give will never thirst; it will become within him or her a spring of water gushing up to eternal life**. This transcends even what was said previously of Wisdom's offer. Her invitation was 'Come to me, you who desire me . . . and those who drink of me will thirst for more' (Sir. 24.19–21). The life-giving revelation Jesus brings will be associated with the Spirit in vv. 23–4 and the link is explicit in 3.5 and 7.38–9. The woman's response is enthusiastic but misses the point, as she continues to operate within a this-worldly horizon – **Sir, give me this water, so that I might not thirst nor keep coming to this place to draw water**. Nevertheless, from within this limited perspective, the woman has made a little progress. Whatever it is she thinks Jesus is offering, she is at least open to receiving it.

16–18 Jesus' instruction that now follows – **Go and call your husband and come back here** – and the woman's response – **I do not have**

a husband – have often been thought to be an abrupt change of topic after the discussion of water, but the betrothal type-scene and the possible sexual innuendoes of the conversation about water allow it to be seen as an integral element in the flow of the dialogue. Initially, it would appear that, since the woman is unmarried, she is an appropriate candidate for betrothal. But Jesus' further words immediately reveal that this is not the case – **you have had five husbands and the one you now have is not your husband; what you have said is true**. They expose the woman's previous marital history and present domestic arrangements. But the force of these words has been hotly debated. Feminist readings of this passage are quite right to warn against importing into the text assumptions about women's sexuality and to point out both that the text passes over the reasons for the woman's marital history and that it is not mentioned in order for Jesus to judge her for it. They also challenge readers to rethink whether that marital history necessarily suggests immorality. Sometimes it is suggested that perhaps she is trapped in the custom of levirate marriage and the last male in the family has refused to marry her. There is elsewhere the trick question put to Jesus by the Sadducees in Luke 20.23–7, based on the levirate custom, about a woman and seven brothers. But that deliberately pushed the custom to absurdity to try to make a point. It does not envisage marriage to six brothers as a likely occurrence. In fact, in first-century Judaism it was quite unusual to have more than three marriages in a lifetime (rabbis only permitted a widow to marry a second or at most a third time) and, in any case, there is no indication that the sixth male here has refused to marry the Samaritan woman, which would be his right under levirate laws; instead, she is living with this man in a sexual relationship. Anyone in the woman's situation would be bound to have been viewed as morally suspect.

Sometimes it is proposed that her history be treated symbolically rather than literally, so that it contains not a reference to her actual husbands at all but to the gods worshipped by the Samaritans, as described in 2 Kgs 17.29–34. Against this approach it is objected that the polemic of the latter passage actually mentions seven gods worshipped by five ethnic groups, or that there is no parallel to the successiveness of the woman's five different husbands. However, the use to which this traditional polemic was later put suggested to Jews that the idolatry of the nations that had settled in Samaria was associated with the number five. Josephus, *Ant.* 9.14.31–2 says that 'each of them, according to their nations, which were in number five, brought their own gods into Samaria, and by worshipping them . . . provoked Almighty God to be angry and displeased at them'. To push the issue of successiveness is to treat the matter of allusion too literally. All that is required is that the woman, in representing Samaria, had a history involving five husbands. That the man she was now living with was not her husband would have suggested the common Jewish view that the

Samaritans' present claim to worship Yahweh was not a valid one. And in pointing out that the man she was with was not her husband, Jesus would be acting in the role of God's prophet, as did, for example, Hosea, when he states on behalf of Yahweh, 'plead with our mother, plead – for she is not my wife, and I am not her husband – that she put away her whoring from her face, and her adultery from between her breasts' (Hos. 2.2).

What has been said already about the evangelist's symbolic use of the betrothal type-scene indicates that there is no need to choose between a more literal and a more symbolic interpretation, but for the latter to work effectively the former needs to be one in which the woman is viewed as morally suspect. There are indeed other clues in the story which confirm that this is how she would have been considered. In the ancient Mediterranean world private space was for women and public space for men. Twice this convention is broken – first by an unrelated male, Jesus, and a female, the woman, talking together alone in a public space and then by the woman when she returns to talk to the men of the town. In addition, the woman is depicted at the well at midday. Women at wells were not unusual but they would only be found there at certain hours, morning or evening, and then in the company of other women. She is there by herself at an unusual hour and this suggests she has been shunned by other women for what they perceived to be deviant behaviour. At the same time, of course, deviant sexual conduct is a frequent image for the people of God's idolatry and failure to remain faithful in its worship of Yahweh, and so the woman can represent what was in Jewish eyes the apostasy of Samaritan religion and the whole of the previous conversation can now be seen also to lead naturally into the topic of authentic worship that emerges in v. 20.

19–20 The woman does indeed treat Jesus' insight as prophetic – **Sir, I see that you are a prophet.** At this point she begins to make the move from her previous, more literal level of understanding to the religious, symbolic level by explicitly introducing the topic of worship and Jewish and Samaritan disagreement about it. **Our ancestors worshipped on this mountain, and you say that in Jerusalem is the place where one must worship.** 'This mountain' remains unnamed but clearly points to Mt Gerizim and draws attention to a specific and distinctive aspect of Samaritan religion. As far as can be ascertained, Samaritans worshipped Yahweh, accepted only the Pentateuch as authoritative, and considered Mt Gerizim rather than Mt Zion in Jerusalem to be the focal point for public worship. In line with this emphasis, they had their own levitical priests, who operated at the Gerizim sanctuary and were deemed to be the legitimate priesthood in contrast to those at the Jerusalem temple. In later Samaritan writings they identify themselves as Israelites rather than Jews. In the first century CE, then, Samaritanism is in all probability to be seen as a rival, and, in certain features, a more conservative, heir to the religion of ancient Israel over against mainstream Judaism.

21–2 In Jesus' reply he first predicts a time when the division between Jews and Samaritans over the proper place for worship will be transcended – **the hour is coming when you will worship the Father neither on this mountain nor in Jerusalem**. A new epoch will be inaugurated which will make possible authentic worship of God, known and addressed as Father, and which will not require adherence to particular cultic sites. At the same time, however, Jesus sides clearly with the Jewish tradition and indicates that the eschatological change will transcend present allegiances in different ways – **You worship what you do not know; we worship what we know, because salvation is from the Jews**. The contrast between Samaritan lack of knowledge and the authentic knowledge of Jesus and those he represents parallels that in the discourse with Nicodemus in 3.10–11. In relation to testimony Jesus asserted, 'we speak of what we know' and now in relation to worship he claims, 'we worship what we know'. In view of the discussion about this Gospel's predominantly negative portrayal of 'the Jews' and its attitude to Judaism, the clause 'because salvation is from the Jews' is clearly highly significant. It constitutes an extremely positive statement, indicating that what Johannine Christians know affirms the validity of the promises of salvation God made to Israel and posits a continuity between those promises and the new epoch of worshipping the Father. As will become apparent from the ensuing dialogue, the statement can be made because in Jesus the Jew (cf. v. 9) the promises of salvation for Israel come to fulfilment. The fourth evangelist can be equally emphatic that salvation comes from the Jews and that those Jews and Gentiles who reject such salvation place themselves under indictment.

23–4 Jesus then announces that the eschatological change, affecting both the previously erroneous Samaritan view and the previously correct Jewish view, is already in the process of being realized – **But the hour is coming, and now is, when true worshippers will worship the Father in Spirit and in truth**. The authentic worship that is no longer tied to particular cultic places entails worship in Spirit and in truth. That the Spirit is the divine Spirit is clear from the comment that precedes the reiteration of the phrase 'in Spirit and in truth' in the following verse – **God is Spirit**. The Spirit is the creative life-giving power of God (cf. 6.63), which, like the wind, 'blows where it wills' (3.8) and cannot be confined to any one place. True worship corresponds to the God who is worshipped and therefore takes place in and through the divine Spirit. It also corresponds to what is true and for the evangelist truth is primarily the revelation of God in Jesus (cf. 14.6; 17.17). Since Jesus is the giver of the Spirit and the embodiment of the truth, worship in Spirit and in truth is also worship centred in and mediated by Jesus. The God who desires a relationship with created humanity is actively seeking those who will worship in this way – **the Father seeks such people as this as his worshippers** – and Jesus as the bridegroom seeking his bride has taken up this mission.

25–6 The arrival of the new epoch of worship is further signalled in Jesus' response to the woman's statement, **I know that the Messiah is coming, who is called Christ. When he comes, he will announce all things to us.** Her words, which reflect the Samaritan expectation of a prophet like Moses as a messianic figure, whom they called the Taheb, fail to recognize both the coming of the eschatological hour, of which Jesus has just spoken, and the identity of the one who inaugurates it. In the betrothal type-scene the stranger reveals his identity, and now Jesus does so in his claim which incorporates but transcends the messianic title used by the woman. He is the Messiah and the sort of Messiah who is one with God, because he can formulate his announcement in the words of the divine self-revelation – **I am, the one who is speaking to you.** This constitutes the first pronouncement by Jesus in the narrative of ἐγώ εἰμι with its remarkable force derived from the Septuagint renderings of the divine declarations in Deut. 32.39; Isa. 41.4; 43.10, 25; 45.18–19; 46.4; 51.12; 52.6. There can be little doubt that the formulation of this seventh and climactic contribution of Jesus to the dialogue is meant to point to Jesus' divine identity (cf. esp. Isa. 45.19 LXX – 'I Am . . . the one who speaks and announces' and Isa. 52.6 LXX – 'Therefore my people will know my name in that day, for I Am he who speaks'). The woman expressed her belief in a figure who will announce all things. Now Jesus claims to be that figure, because, like the incomparable God depicted in Isaiah, he is able to announce decisive events before they occur and has just announced the coming of the time of authentic worship. He could do so, because it is in and through Jesus that God is now revealing God's self and seeking worshippers. Jesus is the new focus of worship, just as earlier he was portrayed as the true place of worship – the new tabernacle (1.14), the new Bethel or house of God (1.51), and the new temple (2.19–22).

27 At this point his disciples came. This comment brings to an end the dialogue with the woman and provides the narrative link for the dialogue with the disciples which will follow in vv. 31–8. The narrator then underlines the shocking nature of what has taken place with his 'inside view' of the disciples – **they were amazed that he was speaking with a woman.** Yet, despite Jesus' break with convention by talking to an unrelated woman in a public space, his disciples refrain from expressing their amazement by questioning him.

28–30 So the woman left her water jar. This action signals both that the woman is not simply about to go home but will return to Jesus and that the previous earthly level of her encounter with Jesus has been abandoned. In the betrothal type-scene the woman would rush off to tell her family. The Samaritan woman hurries off to tell not her family but the citizens of Sychar. Her invitation to them – **Come and see a man who told me everything I ever did** – begins with a formulation that echoes the language of witnesses in this Gospel. Jesus had initiated this by inviting Andrew and an unnamed disciple to come and see in 1.39, and Philip continued the pattern with the same invitation to Nathanael in 1.46. To come to Jesus and to see him both turn out to be functional equivalents in the narrative's discourse for believing in Jesus (cf. e.g. 5.40; 6.35, 37, 40, 44–45; 9.39; 12.40, 45). The woman's witness is to Jesus' knowledge of her marital history, which, in a further breach of convention, she is now willing to discuss publicly. But her witness also extends, albeit tentatively, to the issue of Jesus' identity – **This is not the Christ, is it?** Her lack of certitude does not prevent her from being an effective witness. In fact, this amount of openness to Jesus' revelation of himself far exceeds the attitude of Nicodemus in the previous chapter, who had remained within his own set of certainties. Her testimony arouses sufficient interest that her audience **left the city and came to him.** The consequences of this response will be taken up in vv. 39–42 after the dialogue between Jesus and the disciples has been recounted.

31–3 Meanwhile the disciples were urging him, 'Rabbi, eat.' But he said to them, 'I have food to eat that you do not know about.' The betrothal type-scene ends with the male being given hospitality and a meal, but this will not occur here until the witness to the Samaritans has run its course. Interestingly, when Eliezer after his encounter with Rebekah is first offered food, he refuses to eat until he has accomplished his mission (Gen. 24.33). Jesus also refuses food, stating that he has food, which turns out to be his divine mission, of a different nature and from a different source. The ironies in the dialogue with the woman are now repeated as the disciples make the same mistake as the woman had done initially. This time the misunderstanding has to do not with water and drinking but with food and eating. Their confused response assumes that Jesus has been provided with food from another human source – **No one has brought him something to eat, have they?** – and sets up Jesus' explanation.

34–5 My food is to do the will of him who sent me and to complete his work. The food that sustains Jesus is the mission he has been given by God, who is frequently characterized as the one who sent Jesus. His mission is also designated elsewhere as doing the will and completing the work of God (cf. e.g. 5.30, 36; 6.38–40; 9.4; 10.37–8; 17.4), and his death on the cross will signal its completion (19.30). The imagery now changes from that of food to that of harvest, a traditional biblical image for completion. **Do you not say, 'There are four months yet and then the harvest comes?' Look, I tell you, lift up your eyes and observe the fields, because they are white for harvest already.** But the conventional agricultural wisdom that there is a period of waiting between sowing and harvesting is overturned here. Just as Jesus' presence signified that the time of eschatological worship had arrived (cf. v. 23), so it also means that the eschatological harvest has become a present reality, with the fields that are ripe for harvesting referring in this context to the Samaritans who are about to meet Jesus.

36–8 The harvest imagery is expanded in terms which reflect the language of early Christian mission and ministry (cf. e.g. 2 John 8; 1 Cor. 3.6–8). From a post-resurrection perspective Jesus' followers are seen as those already drawn into his mission as harvesters (cf. 21.1–14, where the imagery of fishing depicts the eschatological mission the disciples share with Jesus). **The harvester receives wages and gathers in the crop for eternal life, so that the sower and the harvester may rejoice together.** Through the mission in which they are involved Jesus' disciples participate in the process of bringing people to eternal life and share in the joy of the harvest with Jesus, the sower who has initiated the process (cf. also 15.11; 17.13 on the notion of sharing Jesus' joy). But a distinction remains between sowing and reaping – **For here the saying is true, 'One is the sower and another is the harvester'.** Indeed, the disciples are to harvest where they have not sown. **I have sent you to harvest that for which you have not laboured. Others have laboured, and you have entered into the result of their labour.** Just as Jesus has been sent on his mission by the Father, so his followers are sent by him to reap the rewards of his mission. As a general principle, later missionary followers will find themselves benefiting from the labours of those who went before them, including Jesus and his first disciples. In this immediate context those who laboured in the sowing that leads to the harvest among the Samaritans in which the disciples are to join are presumably Jesus and the Samaritan woman. This highlights the significant juxtaposition of scenes at this point in the narrative. While the woman is carrying out her witness to the townspeople, Jesus is in dialogue with the disciples, who appear to have been less perceptive than the woman and are told that they need to seize the opportunity for harvesting. This Samaritan woman with a dubious past has, ironically, brought Jesus his true food, in contrast to the disciples (cf. vv. 31–4), by her receptivity to his revelatory mission and by becoming the catalyst for the belief of other Samaritans.

39–40 What was already implied now becomes explicit. The woman has become a witness who bears testimony to Jesus and, like John the Baptist and the Beloved Disciple (cf. 1.7; 19.35), the purpose of her witness is to lead others to belief. **Many of the Samaritans from that city believed in him because of the word of the woman who testified, 'He told me everything I ever did.'** The final scene in the typical betrothal story is that of the man being invited to stay with the family and celebrate the betrothal at a meal. Here Jesus accepts the invitation to stay with the Samaritans from the city: **So when the Samaritans came to him, they asked him to remain with them; and he remained there two days.** The language of 'remaining' recalls what occurred with the first two disciples (1.39) and elsewhere signifies a lasting relation between Jesus and his followers (cf. e.g. 8.31; 15.4–7).

41–2 Even more Samaritans come to believe in Jesus during his two days among them. They now believe **because of his word.** As they say to the woman, **We no longer believe because of what you said, for we ourselves have heard and know that this is truly the Saviour of the world.** This encapsulates the relationship of testimony and belief. The witness that is necessary to point others to Jesus is then completed as those others have an experience of Jesus for themselves. Through the presence of Jesus the Samaritans move from the ignorance of idolatry – 'you [plural] worship what you do not know' (v. 22) – to true knowledge – 'we . . . know that this is truly the Saviour of the world'. Such knowledge perceives that, although salvation comes from the Jews (v. 22), it is not confined to them. The confession of Jesus' universal significance also excludes rival claims, including those made on behalf of the Roman emperor, since the title 'Saviour of the world' was applied in particular to Nero and Hadrian. The universal salvation embodied in Jesus, embracing Jew, Samaritan and Gentile, corresponds to the universal scope of the worship mediated by him, no longer restricted to locations such as Gerizim or Jerusalem (cf. vv. 21–4).

This passage's thoroughly Johannine literary structuring and its concern with characteristic themes, such as water, the Spirit, truth, Jesus as the fulfilment and replacement of Jewish religious institutions, Jesus as the bridegroom and believers as the bride, realized eschatology, the disciples' misunderstanding, and the cosmic scope of Jesus' mission, make it extremely hard to isolate with any precision an underlying tradition and its origins. Yet the details of the story show the evangelist to be well informed about Samaria and Samaritan beliefs. It is by no means impossible that the account has been massively elaborated on the basis of an earlier tradition of an encounter between Jesus and a Samaritan woman. But a mission to Samaritans during Jesus' ministry has no parallel in the Synoptic tradition. Instead outreach to Samaria is depicted as part of the early church's mission in Acts 8.4–24. It may well be, then, that Samaritans

were to be found among Johannine Christians and that this story legit-
imates their presence and encourages further outreach (cf. vv. 35–8) by
reading back a Samaritan mission into the time of Jesus, just as it reads
back the initiation rite of baptism (cf. vv. 1–4).

The main themes of this narrative might be summed up alliteratively
as wedding, water, worship and witness. The betrothal type-scene is
reinterpreted as symbolic of God's betrothal to God's people. Jesus, as the
unique representative of God who is one with God, is presented as the
bridegroom seeking a bride, the new people of God. Represented by the
Samaritan woman, the new bride turns out to include women as well as
men, Samaritans as well as Jews, and those with dubious pasts who would
normally have been considered to be impure. Jesus overturns the usual
conventions in choosing his bride. His new covenant bride transcends
ethnic, gender and purity divisions so that Jesus as bridegroom can be
confessed as truly the Saviour of the world. In this light the water he
offers is neither simply that which quenches thirst nor that which gives
rise to sexual overtones but represents the revelation from God that is
life-giving and that is mediated by the Spirit.

Jesus, as the bridegroom, has taken up the mission of the Father, who
is seeking worshippers who will worship in Spirit and in truth. The Spirit
will be sent in Jesus' name as his fully authorized representative, and the
truth – that God is known in Jesus and that he is one with God – is
disclosed in Jesus' person and mission. Authentic worship in the time of
eschatological fulfilment is made possible, then, through the person and
presence of the one who reveals himself as the Messiah who can take on
his lips the divine name, 'I Am'. To belong to the bride, the new people
of God, is to participate in the worship inaugurated by Jesus being the
new temple in whom the divine presence is now located. It is also to
participate in worship that has clearly trinitarian dimensions, because it
is worship of the seeking Father, mediated by the person of Jesus, and
enabled by the life-giving Spirit.

The Samaritan woman moves through misunderstanding to a level of
insight into Jesus' identity that is sufficient for her to become a witness to the
people of Sychar. The contrasts between her encounter with Jesus and that of
Nicodemus in the previous chapter are instructive. The latter was a named,
male Jew and, as a Jewish teacher, was a leading member of society. She is
an unnamed, female Samaritan and a marginalized member of a heterodox
group. Nicodemus comes to Jesus at night and remains in the darkness of his
own categories. The woman's encounter with Jesus in broad daylight leads to
her increasing understanding and openness to Jesus' revelation. Her testimony
results in the belief of many other Samaritans, who are enabled to encounter
Jesus for themselves. It thereby becomes a model for participation in the
universal mission of eschatological harvesting which Jesus has inaugurated and
instructs his followers to continue.

(vii) Return to Cana and healing of the official's son   *4.43–54*

(43) After the two days he left there for Galilee. (44) For Jesus himself had testified that a prophet is without honour in his own country. (45) When therefore he came to Galilee, the Galileans received him, having seen all that he had done in Jerusalem at the festival, for they too had gone to the festival.

(46) So he came again to Cana of Galilee, where he had made the water wine. Now there was a royal official whose son was ill in Capernaum. (47) When he heard that Jesus had come from Judaea into Galilee, he went to him and asked him to come down and heal his son, for he was at the point of death. (48) Jesus said to him, 'Unless you see signs and wonders, you will not believe.' (49) The official said to him, 'Sir, come down before my child dies.' (50) Jesus said to him, 'Go. Your son lives.' The man believed the word Jesus had spoken to him and went. (51) While he was still on the way down, his slaves met him and told him that his child was living. (52) So he enquired of them at what time he had taken a turn for the better. They said to him, 'Yesterday at the seventh hour the fever left him.' (53) The father therefore realized that it was at that time that Jesus had said to him, 'Your son lives,' and he and his whole household believed. (54) Now again this second sign Jesus did after coming from Judaea to Galilee.

The transitional comments in vv. 43–5 depict Jesus' move from Samaria to Galilee and prepare for his more specific return to Cana, from where he performs the second sign. The account of the sign again takes the traditional form of a miracle story. The setting is provided in v. 46 and the situation of need, giving rise to a request for help, is outlined in vv. 47–9. The miraculous intervention through Jesus' powerful word follows in v. 50 and confirmation that the miracle has taken place is provided in vv. 51–3. The account is rounded off by the narrator's concluding comment in v. 54. In a way that has similarities with 2.1–12 and later incidents, the basic form is elaborated by a typical Johannine feature that underlines Jesus' sovereignty. He does not respond to the situation immediately when asked. The request of the official is met with an initial form of rebuff (v. 48) before the request is repeated and Jesus then decides to respond positively. This is not the only aspect of the account that takes readers back to the opening of the section. They are explicitly reminded in v. 46 of the earlier miracle in the same location of Cana and the enumeration of the later miracle as the second sign in v. 54 reinforces the connection, since the turning of water into wine had been described as the first sign in 2.11. As was noted in the comments on the first sign, it is also closely connected with the second one through the clear verbal and conceptual links with the Elijah tradition in 1 Kgs 17 LXX. In addition, the reference to Jesus' activity in Jerusalem at the festival in v. 45 recalls the episode following the first sign in 2.13–25. In these ways the ending of the section forms an *inclusio* with its opening.

43–5 The temporal marker – **after the two days** – refers back to v. 40 and Jesus' stay among the receptive Samaritans. Now Jesus leaves **for Galilee**, where he has not been since his short stay in Capernaum (cf. 2.12). The move prompts the narrator's comment referring to the traditional saying **that a prophet is without honour in his own country**. Similar sayings are found elsewhere in regard to philosophers (cf. e.g. Epictetus, *Diss*. 3.16, 11; Dio Chrysostom, *Or*. 30.6; Philostratus, *Ep*. 44) and it is employed in varying formulations in the Synoptics (cf. Mark 6.4; Matt. 13.57; Luke 4.24; cf. also *Gos. Thom*. 31) in relation to the offence taken at Jesus' ministry in his home town of Nazareth. Here the saying is treated as part of Jesus' witness – **for Jesus himself had testified** – but it is not stated when the witness is given. It may well be that readers familiar with the Synoptic tradition are meant to recall it as the basis for the narrator's comment. But how the saying functions in its Johannine context is much debated. What is the force of the connective 'for' and how is the logic of the passage to be construed? What in this narrative is the home territory in which Jesus as a prophet is without honour? The answer to these questions depends to a large extent on how one interprets the following verse and its description of the reception of Jesus in Galilee. Does it portray a clearly positive response or one that suggests potentially more negative elements?

Some commentators argue that, since the response on the part of the Galileans appears to be a welcoming one and the Capernaum official believes, it cannot be Galilee in which Jesus is without honour but must be Judaea. After all, Jesus is in Judaea more frequently than in Galilee in this Gospel, has just recently come from Judaea, where he did not receive an adequately positive reception (cf. 3.11, 32 on his testimony not being accepted), and since Jerusalem and the temple are there, at least theologically it ought to have been his own country (cf. 1.11 – 'he came to what was his own and his own people did not receive him').

It may well be the case, however, that Galilee is in view as the home territory in this Gospel also. Jesus has most immediately been in Samaria, where he was recognized as a prophet (4.19). Now he comes to Galilee and it is at this point that the saying about a prophet being without honour in his own country is introduced. Readers have already learned that Jesus is from Nazareth (1.45–6) and that he and his family have a base in Capernaum (2.12), so they would most naturally assume Galilee to be his home territory (cf. also 7.41, 52). To this point his disciples have responded in belief but there has been no indication of a positive response on the part of Galileans in general. What is now said about their reaction is that **the Galileans received him, having seen all that he had done in Jerusalem at the festival, for they too had gone to the festival**. The mention of Jerusalem and the festival deliberately recalls 2.23–5 – 'while he was in Jerusalem during the Passover festival' – and what is said about the Galileans is similar to the response of the many there who 'believed in his name because they saw the signs that he was doing'. Yet that response was clearly evaluated as at best equivocal and at worst quite inadequate, because Jesus' reaction was not to trust himself to them. The link back to 2.23–5, then, indicates that what is said about the Galileans here may well not be as positive as it first appears. The suspicion is confirmed by what Jesus will go on to say in v. 48 – 'Unless you [plural] see signs and wonders, you will not believe.' He imputes to Galileans generally an inappropriate reception based solely on seeing signs. The royal official will prove himself an exception by believing Jesus' word without first seeing the sign. If the 'for' in v. 44 is a weak link illuminating or supporting statements in its context, it simply provides a connection between Galilee, the immediately preceding word, and the saying. If it is taken in its full causal force as providing the motivation for Jesus' move, then the logic would be, in continuity with 4.1, that Jesus wants to withdraw from the unhealthy interest of the Pharisees in his activity and comes to Galilee, where he expects no particular stir to be caused because a prophet does not command that sort of attention among his own people. On this interpretation of Jesus' homeland, its relation to the statement in the prologue is that Jesus' own people who did not accept him are the majority of Jews, both those in Galilee, Jesus' actual home country, and those in Judaea. If the formulation of v. 44 is meant for those who know the Synoptics to recall the saying there, then clearly that would provide further support for the reading of the prophet's home country as Galilee.

46 The return to Cana – **he came again to Cana of Galilee, where he had made the water wine** – and the explicit reminder of the previous miracle raise expectations for the readers in regard to the narrator's next statement – **Now there was a royal official whose son was ill in Capernaum**. The term describing the father – βασιλικός – could be employed with a variety of references – a person of royal blood, a royal official or scribe, or a soldier in royal service. The royal employ in view could be that of either the Herodian kings or the emperor. Given the relation of this story to the Synoptic account about the centurion from Capernaum (see the discussion below), many deem the military reference to be most likely here. But it cannot be ruled out that, even if he knows this version of the story, the evangelist has chosen to present its main character differently. Since the evangelist does not use an explicitly military term, he leaves open the exact nature of this man's occupation and 'royal official' remains the best translation. Also, in distinction from the version of the story in Matthew and Luke, this Gospel does not specify the official's ethnic identity. Someone working for Herod Antipas could have been either a Jew or a Gentile. Scholars have been anxious to decide one way or the other. Some argue that the official is to be seen as a Jew, as one of the Galileans who have just been mentioned, because the evangelist does not view the Samaritans as Gentiles and has a clear schema in which any mission beyond Israel to Gentiles only occurs after Jesus' glorification. No Gentiles are introduced into the narrative until the announcement of Jesus' hour of glorification and the Greeks who wish to see him at this point are not said to have their wish granted (cf. 12.20–6). It is his lifting up on the cross that will enable Jesus to draw all people to himself (cf. 12.32–3). This is not, however, decisive. It has already been noted that the evangelist is capable of setting out such broad schemas only to break them somewhat awkwardly because of the way he will sometimes collapse pre- and post-Easter temporal perspectives. He can, for example, make clear that the Spirit will not be given until Jesus is glorified (7.39) but then have Jesus speak to characters in a way that assumes the Spirit is already on offer (cf. 3.5–6; 4.23–4). Consequently, other scholars have claimed that it is more likely that the royal official is a Gentile and that this would fit with the way this section of the narrative broadens the scope of Jesus' ministry, beginning with dealing with Jews, moving to Samaritans who were seen as neither Jews nor Gentiles, and then ending with a Gentile. It is also argued that those readers familiar with the Synoptic accounts would most naturally assume this Capernaum official was a Gentile. While there are no decisive considerations against his being a Gentile, this view cannot be held with any certainty, and it must be said that it is unlikely that the evangelist intended any particular significance to be attached to the man's ethnic origins, because there would have been simple and obvious ways to make these clear if he had so desired.

47 The official had learned enough about Jesus' powers, either through being in Jerusalem himself (cf. v. 45) or from reports, and his concern about his son was so great, that, **When he heard that Jesus had come from Judaea into Galilee**, he went to Cana and asked Jesus to come down to Capernaum to heal him. His son is described as **at the point of death**. The exact nature of the illness is not specified, although v. 52 will speak of an accompanying fever. In ancient texts, however, fever was not viewed simply as an accompanying symptom but as an illness in itself which could often be fatal (cf. Hippocrates, *Epid.* 1). The length of time a fever had lasted and whether a patient had taken to bed were seen as significant clues to whether death was imminent. Fevers were more likely to prove fatal in the case of children and it is estimated that at this time only 49 per cent of children survived to the age of five. It would not be hard for readers to identify with the plight of this official, who feared that his child was going to die (cf. v. 49), perhaps because he had taken to bed or because of the length of time the fever had already lasted.

48 Yet instead of immediately responding to this desperate human need, Jesus, somewhat surprisingly, replies, **Unless you see signs and wonders, you will not believe**. The statement is addressed beyond the official to 'you' in the plural. Commentators have not agreed on its force. Some have taken it as a positive comment on the role of miracles, in which Jesus underlines that signs and wonders are a necessary preliminary to faith. On this interpretation it would function as a signal that Jesus is therefore about to do what the man asks. Supporters of this view also appeal to the fact that this is the only place in the Gospel where the expression 'signs and wonders' occurs, and, where that phrase is found in the Jewish Scriptures, it is frequently in the context of signs and wonders leading to the acknowledgement of the truth about God (cf. e.g. Deut. 4.34–5). They also appeal to the response of the official's household, whose members do believe on seeing this sign. In addition, it is sometimes suggested that the saying is emphasizing the proper seeing of signs, whereby the significance of the one who performs them is recognized, and that the official by his response shows he has the appropriate sort of sight. But this is to read far too much both into the use of the verb 'to see' in this particular context and into the man's response. It is more likely that the characteristic Johannine pattern of request – rebuff – delayed response, which shapes this account, indicates that Jesus' initial reply is less than straightforwardly positive. It may echo the Synoptic refusal of a demand for signs on the terms of those who request them (cf. Mark 8.11–12 parr.) or, when it is read in the light of the Galileans' response in v. 45 with its taking up of 2.23–5 (see the discussion above), it may express to a general audience beyond the official the evangelist's reservations about the sort of faith based simply on having seen signs. Through Jesus' rebuke of what would be a superficial faith on the part of the Galileans, the readers are addressed and alerted to this issue. The official in his reply takes no obvious notice of what has just been said and will simply repeat his request.

49–50 The official's previously reported request is now given in direct speech – **Sir, come down before my child dies**. It is now also made clear through the diminutive form of the term used that his son is a child. Jesus now responds to the man's need on his own terms. Rather than accompanying the man to Capernaum, he simply says, **Go. Your son lives**. In the Elijah traditions in 1 Kgs 17 LXX, which have points of contact with the two Cana miracles, Elijah, on having restored the widow's son to life, also uses the very same words – 'Your son lives' (17.23). But the difference should not be missed. Jesus' words do not come after physical encounter with the child. It is by these words alone that he heals. The official's reaction to Jesus' response is also surprising. Instead of being disappointed that Jesus does not intend to visit his son, he **believed the word Jesus had spoken to him and went**. As in the earlier sign at Cana, attention is thereby focused on Jesus' powerful word, which is able to effect signs, and the necessity of openness and obedience to that word. The official exercises faith in that word without first having had to see the sign.

51–3 While the official is on his way back to Capernaum, the household slaves come to meet him with the good news that his son is alive. That the recovery was not simply due to the natural course of events is confirmed as the official asks when his son had begun to recover and discovers that it was exactly at the time that Jesus had pronounced the words, **Your son lives**. As a result both **he and his whole household believed**. His household comes to faith as a consequence of the official's initial belief (cf. v. 50). This formulation recalls the conversion of Gentile households in the Acts account (cf. Acts 10.2; 11.14; 18.8). It closes the account of the sign in a way that parallels that of the first Cana sign in 2.11, where the disciples are said to have believed in Jesus. The appropriate response to Jesus' performance of signs is belief in the one who performs them.

54 The narrator's concluding comment – **Now again this second sign Jesus did after coming from Judaea to Galilee** – is seen by some as support for the view that the Fourth Gospel drew on a previous signs source or Signs Gospel. It is claimed that the numbering fits awkwardly, since it fails to account for the other signs said to be performed in Jerusalem (2.22) and is not used again for the further signs related in the narrative. The geographical qualification also appears awkward because there have now been two movements from Judaea to Galilee. The suggestion is therefore made that in the original source this miracle followed immediately upon that of turning water into wine and that that sequence and its numbering have been taken up without being properly integrated into the new context. But these features are insufficient in themselves to point to a signs source. The geographical reference is not as awkward as is suggested, and our translation indicates that it is perfectly possible to take it as stating that, just as Jesus performed the first sign after coming from Judaea to Galilee, so again he performed the second sign after making the same move. On this reading the numbering of the two signs is natural. It is part of the connection the narrator wishes to make between the two Cana signs, which open and close this section of the narrative. There will be no further signs at Cana and so the numbering drops out after this.

In the Synoptics there are two traditions of Jesus healing at a distance and both involve Gentiles. There are only very general correspondences with the incident of the Syrophoenician woman in Mark 7.24–30 (cf. also Matt. 15.21–8). There the woman begs Jesus to cast a demon out of her daughter. Jesus initially rebuffs her but her response to the rebuff is the catalyst for Jesus' words, 'For saying that, you may go – the demon has left your daughter.' The woman returns home and finds the demon has left her child. But the second Cana sign has more obvious connections with the healing of the centurion's servant at Capernaum, which is part of the so-called Q material that Matthew and Luke have in common. In both Matt. 8.5–13 and Luke 7.1–10 Jesus is already in Capernaum and prepared to go to the centurion's house, but it is the centurion who suggests that Jesus is able to heal at a distance and this he then does. The fourth evangelist appears to have creatively adapted this story. Jesus is placed in Cana, the centurion becomes a royal official and the servant a son (though Matthew's account is ambiguous and his term παῖς could mean either servant or son; cf. also John 4.51). It also takes on typical Johannine traits. There is no mention of Jesus' amazement at the man's faith, as in Matt. 8.10 and Luke 7.9. This would underline Jesus' humanity. Instead, as with many of the other signs, whatever the Synoptic Jesus does, the Fourth Gospel's Jesus is able to surpass. It is he in his sovereign initiative who simply decides to heal from a distance and this distance is no longer merely within Capernaum but extends all the way from Cana to Capernaum. Interestingly, the closest points of contact are not with any of the material Matthew and Luke have in common but with distinctive Lukan material at the beginning and distinctive Matthean material at the end. Both Luke 7.2 and John 4.47 have the sick person on the point of death and both Matt. 8.13 and John 4.52–3 stress the synchronicity between the hour of Jesus' word of healing and the hour the healing occurs. There is a further detail at the end that suggests that the fourth evangelist knew Matthew's Gospel. In v. 52b the official's slaves state, 'Yesterday at the seventh hour the fever left him.' There has been no mention of fever earlier in the account and there is only one other place in the Gospels where a sick person suffers from fever. It is in the account of the healing of Peter's mother-in-law, which Matthew has placed immediately after his version of the healing of the centurion's servant in Matt. 8.14–15 and where he uses the formulation 'the fever left her'. It is unlikely then that John has independently adapted the tradition behind Q. It would have to be supposed that it originally contained the points at which Matthew and Luke now differ and that John included these but omitted the bulk of the tradition. It is possible that he knew an independent version of the tradition that circulated orally but highly coincidental that his reproduction of it included parts of Matthew's and Luke's redaction of Q. It seems simpler and more likely than positing an unknown independent tradition to see him as familiar with both earlier writers' versions and as being influenced by parts of both in his own creative rewriting of the miracle story. The observation about the mention of fever in the immediate context of Matthew's version considerably strengthens this likelihood.

The Fourth Gospel employs this story as part of its portrayal of Jesus as the bestower of life. The first sign at Cana with its extravagant provision of wine showed Jesus as the divine giver of the abundant life of the new age. The significance of the second sign is similar. It is stated twice that the child is under the threat of imminent death (cf. vv. 47, 49) and then stressed three times that as a result of Jesus' word he lives (cf. vv. 50, 51, 53). Jesus' giving or restoring of human life in the face of death points to his giving of divine life. What is more, his divine power is revealed in his ability to heal without any physical contact and at a considerable distance from the person involved. In the Logos was life and now through the mere word of the incarnate Logos healing takes place. The official's model response indicates that, if the life Jesus brings is to be experienced, what is essential is belief in his word. This is the sort of faith that entails not merely remaining impressed by the signs but risking trust in the one who performs them.

3. Revelation and Testimony in Controversy with 'the Jews'   5.1—10.42

The first two signs have not been followed by discourse or debate but after the next sign dispute does ensue and there is a lengthy discourse in response to it. This signals a definite change of tone in this next major section of the narrative. In the previous section there has been some questioning and perplexity amidst the generally positive response to Jesus' mission, but from now on both his words and deeds will meet with a significant amount of opposition and rejection, and controversy will dominate the narrative.

(i) Healing of the man at the pool   *5.1–18*

(1) After this there was a festival[1] of the Jews, and Jesus went up to Jerusalem. (2) Now there is in Jerusalem at the Sheep Gate a pool,[2] called in Hebrew Bethzatha,[3] which has five porticoes.

---

[1] Some early witnesses have the definite article before 'festival'. However, the evidence for the reading without an article is stronger and the scribal tendency would have been to make an unnamed festival more clearly one of the three main pilgrimage festivals (probably Passover) by adding the article.

[2] The translation 'Sheep Gate' masks two difficulties with the syntax of the Greek sentence, where the best-attested and more difficult reading seems to have a word

(3) In these lay a great number of sick people, blind, lame and paralysed.[4] (5) A certain man was there who had been ill for thirty-eight years. (6) When Jesus saw him lying there and knew he had already had this illness for a long time, he said to him, 'Do you want to become well?' (7) The sick man answered him, 'Sir, I do not have anyone to put me into the pool when the water is stirred up. While I am on my way, someone else gets down ahead of me.' (8) Jesus said to him, 'Rise, take up your mat and walk.' (9) And immediately[5] the man became well and picked up his mat and began to walk. Now that day was a sabbath. (10) The Jews therefore said to the man who had been healed, 'It is the sabbath and it is not lawful for you to carry your mat.' (11) He answered them, 'The man who made me well said to me, "Take up your mat and walk."' (12) They asked him, 'Who is the man who said to you, "Take it up and walk"?' (13) The man who had been healed did not know who it was, for Jesus had slipped away, since there was a crowd there. (14) After this Jesus found him in the temple and said to him, 'See, you have become well; do

---

missing and the word for 'pool' could be either nominative or dative. If it is read as a nominative, then a literal translation produces 'there is in Jerusalem at the sheep a pool', and if as a dative, 'there is in Jerusalem at the sheep pool' with no resulting predicate. Either way, a word would need to be supplied. Those who take 'pool' as nominative usually supply 'gate,' while those who take it as dative supply 'a place' after 'pool'. The original of Sinaiticus has no preposition and therefore reads smoothly – 'there is in Jerusalem a sheep pool', but it is much more likely that this reflects an adaptation of a difficult text than that other texts would have added a preposition and thereby created a major difficulty. For these reasons the translation has followed those who opt for the more difficult reading and then supply the word 'gate' in order to achieve coherence. For further discussion, see the comment on this verse.

[3] There is considerable divergence in the textual traditions about the name of the pool, with Bethzatha, Bezatha, Belzetha, Bethsaida and Bethesda all being represented. Bethsaida appears to be an assimilation to the name of the town mentioned in 1.44 and Bezatha and Belzetha to be variants of Bethzatha. This leaves a difficult choice between Bethzatha and Bethesda. Recent archaeological activity and the mention of Betheshdathayim in the Copper Scroll at Qumran (3Q15 11.12) have inclined some to support Bethesda, but Bethzatha has the important witness of Sinaiticus (‭א‬) in its favour.

[4] Some manuscripts contain material which is included as vv. 3b–4 in older English translations – 'waiting for the stirring of the water, for an angel of the Lord went down at certain seasons into the pool, and stirred up the water; whoever stepped in first after the stirring of the water was made well from whatever disease that person had.' It is generally agreed, however, that this constitutes a later gloss, added to explain the reference to the stirring of the water in v. 7. The best witnesses (p[66,75] ‭א‬ B C* D) do not contain it, it comes with its own set of variants and it includes a considerable number of words and expressions not found elsewhere in John.

[5] 'And immediately' is omitted in ‭א‬* and 'immediately' is omitted in D W[supp] it[aur,d,l]. Nevertheless, the evidence for the phrase is early and widespread (p[66,75] ‭א‬c A B C K L) and it should be included.

not sin any more lest something worse happen to you.' (15) The
man went away and told the Jews that it was Jesus who had made
him well. (16) For this reason the Jews were persecuting Jesus
because he was doing these things on the sabbath. (17) But Jesus
answered them, 'My Father is working until now and I also am
working.' (18) For this reason the Jews were seeking all the more
to kill him, because he not only broke the sabbath but was also
calling God his own Father, making himself equal to God.

The conventional form of a miracle story has again left its stamp on John's
account of this healing. The scene is set in vv. 1–3, the need of the man is
established in vv. 5–7 and the miracle is recounted in vv. 8–9a. The rest of
the episode, vv. 9b–18, can be seen as a lengthy confirmation of the fact
that the miracle has taken place because of the dispute that it provokes.
But the simple pattern of the miracle story is broken by this final section
because, beginning with v. 9b, the ending of the miracle story becomes
a sabbath controversy story. Only v. 14, in which Jesus meets the healed
man in the temple, is not dominated by the sabbath issue. For this reason
some hold that the saying of Jesus it contains may have formed the
original conclusion of the miracle story. But as the account now stands,
the two sorts of story have been woven into a unified narrative which has
structural correspondences to the story of the man born blind in chapter
9 and need not have had two separate Johannine traditions behind it
(see the discussion below). It unfolds in seven parts – (i) a description
of the setting (vv. 1–3), (ii) Jesus' encounter with the sick man (vv. 5–7),
(iii) Jesus' healing of the man on the sabbath (vv. 8–9), (iv) an exchange
between 'the Jews' and the man (vv. 10–13), (v) an exchange between
Jesus and the man in the temple (v. 14), (vi) an exchange between the
man and 'the Jews' (v. 15), (vii) controversy between 'the Jews' and Jesus
(vv. 16–18). This last part moves away from the specific incident to the
broader relations between Jesus and the authorities arising from his
sabbath activities and accompanying claims.

1–3 The narrator indicates the beginning of a new episode through the
phrase **After this**, and through the change of location – **Jesus went up
to Jerusalem**. The occasion for the visit is **a festival of the Jews**. Jewish
festivals will play an increasingly important role in this section of the Gospel.
This one remains unnamed, however, because, unlike the others, its significance is not taken up in the narrative that accompanies it. The formulation 'a
festival of the Jews' is probably not simply a neutral description but reflects the
present distancing of the evangelist and his community from Jewish institutions. Despite their having emerged from within a thoroughly Jewish milieu,
as a result of their history of conflict with the synagogue they now see such
festivals as belonging to their parent religion.

Some of the difficulties surrounding the narrator's topographical description have been outlined in the notes to the translation. Whether or not the word 'gate' is to be supplied in the light of Neh. 3.1 and 12.39, which speak of Jerusalem's Sheep Gate, and whether or not the place was called Bethzatha or Bethesda, archaeological excavations have shown that there was an area to the north-east of the temple, near the present church of St Anne, which had two large pools and other smaller pools in which people could bathe. The two large pools were built *c.* 200 BCE in the time of the high priest Simeon to supply water to the temple. Most scholars incline to the view that this double pool, which had a central partition, lies behind John's reference to the **five porticoes**, two of which would have been on each side and one in the middle. The adjacent pools were built later to serve as smaller baths, probably for both medicinal and religious purposes. When the two main pools later fell into disuse, they continued to fill with rain and may well have been used to wash the sheep brought for temple sacrifice. Later, by the time of Hadrian in the early second century CE, the area had become a healing sanctuary dedicated to Asclepius or Serapis. This strongly suggests that it had already been associated in Jewish tradition with healing powers. This story certainly assumes such a tradition and mentions here at the outset **a great number of sick people, blind, lame and paralysed**, who were lying in the porticoes. Strabo (8.6.15) gives a similar depiction of those gathered at the Asclepius healing sanctuary in Epidaurus.

5–7 The focus then narrows to one of these people, a man **who had been ill for thirty-eight years**. Some suggest that this precise number may be intended to recall the length of time Israel was in the wilderness, according to Deut. 2.14. The same reference, however, indicates that thirty-eight years was considered to be the lifespan of a generation and the thought may therefore be that the man has been ill for a lifetime. More certainly, it serves to ensure that the healing which will take place will be seen as miraculous, and indeed as more impressive than any of its Synoptic counterparts. There Jesus healed a woman who had been suffering from a haemorrhage for twelve years (Mark 5.25–34 parr.) and a woman crippled for eighteen years (Luke 13.10–17), but here in John this man has been ill for thirty-eight years. The precise nature of the man's illness is not spelled out. From what follows it is clear that he is only able to move with great difficulty and the miracle consists in his being able to stand up and walk. Those who were paralysed or lame have just been mentioned and so either this man was simply badly lame or had a form of paralysis that affected at least his legs. He does not point out his need or ask for healing himself. Instead Jesus perceives the need and takes the initiative. Jesus **knew he had already had this illness for a long time**. This is in line with John's earlier characterization of Jesus in terms of his special knowledge (cf. 1.48; 2.24–5; 4.17, 18, 29). Whether Jesus knew the long time was thirty-eight years is not specified, nor is how much of that time the man had spent lying near the pool. Jesus' question to the man – **Do you want to become well?** – appears strange. If the man had not wanted to be healed, presumably he would not have been at the pool, and readers have just been told of Jesus' special knowledge of this man's situation. Nevertheless, the question can be read as an offer of healing and it provokes a response that indicates the man's plight more specifically and makes clear why Jesus' offer is so pertinent: **Sir, I do not have anyone to put me into the pool when the water is stirred up. While I am on my way, someone else gets down ahead of me.** Behind this reply is the belief that the place is a healing sanctuary and that its pool has healing powers at particular times, signalled by bubbling or stirring of the waters. Evidently it was also held that the healing powers extended only to the first person into the pool on such an occasion. The later gloss in vv. 3b–4 provides just such an explanation for those readers who might have been unfamiliar with these beliefs (see n. 4 above). The man's reply indicates why he has so far not been healed but he does not, of course, recognize what Jesus is offering him. It may therefore be an example of the Johannine device of misunderstanding. The man's response can be read as his treating Jesus' question as an offer of help to get him into the pool rather than as an offer of direct healing.

8–9a Despite this, Jesus does for the man what he so desperately needs. Again, the miraculous intervention is related very succinctly. Contrary to the man's receding hopes, Jesus does not need to employ the powers of the pool but simply exercises the power of his word, as he issues the command, **Rise, take up your mat and walk.** These are precisely the same words used by Mark's Jesus in healing a paralysed man, apart from a connecting 'and' between 'rise' and 'take up' (Mark 2.9, though cf. also 2.11, where in a slightly different formulation the 'and' is omitted between the two imperatives). The healing is instantaneous and is demonstrated through the man's obedience in taking up his mat and walking, as he had been instructed.

9b–10 Only now does the narrator insert the ominous temporal note – **Now that day was a sabbath.** He will use the same technique of mentioning the sabbath setting after the miracle has occurred when he tells of the man born blind receiving his sight (cf. 9.14). Readers are prepared for the controversy that will inevitably follow, as it does in the Synoptic accounts of sabbath healings (cf. Mark 3.1–6 parr.; Luke 13.10–17). The element of conflict is introduced immediately. Jesus is not, however, initially involved, since he has disappeared from the scene. It is the man who has been healed who is accused of sabbath infringement (cf. also 9.15): **The Jews therefore said to the man who had been healed, 'It is the sabbath and it is not lawful for you to carry your mat.'** This is the second time that the term 'the Jews' has been used for the opposition to Jesus' mission in this narrative (cf. 2.18). Again it should be remembered that it cannot refer to all Jewish people, since both the man who has been healed and Jesus, his healer, are also Jews. The negative reference is primarily to the religious authorities who oppose Jesus, as here, though that reference can be broadened so that such opponents and other Jews who resist Jesus' claims become representative of the unbelieving world. Violation of sabbath law was a serious matter and in fact the Torah attached the death penalty to it (Exod. 31.14, 15; cf. also Num. 15.32–6). Carrying a mat or small mattress would have been seen as constituting work. This sort of carrying was classified as work in the later Mishnah (cf. *m. Sabb.* 7.2) and there was earlier precedent for this ruling in Jer. 17.21–2. The saving of life could take precedence over sabbath law but that is not involved here, and since the account gives no reason why the healing could not have waited until the next day, it may well be that the evangelist is suggesting that Jesus' initiative was meant to provoke debate about contemporary sabbath legislation.

11–13 In response to the confrontation from 'the Jews', the healed man quite naturally passes responsibility for his action onto the one who gave him instructions to carry his mat – **The man who made me well said to me, 'Take up your mat and walk.'** Ignoring his extraordinary claim to have been healed, the man's interlocutors concentrate their attention on the perpetrator of the sabbath infringement and ask the identity of the one who gave the command to carry the mat and walk. At this stage the man is ignorant of the identity of his healer, since he had not bothered to ask and **Jesus had slipped away** in the crowd. Readers are left to assume that the Jewish authorities leave the healed man alone in the hope of catching up with his sabbath-breaking healer.

14 As he has done throughout the incident, in which the healing required no request and no recognition of him, Jesus takes the initiative in seeking out the man (cf. also 9.35). Finding him in the temple area, Jesus tells him, **See, you have become well; do not sin any more lest something worse happen to you.** Later, in the case of the blind man, the evangelist will have Jesus subvert the axiom that disease can always be traced directly to a person's sin (cf. 9.3). Some commentators want to keep coherence within the Gospel by claiming that here also the statement does not reflect on the man's past but is simply a warning about future sin. It is hard, however, to avoid the implications of 'any more' and 'something worse', which suggest fairly clearly that there is some connection between past sin and the illness. Significantly, healing from paralysis and forgiveness of sins are also connected in Mark 2.1–12, the Synoptic account with which this passage has most in common. As an aside, it might also be mentioned that a sense of guilt producing paralysis is a phenomenon not unknown in the present day. This interpretation need not be seen as destroying coherence with John 9. A connection between particular sins and a disease is not accepted as a general rule but it is not excluded in specific cases. But what is meant by 'something worse'? It does not seem likely that the man is being threatened with a worse physical disease, something more debilitating than thirty-eight years of immobility. It is possible that physical death is in view but more probable that the eternal consequences of sinning are being raised. After all, in the immediately ensuing discourse Jesus will be presented as exercising the divine prerogatives of both giving life and judging (vv. 21–4). In this way the significance of the sign is being hinted at. Physical healing points to the eternal life Jesus offers but continuing to sin in the face of that offer leads to condemnation.

15 The man went away and told the Jews that it was Jesus who had made him well. It is not made clear within the account how this time the particular words Jesus speaks to the man enable him to know the speaker is Jesus when just a moment earlier Jesus' words to him had left him ignorant of the speaker's identity. Because the account is so brief, interpreters also debate how the man's action of going to 'the Jews' should be evaluated. Some insist that it should not be assumed that it entails cowardice, ingratitude or betrayal and argue for a positive evaluation by pointing out that the verb employed here – 'told' or 'announced' – is found elsewhere in positive contexts (cf. 4.25; 16.13–15) and that the man does not announce that Jesus instructed him to take up his mat but emphasizes that Jesus made him well. But this argument appears somewhat disingenuous. The force of a term depends on its context and whether this particular context is positive or negative is precisely what is debated. More importantly, the dialogue of vv. 11–12 has made clear that the man's declaration to the authorities that Jesus made him well could not be an innocent announcement, because they have already let him know that that is exactly the information they need in order to determine the identity of the one who issued a command that violated the sabbath. Taken in context, then, it is hard to evaluate the man's action in any other way than negatively. But at no stage of the story has the narrator been interested in the man's motivations in relation to Jesus and that does not change here. The main purpose of the narrator's statement is to strengthen the connection between the miracle story and a direct confrontation between Jesus and 'the Jews'.

16–17 The healed man's action of identifying Jesus as the sabbath-breaker provides an explanation for the conflict between Jesus and his opponents, which is formulated in a much more general way, moving beyond this specific incident – **For this reason the Jews were persecuting Jesus because he was doing these things on the sabbath.** What has occurred in this sign is fitted into a broader pattern of similar sabbath actions on the part of Jesus and a hostile response to these on the part of the Jewish authorities. The term translated as 'persecuting' can also have the force of 'prosecuting' and, given the pervasiveness of legal motifs in the defence speech of Jesus which follows in 5.19–47, the forensic connotations attached to the opposition's hostility may well be in view here.

But Jesus answered them, 'My Father is working until now and I also am working.' The where and when of Jesus' response to his critics is not specified. His saying is simply given a general setting in sabbath conflicts. The answer to the implicit accusation that he is working on the sabbath is a plain acknowledgement that this is so. There is no attempted defence in terms of precedents from Torah, traditional practice or other legal arguments, as in the Synoptics (cf. Mark 2.25–6; 4.4; Luke 13.15; 14.5) or later in this Gospel (7.22–3). Instead the response is in terms characteristic of the Johannine Jesus. He claims that in this, as in all he does, he is only imitating his Father. The statement that his Father works is to be seen in the context of Jewish thinking about God's activity, where there was discussion whether God could be said to be working if God rested after the creation and whether, if God did work, such divine activity was broken off on the weekly sabbath (cf. Philo, *Cher.* 86–90; *Leg.* 1.5–6). The general view was that God continued to be active in sustaining the creation and as life-giver and judge. God rested from initial work on the world but not from God's work with humanity and in this was not bound by the sabbath. It will be precisely in terms of these beliefs about God that Jesus' work is explicated in vv. 19–30. His work entails the accomplishment of the judgement of the end time in both its positive and negative aspects. As elsewhere in the narrative (cf. 4.34; 9.3; 17.4), Jesus' work is inseparably bound up with the Father's work and stands for his mission as a whole, and to this the requirements of sabbath law must yield. Also characteristic of the Fourth Gospel's presentation of this work is the temporal note sounded by the phrase 'until now', which suggests that the continuing activity in view will come to an end. Jesus' work or mission is according to a divine timetable (cf. the references to his 'time' or his 'hour'), and that work will be completed in the glorification of his death (cf. 4.34; 17.4; 19.30). In terms of the narrative as a whole there is an eschatological implication. Sabbath rest, with its cessation from work, was one of the images employed in Judaism for the life of the end times. If Jesus' work of judgement and salvation will be completed at his glorification, it is at that point also that the rest, to which the sabbath points, is accomplished.

18 Jesus' linking of his work to that of his Father gives rise to a further charge, which is not explicitly made, but is embedded in the reason given by the narrator for 'the Jews' seeking to kill Jesus – **because he not only broke the sabbath but was also calling God his own Father, making himself equal to God**. Such a formulation of the issue clearly comes from later disputes between the synagogue and Christians over the latter's Christological claims. As will become clear from the defence in vv. 19–47, the Christians' response to this further charge would have involved both an acknowledgement and a denial. The nature of Jesus' relationship to God as Son to Father was such that he was equal to God but he did not make himself equal, since this was a status conferred on him within the relationship. It is also noteworthy that 'the Jews' are portrayed now as not only persecuting Jesus (v. 16) but as **seeking all the more to kill him**. In this way the opposition is depicted as having already determined the verdict in this controversy or trial at its outset. A similar point about the intentions of the Jewish authorities is made after a sabbath healing early in Mark's narrative (Mark 3.6).

The mention of Mark's narrative raises questions about the relation between John's story and the Synoptics and whether John's story is based on independent tradition or rather constitutes another example of the evangelist's creative reworking of material found in a different form in the Synoptics. On one side of the debate, some scholars are impressed by the specificity and accuracy of the topographical setting for the miracle in John and by the significant differences in detail between this account and its closest Synoptic parallel in Mark 2.1–12. They also point to the ambivalent responses of the man involved as unlikely to have been made up and to the probable addition of the sabbath issue to a story which originally lacked this topic. On these grounds they hold that the miracle story itself represents a distinct tradition and one which may reflect some historical incident in Jesus' Jerusalem ministry. On the other side of the debate, the significant correspondences with Mark 2.1–12 can be pointed out. Both involve a man who is in some way paralysed and requires the help of others. In both some connection is made by Jesus between sin and the healing (cf. Mark 2.5, 9–11 and John 5.14). In both the command to rise, take up the mat and walk is given in precisely the same words (cf. Mark 2.9, 11 and John 5.8). It is not sufficient to say that similar circumstances would lead one to expect this coincidence. Matthew's and Luke's variations on the Markan wording indicate that this is not the case. Both Mark and John emphasize the immediacy of the man's response and healing (cf. Mark 2.12 and John 5.9a). Both accounts give rise to a charge of blasphemy (cf. Mark 2.7 and John 5.18). These similarities suggest that at least John was familiar with the Markan account and was influenced by its formulations in the telling of his own miracle story. If, however, one also brings into play the next miracle story in Mark, that of 3.1–6, then the correspondences between Mark and John increase. Mark 3.1–6 depicts a sabbath healing and accompanying controversy. The healing is of a paralysed limb and as a direct consequence of it the opposition (here a combination of Pharisees and Herodians) plot to kill Jesus. It can be argued that the combination of the two Markan miracles provides all the major building blocks for John's story. On this view, it becomes significant that, while the mat is essential to the telling of the Mark 2.12 account, it does not fit as smoothly into John's story despite its centrality. Readers have to assume that the man kept one permanently by the pool, had someone to move it around for him, although he had no one to help him move to the pool, and that it was necessary for him to carry it away after the healing. These minor difficulties simply do not arise from the Markan story. The evangelist then would have woven elements from the two Markan miracles into his own sign narrative, to which he lends verisimilitude by supplying a Jerusalem setting at a well-known healing sanctuary. The resulting story has all the marks of John's literary style and theological motifs. It corresponds in a number of structural elements to the story of the man born blind in chapter 9. The sabbath setting is brought in after the miracle has been recounted. Jesus disappears from the scene while the man is interrogated by 'the Jews'. They cast aspersions on his healer for performing the healing on the sabbath. Jesus later finds the man and is then himself drawn into an exchange with the Jewish authorities. Other characteristic Johannine motifs in the story are its stress on Jesus' sovereign initiative, the portrayal of Jesus as having special knowledge, the man's misunderstanding, the designation of the opposition as 'the Jews', the depiction of Jesus' mission as work and the focus on the implications of Jesus' relation to God in terms of Father and Son. How one assesses the debate over this particular story is likely to depend on whether one is persuaded by other instances that John creatively adapts Synoptic material and on the extent of the creativity one is willing to attribute to him. While the case for this here is reasonably strong, it cannot be proven. To accept it, it should be added, does not necessarily entail any denial of the general historicity of the tradition that Jesus performed healing miracles involving those who were paralysed or lame, and Mark 2.1–12 and the Q saying about the lame walking (cf. Matt. 11.5/Luke 7.22) provide evidence for this sort of miracle being firmly embedded in the earliest tradition.

As do the two Cana signs, this third sign points to Jesus as the giver of life. Jesus' words to the man, 'See, you have become well', and the repetition of the Greek term for 'well' or 'whole' (ὑγιής) underline this. Indeed all six uses of this term in the Fourth Gospel are with reference to this man – one later in 7.23 and five here (vv. 6, 9, 11, 14, 15). The giving of health and wholeness on the physical level points beyond itself to the offer of eternal life. This significance of the miracle is reinforced in two further ways. The man's illness – a paralysis or lameness of the limbs – was associated with death in the ancient world. On some understandings of the body, paralysis was held to entail a loosening of the sinews which nurtured the bones and marrow, containing the soul (cf. Dioscorides 3.78). Loose sinews therefore signalled that the soul was ready to depart. And not only was this so, but withered limbs were also held to be dead already (cf. Aretaeus, *Sign. diut.* 1.7.2). The command to arise (cf. v. 9), addressed to a man whose body was under the threat of death, now takes on connotations which go beyond getting to his feet (cf. 5.21). The warning of something worse happening to the man if he continues to sin also suggests that the eschatological consequences of either life or condemnation are at stake here.

Jesus' offer of life takes on added force from both the spatial and temporal settings of this sign. It takes place at a healing sanctuary where the waters are believed to have therapeutic powers. In the Graeco-Roman world such sites were linked with the major god of healing, Asclepius, and frequently the reports of miracles on the inscriptions from the Asclepius sanctuary at Epidaurus end with the formulation 'and from that moment he became well' (ὑγιὴς ἐγένετο). As noted earlier, this Jerusalem site in particular was later explicitly dedicated to Asclepius. Whether or not there was any association of the pool with Asclepius a little earlier, Jesus' healing at this sanctuary implicitly stakes a claim over against any rival ones for Asclepius, just as his turning of water into wine is to be seen in the light of the claims made for Dionysus. Jesus' superiority is demonstrated by healing the man simply through the power of his command, without the need to be petitioned or to use any powers in the waters or to resort to formulaic invocations. The sign also occurs on the sabbath and provokes controversy with 'the Jews'. In this context the claim is made that Jesus' healing activity is part of the work of his mission and in that mission he is simply doing the continuing work of his Father in giving life and judging. Jesus' provision of life thus takes precedence over the requirements of sabbath legislation. The implied claim about Jesus' relation to God is seized on by the opposition and will be the focus of attention in the discourse that follows.

*(ii) Jesus' discourse on his relation to the Father, judgement
and testimony* 5.19–47

(19) Jesus answered them, 'Truly, truly, I say to you, the Son is able to do nothing by himself, only what he sees the Father doing; for whatever the Father does, the Son likewise does. (20) For the Father loves the Son and shows him everything that he himself does, and he will show him greater works than these so

that you may be amazed. (21) For just as the Father raises the dead and gives them life, so also the Son gives life to whomever he wishes. (22) For the Father judges no one, but has given all judgement to the Son, (23) in order that all may honour the Son just as they honour the Father. The person who does not honour the Son does not honour the Father who sent him. (24) Truly, truly, I say to you, whoever hears my word and believes the one who sent me has eternal life, and does not come under condemnation, but has passed from death to life.

(25) 'Truly, truly, I say to you, that the hour is coming and is now here when the dead will hear the voice of the Son of God and those who hear will live. (26) For just as the Father has life in himself, so also he has granted the Son to have life in himself, (27) and has given him authority to exercise judgement, because he is the Son of Man. (28) Do not be amazed at this, for the hour is coming at which all who are in their graves will hear his voice (29) and will come out, those who have done good to the resurrection of life, and those who have done evil to the resurrection of condemnation. (30) I am able to do nothing by myself; I judge as I hear, and my judgement is just, because I do not seek my own will but the will of him who sent me.

(31) 'If I witness about myself, my testimony is not true. (32) There is another who witnesses about me, and I know that the testimony he gives about me is true. (33) You sent messengers to John, and he has borne witness to the truth. (34) I do not accept witness from a human, but I say these things to you so that you may be saved. (35) He was a burning and shining lamp, and for a while you were willing to rejoice in his light. (36) But I have a testimony greater than John's; the works that the Father has given me to complete, the very works that I am doing, witness about me that the Father has sent me. (37) And this Father who sent me has borne witness about me. You have never heard his voice or seen his form, (38) and you do not have his word remaining in you, because you do not believe the one he has sent. (39) You search the Scriptures, because you think that in them you have eternal life, and it is they that witness about me. (40) Yet you are not willing to come to me to have life.

(41) 'I do not accept glory from humans, (42) but I know you and know that you do not have the love of God in you. (43) I have come in my Father's name and you do not receive me; if another comes in his own name, you will receive him. (44) How can you believe when you receive glory from one another and do not seek the glory that comes from the only God? (45) Do not think that I will accuse you before the Father; the one who

**accuses you is Moses, on whom you have set your hope. (46) For
if you believed Moses, you would believe me, because he wrote
about me. (47) If you do not believe his writings, how will you
believe my words?'**

Jesus' extended discourse in this section is a response to the hostile Jewish
authorities who have just been described as persecuting Jesus and as
intent on killing him (cf. vv. 16, 18). The frequency of the occurrence of
key forensic terms suggests that it can be seen as a defence in an interrogation or trial. 'To judge' (κρίνω) occurs twice (vv. 22, 30), 'judgement'
(κρίσις) is found five times (vv. 22, 24, 27, 29, 30), 'to witness' (μαρτυρέω)
is employed seven times (vv. 31, 32, 33, 36, 37, 39) and 'testimony'
(μαρτυρία) is used four times (vv. 31, 32, 34, 36). The discourse begins as
a defence against the charges that Jesus has broken the sabbath and that in
calling God his Father he has made himself equal with God (vv. 16–18).
In the first part (vv. 19–30) it is made clear that the one who is giving
witness in his own defence is in fact the judge, while in the second part
(vv. 31–47) his witness is shown to conform to the laws of testimony and
then the tables are turned so that the accusers become the accused.

19–20 Jesus introduces his self-defence with the words of solemn oath,
'Amen, amen,' and responds to the charges made by spelling out his
relationship with the Father. What the defence will amount to is that his
activities show that he and his Father are one (and therefore, in terms of
the charge in v. 18, equal), but that this relationship is not one that he
has made for himself but rather one that derives from the intimacy that
already exists between himself as the Son and the Father – **the Father
loves the Son and shows him everything that he himself does**.
These verses stress Jesus' dependence on the Father – **the Son is able
to do nothing by himself** – yet this is in order to assert not so much
his subordination to the Father, though this is assumed, but the complete
unity of his actions with those of the Father – **whatever the Father
does, the Son likewise does**. This constitutes an elaboration of Jesus'
earlier response in v. 17. He could say that his Father was working until
now and that he was working, because as the Son he is simply doing what
he sees his Father doing. The suggestion that behind this formulation
lies a proverb about an apprentice son has some plausibility. Just as the
apprentice son watches and then repeats the work of his father, a skilled
artisan, so in this Christological adaptation Jesus claims that in his works,
such as the healing on the sabbath, he is only imitating what he sees his
Father doing. If his accusers have been surprised by the claims he has
made in regard to such a work, there is, he asserts, further cause for astonishment, because the Father out of his love for the Son **will show him
greater works than these so that you may be amazed**. Since the

greater works will turn out to be the activities involved in judging with its outcomes of the giving of life or condemnation (cf. vv. 21–30), those who have brought charges against Jesus should be amazed because they are in fact facing one who is not simply the accused but the judge.

21 Jesus' claim starts from the traditional expectation of God's end-time activity in the resurrection – **just as the Father raises the dead and gives them life** – and asserts that this giving of eschatological life is also the Son's activity in imitation of his Father and that it is taking place already ahead of time through his sovereign authority – **so also the Son gives life to whomever he wishes**.

22–3 Jesus' giving of life is then set in its context in the whole process of judgement, in which it constitutes the positive verdict. The terms 'to judge' and 'judgment' here are neutral in force. The Son's role in judgement is expressed in the strongest terms. It is no longer a case of copying what he sees the Father doing. Instead **the Father judges no one, but has given all judgement to the Son**. This also underscores that Jesus' status and relation to the Father are not the result of his usurpation but of the Father's bestowal. His relation to the Father is expressed in a different form in the purpose clause – **in order that all may honour the Son just as they honour the Father**. By giving the Son responsibility for judgement, the Father can be seen as vindicating the Son's reputation and reversing the shame that would have been attached to his being accused and condemned by the authorities. Indeed, the role of the Son as the fully authorized representative of the one who has sent him means that **The person who does not honour the Son does not honour the Father who sent him.** Since giving honour or glory to God is equivalent to recognizing God as God (cf. e.g. Rom. 1.21; 1 Tim. 1.17; Rev. 4.9, 11), this amounts to a very strong claim on Jesus' behalf about his oneness with God.

24 This oneness is underlined, as the Son's judging activity is given a present focus. The notions that on one's response to the Son depends the verdict of either life or condemnation and that this verdict is experienced already in this life have been set out earlier in 3.16–19. But in their repetition here the proper response is formulated not simply in terms of believing in the Son but as **whoever hears my word and believes the one who sent me**. Again, therefore, Jesus' word is so completely at one with God's that to accept the former is at the same time to accept the one who has commissioned its speaker. The one who responds in this way **has eternal life, and does not come under condemnation, but has passed from death to life**. The result for such a person is therefore the intended outcome of the judgement process – moving from the negative experience of being under the condemnation of death to the positive experience of the verdict that bestows life.

25 The conviction that a realized eschatology of judgement is taking place through the activity of the Son is repeated – **the hour is coming and is now here** – with the emphasis in what follows on the latter clause, so that in the present those who will **hear the voice of the Son of God** and experience life are the spiritually dead.

26–7 The emphasis that **the Father has granted the Son to have life in himself, and has given him authority to exercise judgement** functions as a further response to the charge of v. 18 that Jesus was making himself equal to God. Because of his relation to the Father, like the Father, Jesus himself is the possessor and giver of life. The depiction of Jesus moves from Son of God in v. 25 to Son in v. 26 and then to Son of Man in v. 27, indicating that, whatever the different nuances of meaning they convey, these titles function as virtual equivalents in the narrative. The authority to judge is associated with the last title here – **because he is the Son of Man** – and this association is not surprising, since one of the three main contexts of Son of Man sayings in the Synoptic tradition is that of the final judgement. What is somewhat surprising is that in the Greek this is the only instance in all four Gospels of the application of 'the Son of Man' to Jesus that omits the usual definite article before both 'Son' and 'Man' (where the second article normally makes this phrase an awkward one). This may well suggest that the origin of the title in Dan. 7.13 LXX, where the phrase 'one like a son of man' also has neither definite article, is more directly in view here. The title 'the Son of God', on which the Greek formulation for 'the Son of Man' may well have been modelled, also normally has an article before both terms, but again there is one instance in John where the definite articles are omitted (19.7; but cf. also Mark 1.1; 15.39; Luke 1.35; Rom. 1.4).

28–9 Jesus' claim to exercise the divine prerogative in judgement is not only made in regard to the present stage of the process but holds for its final stage also. There is no need to assign this material to a later redactor who needed to accommodate the text to early Christian tradition. Despite the narrative's stress on the realized aspect of judgement, there is no incompatibility in its retaining the future final aspect of traditional expectations about the judgement associated with the resurrection of the dead. Here **the hour is coming** stands alone without the accompanying 'and is now here' of v. 25. At that hour it will be the voice of the Son of God (cf. v. 25) or the Son of Man (cf. v. 27) that the physically dead will hear and their resurrection will be either to a verdict of life or to a verdict of condemnation. Just as in 3.19–21, where the judgement provoked in the present by the coming of Christ exposes people's deeds in their true light, so here this final judgement will again be on the basis of people's deeds – whether they have done good or evil. The final verdict functions as a full and visible exhibition of the present verdict. If justice has to be seen to have been done, its public and open demonstration remains important; hence no doubt the notion, found in Dan. 12.2 and familiar in the thought of second temple Judaism, of a resurrection even for condemnation. The mention of Jesus' voice as the agent of resurrection anticipates in the narrative sequence his cry 'with a loud voice' outside Lazarus' tomb resulting in the appearance of Lazarus still wrapped in his grave-clothes (11.43–4), and this in turn anticipates the eschatological resurrection of which this discourse speaks.

30 The first part of Jesus' defence speech ends on an *inclusio* which stresses his dependence on his Father in a similar fashion to his first words – **I am able to do nothing by myself** (cf. v. 19). This time the notion of dependence supports what has become the main claim in his defence, namely, that he is in fact his accusers' judge. Just as his perspective on the deeds that provoked the charge was that they were done in imitation of what he saw the Father doing (v. 19), now his view of his judging is that it is in imitation of what he hears the Father saying – **I judge as I hear**. Such judgement can be said to be **just, because I do not seek my own will but the will of him who sent me**. His will is so fully dependent on, and therefore identified with, the will of the one who has sent him that his judgement is bound to be just – it is God's judgement.

31–2 On the basis of the first part of this trial scene, it could be alleged that Jesus was appearing as the sole witness in his own defence. In terms of Jewish legal conventions this would of course make his testimony invalid. It is in this sense that Jesus' words – **If I witness about myself, my testimony is not true** – are to be understood. Deut. 19.15 rules that three, or at least two, witnesses are needed for valid testimony. For this reason Jesus claims that **There is another who witnesses about me, and I know that the testimony he gives about me is true**. It is not immediately clear to whom he is referring. He will go on to mention a number of types of witness – John the Baptist (vv. 33–5), his own works (v. 36), the Father himself (vv. 37–8), and the Scriptures (vv. 39–40). But these four do not have the same status as witness, and by vv. 36–7 it becomes apparent that the other witness is in all probability the Father (cf. also 8.17–18, where the two witnesses required are Jesus and the Father). Jesus' works, which are given him by the Father, and the Scriptures, which are the Father's word, can then both be seen as the visible aspects of the Father's testimony. Although in this way the requirement for two witnesses is fulfilled, this would not, of course, have actually satisfied the law, where an appeal to a divine witness was not in view.

33–5 This divine testimony is contrasted to the human testimony of the Baptist. Jesus does not directly appeal to this testimony but reminds his accusers that they had instigated the interrogation of John (cf. 1.19) and thereby had provided themselves with a further testimony, because **he has borne witness to the truth**. Having recalled the witness that the opposition has already heard, Jesus then makes clear that this is not the other witness to whom he has referred – **I do not accept witness from a human, but I say these things to you so that you may be saved.** He has only mentioned John's witness by way of concession, to accommodate to the need for human salvation. The thought is that Jesus' relationship with the Father is such that his testimony is really self-authenticating, but, in the same way as the narrative as a whole has John as its first witness, he enlists human witnesses in conformity to human legal conventions so that all means will be employed to enable people to experience the intended outcome of the judgement process and be saved. Indeed John's testimony appeared to have served that purpose – **for a while you were willing to rejoice in his light**. But it is also made clear that John's witness was not the light itself but a derivative brightness. He is described as **a burning and shining lamp** that helps to disseminate the light, reminding readers of the language of the prologue – 'he was not himself the light, but came in order that he might testify about the light' (1.8).

36 The other testimony to which Jesus is willing to appeal is **greater than John's**. It is the testimony of the Father himself (vv. 36–40), and in the first instance this witness consists of **the works that the Father has given me to complete, the very works that I am doing**, works such as the healing of vv. 1–9 which had provoked this particular controversy in the first place. The signs Jesus does are included in the testimony of his works and are properly understood when they are seen as bearing witness to the divine origin of Jesus' mission, to his commissioning as the Father's representative. Their witness about him is **that the Father has sent me**. Jesus will repeat the emphasis on the witness of his works in 10.25 and will then point out in 15.24 that they also play a condemnatory role for those who do not believe.

37–8 And this Father who sent me has borne witness about me. The main clause employs the perfect tense of the verb, indicating that this witness has taken place in the past but has continuing significance. To what, in addition to the works given to Jesus, does this witness refer? The answer becomes clear through the charges Jesus now makes. His accusers would claim that God had provided such testimony, if anywhere, in revealing the law and in its inscripturation. This was when Israel had heard God's voice (cf. e.g. Exod. 19.9; Deut. 4.33; Sir. 17.13) and had seen God (cf. e.g. Exod. 19.11; Deut. 5.4; Sir. 17.13), and Torah was God's word

that remained in their hearts (cf. e.g. Deut. 6.6; 30.14; Ps. 119.11, 34). At
the same time, however, Deut. 4.12,15–18 could also say that Israel had
not seen God's form. But whatever his accusers' claims in regard to this
revelation, Jesus asserts that none of them are true – **You have never
heard his voice or seen his form, and you do not have his word
remaining in you.** The first part of his accusation echoes that of Yahweh
against Israel in Isa. 48.8 ('you have never heard'), and the reason given for
the charges is **you do not believe the one he has sent.** As the Father's
commissioned representative, Jesus is now the repository of God's self-
revelation. As the narrative as a whole makes clear, hearing God's voice,
seeing God and having God's word remain in one are all now associated
with Jesus (cf. e.g. 3.34; 14.9; 15.7).

39–40 The Scriptures constitute the Father's continuing witness, but,
from Jesus' perspective, because they **are not willing to come to me to
have life**, his Jewish opponents fail to see that these Scriptures **witness
about me.** Jesus recognizes that **You search the Scriptures, because
you think that in them you have eternal life**, but he holds such study
to be in vain when it refuses the hermeneutical key provided by God's
present revelation in him and thereby misses out on the verdict of life
which he as judge now renders (cf. vv. 21, 24).

41–4 The clash between Jesus and his accusers is presented as a clash of
perspectives about glory, a topic that had surfaced briefly earlier in the
mention of honour in v. 23. There is also a connection with Jesus' earlier
statement in v. 34. There Jesus had said that he does not accept human
testimony, while here he says, **I do not accept glory from humans.**
To accept the testimony of another about oneself is to be dependent on
the opinion of another for one's reputation or honour. Human honour
or glory is precisely the reputation one has in the eyes of others, and in
refusing such usual human evaluation Jesus is calling into question this
basic cultural value. Because of his relationship with the Father, the only
testimony other than his own that Jesus would accept was that of the
Father. In the same way the only glory he will accept is that which the
Father gives him in vindicating his claims (cf. also 7.18; 8.50; 17.1, 5, 24).
In the context of this discussion, the charge Jesus lays against his accusers
is **you do not have the love of God in you.** If they had, they too
would seek God's glory above all else. Instead they remain on the merely
human level of concern about their honour and reputation in the eyes of
each other – **you receive glory from one another.** Jesus charges that
because they are caught up in the human system of assessing reputation,
if another comes in his own name, you will receive him. Such
a person is dependent on human testimony and thereby colludes with
the system. This system of human glory prevents the opposition from

accepting Jesus – **I have come in my Father's name and you do not receive me**. As the tables begin to be turned and the defendant becomes the prosecutor, the whole criterion for his accusers' judgement is indicated. They purport to be accusing Jesus out of a concern for the reputation of the only God, which they see threatened by Jesus' claims, and they interpret these claims as an attempt by Jesus to make himself equal with the one God. But Jesus' defence questions their deepest motivations and loyalty. If they were truly concerned about **the glory that comes from the only God** rather than human glory, they would believe in the one whose coming in the Father's name and whose total dependence on the Father demonstrate that he seeks only the Father's glory.

45–7 The turning of the tables is now taken further: **Do not think that I will accuse you before the Father; the one who accuses you is Moses, on whom you have set your hope.** Jesus will not need to serve as accuser of his opponents. Contrary to all expectations, Moses has that role. The one on whom they have set their hope, as demonstrated in their observance of the law, the one whose disciples they will later claim to be (cf. 9.28), turns out to be the accusing counsel (ὁ κατηγορῶν) rather than the defending counsel (ὁ παράκλητος). Both Greek terms had specific legal connotations and also became loan words in Hebrew juridical usage. Moses was viewed as Israel's great defender, intercessor and advocate (cf. e.g. *Jub.* 1.20–1; *Test. Mos.* 11.17). But here, in an ironic role reversal, Moses becomes the counsel for the prosecution. The controversy had been fuelled by 'the Jews' using Moses as an accuser against Jesus, charging that he had broken the sabbath law (cf. vv. 10, 16). It finishes with Jesus using Moses as an accuser against unbelieving Jews. And Jesus' presupposition for this latter use of Moses is that **he wrote about me**. This is a point of view that pervades the narrative – that Jesus is the fulfilment of everything in the law, a view that shades over into Jesus being the replacement of everything in the law. The reason for the unbelief of Jesus' opponents can now be portrayed, despite their own avowals, as a lack of true belief in Moses – **if you believed Moses, you would believe me**. The formulation of the final question not simply in terms of Moses but also in terms of his writings – **If you do not believe his writings, how will you believe my words?** – links the final element of Jesus' defence with the main thrust of its second part – the Father's witness to Jesus in Scripture. The writings of Moses, like the rest of the Scriptures (cf. v. 39), testify about Jesus. The narrative will provide its own extended illustration of just how they do so in the immediately following chapter with its discourse on the bread of life that is at the same time a midrashic treatment of Exod. 16 (cf. 6.25–59).

Through this discourse the claims of the evangelist and his community about the relationship of Jesus to God, claims that caused so much dispute with the synagogue, are linked with the controversy of Jesus' healing on the sabbath and framed in terms of a trial scene in which Jesus is at one with and fully represents God the judge. The issues are who is to be the judge of such claims and what are the criteria of judgement. The point of view of this Gospel's narrative emerges through the device of a defence speech in which the defendant is shown to be the judge who at the same time calls for a re-evaluation of the traditional criteria for judgement. For the Fourth Gospel what makes the difference is whether one starts with Jesus and his relationship to God or insists on one's own categories – Moses, Scripture, human glory and human conventions about testimony. Jesus himself has to become the criterion of judgement to which these other categories are subordinated and by which they are transformed. In the light of the divine testimony merely human assessment is to be rejected, but the earlier witness of the Scriptures and of Moses remains significant as long as both are interpreted in terms of God's present and decisive witness in Jesus.

(iii) THE FEEDING OF THE FIVE THOUSAND   6.1–15

(1) After this Jesus went across the Sea of Galilee, or of Tiberias.[1] (2) A great crowd followed him, because they saw the signs he was doing for the sick. (3) Jesus went up the mountain and sat down there with his disciples. (4) Now the Passover, the festival of the Jews, was near. (5) When Jesus looked up and saw that a great crowd was coming towards him, he said to Philip, 'Where are we to buy bread so that these people may eat?' (6) He said this to test him, because he himself knew what he was going to do. (7) Philip answered him, 'Two hundred denarii worth of bread would not be enough for each of them to have a little.' (8) One of his disciples, Andrew, the brother of Simon Peter, said to him, (9) 'There is a boy here who has five barley loaves and two fish. But what are they for so many?' (10) Jesus said, 'Make the people sit down.' Now there was a great deal of grass in the place, so the men sat down, about five thousand in number. (11) Then Jesus took the loaves, and having given thanks, he distributed them to those who were sitting, so also the fish, as much as they wanted. (12) When they had had their fill, he said to his disciples, 'Gather up the pieces left over, so that nothing is lost.' (13) So they gathered them up, and they filled twelve baskets from the pieces of the five barley loaves which those who

---

[1] The most difficult but also best-attested reading has two successive genitives for the name of the sea – 'of Galilee of Tiberias'. Variants have attempted to deal with the difficulty either by omitting 'of Galilee' or by inserting between the genitives an 'and' or the phrase 'to the regions of'. The translation adopted here deals with the awkwardness by inserting an 'or'. The alternative name for the sea will be found later in 21.1.

had eaten had left over. (14) When the people saw the sign he had done, they said, 'This is truly the prophet who is to come into the world.' (15) Since Jesus knew that they were about to come and seize him in order to make him king, he withdrew again to the mountain by himself.

The abrupt change of setting from Jerusalem to crossing the Sea of Galilee has led many to suggest that this new episode would most naturally follow on from the end of chapter 4 and that the sequence of episodes in the narrative must have become disarranged in the course of transmission. On this basis some have transposed the chapter order for purposes of their analysis. There is, however, no actual textual evidence for a different order and this view may well be over-concerned with geographical issues at the expense of thematic links. Whether or not 6.1 was originally linked with some other passage in an earlier edition of the Gospel, it makes excellent sense that the evangelist has placed the self-contained unit of 6.1–71 where he has. As will be seen, it illustrates superbly Jesus' claim in the last part of the previous chapter (5.39, 46–7) that the scriptures bear witness to him and that Moses wrote about him, because the bulk of the discourse consists in a Christological exposition of a scriptural passage from the Pentateuch, namely Exod. 16. In addition, the mention of healings in 6.2 may well presuppose the two previous healing miracles in 4.46–54 and 5.1–18, and it can be claimed that the narrator has already prepared readers for swift moves between Jerusalem and Galilee in 2.12–13 and 4.54.

The healing of the lame man had provided a platform for the discourse that followed, in which Jesus elaborated his defence of this activity on the sabbath in exchange with 'the Jews'. This chapter will follow a similar pattern. The feeding miracle will give rise to the discourse on the bread of life, which will again be conducted in exchanges with those who are designated as 'the Jews' (cf vv. 41, 52). The passage containing the feeding story falls into two parts. There is an extended introduction in vv. 1–4, which is followed by the account of the sign in vv. 5–15. The latter follows the pattern already noted for miracle stories with descriptions of the situation of need (vv. 5–9), of the miraculous act (vv. 10–11) and of the confirmation of and response to the act (vv. 12–15).

1–4 The introductory verses open with a spatial marker. The action that follows takes place in the vicinity of **the Sea of Galilee**. After crossing the sea, Jesus is followed by a crowd **because they saw the signs he was doing for the sick**. In fact, the narrative has only depicted one sign for the sick in Galilee so far, the healing of the official's son in 4.46–54. But there the Galileans have just been depicted as also having been in Jerusalem and seen what Jesus did there (cf. 4.45). No doubt readers are therefore also meant to recall both the Jerusalem healing in 5.1–18 and the mention of the Jerusalem signs in 2.23–5. The latter passage reminds them that seeing the signs is important but needs to lead on to genuine faith, and prepares them for the depiction of the crowd's response later in vv. 15, 26, 30. The other major figures in the feeding and what follows are **the disciples** and they are mentioned next as being with Jesus when he **went up the mountain and sat down there**. The mountain will be referred to again in v. 15 when Jesus withdraws to it, but the narrative fails to indicate prior to this that Jesus and the disciples have come down from it. The inclusion of the mountain in the account may well be intended to invoke the scriptural significance of mountains as loci of revelation. In particular, Moses on the mountain represents the giving of Torah, which could be compared to bread (cf. Deut. 8.3). Now Jesus is on the mountain and will provide bread, through which he will be revealed as the bread of life which fulfils all that Torah represented. The narrator then inserts a temporal note – **now the Passover, the festival of the Jews, was near** – which interrupts the sequential flow. In its more extended chronology of Jesus' ministry this Gospel has three Passovers (2.13; 6.4; and the final one from 11.55 onwards). Like the mention of the mountain, the reference here draws attention to scriptural and Mosaic themes. The Passover is a particularly appropriate setting for the exposition of the exodus events that will follow in Jesus' discourse and for the eucharistic motifs that emerge at its end, since the eucharist was instituted at a meal which, if not itself a Passover meal, was associated from the earliest times with the Passover.

5–7 Instead of the disciples at the end of the day asking Jesus what to do because the crowd is hungry, as in the Synoptic accounts, here the miraculous element and the sovereignty of Jesus over the situation begin to be heightened in typically Johannine style, when, as soon as he sees the crowd coming, Jesus himself poses the question of food to Philip. Since there is no mention of the crowd's hunger, Jesus is presented as having determined simply to act as a gracious host. The question to Philip about food is thus not so much a response to need as a pre-emptive move made on the basis of his special knowledge that he will provide hospitality for those who have come to him. The narrator underlines this with his 'inside view' of Jesus' motivation – **He said this to test him, because he himself knew what he was going to do.** Jesus' question was not a genuine enquiry but a means of testing Philip. Jesus here is very much the divine figure, as later in the Lazarus story, when he can let Lazarus die because he is confident that the desired miracle will be worked. In taking Jesus' question at its face value, Philip fails the test and thereby becomes the victim in this instance of the misunderstanding motif. He responds on the merely human level by stating the practical problems of giving hospitality to such a large group instead of perceiving that, if Jesus could supply wine in abundance (cf. 2.1–11), he can also be the source for the provision of food. Philip clearly represents the disciples as a whole and uses words similar to those attributed to the group in Mark. But again the differences here heighten the miraculous nature of the feeding. In Mark 6.37 the disciples think that two hundred denarii worth of bread would feed the crowd. Since a denarius was the usual wage for a day's work, two hundred denarii represent over a half a year's wages. But here Philip indicates that even this amount would be far too little – **Two hundred denarii worth of bread would not be enough for each of them to have a little**.

8–9 In John's elaboration of the story another named disciple is now introduced, **Andrew, the brother of Simon Peter,** and readers will recall that it is Andrew and Philip in whom the evangelist has shown particular interest already as key figures among Jesus' group of disciples (cf. 1.40, 43–4; cf. also 12.22). Whereas in Mark Jesus tells the disciples to find out how much food there is, here Andrew, also operating on the merely human level, locates a boy, a further addition to the Synoptic version, who has the five loaves and two fish, and then draws the obvious despairing conclusion, **But what are they for so many?** The Johannine details about the boy (παιδάριον) and about the loaves being barley loaves (ἄρτους κριθίνους) suggest the influence of the Elisha story in 2 Kgs 4 LXX, where the prophet miraculously feeds one hundred men with some barley loaves (ἄρτους κριθίνους – v. 42) and has some left over, and where the servant, who objected that the loaves would not be enough for a hundred men, has just been described as the prophet's παιδάριον (vv. 38, 41).

10–11 The amount of food Jesus will use is smaller than in the Elisha story and the numbers he will feed are far greater. Jesus gives instructions that the people are to be made to sit and the narrator comments that **the men sat down, about five thousand in number**. This agrees with Mark's story in seeing the crowd as being made up of men, among whom presumably the youth is to be included. Only Matthew mentions the presence of women and children in addition (cf. Matt. 14.21). John also agrees with Mark in commenting on the state of the grass. Mark notes its greenness (cf. 6.39), while here the narrator states that **there was a great deal of grass in the place**. Both comments indicate that the time of year was spring, and this fits the earlier reference in John's story to Passover (v. 4).

The scene is now set for the miracle of the multiplication of the loaves and fish. **Then Jesus took the loaves, and having given thanks, he distributed them to those who were sitting, so also the fish, as much as they wanted.** The language of taking the loaves, giving thanks and distributing recalls that used in the early church's eucharistic practice. The fish are mentioned almost in passing, and, of course, the remnants that are collected later are all from the loaves, so that the readers' attention is kept on the bread. While the Synoptics have Jesus blessing the loaves, John employs the verb 'to give thanks' (εὐχαριστέω), as do Luke and Paul in the words of institution for the Lord's Supper (cf. Luke 22.17, 19; 1 Cor. 11.24), and thereby creates associations with the term that early on began to be used by Christians for the celebration of the meal (cf. *Did.* 9.1; 10.1, 7). The eucharistic connotations of the feeding will become more explicit through the last part of the following discourse, which expounds its significance (cf. vv. 52–8). In contrast to the Synoptics, which depict the disciples distributing the food to the crowd, here in the Fourth Gospel the focus is on Jesus as the distributor, the host at the meal he has supplied. And while the other versions simply state that the crowd were satisfied, John's account underlines the abundance of Jesus' provision more colourfully by portraying the men as all having 'as much as they wanted'.

12–13 The extravagance of Jesus' supply continues to be underlined. After the men **had had their fill,** the disciples still **filled twelve baskets from the pieces of the five barley loaves which those who had eaten had left over.** In all this the emphasis remains on Jesus' sovereign control. Whereas in the Synoptics the gathering up of the fragments is simply part of the description of the consequences of the miracle, here Jesus himself gives the order to gather up the fragments left over. That the purpose of collecting the remnants is **so that nothing is lost** is also distinctive to John. The verb can also be translated as 'perishes' and the clause has two connotations that will be picked up in the later discourse. In the Exodus story Moses also commanded that all the manna be gathered and none left over. When the people disregarded the instructions, the remaining manna bred worms and became foul (Exod. 16.19–20). The discourse will allude to this in terms of the food that perishes (v. 27). It will also go on to talk of Jesus not losing anything that the Father has given him (v. 39; cf. also 10.28; 17.12; 18.9). This might offer some support for the view that sees in the twelve baskets an allusion to the twelve tribes of Israel and therefore, in this context, to the new people of God. It does appear significant that after the conclusion of the discourse the evangelist will for the first time lay stress on twelve as the number of the disciples who constitute the core of this new people (vv. 67, 70, 71).

14–15 In the Synoptics there is no depiction of the response of the crowd to the feeding and no clear indication that they recognized what had really happened. The Fourth Gospel, however, reports the crowd's acclamation on the basis of what it has seen – **When the people saw the sign he had done, they said, 'This is truly the prophet who is to come into the world.'** There is some debate about whether the end-time prophet Jesus is perceived to be is to be identified with the prophet like Moses of Deut. 18.15. The link with kingship in the following verse might well support such an identification, since in a number of Jewish traditions Moses was seen as a prophet-king. If so, the people view Jesus as preparing for a new exodus and, also like Moses, as supplying them with sustenance. But just as Nicodemus' confession based on Jesus' signs proved inadequate, so does the crowd's acclamation, as its sequel makes clear: **Since Jesus knew that they were about to come and seize him in order to make him king, he withdrew again to the mountain by himself.** Again Jesus has special knowledge – this time of the crowd's intentions. Seeing him as the prophet-king, they want to install him as such. Jesus is a king, as the use of the title in 1.49 has already indicated, but any attempt by humans to make him king in some form of insurrection shows that they have not understood the nature of his kingship. This will be spelled out later in Jesus' dialogue with Pilate (cf. esp. 18.36–7). Meanwhile, in anticipation of the people's intended action, Jesus withdraws to the mountain mentioned earlier in the account. While this is the only clear narrative account in the Gospels of Jesus having to confront popular misunderstanding of his messianic mission, it is plausible to see the evangelist here reading between the lines of the last part of Mark's story. After feeding five thousand men, who have been grouped in military formation in the desert (cf. 6.39–40), Mark's Jesus has to compel his disciples, who had witnessed the miracle, to leave first, so that he can dismiss the crowd himself before withdrawing to a mountain to pray, something he only does in Mark's narrative at times of critical decision for his mission (cf. 6.45–6). Is Mark hinting that this was because of revolutionary zeal on the part of the crowd which the disciples might have fuelled by their knowledge of what had happened? In any case, it is John's account that draws out these political dimensions of the feeding.

Since this is the only miracle story common to all four Gospels, it is not surprising that the relationship among the accounts has generated a huge amount of discussion. On a first comparison of this pericope with its Synoptic counterparts (cf. Mark 6.32–44; Matt. 14.13–21; Luke 9.10–17), it is easy to be so impressed by its differences that one concludes that it must be a quite independent account of the same tradition that lies behind Mark. After all, as is frequently pointed out, the three Synoptic stories have 53 words that are common to all of them, while John has only eight words in common with the others, and they are the ones absolutely necessary to be telling the same story (five, two, five thousand, the loaves, twelve baskets of pieces). However, a different picture begins to emerge when one takes the broader context of John 6 as a whole into account and notes the parallels with the material in Mark 6.32—8.30. The feeding of the five thousand is followed immediately by Jesus' walking on the water (vv. 16–21; cf. Mark 6.45–52). There is a discourse on bread (vv.

25–58; cf. Mark 8.14–21), a demand for a sign (v. 30; cf. Mark 8.11–12), and a confession from Peter (vv. 66–71; cf. Mark 8.27–30). These broader correspondences suggest a clear dependence on the sequence Mark constructed and encourage a closer comparison of their feeding stories.

Mark, of course, has two feeding stories, the first involving five thousand and the second in Mark 8.1–10 involving four thousand. Some claim that the comparison with the Fourth Gospel shows that the latter has been influenced by both accounts. However, there is only one place in John where there is agreement with the feeding of the four thousand – the use of the verb 'to give thanks' before the distribution of the loaves (cf. Mark 8.6 and John 6.11). Interestingly, if there is any influence from the account of the second feeding it is likely to be from Matthew's version, where 'to give thanks' is also employed and where the setting for the feeding of the four thousand places Jesus on a mountain with crowds who have seen his healings (Matt. 15.29–31; cf. John 6.2–3).

The major comparison, then, must be between Mark 6.32–44 and John's account. Now the actual words shared by John and Mark (but not by the other two Gospels) are more than double the previous count and amount to eighteen. In addition to agreement on the basic elements of the multiplication of the five loaves and two fish for a crowd of five thousand men with twelve baskets of fragments being gathered up, both begin with Jesus crossing the sea and being followed by a crowd, both depict the incomprehension of disciples, who talk about two hundred denarii worth of bread, both mention the state of the grass, thereby indicating the time of year, and both conclude with Jesus retiring to the mountain. As has been seen, the variations on the basic structure within the Fourth Gospel's account are all fully explicable as belonging to distinctive Johannine stylistic and theological, especially Christological, motifs. The addition of the two named disciples, Philip and Andrew, cannot be attributed merely to the sort of details that get added on in the transmission of oral tradition. The singling out of these two figures is dependent on the evangelist's own interests as indicated in the account of the gathering of the disciples earlier and the introduction of the Greeks later, where he has made these two prominent in his presentation. The most obvious explanation appears to be that John was familiar with Mark's story and creatively reworked it, heightening the allusions to the Elijah tradition in the process by mentioning the barley and the youth. There is only one strong argument against this. Why, it is asked, if John knew Mark, does John omit Mark's reference to a setting in the desert or wilderness, which would fit so well with his later clear comparison of the feeding to the giving of the manna in the wilderness (cf. vv. 31, 49)? But this objection ignores the context of the passage. Unlike Mark, John needs the same crowd that were present at the feeding as the audience for the following discourse. Having decided to keep the feeding and the walking on the water together, as in Mark, he must therefore find a way of getting the crowd over to the other side of the sea for the next day. He does not want to add to the complications of this transition. It is awkward enough to have to have boats showing up the next day (cf. vv. 22–3). With a wilderness setting John would also need to have the people stay overnight in the wilderness or give some other explanation, but by leaving the setting unspecified he can also leave the arrangements vague and allow readers to imagine that the next day the people have reconvened from their nearby homes before crossing the sea. Those who dispute the dependence of John's account on Mark still end up advocating that the Johannine version is best explained by a tradition similar to the version preserved in Mark 6. In the absence of any hard evidence for such a tradition and in the presence of so many clear indicators of a relationship with the version we do have, it seems more economical and more plausible to conclude that John has reworked Mark and not simply a pre-Markan tradition that looks very much like Mark.

The significance of this sign of the multiplication of loaves and fish will be explicated at some length in the material that follows in 6.26–58, where the focus will be on its pointing to Jesus himself as the bread of life. Here it is sufficient to observe that, like the previous signs, this one does indeed portray Jesus as the giver of life in abundance, this time through its central symbol of bread. The bread more than satisfies the five thousand who are fed and there is plenty left over. Jewish traditions pictured the abundant life of the end times in terms of a banquet at which the manna would again come down from on high (cf. e.g. Isa. 25.6; 2 Bar. 29.5–8). This meal points to Jesus as the supplier of the life of the age to come. At the same time, because grain or bread was essential for survival and frequently in short supply, providing food for the people was an indication of political power. But this was an implication of the sign that Jesus wished to resist, since it failed to move beyond its material level to that to which it pointed, the divine life disclosed in Jesus. Jesus' gracious gift of life cuts across conventional expectations, whether they be those of disciples who are unable to perceive that Jesus has the resources to meet the full spectrum of human needs, or those of the crowd, who want to make the giver fit into their own categories of political power and influence.

(iv) The walking on the sea 6.16–21

(16) When it was evening, his disciples went down to the sea, (17) got into a boat and went across the sea to Capernaum. It had already grown dark and Jesus had not come to them. (18) The sea became rough because a strong wind was blowing. (19) When they had rowed about three or four miles,[1] they saw Jesus

walking on the sea and coming near to the boat, and they were afraid. (20) But he said to them, 'I am; do not be afraid.' (21) Then they wanted to take him into the boat, and immediately the boat reached the land to which they were going.

This episode appears to disrupt the natural thematic flow of the narrative from the miracle of the supply of food to the discourse on the bread of life. The reasons for its inclusion at this point will be discussed below in reviewing its relation to the Markan account. As it stands, the episode can be seen to have its own function in relation to the surrounding material. It is told primarily from the viewpoint of the disciples, who are given a further disclosure of the identity of the one who has just multiplied the loaves and fish. Having withdrawn himself from those who would make him a political figure, Jesus now shows himself to his followers as the divine figure who cannot be reduced to conventional human expectations. While the crowds form the audience for vv. 22–59, it will be the disciples who are addressed in vv. 60–71. This epiphany (an extraordinary appearance of a divine or heavenly figure) forms part of the preparation for the critical decision about continuing to follow Jesus that the twelve will need to make. In addition, Jesus' self-identification with the words 'I Am' in absolute form prepares for the Gospel's first 'I Am' saying with a predicate in the following discourse – 'I am the bread of life' (v. 35).

The miracle of the walking on the water is unlike the three signs that have preceded it in that it is not immediately apparent that Jesus is responding to a clear situation of human need. The disciples are having difficulty rowing because of the weather but there is no suggestion that they are in danger or in need of being rescued from drowning. Their fear is not produced by the strong wind but by the miracle itself – Jesus' appearance on the sea. Nevertheless, the miraculous appearance does meet a basic need, that of being reunited with Jesus as a result of a successful sea crossing, and so the account of the epiphany does have the main elements of a typical miracle story. The setting is depicted in vv. 16–19a, Jesus' deed and word that constitute the epiphany are at its centre in vv. 19b–20, and it is rounded off with the disciples' response to and the further consequences of the miracle in v. 21.

16–19a The details of the setting are recounted rather enigmatically. After the feeding of the five thousand, the disciples get into a boat and begin to cross the sea to Capernaum. Why they have departed without Jesus is not explained. In Mark's account Jesus had instructed them to leave without

---

[1] The text has 'twenty-five or thirty stades'. A stade is just over 600 feet or just under 200 metres; hence the distance here is between three and four miles or between five and six kilometres.

him (6.45–6) and perhaps John expects readers familiar with Mark to supply this information. In contrast to Mark's story, however, the disciples' destination here is Capernaum rather than Bethsaida (cf. Mark 6.45). **It had already grown dark and Jesus had not come to them**. Many commentators want to read Johannine symbolism into the mention of darkness. But it is highly unlikely that the disciples are being depicted as in the darkness of unbelief and alienation from God and preferable to take this as a simple variation on Mark's temporal notes about 'evening' and 'the fourth watch of the night' (cf. Mark 6.47–8). The narration is done from the disciples' perspective. In the darkness they are on the sea and waiting for Jesus to come to them. It is not made clear precisely what the disciples' expectation about Jesus was, whether they were expecting him to take another boat and catch up with them and whether he would do so by himself or accompanied by others. It may be better, therefore, simply to take this clause as a narratorial aside for the benefit of readers, who are being informed that the disciples are still alone. The narrator then proceeds to indicate that the sea was rough, not to suggest the disciples' perilous state but their slow progress – they had only **rowed about three or four miles**, and thus were not much further than the middle of the lake.

19b–20 At this point the disciples **saw Jesus walking on the sea and coming near to the boat, and they were afraid. But he said to them, 'I am; do not be afraid.'** On the surface level of the narrative Jesus' words have the force of 'Don't take fright, it's me!' But the narrator's comments have already made clear that the disciples know it is Jesus. What makes them afraid is that he is walking on the water and it is this that cries out for explanation. This is why the portrayal of Jesus here is not simply a conventional self-identification and instead has all the trappings of a scriptural theophany. Job 9.8 depicts God as Creator trampling the high places of the sea and the LXX version employs similar language to that of John by speaking of God walking on the sea as on dry ground. Later in Job 38.16 LXX God appears to Job in a whirlwind and speaks of having come in creation on the springs of the sea and walked in the recesses of the abyss. Walking on the sea can also be attributed to Wisdom (cf. Sir. 24.5–6). Similar imagery can be used for God's acts of salvation, particularly in the exodus (cf. Ps. 77.19 – 'your way was through the sea, your path through the mighty waters; yet your footprints were unseen'; cf. also Isa. 43.16). In the Jewish Scriptures theophanies evoke fear and their audiences have to be enjoined not to be afraid (cf. e.g. Gen. 15.1; 26.24; 46.3; Judg. 6.23). This, of course, happens here with Jesus' miraculous appearance. But the injunction not to fear is coupled with the divine name revealed to Moses in the appearance in the burning bush. Deutero-Isaiah takes up this formulation and uses 'I Am' (ἐγώ εἰμι) eight times in an absolute way for God's self-identification as the one true God (cf. Isa. 41.4; 43.10, 25; 45.18; 46.4 (twice); 48.12; 51.12 LXX). What is more, throughout the same section of Isaiah there are frequent divine exhort-ations not to fear. John has μὴ φοβεῖσθε, which is found in Isa. 40.9 LXX, while Isa. 41.10, 13; 43.1, 5; 44.2; 54.4 LXX all have μὴ φοβοῦ. This brief portrayal of Jesus is therefore pregnant with meaning. He is being presented as the embodiment of the God who walks on the water and whose self-proclamation is 'I Am; do not be afraid.'

21 Having made this point about Jesus' identity clearly, the narrator concludes the epiphany miracle briefly and enigmatically. The disciples **wanted to take him into the boat.** Whether they succeeded in their intention is not related. Instead, no sooner do they have the intention than **immediately the boat reached the land to which they were going**. It is hard to see this as anything other than a further miraculous consequence of Jesus' presence. There is no mention of the disciples who had been rowing slowly against the wind now quickening their pace and making it speedily to the shore. The arrival at the destination is instantaneous. In Mark's story there is a hint of the miraculous at this point, since the wind dies down as soon as Jesus enters the boat (Mark 6.51). But, as always where there are Synoptic parallels, the Fourth Gospel makes its miracle story even more impressive. In this ending there are also further echoes of motifs associated with the use of the 'I Am' formulation in Deutero-Isaiah LXX, where the divine self-manifestation has saving significance for Israel. Not only has Jesus' appearance on the water shown that he is the one 'who makes a way in the sea, a path in the mighty waters' (Isa. 43.16) and that 'when you pass through the waters, I will be with you' (Isa. 43.2), but it is also now made clear that his presence has 'made the depths of the sea a way for the redeemed to cross over' (Isa. 51.10).

Again there is debate over whether John has made use of his knowledge of Mark 6.45–52 or rather had independent access to a pre-Markan tradition. Those who take the latter view point to the relative brevity of John's account in contrast to Mark's and its lack of typical Johannine embellishments and symbolism and suggest that John may therefore represent a more primitive form of the tradition than Mark. But any common source has to be hypothetical, and it is just as easy to explain John's brevity and differences from Mark in terms of his reworking of the latter as it is to suggest his greater faithfulness to an unknown earlier tradition. It has already been noted that this story makes for an awkward fit in John's narrative sequence. He retains the story in its Markan sequence immediately after the feeding of the five thousand despite the relative disruption of his own move from sign to discourse, because its main theme is so congenial to his overall portrayal of Jesus. At the same time he minimizes the disruption by concentrating on this main theme in Mark's story. On closer examination it can be seen that nearly all Mark's additional wording comes from his including the arrangements by which Jesus dismissed the crowd at the beginning and from his characteristic emphasis on the gross misunderstanding of the disciples, both in the extra details of the depiction of the walking on the sea and in his editorial comments at the end. John has already dealt with Jesus' withdrawal from the crowd in 6.14–15 and in terms, as has been noted, that suggest knowledge of Mark. He does not pursue the misunderstanding of the disciples in the same major way as Mark and is not interested in it at this point. Mark has an extra element from scriptural theophanic accounts, namely, the initially strange formulation – 'he wished to pass by them' (6.48), which employs the same Greek verb as in the LXX versions of the passing-by entailed in various theophanies (cf. Exod. 33.19, 22; 34.6; 1 Kgs 19.11) and angelophanies (cf. Gen. 32.31–2; Dan. 12.1). He also has the disciples thinking that this phenomenon was a ghostly apparition (6.49). So in their incomprehension they mistake a divine revelation for the appearance of some sea spirit. John omits this depiction of mistaken identity plus Mark's closing stress on the disciples' obtuseness in order to concentrate on the essentials of the Christophany. He retains the stripped-down Markan account precisely because it fits so well with his own emphases. The signs all point to the unmistakably divine creative power at work in Jesus and here is a story that again shows Jesus' control of the elements. As has been noted, his distinctive ending, where what amounts to a second miracle is succinctly added, is characteristic of the way his signs always trump any similar Synoptic miracles. But, more importantly, he keeps the self-identication of Jesus from Mark's story in exactly the same words, dropping only the initial exhortation, 'Take heart,' because it contains the 'I Am' formulation, which will be of such significance for his own portrayal of Jesus' divinity. Indeed, it may well be that the Markan account (cf. also Mark 14.62) provided the catalyst which enabled John to develop the potential double meaning of 'I Am' into the major feature it becomes in his own high Christology, in which Jesus is the embodiment of divine self-revelation.

What has already been said about the distinctives of John's account makes plain the force of this epiphany miracle for his narrative. The unlimited power of God as Creator and Saviour in the Jewish Scriptures is now attributed to Jesus, who also walks on the sea as on dry land, demonstrating his control over the forces of nature, thereby reuniting himself with his followers, reassuring them and bringing them across the waters to their destination. In the process Jesus is also presented as taking on his own lips the self-identification of this God in the formula 'I Am; do not be afraid.' As in 2.1–11, where the impact of the sign on the disciples was primary, so here: Jesus' task in this narrative is to make God known (cf. 1.18) and in traversing the sea he displays dramatically to his disciples that he is one with God in deed and word (cf. also 10.31). In this way this tautly recounted episode can be seen not as a distraction from the rest of the chapter but as encapsulating in narrative form what is at the heart of the Fourth Gospel's Christology. As with some of John's earlier signs, the powers here attributed to Jesus were associated in the Graeco-Roman world with other deities. Mastery of the sea by being able to walk across it was a distinguishing characteristic of Poseidon or Neptune (cf. Homer, *Il.* 13.26–30; Virgil, *Aen.* 5.1057–9, 1081–5). Christian claims for Jesus can again be seen to counter implicitly any such rival claims.

(v) Jesus' discourse on the bread of life   *6.22–59*

(22) The next day the crowd that had stayed on the other side of the sea saw that no other boat had been there, just one, and that Jesus had not got into the boat with his disciples but that they had set off by themselves. (23) Then other boats from Tiberias came near the place where they had eaten the bread after the Lord had given thanks.[1] (24) So when the crowd saw that neither Jesus nor his disciples were there, they themselves got into the boats and went to Capernaum searching for Jesus. (25) And when they found him on the other side of the sea, they said to him, 'Rabbi, when did you come here?' (26) Jesus answered them and said, 'Truly, truly, I say to you, you are searching for me not because you saw signs but because you ate of the bread and were satisfied. (27) Do not work for the food which perishes but for the food which remains for eternal life, which the Son of Man will give you. For on him God the Father has set his seal.' (28) So they said to him, 'What must we do to work the works of God?' (29) Jesus answered and said to them, 'This is the work of God, that you believe in the one whom he has sent.' (30) So they said to him, 'What sign will you do then, so that we may see and believe you? What will you work? (31) Our ancestors ate the manna in the wilderness, as it is written, "He gave them bread from heaven to eat."' (32) Then Jesus said to them, 'Truly, truly, I say to you, it was not Moses who gave you the bread from

---

[1] The vast majority of manuscripts contain the last clause of v. 23. However, it is absent from some Western texts (D 086 it[a,d,e] syr[c,s] arm). The use of 'Lord' by the narrator is comparatively rare in this Gospel. Three references are to the post-resurrection Jesus (cf. 20.20; 21.7, 12) and one to the Jesus of the public ministry (cf. 11.2). But because of the earliness and variety of text-type among the witnesses that contain the clause, it should in all probability be regarded as the only other instance of this usage in the narration of the public ministry.

heaven, but it is my Father who gives you the true bread from heaven. (33) For the bread of God is that which comes down from heaven and gives life to the world.' (34) They said to him, 'Sir, give us this bread always.'

(35) Jesus said to them, 'I am the bread of life. Whoever comes to me will never hunger, and whoever believes in me will never thirst. (36) But, as I said to you, you have seen me[2] and yet do not believe. (37) All that the Father gives me will come to me, and whoever comes to me I will never drive out; (38) for I have come down from heaven not to do my own will but the will of him who sent me. (39) This is the will of him who sent me, that I should lose nothing of all that he has given me but should raise it up at the last day. (40) For this is the will of my Father, that everyone who sees the Son and believes in him should have eternal life, and I will raise them up at the last day.'

(41) The Jews therefore murmured about him, because he said, 'I am the bread which came down from heaven.' (42) And they said, 'Is this not Jesus, the son of Joseph, whose father and mother we know? How can he now say, "I have come down from heaven"?' (43) Jesus answered and said to them, 'Do not murmur among yourselves. (44) No one can come to me unless drawn by the Father who sent me and I will raise that person up on the last day. (45) It is written in the prophets, "And they shall all be taught by God." Everyone who has listened to the Father and learned comes to me. (46) Not that anyone has seen the Father except the one who is from God; he has seen the Father. (47) Truly, truly, I say to you, whoever believes has eternal life. (48) I am the bread of life. (49) Your ancestors ate the manna in the wilderness and died. (50) This is the bread that comes down from heaven so that a person may eat it and not die. (51) I am the living bread that came down from heaven. If one eats this bread, one will live for ever; and the bread which I shall give for the life of the world is my flesh.'

(52) Then the Jews disputed fiercely among themselves and said, 'How can this man give us his flesh to eat?' (53) So Jesus said to them, 'Truly, truly, I say to you, unless you eat the flesh of the Son of Man and drink his blood, you have no life in you. (54) Whoever eats my flesh and drinks my blood has eternal life

---

[2] It is difficult to decide whether 'me' should be included as the more likely original reading. Some witnesses (א A it[a,b,e,q] syr[c,s]) lack the personal pronoun as object and thereby allow a more general reference to the preceding sign as the implicit object. The surrounding context is full of uses of the first person pronoun and there might well have been assimilation to the context. On the other hand, the witnesses which include 'me' have among them the older p[66,75vid] and are widespread and varied.

and I will raise that person up at the last day; (55) for my flesh is true food and my blood is true drink. (56) Whoever eats my flesh and drinks my blood remains in me and I in that person. (57) Just as the living Father sent me and I live because of the Father, so whoever eats me, that person will live because of me. (58) This is the bread that came down from heaven, not like that which the ancestors ate and they died; whoever eats this bread will live for ever.' (59) He said these things while teaching in the synagogue in Capernaum.

Before Jesus gives his teaching about the bread of life to the crowds, there is an introduction, which provides the setting (vv. 22–4). It relates how the Galilean crowd who had witnessed the feeding also become the audience for the teaching. Naturally, the passage is also linked to what has preceded it and the crowd's reactions supply confirmation of Jesus' miraculous crossing of the lake. In vv. 25–59 Jesus' teaching is in the form of an exchange between him and the crowd, who in vv. 41, 52 can be termed 'the Jews'. The crowd's questions or comments, which become increasingly negative, serve as prompts for the next stage in the development of Jesus' discourse (cf. vv. 25, 28, 30–1, 34, 41–2, 52). The passage also contains four 'Amen, amen . . .' sayings of Jesus and three of these are immediate responses to what has been said by the crowd. But the shaping of the material as a dialogue or dispute indicates only one aspect of its skilful literary composition. Another major feature is hinted at by the spatial markers that begin and end this material. The obvious impression from the general mention of 'the other side of the sea' in v. 25 is that Jesus carries on his exchange with the crowd who have found him in some open location in or near Capernaum. But the narrator's concluding comment in v. 59 unexpectedly states that the whole exchange has been while Jesus was teaching in the synagogue in Capernaum. What appears on the surface to be simply a piece of awkward editing actually discloses that the exchange with 'the Jews' has in all probability been built up from material in the form of a synagogue homily with its typical midrashic features of commentary on a scriptural text, found here in v. 31. The evangelist has given this form a further twist by making the commentary on Scripture serve as a commentary on Jesus' own saying in v. 27.

In order to appreciate these underlying features of the composition of this section, it is worth explaining and setting them out in a little more detail. In the synagogue services at that time Scripture would be read. There was first a reading from the Torah (the *seder*) and then a reading from the Prophets (the *haftarah*). In the case of John 6 the underlying *seder* is supplied by Exod. 16, the passage about the manna, and the *haftarah* by Isaiah 54.9—55.5. This would be followed by a midrashic homily in which it would be shown how the Scripture spoke to the circumstances in which the synagogue community found itself. There were a variety of formats for the homily, including dialogue form with questioning and answering, or posing a question or problem in the introduction and going on to answer it by means of midrashic commentary. The latter technique was known by the later rabbis as *yelammedenu* but can also be found earlier in Philo (cf. *Quaest. in Gen.*). The basic technique, however, was to weave together part of the *seder* text for the day with a text from the *haftarah* and to apply these in an exposition, which contained additional scriptural citations, was linked to the initial text through catchwords, and concluded with a final text repeating or alluding to the text for the day.

Within the discourse this technique can be seen in operation in regard to the Scripture citation supplied by the crowd in v. 31 – 'as it is written, "He gave them bread from heaven to eat."' The wording is a combination of Exod. 16.4 and 16.15 from the *seder* text (probably formulated here also in the light of Ps. 77.24 LXX; for further discussion of the disputed source of the citation, see comments on v. 31). This is followed in v. 32 by an explanation of the words 'he gave'. Verses 33–48 then contain an extended explanation of 'bread from heaven'. Into this are woven references from the *haftarah*. It is actually cited in v. 45 (cf. Isa. 54.13) and in vv. 35, 37, 40, 44, 45, 47 there are allusions to the language of 'hear . . . come to me . . . so that you might live' (cf. Isa. 55.2b–3a). In addition, the exchange is shaped by the language of 'murmuring' (vv. 41, 43) drawn from the Torah passage (cf. Exod. 16.2, 7–9, 12). The last words from the original citation – 'to eat' – are then explained in the final section of the passage in vv. 49–58. Throughout it there is again allusion to the *haftarah*'s language of 'eat . . . so that you might live' (cf. Isa. 55.2b–3a) and it concludes in v. 58 with a reference back to the citation of v. 31 and its context – 'This is the bread that came down from heaven, not like that which the ancestors ate and they died . . .'

But the material in vv. 25–59 can be seen as supplying a similar sort of commentary on the preceding saying of Jesus in v. 27, to which the commentary on the Torah text is subordinated. This saying is 'Do not work for the food which perishes but for the food which remains for eternal life, which the Son of Man will give you' and itself contains allusions to Exod. 16.18–21 and Isa. 55.2–3, both *seder* and *haftarah*. The exposition of the saying proceeds by elaborating on the significance of terms in its text. First, 'work' is explained as believing in vv. 28–9 and then later in vv. 35b–40 and vv. 44–7 believing is elaborated in terms of coming to Jesus and its relation to 'eternal life' is indicated. Prior to this further elucidation, vv. 30–4 provide an explanation of 'the food . . . which the Son of Man will give you' as the bread from heaven. The bread from heaven is identified with 'the Son of Man' in vv. 35a, 38, 41–3, 48–51a and then with the flesh and blood of the Son of Man in the final section in vv. 51b–8. The last verse of the exposition refers back to its starting point in the saying of v. 27 with 'not like that which the ancestors ate, and they died' alluding to 'the food which perishes' and 'whoever eats this bread will live for ever' alluding to 'the food which remains for eternal life'.

So this passage is structured around an exposition of the saying of Jesus in v. 27, which also involves an exposition of Scripture in the light of the saying and its significance. In its final form it is obviously an exchange between Jesus and the crowd, but, as has already been noted, expositions could in any case take the form of a dialogue of question and answer. The two expositions here are obviously interwoven and overlapping and are joined neatly at the beginning and the end, since v. 27 contains the allusion to the Scriptural passages and v. 58 refers back both to the saying of Jesus in v. 27 and to the scriptural citation in v. 31. In this way, as the exposition of Scripture serves the development of Jesus' saying, the passage spendidly illustrates the perspective set out in 5.39, 46, 47, namely that Scripture, when rightly understood, witnesses to Christ and that Moses or Torah speaks of Christ.

22–4 After Jesus' walking on the sea at night, it is now **The next day** and there is geographical distance between Jesus and the crowds who will form the audience for his exposition of the significance of the sign they had witnessed. The crowd is still **on the other side of the sea** and **near the place where they had eaten the bread after the Lord had given thanks**. In preparation for the following discourse the feeding is here described in terms of the bread and not the fish, and later eucharistic associations are also evoked by talk of 'the Lord' and his giving thanks. The crowd were depicted at the beginning of the feeding sign as following Jesus because of the signs he had done (v. 2) and then after the feeding as wanting to make him king (v. 15). Though Jesus withdrew, they still are determined to find him. But there is mystery. They ascertain that Jesus is no longer around, but they know that there was **just one** boat and that in it the disciples **had set off by themselves**. The narrator's recounting of this provides indirect confirmation of the miracle of the walking on the water. The crowd, unaware of this, can only assume that somehow Jesus too must have crossed the lake. At this point, very conveniently, **other boats from Tiberias** arrive, enabling the crowd to embark for Capernaum and to continue their search for Jesus on the other side of the lake.

25–6 After finding Jesus, the crowd's question to him is the confused one, **'Rabbi, when did you come here?'** In the light of the information supplied by the narrator in v. 22 about there having been only one boat, it is not so much the time but the manner of Jesus' arrival that should have provoked curiosity. Certainly readers, with their knowledge of what was related in vv. 16–21, know it would have been more to the point for the crowd to have asked, 'How did you come here?' In any case, Jesus' reply ignores the actual force of the question. He responds, as he did earlier in the narrative to Nicodemus, with an 'Amen, amen ...' saying which appears to be totally unrelated to what his dialogue partner has said but which immediately takes the dialogue on to another level and challenges the thinking of the one addressed. Here the crowd are asked to rethink why they have followed Jesus at all, as they are told, **you are searching for me not because you saw signs but because you ate of the bread and were satisfied.** This is a familiar Johannine theme. The people have in fact seen the signs with their own eyes (vv. 2, 14) but they have not seen them properly, because they have failed to see past the external sign, which in this case filled their stomachs, to the reality to which it points. To see properly would not be to remain content with the merely earthly benefits supplied but to believe in Jesus as the source of all life. This true sight will be stressed again in vv. 36, 40.

27 What is entailed in true perception of the feeding sign is elaborated in the key saying that follows: **Do not work for the food which perishes but for the food which remains for eternal life, which the Son of Man will give you.** The actual bread which the crowd ate is material food that perishes. Their energies ought to be expended on obtaining the sort of food which is lasting because it holds the promise of eternal life, and this ultimate source of nourishment is also available from the one who supplied the loaves. 'The food which perishes' picks up on Jesus' instructions that none of the food left over from the feeding should be lost or perish (v. 12) and also alludes clearly to Israel's experience in the wilderness with the manna, when that which was left either melted in the sun or bred worms and became foul (Exod. 16.20–1). The saying also alludes through its talk of 'work' and 'life' to Isa. 55.2–3, where the prophet appeals to the people to come for true nourishment ('so that you may live') and not to expend their labour on what is not true bread and does not ultimately satisfy. By raising the issue of true food or bread which does not perish, by alluding to the manna incident as a contrast to the food that is worthwhile, by its talk of 'eternal life' and by its relating of these themes to the Son of Man, the saying sets the agenda for the rest of the passage and provides the interpretative lenses through which the later scriptural citation about the manna is to be viewed.

The additional statement about the Son of Man – **For on him God the Father has set his seal** – recalls the language of 3.33, where acceptance of Jesus' testimony is to set one's seal to or ratify that God is true. The verb could be used technically for sealing and signing as a witness. Here the ratifying or attesting is done by God as the witness (cf. 5.32, 37) and under-lines the authorization given to the Son of Man as God's unique agent in the giving of life. The crowd had previously acclaimed Jesus simply as the prophet like Moses, but the Father's witness is to Jesus as the Son of Man.

28–9 Jesus' saying spoke paradoxically of working for that which is ultimately a gift. The question of the crowd picks up the first element and thereby puts the stress on performance – **What must we do to work the works of God?** Doing or working the works of God was one of the ways of speaking about obeying the law as performing that which God required. Jesus' response reduces the works set out in Torah that are pleasing to God to one requirement – **This is the work of God, that you believe in the one whom he has sent**. Belief in Jesus as God's authoritative agent rather than adherence to Torah is now the central criterion for pleasing God. To talk of belief as a work is to return to the paradoxical content of v. 27, because belief is a unique kind of activity that entails appropriating and receiving what has already been done on one's behalf and is summed up in the one whom God has sent for that purpose. The importance of such belief will be underlined in vv. 35b, 40, 47.

30–1 In their response Jesus' interlocutors continue to play with the term 'work', this time making any belief in Jesus contingent on his work in the sense of his performance of some accrediting sign. Their questions are strange ones in the light of the preceding narrative's account of Jesus' miraculous deeds: **What sign will you do then, so that we may see and believe you? What will you work?** Moses, the mediator of the law, with which belief in Jesus has just been compared, was accredited through various signs. One of these was the giving of manna in the wilderness – **Our ancestors ate the manna in the wilderness, as it is written, 'He gave them bread from heaven to eat.'** It appears that the sign they adduce as typical of what they require from Jesus, if they are to believe him, is analogous to the very one Jesus has just performed and they have already seen yet also failed to see, thus confirming Jesus' words in v. 26. At the same time, however, they did previously in 6.14 recognize the feeding miracle as an accrediting sign that Jesus was the prophet like Moses, so does it make sense that they would be asking for this again? It may be better, then, to see the crowd as having already accepted that Jesus had legitimated himself as the prophet like Moses in the feeding but now requiring that, if he claims to be something more, the Son of Man sent by God and providing eternal life (vv. 27, 29), a further such sign be given to substantiate the claim.

The scriptural citation, like a number of others in the Gospel, does not correspond exactly to any one verse in its source. Our earlier discussion of composition proposed a combination of Exod. 16.4 and 16.15 as the primary text. Some scholars, however, argue that the scriptural source is Ps. 78.24 (77.24 LXX). Indeed one recent ingenious but ultimately implausible interpretation holds that the pattern of the whole psalm is repeated in this discourse. In favour of Ps. 78.24 – 'he rained down on them manna to eat, and gave them bread of heaven' – is that this text in the LXX has 'them' (αὐτοῖς). In favour of a combination of Exod. 16.4 and 16.15 is that in the LXX this combination has bread 'from heaven' (ἐκ τοῦ οὐρανοῦ), not simply 'of heaven' (οὐρανοῦ). It may well be, however, that the evangelist has allowed the wording of the psalm passage to influence his rendering of Exod. 16. What tips the scales for the latter as the primary source, however, is that the rest of the passage contains references or allusions to the surrounding material in Exod. 16 and that in all probability Ps. 78.24 (cf. also Ps. 105.40; Neh. 9.15; Wis. 16.20) is already a reflection of the Torah passage.

32–4 Jesus now begins to provide his interpretation of the citation. In Jewish thought the manna as a source of nourishment and life was seen as symbolizing Torah, so Jesus points out that in any case **it was not Moses who gave you the bread from heaven**; the real source of such life in the past was God. This presumably would not have been disputed by his hearers. That previous gift, however, is surpassed by what is on offer from the same God who is now to be designated as the Father of Jesus – **it is my Father who gives you the true bread from heaven**. Since what the Father gives in the present is the true bread, the previous gift of manna, which was indeed from God, was an ultimately inadequate provision and can only point to the authentic means to life that has come into their midst in Jesus: **For the bread of God is that which comes down from heaven and gives life to the world.** What is more, this gift of bread is not just for Israel but provides life for the world. There is an ambiguity about the force of this sentence, because 'that which', referring to bread, can also be taken as 'he who', referring to Jesus. But the explicit identification of the bread with Jesus still awaits. At this stage the crowd's response – **Sir, give us this bread always** – is probably a misunderstanding, which takes 'bread of God' in earthly terms and requests a permanent supply of bread, just as the Samaritan woman initially requested a permanent supply of the water Jesus offered her, so that she would not need to keep returning to the well (cf. 4.15).

35–6 Now Jesus takes the next step and reveals himself to be the true bread the Father is giving. The formulation employs the language of divine self-identification followed by a predicate – **I am the bread of life.** In it Jesus claims to be the embodiment of the revelation from God which is necessary for life. According to Deut. 8.3, the manna had been given as an object lesson in order that Israel should 'understand that one does not live by bread alone, but by every word that comes from the mouth of the Lord'. The latter clause clearly has in view the Torah in particular (cf. also Wis. 16.20–6). Philo makes a similar connection in *Decal.* 15–17, and elsewhere he can speak of the manna as a type of Wisdom (*Mut.* 259-60; *Congr.* 173–4) or of the Logos (*Leg.* 162). All of these are revelatory concepts. Now, as the divine revealer and giver of the life of the age to come, Jesus claims to fulfil and surpass what Torah, Wisdom and the Logos would have signified for first-century Judaism. This central claim of the discourse relates back both to v. 27 and to v. 31. The food which remains for eternal life and the bread given from heaven are both to be found in Jesus, who is the bread of life.

On these grounds he can assert, **Whoever comes to me will never hunger, and whoever believes in me will never thirst.** The ideas and language of this assertion are strongly reminiscent of the Wisdom tradition and of Wisdom's invitation in Sir. 24.19–21 – 'Come to me, you who desire me, and eat your fill of my fruits . . . Those who eat of me will hunger for more, and those who drink of me will thirst for more' (cf. also Prov. 9.5). Jesus' offer, however, outdoes that of Wisdom in its promise of complete satisfaction for believers. In the parallelism of Jesus' saying, 'to come to' Jesus is synonymous with 'to believe in' him. Jesus' verdict on the crowd, however, is that, although they have seen him, they **do not believe.** This both repeats the judgement on their seeing in v. 26 and anticipates their more explicitly unbelieving responses in vv. 41, 42, 52.

37–8 There turns out to be another factor at work in whether or not people believe – a divine factor: **All that the Father gives me will come to me.** Those who come to or believe in Jesus constitute the Father's gift to him and he will in no way refuse this gift. Indeed, **whoever comes to me I will never drive out.** Being driven out will be the fate of believers at the hands of the synagogue authorities (cf. 9.34–5); with Jesus, however, they have no such fear but rather the assurance of ultimate security. God's intention is that the giving of believers to Jesus be completed, and Jesus' promise of the good keeping of the gift is assured, because his will is perfectly in tune with God's – **for I have come down from heaven not to do my own will but the will of him who sent me.** Indeed the principle of agency, which underlies the formulation of the relationship between God and Jesus here, presumes precisely this – an agent, one who is sent, will carry out his commission completely as the sender requires.

39–40 This will of God, which was previously expressed in the law but which Jesus, as God's specially commissioned envoy, has now come to accomplish, is spelled out further in two overlapping assertions. They contain three elements: (i) **that I should lose nothing of all that he has given me.** This repeats the assurance of believers' security in Jesus' hands. (ii) **that everyone who sees the Son and believes in him should have eternal life.** It is God's will, and Jesus' accomplishment, that all who exercise true sight and therefore believe enjoy the life of the age to come which begins in the present. (iii) **and I will raise them up at the last day.** The notion of resurrection at the last day is found in both assertions. Jesus' keeping of believers finds its fulfilment in their eventual end-time resurrection by him and this also means that the eternal life which begins in the present is not simply about the life of the soul, which will continue after death, but involves the transformation of the body in a future resurrection.

41–2 The response of the crowd to Jesus' teaching to this point is now depicted. Since it is a negative response, Jesus' interlocutors are now for the first time called 'the Jews': **The Jews therefore murmured about him.** The shaping of this passage into the form of a dialogue has also been coloured by its midrashic commentary on Exod. 16, because the crowd are said to murmur or complain and this same term is dominant in Exod. 16.2, 7–9, 12 LXX, where the people are told that their murmuring against Moses and Aaron is ultimately a murmuring against God. A similar point is implicit here in the murmuring of 'the Jews' against Jesus. Their complaint is **because he said, 'I am the bread which came down from heaven.'** Their formulation brings together what Jesus has said in vv. 33, 35, 38, and their problem with it is expressed in their two questions – **Is this not Jesus, the son of Joseph, whose father and mother we know? How can he now say, 'I have come down from heaven'?** The Christological issue, as frequently elsewhere in the narrative, is that of Jesus' origins. How can someone whose earthly origins are known claim to have a heavenly origin? The evangelist and those whom he represents want to maintain the paradox of the incarnation in which both perspectives on Jesus' origins are true, because he is the divine Logos who has become flesh. The Jewish opposition to such Christian claims insisted that the earthly perspective was sufficient to categorize Jesus.

43–4 Jesus rebukes 'the Jews' for their murmuring but ignores its specific content. Instead he asserts that it is impossible for humans to have the proper perspective on his origin and identity unless God takes the initiative and enables them to believe – **No one can come to me unless drawn by the Father who sent me.** The paradoxical Christology, in which Jesus has both human and divine origins, can only be grasped where there is also a paradoxical response, in which believing is a matter both of human responsibility and divine initiative. The theme that God is at work in determining who comes to Jesus is repeated from vv. 37 and 39, and repeated from vv. 39–40 is the notion that the destiny of such believers is their future resurrection – **and I will raise that person up on the last day.**

45–6 The scriptural support for the necessity of God's role in human believing is taken from the same section of the prophets that has already been alluded to in the discourse. **And they shall all be taught by God** is drawn from Isa. 54.13. For Isaiah the source of this divine teaching was the law. Now Jesus claims that **Everyone who has listened to the Father and learned** from this divine teaching **comes to me.** The point is similar to that made in 5.37, 39–40, where it is the Father's testimony through Scripture and Moses that should lead all the people to believe in Jesus. To have listened to the Father does not, however, put believers in precisely the same category as Jesus himself: **Not that anyone has seen the Father except the one who is from God; he has seen the Father.** Jesus remains unique in that only he has seen the Father (cf. 1.18) and so believers' knowledge of God is mediated through him. No one comes to Jesus unless taught by God but no one truly listens to God except through Jesus.

47–51 Jesus now reiterates a number of the themes he has already addressed. The person who **believes has eternal life** now and the source of that life is Jesus, who again identifies himself as **the bread of life** (cf. v. 35). The crowd had earlier spoken of 'our ancestors' eating the manna (v. 31). Now, reflecting the later situation of the evangelist and Johannine Christians in relation to the synagogue, Jesus talks of **your ancestors** who **ate the manna in the wilderness and died**. The manna had only sustained life temporarily and the wilderness gener- ation still died. By contrast the bread now on offer in Jesus means that believers will not die. It is easy to see how such a strong contrast might lead to confusion among Christian believers when, like the wilderness generation, they too experienced physical death in their midst. This passage has already spoken of Jesus raising up believers at the last day, so it ought to be clear that the reference is not to physical death, but other passages will address this issue directly in order to indicate that believers may die physically but will not experience ultimate spiritual death with its separation from the divine life (cf. esp. 11.25–6). The person who in faith appropriates, that is, eats of, Jesus as **the living bread that came down from heaven . . . will live for ever**. The last clause of Jesus' response sounds a new note that sets the agenda for the final section of the discourse – **the bread which I shall give for the life of the world is my flesh.** The bread is now more specifically identified as Jesus' flesh (σάρξ). The incarnate Logos will give his physical life and the beneficiary of the gift is the world. As a result of Jesus giving up his life, the world, which is at present alienated from the divine life, will be enabled to experience the gift of this life. A central theme of the Gospel is sounded here – life for the world is at the expense of death for Jesus.

52–3 The reaction of 'the Jews' signals the next and last stage of the discourse and here the exposition of the scriptural citation from v. 31

– 'He gave them bread from heaven to eat' – is being brought to a conclusion with the phrase 'to eat' now in view. 'The Jews' naturally dispute among themselves what it can possibly mean for Jesus to be speaking not just about the bread of life but about this gift in terms of eating his flesh. Their response is not expressed directly to Jesus, and his next words not only ignore the question but intensify the force of his previous saying and add an element that would be even more offensive – **unless you eat the flesh of the Son of Man and drink his blood, you have no life in you**. The drinking of blood was strictly prohibited according to the law (cf. Lev. 17.10–14). To imagine that Jesus' words were to be taken in any literal cannibalistic sense would be to remain on the purely earthly level of understanding, in the same way that Nicodemus had earlier understood the language of being born again as having to enter the womb a second time (3.4)! Clearly the force is metaphorical and in basic continuity with the previous metaphorical use of language in the discourse, where the verbs 'to see', 'to work' and 'to come' all signify 'to believe'. 'To eat' has already been introduced with this sense in vv. 50–1. The object of such belief to this point has been Jesus as the revelation from God, the bread of heaven, who provides life. But this section of the discourse takes the thought a step further by specifying that the object of belief is Jesus in his flesh-and-blood manifestation. So at a fundamental level the language underlines that the belief which results in life is belief in the incarnation. At the same time, however, there is no escaping the implication that eating the flesh and drinking the blood entail that the flesh has been broken and the blood shed. In other words, this is belief in an incarnate Christ who has given his life in a violent death.

For Christians it was precisely this belief that was vividly represented in the eucharist and it is highly probable that the words of institution from the Synoptic tradition of the Last Supper have influenced the formulation here in the Fourth Gospel, which, of course, does not include a eucharist institution in its supper account. It is the version in Matt. 26.26–8 to which the Johannine statement about eating Jesus' flesh and drinking his blood comes closest – 'Take, eat; this is my body ... Drink from it, all of you, for this is my blood ...' Luke 22.19 speaks of 'my body, which is given for [ὑπέρ] you' and v. 51 of the discourse here has already asserted that the bread is Christ's flesh which he will give for (ὑπέρ) the life of the world. The difference is that, whereas the Synoptics speak of Jesus' body (σῶμα), John speaks of his flesh (σάρξ). Both are appropriate translations of the underlying Aramaic term, but John prefers 'flesh' because it fits better his stress on incarnation.

54–5 Up to this point the verb φάγειν has been used for 'to eat' but now there is a shift to the verb τρώγειν, which can have the force of 'to chew' or 'to munch' (cf. also vv. 56–8). Some see the employment of a verb which emphasizes the physical activity of eating as pointing to the actual eating involved in the eucharistic meal. But to make this a major ground for holding that this verse is now saying that participation in the sacrament is necessary for experiencing eternal life appears dubious. The two verbs can be used synonymously, and even if τρώγειν has more intimate or more down-to-earth connotations, its primary function here remains metaphorical. In any case, Jesus' promise for the one who eats his flesh and drinks his blood is the same as for those who believe (cf. v. 40) – the person **has eternal life and I will raise that person up at the last day**. Life in its fullness now and in the future is the result of belief, **for my flesh is true food and my blood is true drink**. There is an implicit contrast with all other claims to provide spiritual food and drink, including those of Torah and Wisdom. These are relegated to the past now that the genuine source of life, to which they pointed, is present. Whoever partakes of the true food and drink, as v. 35 has indicated, will never be hungry and never be thirsty.

56–7 To believe in the incarnate and crucified Jesus is to be in a relationship with him that involves mutual indwelling – **Whoever eats my flesh and drinks my blood remains in me and I in that person.** In the evangelist's language 'to remain' or to abide or continue in Jesus is essential to true discipleship (cf. e.g. 8.31; 15.4, 6, 9–10). The notion of the mutual indwelling of the believer and Jesus will also become a major theme in the Gospel and here, as later, a parallel is drawn between this relationship and the relationship between Jesus and the Father – **Just as the living Father sent me and I live because of the Father, so whoever eats me, that person will live because of me.** It will become explicit that the believer's union with Jesus not only parallels but participates in the union between the Father and the Son (cf. esp. 17.21, 23). Here that notion is implicit in regard to the concept of life. The divine being described as the living Father is the source of the life of Jesus as the uniquely authorized divine agent. This intra-divine life is mediated to believers through Jesus, who becomes in turn their source of life.

58–9 The final words of the discourse make use of the formulations of vv. 49–51, which in turn had reiterated earlier themes. So the central message is driven home one more time – **This is the bread that came down from heaven, not like that which the ancestors ate and they died; whoever eats this bread will live for ever.** The narrator's following comment that this had been Jesus' synagogue teaching serves as a reminder of the form which underlies the exchange that has taken place, so that, in line with typical synagogue teaching on Scripture, the final verse, as has been noted earlier, refers back both to the citation in v. 31 and to the preceding saying of Jesus in v. 27, which provides the conceptual framework through which the citation will be interpreted.

It has already been noted that John 6 follows the sequence of material in Mark 6.32—8.30 and that that material contains a discourse on bread in 8.14–21. The Markan episode is designed to draw out the meaning of the two feedings that have preceded and to underline the failure of the disciples to 'understand about the loaves' (Mark 6.52). Along with the disciples, readers are invited to see a deeper significance in the bread that has been broken first in a Jewish setting and then in a Gentile one. The reference to the one loaf or one bread that the disciples have with them in the boat (Mark 8.14; cf. 1 Cor. 10.18) is held by a number of interpreters to give the Christological and eucharistic clue to this deeper significance of the feedings. The miracles of the broken loaves point to Christ as the bread that will be broken for both Jews and Gentiles. Whether or not this is the symbolism intended by Mark, it is precisely this direction in the interpretation of the Markan tradition that is taken by the fourth evangelist, as he makes explicit that the feeding sign has in view Christ as the true bread, who gives his flesh not just for Israel but for the world.

In the context of Passover and against the backdrop of the scriptural account of the giving of manna in the wilderness, Jesus proclaims himself in this discourse to be the bread of life. He is both the embodiment and the giver of eschatological life and thereby supersedes Moses, Torah and Wisdom. Just as the manna, of which this bread is a type, came from heaven, so Jesus too has a heavenly origin and has been sent by God into the world as God's uniquely authorized agent. There is a progression in the conveying of this message. First Jesus identifies himself as the life-giving divine revelation, then there is stress on the incarnate nature of this revelation through the mention of his flesh, and finally, as he speaks of the giving of this flesh and of eating his flesh and drinking his blood, it becomes plain that the life-giving revelation includes and indeed climaxes in his violent sacrificial death. In line with this development, the concept of revelation, with its background in Torah and Wisdom, is coloured at the end of the discourse by eucharistic language. Accompanying this Christological focus is an insistence on humans believing if they are to experience the eternal life which begins now, carries them through death and culminates in the resurrection at the last day. This life is a share in the divine life which is mediated by Jesus. The necessity of believing in order to appropriate life is also expressed through a number of synonyms – working, seeing, coming, eating and drinking. Belief is a continuous activity which enables a person to remain in Jesus, and the eucharistic associations of eating Jesus' flesh and drinking his blood point to the visible expression of belief in the efficacy of Jesus' death through ongoing participation in the eucharist. At the same time Jesus makes clear that believing is not simply a human activity but one which God initiates. The notion that it is God who draws believers to Jesus, who in turn guarantees their security, is meant to provide assurance to those who have been told by the synagogue and its actions against them that, in confessing Christ, they have abandoned the covenant, forfeited their election and ultimately been cast out. Christian believers are here told that to come to Jesus is at the same time to be drawn into the divine life and to receive the promise that they will never be cast out.

(vi) Defection of some disciples and Peter's confession   *6.60–71*

(60) Then many of his disciples who listened said, 'This saying is hard to take; who can listen to it?' (61) But Jesus, inwardly aware that his disciples were murmuring about this, said to them, 'Does this offend you? (62) Then what if you were to see the Son of Man ascending to where he was before? (63) The Spirit is the giver of life; the flesh is of no avail. The words I have spoken to you are spirit and life. (64) But there are some of you who do not believe.' For Jesus knew from the beginning those who would not believe and the one who would betray him. (65) And he said, 'For this reason I have told you that no one can come to me unless it is granted to that person by the Father.'

(66) After this many of his disciples turned back and no longer went about with him. (67) So Jesus said to the twelve, 'Do you also want to go away?' (68) Simon Peter answered him, 'Lord, to whom shall we go? You have the words of eternal life. (69) We have believed and have come to know that you are God's Holy One.' (70) Jesus answered them, 'Did I not choose you, the twelve, and one of you is a devil?' (71) He was speaking of Judas, son of Simon Iscariot, for he, one of the twelve, was going to betray him.

This final section of chapter 6 builds on what has preceded it. 'This saying' (v. 60) is a clear reference back to the bread of life discourse. In addition, there is a repetition of some of its language and themes – murmuring, life or eternal life, the Son of Man, flesh, belief, and the Father's part in bringing people to Jesus. At the same time, however, there is a shift in conversation partners and in focus. Whereas in the discourse Jesus has been talking to the crowd who become 'the Jews', now the interlocutors are more specifically those who are disciples, first a more general group (vv. 60–6) and then the twelve (vv. 67–71). The emphasis is on the nature and quality of their response to Jesus' self-revelation.

60 It is not clear how the **many of his disciples who listened** to the discourse are related either to the crowd or to the disciples to whom Jesus appeared on the water. Although the crowd had followed (v. 2) and

acclaimed Jesus (v. 14), their response to him is predominantly uncomprehending and negative and they are designated as 'the Jews' and not
as disciples. It also seems unlikely that the disciples who were in one
boat would be thought of as a broad grouping who could be described
as many and from whom the twelve could then be distinguished. The
primary function of this group may therefore be to represent later Jewish
followers of Jesus who were unable to go all the way with the viewpoint
on Jesus represented by the evangelist. The referent of **This saying** which
many disciples find offensive is also not entirely clear. Some scholars treat
vv. 51c–8 as later redaction and therefore see the reference as the teaching
of vv. 25–51b or particularly its summarizing final statement about Jesus
being the living bread who has come down from heaven. But we have
found no reason why vv. 51c–8 should not be treated as an integral part of
the discourse and there seems to be no particular problem for those who
are disciples in holding that Jesus is the revelation from God that gives
life. It is more likely that what some found hard to take was precisely the
last part of the discourse about eating Jesus' flesh and drinking his blood,
with its emphasis on this revelation taking place in Jesus' flesh and on the
necessity of belief in the efficacy of his sacrificial death.

61–2 The narrator's comment, with its 'inside view' of Jesus – **inwardly
aware that his disciples were murmuring about this** – already
associates the response of these disciples with that of the unbelieving
Jews by repeating the verb 'to murmur', which has overtones of rebellion
against God (cf. vv. 41, 43). Jesus' question to them also already indicates
how he will evaluate their response. **Does this offend you?** contains the
verb σκανδαλίζειν, which has the force of 'to cause to stumble' in such
a way as no longer to continue to follow or believe (cf. 16.1). His second
question is incomplete. It has the protasis, expressing a potential condition
– **Then what if you were to see the Son of Man ascending to
where he was before?** – but without an accompanying apodosis. The
force of the question is not entirely clear. Some have taken it to have
a relatively positive conclusion – 'would that convince you?' It is more
likely that it should be completed by 'would you still be offended?' or,
even more likely, by 'would you not be even more offended?' The notion
of the Son of Man ascending to where he was before involves the full-
blown Johannine belief in Jesus as the Son of Man who returns via death
and exaltation to the pre-existent state of glory he shared with the Father
(cf. also 3.13–14; 8.28; 17.5; 20.17). Those who might want to believe in
Jesus as Messiah but stumble at the offensiveness of the notion of eating his
flesh and drinking his blood will find even more unacceptable the notion
of the crucifixion as integral to this Son of Man's unique relationship with
the Father from whom he has descended and to whom he will ascend.
This is the Johannine version of the saying about seeing the Son of Man

which was found to be blasphemous by the high priest in the Synoptic tradition of the trial before the Sanhedrin (cf. Mark 14.62 parr.).

63 The Spirit is the giver of life; the flesh is of no avail. The words I have spoken to you are spirit and life. The context of this next saying needs to be recalled. The bread of life discourse has stressed that eternal life is appropriated through believing, and this was the primary force of the assertion that eating Jesus' flesh and drinking his blood were necessary in order to have life. Now this saying begins to reflect on the mystery of why some believe but others are unable to accept Jesus and his teaching. The framework for such reflection is provided by the contrast between Spirit and flesh. To understand the contrast, it is necessary to appreciate the reference of the term 'flesh' here. After the positive evaluation that has been given to Jesus' flesh in the preceding discourse, the negative assertion about the flesh here has struck many as contradictory and contributed to various theories of different levels of redaction in the chapter. Others, who also link the use here with its earlier reference to Jesus' flesh, have attempted to soften the contradiction by claiming that Jesus' flesh in and of itself does not have efficacy and needs the Spirit, only given when the Son of Man is ascended and glorified, to work through it before it is able fully to be the vehicle of life. But it is hard to imagine that the stark formulation that the flesh is of no avail is simply a qualification of the emphatic assertion that Jesus' flesh is to be identified with the bread which does avail for the life of the world (cf. v. 51).

The confusion can be avoided when it is observed that the evangelist employs 'flesh' positively when it is linked with Jesus and negatively when it is associated with human response to the divine revelation. In the latter context, the flesh/Spirit contrast has similar associations to that found in the Pauline writings. 'Flesh' refers to the sphere of merely human existence which, without the activity of the Spirit, is alienated from the life of God. Nicodemus was unable to come to true understanding of Jesus because he remained only in the realm of the flesh and was not born of the Spirit (3.6; cf. also 1.13). The unbelieving Pharisees judge Jesus 'according to the flesh' (8.15). Here, too, although Jesus' words are Spirit and life, animated by the divine Spirit and therefore life-giving for those who believe, these disciples in their response remain oriented to the sphere of the flesh and for this reason are unable to accept those words. The flesh is of no avail in evaluating Jesus; merely human categories can only take offence at the claim that the flesh of the divine Son of Man must be offered up in death for the life of the world.

64–6 It is entirely in keeping with this train of thought that Jesus then adds, **But there are some of you who do not believe.** Among would-be disciples of Jesus, there are those who are unable to come to proper belief because their merely natural categories of judgement have not been transformed. The narrator again protects Jesus' sovereignty by adding that he **knew from the beginning those who would not believe and the one who would betray him**. This both recalls the earlier narratorial aside of 2.23–4, in which Jesus is depicted as not willing to entrust himself to the many who believed, because he knew what was in them, and points ahead to Jesus' own statement and the narrator's further explanation about the betrayer in vv. 70–1. Jesus' knowledge about those who will truly believe is in line with the Father's will – **For this reason I have told you that no one can come to me unless it is granted to that person by the Father.** The mystery of belief or unbelief is ultimately in the hands of God. Just as the Spirit has to be at work for humans to be able to transcend their own categories and come to a true recognition of Jesus, so the Father is the one who grants such believing recognition. In the preceding discourse God's activity in bringing humans to belief has been expressed in terms of believers being the Father's gift to Jesus (v. 37) and of the Father drawing them to Jesus (v. 44). Now there is the reminder that belief is not something on which humans can congratulate themselves; it is God's gift to them. However, to refuse the bread of life because of offence at the full implications of the offer is, of course, possible and reveals that it has not been granted to one to remain with Jesus. The theological discussion has been leading up, as an explanation, to the statement that **After this many of his disciples turned back and no longer went about with him.** As will be noted later, this formulation of a crisis of belief leading to defection among Jesus' followers in all probability reflects issues that arose later, in the evangelist's own setting.

67–9 In the narrative the defection of many disciples leads to Jesus now turning to the core group who remain with him. This is the first of only three times that the narrator will speak of **the twelve** (cf. also v. 71 and 20.24). This Gospel assumes the existence of an original twelve but is not particularly interested in them, preferring to speak of Jesus' disciples as an unspecified group. Here, however, the twelve serve to distinguish the smaller group that come to authentic faith from the many who began to follow Jesus but whose belief in him eventually proved to be inadequate. When they are asked whether they too wish to abandon Jesus, Peter responds as their representative with the words, **Lord, to whom shall we go? You have the words of eternal life. We have believed and have come to know that you are God's Holy One.** This is the Johannine equivalent to the Synoptic confession of Peter, also made at a turning point in Jesus' ministry and in response to a question from Jesus (cf. Mark 8.27–9 parr.). Here Peter acknowledges that Jesus alone is worthy of their allegiance. Echoing Jesus' own words in v. 63, he confesses that Jesus has the words that impart life. The verbs in his further confession are in the perfect tense, indicating belief and knowledge that began in the past and continue into the present. The Synoptic confession of Jesus as the Messiah is inappropriate here, since Jesus has been recognized by his close disciples as the Messiah from the start of this narrative (cf. 1.41). Instead the content of this confession focuses on Jesus' divine origin as the Holy One of God. The only other place this title is employed of Jesus is in the demon's correct recognition of Jesus in Mark 1.24 and its parallel, Luke 4.34. In the context of the Fourth Gospel this title signifies that Jesus shares the Father's holiness (cf. 17.11) and has been set apart by the Father in order to be sent into the world (cf. 10.36).

70–1 Peter has spoken for the twelve. In response, Jesus does not directly acknowledge his confession but addresses the whole group – **Did I not choose you, the twelve, and one of you is a devil?** Peter's confession is an indication of Jesus' sovereign choice of his followers, who will be reminded later that they did not choose Jesus but he chose them (15.16). Here the Synoptic tradition of Jesus' choice of twelve disciples as the representatives of Israel is taken up (cf. Mark 3.14 parr.) and yet the devil is able to infiltrate even this group. One disciple can in fact be designated as a devil. The narrator explains that this is a reference to **Judas, son of Simon Iscariot, for he, one of the twelve, was going to betray him**. The name of Judas' father is given only in this Gospel (cf. also 13.2, 26). In the later references in 13.2, 27 the devil or Satan is said to be operative in Judas' intention to betray Jesus, indicating why here, as the betrayer, Judas can be said to be a devil. In that later context Jesus' choice of twelve will be qualified, as Judas is excluded from those who have been chosen (13.18). It is significant that this first reference to Jesus' betrayal by a disciple is in the context of the offence given by his teaching about the necessity of giving his flesh in a sacrificial death for the life of the world.

The final part of chapter 6 continues its pattern of following the Markan sequence. Very shortly after the feeding, the walking on the water and a conversation about bread, Mark has the episode at Caesarea Philippi with Peter's confession (Mark 8.27–33). Immediately after the confession, Jesus begins to instruct the disciples about the sort of Messiah he is by speaking of the necessity of the Son of Man's suffering and death. When Peter is unable to accept such teaching, Jesus addresses him as Satan and he is told that he is thinking in human rather than divine terms. The basic components of the tradition lying behind John 6.60–71 are all here. The fourth evangelist has already incorporated the teaching about the Son of Man's death into the bread discourse, so Peter's confession comes after rather than before such teaching. But the teaching still causes offence among Jesus' disciples. Whereas in Mark this is explained in terms of a divine/human contrast, in John the Spirit/flesh contrast serves the same function. In Mark Peter has a Satanic role, while in John it is Judas who becomes Satan's accomplice. Matthew's additions to Mark are also particularly interesting in terms of the Johannine account. He adds a further title to 'Messiah' in order to emphasize Jesus' divine origins – 'Son of the living God' (16.16), and in John Jesus has just been described as the Son of Man sent by 'the living Father' (cf. v. 57). Matthew's account also has an earlier variation on the divine/human contrast, in which the term 'flesh' appears, as Peter is told, 'Flesh and blood has not revealed this to you, but my Father in heaven' (16.17). It is Matthew who employs the term 'stumbling block' (σκάνδαλον, 16.23) in regard to Peter's viewpoint on Jesus' passion, while John uses the cognate verb (σκανδαλίζειν) for the effect of such teaching on the many disciples (v. 61). It would not be surprising if the evangelist was familiar with both Mark and Matthew at some point in his composition of this section.

As has been noted, his depiction of the defection of many of Jesus' disciples over the issues raised in the bread of life discourse appears to reflect a later setting with its controversy over Christological beliefs. Some have gone so far as to propose four different crises lying behind the exchanges of John 6 as a whole, but this is far too speculative. Even the controversy that is reflected in this final section of the chapter cannot be pinned down precisely. Its general features can only be guessed at on the basis of hints in the Gospel and elsewhere; there then remain two main possibilities. It is clear from elsewhere that there were Jewish Christians in the evangelist's locale who initially believed in Jesus but were ultimately unable to make the full Johannine confession of faith and that the evangelist attributes this failure to their fear of being expelled from the synagogue. To have confessed Jesus as Messiah would not have provoked trouble with the religious authorities but to accept that Jesus was the sort of Messiah outlined in the discourse, who was pre-existent with God, who became incarnate and whose crucified flesh was efficacious for the life of the world would have been precisely the belief that risked persecution and expulsion and which some would have been reluctant to make. The eucharistic formulations at the end of the discourse would have faced such sympathizers with the choice of whether they would participate in solidarity with Johannine Christians in the rite that visibly expressed this controversial Christological belief or remain within their traditional Jewish categories about Messiahship and therefore within the synagogue. The other possible referent is the second crisis faced by the evangelist and Johannine Christians (see the discussion of Setting in the Introduction). The Johannine epistles make explicit that some had withdrawn from the community. In the writer's view, those who seceded had a defective Christology which failed to do sufficient justice to the full humanity of Jesus and its soteriological significance. It was precisely such people who would be liable to take offence at the notion that it was not only Jesus' role as the divine revealer that was important for faith but it was equally important to confess that the flesh in which the divine revelation was embodied and the giving of that flesh in a sacrificial death were essential for salvation and for an authentic experience of eternal life. The final stage of the evangelist's composition of the Gospel appears to have been under way at the same time that this internal crisis was taking place. If so, this passage would belong to the later stage of writing and would be suggesting that both this turning away on the part of those who could not accept the implications of the eucharistic words for their view of Jesus and the diminution of the community as a result had been foreseen by Jesus and was not a development outside his sovereign purposes.

For the evangelist this crisis, whatever its exact nature, and the turning away by those who had previously been followers of Jesus raised acute questions about why some were able to make a full commitment of faith and others were not. In probing the mystery, this section appeals both to the contrast between the realm of the Spirit and the realm of the flesh and to divine election, a notion already drawn on in the earlier discourse. Those who are unable to accept the community's view of the person and work of Jesus have not had their categories of thought and ways of judging transformed by the Spirit and remain within a merely human orientation. This does not free them from responsibility for not responding appropriately but it does provide evidence that they are not among those to whom God the Father has granted belief or those who have been chosen through God's unique agent, Jesus. At the same time no false security for believers is suggested. The disruptive work of the divine adversary goes on even among the chosen twelve, from whom will come a betrayer. Even Peter, who makes the true confession of faith, will have his moments of denial and betrayal and will need to be restored to faithful discipleship, as the later narrative reveals. Election by Jesus does not remove the necessity of continuing to believe.

(vii) Jesus goes to the Festival of Tabernacles   7.1–13

The material in 7.1—8.59 has the Festival of Tabernacles as its setting and draws directly on its imagery, while that in 9.1—10.21 continues with this festival as the implicit backdrop until the setting changes in 10.22 to the Festival of Dedication (Hanukkah). The sequence of argument in chapters 7 and 8 can appear rather disjointed. This may well be because the evangelist has brought together from his tradition smaller units relating various aspects of disputes about Jesus. They are given a certain cohesiveness through their present setting in relation to the festival and through the sense of mounting conflict which they convey, including the note of increasing threat to Jesus' life (cf. 7.1, 19, 25, 30, 32, 44; 8.37, 40, 59).

The Festival of Tabernacles or Booths was the most popular of the Jewish festival pilgrimages. Josephus described it as 'especially sacred and important to the Hebrews' (*Ant.* 8.101). It lasted for eight days from 15 Tishri, which fell in late September or early October. Later traditions about its celebration are preserved in the Mishnah (cf. *m. Sukk.* 1–5). In the first century CE it celebrated the completion of the harvest and was associated with God's guidance of Israel when the people lived in tents during the wilderness experience at the time of the exodus, but it had also become linked with the salvation God would provide at the eschaton (cf. Zech. 14). In addition, at this festival a request was made for an abundance of rain as a sign of God's continuing special provision for Israel. The chief element in the celebration would have been the making of booths, in which the men slept and ate during the first seven days. On these days there was a procession to the Pool of Siloam to gather water and four large menorahs were set up in the court of the women, providing light to enable the celebrants to dance there through the night. Both the water/rain and the light imagery are taken up in the depiction of eschatological salvation in Zech. 14.6–8, 17. Both kinds of imagery would also have been linked with the provision offered by Torah. Here in John the former will be applied to Jesus in chapter 7 and the latter in chapter 8. The manna or bread, also associated with Torah, has just been depicted in chapter 6 as embodied in Jesus and the thematic sequence of the Christological application of bread, water and light imagery makes sense of the present arrangement of chapters, despite the geographical disruption caused by placing the material of chapter 6 between the Jerusalem controversies in chapters 5 and 7.

The controversy in chapter 7 divides into three parts. It is introduced by Jesus' decision, after dispute with his brothers, to go to the festival (7.1–13). There follow two accounts of his teaching and the reaction it provoked in terms of division of opinion and attempts to arrest him (7.14–36; 7.37–52). Some later texts then include the pericope about the woman taken in adultery as 7.53—8.11. This will be discussed in the Appendix at the end of the commentary.

(1) After this Jesus went about in Galilee, for he did not wish to move around in Judaea because the Jews were seeking to kill him. (2) Now the Jewish Festival of Tabernacles was near. (3) His brothers therefore said to him, 'Leave here and go to Judaea, so that your disciples also may see the works you are doing, (4) for no one does something in secret if he wants to be known publicly.[1] If you are doing these things, show yourself to

---

[1] There is a question whether the best text contains a pronoun before the phrase ἐν παρρησίᾳ and if so, whether this is in the masculine nominative or neuter accusative. The omission is not well attested. The neuter accusative (αὐτό) – 'if he wants it to be known publicly' – is supported by p⁶⁶* B W itᵈ Diatessaronⁿ, but there is better external attestation for the masculine nominative (αὐτός), which stresses the subject of the

the world.' (5) For not even his brothers believed in him. (6) So Jesus said to them, 'My time has not yet come, but your time is always right. (7) The world cannot hate you, but it hates me, because I testify about it that its works are evil. (8) You go up to the festival; I am not[2] going up to this festival, because my time has not yet been completed.' (9) Having said these things, he remained in Galilee. (10) But after his brothers had gone up to the festival, then he himself also went up, not openly but[3] in secret. (11) The Jews were looking for him at the festival and saying, 'Where is he?' (12) And there was much murmuring about him among the crowds.[4] Some were saying, 'He is a good man,' while others were saying, 'No, on the contrary, he is leading the crowd astray.' (13) But no one was speaking publicly about him for fear of the Jews.

1–2 The narrator now provides transitional material linking the past action both in Jerusalem and Galilee with the imminent future action back in Jerusalem. Jesus is depicted as still **in Galilee**, where he was for the bread of life discourse in chapter 6, and his motivation for staying there – **for he did not wish to move around in Judaea because the Jews were seeking to kill him** – reminds the reader of the aftermath of Jesus' earlier sabbath healing in Jerusalem, where 'the Jews were seeking all the more to kill him' (5.18), and the referent for 'the Jews' is clearly the Jerusalem religious authorities. The temporal note that **the Jewish Festival of Tabernacles was near** suggests a possible occasion for Jesus' return to Jerusalem, despite what has been indicated about its dangers.

3–5 The urgings of Jesus' brothers that he go to Judaea probably presuppose that they are ignorant about the threats to his life rather than that they are being deliberately malicious and wanting to see him meet his end. (On their apparent ignorance that Jesus has already performed his works in Jerusalem, see the discussion of the composition of the Gospel in the Introduction). They are aware of his extraordinary activities. The one

---

second clause – 'if he (himself) wants to be known publicly' – and is found in p[66c,75] ℵ E[c] K L it[a,aur,c,f] vg syr[p,h,pal] cop[sa.]

[2] Some early witnesses have 'not yet' (οὔπω) instead of 'not' (οὐκ), but this looks like a clear attempt to alleviate the difficulty posed by the contradiction between Jesus' words and his subsequent action.

[3] Many of the same early witnesses, including p[66,75] B, have ἀλλ᾽ ὡς, 'but as it were'. Again, this looks like a gloss to soften the contradiction with Jesus' words in v. 8. It is omitted by ℵ D it[a,b,d,e] syr[c,s] cop[sa] Diatessaron[n].

[4] Some manuscripts have the singular ὄχλος, 'crowd', and the rest of the passage consistently employs the singular noun. But the plural is well attested (p[75] B K L) and, as the more difficult reading, may well be the earlier.

earlier reference to the brothers (2.12) implies that they had been present at the first sign, the turning of water into wine. **If you are doing these things** does not indicate scepticism, as some commentators suggest. After all, his miraculous acts form the basis of the argument they have made in v. 3b. The focus of their comments is, instead, on what would constitute a successful mission. In their view, there is no point in Jesus working **in secret**; he should display his acts on as broad a public platform as possible, not only before his followers in Judaea but before **the world**. Their advice, however, is seen as reflecting their unbelief – **for not even his brothers believed in him**. They fail to recognize that Jesus' mission is not congenial to the world and that his aim is not to achieve publicity for himself but to do the will of the one who sent him.

6–8 Accordingly, Jesus' response stresses his very different perspective. Earlier he had told his mother that his hour had not yet come (2.4); now he tells his brothers, **My time has not yet come, but your time is always right**. Their orientation is such that they act in whatever way suits their interests at the time, but Jesus' schedule is dictated by his Father's will and informed readers know that this is to culminate in his hour of glory through death. In the meantime Jesus faces the hostility of the world. The attitude of his brothers is shaped by the world, to which, it is implied, they belong, and so he can say, **The world cannot hate you**. In sharp contrast, the world does hate Jesus, because his mission of salvific judgement entails that he **testify about it that its works are evil**. The world that hates Jesus has its chief representatives in the Jewish religious authorities who seek to kill him. His witness to a world that is alienated from its source of life can result in people believing and coming out of the world or it can have the effect of arousing its hatred when its evil is exposed (cf. also 3.19–20; 15.18, 24–5). Having shown the incompatibility between his brothers' advice and his own attitude to his mission, Jesus tells them to go to the festival but says, **I am not going up to this festival, because my time has not yet been completed**. The stress on *this* festival may be intended to indicate that Jesus is already aware that there will be a future festival – Passover – at which the divine timing for the accomplishment of his mission is to be fulfilled.

9–10 As might have been expected after such a response from Jesus, the narrator reports that **he remained in Galilee**. Yet in the next breath he surprises readers by relating that, **after his brothers had gone up to the festival, then he himself also went up, not openly but in secret**. This amounts to a drastic change of plan, clearly contradicting the announcement Jesus had just made. It does, however, fit an emerging pattern in the characterization of Jesus. A request or suggestion is made to him and he rebuffs it, but then in a delayed response he accedes to it, yet on his own terms. This pattern was at work in his responses to his mother in accomplishing the first sign (2.3–10) and to the official from Capernaum in the second sign (4.47–53) and will recur in his reaction to the message from Martha and Mary in the account of the raising of Lazarus (11.3–15). Here Jesus refuses to act in accordance with his brothers' agenda and timetable. He does eventually go the festival but it is now a decision that is taken in line with the divine schedule. It is also on his own terms. His brothers had urged him to show himself publicly, but Jesus does not go up as part of the public pilgrimage but rather travels in secret and only puts in an appearance halfway through the festival (cf. v. 14).

11–13 Until this point there has been discussion about Jesus' attendance at the feast from his own and his brothers' perspective in Galilee. Now the focus shifts to speculation about him in Jerusalem: **The Jews were looking for him at the festival**. Since they are distinguished from the crowds (v. 12), 'the Jews' here are the religious authorities and their intention in looking for Jesus is supplied from the earlier reference in v. 1 about their seeking to kill him. At the same time **there was much murmuring about him among the crowds**. The term translated as 'murmuring' is the same as in 6.41, 43, 61, but here it does not have the overtones of complaint but refers to suppressed discussion, as the explanation – **no one was speaking publicly about him for fear of the Jews** – makes clear. For the first time the religious authorities are depicted as a threat not only to Jesus himself but also to those who might voice favourable opinions about him, and the phrase 'for fear of the Jews' will recur with a similar force in 9.22; 19.38; 20.19. The crowd's subdued debate about Jesus involves a division of opinion (cf. also 7.40–3). Some hold that Jesus' deeds and words indicate he is good and reliable, but others suspect him to be a false prophet, who **is leading the crowd astray**. The notion of leading astray or deceiving the people picks up on what is said about false prophets in Deut. 13.5, 10, 13 and it became part of the charge later made against Jesus in Jewish polemic (cf. Justin, *Dial.* 68.8–9; *m. Sanh.* 43a).

The disjunction between Jesus and his unbelieving brothers during his ministry would have been familiar to the evangelist from the Synoptic tradition, especially Mark, and here he employs it to convey his own perspective on Jesus' operating according to the Father's timing for his mission. Mark's version of the saying about a prophet without honour (cf. John 4.44) had spelled out the implications for family realtionships – 'Prophets are not without honour, except in their home town, and among their own kin, and in their own house' (6.4) – and earlier in 3.21, 31–5 the attitude of Jesus' mother and brothers is associated with that of the Jerusalem scribes who believe him to be possessed. Here in John 7 too the discussion with the brothers is set against the backdrop of the Jerusalem authorities seeking to kill him (v. 1) and the brothers are associated with the world that hates Jesus (v. 7). The charge that Jesus has a demon will be taken up later by the crowd in v. 20. The statement that 'not even his brothers believed in him' (v. 5) suggests that Jesus has met with widespread unbelief (cf. also Mark 6.5–6) and fits with the immediately preceding depiction of many of his followers in Galilee having turned away from him (cf. 6.66). Also developed from Mark's narrative is the notion of a hiddenness or secrecy to Jesus' mission. In what has come to be called 'the messianic secret' motif, throughout Mark's story Jesus insists that what he does should not be publicized widely. The sort of messianic figure he is will not be able to be appreciated fully before his death and resurrection (cf. esp. Mark 9.9–13). Similarly in John, despite Jesus' signs, there is a sense in which during his mission the nature of his glory remains elusive. Paradoxically, the full public display of glory still awaits the crucifixion and exaltation.

The narration of the prelude to Jesus' attendance at the Festival of Tabernacles deals with the issues of the nature of Jesus' mission and of his identity and these will be developed in the rest of the chapter. The dialogue with his brothers indicates that his mission will not be one in which he seeks publicity for himself and v. 18 will spell out that he does not seek his own glory but the glory of the one who sent him. That glory has its own public hour and, in line with this, Jesus has made clear that his time has not yet come and he will only act in relation to the divine timetable. Despite his travelling to Jerusalem in secret, however, his identity has already become a topic at the festival. Through the dialogues that follow readers will continue to be presented with the crucial importance of the decision whether Jesus is a false prophet or the true prophet, the Messiah, the one sent by God.

(viii) Jesus' teaching on the law and the Messiah and the response   7.14–36

(14) When the festival was already half over, Jesus went up into the temple and began to teach. (15) Then the Jews were astonished, saying, 'How does this man have such learning without having studied?' (16) Then Jesus answered them and said, 'My teaching is not mine but his who sent me. (17) If any one wants to do his will, that person will know whether the teaching is from God or whether I am speaking on my own. (18) The one who speaks on his own seeks his own glory; but the one who seeks the glory of him who sent him is true and there is no falsehood in him. (19) Did not Moses give you the law? Yet none of you keeps the law. Why are you seeking to kill me?' (20) The crowd answered, 'You have a demon. Who is seeking to kill you?'

(21) Jesus answered and said to them, 'I did one work and you are all astonished. (22) Moses gave you circumcision – not that it is from Moses but from the patriarchs – and you circumcise a man on the sabbath. (23) If a man receives circumcision on the sabbath in order that the law of Moses may not be broken, are you angry with me because I made an entire man well on the sabbath? (24) Do not judge by appearances, but judge with just judgement.'

(25) Now some of the people of Jerusalem were saying, 'Is this not the man they are seeking to kill? (26) And here he is speaking publicly and they say nothing to him. Can it be that the authorities have indeed recognized that this is the Christ? (27) But we know where this man is from, yet when the Christ comes, no one will know where he is from.' (28) Then Jesus cried out as he was teaching in the temple and said, 'You know me, and you know where I am from. I have not come on my own, but the one who sent me, whom you do not know, is true. (29) I know him because I am from him and he sent me.' (30) Then they tried to arrest him, but no one laid a hand on him because his hour had not yet come. (31) Yet many of the crowd believed in him and were saying, 'When the Christ comes, will he do more signs than this man has done?'

(32) The Pharisees heard the crowd murmuring such things about him, and the chief priests and the Pharisees sent guards in order to arrest him. (33) Then Jesus said, 'I am with you for a little time still, and then I am going to him who sent me. (34) You will seek me and you will not find me, and where I am you cannot come.' (35) So the Jews said to one another, 'Where does this man intend to go in order that we will not find him? Does he intend to go to the dispersion among the Greeks and to teach the Greeks? (36) What is this saying he spoke, "You will seek me and you will not find me, and where I am you cannot come"?'

The composition of the audience for Jesus' teaching in this section is not always clear and this may well be a further sign that disparate traditions have been brought together by the evangelist. In the previous section 'the Jews', as the religious authorities, were distinguished from the crowds (vv. 11–13), but here the two appear to merge more closely. The astonished response to Jesus' teaching in v. 15 is said to come from 'the Jews' and, given vv. 11–13, one would expect these again to be the authorities. But one would also expect the audience to be the pilgrims at the festival and indeed, after Jesus responds to 'the Jews', it is said to be 'the crowd' who answer him back and become his dialogue partner (vv. 20–1). Then in v. 25 the respondents are designated 'some of the people of Jerusalem' (does this include pilgrims from elsewhere?) who distinguish themselves from 'the authorities' (v. 26). These Jerusalemites appear to be the antecedent for the subject of 'they tried to arrest him' (v. 30) and they are then distinguished from the many in the crowd who believed (v. 31). To add to the confusion, in v. 32 'the Pharisees' are introduced, distinguished from the crowd, and, along with 'the chief priests', are those who send guards to arrest Jesus. Finally, in v. 35, the audience for Jesus' last saying in the section is again 'the Jews'. The impression given, here as in other places in the narrative, is that the evangelist is not much concerned with hard-and-fast categories. Distinct groups from the time of Jesus, the Pharisees and the chief priests, can be brought together and, in the light of the circumstances of the evangelist's own time, can be labelled 'the Jews', the hostile authorities, but at the same time the unbelieving response to Jesus in both sets of circumstances can be said to come from 'the Jews' as a broader group and the crowd, depending on its particular response, can move in and out of this category (cf. also 6.41, 52).

14–15 Jesus does not come out into the open until **the festival was already half over** and then he begins to teach in the temple. In the Synoptics Jesus teaches in the temple and is thereby engaged in controversy with the religious leaders shortly before the Passover festival (cf. Mark 11—12 parr.), while here in John his main temple teaching is given during Tabernacles. The initial response on the part of 'the Jews' is one of astonishment. In the Synoptics a similar response to Jesus' teaching is found at various points. Mark 1.22 relates that 'they were astounded at his teaching, for he taught them as one having authority and not as the scribes' (cf. also e.g. Matt. 7.28–9). Here the question, **How does this man have such learning without having studied?**, makes much the same point. It is not simply an observation about Jesus' teaching skills despite his lack of formal education. It refers to the mastery of the law his teaching reflects despite his not having studied under teachers of the law in such a way as to pass on their traditions and cite their authority.

16–17 In response Jesus attributes his teaching to the highest possible authority – **My teaching is not mine but his who sent me**. This also constitutes a response to the earlier charge about his being a false prophet (v. 12). According to Deut. 18.15–22, the true prophet like Moses, whom the people are to heed, will be one into whose mouth God's words will be put and 'who shall speak to them everything that I command'. It has already been stressed that Jesus does nothing on his own account but that, as the one whom God has sent, he speaks the words of God (3.34; 5.30). Since Jesus has claimed only to be doing the will of God (cf. 5.30; 6.38), he can also assert, **If any one wants to do his will, that person will know whether the teaching is from God or whether**

I am speaking on my own. Whether Jesus' teaching is from God can ultimately only be known by one who has made a commitment to wanting to know God's will. The argument is necessarily in some sense circular. If Jesus' teaching does represent God, there can be no other, superior criteria by which to validate or prove his claim. The truth of the claim can only be discovered by a willingness to participate in it through being open to belief, and 6.29 has already made clear that to do the work or the will of God is to 'believe in him whom he has sent'.

18 Although the formulation of this verse is in the third person, it is clear, because of the way the language of the two preceding verses is taken up, that Jesus is referring to himself. If he were simply speaking on his own account, he would be seeking **his own glory** or honour and attempting to curry popular favour. But because he **seeks the glory of him who sent him**, he **is true and there is no falsehood in him**. This takes up from 5.41–4 the discussion of the difference between human and divine ways of reckoning honour and applies it to the issue of whether Jesus is to be deemed a true or false prophet. His overriding concern for God's reputation is such that not only his teaching but also he himself constitutes the true revelation in which no deceit or falsehood is to be found (cf. also 14.6).

19–20 Seemingly abruptly, Jesus now raises the topic of Moses and the law. Its relevance becomes clear, however, once it is remembered that the opposition draws its criteria for judging Jesus from what Moses says about true and false prophecy and would appeal to the law imposing the death penalty on a false prophet. Jesus, however, claims, **none of you keeps the law. Why are you seeking to kill me?** The counter-charge is made that, in seeking to kill Jesus, they have misunderstood and are violating the law they think they are upholding. Their seeking to kill Jesus refers back to their action in 5.18 in response to Jesus' healing on the sabbath, but from Jesus' perspective such a response is a setting aside rather than a keeping of the law. His reasoning will become clear in vv. 21–4. But first the crowd intervene with a response. The genuineness of their ignorance of the authorities' intention to put Jesus to death has to be in question after the narrator's earlier comment in v. 13 about their 'fear of the Jews', and their accusation – **You have a demon** – aligns them at this point with the hostile attitude of 'the Jews'. On one level it is a way of stating that they think Jesus is insane, since madness was frequently attributed to possession and social deviants were demonized, but at another level it also serves to associate Jesus with false prophecy and sorcery (cf. Deut. 13.1–11; 18.9–14). A similar charge is made against Jesus in Mark 3.21–2.

21–3 Jesus directs their attention back to the cause of all the hostility – **I did one work and you are all astonished** – a reference to the healing of the paralysed or lame man on the sabbath (5.1–18). He then demonstrates the faulty nature of their interpretation of the Torah in their accusations against him. He has acted once in an apparent breach of the sabbath law, but this is something that they do constantly. The Torah has two commandments that appear to clash – sabbath keeping and circumcision on the eighth day – but in fact it was perfectly acceptable to **circumcise a man on the sabbath**. Like a number of other commandments, circumcision was seen to override the sabbath and this was a long-standing principle of legal interpretation. Jesus can then employ a further common interpretive rule – the argument from the lesser to the greater: **If a man receives circumcision on the sabbath in order that the law of Moses may not be broken, are you angry with me because I made an entire man well on the sabbath?** The force of the argument is clear. If the sabbath could be overridden in order to deal with a single part of the body, how much more in order to heal the whole body? In fact, just this sort of interpretation of sabbath law can be found in later rabbinic tradition (cf. e.g. *t. Sabb.* 15.16; *b. Yoma* 85b) and the principle it enshrined – that the protection of life took precedence over the sabbath commandment – was no novelty.

24 On this basis Jesus now challenges his audience: **Do not judge by appearances, but judge with just judgement**. It is incumbent on Jesus' accusers to read and weigh Torah rightly and not to leap to a superficial conclusion by taking one isolated aspect of it. As Jesus has already made clear, those who judge falsely by employing Moses and the law against him will discover that Moses functions not as their advocate but as their accuser (5.45–6). The opposition's application of the law to Jesus is part of their judging by human standards, which is here labelled 'by appearances' and later 'by the flesh' (8.15). In the context of the passage and of the narrative as a whole, to judge with just judgement entails appropriating the evaluative norm provided by Jesus' own witness (cf. v. 18; also 8.16) and this will result in interpreting Moses and the law in the light of that witness.

25–7 A series of reactions are now attributed to **some of the people of Jerusalem**. If they are to be distinguished from members of the crowd who are pilgrims from elsewhere, this may explain why they are portrayed as privy to the intentions of the authorities and as willing to speculate about why these are not being carried out. They know that the plan is to kill Jesus but cannot understand why **he is speaking publicly and they say nothing to him**. They wonder, therefore, whether this signals a re-evaluation of Jesus on the part of the authorities – **Can it be that the authorities have indeed recognized that this is the Christ?** The people themselves, however, are dubious about Jesus being the Messiah, because **we know where this man is from, yet when the Christ comes, no one will know where he is from**. This reflects a strand of messianic expectation in which it was thought that the origin and identity of the Messiah would remain concealed until he was publicly revealed (cf. *1 Enoch* 46.2–3; *4 Ezra* 7.28; 13.32). It also reflects the sort of debate between early Christians and Jews in which Johannine Christians are likely to have been involved and which is evidenced later in Justin, *Dial.* 8.4. In the context of the Fourth Gospel there is considerable irony about this objection, since its proponents profess knowledge of Jesus' origins (from Galilee) but it is a consistent theme of the narrative that the opposition are ignorant of Jesus' true origins (from above or from God).

28–9 This is precisely the point Jesus now spells out in challenging the Jerusalemites' speculations. He contrasts their presumed knowledge with his own knowledge and in the process accuses them of an ultimate ignorance. Theirs is another case of judging by appearances. They think they know Jesus' identity and origins on the basis of some pieces of data about his earthly life. But this is to remain ignorant of his true origins: **I have not come on my own, but the one who sent me, whom you do not know, is true. I know him because I am from him and he sent me**. Essential to understanding Jesus' identity is recognition of his divine agency. He is from God (παρ' αὐτοῦ cf. also 1.14; 6.46; 9.33; 16.27–8; 17.8) and has been sent by him, and since the sender is true, the sent one, who is the uniquely authorized agent, shares in that truth (cf. v. 18). What is striking is the radical claim that the opposition do not know the one who sent Jesus (cf. also 8.19, 55). It is not simply that common knowledge of God can be assumed and that the dispute is about Jesus' relationship to this God. Rather Jesus' relationship to God is such that not to know him is to show that one also does not know God. For the Fourth Gospel Jesus has become the decisive criterion for knowledge of the true God. What is required is to share in Jesus' knowledge ('I know him') and this, according to the prologue, is what Jesus' mission is about; as 'the only God, who rests in the lap of the Father, he has made him known' (1.18).

30–1 The narrator suggests that something of the force of this absolute claim was perceived and found offensive, because **they tried to arrest him**. Who attempted the arrest is not clear – presumably some of the Jerusalemites among the crowd. A theological reason is given for the failure of the attempt – **his hour had not yet come**. Others among the crowd are more sympathetic. The Davidic Messiah was not necessarily expected to perform miracles, and so the signs Jesus has done are seen as demonstrating that he has more than fulfilled messianic hopes. Yet, as the earlier reference to popular belief on the basis of Jesus' various signs indicates, a question mark hangs over whether such belief will become authentic (2.23–5).

32 What appears to be a further and more official attempt to arrest Jesus now ensues. The more positive response of the crowd is again described as 'murmuring' because it is not made openly (cf. v. 12), but the religious leaders in the shape of **the Pharisees** are still said to have heard it and therefore to have decided to act in combination with **the chief priests** in having the temple police take Jesus into custody. The combination of Pharisees and chief priests was not a natural one and in the Synoptics is found only in Matt. 21.45; 27.62. The prominence of the Pharisees in the hostile alliance described in John may well reflect their role after 70 CE and in the opposition to Johannine Christians. The outcome of the opposition's plans here will not be mentioned until vv. 45–9.

33–4 Meanwhile Jesus continues his teaching and stresses the brevity of the remaining time of his mission – **I am with you for a little time still** – and therefore the urgency of believing in him while there is still time and he is still accessible. But to believe in him is to recognize both his origin and his destiny, and he speaks of the latter in enigmatic fashion – **I am going to him who sent me. You will seek me and you will not find me, and where I am you cannot come.** This will be one of the main topics in the farewell discourses to the disciples, who will have equal difficulty in comprehending it.

35–6 The bemusement of Jesus' hearers, now labelled again as 'the Jews', is indicated by their questions to one another. They repeat the words, asking what they mean, after having unconfidently raised the possibility that he might be talking about intending **to go to the dispersion among the Greeks and to teach the Greeks**. Irony may be intended here, since readers will know that in fact one result of Jesus' going away to the Father was the spread of his teaching beyond Israel to the Greeks (cf. also 10.16; 11.52; 12.20–3).

Amid speculation about his Messiahship, divided opinion, and outright hostility Jesus teaches about his own identity. Both the nature and content of that teaching arouse astonished questioning. Without having been instructed by other rabbis, he displays knowledge and is able to interpret the law in such a way that he turns it back on his accusers. At the same time he claims that his teaching is true because it is God's teaching. It is assumed that Jesus meets the criteria for Messiahship but his claims of coming from and going to God and of his knowledge of this God in contrast to the people's ignorance break the bounds of traditional messianic categories. Indeed his person and teaching become the measure of any true knowledge of Israel's God. When it comes to human discernment and appropriation of such knowledge, two elements in this passage are crucial. One has to be prepared to do God's will, that is, to be open to belief. Whether in theology or Christology (and the two are inseparable in this Gospel), it is faith that leads to understanding. The exhortation not to judge by appearances but to judge with right judgement reinforces this by inviting readers, like Jesus' hearers, to be willing to suspend usual and merely human ways of evaluation, which place Jesus within fixed preconceived categories, and to risk seeing him as one in whom God is uniquely represented in the world and who therefore is able to transform and redefine previous structures of judgement, even those about God.

(ix) Jesus' teaching on living water and the response   *7.37–52*

(37) On the last great day of the festival Jesus stood and cried out, saying, 'If any one is thirsty, let that person come to me,[1] (38) and let the one who believes in me drink. As[2] the scripture said, "Out of his belly shall flow rivers of living water." ' (39) Now he said this about the Spirit which those who believed[3] in him were to receive; for there was no Spirit as yet, because Jesus had not yet been glorified.

(40) Some of the crowd who heard these words said, 'This man is truly the prophet.' (41) Others said, 'This man is the Christ.' But others said, 'Surely the Christ does not come from Galilee, does he? (42) Did not the scripture say that the Christ comes from the seed of David and from Bethlehem, the village where David was?' (43) So a division arose in the crowd because of him. (44) Some of them wanted to arrest him, but no one laid hands on him.

(45) Then the guards went to the chief priests and Pharisees, and the latter said to them, 'Why did you not bring him?' (46) The guards answered, 'Never has a man spoken like this.'[4] (47)

---

[1] Some early manuscripts (p⁶⁶* ℵ⅂* D it^{b,d,e}) omit πρὸς με, 'to me'. But it has strong and wide attestation, including p⁷⁵ and B, which read ἐμέ, and 'come to me' is a frequently used Johannine phrase on Jesus' lips (cf. e.g. 5.40; 6.35, 44, 45, 65), so the omission may well be due to a scribal oversight.

[2] There are two major ways of punctuating the text and the translation above represents one of these. For discussion of the options, see the comments on these verses.

[3] Some manuscripts, e.g. p⁶⁶ B, have the aorist participle, πιστεύσαντες, while others, e.g. ℵ D, have the present participle, πιστεύοντες. The former agrees with the aorist form of the main verb and it appears more likely that this would have been altered to the latter rather than vice versa, possibly in an attempt to relate the saying more directly to later readers.

[4] The translation of the guards' answer represents the shortest form of the text. It is this shortest form that provides the best explanation for a number of other manuscript traditions which are all longer and spell out in various forms that the force is 'never has a man spoken in the way that this man speaks'.

Then the Pharisees answered them, 'Have you also been led astray? (48) Has any of the leaders or of the Pharisees believed in him? (49) But this crowd, which does not know the law, is accursed.' (50) Nicodemus, who had come to him earlier and was one of them, said to them, (51) 'Our law does not judge a person before first hearing from him and learning what he is doing, does it?' (52) They answered and said to him, 'You are not from Galilee too, are you? Investigate and you will see that a prophet does not arise from Galilee.'

37–8 There is disagreement among scholars whether **the last great day of the festival** refers to the seventh or the eighth day. Those who argue for the seventh day do so on the grounds that it was the greatest day in terms of the festival rituals. On this day the priests processed around the altar with the water drawn from the Pool of Siloam not just once but seven times, and on the following day the water drawing and the dancing in the light of the menorahs did not take place. The seventh day would therefore be the most dramatic occasion for Jesus' announcements about water and light. But this argument does not take seriously enough the narrator's own description of the day as last and great. The last day is most naturally taken as the final, eighth day, which was a sabbath, and 'great' fits best both the depiction of this eighth day in Lev. 23.36 as a holy convocation and solemn assembly and the narrator's own later designation in 19.31 of the sabbath of the Passover as a great day, that is, one of special solemnity. It would be no less dramatic for Jesus, after the specific rituals had all been carried out, to announce in the midst of the final great sabbath convocation that the festival's symbols find their true significance in him.

Precisely what Jesus is presented as saying about the water symbolism is one of the most disputed syntactical and exegetical issues in the whole Gospel. There are three interrelated questions that require attention. How are vv. 37b–38a to be punctuated? Are the streams of living water being said to flow from Christ or from the believer? From which source or sources is the scriptural citation drawn? The major factors relevant for a decision on these matters will be treated briefly.

In the Greek text καὶ πινέτω, 'and let [that person] drink', follows **let that person come to me** and precedes **the one who believes**, which is then followed by **as the scripture said**. The main punctuation options are to place a full stop after 'let drink', which directly connects it with coming to Jesus and makes 'the one who believes' the antecedent for the scripture citation, or to place the full stop after 'the one who believes', which makes this clause the subject of 'let drink' and allows the scripture quotation to refer to the source of the believer's drink, namely, Christ. In other words, these two options are represented in translation as (i) 'let that person come to me and drink. The one who believes in me, as the scripture said, "Out of his belly shall flow rivers of living water."' and (ii) 'let that person come to me, and let the one who believes in me drink. As the scripture said, "Out of his belly shall flow rivers of living water."' The grammatical and syntactical arguments for each are inconclusive. The first results in a suspended subject which is only picked up awkwardly by the genitive 'his' in the actual quotation, but this is not an impossible construction and 'the one who believes in me' is frequently found in John as the beginning of a sentence, though not in this type of construction. The second produces a balanced parallelism – 'If anyone is thirsty, let that person come to me; and let that person drink, who believes in me.' Being thirsty and drinking match each other (cf. also 4.13–14a), and coming to Jesus and believing in him are synonymous elsewhere in John (cf. e.g. 6.35; 6.37, 40; 6.44–7). On the other hand, the few other scriptural citation formulae in John which are introduced by καθώς, 'as', come after the subject to which they most directly refer. Similarly, the evidence is divided in regard to how early readers deciphered the text. Some early manuscripts with punctuation follow the first option with its primary reference to the believer, as do Origen and Athanasius, while Justin, Hippolytus, Tertullian and Irenaeus read it as referring to Jesus, as in the second option.

This second option has been preferred in the translation offered here, because it is judged that considerations of context and of the likely sources of the citation favour the view that the streams of living water are presented as flowing from Jesus rather than from the believer. As has been noted, the focus of the narrative of John 7 up to this point has been on Jesus and his identity and origins. One would therefore expect that this focus would be maintained in these verses rather than shifting to the believer. If the water and light symbolism of Tabernacles is kept to the fore, then the fact that Jesus applies the light imagery directly to himself in 8.12 makes it likely that he does the same with the water imagery. Some, however, point to the earlier water imagery in 4.14 as a precedent for the reference to the believer. It is true that there it is applied to the believer, but the imagery is not quite the same. In 4.14 Jesus is clearly the source of the water ('the water that I give') and the spring of water gushing up to eternal life is within the believer, while here the streams of living water flow out from the person's belly as a source of life for others. In addition, if, as v. 39 makes clear, this living water is a reference to the Spirit which believers receive, then elsewhere in John Jesus is the source or origin of the Spirit for others (cf. 1.33; 15.26; 16.7, 14; 20.21) and this would lead us to expect that the one from whose belly the water of the Spirit flows out is most definitely Jesus rather than the believer. Water flowing from Jesus' belly is also in line with the crucifixion account in this Gospel, where blood and water flow from Jesus' side (cf. 19.34).

There is no known source in the Jewish Scriptures which has the wording or even the combination of ideas of the quotation. It is, therefore, generally agreed that this is one of the evangelist's composite citations and in it various types of scriptural material about living water have been combined. One type of material is the exodus motif of the water flowing from the rock struck by Moses in the wilderness in order to be drunk by the people. John 6 had taken up the manna in the wilderness from Exod. 16 (cf. also Ps. 78.24) and now John 7 takes up Exod. 17.6, and the rehearsal of this incident in Ps. 78.16,20 (Ps. 77.16, 20 LXX) employs two of the same terms as here, 'rivers' (ποταμοί) and 'flow' (ῥέω), in its description of the emerging water. In Deutero-Isaiah this exodus motif is used to depict future salvation. In this way the new thing God will do, according to Isa. 43.20, will include giving 'water in the wilderness, rivers in the desert, to give drink to my chosen people', and in Isa. 44.3 the pouring out of water is linked with the pouring out of God's Spirit. Another type of eschatological material that speaks of the provision of water in the future has the Jerusalem temple as the water's source. In Ezek. 47.1–12 water flows out from below the threshold of the temple, becomes a river, and gives life. Most interesting, however, is Zech. 14, which also uses Feast of Tabernacles imagery for the eschaton (cf. esp. 14.16–19), takes up light and water symbolism (cf. 14.7–8) and, in developing the latter, like John 7.38, describes the water as 'living' – 'on that day living water shall flow out from Jerusalem'. It looks, then, as though the Fourth Gospel here in its water imagery may well be associating the flow of water out of the rock from Exod. 17 and Ps. 78 with the flow of water out of the Jerusalem temple from Zech. 14, which had already been linked with the Festival of Tabernacles. In support of this hypothesis is the fact that some later Jewish traditions, including some connected with the Festival of Tabernacles (e.g. *t. Sukk.* 3.3–18), associate the wilderness rock with the rock at the foundation of the Jerusalem temple. If this is the background of the water imagery, then its most natural application is to Jesus rather than the believer. The exodus motif also lies behind the reference to blood and water flowing from Jesus' side (see comment on 19.34) and elsewhere in early Christian thinking Christ is identified with the rock from which the people drank (1 Cor. 10.4), while earlier in this Gospel's narrative Jesus has already been depicted as the replacement of the Jerusalem temple (cf. 2.19–21; 4.21–6).

But one part of the scripture citation still remains unaccounted for – **Out of his belly**. There appear to be no scriptural texts that have living waters flowing from a person's belly. The issue is not solved by simply stating that 'belly' is likely to be a synonym for 'heart'. Prov. 4.23 does state that from the heart flow the springs of life, but this is not a text with any clear links to the other probable sources of the citation, and the evangelist could have chosen to use 'heart' (καρδία) but instead for some reason has preferred 'belly' (κοιλία). It is also true that there are links between v. 38 and 19.34 and that the physicality of the term 'belly' prepares for the mention of Jesus' side in the latter text, but this is insufficient explanation for the choice of the term in the first place. One suggestion that does provide more links with the rest of the citation is that 'belly' is an allusion to the Jewish tradition that Jerusalem and its temple were considered to be the navel of the earth, imagery found early on in Ezek. 38.12 and *Jub.* 8.19. Another possibility remains. The term κοιλία is found elsewhere in John with one of its common connotations, namely, 'womb', and in a context which speaks of new life through birth by water and the Spirit (cf. 3.4–5). At first sight this observation seems unpromising. What could a reference to *his* womb mean and how could birthing imagery, appropriate enough for water and the Spirit, be connected to the notions of the wilderness or temple rock? The answers are not in fact that hard to find. In Exod. 17 God stands on the rock and becomes identified with it as Moses strikes it, and Rock becomes a name frequently used for God. The Song of Moses can in one place use the startling imagery of 'the Rock that bore you, the God who gave you birth' (Deut. 32.18). Ps. 78, which recounts that 'he made streams come out of the rock, and caused waters to flow down like rivers' (v. 16), goes on to say that 'they remembered that God was their rock' (v. 35). The link between this imagery and the Jerusalem temple is found in Isa. 30.29, where Zion is 'the mountain of the Lord . . . the rock of Israel'. Finally, these associations come together in the cluster of images in Isa. 43.14—44.8, to which reference has already been made in connection with the rest of the citation. In the depiction of the newness of future salvation God will give water in the wilderness, rivers in the desert, as drink for the chosen people whom God has formed in the womb (ἐκ κοιλίας), and will pour water, streams and the Spirit on this people, so that they will be witnesses that there is no other god, no other rock (cf. 43.19–21; 44.2–3, 8). In this light the implications of John's citation, therefore, are that Jesus is now the rock, from whose womb come the waters of new life, the waters of the Spirit, the agent of new birth (cf. 3.5–6, 8; also 1.12–13).

39 The narrator now spells out that Jesus **said this about the Spirit which those who believed in him were to receive**. 'This' refers particularly to the flow of living waters (see 3.5 and the comments there on the background of the association between water and the Spirit). The temporal perspective at this point is future; those who believed were yet to receive the Spirit from Jesus. From this vantage point, that of the experience of those who accepted Jesus during his ministry, it can even be said that **there was no Spirit as yet, because Jesus had not yet been glorified**. The statement is clearly not to be taken absolutely, since Jesus himself is depicted as experiencing the Spirit (cf. 1.33; 3.34). Only after Jesus' death and exaltation is the Spirit made available to others (cf. 19.30b, 34; 20.21). The same perspective is maintained in the farewell discourses, where the coming or the sending of the Spirit is still future and awaits Jesus' departure. Despite this emphasis, the narrative is not consistent. Being born of the Spirit appears to be a possibility for Nicodemus in the present (3.5–6), Jesus tells the Samaritan woman that the time for worship in the Spirit is now here (4.23–4), and to accept Jesus' words is to receive the Spirit and life that they mediate (6.63). This phenomenon is part of the Gospel's combination of temporal perspectives, in which what was in fact experienced after the resurrection is retrojected into the time of Jesus and thus in the story line anticipates the post-glorification period.

40–2 In the crowd's response the previous discussion about Jesus as the prophet and the Messiah is again taken up. The positive reaction –**This man is truly the prophet** – presumably has in view the prophet like Moses. Since Moses was instrumental in giving people water to drink in the wilderness, Jesus' claim to provide water may have convinced some that he was Moses' prophetic successor. Similarly, the other positive response, **This man is the Christ**, may have been provoked because some strands of messianic expectation associated the Messiah with springs of wisdom from which all were able to drink (cf. *1 Enoch* 48.1, 10; 49.1). An opposing view is expressed, however – **Surely the Christ does not come from Galilee, does he? Did not the scripture say that the Christ comes from the seed of David and from Bethlehem, the village where David was?** How the evangelist would expect readers to respond to this objection is disputed. Is the force that any such speculation about Jesus' place of earthly origin is beside the point, because Jesus' real place of origin is above? Or is there irony because readers know from their acquaintance with other Gospel traditions that what appears to be an objection is not, since Jesus' birthplace was in fact Bethlehem and not Galilee? The issue is difficult to decide. Elsewhere this Gospel makes it clear that Jesus' earthly place of origin is Nazareth, and at its outset this presents a scandal for Nathanael, yet he is able to make the confession that Jesus is the royal Messiah, 'the King of Israel', without that being dependent on knowledge of Jesus coming from elsewhere (cf. 1.46–9). Yet how likely is it that the evangelist would raise an objection based on a specific scripture, in this case Mic. 5.2, if he did not think that the objection could be met and that Jesus had actually fulfilled this scripture? It could be, then, that the evangelist is aware of the tradition behind Matthew and Luke or of the actual birth narratives, although having Jesus born in Bethlehem is not at all necessary for his own distinctive Christological perspective. If so, the point here may be that the objectors misunderstand what the real question about Jesus' origin is, and, even when they formulate their own inadequate question, are unaware that that question is one to which Christian believers have already given considerable reflection.

43–4 The division within the crowd reflected by these different opinions is then intensified, because not only are there some who raise objections to Jesus' messiahship but **some of them wanted to arrest him** (cf. v. 30).

45–6 The narrator now returns to the more official attempt to arrest Jesus, which he had introduced in v. 32. The temple guards go back to the chief priests and Pharisees, having failed to carry out their instructions. When asked for an explanation, **The guards answered, 'Never has a man spoken like this.'** They are clearly impressed by the boldness of the claim they have heard Jesus make and thus their response, which is similar to that of 'the Jews' in v. 15, serves as a witness to the power of Jesus' words.

47–9 The Pharisees take this as an indication that, like some of the crowd (v. 12), the guards **Have . . . also been led astray** by this false prophet. They contrast themselves and the religious leaders, whose knowledge of the law would never allow them to be so easily persuaded, with **this crowd, which does not know the law**, and **is accursed**. This reflects a common Pharisaic attitude of despising 'the peoples of the land', who were not well trained in the law and less than meticulous in observing some of its instructions. For the Pharisees such people merited the law's curse on those who failed to observe it (cf. Deut. 27.26). On their view, those who were so lax about the law's requirements were clearly in no position to assess Jesus' teaching properly. The obvious implication is that only they, the Pharisees and the chief priests, were competent to judge Jesus. The last section of the passage attempts to undermine this assumption in two ways.

50–2 First, Nicodemus is brought back onto the scene for a brief appearance in order to point out that those who claim to know the law are not in fact carrying it out in this case. There is a reminder of the previous appearance of Nicodemus and of his depiction there – he **had come to him earlier and was one of them**, i.e. a Pharisee, a leader of the Jews (cf. 3.1). Despite his sympathy for Jesus both there and here, he continues to be designated as 'one of them' and not as 'a disciple of Jesus who was also a Pharisee and Jewish leader'. His sympathy shows itself here in his fairness and concern for due process – **Our law does not judge a person before first hearing from him and learning what he is doing, does it?** His question calls into question the Pharisees' knowledge of the law by reminding them of such passages as Deut. 1.16–17, with its injunctions to give a fair hearing, to judge rightly, not to be partial, and to hear out the small and great alike.

But the Pharisees are not prepared to be corrected. They respond with further prejudice – **You are not from Galilee too, are you? Investigate and you will see that a prophet does not arise from Galilee**. They attempt to associate Nicodemus with Galilee, which they treat with contempt, just as they have done the common people. More substantially, they appeal to

Scripture and claim that no prophet comes from Galilee. Strictly speaking, they are wrong, since the prophet Jonah was from Galilee, according to 2 Kgs 14.25. If what they meant was that there is no prediction that the prophet like Moses or the Messiah will come from Galilee, then they ought to have been aware – as is the evangelist, who will allude to it at the beginning of the next section in 8.12 – of the messianic prophecy about Galilee in Isa. 9.1, 2. Either way, for a second time their competence in the law is exposed as deficient.

Jesus claims to fulfil that which the Festival of Tabernacles signified in its water symbolism by being the source of the living water of the Spirit for those who are thirsty. This again produces division and the attempt to arrest him. The forensic motifs introduced earlier in the chapter are developed, as Jesus' exhortation to judge not by appearances but with right judgement (v. 24) is played out through the divided opinions, through the charges brought against messianic claims made on Jesus' behalf, and particularly through the portrayal of the Pharisees and religious leaders, who claim to be able to judge because of their knowledge of the law but are shown to be incompetent and unjust judges. Jesus' offer of water is by no means unrelated to the judgement theme. The scriptural citation he employs draws on texts about waters flowing from the wilderness and temple rock. The source of the former in Exod. 17.1–7 has as its context the people bringing a suit against Moses and, by implication, God. Indeed Moses is told to take his rod of judgement and to strike the rock on which God now stands. God, the true judge, receives the sentence the rebellious people wish to carry out on Moses and which they deserve, and, in doing so, provides the water they need, as it gushes out of the rock. Through the scripture citation Jesus is now presented as the rock from whom living waters flow. Its rich allusions show Jesus as the fulfilment also of temple and birthing imagery. But by pointing to his glorification as the time when the promise of the citation will be accomplished, the narrator makes clear in particular that in the case of Jesus too the life-giving water of the Spirit will be made available through his undergoing the judgement of death. The crucifixion account will depict blood and water, the symbols of life, flowing from his side (cf. 19.34), as the true judge who is judged becomes the source of the new life of the Spirit for those who believe.

(x) Jesus' teaching on the light, his departure, true discipleship and
Abrahamic descent   8.12–59

(12) Again Jesus spoke to them, saying, 'I am the light of the world. Whoever follows me will never walk in darkness but will have the light of life.' (13) The Pharisees therefore said to him, 'You are witnessing about yourself; your witness is therefore not

true.' (14) Jesus answered, and said to them, 'Even if I witness about myself, my witness is true, because I know where I came from and where I am going. But you know neither where I come from nor where I am going. (15) You judge according to the flesh; I judge no one. (16) And even if I do judge, my judgement is true, because I am not alone, but it is I and the Father who sent me. (17) In your law it is written that the witness of two people is true. (18) I am the one who witnesses about myself and the Father who sent me witnesses about me.' (19) They said to him, 'Where is your father?' Jesus answered, 'You know neither me nor my Father. If you knew me, you would also know my Father.' (20) He spoke these words in the treasury, while he was teaching in the temple. And no one arrested him, for his hour had not yet come.

(21) Again he said to them, 'I am going away and you will seek me, but you will die in your sin. Where I am going, you cannot come.' (22) The Jews therefore said, 'Is he going to kill himself, because he said, "Where I am going, you cannot come"?' (23) He said to them, 'You are from below, I am from above. You are of this world, I am not of this world. (24) Therefore I told you that you would die in your sins; for unless you believe that I am, you will die in your sins.' (25) So they said to him, 'Who are you?' Jesus said to them, 'Why do I even speak to you at all?[1] (26) I have much to say about you and to judge. But the one who sent me is true, and what I have heard from him I speak to the world.' (27) They did not know that he was speaking to them about the Father. (28) So Jesus said, 'When you have lifted up the Son of Man, then you will know that I am, and that I do nothing on my own but speak these things as the Father taught me. (29) And the one who sent me is with me; he has not left me alone, because

---

[1] The most ancient manuscripts agree on the text at this point, but because they contain no division between words or punctuation, different translations are possible. The text can be read as either ὅτι or ὅ τι. In the former case ὅτι can be translated as 'why?' and τὴν ἀρχήν as 'at all' to give 'Why do I even speak to you at all?' In the latter case ὅ τι could be either part of an exclamation ('That I speak to you at all!') or, if τὴν ἀρχήν is taken as 'from the beginning', part of an answer to the preceding question, 'Who are you?' ('That which I am also telling you from the beginning.') Although the last of these options appears to do most justice to the context by supplying an answer to the opponents' question, it is the most difficult to support in terms of normal Greek syntax and usage. If 'from the beginning' was meant, one would have expected a prepositional phrase such as ἐν ἀρχῇ or ἀπ' ἀρχῆς. The adverbial use of τὴν ἀρχήν as 'at all', however, is fairly common in Greek. This makes the first or second translation option preferable. Of the two, probably the first is more likely. Its clear question, expressing momentary exasperation, then serves as a counter to the previous question.

I always do what is pleasing to him.' (30) As he was saying these things, many believed in him.

(31) Then Jesus said to the Jews who had believed in him, 'If you remain in my word, you are truly my disciples, (32) and you will know the truth, and the truth will set you free.' (33) They answered him, 'We are descendants of Abraham and have never been enslaved to anyone. How can you say, "You will become free"?' (34) Jesus answered them, 'Truly, truly, I say to you, everyone who commits sin is a slave of sin. (35) The slave does not remain in the household for ever; the son does remain for ever. (36) If then the Son sets you free, you will indeed be free. (37) I know that you are descendants of Abraham; but you are seeking to kill me, because my word finds no room in you. (38) I speak of what I have seen in the Father's presence; you therefore should do what you have heard from your father.'[2]

(39) They answered and said to him, 'Our father is Abraham.' Jesus said to them, 'If you were Abraham's children, you would be doing the works of Abraham.[3] (40) Yet now you are seeking to kill me, a man who has spoken to you the truth I have heard from God. Abraham did not do this. (41) You are doing the works of your father.' They said to him, 'We were not born illegitimately; we have one father, God.' (42) Jesus said to them, 'If God were your Father, you would love me, for I came out from God and am here. I did not come on my own, but he sent me. (43) Why do you not understand what I say? Because you are not able to hear my word. (44) You are of your father, the devil, and you want to do your father's desires. He was a murderer from the beginning, and he does not stand in the truth, because the truth is not in him. When he tells a lie, he is speaking in character, because he is a liar and the father of lies. (45) But because I speak

---

[2] There is a textual question whether 'father' in both parts of the verse should be accompanied by a possessive. The oldest manuscripts ($p^{66,75}$) omit the possessives in both cases, but a number of variant readings have added 'my' in the first part of the verse and 'your' in the second in an attempt to clarify what they take as a contrast. If the possessives are omitted, there remains a question as to the reference of the second mention of 'father'. It could be that this refers to the Father these Jews share with Jesus. But since they have already indirectly claimed Abraham as father and this notion has just been reiterated by Jesus in the context of a charge that they are seeking to kill him and his word finds no room among them (cf. v. 37), it appears more likely that the second reference is to Abraham and anticipates the discussion that follows in vv. 39–40. The translation, therefore, adds 'your' to reflect this interpretation.

[3] The oldest textual witnesses are fairly evenly divided between the imperfect, ἐποιεῖτε, and the present imperative, ποιεῖτε. The original reading is most likely to have been a mixed conditional sentence with the imperfect, which was changed to an imperative in an attempt to smooth out the syntax.

the truth, you do not believe me. (46) Which of you convicts me of sin? If I speak the truth, why do you not believe me? (47) The one who is from God hears the words of God; the reason you do not hear is that you are not from God.'

(48) The Jews answered and said to him, 'Are we not right in saying that you are a Samaritan and have a demon?' (49) Jesus responded, 'I do not have a demon, but I honour my Father and you dishonour me. (50) But I do not seek my own glory; there is one who seeks it and he judges. (51) Truly, truly, I say to you, whoever keeps my word will never see death.' (52) The Jews said to him, 'Now we know that you have a demon. Abraham died, as did the prophets, and you say, "Whoever keeps my word will never taste death." (53) Are you greater than our father Abraham, who died? The prophets also died. Who do you make yourself out to be?' (54) Jesus answered, 'If I glorify myself, my glory is nothing. It is my Father who glorifies me, the one of whom you say, 'He is our God,' (55) although you do not know him. But I know him. If I were to say that I do not know him, I would be a liar like you. But I do know him and keep his word. (56) Your father Abraham rejoiced that he would see my day, and he saw it and was glad.' (57) Then the Jews said to him, 'You are not yet fifty years old and have you seen Abraham?' (58) Jesus said to them, 'Truly, truly, I say to you, before Abraham came to be, I am.' (59) So they picked up stones to throw at him. But Jesus hid and left the temple.

In most English translations the story of the woman taken in adultery is placed in parentheses between the previous section and this one. This passage, a later addition to the original Gospel, will be treated in the Appendix at the end of the commentary. Its insertion here tends to obscure the fact that the extended debate in 8.12–59 has the same narrative setting as that of 7.14–44. It is at the time of the Feast of Tabernacles and in the environs of the temple. The forensic aspects of the previous dispute have been noted. These now become more concentrated, as a number of themes already treated in the previous section are developed here. Some of the features in Jesus' defence speech of 5.19–47 are also taken up again.

The varying ways in which Jesus' debating partners or accusers are described help to mark the main divisions of this passage. In vv. 12–30 the opponents are designated first as 'the Pharisees' (v. 13) and then as 'the Jews' (v. 22). The two designations also indicate that this material falls into two parts – vv. 12–20, which is rounded off by the narrator's comments about the setting, and vv. 21–30, which concludes with the narrator's remarks about the response of belief on the part of many. In vv. 31–47 there is apparently a change as the audience becomes the Jews who had believed in Jesus (cf. v. 31), while in vv. 48–59 the opposition is again simply 'the Jews' (vv. 48, 57). The differing designations of these groups may well mean that controversies from various stages in the community's history have been brought together in this chapter. There is considerable scholarly debate about whether in this final form the reader is meant to take 'the Jews' in vv. 48–59 as the same group described as 'the Jews who had believed in him' in v. 31 or whether this latter verse is to be treated simply as a transitional gloss. The present form of the narrative seems designed to be read as a continuous debate. The most straightforward way of doing so is to read the dispute of vv. 31–47 as indeed one with Jews who have believed but to see their belief as so deficient that by the time v. 47 is reached it has become exposed as hostile unbelief. Since, in the narrator's view, this group has now been shown to be in reality unbelievers, its members simply fall back into the category of those designated as 'the Jews'. That the opponents in vv. 48–59 are to be identified with the group in vv. 31–47 is indicated by Jesus' comment in v. 55 – 'I would be a liar like you' – which takes up from v. 44 implicit accusation that Jesus' opponents are liars.

The changing designations of the opposition are, however, not as important as the consistent character of the overall dispute, which again has the features of a trial or lawsuit. The varying strands of Jewish opposition are the accusers who interrogate Jesus and bring charges against him. At the beginning his accusers are also his judges, but, as in 5.17–49, Jesus starts as a witness in his own defence and then the roles become reversed, as he becomes prosecutor and judge of the opponents, levelling counter-accusations and charges against them. At issue again are Jesus' claims about his identity, and, typical of Jewish legal process, crucial for the outcome is the establishment of the veracity and character of the witnesses on either side.

12 Jesus' self-identification – **I am the light of the world** – is part of the motif of his replacement of the significance of the Feast of Tabernacles, with its water and light imagery (cf. also 7.37–9). The Mishnah speaks of the four large lampstands in the Court of Women that were lit up at the end of the first day of the festival. The illumination was not only enough for the celebrations and dancing but was said to be so bright as to extend its light over the rest of the city (cf. *m. Sukk.* 5.2–4). Jesus' claim is to be the light not only of Jerusalem but also of the world. It employs the 'I Am' formulation, which occurs in 8.18, 24, 28 and is found again at the end of the passage in 8.58, forming an *inclusio* for this passage as a whole and signalling clearly that the question of Jesus' identity will be the focus of the dispute.

Jesus' assertion is not entirely unconnected with the immediately preceding discussion, where the issue of whether the Christ or a prophet was to come from Galilee has been raised (7.41, 52). Isa. 9.1–2 had said of 'Galilee of the nations' that 'the people who walked in darkness have seen a great light; those who lived in a land of deep darkness – on them light has shined' (cf. also Matt. 4.14–16). This Gospel's prologue has already identified the Logos with light (cf. 1.4, 9) and now the incarnate Logos himself makes this identification explicitly. Readers have also already been shown that light is intimately associated with the motif of judgement (cf. 3.19–21) and are reminded of that association here by Jesus' further claim that whoever follows him **will never walk in darkness but will have the light of life**. In the judgement provoked by the presence of the light there is the negative effect of revealing and condemning what belongs to the darkness and the positive effect, which is in view in this claim, of the illumination producing life, the salvific verdict in the cosmic trial. Through the use of the symbolism of light Jesus is depicted not only as fulfilling a central feature of the Feast of Tabernacles but also as fulfilling all that Wisdom and Torah, which were also associated with light (cf. Ps. 119.105; Wis. 7.26) and life (cf. Deut. 30.15–20; Sir. 17.11; Prov. 8.35), signified. His claim will be taken up again in the following chapter and substantiated through the healing of the blind man (cf. 9.5).

13–14 Jesus' claim to be the light functions as a foil for the discussion of testimony that now follows. The Pharisees respond to Jesus' extraordinary assertion by claiming that it cannot be true, since it is testimony about himself and therefore invalid according to the laws of testimony. In 5.31, as has been noted, Jesus himself conceded this point and immediately appealed to his Father's testimony on his behalf as a second witness. Here he delays before making such a concession to the law (cf. vv. 17–18). This time he first wants to make quite clear that the exceptional identity of the one who is testifying about himself makes his witness valid anyway – **Even if I witness about myself, my witness is true** (cf. also 7.17–18). His statement about his identity is in terms of knowing where he has come from and where he is going. His origin and destiny are key elements in the narrative's depiction of Jesus' distinctive identity. He has come from and is going to God, the Father, heaven, above, glory – these terms are all functional equivalents in underlining his divine origin and destiny. So the claim is that he is so at one with God that his witness is self-authenticating, for by definition God needs no one to validate God's testimony.

15–16 By their failure to allow that in Jesus' case testimony about himself is valid, a failure that in turn rests on the failure to recognize his divine origin and destiny, the Pharisees lay themselves open to the charge Jesus now levels against them – **You judge according to the flesh**. This indictment involves more than that they are simply following the human conventions of Jewish forensic process or judging according to appearances (cf. 7.24). As has become clear from its earlier usage (cf. 1.12; 3.6; 6.63), 'flesh' can have the negative connotations of the sphere which is opposed to God and the Spirit. It is equivalent to the world, earth or below in contrast to God, heaven or above. So the charge is that the Pharisees in pursuing their judgement against Jesus are doing so in a manner that demonstrates their captivity to the realm of hostile unbelief and its values. Jesus then asserts in stark contrast, **I judge no one**. The assertion raises difficulties for interpretation because it also stands in contrast to Jesus' clear earlier statement about his judging activity in 5.30 and to the declaration that follows later in this context in v. 26. But those who take the contrast as a straightforward aporia ignore the fact that in its most immediate context this assertion is qualified both by what precedes it in v. 15a and by what follows it in v. 16. So it may well be that it should neither be taken as an outright denial of any judging activity on Jesus' part nor harmonized by interpreting judging as condemning and thereby seeing the assertion as in line with the statement about the primary purpose of Jesus' mission in 3.17. Rather, Jesus is indicating that by ordinary criteria his activity is not really judging, because it is not according to worldly values and is not exercised as an independent human judgement. The latter point is underlined by the immediate qualification – **even if I do judge, my judgement is true, because I am not alone, but it is I and the Father who sent me**. This explicitly makes his judgement a divine activity, thereby removing it from the whole sphere of the flesh and setting it in the context of the cosmic trial, in which, as the uniquely authorized divine agent, he is engaged in a joint enterprise with the Father who sent him. What is said about Jesus' judging activity in v. 16 parallels what has been said about his witness in v. 14. In both cases Jesus claims that his violation of the expectations and conventions of the human forensic process is justified by his participation in the greater cosmic trial and by his unique relationship to its instigator.

17–18 Jesus now reverts to the topic of testimony. The shifts back and forth between Jesus as witness and Jesus as judge would appear sudden and awkward if the dispute in chapter 5 had not already prepared readers for the irony of Jesus' dual role, which in turn reflects Yahweh's functioning as both witness and judge in the trial scenes of Isa. 40—55. Having stressed his self-authenticating witness, Jesus can now return to the conventions of ordinary Jewish trials – **In your law it is written that the witness of two people is true**. As he did in 5.31–7, he again accommodates himself to the law's requirements (cf. Deut. 19.15). But the concession to the opponents' standard of judgement ('*your* law') is ironic. The law required two witnesses, not including the accused, and an appeal to God is not envisaged as one of these. The force of Jesus' mention of the law appears to be that if the law demands two human witnesses, then he will supply two divine witnesses – himself and the Father. In the end, however, Jesus' witness to himself and his and the Father's joint witness amount to the same thing because of the unity between the Son and the Father who sent him. It should be noted that, in speaking of himself, Jesus uses a periphrastic construction with ἐγώ εἰμι – **I am the one who witnesses about myself** – in order to stress his identification with the role of the witness. Again Isa. 40—55 may well provide the background. Isa. 43.10 LXX, which employs the 'I Am' formulation, also speaks of two witnesses, Yahweh and Israel, the servant, who has just been portrayed as a light to the nations (Isa. 42.6). Through his claims here to be both the light of the world and the one who bears witness, Jesus can also be seen as taking on the role envisaged for the servant in God's lawsuit with the world.

19 The gulf between Jesus' and his opponents' perspectives is again immediately made plain through the narrative's typical device of misunderstanding. Jesus has referred to his Father and now the Pharisees ask, **Where is your father?**, as if they want him to produce his physical father as a witness on the spot. This enables Jesus to declare that such a question is evidence that they know neither him nor his Father. From his perspective the unity between himself and his Father is such that **If you knew me, you would also know my Father.** So his indictment is a radical one. For all their zeal to carry out the law in prosecuting Jesus, his opponents do not really know the one who gave them that law in the first place.

20 The narrator's note about the location of this confrontation – **He spoke these words in the treasury** – also provides a reminder of its setting at the Feast of Tabernacles, since the temple treasury was next to the Court of Women, in which the light celebration took place. As in 7.30, there is a further reminder of the divine timetable for Jesus' mission. This interrogation of Jesus would not result in his arrest, **for his hour had not yet come**.

21 The second stage of the dispute in vv. 21–30 develops two themes already found in the first. In v. 14 Jesus had spoken of his origin and destiny. Now the focus is on the latter as he speaks of his going away. In vv. 12, 18 Jesus had identified himself by using the ἐγώ εἰμι, 'I Am' formulation with a predicate. Here the question of his identity is raised particularly by means of two absolute 'I Am' statements (vv. 24, 28). After declaring that he is going away, Jesus states, **you will seek me, but you will die in your sin**. The reference to 'sin' in the singular underlines that what is in view is not so much individual actions but rather the decisive sin of unbelief. Failure to believe in Jesus entails separation from the source of life and therefore results in death. As has been made clear, it is believing in Jesus or receiving his testimony that enables a person to be born from above, not to perish, and to have eternal life (cf. 3.3–16).

22–3 Once again the device of misunderstanding is employed to illustrate the great divide between the perspective of Jesus and that of 'the Jews'. When Jesus says, **Where I am going, you cannot come,** in contrast to their response to the similar statement in 7.33–5, they at least recognize that his going away has something to do with his death. But they take him to be talking about suicide, and Jesus uses this gross incomprehension as evidence of the totally opposite origins of himself and his opponents. Whereas he is **not of this world** but **from above** (cf. 3.31), they are **from below** and **of this world**. Origin in the divine sphere and origin in the sphere of this world hostile to God define the two parties and explain their opposing perspectives. In this Gospel's discourse what is needed if humans who are caught up in this world are to change their perspective is a transference of spheres through the belief in Jesus that enables them to be born of God (1.12) or born from above (3.3, 7).

24 Unless you believe that I am, you will die in your sins is the way Jesus now formulates this necessary change. The shift in terminology to the plural 'sins' (cf. v. 21) may be no more than stylistic but also indicates that the primary sin of unbelief is exhibited in a variety of actions. The means of escaping the sphere of this world, characterized by its sins and death, is to 'believe that I am'. This object of belief is ambiguous at the level of the hearers in the narrative, as their question will indicate (v. 25). It is possible that 'from above' in v. 23 is the antecedent that is meant to supply an implied predicate, but it is much more likely that again Isaiah provides the background which enables the reader to take the 'I Am' as it stands, absolutely, and to understand it adequately. Indeed the very same words from Jesus' formulation are found in Isa. 43.10 LXX – πιστεύσητε …ὅτι ἐγώ εἰμι, 'believe … that I am'. There the combined witness of Israel and Yahweh is meant to lead to the belief that 'I Am', where the phrase stands for Yahweh's claim to be the only God and the only Saviour of Israel (cf. 43.10c–13). Now Jesus is depicted as applying Yahweh's words of self-identification to himself, and, in so doing, calling the representatives of Israel in his day to believe that their one God and their Saviour from sin and death is to be identified with himself.

25–7 At this point such claims are lost on Jesus' audience. Their uncomprehending question, **Who are you?**, provokes frustration on the part of Jesus, who, on the most likely construction of a difficult sentence, asks why he is speaking to them at all. Nevertheless their incomprehension is not permitted to frustrate his mission more than temporarily. Jesus still has much to say about his listeners and what he has to say is in his role as judge. The truth of that judgement must be heard and must prevail, and this is reinforced by the reminder of his role as the fully authorized representative of the one true judge – **the one who sent me is true, and**

what I have heard from him I speak to the world. In the lawsuit against the world Jesus simply tells the world what he has heard from the source of its true judgement (cf. also v. 16). The narrator then underlines the audience's incomprehension of Jesus' words with the observation that **They did not know that he was speaking to them about the Father.**

28–9 In the face of such a response Jesus announces to his hearers that there will come a time when they will understand the intimate relationship he has with the Father, in which **the one who sent me is with me** and there is such harmony with the Father's will that **I do nothing on my own but speak these things as the Father taught me** and **always do what is pleasing to him**. That crucial time is when they **have lifted up the Son of Man**, which, as was noted in regard to 3.14 (cf. also 12.32–4), is the time of Jesus' exaltation to glory by means of his death by crucifixion. Of the three references to 'lifting up' in the narrative, this is the one that lays stress on the human agents. The appropriate response to this event – realizing what it reveals of Jesus' relationship to the Father – is once more formulated in terms of 'I Am' – **then you will know that I am**. Again it is just possible, though a somewhat awkward possibility, that the implied predicate is the Son of Man. But in the light of v. 24 and the Isaiah background it is more likely that we have another absolute use of the expression. The wording is paralleled in Isa. 43.10 LXX, which has γνῶτε . . . ὅτι ἐγώ εἰμι, while John 8.28a has γνώσεσθε ὅτι ἐγώ εἰμι. Not only the 'I Am' formula but also the language of 'lifting up' (cf. Isa. 52.13) has been taken from Isa. 40—55. The reworking of these elements now indicates in striking fashion that it is the lifting up on the cross that will be the means by which the divine identity and glory of Jesus, who is also the servant-witness, will be revealed. The key moment of the divine verdict in the trial, the vindication of Jesus' claim, is to be the same moment at which the opposition appear to have had their way, namely, their crucifixion of Jesus. So far from such a death being Jesus' humiliation, it is to be seen as his exaltation. So far from it involving his abandonment by the Father, it is to be seen as confirmation that the Father **has not left me alone**.

30 Somewhat surprisingly in the light of the previous comments about the audience's incomprehension of Jesus' words, the narrator now indicates that **many believed in him**. This combination of incomprehension about Jesus' relationship with the Father and yet belief in Jesus may, however, prepare the reader for the exposure of the grave deficiencies of such a belief in the passage that follows. It may well be also that the response of some Jewish believers, which, from the narrator's perspective, is to be seen as pseudo-belief, reflects the evangelist's experience in the setting from which the Gospel emerged. There, some who initially believed were not able, when the time of testing from the synagogue came, to confess openly the community's distinctive belief about Jesus' unique relationship as Son of God to the Father and so became a major cause for disappointment and then disapprobation as apostates.

31–2 The vocabulary of witness and judging now recedes (though cf. v. 50), but the overall trial framework is continued through the accusations and counter-accusations that follow. They again revolve around Jesus' identity and his opponents' inability to accept his claims about himself. In vv. 31–47 the issues are formulated primarily in terms of truth, while in vv. 48–59 they will focus more on Jesus' glory or honour.

The question whether those Jews who have believed in Jesus have exercised true faith is immediately raised by the way in which Jesus addresses them – **If you remain in my word, you are truly my disciples**. In fact, the test of true discipleship is a continuing allegiance to Jesus' teaching, a knowing of the truth which is able to liberate one from the sphere of sin and death – **you will know the truth, and the truth will set you free**. As the similar statement about freedom in v. 36 will make clear, this liberating truth can be summed up as God's revelation embodied in Jesus (cf. also 14.6).

33 The Jewish believers immediately cast doubt on the nature of their belief by the lack of understanding exhibited in their response. They appear to show more concern about the ethnic aspect of their identity – **We are descendants of Abraham** – than about being followers of Jesus and they deny the need for liberation with the claim that they **have never been enslaved to anyone**. There is obvious irony on the political level about such a claim being made by those under Roman occupation, but presumably they intend it more as an expression of their internal religious freedom, including freedom from idolatry (cf. also 5.41), on the basis of their relation to God through the covenant with Abraham.

34–6 Jesus does not allow them to get away with their claim even on this level, drawing them back to his notion of captivity to the sphere of sin and death by pointing out that **everyone who commits sin is a slave of sin**. He then makes use of an everyday analogy, contrasting the slave, who has no permanent right to remain in the household, with the son, who remains for ever. On the one hand, this is an immediate reminder of the opening of this section of the argument. The condition for being a true disciple is to remain in Jesus' word. The one who commits sin is the slave who does not remain in the house and, by extension, does not remain in Jesus' word. On the other hand, in the light of the claim on the part of the audience to be Abraham's descendants, there is also a reminder of the Genesis narrative in which there are two sorts of descendant from Abraham – a slave son and a free son, Ishmael and Isaac (cf. Gen. 16.15; 21.9–21). This is an aspect of the narrative Paul had exploited in his polemic against Jewish Christian opposition in Gal. 4.21–31. Here, however, while 'the Jews' are the slave descendants, it is Jesus himself who is primarily in view as the free son who is able to liberate others – **If then the Son sets you free, you will indeed be free.** For those willing to acknowledge their sinful condition and need of liberation, the Son of God is able to constitute them as permanent members of the household, as free children of God (cf. 1.12).

37–8 In his role as prosecutor and judge, Jesus goes further and, while acknowledging his hearers' physical descent from Abraham, charges his audience with seeking to kill him, and this charge is, of course, confirmed by their action at the end of this exchange (cf. v. 59). Their lethal intent is directly connected to their attitude to Jesus' witness. It is **because my word finds no room in you.** Their way of identifying themselves leads to their becoming closed in on themselves so that they can allow no space within themselves for Jesus' word. True discipleship can be depicted, then, in terms of people either remaining in Jesus' word (v. 31) or, as here, as making room for that word to remain in them. And true identity as Abraham's descendants is to be judged now by people's response to Jesus. Jesus presses further this issue of true paternity. For his part, he claims to speak what he has seen in the Father's presence and then urges his inter-locutors to do what they have heard from the one they invoke as father.

39–40 Their answer makes explicit that it is Abraham who is in view here – **Our father is Abraham.** So, again, Jesus makes the test for such paternity what a person does. A similar sort of discussion is found in Matt. 4.9 and Luke 3.8, where John the Baptist makes repentance and its fruits the criterion for the validity of any claim to have Abraham as one's ancestor. Here Jesus indicates that his opponents' attempt to kill the one who has told them the truth he has heard from God simply shows no affinity with what Abraham did. Presumably in view here is Abraham's reception of and hospitality to God's messengers in Gen. 18.1–8.

41–2 His hearers' refusal to hear the truth and intent to kill him lead Jesus to raise the issue of ultimate spiritual paternity – **You are doing the works of your father.** But before Jesus can make his point explicitly, they interject, **We were not born illegitimately; we have one father, God.** There has been some discussion whether the assertion that they were not born illegitimately (ἐκ πορνείας) is meant as an attack on Jesus because of rumours that may have circulated about the abnormal circumstances of his birth. At this stage, however, the hearers appear to be more concerned to defend their perspective on their own ancestry and to deny any suggestion that it is other than it should be. They will turn to attack Jesus, but in other terms, later in v. 48. Since 'fornication' is often a metaphor used of idolatry in the Jewish Scriptures, the assertion here is best taken as a claim they are not unfaithful idolaters (cf. Hos. 1.2; 2.4–5 LXX) but are faithful to the one God of the Shema (cf. Deut. 6.4). Jesus' response is again to point to a mismatch between their paternity claims and their behaviour, by alleging that if God were truly their Father, they would love him, since he has been sent from God. True love for God would manifest itself in love for the one who has come as God's uniquely qualified representative.

Jesus' formulation about himself goes beyond the language of being sent as a representative – **for I came out from God and am here**. This is what makes him uniquely qualified; he himself has a divine origin. Christian theology has rightly seen this language of coming out from or proceeding from God, which is used also of the Spirit in 15.26, as foundational for its notion of trinitarian relations with their divine processions. God produces God, both Son and Spirit, in a way that manifests internal differentiation within the one God.

43–4 Jesus' rhetorical question makes clear that, as it is, however, those whom he addresses continue in their failure to comprehend his claims. This is, he alleges, **Because you are not able to hear my word** (cf. v. 37). Origin is then seen as determining behaviour. Misunderstanding is caused by an inability to hear appropriately and that inability derives from a relationship to the source of evil rather than a relationship with God – **You are of your father, the devil, and you want to do your father's desires.** The opposition's paternity is attributed to an ultimate personal power of evil, designated here as the devil (cf. also 6.70; 13.2) and elsewhere as the ruler of this world (cf. 12.31; 14.30; 16.11), who, in an allusion to the role of the serpent in the story of the fall in Gen. 3, is seen as both the source and the epitome of all that is contrary to love and truth – **He was a murderer from the beginning . . . he is a liar and the father of lies**.

Although it is directed against a group who are said to want to kill Jesus, the fierceness of the polemic, especially at this point, offends modern sensibilities and indeed this verse is often considered a *locus classicus* of Christian anti-Semitism. Its rhetoric, however, should first be heard from within its first-century context. The accusations in this passage would not have sounded any different from some of the fierce indictments of Israel in its own Scriptures. Most of the charges Jesus makes in this chapter reflect those found in the prophets, in particular, those made by Yahweh against the people in Isaiah. Their lack of knowledge (vv. 14, 19, 55; cf. Isa. 48.8), their being from below (v. 23; cf. Isa 55.9), their being slaves because of sin (vv. 33–4; cf. Isa. 50.1) and their not hearing (vv. 43, 47; cf. Isa. 42.18, 20) are indicted in both Isaiah and John. In addition, in Isaiah

Yahweh had told Israel that its ancestor was a transgressor (Isa. 43.27), that from birth it too had been a rebel (Isa. 48.8), that it was involved in idolatry (Isa. 44.9) and that such idolatry was participation with the devil (cf. Isa. 65.11 LXX – 'you are those who have left me, and forget my holy mountain, and prepare a table for the devil'). Intra-Jewish polemics continued in this vein, so that in *Jub.* 15.33 the children of Israel were identified as 'sons of Belial', *T. Dan* 5.6 – 'your prince is Satan' – is an accusation of Dan against his children who, he believes, are abandoning the Lord, and one rabbi can later call his brother 'the firstborn of Satan' for giving a ruling with which he disagreed (*Yebamot* 16a). This was typical of ancient debate in general, where terms of abuse were expected and functioned as ways of labelling one's opponents as opponents. And, of course, this is reflected elsewhere in early Christian argumentation, where Jesus can tell Peter, 'Get behind me, Satan!' (Mark 8.33) or Paul can call other Jewish Christian missionaries false apostles, deceitful workers, and servants of Satan (2 Cor. 11.13–15). So this sort of language could be employed for those who would have considered themselves Christian believers but whose stance other believers found objectionable. Precisely this appears to be the case here. As has been observed, 'You are of your father the devil' is addressed to Jews who had believed in Jesus but did not continue in their belief in a way the evangelist and his community found satisfactory. When the test came, and persecution and death became real options, they appear to have remained in the synagogue instead of identifying with those who made the full Johannine confession. Elsewhere in early Christianity apostates could also be thought of as crucifying again the Son of God (cf. Heb. 6.6).

The dualism of this Gospel's rhetoric in which 'the Jews' are associated with this world, below, the flesh or the devil, while believers are not of this world and are linked with above, the Spirit and God should not be read as an ontological dualism, referring to a person's essential nature or the origin of his or her being. Instead, this dualism is an epistemological and ethical one (cf. 1.10–12; 3.19–20). It is the distinction between belief and unbelief that determines on which side of the dualism a person is found, with each side representing a different set of values that leads to different criteria for knowing, judging and behaving. What is more, it is clear that, according to this Gospel, both the positive and the negative sides of such dualism can apply to all kinds of people, regardless of their ethnic identity. In reading this type of polemic, it should be remembered that the similarly fierce indictments by the prophets or by the *Testament of Dan* were also not so much ontological statements as judgements aimed at producing repentance. For the Fourth Gospel it is perfectly compatible to see a division taking place within Judaism and humanity as a whole over the claims of Jesus and still to hold that the God of Jesus loves the world and has its salvation as the primary purpose of the Son's mission (cf. 3.16–17). So this rhetoric from intra-Jewish, and in all likelihood intra-Jewish Christian, dispute in the first century is far removed from anything that could be properly labelled anti-Semitism, where that term is understood to denote hatred of the Jewish people as a group because they are Jewish.

45–7 In contrast to the devil, Jesus is the representative of the truth rather than the lie, the innocent victim – **Which of you convicts me of sin?** – rather than the murderous perpetrator of violence. So this section of the dispute, which began by emphasizing that real belief involves knowing the liberating truth that Jesus reveals about himself (vv. 31–2), concludes with his condemnation of his hearers for not believing the truth he is telling them – **because I speak the truth, you do not believe me.** By now it has been made perfectly plain that the supposed Jewish believers in Jesus are bereft of genuine belief and therefore also of a right relationship with God – **the reason you do not hear is that you are not from God.** Indeed the harshest polemic in the narrative has been reserved for them. Not only are they not true followers of Jesus, they are not true sons of Abraham, they are not even sons of God but their paternity has to be traced to the devil. All this underlines that, from the narrator's point of view, in the overall trial process a verdict about Jesus is at the same time a verdict about God. When this passage is seen in the light of the conflict between the evangelist's community and the synagogue, what emerges is the claim that to have an initially positive attitude to Jesus which does not progress to recognizing the truth that behind the 'I Am' of Jesus lies the 'I Am' of Israel's one God is not simply to apostasize or to remain in the synagogue but to call into question one's relationship to God (cf. also vv. 54–5), and thereby to place oneself among those whom Isaiah had earlier indicted, those 'who are called by the name of Israel . . . and invoke the God of Israel but not in truth or right' (Isa. 48.1).

48 The counter-accusation of the hearers, who are now no longer called the Jews who had believed but simply 'the Jews', is equally fierce – **you are a Samaritan and have a demon.** If Jesus has accused them of apostasy and charged them with having the devil as their father, they now allege that he is a Samaritan, and so is the one who is an outsider to the covenant, an apostate from Israel, and that he has a demon (cf. also Mark 3.22) and so he is the one who is possessed by the devil. From the evangelist's point of view these accusations are seen as confirming Jesus' hearers' alienation from God and, because they are lies (cf. v. 55), their relationship to the liar and the father of lies.

49–50 Jesus ignores the allegation that he is a Samaritan, but denies that he has a demon and maintains instead that he is honouring his Father. His claims cannot be dismissed as demonic blasphemy that would dishonour God. At the same time he is concerned about the slight to his own honour resulting from the opposition's accusations – **I honour my Father and you dishonour me** (cf. also 5.23). This does not mean, however, that he is simply concerned about his own glory. It is the one whom the opponents claim as their God, but without truly knowing this God, who seeks Jesus' glory – **there is one who seeks it and he judges.** As Jesus asserts that his own honour will be upheld and vindicated by the ultimate judge, God, the dispute's accusations and counter-accusations are now explicitly placed in the context of the cosmic trial, and the reminder of this motif underlines in particular that the opponents are being judged, as their accusations expose their unbelief.

51–3 Despite this, Jesus under solemn oath continues to offer the positive verdict of life – **Truly, truly, I say to you, whoever keeps my word will never see death.** Those who evidence true belief by holding on to Jesus' word come what may (the equivalent to 'remain in my word' in v. 31) will escape condemnation by having passed from death to life (cf. 5.24). This double 'Amen' saying may well be a Johannine version of the Synoptic saying found in Mark 9.1 (cf. Matt. 16.28; Luke 9.27) – 'Truly, I say to you, there are some standing here who will not taste death before they see the kingdom of God come with power.' If so (and see the comments on 21.22–3 for further indications that this text was known in Johannine circles), the fourth evangelist has reworked the saying to eliminate the problematic time reference and to show that the death in view is spiritual and not physical. The promise offered in the saying here confirms for the hearers their accusation about Jesus having a demon, since someone who claimed to mediate immortality would be making himself equal to God in God's prerogative as life-giver. The possibility of the truth of such a claim is not entertained. Instead its hearers concentrate on what appear to be its pretensions of being greater than both Abraham and the prophets, who died, and ask, **Who do you make yourself out to be?** The wording of the question in terms of Jesus making himself to be someone connects it with the charge elsewhere that Jesus is making himself equal to God (cf. 5.18; 10.33; 19.7).

54–5 Jesus, however, is not in the business of self-aggrandizement, of having to make himself something he is not. His response, as in v. 50, is that it is God who establishes his identity and reputation – **It is my Father who glorifies me.** By speaking of **the one of whom you say, 'He is our God,' although you do not know him,** Jesus again makes clear what is at stake in his mission. The issue is that of how the one true God is known. Now that Jesus has come, God is to be known through the revelation that takes place in him. To refuse Jesus, therefore, is also to forfeit any genuine knowledge of God. It is Jesus' uniquely intimate knowledge of God that qualifies him to be the bearer of true knowledge to others – **But I know him. If I were to say that I do not know him, I would be a liar like you** (cf. also e.g. 1.18; 7.29; 14.7; 17.25–6).

56–8 Jesus now takes up his interlocutors' most recent reference to Abraham (cf. vv. 52–3), asserting that **Your father Abraham rejoiced that he would see my day, and he saw it and was glad.** Abraham functions here similarly to Moses in chapter 5. He is introduced as a witness for the opposition against Jesus but then the tables are turned and he becomes a witness for Jesus in his prosecution of the opposition. Jewish tradition held that Abraham had been shown the end times by God (2 Esd. 3.14) and his laughter in Gen. 17.17 was interpreted as rejoicing (Philo, *Mut.* 154; cf. also *Jub.* 15.17; *T. Levi* 18.14), and these elements are now combined in a Christological application. Typically, 'the Jews' are portrayed as totally misunderstanding Jesus by remaining on the earthly level. They can only mock at the difference between Jesus' relatively short lifespan and the age he would have to be in order to have encountered Abraham – **You are not yet fifty years old and have you seen Abraham?** Their incomprehension provides the foil for Jesus' climactic statement about himself, in the light of which the earlier question about Jesus' identity – 'Are you greater than our father Abraham, who died?' (v. 53) – turns out to be a highly ironic one.

With the astounding claim **before Abraham came to be, I am**, Jesus rounds off the discussion of Abraham and, more significantly, brings to a conclusion the dispute about his identity, which had begun with the 'I Am' saying with a predicate in v. 12, continued with the claim of v. 18, and intensified with the absolute 'I Am' sayings of vv. 24, 28. This final saying clearly contains an absolute use of 'I Am', whose present tense contrasts with the aorist infinitive (γενέσθαι) that expresses the coming into existence of Abraham, and indicates that more than a claim to pre-existence is being made. As with the earlier absolute uses of 'I Am' in vv. 24, 28, a reference to Isa. 43.10 LXX with its lawsuit context again appears to be in view. Significantly, there Yahweh's self-predication in terms of ἐγώ εἰμι is also contrasted with the temporal existence of another being, of whom the aorist tense of γίνομαι is employed – ἔμπροσθέν μου οὐχ ἐγένετο ἄλλος θεός, 'before me no other god came into existence'. Jesus' claim to be the self-revelation of the one true God is now unmistakable.

59 Even Jesus' narrative audience now recognizes his meaning. The narrator's comment is **So they picked up stones to throw at him,** which leaves the reader to assume that they have interpreted his words as a blasphemous identification with God (cf. 10.31, 33) and believe themselves to be carrying out the legal ruling of Lev. 24.16. This audience has reached its verdict, and, ironically, in the attempt to carry it through has proved the charge that Jesus had levelled against them (cf. v. 40). **But Jesus hid and left the temple.** These closing words of the narrator offer no explanation as to how Jesus' evasive activity was possible. What is more important is to see that this is the necessary narrative outworking of the plot's theological framework, in which Jesus' hour, the time for the final human verdict that will coincide with the decisive announcement of the divine verdict, has not yet arrived.

As has been noted, the history of interpretation of this chapter raises painful questions about Christian attitudes to Judaism and about the use of religious invective. Once there has been a reminder of the original setting, in which the language functioned as the apologetic of a minority group of Jewish Christians who had been faced with expulsion by the more powerful Jewish majority, these questions still deserve further extensive discussion. Yet in the end such reflection should not deflect from attention being paid to the Christological beliefs and their implications that provoked the first-century conflict and that remain to be negotiated by later readers. Throughout this passage, and in a number of ways, Jesus has claimed to be the unique locus of God's revelation. Those in dispute with him, though temporarily portrayed as believing, are depicted, on account of their basic unbelief, as uncomprehending, enslaved to sin, unable to receive Jesus' message, hostile in intent and alienated from God. The refusal to recognize the claims of Jesus is shown, therefore, to have profound repercussions. It casts doubt on any claim to be a free descendant of Abraham and to know the one true God of the covenant. For this Gospel, such claims are now to be judged in terms of whether or not they facilitate belief in the one who is presented as so identified with the divine sphere that he is able to take upon his own lips the 'I Am' formulation that had functioned in the Jewish Scriptures as Yahweh's self-designation.

(xi) The healing of the man born blind   9.1–41

(1) As he was walking along, he saw a man blind from birth. (2) And his disciples asked him, 'Rabbi, who sinned, this man or his parents, that he was born blind?' (3) Jesus answered, 'Neither this man nor his parents sinned, but this happened so that the works of God might be revealed in him. (4) We[1] must work the works

---

[1] Some manuscripts have the first person singular instead of the plural. The latter, however, has the better external support, including p^{66,75} ℵ* B.

of him who sent me[2] while it is day; night is coming when no one is able to work. (5) While I am in the world, I am the light of the world.' (6) Having said these things, he spat on the ground and made mud with the saliva, and he spread the mud on his eyes (7) and said to him, 'Go and wash in the Pool of Siloam' (which means Sent). Then he went away and washed, and came back seeing.

(8) Then the neighbours and those who had seen before that he was a beggar said, 'Is this not the one who was sitting and begging?' (9) Others said, 'It is he,' but still others said, 'No, but it is someone like him.' He said, 'I am he.' (10) Then they said to him, 'How then were your eyes opened?' (11) He answered, 'The man called Jesus made mud and spread it on my eyes and said to me, "Go to Siloam and wash." Having then gone away and washed, I gained my sight.' (12) They said to him, 'Where is he?' He said, 'I do not know.'

(13) They led to the Pharisees the man formerly blind. (14) Now it was a sabbath on the day Jesus made the mud and opened his eyes. (15) Again therefore the Pharisees also asked him how he had gained his sight. He said to them, 'He spread mud on my eyes, and I washed, and now I see.' (16) Some of the Pharisees therefore said to him, 'This man is not from God, because he does not keep the sabbath.' Others said, 'How can a sinful man do such signs?' And there was a division among them. (17) So they said to the blind man again, 'What do you say about him, since he opened your eyes?' He said, 'He is a prophet.'

(18) Now the Jews did not believe that he had been blind and had gained his sight, until they summoned the parents of the one who had gained his sight (19) and they asked them, 'Is this your son, who you say was born blind? How then does he now see?' (20) His parents therefore answered, 'We know that this is our son and that he was born blind. (21) How he now sees we do not know and who opened his eyes we do not know. Ask him, he is of age; he will speak for himself.' (22) His parents said these things because they feared the Jews, for the Jews had already decided that if anyone confessed him as the Christ, that person would be expelled from the synagogue. (23) For this reason his parents said, 'He is of age, ask him.'

(24) So for a second time they summoned the man who had been blind and said to him, 'Give glory to God; we know that

---

[2] Again there is a question whether the better reading employs the first person plural or singular. 'The one who sent me' is a characteristic Johannine expression and the plural formulation, which does not occur elsewhere in the Gospel, may well have been introduced to conform to the plural in the first part of this verse.

this man is a sinner.' (25) He answered, 'I do not know whether he is a sinner. One thing I know; I was blind and now I see.' (26) They said to him, 'What did he do to you? How did he open your eyes?' (27) He answered them, 'I have told you already and you did not listen. Why do you want to hear it again? Do you also want to become his disciples?' (28) They reviled him and said, 'You are that man's disciple, but we are disciples of Moses. (29) We know that God spoke to Moses, but we do not know where this man is from.' (30) The man answered them, 'This is what is amazing; you do not know where he is from and yet he opened my eyes. (31) We know that God does not listen to sinners, but if anyone is devout and does his will, he listens to that person. (32) Since the world began it has never been heard that someone opened the eyes of one who was born blind. (33) If this man were not from God, he could do nothing.' (34) They answered him, 'You were born entirely in sins, and do you want to teach us?' And they drove him out.

(35) Jesus heard that they had driven him out, and when he found him, he said, 'Do you believe in the Son of Man?' (36) He answered, 'And who is he, sir[3], that I may believe in him?' (37) Jesus said to him, 'You have seen him and the one speaking to you is he.' (38) He replied, 'I believe, Lord.' And he worshipped him.

(39) Jesus said, 'I came into this world for judgement, so that those who do not see might see and those who see might become blind.' (40) Some of the Pharisees who were with him heard this and said to him, 'Surely we are not blind also, are we?'(41) Jesus said to them, 'If you were blind, you would not have sin; but now that you say, "We see," your sin remains.'

The dispute with and condemnation of Jesus in 8.12–59 is followed by this account of a dispute with and condemnation of the man who had been blind. Jesus had been under interrogation for claims about his identity, particularly the claim to be the light of the world, which is repeated here immediately before the account of the healing in 9.5. Part of Jesus' earlier claim in 8.12 was 'Whoever follows me will never walk in darkness but will have the light of life.' Now the confirmation of this claim through the giving of sight to the blind man leads to this man's interrogation. The force of the narrative sequence is clear. If the one who is the light is subjected to opposition, trial and rejection by those who

---

[3] Here and in v. 38 the term κύριε can be translated as either 'sir' or 'Lord'. The translation offered recognizes a growth in the man's perception.

represent the darkness, it will be no different for his followers who have experienced the light of life.

Although 9.1–41 is treated here as a separate section for comment, it should also be seen as part of a more extended unit that is completed in chapter 10, where Jesus talks about his relationship to his followers in terms of shepherd and sheep, contrasting this with the role of the religious authorities, and where there is not only reference back to the episode with the blind man (cf. 10.21) but also a continuation of the themes of interrogation and judgement in 10.22–39.

The literary features and dramatic effectiveness of this account are impressive. The author's fondness for sevenfold arrangements is evident in the structuring of the episode into seven scenes (vv. 1–7; 8–12; 13–17; 18–23; 24–34; 35–8; 39–41). In accord with the conventions of biblical narrative, each scene is primarily an exchange between two characters or groups. As the central scene, 9.18–23 is particularly important, making explicit the later experience of Christian believers from which the episode is to be viewed. Readers who have known the cost of becoming Jesus' followers are thereby enabled to identify with what happens to the blind man as a consequence of gaining his sight. Two other distinctive features of this account underline the man's role as a model disciple. The focus throughout the rest of the Gospel's narrative is firmly on Jesus as the protagonist, but here curiously Jesus disappears from the scene in vv. 8–34 and the man born blind is instead the centre of attention. In this respect the account of this sign is quite different from that of the healing of the lame man in chapter 5, who quickly fades into the background. The man born blind not only speaks in 13 of the 41 verses but uses irony and sarcasm, some of the implied author's characteristic devices, and takes the initiative as he lectures the religious authorities on some basic theological points. In the process his character undergoes greater development than that of any other figure in the Gospel.

1–3 The two main characters in the opening scene are introduced – Jesus and the man born blind. The disciples are really present only as foils. Their question assumes that the man's blindness must be punishment for sin, either his own or his parents. But the assumption is immediately dismissed by Jesus, who offers a quite different perspective – **this happened so that the works of God might be revealed in him**. Instead of treating the man's blindness as an occasion for speculating about blame, Jesus views it as an occasion for carrying out his mission of performing God's life-giving works and overcoming the blindness. Although the disciples' question about sin is ignored in the immediate context, 'sin' does become a recurring motif later in the chapter – the issue of whether Jesus is a sinner is raised (vv. 16, 24–5, 31), the authorities return to the notion of the man's blindness indicating his being born in sins (v. 34), and finally the

Pharisees' sin is said to remain (v. 41). Sin will be seen to be not so much a moral transgression of the law that incurs physical punishments as the negative response to the revelation of God's works through Jesus.

4–5 Jesus indicates that there is an urgency to the mission he has been given – **We must work the works of him who sent me while it is day; night is coming when no one is able to work.** In this Gospel's narrative Jesus is working according to a schedule, characteristically designated as 'the hour', and this overrides other divisions of time, such as the sabbath (cf. 5.17), and the sabbath issue will reappear here in v. 14. Although the reference to the coming night alludes to Jesus' death negatively (cf. also 13.30), the narrative as a whole views Jesus' death on the cross as the successful completion of his work schedule (19.30). With its talk of day and night, v. 4 also helps to establish the dominant symbolism in the passage and leads into the repetition of the 'I Am' saying from 8.12 – **I am the light of the world.** This also recalls both what was said about the Logos in the prologue in 1.4, 5, 9 and the association of Jesus' coming in both positive and negative judgement with the coming of the light into the darkness in 3.19–21. Here the contrast between night and day and the implied contrast between darkness and light will be tied through the healing miracle to the opposition between the blindness of remaining in night and darkness and the sight that results from receiving the light.

6–7 The healing itself is recounted exceedingly briefly. Clearly the narrator is far more interested in the consequences. There is no exchange between Jesus and the man prior to Jesus' action, which follows immediately from his claim to be the light of the world. Jesus' use of spittle (cf. also Mark 7.33; 8.23) is in line with the practice of healers of his time, in which spittle was widely held to have curative powers (cf. Pliny, *Nat.* 28.7.36–9). Tacitus' account of the blind man who asked Vespasian to cure his blindness in this way provides one of the best-known parallels (*Hist.* 4.81). Here, however, Jesus combines spittle with dust to make a muddy paste that is spread on the man's eyes and then instructs him, **Go and wash in the Pool of Siloam.** As in the case of Elisha's healing of Naaman the Syrian (cf. 2 Kgs 5.1–19), the healing is not completed until the washing occurs and so does not take place in the presence of Jesus (cf. also the healing of the official's son in 4.46–54). In fact, there will be no further encounter between Jesus and the man he has cured until v. 35. After the mention of Siloam, the narrator adds (**which means Sent**). His translation of the Hebrew name of the pool into a Greek equivalent indicates that he considers its derivation significant. He expects readers to make a connection with his distinctive characterization of Jesus in terms of the one who is 'sent' as the Father's uniquely authorized agent, and they have just been reminded of this formulation in v. 4 – 'We must work

the works of *him who sent me*.' Through this play on etymology the point
is underlined that the man's enlightenment comes both via a source that
means 'sent' and ultimately from a source who is the sent one par excellence, sent to carry out the life-giving works of God.

8–9 Typically, miracle stories follow a threefold pattern – a need is established, a miracle is performed to alleviate the need, and the miracle is then
attested. The narrator now elaborates on the last element, turning it into a
second scene in which the man's neighbours and previous acquaintances
are introduced and the tone of interrogation that will follow in the rest
of the narrative is anticipated. Initially opinion is divided on whether this
seeing person can be the same blind beggar that they had known. But
the man's identity is established by his insistence **I am he,** which is a
derivative echo of Jesus' earlier self-identifications, but without, of course,
their divine connotations.

10–12 The issue then shifts to how the miracle has happened, and
the man repeats the essentials of what the narrator has already told
the readers, identifying Jesus as the initiator of his reception of sight.
Finally, the questioning turns to where this Jesus is. At this point the man
confesses his ignorance – **I do not know.** This exchange draws attention
to the long absence of Jesus from the narrative but it also touches on this
Gospel's link between seeing and knowing. To see is to perceive or know
truly, and the newly sighted man will be shown to grow in his perception.
Having begun by simply confessing his ignorance about Jesus' whereabouts, he will end the episode in full perception of his relation to Jesus.

13–14 In this third scene (vv. 13–17) the main antagonists enter the
story, as the man is taken by the neighbours to the Pharisees. The earlier
questioning pursued by the neighbours and acquaintances can be seen
as motivated by natural curiosity, but something more negative in their
attitude appears to emerge in this action. Ominous overtones are also
suggested, especially in the light of 5.1–18, by the narrator only now
revealing that it was a sabbath day when Jesus had healed the man. The
indications are, therefore, that the man has been taken to the Pharisees for
a ruling because some suspect that something is amiss about the incident.
It could be claimed that a double violation of sabbath law had taken place,
since Jesus had performed a healing and had done so by making clay.

15–16 In answering the Pharisees' question about how the healing had
happened, the man testifies to the fact of his sight – **and now I see**
(to this point the sixth reference to the man having gained his sight).
His account provokes a divided judgement on the key issue of Jesus'
relationship to God. Some of the Pharisees are said to have immediately

reached their conclusion. Concentrating on the transgression of the sabbath, they decide **This man is not from God**. Others, however, focus on the sign and ask, **How can a sinful man do such signs?**

17 This scene closes with the interrogation of the man born blind. He is prodded into making a confession about Jesus' identity – **He is a prophet** – thereby taking a first faltering step on the way to full spiritual sight. It is a step that at least recognizes that Jesus is 'of God' in the sense that would have been posited of Jewish prophets, namely, that he has God's approval of his mission.

The essential elements for an overall depiction in terms of an interrogation or mini-trial are now in place. A verdict about Jesus' action of healing on the sabbath needs to be reached – is he a sinner or is he from God? The absent Jesus has been the subject for the Pharisees' interrogation and the man who was blind has functioned as a witness who is cross-examined. In the next scene it will be the healed man's parents who are summoned as witnesses (vv. 18–23). By the time the man himself is called back for a second interrogation (vv. 24–34), the verdict on Jesus has been reached (cf. v. 24) and then gradually the man's own witness to Jesus becomes the focus of the trial, as, like Jesus in earlier episodes, the witness becomes the accused, and eventually a negative verdict is pronounced on him (v. 34). After the short scene in which Jesus and the man born blind are reunited and which functions as this man's vindication (vv. 35–8), in a final dramatic and ironic reversal the conclusion contains a verdict of judgement pronounced this time not by the Pharisees on Jesus but by Jesus on the Pharisees (vv. 39–41).

18–21 In this central scene the designation of the authorities changes. The sympathetic Pharisees disappear and instead the antagonists are called 'the Jews'. There is also a change of tactics on the part of these authorities. Convinced that the man can see, they now question whether he was ever blind in the first place. They call his parents and ask, **Is this your son, who you say was born blind?** The parents confirm the central fact that he was born blind but are evasive about the significance of his present sight, professing ignorance about how this has happened and who did it. It is significant that the parents have not in fact been asked who performed the healing and yet they realize that this is the underlying issue in the interrogation.

22–3 Their equivocation and unwillingness to identify Jesus as the healer, explains the narrator, is **because they feared the Jews**, and this fear overrides any responsibility for and solidarity with their son. The formulation again underlines this narrative's distinctive use of the designation 'the Jews'. The parents are themselves ethnic Jews, of course, and yet they are said to fear 'the Jews'. The term here has to be taken to refer to the representatives of the hostile world in the persons of Jewish religious authorities who reject Jesus. The narrator supplies a further explanation as part of an 'inside view' of the parents' fear – **for the Jews had already decided that if anyone confessed him as the Christ, that person would be expelled from the synagogue**. All the elements of this assertion are anachronistic. They reflect a time later than that of the mission of the earthly Jesus – a situation in which it could be expected that people would make a formal confession of Jesus as the Christ, in which there had also been a formal agreement on the part of Jewish religious authorities about what to do in response to such confessions, and in which that response took the form of excommunication from the synagogue. The anachronistic nature of the narrator's comment provides an important clue for reading this account, and by extension the Gospel as a whole, as a two-level drama, in which the blind man is not only someone healed by Jesus but also the representative of those Jewish Christians who have been expelled from the synagogue because of their confession about Jesus. In this way the two temporal perspectives at work in the narrative – the pre-resurrection perspective of the basic story line about the earthly Jesus and the post-resurrection perspective of the evangelist – are telescoped together in the telling of the story. In 16.2, as Jesus looks to the time after his departure, the expulsion from the synagogue can be thought of as still future, but here and in 12.42 it already colours heavily what takes place in the story line about Jesus' mission. It is unlikely that the historical referent of this expulsion from the synagogue can be linked directly, as some have held, to the twelfth of the eighteen Synagogue Benedictions that were thought to be promulgated around 85 CE (see the discussion of the Setting and Purposes of John's Gospel in the Introduction). Nevertheless, the narrator's explanation for the parents' behaviour gives insight into the setting of the evangelist and the life of the community he represents and the severe costs for Jews who confessed Jesus and suffered the consequences of expulsion from their cherished community. Just as Jesus' mission produced division within his family (cf. 7.3–8), so witnessing to him in the context of the conflict with the synagogue could produce alienation within the families of his followers. Here, aware that in all probability he will have to face the consequences of which they are afraid, the parents put their son back in the dock – **He is of age, ask him**. But their fear and reluctance to risk what could be construed as a public confession become the foil for the actions of the man himself in the next scene where he boldly confronts the authorities.

24–5 Summoned back before the Jewish authorities, in the long fifth scene the man who had been blind comes into his own as a character. The authorities have reached a definite verdict about Jesus – **we know**

that this man is a sinner – and enjoin the man, **Give glory to God**. This language functions as a call to confess or admit the truth, putting the witness under solemn oath (cf. Josh. 7.19; 1 Esd. 9.8; *m.Sanh* 6.2). At the same time there is an irony in the formulation, since readers know that the way to give glory to God in this Gospel's narrative is to believe that Jesus in his signs is the revealer of God's glory. The man's witness begins in a low-key fashion. He claims not to know whether Jesus is a sinner (but cf. vv. 17, 31) and concentrates on what he is absolutely sure of – his own experience. **One thing I know; I was blind and now I see.** In terms of its symbolic force for readers, this is the language of enlightenment and conversion, later taken up most famously in John Newton's hymn 'Amazing grace' – 'I once was lost, but now am found, | was blind, but now I see.'

26-7 When the authorities cast doubt on the credibility of his witness by asking for a third time how this has happened, the man grows more confident in the face of their stubborn refusal to believe his account. The one born blind can now accuse his interrogators of being deliberately deaf – **I have told you already and you did not listen.** This echoes Jesus' own counter-accusations in the preceding interrogation (cf. 8.43, 47). Emboldened, the man turns to wit and sarcasm – **Why do you want to hear it again? Do you also want to become his disciples?** – and in the process reveals his own commitment – he is one of Jesus' disciples.

28-9 The authorities take the bait and respond by reviling him and making clear their own allegiance. The contrast – **You are that man's disciple, but we are disciples of Moses** – goes to the heart of the conflicting claims operative in the narrative and already anticipated in the prologue's contrast between Jesus and Moses (cf. 1.17). The formulation 'disciples of Moses', used here as a self-designation of 'the Jews', is found later in a rabbinic source (*b.Yoma* 4a), where it distinguishes Pharisaic from Sadducean teachers. In line with the formal decision mentioned in v. 22, the authorities have determined that it is incompatible for a Jew, like the formerly blind man, to be a disciple of Jesus and also a disciple of Moses. In effect, they have attempted to define true Jewish identity in terms of their perspective on adherence to Torah. The Jewish authorities link Moses and God through their assertion that **God spoke to Moses**. The evangelist's rival claim holds not only that God has spoken to Jesus (cf. 8.26, 28) but also that Jesus speaks God's words (cf. 3.34; 7.16; 12.49–50) and in fact that he embodies God's word as the Logos (cf 1.1, 2, 14). It also holds that truly to believe Moses is to believe Jesus, because Moses wrote about Jesus (5.46). From the evangelist's perspective, being a disciple of Moses is only incompatible with being a disciple of Jesus if the former is thought to entail rejection of Jesus' claims. The authorities here assert that they do not know where Jesus is from, which conceals their earlier implicit claim that they know where he is not from – he is not from God (cf. v. 24). The term πόθεν, 'from where', which is employed here, is significant elsewhere in the debate about Jesus' identity (cf. 7.27–8; 8.14; 19.9). It focuses on his origin, which from the evangelist's perspective can be formulated as either from above or from God.

30–3 The authorities have failed to perceive the amazing nature of the sign and the man finds this failure itself amazing, exclaiming ironically, **This is what is amazing; you do not know where he is from and yet he opened my eyes.** He then provides some theological reflection on his experience. Starting with an agreed premiss – **We know that God does not listen to sinners** but to those who do God's will – he reminds them that it is totally unprecedented for someone to heal a person born blind, and then concludes that for someone to have done this he has to have been **from God.**

34 The authorities had earlier asked the man for his view of Jesus. Now they do not appreciate this fuller version of that for which they had asked. They are reduced to abusing the man in terms of their theology that his blindness was caused by sin, a perspective earlier dismissed by Jesus in his conversation with the disciples (cf. vv. 2–3), and they rebuke him for daring to try to teach them his theological insights. For the evangelist this man's ability to teach the teachers would in all probability be seen as part of the fulfilment of the scripture that was cited in 6.45 – 'And they shall all be taught by God' (Isa. 54.13). Finally, **they drove him out.** ἐκβάλλω, the Greek verb used here, can mean 'to expel from a group' and therefore takes on the force of the earlier notion of expulsion from the synagogue in v. 22. The excommunication his parents had feared is precisely the outcome of his witness.

35–8 At this point Jesus reappears on the scene. He finds the one who has been driven out. The contrast between rejection by the synagogue and acceptance by Jesus would have resonated with contemporary readers, who might well also recall Jesus' earlier promise – 'anyone who comes to me I will never cast out' (6.37). In the company of Jesus the man quickly develops his Christological insight. Jesus draws out his faith with a question. Initially, the man's reply to **Do you believe in the Son of Man?** shows a mixture of openness and misunderstanding, the familiar Johannine motif that is accompanied by irony. **And who is he, sir, that I may believe in him?** he asks of the Son of Man standing before him. Jesus can then say, **You have seen him** (with perhaps a hint that this is a sight that is more than merely physical) **and the one speaking to you is he.** The title 'Son of Man,' which can sometimes be virtually synonymous in this Gospel with 'Son' and 'Son of God', appears to have been chosen here for two reasons. First, as in the discussion with Nicodemus, it underlines the issue of Jesus' identity as 'from God', because, as 3.13 put it, the Son of Man is the one who descended from heaven, from God. And second, 'Son of Man' has close links with judgement, the theme that is taken up shortly in v. 39. As Son of Man, Jesus is the one who has been given authority to judge with the verdict of either life or death (cf. 5.25–9, esp. 5.27 – 'and he has given him authority to execute judgement, because he is the Son of Man'). The Son of Man with authority to judge is outside the synagogue in the company of the one judged and condemned by human religious authorities. The scene ends with the man's completed spiritual sight, his full-blown Johannine confession of faith – **I believe, Lord** – and accompanying act of worshipping Jesus. As noted in the translation, the context suggests that the second time round κύριος, which can mean either 'sir' or 'Lord', has its full Christian connotations. The verb 'to worship' (προσκυνεῖν) can mean 'to have profound respect for', 'to pay homage to' or 'to offer worship to', where in this last case the appropriate object is God. After the acclamation of Jesus as Lord and in the context of this Gospel's conception of Christ as one with God, it may well be that the man's worship is meant to be understood in the strongest sense of the word, so that the accompanying act makes his confession equivalent to the later one by Thomas – 'My Lord and my God' (20.28).

39 The final scene opens with Jesus' solemn pronouncement – **I came into this world for judgement, so that those who do not see might see and those who see might become blind.** The last part of this mission statement has affinities with the saying of Mark's Jesus that for those outside 'everything comes in parables, in order that they may indeed see but not perceive' (Mark 4.11–12). Here in the Fourth Gospel Jesus' mission as judge has both positive and negative outcomes. The positive aspect has been clearly demonstrated in the blind man's reception of sight and now the negative aspect will be underlined in regard to the religious authorities. Although the actual term 'judgement' (κρίμα) is withheld until here at the end, the whole incident is in fact a narrative embodiment of Jesus' earlier words about the judgement produced by the light coming into the world in 3.19–21.

40–1 The narrator gives no indication of how they came to overhear this conversation with the man born blind, but adds that some of the Pharisees (this is a return to the earlier designation of the authorities) pick up on Jesus' pronouncement. They ask the ironic question, **Surely we are not blind also, are we?** The form of the question anticipates a negative response and readers are set up to expect either Jesus to tell these Pharisees that they are indeed blind or simply to be left to savour the irony. But the irony is prolonged and deepened, as Jesus appears to agree with them that they are not blind: **If you were blind, you would not have sin; but now that you say, 'We see,' your sin remains.** The blindness Jesus refers to is the kind of blindness that knows it is blindness – the blindness of the blind man who was ready to obey in order to receive sight. What these Pharisees are suffering from is in fact an illusion of sight and this has caused a far deeper darkness than they are aware of, the darkness of refusing to acknowledge one's blindness and therefore of being unable to accept the light when it is offered. 'The Jews' had linked the man's blindness with sin (v. 34), as had the disciples earlier (v. 2), but now sin is said to be truly the cause of these Pharisees' deeper spiritual blindness of an illusion of sight. The episode is completed and the tables turned with the final judgement of condemnation – **your sin remains.** 'To remain or abide' (μένειν) is part of the Gospel's characteristic vocabulary and generally has favourable connotations, but the force here is reminiscent of its negative context in 3.36, where again in a pronouncement of judgement Jesus asserts that 'the one who disobeys the Son will not see life, but the wrath of God will remain on that person'.

The basis for this skilfully elaborated account is provided by stories of a healing of a blind man (vv. 1, 6, 7) and a controversy with the Pharisees about sabbath healing (vv. 14–16). Many hold that the evangelist had an independent tradition about this Jerusalem miracle, pointing to differences of detail from Synoptic parallels and to the topographical accuracy in this account of the mention of the pool at Siloam (v. 7). On the other hand, Mark has two stories of the healing of a blind man which may have influenced the Fourth Gospel's account, Mark 8.22–6 and Mark 10.46–52, and Mark 3.1-6 contains a controversy with Pharisees over healing on the sabbath. In Mark 8.22–6 Jesus also employs spittle in the healing and in Mark 10.46–52 blind Bartimaeus is a beggar (a detail revealed about the blind man in John's story in v. 8) and becomes a follower of Jesus on the way to Jerusalem and the cross. It could well be that John has put these basic elements to his own use. Matthew and Luke both omitted the first Markan story, presumably because of the offensiveness of Jesus spitting straight into the eyes of the man and the embarrassment of a miracle that took two attempts. John changes the use of saliva so that it becomes part of a muddy paste for anointing the eyes and of course makes no mention of any half-successful attempt at healing. Instead the two stages in the actual miracle become the anointing of the eyes and then the washing in the pool, and the notion of a progressive coming to sight is taken up in terms of the character's developing spiritual insight. John had included a Jerusalem pool in the setting for the miracle in 5.1–18 and the many structural parallels between that account and this one were noted in the earlier discussion of that passage. This pool has the advantage of a name that has key symbolic significance for John's distinctive Christological formulations. As might be expected from the evangelist's stress on Jesus' sovereignty, the initiative for the healing does not come from requests from others, as in Mark's two stories, but from Jesus himself. And as in the case of other parallels to Synoptic miracle stories where this Gospel heightens the miraculous element, John ensures that his account of the healing of a blind person is even more impressive than the Markan parallels because only here has the person whose sight is restored been blind from birth. This traditional material is immediately related to the major Johannine themes of light and Jesus' work (vv. 2–5) and then gradually becomes more and more coloured by issues from the evangelist's own time and setting. In particular, in the description of the opposition, the Pharisees from Jesus' time shade over into 'the Jews' in vv. 18–34.

In the story as it now stands Jesus enacts his role as the light, the symbol of revelation as judgement with its effects of enlightenment and exposure. The light's judgement is primarily salvific, as Jesus carries out God's life-giving work of just judgement on behalf of humanity, rescuing it from its plight of darkness and blindness. Yet there is also a possible negative consequence, since light exposes darkness for what it is and can blind. Light and darkness are universal symbols, but within Judaism light has more particular connotations through its associations with Torah – 'Your word is a lamp to my feet and a light to my path' (Ps. 119.105). The claim that Jesus is the light, therefore, contains an implicit claim about his relationship to Torah, and so it is not surprising that a dispute between Jewish Christians and other Jews colours this episode and that at the heart of this dispute is the issue of Jesus in relation to Moses (cf. vv. 28–9). For the Fourth Gospel, since Jesus is now the light, the light of Torah has to be seen in the light of *the* Light. To operate the other way around – to use Torah to judge Jesus as a sinner – is, for the evangelist, to make Torah an instrument of darkness rather than light.

If interrogation and judgement provide the theme of the passage, it is the development of two sorts of judgement about Jesus as the bringer of light that provides the movement and irony of the narrative. The judgement of the man born blind, with its progressive knowledge and bold confession of who Jesus is, has increasing clarity of sight. The previously blind man judges Jesus on the basis of his experience of receiving sight. He begins by perceiving Jesus as the man who healed him (v. 11), moves to acknowledging him as a prophet (v. 17), then confesses that he is Jesus' disciple (v. 27), and that Jesus is from God (v. 33), and that he is Lord and Son of Man (v. 38a), and finally he worships Jesus (v. 38b). The Pharisees judge Jesus on the basis of their interpretation of the law (cf. vv. 16, 29) and are unable to see that if they believed Moses, they would believe Jesus (cf. 5.46). This contrasting judgement of the religious authorities develops into deeper blindness. It starts with a divided verdict about Jesus' act of healing (v. 16), and an apparent willingness to hear the healed man's judgement (v.17), but then turns into an unbelieving attempt to discredit the healing (vv. 18–19), a verdict that Jesus is a sinner (v. 24), a reviling of the man for his confession (vv. 28, 34a) and a casting of him out of the synagogue (v. 34b). Finally, for the evangelist, their claim not to be blind exposes the desperate darkness of the sin in which they remain (vv. 39–41).

It is significant that both the developing Christological insight and the hardening of the opposition take place through the clash of claims. The blind man's understanding of Jesus' identity grows through the process of witness, conflict, interrogation, trial and rejection. At the same time the religious authorities increasingly define themselves in opposition to the claims that emerge. Again this appears to mirror the experience of Johannine Christians in their conflict with the synagogue authorities, in which claims about the significance of Jesus would not only have sparked off conflict in the first place but would have been elaborated and refined in the continuation of the conflict, provoking further counter-claims in the process. In this narrative, perception of the identity of Jesus is not only the subject matter of the conflict but is itself shaped and formed by means of the conflict. For readers who face similar conflicts the extensive treatment of the man who was formerly blind provides a model for the courageous witness that is required.

(xii) Jesus' discourse on the sheepgate and the shepherd   10.1–21

(1) 'Truly, truly, I say to you, whoever does not enter the sheepfold through the gate but climbs in some other way is a thief and a bandit. (2) The one who enters through the gate is the shepherd of the sheep. (3) The gatekeeper opens the gate for him and the sheep hear his voice; he calls his own sheep by name and leads them out. (4) When he has driven out all his own, he goes ahead of them and the sheep follow him, because they know his voice. (5) They will not follow a stranger but will run away from him, because they do not know the voice of strangers.' (6) Jesus used this figure of speech with them, but they did not know what he was saying to them.

(7) So Jesus again said, 'Truly, truly, I say to you, I am the gate for the sheep. (8) All who came[1] are thieves and bandits, but the

---

[1] Some manuscripts (including p⁶⁶ ℵᶜ A B D itᵈ) have the phrase 'before me' after 'came', while others (Θ f¹ arm geo) have it before the verb. The reading which omits this phrase has impressive support, including p⁴⁵ᵛⁱᵈ,⁷⁵ ℵ* E F G Δ itᵃ,ᵇ,ᶜ vg syrˢ,ᵖ,ʰ copˢᵃ goth. Since this is the shorter reading, it is to be preferred, and the division of the

sheep did not listen to them. (9) I am the gate. Whoever enters through me will be saved and will go in and come out and find pasture. (10) The thief comes only to steal and kill and destroy. I have come that they may have life and have it in abundance. (11) I am the good shepherd. The good shepherd lays down[2] his life for the sheep. (12) The hired hand, who is not the shepherd and whose sheep are not his own, sees the wolf coming and leaves the sheep and runs away – and the wolf seizes and scatters them – (13) because he is the hired hand and he cares nothing for the sheep. (14) I am the good shepherd, and I know my own and my own know me, (15) just as the Father knows me and I know the Father. And I lay down[3] my life for the sheep. (16) I have other sheep that do not belong to this fold. I must lead them also and they will hear my voice, and there will be one flock, one shepherd. (17) For this reason the Father loves me, because I lay down my life in order to take it up again. (18) No one has taken[4] it from me, but I lay it down of my own accord. I have authority to lay it down, and I have authority to take it up again. I have received this command from the Father.'

(19) Again a division arose among the Jews because of these words. (20) Many of them were saying, 'He has a demon and is raving. Why do you listen to him?' (21) Others were saying, 'These are not the words of one who is demon-possessed. Can a demon open the eyes of the blind?'

Whatever the pre-history of this passage, in its present position Jesus' initial teaching about the sheepgate and the shepherd are now a continuation of his address to the Pharisees from the end of the previous chapter

---

witnesses about the position of the longer reading confirms that the latter is likely to be secondary.

[2] A majority of the Greek texts have τίθησιν, 'lays down', while a minority read δίδωσιν, 'gives'. The latter includes p[45] ℵ* D it[c,d] vg. The former is well and widely attested – p[66,75] ℵ[c] A B K Δ Θ it[a,aur] syr[p,h] cop[sa] – and is in line with Johannine usage elsewhere (cf. 10.17–18; 13.37–8; 15.13; 1 John 3.16), while 'gives' may involve harmonization with Synoptic formulations (cf. Mark 10.45; Matt. 20.28).

[3] Again the readings divide between the majority 'lay down' and the minority (which this time includes p[66]) 'give.' The same factors as in v. 11 are involved in the decision about the most likely original here.

[4] Most textual witnesses have the present tense of the Greek verb, but a few of the best early manuscripts – p[45] ℵ* B – have the aorist tense. These manuscripts represent the Egyptian textual tradition and so do not have a wide attestation but may nevertheless still convey the earliest reading. The aorist form is the more difficult reading and the present tense would be an assimilation to the present tense in the second part of the sentence. It is harder to find an explanation for an alteration from the present to the aorist.

(cf. v. 6). The various hypotheses that have been proposed for rearranging the sequence of the materials in chapter 10 will not be discussed here. Although the change of topic at first appears abrupt, Jesus' words are clearly relevant to what has just taken place, and the response of the crowd at the end makes reference to the opening of the eyes of the blind (cf. v. 21). The Pharisees are the Jewish religious leaders who have just exercised their authority by driving the man born blind out of the synagogue. Jesus now uses traditional imagery for the people of God and its leaders – sheep and shepherds – to provide a framework that both criticizes their actions by implication and sets up his own contrasting role as a true leader of the people of God. The same verb 'to drive out' which was employed of the synagogue leaders' activity in the previous incident (9.34) is in fact now used of the good shepherd's action in relation to the sheep (10.4) but it takes on quite different connotations in its new context, where it refers to the shepherd driving out the sheep into pasture and where this true shepherd goes ahead of his sheep.

Although the imagery would have been familiar in the Graeco-Roman world, where deities, heroes, kings and other leaders were often portrayed as shepherds, it takes its primary force, as has been suggested, from traditional Jewish ways of viewing the relationship between God and God's people or between divine mediators and the people. In Num. 27.12–23 Joshua is appointed as Moses' successor so that the people 'may not be like sheep without a shepherd', an image for the leaderless nation that recurs in 1 Kgs 22.17; 2 Chron. 18.16; Zech. 10.2. Whether it be Joshua, judges, kings or prophets, a variety of Israel's leaders can be depicted as shepherds (cf. e.g. 1 Chron.17.6; Jer. 3.15; 10.21; 12.10; 23.1–4; Isa. 56.11; Zech. 10.3; 11.3–17). Chief among these, however, remains David, the shepherd who was taken from tending the sheep to become the shepherd-king (cf. 2 Sam. 5.2; 7.7–8; 1 Chron. 11.2; Ps. 78.70–1) and who becomes the model for the future messianic shepherd-king (Ezek. 37.24; Mic. 5.2–4). The entire history of the Jewish people from the flood to the period of the messianic kingdom is told as an allegory about sheep and shepherds in the dream visions in *1 Enoch* 89.10—90.39. Philo also treats Moses as the shepherd of God's people (*Mos.* 1.60–2) and, interestingly, depicts the Logos as well as God as shepherd (*Agr.* 50–4; *Mut.* 116). Whatever the state of the flock under its human shepherds, however, it is God who is seen as the one constant shepherd, ruling, judging, rescuing and tending the people (cf. e.g. Gen. 48.15; 49.24; Ps. 23.1; 28.9; 74.1; 80.1; 95.7; Isa. 40.11; Jer. 23.3; 31.10; Mic. 2.12; 7.14). One extended passage, Ezek. 34, brings all these images together and has particularly influenced the thought and language of John 10. Because Israel's leaders have been unfaithful in their task of shepherding God's sheep, they will be judged (vv. 1–10b). God, as the ultimate shepherd, will rescue, feed and care for the sheep, judging between them (vv. 10c–22), and God will set up one shepherd – a Davidic king – so that the sheep will have peace and security (vv. 23–31).

When Jesus' address to the Pharisees takes up such concepts, it opens with what the narrator describes as a figure of speech which involves a sheepfold, its gate, the sheep, their shepherd and intruders (vv. 1–6). Its content functions both to set up a critique of the actions of the Jewish religious leaders depicted in chapter 9 and to supply a cluster of images which will be developed in two main ways. In the first Jesus is featured as the gate in two 'I Am' sayings (vv. 7–10) and in the second he is the shepherd and two further 'I Am' sayings are employed (vv. 11–18). The episode concludes with the by now familiar division of opinion over Jesus' claims (vv. 19–21).

1–3a The parabolic language in the first five verses of the discourse deals with two aspects of a shepherd's relation to the sheep and contrasts both with the roles of others who come into contact with the sheep. Here the first aspect is presented – it is the shepherd who has valid access to the sheepfold and its sheep. The opening **Truly, truly** (Amen, amen), **I say to you** not only signals a change from dialogue to monologue and to a new stage of argument but may also indicate that the material employed is traditional. The Palestinian sheepfold in view is likely to have been adjoining a house and to have had its own separate gate which gave access to the sheep. A large-enough flock would have required an undershepherd or hired watchman to guard it at night and serve as a gatekeeper. Anyone who attempted to gain access by some other means such as climbing over a wall or fence is likely to have been immediately identified as **a thief and a bandit**. Although the term for the latter – ληστής – was frequently used by Josephus of insurrectionists and political revolutionaries (e.g. *B. J.* 4.138) and may well have those connotations when used later of Barabbas in 18.40, it retained its common reference to robbers or bandits, who are in view here. Thieves would primarily have been thought of as those who broke into homes and bandits as itinerant robbers who operated on and from the roads through the countryside. In the context of unauthorized entry into sheepfolds and stealing sheep the two types of activity were equivalent in their effect. Here their activity simply provides a foil for the notion that it is the shepherd himself who has valid access to the fold, which is illustrated through his entry through the gate and his recognition by both the gatekeeper and the sheep.

3b–5 The second aspect of the initial parabolic material treats the intimacy and confidence in the relation between a shepherd and his sheep. It picks up on the formulation of v. 3a that **the sheep hear his voice** and links this to the way the shepherd **calls his own sheep by name and leads them out**. With average-sized flocks of around a hundred sheep the shepherd would usually assign special names to each sheep and could train them to respond to his call by name when he wanted to move them. Having brought the sheep out of the fold, the shepherd would walk ahead of them and **the sheep follow him**, continuing to respond to his voice. **A stranger** would be able to exercise no such control, because the sheep **do not know the voice of strangers**. In this context the stranger in view is likely to be an intruder, such as the thief or the bandit.

6 The narrator now describes the preceding material about the shepherd and the sheep as a **figure of speech** which Jesus' audience fail to understand. This translation provides a helpful compromise in a long-standing debate whether the term παροιμία refers more specifically to a parable or an allegory. The discussion arose from the recognition that this Johannine material is unlike the Synoptic parables, which were generally viewed as having one major point as distinct from allegories, where a number of one-to-one correspondences are intended between the story and the reality to which it points. But there is increasing scholarly agreement that such a distinction was much too sharp and that the two forms can overlap considerably. In any case, the term παροιμία is often used synonymously with παραβολή, 'parable', and in the LXX both translate the Hebrew term *mashal*, which can apply to a variety of forms of comparison, including proverbs, allegories and riddles, and not simply story-length parables. When παροιμία is employed later in 16.25, 29, it refers to material that includes a riddling saying – 'a little while and you will no longer see me, and again a little while and you will see me' – and a comparison to a woman in childbirth, and it is contrasted with speaking plainly or openly. Here too the point is that Jesus' use of the shepherd and sheep imagery is allusive: its meaning does not lie simply on the surface and it can conceal as much as reveal, depending on the receptivity of the hearers.

Rather than isolating two separate Synoptic-like parables behind vv. 1–5 and seeking their original meaning in the ministry of the historical Jesus, as some have done, it may be more helpful to concentrate on the function of these verses in their present context in the Gospel, where they are treated as one figure of speech. For the narrator, the Pharisees **did not know what he was saying to them**, not because they did not understand the words but because they missed the point. In their role as teachers and leaders, they would have construed themselves as shepherds rather than as thieves, bandits or strangers, and are likely to have cast Jesus as an intruder and a sheep-stealer in his encouragement of the man born blind to believe in him and become one of his followers. Yet their mistreatment of the healed man, culminating in reviling him and driving him out, and Jesus' very different response to and relation with the man have made clear to readers the appropriate referents for the figures in the parabolic material. What is more, the Pharisees' lack of understanding can be seen as showing that in their response to Jesus' words they are spiritually deaf, just as in their response to his deed, they were deeply spiritually blind (9.39–41).

7–9 In what follows Jesus attempts further explanation by making the application of the pastoral imagery more explicit. Although the audience in the narrative world remains the same, the content indicates that the evangelist now has his own audience more directly in view. The elaboration also does not keep the original material strictly in view. Some of the features of vv. 1–5 are not explained, such as the gatekeeper or the stranger, and new features are brought into play, such as the hired hand, the wolf and the shepherd's death.

Even the first new saying – **I am the gate for the sheep** – produces a disjunction with what has preceded. The expectation is that Jesus would spell out his own role as shepherd, but that still awaits. Instead he identifies himself with what had been an ancillary part of the earlier imagery. The disjunction is not eased by the observation that sometimes a shepherd might sleep across the opening of a sheep enclosure, thus acting as the door. Such a custom simply does not inform the earlier picture of a gatekeeper opening an actual door. The expanded discourse picks up individual terms from the earlier material and is not afraid of mixing metaphors in the process. Whereas previously Jesus could be seen as the shepherd with valid access to the sheep, now the thought is that he himself embodies access to the sheepfold. References to the gate to heaven (Gen. 28.17) and other heavenly portals in apocalyptic literature are not really to the point as parallels. Here the focus is on Jesus as the gate or door to salvation for the sheep – **Whoever enters through me will be saved and will go in and come out and find pasture.** The 'I Am' statement can be seen as a Johannine Christological application, in the context of pastoral imagery, of the Synoptic saying of Jesus about the narrow gate that leads to life (Matt. 7.13–14) or salvation (Luke 13.23–5). A number of scriptural texts may also have contributed to the formulation. In Ps. 118.19–21 the righteous enter through the gate of the Lord to find righteousness and salvation, while in Num. 27.16–17 Joshua, as the new shepherd of the sheep, will 'lead them out and bring them in'. Elsewhere God as shepherd provides salvation and pasture (cf. esp. Ezek. 34.10c, 12b, 14, 22, 31; Ps. 23.2). Jesus not only fulfils expectations about Israel's faithful leaders but also the role of the divine shepherd. As 14.6 will make plain, as the one who uniquely represents the Father, he is the way, the access to the Father, and therefore also the embodiment of salvation as the truth and the life.

Jesus' identity and role are in contrast to those of unfaithful and illegitimate leaders. **All who came are thieves and bandits** cannot be a general reference to Israel's previous leaders. The evangelist views

figures such as Abraham, Moses and the prophets, when rightly interpreted, as supportive of Jesus' claims (cf. 5.45–6; 8.56). It is also unlikely in
this context that messianic pretenders are in view. As in v. 1, the primary
referent is the Jewish leaders, such as the Pharisees in chapter 9 who have
refused Jesus' witness and whose attempt to gain access to the sheep by
unauthorized means entails that **the sheep did not listen to them**.

10 As if depicting such leaders as thieves and bandits were not offensive
enough, their intent with regard to the sheep is said to involve death and
destruction – **the thief comes only to steal and kill and destroy**
(cf. 8.40, 44; 16.2). This serves as a foil for Jesus' own mission statement
– **I have come that they may have life and have it in abundance.**
The whole thrust of his mission has to do with bringing about the
well-being of God's flock. The formulation echoes other statements of
this motif of the bringing of life (cf. e.g. 3.16; 4.14b; 5.24; 6.33, 40, 51;
11.25) and provides a parallel with the notion of 'being saved' in v. 9 (cf.
also 3.16–17). The revelation and salvation Jesus offers entail the positive
judgement of life, and the signs of turning water into wine and feeding
the five thousand have demonstrated that this life is given in abundance.

11 This depiction of Jesus' mission forms a natural transition into the
next stage of exposition of terms from the opening pastoral imagery. Now
comes the self-identification that had been expected – **I am the good
shepherd.** The term καλός, translated here, as is customary, as 'good', can
also be interpreted as 'beautiful', 'noble', 'honourable' or 'ideal', and so has
some similarities to the force of the adjective 'true' in Jesus' identification
of himself as the true bread and the true vine (cf. 6.32; 15.1). More telling,
however, is the observation that the opposite of καλός is not so much 'bad'
or 'evil' but more frequently 'shameful' or 'disgraceful', so that the terminology belongs to the honour/shame field of discourse that is pervasive in
the Fourth Gospel and will now affect the way the shepherd is depicted.
In the Scriptures, and particularly in Ezek. 34.11–16, 25–31, God is the
ideal shepherd in seeking, rescuing, feeding, caring for and protecting
his flock and now Jesus identifies himself as fulfilling this divine role. Yet
here what distinguishes the noble shepherd is that he **lays down his life
for the sheep**. The life of a shepherd could involve risk and danger, and
resisting thieves or wild animals (cf. 1 Sam. 17.34–7) might on occasion
lead to a shepherd's death. But defining the good shepherd in terms of
his actual death on behalf of the flock goes well beyond all the scriptural
imagery about the shepherd's relation to the sheep and is shaped by both
Greek traditions about what constitutes a noble or honourable death and
Christian belief about the significance of Jesus' death.

Greek discussions of epideictic rhetoric and Graeco-Roman handbooks
in their rules for the encomium set out what are considered to be noble

(καλάι) actions, and Athenian funeral speeches specify what is involved particularly in dying nobly (καλῶς). That this understanding had already penetrated Jewish literature written in Greek is clearly demonstrated in the way the actions and particularly the deaths of the Maccabean heroes are described in 1, 2 and 4 Maccabees. Two of the major criteria for such actions or deaths are reflected in this verse's formulation about Jesus' death. In order to be praiseworthy or honourable, they should be voluntary and for the sake of others. The notion of choosing a glorious or noble death in preference to life or to bringing shame on others is found in e.g. Plato, *Menex.* 246d; Isocrates, *Evag.* 3; Thucydides, *Hist.* 2.42.4, 2.43.4; 2 Macc. 6.19, 28; 7.14, 29 and *4 Macc.* 5.23; 11.3; 14.6. Here the good shepherd lays down his life − a deliberate and willing action, whose voluntary nature will be emphasized by a threefold repetition of the thought in vv. 15, 17, 18. 'Noble actions are those which we do for the sake of others and not ourselves' (Theon, *Prosgymnata* 9.25) and the deaths of Athenian soldiers were considered noble because they benefited their city and the rest of Greece and 'they gave their lives for the sake of [ὑπέρ] the freedom of the Greeks' (Hyperides, *Funeral Speech* 9, 16). Similarly, the Maccabean martyrs are said to have died nobly because their deaths were suffered on behalf of their kindred or the nation and in order to save them (cf. e.g. 1 Macc. 6.44; 9.10; 13.4; 2 Macc. 8.21; *4 Macc.* 17.10, 20–2). Here the shepherd dies nobly 'for the sake of' or 'on behalf of' (ὑπέρ) the sheep. The same preposition is used of Jesus' death in 6.51 and 11.50–2 and has sacrificial connotations.

12–13 The negative foil for the role of the good shepherd is that of **the hired hand**, who, because he acts primarily for monetary reward, has no real loyalty or care for the sheep. He is likely, therefore, in face of a wolf's attack, not to feel any responsibility to risk danger to himself but to run off and leave the sheep to be seized and scattered. Such cowardly action in the face of danger would be deemed disgraceful or shameful. What happens to the sheep under the hired hand who is not a true shepherd corresponds most closely to the situation under the false shepherds in Ezek. 34.2–10 (cf. also Zech. 11.15–17) who are indicted for being more concerned for their own welfare than that of the flock and are held accountable for the sheep being scattered and becoming prey for the wild animals.

14–15 The hired hand's behaviour indicates a lack of any real relation to the sheep. By contrast, the repetition of the self-identification of Jesus as the noble shepherd picks up on the original formulation about the mutual knowledge of shepherd and sheep in vv. 4–5 and maintains, **I know my own and my own know me**. Jesus is the good shepherd because of the personal and mutual relationship between himself and those who belong to him. The mutual knowledge that was meant to characterize the covenantal relation between God and Israel is now to be found in the recognition and love between Jesus and his own, and the latter parallels and is modelled on the relationship between Jesus and the Father – **just as the Father knows me and I know the Father.** What was said about the noble shepherd's death in v. 11 is now more explicitly linked to Jesus' mission – **I lay down my life for the sheep.** In the present context this act follows from Jesus' intimate concern for his followers and from his relation to the Father (cf. also vv. 17, 18c). Again this can be seen as reflecting a further aspect of the convention about a noble death. Such a death displayed the virtue of justice because it honoured duty towards others and expressed piety towards the gods (cf. e.g. Isocrates, *Evag.* 8, 23, 25; Hyperides, *Funeral Speech* 11, 16, 24; 1 Macc. 9.10; *4 Macc.* 12.14).

16 I have other sheep that do not belong to this fold most probably refers to those who do not belong to the Jewish people but who are Gentile believers in Jesus. The notions of 'leading' and 'hearing' from v. 3 can now be applied to them: **I must lead them also and they will hear my voice, and there will be one flock, one shepherd.** The gathering of scattered sheep under the rule of the one shepherd, the Davidic king, in Ezek. 34.23; 37.24 has reference to diaspora Jews, but they are not described as 'other sheep' and so here the evangelist has broadened the reference to include Gentiles, who form a significant part of his intended audience (cf. the similar move in 11.52 in speaking of 'not for the nation only, but to gather into one the dispersed children of God'). Jesus, the one shepherd, will bring about the one flock of Jews and Gentiles, whose distinguishing mark is their willingness to listen to their shepherd's voice (cf. also v. 27). The importance of the oneness of his followers will be emphasized later in 17.21–2.

17–18 In these closing verses of the discourse the shepherd imagery can be left behind as Jesus now speaks directly both about his mission and his relation to the Father. **For this reason the Father loves me, because I lay down my life in order to take it up again.** Here Jesus sees both his death and his resurrection as at the heart of that mission and as acts that he undertakes in sovereign freedom. Elsewhere in the New Testament in formulations about the resurrection Jesus is usually the object of God's act rather than the subject of his own act. Here he chooses to lay down his human life (ψυχή) temporarily in order then to embrace it anew in resurrection form in his divine life. Again the evangelist's distinctive post-resurrection perspective is reflected in this formulation, as Jesus is viewed as the Logos/Son who has life in himself (cf. 1.4; 5.26) and his mission as emanating from the mutual love between Father and Son. It would be out of place to take 'For this reason' as indicating that the Father's love for Jesus is conditional on the latter's earning it through his self-sacrificial mission. Both his death and his victory over death in resurrection reflect the Father's loving will for Jesus and the world and to this extent are a **command from the Father** which Jesus obediently receives. Yet at the same time that obedience is freely chosen by one who has been granted power over life and death (cf. 5.26–7) – **I have authority to lay it down, and I have authority to take it up again** – and who exercises his own will in complete union with the Father's will. The giving of his life is a sovereign decision that embodies the divine purpose – **No one has taken it from me, but I lay it down of my own accord.** This post-resurrection Christological perspective also has an apologetic thrust. Jesus' death is not to be seen as that of an unwilling victim whose opponents have triumphed nor does it undermine claims about his divine status. In the convention about a noble death not only is such a death voluntary but those who suffer it can also be said to be unconquered and to triumph (cf. Lycurgus, *Leocrates* 48–9; *4 Macc.* 1.11; 7.4; 11.27). In a unique way, because he claims to have the divine prerogative of power over life and death, Jesus in his death is not the vanquished but the vanquisher and so, contrary to normal evaluation, his crucifixion is not a matter of shame or disgrace but a noble or honourable death.

19–21 In the narrative this discourse meets with the divided reaction that has occurred at earlier stages of Jesus' mission (cf. 7.12, 40–3; 9.16). Some maintain that Jesus should not be listened to because **He has a demon and is raving**, a charge already made against him in 7.20 and 8.48. Others remain impressed by the miracle which has been the catalyst for this whole controversy, namely, the opening of the blind man's eyes, and are not inclined to attribute either this or Jesus' teaching to demonic influence – **Can a demon open the eyes of the blind?** Although the reference to 'the blind' here is in the plural and thus has generalized from the particular report in John 9, this conclusion to the passage reinforces that its discourse is to be linked with and interpreted in the light of the contrasting attitudes of Jesus and the religious leaders to the blind man in the previous episode.

The Synoptic background for Jesus' self-identification as the gate or door has been mentioned in the comments, but of course there are also, references to sheep and shepherds among Jesus' sayings in the Synoptic tradition. In Matthew Jesus speaks of 'the lost sheep of the house of Israel' (10.6; 15.24) and sends his disciples out as 'sheep into the midst of wolves' (10.16), while in Luke he addresses them as 'little flock' (12.32). The parable about a lost sheep is related in different forms in Matt. 18.10–14 and Luke 15.4–7. Perhaps most influential for the Fourth Gospel's portrayal of Jesus himself as the shepherd is Jesus' prediction in

Mark 14.27 and Matt. 26.31 about the desertion of his disciples, in which he identifies himself with the shepherd of Zech. 13.7 – 'I will strike the shepherd and the sheep will be scattered.' In addition, the narrator in both Mark 6.34 and Matt. 9.36 depicts Jesus' compassion for the crowds in terms of their being 'like sheep without a shepherd' (cf. Num. 27.17) and Matt. 2.6 already applies the prophecy in Mic. 5.2 about the messianic shepherd-ruler to Jesus' birth. The material that constitutes the figure of speech here in vv. 1–5 might derive from additional parabolic teaching in the ministry of Jesus but in its present form already deals with distinctively Johannine issues. Nevertheless, the basic concepts of Jesus as the shepherd and his people as the sheep clearly have their roots in the Synoptic tradition and what is found here in the bulk of the discourse represents expansion on that tradition in the light of both the Jewish Scriptures, especially Ezek. 34, and Johannine Christological and ecclesiological concerns. Whereas the typical formulation of the Synoptics is 'the kingdom of God is like . . .', here, as elsewhere, the Fourth Gospel focuses on Christological application with 'I Am' statements, seeing Jesus himself as embodying the various aspects of life under God's rule. The mutual knowledge between Jesus and his followers, which is analogous to that between Jesus and the Father (vv. 14–15), may well be derived from the Synoptic saying in Matt. 11.27 and Luke 10.22, which has precisely these elements but is now placed in this new context where it can illuminate the relation between the noble shepherd and his sheep.

It is not surprising that this last extended discourse in the public mission of Jesus looks forward to the passion by making the distinguishing mark of Jesus' role as the noble shepherd his sacrificial death. In the depiction of that death as a noble or honourable one, this passage contributes to the pervasive motif whereby his crucifixion is seen not as shameful but as the place of his lifting up in exaltation and as the hour of his glory or glorification. As has been noted, the scriptural background of the shepherd imagery for leadership of God's people links it with kingship and judging. In John the king who will rule from the cross and the judge who will experience the judgement of crucifixion is now also the shepherd who lays down his life for the sheep. This death and the resurrection that completes it are part of Jesus' mission carried out in union with the Father and not merely the results of the actions of human antagonists. Jesus' mission as the good shepherd who desires the well-being of the sheep has as its goal the production of life in abundance, already signified in the abundance of wine at the wedding in Cana and the abundance of food left over at the feeding of the five thousand. Just as on these previous occasions there were clear hints that this life would paradoxically come through death, so now this motif is further underlined. The giving of life for all is effected through the giving of this particular life. Such an achievement is possible because this good shepherd not only fulfils the task of Israel's faithful leaders and its awaited messianic shepherd-king but also embodies God's own role as the shepherd of the flock.

It is illuminating to compare the Fourth Gospel's use of the shepherd imagery not only with the scriptural material but also with that of 2 *Baruch*, a roughly contemporary apocalyptic text, where, in the struggle to come to terms with the fate of Jerusalem and the nation after 70 CE, the people are presented as lamenting that 'the shepherds of Israel have perished, and the lamps which gave light are extinguished, and the fountains from which we used to drink have withheld their streams'. Baruch replies, 'Shepherds and lanterns and fountains came from the Law and when we go away the Law will abide. If you, therefore, look to the Law and are intent upon wisdom, then the lamp will not be wanting and the shepherd will not give way and the fountain will not dry up' (77.13-16). Both the Fourth Gospel and 2 *Baruch* take up major symbols from the tradition in their concern for the renewed identity of God's people. 2 *Baruch* sees the faithful shepherding Israel needs as dependent on renewed attention to Torah. The Fourth Gospel claims that the renewed people of God from both Jews and Gentiles find their identity in looking to Jesus not only as the source of water and light (chapters 7–9) but now also as the faithful shepherd.

Though the image of God's people as a flock was pervasive in the Jewish Scriptures, present-day readers are not likely to find being compared to sheep an immediately attractive notion. Nevertheless the depiction of the flock in this passage is primarily determined by the identity and mission of Jesus. Believers have a corporate identity as those who have found access to salvation and life only through Jesus as the gate. At the same time there is an individual aspect to the imagery, since here the shepherd calls each sheep by name. The members of this flock are not mindless followers but discerning sheep, those who recognize and listen to the voice of Jesus, the shepherd, rather than any other would-be leaders, and whose intimate relationship with Jesus is patterned on that between Jesus and God. Some of these aspects of the believing community's identity and life will be treated later in the farewell discourse section of the narrative. There also Peter will echo the words of the noble shepherd by speaking of laying down his life for him (13.37). However, his subsequent actions will display the cowardice and shame of the hired hand (cf. 18.15–18, 25–7). Only at the end of the narrative will Peter be commissioned as the flock's undershepherd, whose tending of the sheep will also culminate in his own noble death (21.15–19).

(xiii) Jesus at the Festival of Dedication   *10.22–39*

(22) Then the Festival of Dedication took place in Jerusalem. It was winter, (23) and Jesus was walking in the temple, in the

portico of Solomon. (24) So the Jews surrounded him and said to him, 'How long will you keep annoying us? If you are indeed the Christ, tell us openly.' (25) Jesus answered them, 'I told you and you do not believe. The works that I do in my Father's name testify about me. (26) But you do not believe because you do not belong to my sheep. (27) My sheep hear my voice, and I know them and they follow me. (28) I give them eternal life and they will never perish, and no one will snatch them from my hand. (29) My Father, in regard to what he has given me, is greater than all,[1] and no one is able to snatch from the Father's hand. (30) I and the Father are one.' (31) Again the Jews took up stones to stone him.

(32) Jesus answered them, 'I have shown you many good works from the Father. For which of these are you going to stone me?' (33) The Jews answered him, 'We are not stoning you for a good work but for blasphemy, because you, though a human, are making yourself God.' (34) Jesus answered them, 'Is it not written in your law, "I said, you are gods"? (35) If it calls those gods to whom the word of God came – and the scripture cannot be annulled – (36) are you saying of the one whom the Father consecrated and sent into the world, "You blaspheme," because

---

[1] The text-critical decision about the wording and syntax of this clause is a difficult one. The clause begins with 'my Father' in the nominative case but then the various manuscripts disagree about whether the following relative pronoun is masculine (ὅς) or neuter (ὅ) and whether the comparative adjective 'greater' is masculine (μειζών) or neuter (μεῖζον) and they have these variations in different combinations. (i) B* has the neuter in both cases and is supported by it^{b,c} vg cop^{bo} goth Ambrose, which simply have 'all' and 'greater' in reverse order. This would give the translation 'As to my Father, what he has given me is greater than all.' (ii) ℵ D L W Ψ have the neuter in the first instance followed by the masculine in the second. This is difficult to translate but might be rendered by 'my Father, in regard to what he has given me, is greater than all.' (iii) p^{66} (though it changes the tense of the verb) and some later manuscripts (K Δ Π f^1) have the masculine in both instances and provide the most straightforward reading – 'My Father who has given (them) to me is greater than all.' (iv) A Θ syr^{pal} have the masculine followed by the neuter, which could be translated 'My Father who has given (them) to me is a greater entity or power than all.' If reading (iii) were original, it is hard to explain how the other readings came about. Reading (iv) requires a degree of speculation to find a referent for the neuter form of 'greater'. The difficulty of reading (i) is primarily internal. It depicts the sheep, rather than the Father, as 'greater than all'. This, combined with the unexpected neuter relative pronoun following 'My Father', could have produced alterations in the manuscript tradition. But it may well be the case that reading (ii), which is well supported and is the most difficult syntactically, has the best claim to be original. It has the unexpected neuter relative pronoun following 'my Father' but also combines this with the masculine form for 'greater'. It would explain best why the attempts to smooth out the syntax move in both directions, consistency with the neuter and consistency with the masculine.

I said, "I am God's Son"? (37) If I am not doing the works of my Father, do not believe me. (38) But if I do them, even if you do not believe me, believe the works, so that you may know and understand² that the Father is in me and I am in the Father.' (39) Then they sought again to arrest him, but he escaped from their hands.

The material in 7.1—10.21 has had the Festival of Tabernacles as its backdrop. This next episode is set at the following feast, the Festival of Dedication, some two to three months later. There is, however, broad thematic continuity, since the claims of Jesus and his relation to God the Father remain central, and, more specifically, the sheep and shepherd imagery from 10.1–21 is taken up again in vv. 26–9 in a way that appears to presuppose the same audience. As always, the evangelist's eye is as much on his own audience as on what is appropriate for the audience in the narrative. The latter audience can again be designated simply as 'the Jews' and the hostility between these religious authorities and Jesus that was evident in the previous section and erupted into an attempted stoning in 8.59 is, if anything, intensified in this brief section, which contains another attempted stoning and then an attempted arrest of Jesus.

The episode is another interrogation or trial scene and, as will be discussed later, the evangelist in fact incorporates into it the issues dealt with in the Synoptic tradition of Jesus' trial before the Sanhedrin. The stated purpose of the Gospel as a whole is to further belief in Jesus as the Christ, the Son of God (20.31), and its narrative sets out what such an identification of Jesus entails. Here the appearance of each of these titles and the treatment of their implications can be seen as contributing to the structure of the passage and its two main parts. First, however, a setting is provided in vv. 22–3. Then, in vv. 24–31, the question of Jesus' Messiahship is raised. Jesus responds in a way that takes matters far beyond this traditional concept, culminating in the assertion that he and the Father are one (v. 30) and provoking the response of an attempted stoning on the part of 'the Jews' (v. 31). In the second main section, vv. 32–9, the issue of Jesus' relation to God is pursued and he talks of himself as God's Son. Again the understanding of Son of God is pushed beyond traditional connotations, culminating in Jesus' statement that the Father is in him and he is in the Father (v. 38) and provoking the response of an attempted arrest by the audience (v. 39).

---

² Some manuscripts do not contain καὶ γινώσκητε, 'and understand', and others replace it with καὶ πιστεύσητε, 'and believe'. But the support for καὶ γινώσκητε is early and wide (p⁴⁵,⁶⁶,⁷⁵ B L Θ) and both the omission and replacement can be explained on the basis of copyists attempting to improve what they considered redundant wording.

22–3 The Festival of Dedication (Hanukkah) commemorated the freeing of Jerusalem from its Syrian oppressor, Antiochus Epiphanes, and in particular the dedication or consecration of the temple and its altar at the time of the Maccabees in 165 BCE. The latter act had been necessary, because two years previously, in what became known as 'the desolating sacrilege', Antiochus had defiled the temple by setting up an altar to his own gods (1 Macc. 1.41–61). 1 Macc. 4.36–59 describes the cleansing and dedication at the original event and also the decision that the eight-day celebration should become an annual festival during the month of Chislev. The significance of the festival will be reflected in the fact that explicit discussion about the Messiah, Israel's expected deliverer, takes place when the nation's deliverance was being celebrated and then later in the formulation about Jesus in v. 36. Here its time of year is mentioned – **it was winter** – and this may be linked to the spatial indicators that follow. As in the case of the episodes related to the Festival of Tabernacles, the action takes place in the temple environs (cf. also 7.14, 28; 8.20, 59), but here the **portico of Solomon** is specified, and this area at the south-east end of the outer court would have provided most protection from winter weather.

24–5 Here Jesus is interrogated by **the Jews**, presumably representatives of the unbelieving religious establishment as in the previous episode (cf. 10.19), who **surrounded him**. The question they pose is not simply a reflection of their curiosity but of their hostility. Some translations take it as 'How long will you keep us in suspense?' but there is very little evidence for such a meaning for what would literally be translated as 'How long are you taking away our life?' The force of the idiom in modern Greek is **How long will you keep annoying us?** and there are loose parallels to its wording with similar force in Sophocles, *Oedipus Rex* 914 and Euripides, *Hecuba* 69–70. The interrogators are irritated by what appears to them to be Jesus' elusive way of talking and want a clear statement as to whether he is claiming to be the Messiah – **If you are indeed the Christ, tell us openly.** The issue has been raised previously by the Jerusalem crowd, who are divided in their opinion (cf. 7.26–7, 31, 41–2) but, although Jesus has spoken of himself as the Son of Man, the Son and the one who has come from heaven or from God, he has not directly asserted his Messiahship to the religious authorities. He has, however, performed the signs that are expected of a future messianic figure and in the previous episode on the basis of the enigmatic *paroimia* has talked of himself as shepherd in terms employed of the Davidic Messiah. It is appropriate, therefore, that the authorities should be depicted as now demanding some plain talking. From as early as 1.41, with Andrew's testimony to his brother, readers know that Messiahship is indeed part of Jesus' identity, but as is clear from his 'I Am' in response to the Samaritan woman, Jesus' acknowledgement of the title claims far more (cf. 4.25–6, 29), and so will his reply to his interrogators here.

He begins by saying **I told you and you do not believe**, emphasizing that, if they had been open to his teaching, they would have understood that it had already answered their question (cf. also 5.38, 44, 47). What Jesus goes on to say underlines this, because it echoes statements he has previously made to 'the Jews'. **The works that I do in my Father's name testify about me** is a restatement of the saying in 5.36. These works include the miraculous signs but also extend to the whole of his activity and take in his teaching. They point to being done 'in the Father's name', that is, to his role as the Father's fully authorized representative.

26–7 Jesus then provides the explanation for his interrogators' failure to believe – it is **because you do not belong to my sheep**. This returns to the pastoral imagery of the preceding discourse and to the paradox of belief or unbelief that has been encountered earlier in the Gospel. Humans have the responsibility to believe, yet at the same time the ability to do so is ultimately the result of God's mysterious working – 'No one can come to me unless drawn by the Father who sent me' (6.44; cf. also 6.65). It is those who have been drawn into Jesus' flock and have become his sheep who can acknowledge his claims – **My sheep hear my voice, and I know them and they follow me**. Here the language of 10.3, 4, 14, 16 is taken up again.

28–9 I give them eternal life and they will never perish picks up on the thought of 10.10 that instead of allowing the sheep to experience death and destruction, Jesus has come that they may have life in abundance. Here the variation through the use of 'to perish' also takes up the earlier formulation from 3.16 – 'that everyone who believes in him may not perish but have eternal life'. Mention of the secure future destiny of those who believe in Jesus remains within the context of pastoral imagery in the assurance that **no one will snatch them from my hand**. This shepherd will not permit anyone to seize or steal his sheep (cf. 10.10a) and more general assurances to the effect that Jesus will lose none of those given to him have already been provided in 6.37–40. There it was stressed that Jesus was at one with the Father's will in this matter and this point is now reiterated.

My Father, in regard to what he has given me, is greater than all, and no one is able to snatch from the Father's hand. The assurance of the ultimate security of Jesus' sheep, because no one will snatch them from his hand, is strengthened by this reference to the Father. The sheep also belong to the Father, who has given them to Jesus. The reference to believers as a gift from the Father, employing a neuter singular formulation, is also found in 6.39 and 17.24. Since the Father is greater than all in power, it is impossible that anyone could prise the sheep from his strong grip.

30–1 The implication of these assertions is now drawn – **I and the Father are one.** When this statement is taken strictly in the context of the discourse, its force is that Jesus and the Father are one in securing the safety of the sheep in their care. There may be two agents but their protecting hand is one. The Father can be said to be greater (cf. also 14.28), but the Father and Jesus are completely one in the salvation they provide, because Jesus fully shares in God's work and will (cf. also 10.18). If this is the case, however, there are further implications for Jesus' identity, and so later Christians who used this text in Christological debates and formulations about the metaphysical unity of the Father and the Son need not be faulted as totally misguided. Indeed, once the text is read in the context of the whole Gospel and particularly its prologue's assertions about the relation of the incarnate Logos to God, it invites further reflection on its implications for Jesus' ontological status of equality with God. Father and Son are united in the work of salvation because they are united in their being. The immediate point, however, in response to the interrogators' question is that it is not enough simply to attempt to fit Jesus into the category of Messiah. That category is transformed in the light of his unique relationship to God.

Ironically, in the narrative setting Jesus' audience take his words as entailing the full Johannine notion of his equality with God, but within their framework such a claim can only be interpreted as blasphemy and so **Again** (as in 8.59) **the Jews took up stones to stone him.**

32–3 Jesus forestalls their action by his response which opens the second half of the passage. As he has just done, he points to the witness of his works – **I have shown you many good works from the Father.** The adjective accompanying 'works' in these verses is καλός and may well pick up on the connotations of its earlier use in relation to the shepherd. Jesus has carried out many honourable or noble deeds, which have benefited others, have displayed his unique power, and have been for God's glory, and so he demands to know which of them merits his death – **For which of these are you going to stone me?** His question allows the opposition to make explicit the reason for wanting to stone him – **We are not stoning you for a good work but for blasphemy, because you, though a human, are making yourself God.** Despite his similar teaching in the past, this is the only time in the narrative that Jesus is explicitly accused of blasphemy. This was, however, the implicit accusation that lay behind the previous attempt at stoning him in 8.59, where Jesus could be viewed as having pronounced the divine name with his preceding 'I Am' statement, this then being seen as in breach of Lev. 24.26 (cf. also *m. Sanh.* 7.5). There is no pronunciation of the divine name here, however, and instead the charge is similar to that for which the narrator has said in 5.18 that 'the Jews were seeking . . . to kill him', namely, that because of the relationship to God which Jesus was asserting, he was 'making himself equal to God'. Here the formulation 'making yourself God' reflects the dispute between the synagogue and the claims of Johannine Christians about Jesus' identity. Because Jewish believers were prepared to speak of Jesus in terms used of God, this attracted the fierce objection that they were making him God and that this amounted to blasphemy. But from the evangelist's perspective there could be no question of either Jesus making himself God or Christians making him God; this was simply the status he already had by virtue of his relation to the Father.

34–6 The debate between those who accepted and those who rejected the claim that Jesus was divine was conducted at a variety of levels. Since for both sides Scripture was a final authority, the current conventional means of appealing to Scripture for support came into play and now one of the arguments employed by Christians is attributed to Jesus. Much has been written about his use of the citation from Ps. 82.6 – **I said, you are gods**. The discussion may have been unnecessarily complicated by the assumption that, in order to understand the argument, the reader needs to know the identity of those who are called 'gods' in this verse. The problem is that there is no agreement about the referent in the original psalm or, more importantly, about how it would have been interpreted in first-century Judaism. In regard to the original referent, many suppose, perhaps out of a reluctance to find any belief in the existence of a plurality of gods in the Scriptures, that *elohim* in vv. 1, 6 has Israel's judges in view. But the far more obvious interpretation is that Israel's God is addressing the gods of the nations, who are indicted for failing to exercise justice and allowing oppression and chaos to prevail. It should be clear from v. 7, which pronounces the true Judge's verdict – 'you shall die *like* mortals' – that beings other than mortals are designated. In the final verse, in contrast to the gods who will fall, God is called on to rise up and judge, since all the nations belong to this God rather than to the other gods. By the first century CE, however, Jewish interpretation of the psalm had moved in various directions, in which the main candidates for 'the gods' had become (i) the angels, (ii) Israel's leaders or judges, and (iii) the Israelites at Sinai. The first tradition – angelic beings with responsibilities for the nations – is a variation on the most likely original meaning. The second – Israel's judges – holds that they can be called 'gods' because the exercise of judgement is a divine prerogative granted to particular humans, despite their propensity to misuse this power. The third interpretative tradition – Israel at the time of the giving of the law at Sinai – claimed that the law made its recipients holy and immortal, the qualities of 'the gods', but that with the sin of the golden calf the Israelites lost this status and once again became doomed to die as mortals.

Yet once one sees that typical conventions of midrashic exegesis are involved (such as the validity of isolating a single word from its context and the argument from the lesser to the greater – *qal wahomer*), the coherence of the argument is clear from its surface features. It runs as follows. In the law to which 'the Jews' appeal in their judgement of Jesus – **your law** – and which constitutes Scripture that **cannot be annulled**, those addressed by this word from God are designated 'gods'. How can it, therefore, be blasphemy when, not those addressed by God but the one who embodies God's address to the world, because God the Father consecrated and sent him into the world, declares **I am God's Son?** The charge is that Jesus makes himself God. The defence is scriptural and moves from the lesser – **those . . . to whom the word of God came** – to the greater – Jesus' unique representation of God as **the one whom the Father consecrated and sent into the world**, who is thereby the Word of God itself (cf. 1.14). 'Sent into the world' implies Jesus' pre-existence in divine reality and thereby evokes the earlier notion of the Logos who becomes incarnate. If the lesser can be called 'gods', then not only is it baseless to dispute the validity of the greater calling himself Son of God but this would also be to dispute Scripture itself. The advantage of this reading is not only that it does not require specific knowledge of detailed interpretation of the psalm but also that, for this reason, it would have been intelligible to the Gospel's Gentile readers.

If, however, fuller knowledge of Ps. 82 and its interpretation is being presupposed, so that it is not simply the fact of being recipients of an address by God but also the identity of such recipients that is important, how might the various options add to the thrust of the argument? First of all, it can be pointed out that in the synonymous parallelism of Ps. 82.6, a line not cited here in John, 'sons of the Most High' becomes the functional equivalent of 'gods', and so Jesus' use of 'Son of God' as a self-designation by no means distances his response from the terms of the text. If the use of the psalm here has the gods of the nations in view as the recipients of God's address, then the psalm's dispute between Yahweh and the gods of the nations can be seen to have affinities with the cosmic trial motif from Isa. 40—55, which informs so much of the conceptual world of the Fourth Gospel's narrative, and helps to explain why in this further trial scene Ps. 82 would have come to mind. If God can even address such rival entities as 'gods', then there should be no problem about the uniquely authorized representative of this God being designated as Son of God. If Israel's judges are in view as receiving God's word, this would make the *ad hominem* aspect of the argument here in John even more pronounced, since the Jewish religious authorities interrogating Jesus would see themselves as the contemporary representatives of such a group. It is just such a group as themselves who were called 'gods', so how can they justifiably object to God's uniquely qualified envoy being considered Son of God? This would contribute to the frequent pattern in this Gospel, in which those who attempt to judge Jesus have their judgement turned back on themselves. The rest of the content of the psalm could also be seen by readers of John as indicting such judges and therefore as in continuity with the criticism of Israel's leaders that has been part of the earlier shepherd discourse in vv. 1–21. Finally, if it is Israel at Sinai that is in view, then the added force of the argument is that if God made those who received the law holy and immortal and able to be called 'gods', then how much more should the one whom God has sanctified and sent be seen as made Son of God not by himself but by God.

The details of the scriptural argument should not be allowed to obscure the significance of the unusual Christological formulation in v. 36. Everywhere else in the Gospel God or the Father is the one who has sent Jesus and Jesus is the one whom God has sent. Here, however, this pervasive form of wording is altered and Jesus becomes the one whom the Father has *consecrated* and sent. This links Jesus to the central theme of the Festival of Dedication – the consecration of the temple altar. In doing so, it feeds into two major motifs in the Gospel. The first is Jesus as the fulfilment or replacement of the significance of the Jewish festivals. Just as he can be seen as the true Passover lamb and the true water and light of Tabernacles, so now he is the true focus of dedication. This in turn contributes to the second motif of Jesus' relation to sacred space. Not only is he the true house of God (1.28), the true temple (2.19–21), and the one who supersedes both Mt Gerizim and Jerusalem as the place of worship (4.21–6), but he is also the truly consecrated temple altar.

37–8 The controversy now returns to the level of the significance of Jesus' works (cf. vv. 25b, 32). What someone does expresses who they are. Jesus has employed this notion earlier to undermine the claim of 'the Jews' to have Abraham as their Father and to be his children; their actions were not consonant with their words (cf. 8.39–41). Now he invites the same standard of judgement in regard to himself – **If I am not doing the works of my Father, do not believe me** (when I say I am God's Son). He expresses confidence that his deeds will stand scrutiny as fully in line with the Father's will for the flourishing of human life. So even if the interrogators do not believe his claim, they should **believe the works**, because these point inescapably to the same conclusion about Jesus' relation to God, namely, that **the Father is in me and I am in the Father**. This time Jesus' unity with the Father is formulated in terms of their mutual indwelling, a notion that will be repeated in the farewell section in 14.10–11 and 17.21. Again readers are confronted with the paradox of the interpenetration of human responsibility and divine initiative, so that those who have been told they do not believe because they do not belong to Jesus' sheep (v. 26) can still be invited to believe, because it is assumed that they are capable of so doing.

39 Again this talk of Jesus' oneness with the Father produces a hostile reaction – **they sought again to arrest him** (cf. 7.30). Jesus, however, remains elusive – **he escaped from their hands**. The narrator's comment recalls Jesus' language in vv. 28–9. Just as the destiny of Jesus' sheep is secure in the Father's hand, so is Jesus' own destiny and human hands will have no power over him until the divinely permitted time.

This trial scene reflects knowledge of the trial before the Sanhedrin in the Synoptic tradition, which is not found in John's passion narrative, and the similarities are the result of the evangelist's decision to incorporate elements of that tradition into his structuring of the public mission of Jesus in terms of a trial before the Jewish religious authorities. Earlier evidence of knowledge of the Sanhedrin trial was found in the Fourth Gospel's account of the temple incident, where, instead of the false witnesses of Mark 14.58 making the accusation that Jesus had threatened to destroy the temple and build another in three days, Jesus makes a similar assertion himself in John 2.19. In this Gospel also the role of the high priest, Caiaphas (according to Matthew), in securing the agreement of the Sanhedrin in calling for Jesus' death in the Synoptic Jewish trial will be set out in advance after the raising of Lazarus in 11.47–53 (cf. 18.14). The present passage takes up the question and answer about Jesus as Messiah and Son of God and the issue of blasphemy found in Mark 14.61–4 and its parallels in Matt. 26.63–6 and Luke 22.67–71 (though Luke omits any mention of blasphemy). John's account has 'if you are indeed the Christ' (v. 24), the claim to be 'Son of God' (v. 36) and the issue of 'blasphemy' (vv. 31–3, 36) and in fact resembles most closely the Lukan redaction, which has divided the question about Jesus as Messiah and Son of God into two separate issues. The opening of the dialogue in vv. 24–5 – "'if you are indeed the Christ, tell us plainly." Jesus answered them, "I told you, and you do not believe"' – again has the closest verbal links with Luke 22.67–8 – "'If you are the Christ, tell us." He replied, "If I tell you, you will not believe."' Here in v. 36 Jesus asks, 'Are you saying . . . "You blaspheme," because I said, "I am God's Son"?' Mark has 'Are you . . . the Son of the Blessed?' and Jesus replying 'I am' (14.61–2), while Luke formulates this as 'Are you the Son of God then?' with Jesus replying, 'You say that I am' (22.70). Just as in Mark 14.63–4 the high priest accuses Jesus of blasphemy and then all condemn him as deserving death, so here in vv. 31–3 'the Jews' accuse Jesus of blasphemy and attempt to stone him to death. Some argue that John obtained the same material found in Mark and Luke from an independent tradition. But not only is this not susceptible to verification but it is also not the most obvious explanation. The simpler conclusion is that John knew of the Markan and Lukan traditions and reworked them and placed them in a different setting.

This passage's trial scene depicts issues that reflect some of the evangelist's deepest concerns and convictions. In many ways it presents readers with the Fourth Gospel's controversial Christology in a nutshell, forcing reflection on the appropriate identification of Jesus. As has been noted, whether he is the Messiah is at the centre of the first part of the interrogation and his claim to be Son of God plays a key role in the second part, and these are the two titles that feature in the Gospel's statement of purpose (cf. 20.31). In each part the dispute leads to a statement about Jesus' relationship with God which presupposes the title but clarifies its proper understanding – first, 'the Father and I are one,' and then, 'the Father is in me and I am in the Father'. The consequence of such a presentation is that Jesus' opponents are faulted for thinking they can make him fit into the religious categories they already have. For the evangelist, Jesus' unique relationship of oneness and equality with God transforms existing criteria of judgement rather than merely accommodating itself to them. His Messiahship is not simply that of a greater national liberator than Judas Maccabeus, who would be remembered at this Festival of Dedication. Instead he brings a more ultimate salvation for his people, in the accomplishment of which he and God the Father are completely one. Similarly, when Jesus says, 'I am God's Son', he is not simply claiming to be a righteous Israelite or a royal figure or even an angelic being. Instead this is the sort of Sonship to the Father that entails a mutual indwelling, a co-inherence, a perfect fellowship. If these sort of Christological claims are to be rightly understood, again categories of judgement need to be transformed. Within their own criteria, Jesus' interrogators can only interpret them as blasphemy. What the evangelist wants readers to understand is that the total unity of Jesus' mission with that of the Father is not that of a human making himself God but originates with God in the first place. God gives Jesus his unique identity and mission. This is the force of the formulation in v. 36 about Jesus as the one whom God has sent into the world – he has come from the sphere of divine reality and is in the world as the divinely consecrated one. Against the backdrop of Hanukkah and its celebration of the consecration of the temple altar, this perspective on Jesus' mission also means, in line with the evangelist's thought elsewhere, that Jesus now embodies what the temple altar represented, the consecrated locus of the very presence of God.

In the Fourth Gospel the right identification of Jesus is inextricably linked to the issue of belief. That link is clear in its statement of purpose in 20.31 and it is to the fore in both main parts of this passage – in vv. 26–7 and vv. 37–8. How is it that some have their previous categories transformed so that they see in Jesus the presence of God and acknowledge the co-inherence of this Son with the Father, and why do others fail to attain this insight? This passage's explanation appears rather circular. Jesus' interrogators are told they do not believe because they do not belong to his sheep, yet they are still invited to believe and are held responsible for not doing so. His followers believe because they are the sheep whom God has given to Jesus and who have been enabled to recognize his voice. But such circularity may be all that is available. Believers cannot take the credit for their own faith and they experience it as God's gift. And why at this point others do not acknowledge the truth of Jesus' claim that 'I and the Father are one' is left as a mystery that only God can fathom and resolve. But in their context these formulations are meant primarily as encouragement and assurance for believing readers. Through a belief that was not of their own doing, they find themselves in the secure hand of Jesus, the noble Shepherd, and, because he and his Father are one, those in Jesus' hand are in the hand of the one who is sovereign over all and who will not let them be snatched from its loving embrace.

(xiv) Transition: Jesus beyond the Jordan   10.40–2

(40) He went away again across the Jordan to the place where John had been baptizing at first, and he remained there. (41) Many came to him and were saying, 'John did no sign, but everything John said about this man is true.' (42) And many believed in him there.

The last three verses of this chapter constitute both a spatial and chronological transition in the narrative and indicate that the response to Jesus on the part of the populace could be quite different from the hostile treatment he has just received from the religious authorities. This short section looks back to the start of Jesus' public ministry and forward to the story of the last sign in that ministry.

40 Jesus leaves Jerusalem and returns to **the place where John had been baptizing at first.** This location **across the Jordan** was specified earlier in 1.28 as Bethany. Its identification with reference to John's baptizing activity rounds off Jesus' ministry at this stage by pointing back to its beginning. Moving Jesus away from Judaea also enables the narrator to have Jesus absent from the area when he receives the news of Lazarus' illness in the next episode and to have the return to Judaea be a return to the threat of death that Jesus has just experienced.

41–2 The words of those who come to Jesus in this new setting both set up a final contrast between Jesus and John and recall and endorse the latter's testimony. The statement that **John did no sign** underlines by contrast that Jesus' mission is characterized by signs and functions similarly to John's denial in 1.20 that he is the Christ. The previous trial scene has spoken of Jesus' 'works'. Reintroducing the notion of 'signs' prepares readers for the next great sign, the raising of Lazarus. In this last reference to John, he still plays his role as witness, although that terminology is not employed – **everything John said about this man is true**. The people's endorsement of John's witness as true (cf. also 5.33) is part of a positive response that contrasts with the reception of Jesus by 'the Jews' in Jerusalem. While their unbelief was indicted, here the people's belief is emphasized – **Many came to him . . . And many believed in him there.** Earlier references to many believing are linked with their interest in the signs Jesus performs (cf. e.g. 2.23; 7.31). In the present context the contrast with John implies that Jesus was performing signs, so that both the witness of the signs and the remembered witness of John form the basis for the belief that the narrator depicts. There are two sides to his perspective on faith resulting from signs. Jesus has just invited belief in his works, which include signs (10.38), and there is no criticism of the faith described here. Nevertheless, other passages (e.g. 2.23; 4.48) indicate that believing on the basis of signs can prove to be inauthentic because it fails to see their implications for Jesus' true identity in relation to God.

4. Conclusion: Move Toward the Hour of Death and Glory   11.1—12.50

(i) The raising of Lazarus   *11.1–53*

(1) Now a certain man was ill, Lazarus of Bethany, the village of Mary and her sister, Martha. (2) Mary, whose brother Lazarus was ill, was the one who anointed the Lord with ointment and wiped his feet with her hair. (3) So the sisters sent word to him, saying, 'Lord, the one whom you love is ill.' (4) But when he heard this, Jesus said, 'This illness is not to lead to death but is for the glory of God, so that the Son of God may be glorified through it.' (5) Now Jesus loved Martha and her sister and Lazarus. (6) When, therefore, he heard that he was ill, he remained two days in the place where he was. (7) Then after this he said to his disciples, 'Let us go to Judaea again.' (8) The disciples said to him, 'Rabbi, the Jews were just now seeking to stone you, and are you going there again?' (9) Jesus answered, 'Are there not twelve hours in the day? If one walks in the day, one does not stumble, because one sees the light of this world. (10) But if one walks in the night, one stumbles, because the light is not in one.' (11) He said these things and after this told them, 'Our friend Lazarus has

fallen asleep, but I am going to awaken him.' (12) His disciples therefore said to him, 'Lord, if he has fallen asleep, he will be restored to health.' (13) But Jesus was talking about his death. They thought he was talking about the sleep of actual slumber. (14) So then Jesus said to them plainly, 'Lazarus has died. (15) And I am glad for your sake that I was not there, so that you may believe. But let us go to him.' (16) So Thomas, who was called the Twin, said to his fellow disciples, 'Let us also go in order that we may die with him.'

(17) When he arrived, Jesus found that Lazarus[1] had already been in the tomb four days. (18) Now Bethany was near Jerusalem, about two miles[2] away. (19) Many of the Jews had come to Martha and Mary to console them about their brother. (20) When Martha heard that Jesus was coming, she went to meet him; but Mary sat in the house. (21) Martha said to Jesus, 'Lord, if you had been here, my brother would not have died. (22) But even now I know that whatever you ask of God, God will give you.' (23) Jesus said to her, 'Your brother will arise.' (24) Martha said to him, 'I know that he will arise in the resurrection on the last day.' (25) Jesus said to her, 'I am the resurrection and the life. The one who believes in me, even though that person dies, will live, (26) and everyone who lives and believes in me will never die. Do you believe this?' (27) She said to him, 'Yes, Lord. I believe that you are the Christ, the Son of God, the one coming into the world.'

(28) When she had said these things, she went away and called Mary her sister and said to her privately, 'The teacher has come and is calling for you.' (29) When she heard this, she got up quickly and went to him. (30) Now Jesus had not yet come to the village but was still at the place where Martha had met him. (31) So the Jews, who were with her in the house and consoling her, having seen Mary get up quickly and go out, followed her, thinking that she was going to the tomb to weep there. (32) When Mary came to where Jesus was and saw him, she fell at his feet and said to him, 'Lord, if you had been here, my brother would not have died.' (33) When Jesus saw her weeping and the Jews who had come with her weeping, he became angry in spirit and was greatly agitated, (34) and he said, 'Where have you laid him?' They said to him, 'Lord, come and see.' (35) Jesus wept. (36) Then the Jews said, 'See how he loved him.' (37) But some

---

[1] 'Lazarus' has been specified for the sake of clarity, since the Greek simply has the third person pronoun.

[2] In Greek the distance is given as fifteen stadia.

of them said, 'Could not this one who opened the eyes of the blind man have done something so that this man would not have died?'

(38) Then Jesus, having again become angry in himself, came to the tomb. It was a cave, and a stone was lying against it. (39) Jesus said, 'Take away the stone.' Martha, the dead man's sister, said to him, 'Lord, there is already a stench, because it is the fourth day since he died.' (40) Jesus said to her, 'Did I not tell you that if you believe you will see the glory of God?' (41) So they took away the stone. Jesus looked upwards and said, 'Father, I thank you that you have heard me. (42) I know that you always hear me, but I have said this for the sake of the crowd standing by, so that they might believe that you have sent me.' (43) And when he had said these things, he cried out in a loud voice, 'Lazarus, come out!' (44) The dead man came out, with feet and hands bound in bandages and his face wrapped in a cloth. Jesus said to them, 'Unbind him and let him go.'

(45) Many of the Jews, therefore, who had come to Mary and had seen what he had done, believed in him. (46) But some of them went to the Pharisees and told them what Jesus had done. (47) The chief priests and Pharisees therefore convened a meeting of the council,[3] and said, 'What are we doing about the fact that this man is performing many signs? (48) If we allow him to go on like this, all will believe in him and the Romans will come and take away both our place[4] and our nation.' (49) But one of them, Caiaphas, who was high priest that year, said to them, 'You know nothing; (50) you do not consider that it is advantageous for you that one man should die for the people and that the whole nation should not perish.' (51) Now he did not say this on his own, but, being high priest that year, he prophesied that Jesus was about to die for the nation, (52) and not for the nation alone but also to gather into one the dispersed children of God. (53) So from that day on they resolved to kill him.

This seventh and climactic sign is given far more attention and space in the narrative than any other. It stands apart from the preceding six signs not only because of its subject matter. Whereas the others are paired in terms of their setting, with two in Cana (cf. 2.1–11 and 4.46–54), two in Jerusalem (cf. 5.1–18 and 9.1–41) and two in Galilee (cf. 6.1–15 and

---

[3] The Greek word συνέδριον is often simply translated as a technical term, 'Sanhedrin', with reference to the official Jerusalem council.

[4] Most probably a reference to the temple as holy place.

6.16–21), the seventh stands alone in its Bethany setting. It is distinctive for two further reasons. This is the only sign in which the recipient of Jesus' action is named and said to be in a close personal relationship with Jesus, and it is the only one where the discourse or dialogue that interprets its significance comes before the miraculous action. There are, however, links with the first sign through the mention of Jesus' glory and the disciples' belief (vv. 4, 15; cf. 2.11) and with the sixth sign through the mention of the opening of the eyes of the blind man (v. 37; cf. 9.1–41) and the imagery of light (vv. 9–10; cf. 9.4–5). Whereas a number of the earlier signs have presented Jesus as life-giver in dealing with situations that could lead to death or are associated with death, the seventh sign now brings Jesus into direct confrontation with death and its consequences.

But how far does the account of this sign extend? Many see the Lazarus episode as reaching only as far as v. 44, but this is to cut it off too abruptly. Part of the reason discussions often stop at this point is that the actual miracle is so delayed in this sign story that when it happens interpreters are inclined to think that the story has finally reached its conclusion, forgetting that, as in other miracle stories, the response, which also confirms that a miracle has taken place, is an integral part of the account. Here the response is a divided one and its negative aspect extends to v. 53. Others suggest that the episode continues as far as 12.11, since the anointing of 12.1–8 has as its setting a dinner for Lazarus and 12.9–11 tells of Lazarus having become the focus of attention for the crowd and for the chief priests who plan to kill him. Others still hold that this is also to stop too soon, since the final mention of Lazarus occurs in the next account, that of the entry into Jerusalem in 12.12–19, where in vv. 17–18 the crowds who meet Jesus are linked with the crowd at the tomb of Lazarus. The last two options are enticing not only because they would account for more or all of the Lazarus references but also because they provide a balance between the roles of the two sisters in the story. Whereas in the lead-in to the raising of Lazarus Martha has the more prominent and positive part, in the anointing scene this is reversed and Mary now exhibits theological insight through her actions with Martha serving at table in the background.

One would be tempted to embrace the view that the Lazarus episode ends at either 12.11 or 12.19 were it not for the material in 11.54–7, which is often passed over too quickly or subsumed as part of a scene that runs from 11.45 to 11.57. The meeting of the council implicitly has a new spatial setting but is related as part of a chain reaction initiated by those who respond negatively to the Lazarus miracle. An explicit change of spatial and temporal markers is found first in 11.54–7, where Jesus and his disciples move to Ephraim and have to return to Bethany later in 12.1, and then a new temporal indicator is introduced with the mention of the Passover and the preparations for it in Jerusalem. This is the third Passover

mentioned in the narrative. Readers have just been told that the council
has now planned to put Jesus to death and so the mention of Passover
raises the obvious question whether this is likely to be Jesus' last Passover
attendance. Everything in 11.54–7 drives home this question. Jesus' move
to Ephraim near the wilderness region with the disciples for an indefinite
period is a move to a less threatened location. Is this temporary? Will he
risk returning to the Jerusalem area, where he can be seized? This question,
raised already at the beginning of the Lazarus episode in vv. 8, 16, is asked
explicitly in v. 56 by the pilgrims already assembling in Jerusalem for the
Passover, and the narrator makes clear that this is against the backdrop of
orders having been given that anyone knowing Jesus' whereabouts should
inform the authorities so that they can arrest him (cf. v. 57). So 11.54–7
mark a definite break and point forward to the last Passover in Jesus'
mission. From this point on all the action is played out in relation to the
Passover setting, which is not in view in the actual story of the raising of
Lazarus. Jesus' return to Bethany is explicitly said to be six days before the
Passover (12.1) and signals the answer to the question about whether he
will return to Jerusalem for the festival, and the account of the entry into
Jerusalem underlines the connection with the festival (12.12). Further
references to the festival punctuate the narrative that follows (cf. 12.20;
13.1; 18.28, 39; 19.31, 42). Although the raising of Lazarus takes place
some time before the action of the final Passover begins, the evangelist
is at pains to show that it is the catalyst for the arrest, interrogation, trial
and death of Jesus, which happen during the festival, and so the further
substantial references to Lazarus as the one whom Jesus had raised from
the dead (cf. 12.1, 9, 17) colour the accounts of Jesus' progress to his last
festival attendance in Jerusalem in 12.1–19. For these reasons the material
in 12.1–19 should inform the interpretation of the account of the raising
of Lazarus but is not to be considered part of the Lazarus episode proper,
which is constituted by 11.1–53. The episode begins with Lazarus' illness
and death, moves to Jesus' raising him from the dead and ends on the note
that the one who is the giver of life now himself faces death.

It divides fairly naturally into six scenes – (i) the setting of the story, with
Lazarus' illness and Jesus' delay in responding (vv. 1–6); (ii) Jesus' dialogue with
the disciples (vv. 7–16); (iii) the arrival at Bethany and the encounter with
Martha (vv. 17–27); (iv) the encounter with Mary and 'the Jews' (vv. 28–37);
(v) Jesus' arrival at the tomb and his raising of Lazarus (vv. 38–44) and (vi) the
divided response to the miracle and its aftermath for Jesus (vv. 45–53).

1–2 The three main characters other than Jesus are all introduced in
v. 1. Lazarus is introduced in two ways, both connecting him with his
sisters, and suggesting that they are more likely to be known already to
the implied readers. First, it is said that **a certain man was ill**, who is
then specified as **Lazarus of Bethany**, and Bethany is characterized

by its association with the two sisters – **the village of Mary and her sister, Martha**. Secondly, the reader is reminded that this Mary is **the one who anointed the Lord** and told again that the Lazarus who is ill is her brother. In terms of the present narrative of the Gospel v. 2 is a prolepsis of 12.1–8, since the anointing has not yet been recounted. The formulation may also suggest that in fact the reader is expected to be already familiar with this incident. In terms of the Gospel's composition it might indicate either that in an earlier edition of the Gospel the story of the anointing had already been told or that the final writer glossed an earlier edition to help clarify the identity of Mary. As the narrative now stands, this advance notice of Mary anointing Jesus' body for burial signals that the later pericope is to be closely related to the raising of Lazarus and serves the purpose of introducing right from the start one of the main motifs of the story, namely that the raising of Lazarus to life is bound up with the movement of Jesus toward death.

3–4 How Jesus becomes involved in the story is explained, as the narrator reports that **the sisters sent word to him, saying, 'Lord, the one whom you love is ill.'** This further description of Lazarus has prompted some to identify him with the Beloved Disciple who is introduced in 13.23 as 'he whom Jesus loved'. But then it would be very strange that, having named him here, the evangelist is at great pains to preserve his anonymity in the rest of the Gospel. Leaving aside the major questions of historicity surrounding this episode, the identification runs into other problems even on the narrative level. If the other disciple in 18.15 is also to be identified with the Beloved Disciple, as many hold (see the discussion at 18.15), then it makes little sense that in the Lazarus story the chief priests are out to kill Lazarus, while in the later incident the other disciple has privileged access because he is known to the chief priest. Interestingly, the formulation 'the disciple whom Jesus loved' employs the verb ἀγαπάω. This is used for all three family members in v. 5, but when Lazarus is singled out here in v. 3 the verb φιλέω is used, and in v. 11 Lazarus is described as 'our friend' (φίλος). This suggests the influence of a major Johannine motif found in 15.12–14. There, in connection with the love commandment, Jesus says, 'No one has greater love than this, to lay down one's life for one's friends.' There is an immediate indication that this general statement can also be interpreted as a self-description, as he adds, 'You are my friends.' Jesus' laying down of his life is to be seen as for his friends. Jesus has also just spoken of the good shepherd as one who lays down his life for the sheep (10.21). Now what will emerge in the Lazarus story is the dramatic enactment of this motif from 15.13, with Jesus showing his readiness to perform an act for one particular friend which will result in the laying down of his life.

Jesus' response to the sisters' message is enigmatic. He declares that

Lazarus' **illness is not to lead to death but is for the glory of God**. This initially sets readers up for a further sign that would entail a healing, since the illness is said not to be one that results in death. But, given Jesus' response in what follows, this expectation is almost immediately thrown into question, and, given that Lazarus' illness does in fact lead to his death, readers who keep this saying in mind and who have been convinced of the reliability of Jesus' viewpoint are alerted to this death therefore not being the ultimate outcome of the episode and to the illness somehow serving the greater purpose of God's glory. In this way the saying anticipates the thrust of the rest of the narrative by already putting a question mark against usual attitudes to death as the end of physical life. As earlier in the narrative, the glory of God is linked to the glory of Jesus – **so that the Son of God may be glorified through it**. The saying thus makes clear that what will unfold in this episode is a further disclosure of Jesus' identity which is in turn a disclosure about God. Its formulation also underscores that there is a sign in the offing, since the narrator had made clear that the very first sign entailed Jesus' revelation of his glory (2.11). Because Jesus' glorification in this narrative is inextricably linked to his death and exaltation (cf. 7.39; 12.16, 23, 28; 13.31–2), a connection is established between the coming sign and Jesus' own destiny that is highly ironic. Lazarus' illness will not end with his death, but it will be a catalyst for Jesus' death.

5–6 That there is more to the saying of v. 4 than might at first appear is underlined by the report of Jesus' strange decision. Although Jesus loved the two sisters and their brother, and although Jesus had received the message that Lazarus was ill, **he remained two days in the place where he was**, which is presumably still the other Bethany mentioned in this Gospel (10.40; cf. 1.28), Bethany in Perea. In terms of the details of the story, since the two Bethanys were about one day's journey apart and, assuming that Lazarus died almost immediately after the sisters had sent their message, a further stay of two days is the minimum time necessary for it to be possible for Lazarus to have been dead four days when Jesus arrives on the scene (cf. v. 17). In terms of the bigger question of why Jesus stayed at all after receiving the message, the implication is clear. Jesus' delay and absence are to be seen as compatible with his love. They are in fact the way of expressing his love, as the **therefore** at the beginning of v. 6 confirms. The explanation for this unusual expression of love is suggested in Jesus' saying that has just preceded his decision. His deliberate delay, incomprehensible for normal human timetables, is to be understood, in line with similar responses to his own mother and brothers in 2.4 and 7.6–8, as an indication that Jesus is operating according to a divine timetable and plan for his mission that involves his and the Father's glory.

7–10 That plan and timetable are the explicit topics of the conversation between Jesus and the disciples that now ensues. This is the only section of the story in which the disciples appear and the dialogue with them here serves as an interpretative backdrop for the later action. Jesus indicates his readiness to return to Judaea and invites the disciples to accompany him. The narrator has given no indication of the lapse of time between the action in Jerusalem recorded in the previous chapter and the receipt of the message from the two sisters. The disciples, however, formulate their objection to Jesus' proposal in terms of narrative time and remind him that **the Jews were just now seeking to stone you** (cf. 10.31). So their question – **and are you going there again?** – points to their sense of the danger in what appears to be Jesus' courting of death. From the perspective of 9.4 – 'We must work the works of him who sent me while it is day; night is coming when no one is able to work – Jesus' reply with a further question – **Are there not twelve hours in the day?** – suggests that it is still day, and so he and his disciples must be about God's work whatever danger might lie ahead. The formulation of the rest of the saying in terms of seeing the light and having the light in one is such that it must be his followers rather than Jesus who are primarily in view. In it Jesus attempts to switch their preoccupation with the matter of death to a concern about the more significant danger of stumbling. To stumble or fall is to give up in the face of a threat such as death (cf. also 16.1–2). The positive statement – **If one walks in the day, one does not stumble, because one sees the light of this world** – indicates that, through their relation to Jesus as the light, the disciples are to see themselves as not only included in the working out of the divine timetable for Jesus' mission, as his invitation to them– **Let us go to Judaea again** – has just implied, but also as having the resources to overcome fear of the possible death that this might entail for them.

11–13 The supernatural knowledge attributed to Jesus in this Gospel comes to the fore again as Jesus now tells the disciples that he knows that Lazarus is dead. However, the narrator extends this announcement by introducing his typical device of misunderstanding, which is facilitated by Jesus first saying **Our friend Lazarus has fallen asleep, but I am going to awaken him,** which may well be a reminiscence of Mark 5.39, where Jesus, to the amusement and scorn of the mourners, tells Jairus, 'The child is not dead but sleeping.' But 'falling asleep' was a common euphemism for death in both Judaism and the Greek world and so the device of misunderstanding appears to be employed rather heavy-handedly, especially since the narrator then feels it necessary to explain the misunderstanding. The disciples are portrayed here as so dense as not to be able to understand the most obvious metaphor. It is the most damaging assessment of them so far in the narrative and prepares the ground for some of their further obtuse responses to Jesus' sayings in the farewell discourses. Elsewhere in the narrative characters who are the victims of misunderstanding serve as foils to enable the reader to come to the right interpretation, and given the way that this misunderstanding is underscored so heavily, it is likely that this instance is no exception. Despite the common use of the metaphor, the evangelist intends to emphasize its significance. The disciples have taken sleep literally as normal physical rest – **the sleep of actual slumber** – but readers are meant to ponder the perspective of Jesus' words that death is sleep. This is supported by the fact that this euphemism, though by no means distinctive to early Christianity, was employed as a characteristically Christian way of speaking of death, once it was held that Jesus' resurrection had removed death's sting (cf. Acts 7.60; 1 Cor. 7.39; 11.30; 15.6, 18, 20, 51; 1 Thess. 4.13–15). In such usage it was not meant to indicate the actual state of those who had died as some sort of unconscious existence but was a metaphor that stressed the temporary and reversible effect of death. Given this Christian usage, talk of Lazarus sleeping suggests not only the reversibility of Lazarus' death but also that the believing dead, whom Lazarus represents in this story, will be awakened by Jesus to life at the final resurrection.

14–15 After using plain language – **Lazarus has died** – Jesus compounds the strangeness of his delay by adding, **And I am glad for your sake that I was not there, so that you may believe.** While he does not say precisely that he is glad that Lazarus is dead, this does seem to be implied in that his gladness is for the sake of the disciples' believing on the basis of what Jesus will do about the death. In line with v. 4, normal human reactions are not the point but give way to the sign that will disclose Jesus' glory. That a sign is in the offing is this time indicated by the mention of the disciples' belief, which points back again to the narrator's summarizing conclusion to the first sign in 2.11. Clearly then this reference to their belief does not indicate initial belief but a further boost to the process of believing. In v. 7 Jesus had exhorted, 'Let us go to Judaea again'; now Lazarus himself becomes the focus of the journey, as Jesus exhorts, **let us go to him**.

16 For the first time in the Gospel Thomas is now mentioned. Elsewhere in the New Testament he is simply listed among the disciples (cf. Matt. 10.3; Mark 3.18; Luke 6.15; Acts 1.13). The Fourth Gospel is the only canonical text to give him a distinct narrative role (cf. also 14.5; 20.24–9) and to supply him with the further Greek name, Didymus (cf. also 20.24; 21.2). The earlier mention of Judaea had raised the spectre of Jesus' death, and Thomas' statement of resigned bravado and loyalty – **Let us also go in order that we may die with him** – brings together the earlier fear about a trip to Judaea in general (cf. v. 8) with the consequences of a visit to Lazarus in particular. Indeed his words are ambiguous. Since it is Lazarus' death that has just been mentioned, they could just as well be taken as a reference to dying with Lazarus as to dying with Jesus. Either way, their force is still that to go to Lazarus entails the probability of death, because it is to go to Judaea, where Jesus will inevitably encounter those who have already tried to kill him. Thomas' comment is truer than he suspects. In the case of Jesus what he does not yet know but what the narrator will recount is that it is precisely Jesus' act of raising Lazarus that will trigger off the events that finally lead to his death. Thomas also does not know that this will trigger off a situation in which disciples will also be faced with death (cf. 12.9–11; 16.2; 21.18–19). This, of course, has already been intimated in Jesus' earlier inclusion of the disciples in his mission (vv. 9–10) and his invitation to them to accompany him back to Judaea and its perils (v. 7).

17–19 The third section of the Lazarus episode moves immediately to Jesus' arrival and subsequent meeting with Martha. But the narrator supplies some further details before recounting the meeting. The first of these is Jesus' discovery that Lazarus **had already been in the tomb four days**. In Jewish custom the body was buried immediately after death, and this note plays on the popular Jewish belief that the soul then departed finally from the body after three days. It therefore underlines that Lazarus is truly dead. What will be needed is not some reanimation but an actual resurrection. For the first time in this narrative the location of Bethany, where Lazarus and his sisters reside (cf. v. 1), is now described. It is said to be fifteen stadia or some two miles from Jerusalem, alerting the reader to its proximity to the previous location of intended violence toward Jesus. This note with its reference to Jerusalem may also suggest the place of origin of **Many of the Jews**, who are said to have **come to Martha and Mary to console them about their brother**. The presence of other mourners and an initial reference to 'the Jews', which is by no means hostile, are not out of place at this point, but more is involved in their introduction into the story. Some will believe (v. 45) but others of them will hurry to report the incident to the Pharisees (v. 46). What happens at Lazarus' tomb, therefore, is not allowed to remain a private affair and the role of these other Jews in the story enables there to be both a public witness to the sign and the necessary link leading from the sign to the decision of the religious authorities to put Jesus to death. A favourable reference to 'the Jews' here need by no means preclude, as some hold, a two-level reading of the narrative in the light of later Jewish Christian experience of expulsion from the synagogue. 'The Jews' in this Gospel include both those who are overtly hostile to Jesus' mission and those who are initially sympathetic and can even be said to believe on the basis of the signs but whose response is not deemed adequate. In the later situation, of course, despite any official ban, relationships between Jewish

Christians and other Jews would not necessarily have been uniformly hostile, and deaths in the family would have been occasions when ordinary human sympathies came to the fore.

20–2 The narrator had already spoken of Jesus' arrival in Bethany in v. 17, but now moves back to a point just prior to this in order to be able to relate separate encounters with the two sisters while Jesus is on his way (cf. v. 30). Martha's first words to Jesus, expressing her regret at his absence, also have overtones of complaint at his delay – **Lord, if you had been here, my brother would not have died.** They also, of course, indicate her belief in Jesus' healing powers. In comparison with Mary's repetition of these words in v. 32, Martha's belief in Jesus appears to go further: **But even now I know that whatever you ask of God, God will give you.** The formulation is reminiscent of the Synoptic saying in Matt. 7.7 and Luke 11.9 – 'ask, and it will be given you' – which has also influenced other Johannine sayings about prayer (cf. 15.16; 16.23–4). It was generally held that the prayers of a righteous or holy person would be answered (cf. also 9.31), and in these circumstances ('even now') Martha's affirmation suggests she has not lost all hope for her brother.

23–5a Jesus assures her, **Your brother will arise.** Despite her affirmations about Jesus, Martha is not prepared for the true sense of such an assurance. The device of misunderstanding is again operative, as she takes Jesus' words to be a reference to Lazarus' participation in the end-time resurrection. Her misunderstanding serves as a foil for the key self-identification of Jesus in the 'I Am' saying which follows. In claiming **I am the resurrection and the life,** Jesus declares himself to be the fulfilment of traditional Jewish eschatological expectations. 5.19–30 has already indicated that those expectations still hold but now have their focus in Jesus, who has already been given the authority to give life and to judge, the activities God was expected to carry out only at the end of history. In 5.28–9 agency in a general resurrection at the end is also ascribed to Jesus as Son of Man. The formulation here in v. 25a indicates that resurrection and life are not simply synonyms, because the general resurrection is coincident with a final judgement and entails either a resurrection of life or a resurrection of condemnation. So in claiming to be the resurrection and the life, Jesus is claiming to be both the one who embodies the power to raise from the dead and the one who is the source of the positive verdict of life. That the claim takes the form of an 'I Am' predication, with its connotations in this Gospel of the divine self-identification, underscores that raising the dead and giving life were considered to be divine prerogatives and that Jesus is once again disclosing his unity with the Father. Indeed in 5.21 Jesus had claimed to be acting in imitation of the Father who 'raises the dead and gives them life' and that formulation may well have shaped Jesus' claim here that in and through him both resurrection and life are made available in the present and no longer reserved for the last day.

25b–6 The significance of the 'I Am' saying is elaborated in the following parallel clauses – **The one who believes in me, even though that person dies, will live, and everyone who lives and believes in me will never die.** Both stress the necessity of believing in order to appropriate the resurrection and the life available in Jesus, the first clause focusing more specifically on resurrection and the second more specifically on life. Their force turns around the different meanings of 'to die'. Believers in Jesus may undergo physical death but that cannot deprive them of the experience of the resurrection. They will live beyond death because belief in Jesus guarantees resurrection life. In fact, asserts the second clause, to believe in Jesus is to have that life now and means that believers will never experience spiritual death, because the quality of the life they enjoy is eternal. Some interpreters would claim that the meaning of the two clauses is more complex than we have suggested because not only 'to die' but also 'to live' have different senses so that the reference in v. 26a to 'everyone who lives' has in view the one who has physical life. Since the one who believes must of necessity be physically alive, such a reference would appear to be completely superfluous. It is far less strained to hold that 'everyone who lives' picks up immediately on the preceding 'will live' and for this reason comes before the mention of believing. It gives the reference to resurrection life a present dimension, just as 5.25 had already transposed this language to the present experience of eternal life – 'the hour is coming and is now here when the dead will hear the voice of the Son of God and those who hear will live'. The final question to Martha – **Do you believe this?** – underlines both that belief is essential and that Jesus' preceding words are the key to a true understanding of the episode. For this reason, the question can be seen as addressing not only Martha but also the reader.

27 But does Martha really believe *this?* She answers positively and makes a full-blown Johannine Christological confession – **Yes, Lord. I believe that you are the Christ, the Son of God, the one coming into the world.** This is precisely what, according to 20.31, the evangelist wants the reader to believe about Jesus and, significantly, this confession of faith is here made by a woman. Jesus was acclaimed as Messiah in 1.41 and as Son of God in 1.49, and throughout the narrative it is made clear that he is the sort of Messiah whose unique relationship to God is only adequately grasped in terms of divine sonship. Martha's third description of Jesus as **the one coming into the world** takes up the messianic formulation about the coming one (cf. Matt. 11.3; Luke 7.20) and adds to it the further Johannine notion that this one who comes into the world has his origin in the divine world (cf. 1.9; 18.37; cf. also e.g. 3.31; 6.51;

8.23). It is striking, however, that, complete as Martha's Christological confession is, it makes no explicit reference to what Jesus has said about resurrection and life. Is Jesus' embodiment of resurrection and life to be seen as entailed in the full implications of the titles Martha has used? Or is Martha to be viewed as a representative of Johannine Christians who can make the appropriate confession about Jesus but still have not seen the significance of such a confession for the death of a believer? That Martha, for all her insight, still has not seen her confession's significance for the raising of her brother may well be indicated by her later reaction to Jesus' command that the stone be removed from the tomb and by Jesus' response to her in vv. 39–40.

28–9 The fourth scene (vv. 28–37) brings Jesus together with Mary and 'the Jews' and moves the focus of the narrative closer to Lazarus' tomb (cf. vv. 30, 34). It opens with Martha conveying to her sister a message that the teacher is calling for her and with Mary responding quickly. This calls to mind the language of the previous chapter about the shepherd who calls his sheep (10.3) and the sheep who listen to his voice (10.16), placing Mary clearly among the sheep who belong to the good shepherd. That Jesus' message is conveyed to Mary **privately** distinguishes her relationship to Jesus from that of even the sympathetic Jews in the story. As a narrative device, having 'the Jews' ignorant of what Mary intends to do ensures that they will follow her and be with her as an audience when Jesus eventually goes with her to the tomb.

30–1 The note that **Jesus had not yet come to the village** also serves to underline the differing relation to Jesus of the two sisters and 'the Jews'. In the absence of the mourners Jesus has imparted to Martha the real significance of what is about to happen and intends to encounter Mary in similar fashion. But Mary is unable to shake off the Jewish mourners who follow her to the place where Martha had left Jesus. This action is described from the perspective of 'the Jews' who pursue Mary, believing she is going to the tomb to weep.

32 It is often observed that Mary in her encounter with Jesus does not come off well in comparison with Martha, and that whereas Martha moves well beyond her initial reproach of Jesus for not having been there when it mattered to real Christological insight, Mary does not. But the contrast should not be drawn too sharply. A full comparison of the characterization of the two sisters must take into account the extended narrative and that includes Mary's anointing of Jesus in 12.1–8, which displays her own devotion and insight and which has been referred to at the beginning of this episode (cf. v. 2). But also this fourth scene has a different function from the previous one. There would be little point in repeating the theological dialogue, and, besides, this turns out not to be simply an encounter between Jesus and Mary in the way the previous scene brought together Jesus and Martha. So despite Mary's coming and falling at Jesus' feet (cf. Luke 10.39) and repeating her sister's words, **Lord, if you had been here, my brother would not have died,** the conversation does not develop on similar lines as before, because Jesus is now confronted with a quite different public scene of Mary and the accompanying Jews weeping. Mary is no less a representative figure for the believing reader than is Martha. While Martha serves to highlight the Christological and eschatological concerns readers face when other believers die, Mary represents the reality of the suffering that has raised such issues about Jesus' delay and absence and which does not simply disappear even when they are answered by Jesus' revelation of himself.

33–5 Intriguingly, it is in this public setting that Jesus reveals his deepest personal emotions. The change in the characterization of Jesus is striking. The one who from the beginning of the episode has displayed detachment from the death of his friend, Lazarus, so that God's glory could be revealed, the one who has exhibited supernatural knowledge, the one who has proclaimed his sovereignty over death and his embodiment of life, is now by contrast described as profoundly human in his response. At the weeping of Mary and 'the Jews' **he became angry in spirit and was greatly agitated**. Some interpreters and translations avoid the notion of Jesus' anger here or find it inexplicable in the context and therefore subsume the first verb under the meaning of the second, taking it as 'greatly disturbed' (NRSV) or 'deeply moved' (NIV). But the verb ἐμβριμάομαι consistently refers elsewhere to expressing anger or indignation (cf. Dan. 11.30 LXX; Matt. 9.30; Mark 1.43; 14.5). Once this is accepted, commentators are still divided over what produces the anger and agitation in Jesus. Some suggest that Jesus is angry at the intrusion of 'the Jews' into what was meant to be a private occasion. But this does not do enough justice to the fact that it is Jesus seeing both Mary's weeping and that of 'the Jews' that triggers this response. Since it appears to be evoked by the grief of Mary and 'the Jews', some see Jesus' emotion as a reaction to the unbelief they consider to be behind this grief. A variation on this suggestion makes a rather forced distinction between Mary and 'the Jews' and claims that Jesus is angry with Mary for joining 'the Jews' in weeping, despite the fact that Mary's weeping is actually mentioned first. Others see Jesus' emotions as a reaction to the phenomenon of death that has produced the grief. Others still, taking up a suggestion of Chrysostom and reading between the lines, claim that Jesus is angry and agitated at the prospect of his own death.

What follows in the account should be allowed to be determinative for the interpretation here. After enquiring where Lazarus has been buried, Jesus is invited to **come and see**, and at this **Jesus wept**. This strongly favours the interpretation that Jesus' anger and agitation that turn into open weeping are, first and foremost, his response to death and the pain that it causes rather than to unbelief in his miraculous powers. If the weeping of Mary and 'the Jews' were meant to be interpreted as a symptom of their unbelief, it would make no sense to have Jesus then join in their weeping – the use of a different verb for Jesus' weeping is stylistic and not to be read as signifying something other than grief. Jesus, then, is identifying with the grief caused by the loss of a loved one. In the immediate context his anger is in regard to the death that has caused such a loss. But Chrysostom's view may not be as far-fetched as it might at first appear. Readers have been given numerous indications throughout the episode that the raising of Lazarus is linked with Jesus' death. Since Mary, who will anoint Jesus for burial, as readers already know (v. 2), is weeping at his feet, the same position she will occupy in the anointing story, Jesus' own death and burial may well be evoked. What is more, the other verb, 'to be greatly agitated', is employed again in John for Jesus' emotions in the face of his forthcoming betrayal and death (12.27; 13.21), and sorrow and agitation characterize the Synoptic Jesus in Gethsemane (cf. Mark 14.33–4; Matt. 26.37–8). So while the immediate cause of Jesus' indignation, agitation and weeping is Lazarus' death, there are enough hints to make it plausible to view Jesus' response to Lazarus's death as also anticipating his response to his own death. Such a portrayal of Jesus is not so much a contradiction of the earlier stress on his knowledge and gladness that what will ensue will be a revelation of God's glory and of his own power over death as it is part of the narrative's paradoxical depiction of the Logos who has become flesh. As the divine Logos, he displays sovereignty in the face of death, but, as the incarnate Logos, he also shows human anger and sorrow when presented with the consequences of death's disruptive power in the case of this one whom he loves and, by extension, in his own case.

36–7 Jesus' weeping produces both a more positive and a more negative reaction among 'the Jews'. But even the more positive interpretation of Jesus' grief as showing how much he loved Lazarus is not totally reliable but remains on the surface. As has been suggested, Jesus' emotional response entails much more than this and is directed at the death to which Lazarus has succumbed. Some have taken the response of the other Jews as also positive and concentrated on its assumption that Jesus had already opened the eyes of the blind man (cf. 9.1–41). But, given other instances of divided responses to Jesus earlier in the Gospel (cf. 7.12, 40–2; 9.16; 10.19–21), it is more likely that it is to be interpreted as casting aspersions on the ability of this miracle worker when faced with mortal illness. In any case, it sets up the act of power that follows in the next scene (vv. 38–44).

38–40 As Jesus now at last comes to the tomb in the fifth scene, the narrator highlights once more his emotion of indignation – **having again become angry in himself**. This time his anger drives him to positive action, as he commands, **Take away the stone**. But before the stone is removed from the entrance to the cave that forms Lazarus' tomb, the suspense is heightened by Martha's objection. Described as **the dead man's sister**, which seems superfluous at this stage of the account, she shows she is not prepared for what is about to take place and points out the stench that already exudes from one who has been dead for four days (cf. also v. 17). The reality of the death and therefore also the magnitude of the imminent miracle are highlighted in her intervention. In turn, Jesus' response appears to underline that there was still an element missing from Martha's earlier confession of faith – **Did I not tell you that if you believe you will see the glory of God?** In fact, strictly speaking, Jesus has not told Martha this. His words about Lazarus' death leading to the glory of God were addressed to the disciples in v. 4. The repetition of this theme here reminds the reader of the purpose of the miracle that will follow. It is a sign of God's glory disclosed through Jesus, and what is more it will lead inextricably to the further climactic revelation of that glory through Jesus' death. The fact that, in order to make sense of Jesus' reply, the reader has to put together what was said to the disciples in v. 4 with what was said to Martha in vv. 25–6 makes clear that Martha serves here as representative of the reader, who is also being addressed by Jesus' question.

41–2 Finally the anticipated event gets under way. In accord with Jesus' instructions, the stone is now removed from the tomb, but there is a further building of suspense as Jesus now pauses to pray. Little in this account has proceeded as one might have expected, and this prayer is no exception. It is not a prayer of petition, asking God to intervene and to act through Jesus. Instead it is a prayer of thanksgiving before the event. In fact, its first words echo the words of Ps. 118.21 and are taken from a psalm of thanksgiving celebrating God's steadfast love and the victory of God's salvation. Later in 12.13 the evangelist, in common with the Synoptic accounts of Jesus' entry into Jerusalem, will take up Ps. 118.25–6. Interestingly, the words of thanksgiving from Ps. 118.21 – 'I thank you that you have answered me' – follow the psalmist's exultation that 'I shall not die, but I shall live; . . . The Lord . . . did not give me over to death' (Ps. 118.17–18). Now before the demonstration that Lazarus has not been given over to death, Jesus looks up and addresses God – **Father, I thank you that you have heard me**. Underlining his sovereignty over the situation, which comes from his relationship to the Father, Jesus goes on to make clear that, since he knows that the Father always hears him, this prayer is actually for the sake of the crowd – **I have said this for the sake of the crowd standing by, so that they might believe that you have sent me**. Jesus' unity with the Father is such that explicit prayer, even of thanksgiving, is not strictly necessary for Jesus – even when raising someone from the dead. His addressing God in prayer has been so that others may see the true significance of the sign about to be performed and believe in Jesus' true identity as the one sent by the Father. His earlier words – **I know that you always hear me** – not only suggest that his relationship with God entails a continual communication which does not need to come to expression in words, but also serve as a further demonstration of the statement in 5.19–20 that, because of his unique relationship to his Father, the Son does nothing on his own.

43–4 The sign itself is accomplished swiftly and narrated briefly – **he cried out in a loud voice, 'Lazarus, come out!'** These words carry echoes from earlier in the narrative discourse. In particular, 5.28–9 – 'for the hour is coming at which all who are in their graves will hear his voice and will come out' – now takes on narrative form. But the personal address of the call also reminds the reader of 10.3b – 'He calls his own sheep by name and leads them out.' The emergence of Lazarus from the tomb is suitably dramatic. Still described as **The dead man**, he comes out **with feet and hands bound in bandages and his face wrapped in a cloth.** As some have observed, Lazarus' ability to exit from the tomb, despite being bound and unable to see, appears to involve a second, minor miracle in addition to his raising! But to focus on this detail reduces the impact of the episode to the farcical and its application of an excessively literal perspective to ancient storytelling is in danger of obscuring the main point the story symbolizes. After Lazarus' emergence, Jesus then only has to give the further obvious instructions to **Unbind him and let him go.** His delivery from the constraints of the grave-clothes further symbolizes his rescue from the bondage of death. The mention of the resurrected Lazarus' attire as he exits from the tomb points forward in contrast to the description of Jesus' resurrection in 20.6–7, where the grave-clothes of Jesus have been left behind and rolled up, indicating his own sovereignty in his resurrection, unlike Lazarus' dependence on Jesus and others.

45–6 At the beginning of the concluding section (vv. 45–53), there is a typically divided response to this sign as to other aspects of Jesus' mission. But it is significant that the majority response among 'the Jews' is belief – **Many of the Jews, therefore, who had come to Mary and had seen what he had done, believed in him** (cf. also 12.11, 17). This further undermines the suggestion that Jesus' earlier anger was provoked by their understandable prior lack of belief. But it is the response of a substantial minority that moves the action along. Some report back to the Pharisees what has happened, and it will now become unmistakably clear that the raising of Lazarus precipitates the coming of Jesus' hour, to which the whole action of the plot has been moving.

47–8 The Pharisees and chief priests convene a meeting of the Sanhedrin and confront a dilemma – **What are we doing about the fact that this man is performing many signs?** The fear is that to allow Jesus to continue to perform signs like that of raising Lazarus will lead to mass belief and the transformation of the nation as it now is, so that the Romans will no longer find it acceptable and **will come and take away both our place and our nation**. Ironically, as readers will know, the destruction of the temple is precisely what happened anyway, despite the decision to put an end to Jesus' working of signs.

49–52 Caiaphas, who, though elected not for a year but for life, is remembered here as the high priest in the year of Jesus' death, claims insight superior to the ignorant fear that has been expressed – **You know nothing; you do not consider that it is advantageous for you that one man should die for the people and that the whole nation should not perish.** Caiaphas' solution for dealing with Jesus by making him a scapegoat contains at the same time, however, a revelation of an important truth about Jesus' death. It will indeed be 'on behalf' or 'for the sake' of the people, and that people will not only include Israel. The narrator makes this insight explicit. Assuming the tradition that by virtue of his office the high priest also received the gift of prophecy (cf. Josephus, *A. J.* 6. 115–16; 11.327; 13.282–3), the narrator holds that Caiaphas unknowingly **prophesied that Jesus was about to die for the nation, and not for the nation alone but also to gather into one the dispersed children of God.** Readers are meant to savour the irony that Caiaphas' words are therefore truer than he knows and to understand their significance as an interpretation of Jesus' death. In line with 10.11–18, Jesus' death is a noble or honourable one, because actions undertaken for the sake of one's country were considered noble (cf. Aristotle, *Rhet.* 1366b) and deaths suffered for one's nation were praised as worthy of honour (cf. Hyperides, *Funeral Speech* 9). That Jesus can be truly said to die for the nation should not be overlooked in favour of the universalizing of the benefits of his death that follows. Unlike the notion of 'the children of God', the term for 'nation', ἔθνος, is not spiritualized here or in its usage in 18.35. It is the Jewish nation that is in view. It is significant that in this Gospel, which has hostile references to 'the Jews' and is alleged to reflect anti-Judaism, Jesus' death and its benefits are depicted as for the nation of Israel. The notion of gathering the dispersed children of God takes up the language used in the prophets for the expectation of the end-time salvation of diaspora Jews (cf. e.g. Isa. 11.12; Jer. 23.2–3; Ezek. 11.17; 20.34), but this Gospel has already transformed the concept of the children of God so that it now refers to those who believe in Jesus (cf. 1.12–13). Jesus' death, then, is here seen as on behalf not only of Israel but of all who believe, both Jews and Gentiles. The expansion of those

who will benefit from his death would have also been seen as increasing
the honour it deserves. As Jesus has stated in 10.16–17, 'I have other sheep
that do not belong to this fold. I must bring them also . . . So there will
be one flock'. The fulfilment of this universal plan of salvation to produce
one people of God has now, in fact, been set in motion by Caiaphas' plan,
which was of course precipitated by the raising of Lazarus.

53 Caiaphas' plan is accepted by the Sanhedrin and from this point on
Jesus lives under the sentence of death. In one sense this only confirms
the intentions of Jesus' opponents that have been in view from as early as
5.18 (cf. also 7.32, 45; 8.59; 10.31, 39). But now their previous informal
attempts to have done with Jesus are given official sanction. In the
absence of Jesus, the defendant, and without any formal legal procedures,
the religious authorities have already reached their verdict on his fate. But
the Sanhedrin's decision to put Jesus to death can also now be seen as
having been made in the shadow of Jesus' demonstration of his claim to
be the resurrection and the life. In the light of what the preceding scenes
have demonstrated about Jesus' identity, there is a sense of profound
irony about the decision-making of the agents of death, a sense of their
ultimate impotence before the force of life that is operative in Jesus. Their
scheming can only contribute to the life that will flow from Jesus' death
and to the vindication of that death in his resurrection.

Whereas in the story line of the Synoptic Gospels the temple incident
is the event that provokes the protagonist's arrest and condemnation, in
the Fourth Gospel it is the raising of Lazarus that causes the religious
authorities to reach their decision to do away with Jesus. The Synoptics
clearly do not know of this supposedly major catalyst in producing the
death sentence on Jesus, and in terms of historical plausibility the temple
incident is a far more likely candidate for this role. But are there any
grounds for holding that the miracle story itself, when its role in the
Fourth Gospel's plot is discarded, might have some claims to historicity?
Both the occurrence of this account in the Fourth Gospel alone and
the nature of the miracle it relates lead many to the view that it must
be a wholesale invention of the evangelist. After all, if it was in an early
tradition and therefore known to any of the Synoptic evangelists or their
sources, it seems exceedingly strange that they would have omitted such
a striking sign of Jesus' power carried out for a family that are said to be
particularly close to him. But the view that such a resurrection story has
to be a complete fiction needs qualification, despite the obvious signs of
its literary artistry and invention. It ignores the possibility that if there was
a tradition behind John's account, it would not necessarily be any more
striking than the Synoptic raisings and may well not even have originally
involved a family said to be close to Jesus. It also ignores the fact that the

Synoptic Gospels do know and tell of resurrections from the dead by Jesus. The raising of Jairus' daughter is found in Mark 5.21–43 and taken over in Matt. 9.18–26 and Luke 8.40–56, and Luke 7.11–17 contains an account of the raising of the son of the widow of Nain. In addition, the report of Jesus' ministry to be relayed to the imprisoned John the Baptist, according to Luke 7.22 and Matt. 11.5, mentions that 'the dead are raised'. Evidently then traditions about Jesus' power to raise the dead circulated from an early stage. John's narrative could be an extensive elaboration on one such tradition.

Many scholars, with varying degrees of confidence, believe that they have been able to isolate such a traditional source behind the present Johannine narrative. The reconstructed source differs significantly from one scholar to another, but most would include in it vv. 1, 3, 6, 17, 19, 29, 31–4, 38, 39a, 41a, 43–4. The relative consensus about this core might seem impressive, yet the hazardous nature of attempts to isolate tradition from redaction in a text so thoroughly pervaded by its author's own vocabulary, style and theology becomes apparent on closer examination of this stripped-down core tradition. The details within the very first verse can all be disputed. Some consider the place, Bethany, and the names of at least Lazarus and Mary to be part of the bedrock of the tradition. But there is a strong case for claiming that the evangelist has provided the Bethany setting because this is where Mark 14.3 places the anointing of Jesus with pure nard by a woman, which follows on from the Lazarus story and is coloured by it. John makes the woman Mary and provides her with a home and family. Whether the name Lazarus was part of a traditional source is, of course, even more disputed, producing a complex series of arguments and counter-arguments. Some suggest that the source for John's story at this point was the parable involving a poor man in Luke 16.19–31. This has some plausibility, since not only does the Lukan parable have the name Lazarus for this man and tell of his death, but it also has a striking punch line. When the rich man asks that Lazarus go back and warn his brothers, believing that they would be brought to repentance by his return from the dead, Abraham replies, 'If they do not listen to Moses and the prophets, neither will they be convinced even if someone rises from the dead' (16.31). This appears to be tailor-made for the fourth evangelist's theological perspective. He has already made the point that 'the Jews' fail to listen to or believe Moses (cf. 5.46) and now he actually has Lazarus rise from the dead to demonstrate that such a sign will make no difference to those in hardened unbelief. The last point of this proposal, however, needs to be qualified and expanded, since in John's account 'Many of the Jews' are in fact said to believe on the basis of Lazarus' resurrection (cf. 11.45; 12.10, 11, 17). Nonetheless, readers have learned to be suspicious of responses of belief based on seeing signs, and among those labelled 'the Jews' are included characters and crowds who are sympathetic to Jesus and his signs but whose faith does not progress beyond this and is therefore deemed ultimately inadequate (cf. 2.23–5; 3.2; 4.48; 6.26, 30; 7.31; 10.41; 12.37–43). There is little reason to think that 'the Jews' in 11.45 who are later identified with the crowd (cf. 12.17–18) are viewed as having more satisfactory belief. But against the view that the name Lazarus is imported from Luke, it is pointed out how unusual it is for any of Jesus' parables to give its characters names; indeed, this Lukan parable is the only one in the Synoptics to do so. The claim can therefore be made that it is just as likely that a tradition about the raising of Lazarus was already in circulation and known to Luke or his source and that the name 'Lazarus' entered the parable due to the influence of that tradition. On the other hand, this is also the only sign in the Fourth Gospel where the recipient of the miracle is named. This may not be so much evidence of historical tradition as part of the evangelist's concern to provide a graphic account. After all, he introduces the named characters of Andrew and Philip into the feeding of the five thousand and that of Judas into the story of the anointing that follows the Lazarus episode. Any underlying tradition could equally well have been about an unnamed character and in reworking it the evangelist introduced Lazarus, Mary and Martha to give his story colour. It is noteworthy that the manner of this introduction suggests that the only character with whom the readers are not expected to be familiar is Lazarus. Whatever the decision about Lazarus, Mary and Martha do appear to have been introduced into the story from Luke 10.38–42, where there is, of course, no mention of them having a brother Lazarus who is a particular friend of Jesus, but where they have the same basic character traits as here and in John's anointing story, with Mary consistently positioned at Jesus' feet and Martha doing the serving.

Other elements in the reconstructed source are no more secure than its first verse. As has been suggested in the comments, the formulation of v. 3 may have been shaped by specifically Johannine tradition, and v. 6 is part of the typically Johannine pattern of (implied) request followed by rebuff and then a delayed response on Jesus' own terms. Verse 17 with its mention of Lazarus having been in the tomb for four days can be seen as part of the evangelist's characteristic heightening of the miraculous in his signs when there are similar Synoptic incidents. None of the dead raised in the Synoptics had reached the tomb, let alone been in it for four days. The sympathetic Jews in vv. 19, 31–4 are not a remnant from the tradition. As has been noted in the discussion of the influence of the Lukan parable, these Jews fit the overall Johannine categorization of 'the Jews' and they have a clear function in John's overall plot, enabling him to make the necessary link between a private family affair in Bethany and both the council's decision to kill Jesus and Jesus' entry into Jerusalem. The emotional agitation attributed to Jesus in vv. 33, 38 can be seen as

John's transposition of similar emotions from the Synoptic Gethsemane account, where Jesus was facing his own death (cf. also 12.27). Even the formulation of the actual raising of Lazarus in vv. 43–4 has been shaped by the saying of the Johannine Jesus earlier in 5.25, 28–9a.

It has to be concluded that the hypothetical tradition behind John 11 will not bear the weight many give to it. There is no way of telling whether the evangelist in composing this story is building on any one specific tradition. The most that can be said is that he has chosen for his own theological purposes to tell the story of Jesus raising someone from the dead, an ability Jesus was believed to have in the earliest Christian traditions, to do so as dramatically as possible, and to give the story a distinctive and pivotal role in his overall plot. It appears most likely that in the process he has creatively worked into his story material known to him from the Synoptic Gospels and skilfully made its details and dialogue the vehicle of distinctive Johannine theological themes. Characteristically, the evangelist heightens the miraculous element in his version. Only in the Fourth Gospel's account of Jesus raising someone has the corpse been buried for four days and begun to stink.

Finally, it should be noted that John's account of the Sanhedrin meeting with Caiaphas has its parallel in the religious authorities' plot to kill Jesus which is mentioned in Matt. 26.1–5 and Mark 14.1–2 (cf. also Luke 22.1–2), set just before Passover, and placed immediately prior to their account of the anointing. Here John has closer links with the more elaborate Matthean version, which, unlike Mark, mentions that the meeting was convened in Caiaphas' palace and contains the language of 'taking counsel . . . in order that they might kill him' (Matt. 26.3–4; cf. John 11.53). In addition, John replaces the Synoptic 'chief priests and scribes' or 'chief priests and elders of the people' with his own 'chief priests and Pharisees' and gives Caiaphas a dominant role in the proceedings, similar to that which he will have in the Synoptic account of the Sanhedrin trial (cf. Mark 14.55–65; Matt. 26.57–68), which John will omit. Instead the evangelist deals with the main issues and outcome of that trial in 10.24–38 and in this scene.

In terms of the Gospel's overall plot, the Lazarus episode provides the pivot between the action in Jesus' public mission in the first part of the story and the events that unfold at the final Passover in its second part. Why choose this rather than the temple incident as the catalyst for Jesus' death? For the evangelist, it makes even clearer than the Synoptics that Jesus' mission posed not only a threat to the religious establishment and its political arrangements but also a challenge at a deeper level. The Synoptic temple incident has obvious Christological implications but in the Lazarus episode Christological claims are explicitly and dramatically foregrounded. With the advantage of hindsight and the perspective of his own setting, the evangelist perceives that it is the issue of Jesus' identity, which in turn raises the question of the identity of God, that presented the ultimate challenge and was the reason for his death. Having the opposition plan to kill him as the result of an episode in which he displays the life-giving powers which are the prerogative of God and claims to embody the resurrection and the life is a powerful narrative vehicle for this insight. The evangelist's creative composition and literary artistry combine to produce a striking narrative which shows the relation of Jesus to the great issues of life and death. If it can be said that the Fourth Gospel is the gospel of life, then this episode is the Fourth Gospel in miniature. Jesus' saying, 'I am the resurrection and the life', provides the main key to its interpretation. The demonstration of this claim in the return of Lazarus to human mortal life is a sign of the giving of eternal life and of the death and resurrection of Jesus, on which such life is predicated. In the Lazarus episode the one who embodies life moves under his own timetable and inexorably toward the location of death, Lazarus' tomb, and produces life out of death. But the forces of death are not done with. This is a temporary and partial victory. Both the giver of life and the receiver of life (cf. 12.9–11) face the further imminent threat of death. As a result of the initial overcoming of death for Lazarus, the one who is the resurrection and the life is himself put under the sentence of death. Only in his own death and resurrection to life will the decisive defeat of the great enemy, death, take place. Lazarus' resurrection, then, is a sign that points ahead to the final resurrection, precipitates the death of Jesus – life for Lazarus means death for Jesus – but also anticipates the vindication of that death in Jesus' own resurrection. The one who claims to embody the resurrection will make good that claim as he takes up his own life after laying it down. In this way Jesus' movement towards Lazarus' tomb to give life to Lazarus is at the same time Jesus' movement toward his own death and resurrection to give life to believers.

The Lazarus story can also be seen as the evangelist's means of dealing with the issue of the death of believers, who are meant to have eternal life, during the time of the delay or absence of Jesus. As the dialogue with Martha indicates, for believers death does not disrupt the experience of eternal life until the final resurrection. The life they already possess through Jesus is such that they will never die spiritually and be separated from the life of God (cf. 11.25b–6). At the same time, physical death remains a reality until the final resurrection and so the weeping of both Mary and Jesus are regarded as totally appropriate to the loss of a loved one. No denial of the reality or pain of death is encouraged. Belief in Jesus as both the resurrection and the life displaces doubt and hopelessness in the face of death but does not at present remove pain and tears.

(54) Jesus therefore no longer went about openly among the Jews but went away from there to the region near the desert, to a town called Ephraim, and stayed there with his disciples. (55) Now the Passover of the Jews was near, and many went up from the country to Jerusalem before the Passover in order to purify themselves. (56) They were looking for Jesus and saying to each other as they stood in the temple, 'What do you think? Surely he will not come to the festival, will he?' (57) Now the chief priests and the Pharisees had given orders that anyone who knew where he was should report it so that they might arrest him.

54 The hour of Jesus' death, although precipitated by the raising of Lazarus, is not yet. As was pointed out in the discussion about the extent of the Lazarus episode, this transitional section marks a definite spatial and temporal break from the previous incident. It heightens suspense as readers wonder when and how the plan to be rid of Jesus will work itself out. Jesus has already eluded a number of attempts to seize or kill him and at this point the narrative raises the possibility that this might happen again, because Jesus makes a strategic retreat with his disciples: he **therefore no longer went about openly among the Jews but went away from there to the region near the desert, to a town called Ephraim.** Ephraim, just over twenty miles to the north-east of Jerusalem, would have provided a somewhat safer environment, removed from the more immediate scrutiny of the religious authorities.

55–7 But meanwhile, back in Jerusalem, suspense about Jesus builds within the narrative itself, as **the Passover of the Jews was near, and many went up from the country to Jerusalem before the Passover in order to purify themselves**. In the midst of their preparations for the festival the attention of pilgrims in the temple is devoted to Jesus and the speculation that preoccupies them is **What do you think? Surely he will not come to the festival, will he?** (cf. the earlier reference in 7.11 to people looking for Jesus and asking about him at the Feast of Tabernacles). And this speculation about the unlikelihood of Jesus' appearance, the narrator underlines, is fuelled by the orders issued by the religious authorities, depicted as the historically improbable association of chief priests and Pharisees, **that anyone who knew where he was should report it so that they might arrest him**. The Lazarus episode had no specific chronological setting. It is some time after the Festival of Dedication in the narrative sequence. Jesus' stay in Ephraim with his disciples follows next and is for an unspecified length of time. It is the mention here of the Passover preliminaries that signals its end. From this point on the action will all be set against the backdrop of Jesus' last Passover, during which the attempt to arrest Jesus will finally succeed.

(iii) The anointing at Bethany   *12.1–8*

(1) Six days before the Passover Jesus went to Bethany, where Lazarus was, whom Jesus had raised from the dead. (2) They gave a dinner for him there, and Martha was serving and Lazarus was one of those reclining at table with him. (3) Mary, having taken a pound of costly ointment made of pure nard, anointed Jesus' feet and wiped his feet with her hair. The house was filled with the scent of the ointment. (4) Then Judas Iscariot, one of his disciples, who was about to betray him, said, (5) 'Why was this ointment not sold for three hundred denarii and the money given to the poor?' (6) He said this not because he cared about the poor but because he was a thief and, being in charge of the money-box, used to take what was put in it. (7) So Jesus said, 'Leave her alone; the purpose was that she might keep it[1] for the day of my burial preparation. (8) You always have the poor with you, but you do not always have me.'

1–2 The setting of this episode is Jesus' return six days before Passover to Bethany and to the home of Lazarus. The narrator ensures that readers will see the links with what has preceded it by an explicit and somewhat heavy-handed identification of Lazarus as the one whom Jesus had raised from the dead and by the mention of Lazarus as one of those at the table with Jesus for a meal at which Martha serves. Whereas in the earlier scenes of the two sisters Martha had been given more attention, now she has a background role, while Mary will take centre stage.

3 Mary, having taken a pound of costly ointment made of pure nard, anointed Jesus' feet and wiped his feet with her hair. As in her earlier appearance (cf. 11.32), Mary is found at Jesus' feet, but this time for a different purpose. That Jesus' feet and not his head are anointed indicates that it is mistaken to interpret the episode as a royal or messianic anointing. The cost and extravagance of Mary's act are underlined. The perfume of pure nard was probably worth a year's wages for a labourer

---

[1] The Greek syntax is difficult to interpret. Translated literally, the clause is 'in order that she might keep it for the day of my burial preparation'. This could be taken as an implied directive that Mary keep some of the ointment for Jesus' burial. But this would appear to contradict the point of Judas' objection, which suggests the ointment has already been used. It is better therefore to take the clause as providing an explanation of what has already taken place and to emphasize its purpose element. See also the comments on this verse.

(cf. Judas' estimate of its value in v. 4) and a 'pound' was an extraordinarily large amount to use for this purpose. She wipes Jesus' feet not with a towel but with her own hair, shaken loose as a sign of her deep grief. The cost and extravagance of her action can be seen to correspond to those involved in Jesus' prior action, which entailed the willingness to sacrifice his own life for the sake of Lazarus. The mention of the odour emanating from the anointing – **The house was filled with the scent of the ointment** – is striking in the context of the whole Lazarus episode. Whereas in the case of Lazarus the overpowering odour was the stench of death and decay (11.39), now in the case of what v. 7 will reveal as the anticipation of the anointing of Jesus' whole body for burial there is a pervading fragrance that fills the house. Mary's wiping of Jesus' feet with her hair also anticipates Jesus' washing of the disciples' feet (cf. 13.1–20). In fact, the particular term for wiping occurs in this Gospel's narrative only in connection with Mary's action (cf. 11.2; 12.3) and Jesus' action (cf. 13.5). In the account of the footwashing Jesus will command the disciples to wash one another's feet. Without being asked and ahead of time, Mary performs an act that is a distinguishing mark of the community of disciples. Just as her sister, Martha, has been the first to anticipate the full Johannine confession of faith in Jesus' identity, so now Mary, another female follower of Jesus, is the first to anticipate the full Johannine model of costly loving discipleship.

4–6 The response of Judas Iscariot is introduced as a negative foil to the true understanding of Mary's act. In itself, his reaction – **Why was this ointment not sold for three hundred denarii and the money given to the poor?** – appears unobjectionable. But the reader is alerted to the unreliable and hostile nature of this comment by the surrounding framework and its characterization of Judas. The question is introduced by a reference to him **as one of his disciples, who was about to betray him** and followed by an aside that underlines the hypocrisy of his concern for the poor by pointing out that **he was a thief and, being in charge of the money-box, used to take what was put in it**. It may well be that the characterization of Judas as a thief is another of the details that points to the evangelist expecting his readers to be aware of the Synoptic tradition. There, of course, it is made clear that the immediate motivation for Judas' betrayal of Jesus is the offer of money (Mark 14.10–11), specified in the later tradition as thirty pieces of silver (Matt. 26.14–16). For those aware of the tradition the note here that he was a thief, who helped himself to the communal resources, makes plain that his avarice had been in operation not only at the point of betrayal but all through Jesus' mission. John's additional note seems unlikely to be reliable historical tradition, because it raises the obvious question of why Judas was left in charge of the money-box if it was known that he was in fact stealing from it. The labels 'thief' and 'bandit' are employed for the opposition to Jesus in the Gospel's narrative (cf. 10.1, 8, 10). Just as Barabbas will later be called a 'bandit' (18.40), thereby linking him with those who play an illegitimate role in regard to the true people of God, the sheep of the good shepherd, so the labelling of Judas as a 'thief' has a similar function. Primarily, however, his response in this episode is to be seen as a complete lack of insight into what he has witnessed. Judas will always be able to demonstrate his concern for the poor (cf. v. 8a), but what he has not understood, despite his own future role in bringing it about, is that Jesus' death is now imminent as a result of Lazarus' resurrection.

7–8 Mary's act, however, has not simply been an extravagant expression of her love for Jesus; it has penetrated to the significance of the episode with her brother and therefore to the heart of Jesus' mission, which culminates with his death. Jesus' own response is **Leave her alone; the purpose was that she might keep it for the day of my burial preparation.** Just as in the earlier parts of the Lazarus episode numerous connections had been suggested between what was occurring and Jesus' impending death, so now Mary's act of devotion is clearly linked to the latter event. Indeed, as a result of the raising of Lazarus and the ensuing meeting of the Sanhedrin, Jesus is already under a death sentence as the anointing takes place. With this act of devotion Mary shows an insight into Jesus' departure that the disciples will be lacking even after they have been taught about it in the farewell discourses. Jesus' interpretation of her act suggests that it shows an even greater insight into his identity and mission than Martha's earlier confession. It recognizes that in raising Lazarus Jesus has been willing to go to his own death and that therefore the day for his burial preparation has already arrived. This interpretation only makes sense once it is realized that the term ἐνταφιασμός and its cognate verb can refer not only to burial itself but also to preparation for burial (cf. 19.40; Gen. 50.2–3 LXX; Matt. 26.12). Translations that simply have 'burial' here make Jesus' words more difficult to interpret than is necessary. This occasion is seen as anticipating the preparation for burial, not the actual burial, and Mary is viewed as having kept the ointment for this day of preparation.

Jesus' final words – **You always have the poor with you, but you do not always have me** – have sometimes been taken as evidence of a lack of concern for social and political issues in the ethics of this Gospel. But this is to ignore their context. The saying assumes the continuing validity of traditional Jewish obligation to the poor; cf. esp. Deut. 15.11 – 'Since there will never cease to be some in need on the earth, I therefore command you, "Open your hand to the poor and needy neighbour in your land."' It draws attention, however, to the significance of Mary's deed by underlining the urgency and brevity of the time left for responding appropriately to the presence of the incarnate Logos, who is on the earth for a brief span and now approaches his imminent death.

It was suggested earlier that the account of the raising of Lazarus has been shaped through John's knowledge of the Synoptics. There are further indications of such knowledge in this related episode involving Mary's anointing of Jesus. This explanation of the pericope's relation to other Gospel accounts of an anointing is preferable to that of positing the evangelist's use of an independent hybrid oral tradition. Awareness of Luke 10.38–42 is again suggested because, as in Luke, Martha is depicted as the one who serves and Mary as the one at Jesus' feet. John's anointing scene involves creative use of elements from the anointing account in Mark 14.3–9 supplemented by important details from the account in Luke 7.36–49. From the Markan account John has taken indicators of temporal setting – just before Passover – and spatial setting – a meal table in a house in Bethany. Highly significantly, John has exactly the same rare expression for the ointment used – 'pure nard' – as does Mark. But instead of Mark's anonymous woman pouring the ointment over Jesus' head, John has Mary doing what Luke's sinful woman does, namely, anointing Jesus' feet and then wiping Jesus' feet with her hair (cf. Luke 7.37–8). In the ensuing dialogue the objections of Mark's anonymous 'some' are placed by John in the mouth of Judas, who is characterized in a way that presupposes the immediately following Markan pericope about the betrayal by Judas (cf. Mark 14.10–11). The question why the ointment was not sold for three hundred denarii and the money given to the poor is repeated, as is Jesus' reply that the woman is to be left alone, because the poor are always with them, while he is not. Into the latter reply John inserts the explanation of the woman's act, which follows in Mark 14.8 – it has been an anointing for burial ahead of time.

The commentary has entitled this overall section from 11.1—12.50 'Move Toward the Hour of Death and Glory'. All the main features of this episode – Mary's act of devotion, the focus of this act on Jesus' burial preparation, and the characterization of Judas in his hostile reaction – reflect this forward movement of the plot. They point ahead, as did the preceding story of Lazarus' raising, to aspects of the hour that will be the culmination of Jesus' mission. Here, in particular, there are anticipations of the farewell teaching about discipleship and footwashing, the betrayal, and the preparation for burial. Mary's anointing of Jesus' feet completes this narrative's positive characterization of the two sisters. While Martha's Christological insights are primarily in the context of issues of resurrection, Mary's special perception is associated with concerns about death. In this passage Jesus' statement about the significance of her act as preparation for his burial means that it represents her awareness that in raising Lazarus Jesus has guaranteed his own death. But, as has been noted, her act not only has Christological significance, it also points to a feature of discipleship. Jesus' disciples, out of love for one another, are to wash one another's feet (13.14, 34–5). This female follower has already done this for Jesus himself, and the way she did it – not with water but with an extravagant amount of extremely expensive ointment, not with a towel but with her hair – makes unmistakably clear that this is an act of costly love, the sort of devotion to Jesus that in future is also to express itself in his followers' love for one another (cf. 14.15; 15.12–13).

(iv) The plot to kill Lazarus   *12.9–11*

(9) A large crowd of the Jews learned that he was there and came not only on Jesus' account but also to see Lazarus, whom he had raised from the dead. (10) The chief priests then resolved to kill Lazarus also, (11) because on his account many of the Jews were going away and believing in Jesus.

9–11 In this brief episode the story of Lazarus himself is given an extraordinary final twist. Jesus' raising him from the dead has been such a climactic sign and had such an impact – many believed (11.46) and this provoked the fear on the part of the religious authorities that all would believe (11.48) – that Lazarus himself becomes the object of a death plot. The pericope appears so strange that many commentators hurry over it or only pause to provide brief observations on the difficulties into which the evangelist's storytelling has led him, if it has the consequence of Lazarus also being under the threat of death. But Lazarus has not only attracted, on the negative side, a parallel death plot, he has also, on the positive side, become almost a rival object of attention to Jesus! **A large crowd of the Jews** came to Bethany **not only on Jesus' account but also to see Lazarus, whom he had raised from the dead.** The resurrected Lazarus is the primary public exhibit of Jesus' extraordinary powers. The language employed for the effect produced by Lazarus may reflect the later situation of the rivalry between the synagogue and the Johannine community – **on his account many of the Jews were going away and believing in Jesus.** To put a stop to this desertion to the cause of Jesus, the chief priests are depicted as planning to put Lazarus to death as well as Jesus. This also makes the point, especially relevant to the later period, that followers of Jesus can expect to face the threat of death from the religious authorities (cf. 16.2–3).

So, shortly after his extended account devoted to the raising of Lazarus from the dead, the evangelist raises the possibility of this character being killed! But whereas the plot to kill Jesus is followed through in the narrative, the plot to kill Lazarus is left hanging. The episode serves, nevertheless, as a sharp reminder that Lazarus' resurrection is only temporary. He could die again, not peacefully but violently, and after only a relatively brief experience of new life. In fact, there is a sense in which he returns to the situation he occupied at the beginning of chapter 11 – he is again under threat of death. All this ensures that readers will not miss the force of the earlier account of the raising of Lazarus. It has not been told simply for the sake of this miracle that can so easily be reversed. It is a sign, but only a sign. By associating the plot to kill Lazarus with that to kill Jesus, the narrator underlines the point made at the very beginning of the Lazarus episode that life and death are inextricably linked, not only because Lazarus himself moves from death to life and back to the possibility of imminent death but also, and more especially, because the account of that movement foreshadows Jesus' move from life to death and back to life.

(v) The entry into Jerusalem 12.12–19

(12) On the next day, when the great crowd that had come to the festival heard that Jesus was coming to Jerusalem, (13) they took branches of palm trees and went out to meet him, and they cried out, 'Hosanna! Blessed is the one who comes in the name of the Lord, the King of Israel.' (14) When Jesus found a young donkey, he sat on it, as it is written: (15) 'Do not be afraid, daughter of Zion. Look, your king is coming, seated on a donkey's colt!' (16) His disciples did not understand these things at first, but when Jesus was glorified, then they remembered that these things had been written about him and that they had done these things to him. (17) So the crowd that had been with him when he called Lazarus from the tomb and raised him from the dead continued to testify. (18) For this reason also the crowd went to meet him, because they heard that he had done this sign. (19) So the Pharisees said to one another, 'You see, you are of no help at all. Look! The world has gone after him.'

The Fourth Gospel's account of Jesus' final entry into Jerusalem falls into three main parts – (i) a brief recounting of Jesus' reception by the crowd and his response in vv. 12–15, (ii) the narrator's comment about the disciples' understanding of this in v. 16, and (iii) a linking of this event to the Lazarus episode through the depiction both of the crowd and of the Pharisees' response to Jesus' popularity in vv. 17–19.

12–13 It is extremely difficult to determine which precise day of the week is meant by **On the next day**, and scholars make a variety of suggestions. The previous temporal reference has been to the day of the anointing, and this is said to have been six days before the Passover (cf.

12.1). The Fourth Gospel appears to hold that the Passover (15 Nisan) started on a Friday evening, but is the reckoning in 12.1 inclusive of the Passover or not? If the Passover was from Friday sunset to Saturday sunset, then, reckoned non-inclusively, six days before would be from Saturday to Sunday, but if the meal was in the evening, as seems likely, that would involve Jesus travelling to Bethany during the daytime, which would still have been part of the sabbath, and that is unlikely. The Jewish reckoning of days was probably inclusive, and both this and the previous consideration would suggest that the meal was on the Sunday evening that began the Monday. If 'the next day' is taken in its strict meaning, that would make it a reference to the daytime of the Tuesday. If, as seems less likely, the phrase is taken far more loosely, it might then refer to the daylight hours of the Monday. But on none of these reckonings does the Fourth Gospel have the entry into Jerusalem on a Sunday, the day the event is remembered in the Christian calendar.

Although all four Gospels relate the entry into Jerusalem, John's account is the only one to mention that the festival crowd **took branches of palm trees** and therefore in this respect, if not in terms of the day of the week, it is the one that supplies the name for the Christian liturgical celebration of Palm Sunday. Since the regaining of Jerusalem and the rededication of the temple at the time of the Maccabees, the palm had been associated with national liberation and functioned as a symbol for Israel (cf. 1 Macc. 13.51; 2 Macc. 10.7; cf. also *T. Naph.* 5.4). Here too the palm branches serve a similar purpose for the crowd, who treat Jesus as a national hero. They **went out to meet him**, and the term employed for 'meeting' (ὑπάντησις) reinforces this impression, since it was used for occasions when a victorious leader or king returned to a city, or a visiting dignitary came to it, and its populace went out to greet him in order then to accompany him back into the city. The crowd's cry makes these associations explicit – **Hosanna! Blessed is the one who comes in the name of the Lord, the King of Israel.** The first part of this acclamation draws on the festal greeting of the royal victor on his return to the temple in Ps. 118.25–6, with 'Hosanna' as a transliteration of the Hebrew of the psalm's 'Save us' or of its Aramaic equivalent. The last part, specifying the one who comes in the name of the Lord as 'the King of Israel', is an addition by the evangelist. This may well have been under the influence of Zeph. 3.15, where the community of Jerusalem is summoned to rejoice, because God has dealt with its enemies and 'the King of Israel, the Lord, is in your midst'.

14–15 Once before in this narrative a crowd – the Galilean crowd – had acclaimed Jesus and tried to make him king, but his reaction – retreat to the mountain – indicated that this was not an appropriate interpretation of his kingship (cf. 6.14–15). Jesus' response here makes a similar point, and the evangelist alters the Synoptic sequence of events in order to underline this. The other Gospels have Jesus already riding on a donkey before the crowd's acclamation of him, but here **When Jesus found a young donkey, he sat on it** is an action undertaken in the light of the acclamation and meant to function as an interpretative key, indicating the sense in which Jesus is prepared to be acknowledged as King of Israel. The narration spells this out by seeing the act as a fulfilment of Scripture – **as it is written: 'Do not be afraid, daughter of Zion. Look, your king is coming, seated on a donkey's colt!'** The bulk of the citation is taken from Zech. 9.9 with its promise of a future king for Jerusalem who will bring about peace and justice for all nations. Omitted from the original text are the words 'triumphant and victorious is he, humble and . . . on a donkey.' Whether those words are meant to be recalled or not, the paradox of triumph through humility is nonetheless retained, simply through the image of a king who arrives seated on a donkey's colt. This is not a warrior on a charger.

The opening of the citation has been altered. Zech. 9.9 had 'Rejoice greatly, daughter of Zion!' whereas this version has 'Do not be afraid', which occurs frequently in the Jewish Scriptures in the contexts of theophanies or promised theophanies and announcements of God's reign. Again the passage most likely to have influenced the wording here is from Zeph. 3 (see the comment on v. 13), because there, in the verses surrounding the reference to the King of Israel, the summons to daughter Zion to sing aloud and to daughter Jerusalem to rejoice and exult in v. 14 becomes in v. 16 'do not be afraid, O Zion'. The opening of the Fourth Gospel's mixed citation reinforces the evangelist's perspective that the King of Israel who is now in their midst is none other than the Lord.

16 There follows an explicit acknowledgement that such a perspective on Jesus' kingship was not one that was possible during his actual ministry but has come about as a result of the completion of his mission through his death and exaltation: **His disciples did not understand these things at first, but when Jesus was glorified, then they remembered that these things had been written about him and that they had done these things to him.** As has been frequently noted, the point of view of this Gospel's narrative is predominantly a post-resurrection one and the narrator spelled this out clearly as early as 2.22. It is not that at the time the disciples failed to recognize that the event was interpreted by the crowd in terms of royal messiahship, but that they did not see it as the fulfilment of a particular scripture nor did they understand the nature of Jesus' kingship. In the light of his completed mission, in which glorification was by means of the cross, Scripture and what had happened could be brought together in mutual illumination of Jesus' kingship as one that both fully represented God's kingship and would be carried out not by force and liberation armies but through apparent weakness, not by violent overthrow of the Romans but through defeating the forces of death and evil in his own death (cf. 12.31–3).

17–19 In the Synoptic tradition the main event that accompanies Jesus' entry into Jerusalem is the temple incident. This Gospel, of course, has placed the latter incident at the beginning of Jesus' mission and replaced it with the raising of Lazarus as the catalyst for Jesus' death. It is not surprising then that the Lazarus episode helps to shape the whole of 11.1—12.19 and that here, after the entry, it should be mentioned again for the last time. The attempt to integrate it into this part of the story line is, however, not without its awkwardness: **So the crowd that had been with him when he called Lazarus from the tomb and raised him from the dead continued to testify.** Some have taken this as a reference to a separate crowd that has come with Jesus from Bethany, so that this group and the crowd that come out from Jerusalem to meet Jesus converge. But this is highly unlikely. The natural implication is that the original crowd at the resurrection (cf. 11.42, 45) had dispersed well before now, and in any case the narrative has since introduced another crowd of Jews who had gone to Bethany to see Lazarus (cf. 12.9). Since the narrator continues, **For this reason also the crowd went to meet him, because they heard that he had done this sign,** the best explanation is probably that he has already merged the crowds in his description. A large number of those who were present in Bethany originally are now among the crowds assembling for the festival and are bearing their own witness to others about what has happened. This enables the narrator to supply a reason for the crowd going out to meet and acclaim Jesus. Just as earlier the Galilean crowd had wanted to acclaim Jesus as king on the basis of a sign (cf. 6.14), so now does this Jerusalem festival crowd.

After the raising of Lazarus the Pharisees and chief priests were portrayed as fearful that everyone would believe in Jesus (11.48). Now, at the sight of the crowds acclaiming Jesus, the Pharisees are made to say to each other, **You see, you are of no help at all! Look the world has gone after him.** Their comment with its hyperbole is, of course, highly ironic. In effect, they declare their inability to prevent the success of Jesus' mission in drawing all people to himself as Saviour of the world (cf. 4.42; 12.32). Their response also recalls Deut. 13.1–11, with its discussion of the false prophet who leads the people astray from the command to go after the Lord their God (cf. Deut. 13.5 LXX), and indicates that they see Jesus' popularity as a sign of the false prophet.

If an authentic historical tradition lies behind the earliest Gospel witness – Mark's account – then it is likely to have been elaborated in the telling. The original event would have been a symbolic act on the part of Jesus which made an implicit claim about his messianic role and its nature. But the event would have to have been on a much smaller scale than is depicted in the Gospels, if Jesus were not to have been immediately arrested by the authorities for stirring up the crowds in an inflammatory nationalistic gesture at the time of an important festival. If, instead of great crowds who accompany or meet him, it was a more modest group of followers for whom the symbolism was intended, then such an event need not have attracted mass attention and an accompanying clampdown by the authorities. At the same time, after the temple incident had aroused the ire of the authorities, reports of the manner of Jesus' entry into the city and of his teaching about God's kingdom might well have contributed to the charge against him, passed on to Pilate, that he was a would-be king.

In comparison with the Synoptics, the Fourth Gospel has a much briefer version of the entry into Jerusalem. It omits the preliminary description of Jesus sending disciples from the Mount of Olives to go and find the colt that will be ready to fulfil Jesus' purposes, and, as noted above, in contrast to the Synoptic accounts, it has Jesus sit on the donkey after the crowd's acclamation and not before. It alone, of course, then extends its abbreviated version by commenting on the disciples' understanding of the event and by associating the crowd with the Lazarus episode. In its account of the entry, while Mark 11.8 and Matt. 21.8 have people cutting branches from trees and spreading them on the road, in v. 13 it simply has them taking branches of palm trees with which they go to meet Jesus. In the Synoptics a crowd materializes on the way from the Mount of Olives and accompanies Jesus into the city, whereas in John the crowd that had gathered for the Passover festival go out from Jerusalem to greet him. The crowd's cry in v. 13, using Ps. 118.25–6, has the same wording as in Mark 11.9, where in the parallel accounts Matthew adds 'to the Son of David' after 'Hosanna' and Luke omits 'Hosanna' altogether. But instead of continuing with Mark's reference to the kingdom of David, John has 'the King of Israel', and at this point is closer to the version of the cry in Luke 19.38 – 'Blessed is the King who comes in the name of the Lord.'

After Jesus has simply found the donkey and sat upon it, the fourth evangelist cites Zech. 9.9 as the scripture that is fulfilled and this citation is found, with slightly different wording, only in Matthew, where it is part of the evangelist's distinctive fulfilment citations. Finally, Luke is the only one of the Synoptics to conclude the episode with a comment from the Pharisees about the response of the crowd of Jesus' followers (cf. 19.39, 40). John, in v. 19, has his own version of the Pharisees' comment. The Fourth Gospel, therefore, contains parallel elements from all the Synoptic accounts, where the three diverge, and some of these are clear redactional features of Luke and Matthew. This makes explanations in terms of similarities between independent pre-Synoptic and pre-Johannine traditions look very weak. It is much more likely that here again John knew all three accounts in some form and that his correspondences with and divergences from them are due to his creative reworking of the material for his own purposes.

The focus of this account is on what it means for Jesus to be king. That Jesus is rightly acknowledged as Israel's king is clear from Nathanael's confession in 1.49, but that there is a right and wrong way of viewing his kingship is equally apparent from Jesus' interaction with the Galilean crowd in 6.14–15. Here the Jerusalem crowd's acclamation is put in the appropriate perspective by the portrayal of Jesus seated on the donkey's colt rather than leading armed resistance on a warhorse. A similar point will be made in Jesus' dialogue with Pilate, where his kingship is subordinated to his witness to the truth, and in the crucifixion account, where he reigns from and by means of the cross. In sum, Jesus is king but the identity and mission of Jesus must be allowed to define that kingship. The comment about the disciples' later understanding in v. 16 underlines the evangelist's retrospective point of view, in which Jesus' glorification through his death and exaltation make clear the nature of his mission and therefore of his kingship. That perspective makes possible a proper remembering of the past in which Scripture and a particular incident can be linked in such a way that the true significance of each for identifying and understanding Jesus is drawn out. The farewell section will add that it is the role of the Paraclete to make possible this sort of remembering (cf. 14.26), a remembering that characterizes this Gospel's narrative as a whole.

(vi) The Greeks and the coming of the hour   *12.20–36a*

(20) Now among those who went up to worship at the festival were some Greeks. (21) They came to Philip, who was from Bethsaida in Galilee, and requested of him, 'Sir, we wish to see Jesus.' (22) Philip went and told Andrew. Then Andrew and Philip went and told Jesus. (23) Jesus answered them, 'The hour has come for the Son of Man to be glorified. (24) Truly, truly, I say to you, unless a grain of wheat falls into the ground and dies, it remains a single grain. But if it dies, it bears much fruit. (25) Whoever loves his life loses it, and whoever hates his life in this world will keep it for eternal life. (26) Whoever serves me, let that person follow me, and where I am there my servant will also be. Whoever serves me the Father will honour.

(27) 'Now my soul is troubled. And what should I say – "Father, save me from this hour"? But it is for this reason I have come to this hour. (28) Father, glorify your name.' Then a voice came from heaven: 'I have glorified it and I will glorify it

again.' (29) The crowd that was standing there and heard it said there had been thunder. Others said, 'An angel has spoken to him.' (30) Jesus answered and said, 'This voice came not for my sake but for yours. (31) Now is the judgement of this world; now the ruler of this world will be driven out. (32) And when I am lifted up from the earth, I shall draw all people to myself.' (33) He said this to indicate the kind of death he was to die. (34) Then the crowd answered him, 'We have heard from the law that the Christ remains for ever; how then can you say that the Son of Man must be lifted up? Who is this Son of Man?' (35) Jesus said to them, 'The light is among you for a little time yet. Walk while you have the light, so that the darkness does not overcome you. The person who walks in the darkness does not know where he is going. (36a) While you have the light, believe in the light, so that you may become children of light.'

In the overall Move Toward the Hour of Death and Glory (11.1—12.50), it is in this passage that Jesus announces for the first time that this hour has arrived and proceeds to offer hints about what his death as glory will entail. They are presented as a response to the coming of some Greeks (vv. 20–2) and fall into three parts – (i) vv. 23–6, emphasizing the necessity of his death, (ii) vv. 27–30, depicting his internal struggle in the face of that death, and (iii) vv. 31–6a, outlining the universal impact of his death and responding to the crowd's lack of comprehension.

20–2 Now among those who went up to worship at the festival were some Greeks. The preceding pericope concluded with the hyperbolic comment of the Pharisees that the world had gone after Jesus. Now the introduction of non-Jews into the narrative indicates that again Jesus' opponents have spoken more truly than they know. Some have taken 'Greeks' ("Ελληνες) to refer to Greek-speaking Jews, but the term used for the latter in Acts is 'Ελληνίσται (cf. 6.1; 9.29; 11.20) and this Gospel's earlier use of the former term in 7.35 refers to Greek-speaking Gentiles. Their presence at the Passover suggests that these Greeks are thought of as either proselytes or so-called God-fearers. Josephus speaks of a large number of foreigners being present for Passover but of their not being permitted to partake of the sacrifice (cf. *B. J.* 6.426–7). Their request – **Sir, we wish to see Jesus** – suggests they are to be seen as anticipating the coming of Gentiles into the believing community as part of the universal scope of Jesus' saving death (cf. v. 32). The request is made to Philip, who relays it to Andrew, and then the two tell Jesus. Philip and Andrew both feature in the account of the feeding of the five thousand in 6.5–9 and earlier were more closely linked in the call stories of 1.40–6. Here Philip is described as being **from Bethsaida in Galilee** and in the similar description of him previously Bethsaida is also said to be the city of Andrew and Peter (1.44). It has been suggested that Andrew and Philip are singled out again here as intermediaries for the Greeks because they were the only two disciples known by distinctively Greek names. It may be, however, that their presence at this point functions more as a reminder of the earlier call narratives, because there each acted as an intermediary between Jesus and another potential disciple, with Philip issuing the invitation to Nathanael to come and see. Now there is the coming of the first Gentile disciples who want to see Jesus. The narrator does not state whether their wish is granted. The reader is left to presume that it is not, because this incident only prefigures the Gentile mission, which awaits the completion of Jesus' hour.

23–4 Jesus' response to their request to see him suggests that their arrival does, however, mean that that hour, previously said to be on its way (cf. 2.4; 4.21, 23; 5.25; 7.30; 8.20) has now begun – **the hour has come for the Son of Man to be glorified**. And whereas in the Synoptics the Son of Man's glory is a future matter associated with the parousia, in this Gospel his suffering and glory coincide, since the moment of his glorification involves his death. The words that follow elaborate on the necessity of this death with an analogy: **Truly, truly, I say to you, unless a grain of wheat falls into the ground and dies, it remains a single grain. But if it dies, it bears much fruit.** The double Amen introductory formula may again indicate that this saying and those in vv. 25–6 are rooted in the tradition of Jesus' sayings. As Mark 4 indicates, Jesus employed parables about seeds which bear fruit to speak of the kingdom of God and it could be that this saying reflects one about the necessity of a seed being sown in the ground before it can bring forth a harvest. The image could be used to make a variety of points about the resurrection life of the age to come. In 1 Cor. 15.35–44 Paul also speaks of the need for a seed to die before it can come to life in connection with the resurrection body. Jesus' original parabolic saying may even have employed the image with specific reference to martyrdom, since in Jewish thought the death of a martyr was seen as bearing fruit by benefiting others or the nation (see the earlier discussion of 10.11). In any case, the Fourth Gospel develops the saying further in this direction. A single seed or grain has to disintegrate in the ground before it can not only be renewed but also reproduce life. Jesus' death has just been implied through the notion of glorification. Like the martyr's death but on a greater scale, it will produce 'much fruit' – a worldwide community participating in the salvation and life it achieves (cf. v. 32). In this way the saying also reinforces the point that the coming of the Gentiles to Jesus, anticipated in the request of the Greeks, awaits his imminent death.

25–6 The next saying – **Whoever loves his life loses it, and whoever hates his life in this world will keep it for eternal life** – reflects an aphorism found in a number of forms in the Synoptics. Mark 8.35 has 'Whoever wants to save his life will lose it, and whoever loses his life for my sake and the gospel's will save it.' 'For my sake and the gospel's' is usually considered Markan redaction, and this form of the saying has parallels in Matt. 16.25 and Luke 9.24, where each evangelist has his own minor modifications. The other form of the saying is found in Matt. 10.39 – 'Whoever finds his life will lose it, and he who loses his life for my sake will find it' – and Luke 17.33 – 'Whoever seeks to gain his life will lose it, but whoever loses his life will keep it' – and many consider this to have been part of the Q source. In this teaching on discipleship, to save, find or gain one's life is to attempt to live one's life as though one owned it and it is an enterprise doomed to failure because life is a gift from God, who can also take it away. On the other hand, to lose one's life is to renounce the attempt to secure life for oneself and, instead, to spend it in the service of God and others. Those who lose their lives in this way find that they receive those lives back from God. The Johannine version of the saying employs the language of love and hate for the two orientations towards one's life. To hate one's life in this context is to have a higher, more all-encompassing allegiance than that to one's own survival and does not mean to despise one's life as having no value. This language is also used of the demands of discipleship with reference to family and life in Luke 14.26 (cf. also 16.13). The Fourth Gospel's version also underlines the eschatological dimensions of the saying by adding in characteristically Johannine language the contrast between 'in this world' and 'for eternal life'. To love one's life is to be caught up in the realm of humanity opposed to God, while to refuse to cling to it at all costs is to begin now to receive it back as part of the life of the age to come bestowed by God.

But just as this Gospel interprets the Synoptic presentation of Jesus' teaching about the kingdom Christologically, so here it gives a Christological interpretation to the Synoptic account of his teaching on discipleship. Following the statements about Jesus' death in vv. 23–4, the saying functions no longer merely as an aphorism that applies to all but as one of which Jesus is the supreme paradigm. It is fulfilled in his death and resurrection. By being willing to lay down his life (cf. 10.11, 15, 17, 18), Jesus will keep it for eternal life, because he receives it back from his Father in resurrected form. But the call to discipleship is not drowned out. Jesus is the paradigm that is to be followed – **Whoever serves me, let that person follow me, and where I am there my servant will also be.** Again this has its Synoptic equivalent in Jesus' invitation to take up one's cross and to follow him. Indeed, in the triple tradition this is the saying that accompanies the one about saving and losing one's life (cf. Mark 8.34–5 parr.). Here it is framed in the language of servanthood (cf. Mark 9.35; 10.43–4), and in 13.15–16 Jesus' paradigm of washing the disciples' feet is one to be followed because 'servants are not greater than their masters'. One who serves Jesus will follow him in self-giving, even if that leads to death. But just as Jesus' death will be his glory, so that pattern will be reproduced for his followers. The promise is that they will be where he is, seeing and sharing in his glory (cf. 14.3; 17.24). The Father not only glorifies and honours the Son but also those who belong to the Son – **Whoever serves me the Father will honour.**

27–8 The focus now reverts to Jesus' own destiny with the Fourth Gospel's equivalent to the Synoptic Gethsemane experience of Jesus, which, unlike the latter, is found before, instead of after, the last meal with the disciples. At the prospect of what lies ahead, Jesus concedes, **Now my soul is troubled.** Mark 14.34 has Jesus echoing the LXX language of the refrain in Ps. 42.5–6, 11 and Ps. 43.5 – 'My soul is overwhelmed with grief.' Apparently alerted to these psalms by Mark's account, John employs the language of the parallel line in the refrain about the soul being disquieted or troubled (cf. also 11.33; 13.21). But Jesus' distress immediately recedes into the background and the internal dialogue of his prayer distances him somewhat from the very human figure of the Synoptic Gethsemane acccounts. Indeed, he explicitly rejects the sort of prayer with which the Synoptic Jesus began his agonizing struggle in the garden to conform his will to that of his Father. In the Synoptic tradition Mark 14.35 alone has Jesus praying that the hour might pass from him and all have him asking his Father to 'Remove this cup from me' (Mark 14.36; cf. Matt 26.39; Luke 22.42), but John's Jesus reasons, **And what should I say – 'Father, save me from this hour'? But it is for this reason I have come to this hour.** This Gospel has not only taken up the notion of 'the hour' from Mark here, but also, as has been seen, made it into a structural feature of the plot's movement, so that Jesus has been conscious from the start of his mission that it is all moving towards his 'hour', the supreme point of fulfilment, and that that hour entails both his death and his glory. Because of Jesus' unique relationship with God, for Jesus to be glorified is at the same time for God to be glorified (cf. 13.31). For this reason the only appropriate prayer is that which Jesus now utters – **Father, glorify your name.** This appeal to God's name and glory is typical of Israel's prayer, where it frequently functioned as the motive for an appeal for God's help (cf. Pss. 25.11; 31.3; 79.9; 109.21; 143.11; Jer. 14.7, 21). But Jesus refuses the appeal for deliverance. Instead his sole concern is with his Father's reputation, which is paradoxically to be established through both non-deliverance and what appears to be the very opposite of glory by human standards, namely Jesus' death by crucifixion. There is an answer to his prayer – **a voice came from heaven: 'I have glorified it and I will glorify it again.'** God's name has already been glorified, primarily through the signs, and it will be glorified again, through the death that is now imminent. On two occasions in the Synoptics a voice from heaven attests to Jesus – at his baptism and at his transfiguration, the latter occasion serving as an anticipation of his glory.

29–30 The depiction of the responses to the voice from heaven is not entirely clear: **The crowd that was standing there and heard it said there had been thunder. Others said, 'An angel has spoken to him.'** So the majority of the audience mistake it for thunder but some interpret it as an angelic voice, although even here it is not spelled out whether the angelic voice spoke Aramaic and whether the content of what was said to Jesus was understood. Yet Jesus' explanation, **This voice came not for my sake but for yours,** appears to assume that the crowd has understood the words, since they were for its benefit. Perhaps, however, the precise words are not in view and the narrator assumes that, whether the crowd experienced thunder as a confirmatory portent (cf. e.g. Exod. 19.19; 1 Sam. 12.17–18; Sir. 46.16–17) or thought of the noise as an angelic voice, both phenomena were interpreted as divine approval of Jesus' words. In regard to Jesus himself, however, the point is clear. Whereas in the Lazarus episode Jesus' prayer was not really necessary for him, now an answer to his prayer is not really required for one who is aligned to the will of his Father. The voice from heaven is an accommodation to the crowd, who still need to be convinced of his true relationship to the Father.

31–3 The voice has confirmed that God's reputation is inextricably bound up with that of Jesus, and Jesus proceeds to explain the significance of this for the vindication of his claims – **Now is the judgement of this world; now the ruler of this world will be driven out.** In the trial that is constituted by his public mission, Jesus has been judged and condemned by this world and its powers, but when that trial is seen in cosmic perspective, the reverse is true. The hour of his death and glory that is now beginning is in fact God's judgement of this world in its alienation from and opposition to God (cf. also 16.33). Not only is the world judged but so also is its ruler (cf. 14.30; 16.11), designated in 8.44 and 13.2 as the devil and in 13.27 as Satan. Here again there is a reversal. The one behind the world's driving-out of Jesus and the synagogue's driving-out of Jesus' followers (cf. 9.34) is himself driven out. The hour of the Son of Man's glorification in death, the time of the great reversal, is now described in different terms – **when I am lifted up from the earth, I shall draw all people to myself.** This is the third use of the double entendre of 'to be lifted up' (cf. also 3.14; 8.28) and its language again echoes what is said of the suffering servant-witness in Isa. 40—55 who is to be lifted up and glorified (cf. Isa. 52.13 LXX). For the first time, however, the narrator spells out that this terminology is **to indicate the kind of death he was to die,** namely, being raised up on a cross in a Roman execution, and thus puts beyond doubt that its double meaning brings together Jesus' crucifixion and his exaltation as a single thought. As in 3.14–15, the focus is on the result of this event. The earlier passage is couched in terms of those who believe in him having eternal life, while here the salvific consequence is depicted as universal in scope with the exalted Jesus drawing all people to himself (cf. also 6.44).

34 As in v. 29, there are questions about the coherence of the crowd's response within the narrative, underlining that the writer's concern is more with his dialogue with his readers than with the dialogue between his characters. The response is **We have heard from the law that the Christ remains for ever; how then can you say that the Son of Man must be lifted up? Who is this Son of Man?** There are three problems here. First, Jesus has not actually just said that the Son of Man must be lifted up, although he used the term 'Son of Man' back in v. 23. The crowd's reply in fact relies on the two earlier references to lifting up in 3.14 and 8.28, where the term 'Son of Man' appears. Secondly, the crowd assumes that 'Son of Man' is a messianic title, which is a Christian notion. Thirdly, since they talk of the Christ remaining for ever, their reply appears to presume that Jesus as Son of Man will not, which in turn implies that they have understood the double meaning of the Greek verb for 'to lift up' and that it entails Jesus' death. The substantial point, however, is a variation on the standard Jewish objection to Christian claims about Jesus – Jesus as Son of Man cannot be the Messiah, because the Messiah will not die but will establish his rule permanently (cf. e.g. Trypho's objection in Justin, *Dial.* 32). The support from the law for this objection is likely to be those scriptural texts that speak of David's descendant being established for ever (e.g. Pss. 89.3–4, 36–7; 110.4; Ezek. 37.25).

35–6a In response, Jesus does not become embroiled in debate about his identity in relation to the law. That sort of dispute is found earlier, in chapter 7. Instead, he takes as given the identity he had claimed in that context – that he is the light of the world who fulfils the function of Torah (cf. 8.12) – and uses this to draw a quite different consequence from the fact that he will not physically remain for ever: **The light is among you for a little time yet. Walk while you have the light, so that the darkness does not overcome you. The person who walks in the darkness does not know where he is going.** As Jesus had said in his earlier demonstration of his claim, 'While I am in the world, I am the light of the world' (9.5). Since he will not always be in the world, advantage has to be taken of the time that still remains. The imperative is to live and act now in recognition of who Jesus is. The prologue had spoken of the darkness not overcoming the light (1.5), but here the warning attached to the imperative has a more personal application – 'so that the darkness does not overcome *you*'. The danger of not responding appropriately to the presence of the light in Jesus is that one ends up engulfed by the darkness and is no longer able to see, the condition of the Pharisees indicted in 9.39–41. Such people grope around in the darkness, not knowing where they are going. In contrast, Jesus has frequently asserted that he knows where he is going – to the one who sent him. His followers also know the way and he will take them with him (14.3–6). Not to recognize the light, then, is to be left to the destructive powers of darkness and to be alienated from the light of life. The present situation, created by the coming of the light into the world, is therefore an urgent and critical one – **While you have the light, believe in the light, so that you may become children of light.** Despite its frequent references to the light, only here does the Fourth Gospel employ the expression 'children of light'. In the Qumran literature the members of the community were viewed in this way, especially in 1QM with its 'War of the Sons of Light against the Sons of Darkness' (1.1–16; cf. also 1QS 1.10; 3.13–4.26) and the same terminology is found elsewhere in the New Testament in Luke 16.8 and 1 Thess. 5.5 (cf. also Eph. 5.8). In such contexts the dualism of light and darkness is primarily an ethical one and concerns two ways of life. But whereas in the Qumran writings it is rigorous adherence to the law that distinguishes the children of light, here in John it is their relation to Jesus as the light that gives them their distinctive orientation and produces behaviour in accordance with the will of God. Significantly, this final encounter of Jesus' public ministry not only sets it in cosmic perspective with the light symbolism (cf. 1.4–9; 3.19–21) but also continues the pressing invitation to believe in the one who embodies that symbolism's significance.

Gathered together in this section are a number of Johannine insights into the significance of Jesus' imminent death and its consequences for humans. Far from being an occasion of shame, his death is the crucial moment in the hour of the Son of Man's glorification. God's reputation and honour are intertwined with those of Jesus and so Jesus' death is also the point at which God's name is supremely glorified. In a reversal of values, the crucifixion is not to be seen as undermining the claims of Jesus to Messiahship and divine sonship; rather, in its apparent humiliation the glory of both Father and Son is most clearly established. In the comments above, the evangelist's creative reworking of various aspects of the Synoptic tradition has been indicated. The perspective on Jesus' death as glory is one of the main features of that reworking. In the Synoptic tradition there are sayings about the Son of Man's present suffering and other sayings about his future glory. This Gospel combines the two aspects into one in its view of Jesus' death. Typical of such a combination is also the way the evangelist has linked together in the same episode his equivalent of the Gethsemane account, with its mention of Jesus' soul being troubled, and material recalling the Synoptic transfiguration account through its voice from heaven confirming Jesus' glorification. There can be no mistaking the centrality of the motif of death as glory, for this passage also features the third and final use of the 'lifting up' language in regard to Jesus' destiny. His being raised up on a cross to be executed by the Romans is also his being raised up in exaltation by God. The Gospel's forensic themes are also in play here. Jesus' death is not, as it would appear, simply this world's judgement on him, but, because it is the ultimate judge who undergoes this condemnation, his crucifixion turns out to be also a verdict of judgement on this world and the power of evil that lies behind it. More positively, through the giving of Jesus' life in death much fruit will be borne; indeed there will be universal consequences, as in his death as exaltation Jesus draws to himself all people, foreshadowed in this pericope by the Gentiles who ask to see him. Because of the one who undergoes it and because of its salvific effects, Jesus' departure from this world is unique, yet at the same time its pattern of death as glory is to be replicated among his followers, who are willing not to cling to their lives for themselves but to give them in his service.

(vii) Summary statement about the response to Jesus' signs
    and words   *12.36b–50*

(36b) Jesus said these things, and, when he had gone away, he hid from them. (37) Although he had done so many signs in their presence, they did not believe in him, (38) so that the word which was spoken by Isaiah the prophet might be fulfilled, 'Lord, who has believed our message, and to whom has the arm of the Lord been revealed?' (39) For this reason they could not believe, because again Isaiah said, (40) 'He has blinded their eyes and blinded[1] their heart, so that they might not see with their eyes

---

[1] The main issue in regard to the text is whether the verb to be read here is ἐπήρωσεν, 'blinded' (p⁶⁶,⁷⁵ ℵ K W Π) or ἐπώρωσεν, 'hardened' (A B* L X Θ Ψ). A large number of later manuscripts have the perfect tense of the latter and a few have the perfect tense of the former, but both of these traditions are clearly attempts to bring the second verb of the citation into line with the first in terms of tense. Since the verbs differ in only a single letter, they are easy for a scribe to confuse. The former verb means 'to disable or maim', but, in regard to the eyes or the mind, it has the force of 'to blind'. The latter means 'to make dull or harden' and is more frequently used with the heart as its object (cf. Mark 6.52; 8.17; also Mark 3.5; Eph. 4.18). ἐπήρωσεν has the slightly stronger early attestation and is the somewhat more difficult reading, since it repeats the notion of blinding, though using a different verb. In addition, although the heart, as the seat of perception, can be blinded, the more usual language in relation to the heart would have been that of hardening. It seems more likely, therefore, that a scribe would have either inadvertently read ἐπήρωσεν as ἐπώρωσεν or consciously changed the former to the more customary usage, thinking that the text before him was mistaken.

and perceive with their heart and turn, and I would heal them.' (41) Isaiah said these things because he saw his glory and spoke about him. (42) Nevertheless, many, even of the authorities, believed in him, but because of the Pharisees they would not confess it lest they be put out of the synagogue; (43) for they loved human glory more than the glory of God.

(44) Jesus cried out and said, 'The person who believes in me does not believe in me but in him who sent me, (45) and the one who sees me sees him who sent me. (46) I have come as light into the world, so that everyone who believes in me should not remain in the darkness. (47) And if anyone hears my words and does not keep them, I do not condemn that person, for I came not to condemn the world but to save the world. (48) The person who rejects me and does not receive my words has that which condemns him; the word that I have spoken will condemn him on the last day. (49) For I have not spoken of my own accord, but the Father who sent me has given me a commandment about what to say and what to speak. (50) And I know that his commandment is eternal life. What I speak, therefore, I speak just as the Father has told me.'

This section serves to bring the public work of Jesus to a conclusion, providing a summing up in regard to the response to that work. The conclusion is in two parts. In vv. 37–43 the narrator summarizes the response to Jesus' signs, while in vv. 44–50 Jesus himself summarizes what has been at stake in the response to his words. The forensic motif that has been to the fore previously continues here. The narrative of the public mission that began with the witness of John the Baptist closes with both the negative and positive aspects of judgement (cf. vv. 47, 48, 50). In terms of that overall motif this passage can be seen as forming an initial summing up in the trial of the public ministry. In its first part the narrator acts as counsel for the defence, as he provides an explanation for the deficient response to Jesus' deeds, and in the second part the protagonist, who has been on trial, is given the opportunity to make a final statement about his teaching and its significance.

36b–8 The narrator provides a transitional statement. After Jesus' encounter with the crowd and his closing invitation to believe, **he hid from them**. This underlines the limited nature of the time in which to believe in the light (cf. vv. 35a–6). Earlier Jesus hid himself when it appeared he was going to be stoned (8.59) and so his action here does not suggest he was expecting a positive response to his invitation to believe. In fact, the narrator uses it to lead into the summary of the negative response to Jesus' mission as a whole – **Although he had done so many signs in their**

presence, they did not believe in him. The particular signs that have been related have been performed in a variety of settings, some in Galilee and some in Jerusalem and its surrounds. But mention has also been made of other signs that are not recorded in the narrative (cf. 2.23; 3.2; 6.2, 26; 7.31; 10.32; 11.47). Again, the setting for these has been both Jerusalem and Galilee, so this comment about unbelief in the face of so many signs appears to apply not just to the previous audience of a Jerusalem crowd but to the reception of Jesus on the part of people of Israel in general. In this way it expands on the prologue's statement that the Logos came to what was his own but his own people did not receive him (1.11). At this point appeal is made to Scripture, and in particular Isaiah, to demonstrate authoritatively that this negative response of unbelief does not mean that Jesus' mission has been out of line with God's will. To the contrary, it fulfils that will as revealed in Scripture – **so that the word which was spoken by Isaiah the prophet might be fulfilled, 'Lord, who has believed our message, and to whom has the arm of the Lord been revealed?'** This citation from Isa. 53.1 LXX is part of an *inclusio* between the end and the beginning of the public ministry in regard to Isa. 40—55 as major interpretative backdrop. At the beginning John the Baptist had quoted Isa. 40.3 LXX in the course of his witness. Here in the conclusion the words from Isa. 53 indicate that the response to Jesus is the same as the unbelieving response to the words ('our message') and actions of God ('the arm of the Lord') through the servant-witness. What has happened in the case of Jesus, therefore, can be viewed as the fulfilment of what was predicted in Scripture.

39–41 For this reason they could not believe. The reason for the majority of Israel's failure to believe is given in what follows – a further citation from earlier in Isaiah: **He has blinded their eyes and blinded their heart, so that they might not see with their eyes and perceive with their heart and turn, and I would heal them.** While the previous citation followed the LXX, this one, from Isa. 6.10, corresponds to neither the LXX nor the Masoretic text. It has been considerably reworked. While the LXX puts what has happened to the people in the passive and the MT attributes it to the prophet's message, here, although the subject of the verbs for blinding is not explicitly stated, it is highly unlikely to be anyone other than God. This modified citation also drops the references to 'ears' in both parts of the original verse. Since the subject of this part of the summation is response to the signs, it is sight and not hearing that needs to be stressed, and Jesus has just issued the invitation to believe in the light (v. 36a), which also makes seeing or perceiving the appropriate focus of any explanatory scriptural citation. It is not surprising, therefore, that the original text of v. 40 would have used two different verbs for blinding (see the note on the translation). Here,

as in the narrative as a whole, God's sovereignty and human responsibility are held together. Unbelieving blindness to the signs is wilful and
culpable but not beyond the realm of God's sovereignty over the world
and indeed can be seen as part of God's overall purposes (cf. also the use
of this citation in Mark 4.12 parr.; Acts 28.26–7). There are echoes of the
negative side of Jesus' earlier statement of the dual purpose of his mission
– 'I came into this world for judgement, so that those who do not see
might see and those who see might become blind' (9.39). As elsewhere in
the New Testament, divine hardening or blinding of humans is not necessarily the final word (cf. Rom. 11.25–6), and indeed here the final words
of the citation, now seen as applicable to Jesus, are 'and I would heal
them'. For the evangelist, the invitation is still to be extended to those in
the darkness of blindness to believe and be healed (cf. also v. 46).

The context of the citation from Isa. 6 means that a more positive
appeal can also be made to Isaiah as part of Scripture's witness to Jesus
and his mission – **Isaiah said these things because he saw his glory
and spoke about him.** What Israel as a whole failed to see – the divine
glory, to which the signs pointed – Isaiah had already seen. The allusion is
to Isaiah seeing the Lord (Isa. 6.1, 5), the one whose glory filled the whole
earth (Isa. 6.3). The Targum on Isa. 6.1, whose date may be later than
the first century CE, conflates these verses in similar fashion and speaks
of Isaiah seeing 'the glory of the Lord'. Just as in 8.56 Abraham's seeing
of the end-times could be given a Christological application, so too can
Isaiah's seeing of the Lord's glory. In this case the thought is presumably
that, since Christ as the pre-existent Logos shared God's glory (cf. 1.1, 14;
17.5), all previous sightings of God's glory were also visions of Christ's
glory.

42–3 It appears initially that the narrator's next statement – **Nevertheless,
many, even of the authorities, believed in him** – will introduce the
positive response to Jesus' mission. But it immediately becomes clear
that this is, from the narrator's perspective, a pseudo-belief, a belief that
does not come to expression in public witness – **but because of the
Pharisees they would not confess it lest they be put out of the
synagogue.** The many who are reported as having believed in Jesus
include many of the religious authorities, who, in the time of Jesus, would
have been primarily those of the Sadducean priestly class but could also
include Pharisees (cf. 3.1), yet the chief priests would have had more
power than the Pharisees at this stage and the Pharisees among these
authorities are said to be among those not to have confessed their faith
because of 'the Pharisees'. The awkwardness of the formulation points to
the anachronism of the state of affairs being reflected here, namely the later
situation when the successors of the Pharisees were the group who could
exercise jurisdiction over synagogue life (see the discussion of 9.22). As

early as 2.23–5 the narrator had mentioned many who believed but whose faith was deemed to be inadequate. Sometimes this judgement appears to be because such initial believers failed to see beyond the sign to that which it signified. Here, however, another reason is given for the negative evaluation of their faith. Such belief is fearful of the consequences of making a full confession about Jesus, afraid of the actions of the religious authorities who would excommunicate them from the synagogue. To undergo such a ban would not necessarily lead to their physical death but it would be to experience a form of social death, and so there were many in the evangelist's time who were sympathetic to Jesus' claims but chose to remain in the synagogue and keep their form of belief secret. They are represented in the narrative elsewhere by the parents of the blind man (9.22), by Nicodemus, who comes to Jesus at night (3.2), and by Joseph of Arimathea, who is associated with Nicodemus and described as a secret disciple because of his 'fear of the Jews' (19.38–9). The Gospel's general judgement on those who remain secret believers, however, appears to be that they are ultimately no different from unbelievers. Here the narrator draws attention to the social dimension of their inadequate belief and indicts them by attributing their fear to the fact that **they loved human glory more than the glory of God.** They should not only have seen but been willing to confess openly the glory of God that had come to expression in Jesus' signs. Like 'the Jews' accused in 5.44, they have not fully realized that what is at stake in Jesus' person and mission is the glory of God. They merit the same accusing question that exposes the cause of their ultimate unbelief – 'How can you believe when you receive glory from one another and do not seek the glory that comes from the only God?' Considerations about their reputation and honour in the synagogue and in Jewish society as a whole ought to have paled into insignificance in the light of the reputation and honour that belongs to God and that God has bestowed on Jesus. In contrast to Jesus, who does not seek glory from humans (5.41) but relies on God to seek his glory and to glorify him (8.50, 54), they put a higher premium on the good opinion of humans than on what promotes God's honour. Any belief in Jesus that they have entertained is therefore judged as failing to have come to genuine expression.

44–5 Jesus' last speech on his own behalf in his public ministry summarizes his identity and role, drawing together a number of themes that have featured earlier. There is no indication that Jesus has come out of hiding (cf. v. 36b) and so, on a straightforward reading, it is awkward to have him now make a public statement. The awkwardness is likely to be another indication that stages of composition have left their mark on the final narrative. The first words of his proclamation underline that it is God and the divine glory that have been at stake in his mission, and they continue the notion of seeing that has dominated the narrator's comments in the preceding verses:

The person who believes in me does not believe in me but in him who sent me, and the one who sees me sees him who sent me. Since Jesus is God's fully authorized representative (cf. 13.20), to believe in Jesus is to believe in God and to see Jesus is to see God.

46–7 Jesus' mission statement – **I have come as light into the world** – picks up for a final time on the light motif of earlier passages (cf. esp. 8.12; 9.5; 12.35–6a), and, as elsewhere (cf. e.g. 3.19), this imagery conveys connotations of judgement. Initially the positive effects of the light's judgement are in view – **so that everyone who believes in me should not remain in the darkness.** In fact, Jesus can go on to say, **if anyone hears my words and does not keep them, I do not condemn that person, for I came not to condemn the world but to save the world.** His mission as the light has the primary purpose of giving the light of life and his mission of judgement has the primary purpose not of condemnation but of rescue and restoration to well-being, that is, salvation. In this way the assertion of 3.17 is repeated but now with Jesus as its subject rather than God.

48–50 Having said that he does not condemn those who fail to respond positively to his word, Jesus nevertheless announces, **The person who rejects me and does not receive my words has that which condemns him; the word that I have spoken will condemn him on the last day.** Here unbelief is a choice for which humans are held accountable, complementing the notion of unbelief as the result of divine activity in vv. 39–40. The assertion about condemnation, however, appears to contradict the previous statement in v. 47 (see the similar difficult juxtaposition in 8.15–16 of an assertion about Jesus not judging with those about his judging). Is the distinction being made here one between Jesus and his word, a strange one for a Gospel that can call Jesus the Logos, or one between present and future, again a strange one for a narrative that can speak of condemnation taking place already in the process of making an unbelieving response (cf. 3.18)? It is more likely that the distinction is again that between the primary purpose and the secondary consequence of Jesus' mission. The point here, in any case, is that the secondary consequence will be a judgement of condemnation on the last day for those who fail to receive Jesus' word and it will be precisely the word that Jesus has spoken that will function as the judge. His word can function in this way because it is none other than the word of judgement God would pronounce (cf. 5.27, 30).

Jesus goes on to claim here just such a relation between his word and God's word – **For I have not spoken of my own accord, but the Father who sent me has given me a commandment about what to say and what to speak.** Because of his total dependence on the Father, his words not only witness to the truth but also serve as the final arbiter of that truth. The formulation here also recalls the dispute about whether Jesus is the true or a false prophet. Jesus' words contain unmistakable allusions to Deut. 18.18–19. He is claiming to be the true prophet, the prophet like Moses, of whom God says, 'I will put my words in the mouth of the prophet, who shall speak to them everything that I command. Anyone who does not heed the words that the prophet shall speak in my name, I myself will hold accountable.' As the one who speaks the words that God has commanded and to which all will be held accountable, Jesus' assertion is that, far from being a false prophet, he fulfils all the criteria for the true prophet like Moses. What is more, as regards God's words, Jesus knows **that his commandment is eternal life**. This saying recalls the earlier assertions of Jesus – 'anyone who hears my word and believes him who sent me has eternal life' (5.24) and 'the words that I have spoken to you are spirit and life' (6.63), and also Peter's response – 'You have the words of eternal life' (6.68). Jesus' words of eternal life have had the direct backing of God. God's commandments to Moses were the means of life – long life in the land (Deut. 32.45–7; cf. also 8.3), but now God's commandments to the prophet like Moses are the means of eternal life. The opposition to Jesus has been judging on the basis of its interpretation of Moses' commandments and has failed to realize that those commandments now have to be read in the light of the commandments given to Jesus, which have become the criterion for judgement and the means of life. This is part of their failure to see that Moses wrote about Jesus (5.46). Talk of eternal life enables the judgement motif that runs throughout the ministry to end on a positive note. Jesus' words as an expression of God's commandment are meant to provide the judgement of life, life which has the quality of the age to come (cf. v. 47b). The final assertion – **What I speak, therefore, I speak just as the Father has told me** – underlines for a final time that the witness of Jesus' word expresses precisely God's word (cf. 7.17–18; 8.28, 46–7) and indicates that the conclusion of the public ministry forms an *inclusio* with the prologue. Not only is the dual outcome of the ministry anticipated in 1.10–12, but Jesus' word as the complete expression of the Father's word also, of course, recalls the Logos of 1.1, 14, in whom are life and light and glory (cf. 1.4, 5, 14).

All the themes in this passage have been sounded before in the ministry. Now they are brought together as a summation of Jesus' case and additional scriptural support is supplied through the two citations from Isaiah. The narrator's summary in vv. 37–43 seeks to provide an explanation for the negative outcome of Jesus' mission in Israel as a whole, depicting two kinds of negative judgement about Jesus that have resulted – that of outright unbelief in the face of the evidence provided by Jesus' signs, and that of inadequate belief, the response of secret sympathizers. As the summation on Jesus' lips in vv. 44–50 moves to its close, it is dominated by the theme of judgement. In line with the earlier treatment of this motif, light and darkness provide the cosmic backdrop for the interaction between God and the world, and the witness of Jesus' word turns out to be the judge. As the section as a whole makes plain, if the response is unbelief, the judgement will be negative, but Jesus' mission is salvific and its intended outcome is the positive verdict of eternal life.

It is also made unmistakably clear that the issue that is at the centre of the process of judgement and that makes Jesus' mission so controversial is his relation to God. Because of the nature of that relationship, an inappropriate response to Jesus' signs is unbelief in the God who confirms people in their refusal to see what is before their eyes, and it is a failure to make God's glory or reputation the supreme motivating force in one's life. Because of the nature of that relationship, to believe in and see Jesus is to believe in and see God, and to respond to Jesus' word is to respond to God's commandment. Because of the nature of that relationship, Jesus' word and God's word both function as the judgement that effects either life or condemnation.

The discussion of this central issue could all have been handled by the narrator, but instead the last part is placed on the lips of Jesus himself. In this way he enacts the content of his summation by having the last word, making the final judgement on what is at stake in his own mission. Because it has no geographical setting or specific audience in the narrative, this part of the summation creates the effect of Jesus speaking directly to readers and their own situation and confronting them with the implications of his identity. At the same time this section points ahead. Jesus will develop some of its themes yet again in his farewell discourse. And readers are prepared to reflect on the passion narrative, having been left in no doubt about the identity of the one who will experience suffering and death.

C. JESUS' FAREWELL, PASSION AND RESURRECTION (DEPARTURE AS GLORY)   13.1—20.31

1. The Farewell   13.1—17.26

The hour of Jesus' departure and glory, to which the narrative has been leading, is now fully upon him. But before the accounts of the passion and resurrection, the narrator presents Jesus making full preparations for his followers, as he takes an extended farewell. For the most part this section contains material distinctive to the Fourth Gospel, although it has functional equivalents in the Synoptic accounts of Jesus' apocalyptic discourse and of the Passover meal at which the Lord's Supper is instituted. If the material is taken in its present form and the narrator's markers are followed, then it divides into five parts. The farewell is set at a final meal and opens with Jesus washing the disciples' feet (13.1–20). He then predicts his betrayal and initiates it by his words to Judas (13.21–30). Some treat the material in 13.31–8 as a separate unit and see the farewell discourse beginning at 14.1, but there is no break in the dialogue at this point and the content of 13.31–8 introduces topics to be developed in what follows, and so it is preferable to take the discourse as opening in 13.31. Scholars often talk of two or three farewell discourses and indeed the discourse material here may well have come from three different stages in the tradition, but in their present form they constitute one major speech, running from 13.31 to 16.33. Jesus' words in 14.31 – 'Rise, let us go from here' – indicate a break or pause, dividing the farewell speech into two major parts – 13.31—14.31 and 15.1—16.33. Jesus' prayer in 17.1–26 then forms a clear concluding unit for the farewell.

(i) The footwashing   *13.1–20*

(1) Before the festival of the Passover Jesus, knowing that his hour had come to pass from this world to the Father, having loved his own who were in the world, loved them to the end. (2) It was supper, and the devil had already put it into the heart of Judas, son of Simon Iscariot, to betray him. (3) Jesus, knowing that the Father had given all things into his hands and that he had come from God and was going to God, (4) got up from supper and took off his outer garments, and, taking a towel, tied it around himself. (5) He then poured water into a bowl and began to wash the disciples' feet and to wipe them with the towel that was tied around him. (6) He came to Simon Peter. He said to him, 'Lord, are you going to wash my feet?' (7) Jesus answered and said to him, 'You do not know now what I am doing, but after these things you will understand.' (8) Peter said to him, 'You will never wash my feet.' Jesus answered him, 'Unless I wash you, you have no participation with me.' (9) Simon Peter said to him, 'Lord, not only my feet but also my hands and my head.' (10) Jesus said to him, 'The one who has been bathed has no need to be washed, except for the feet[1], but is entirely clean. And you

---

[1] The textual tradition offers two major options, although one of these has also given rise to a number of minor variants. Some witnesses do not contain the phrase εἰ μή τοὺς πόδας, 'except for the feet'. These are ℵ it^{aur,c} vg^{ww} Tertullian Origen. The majority of witnesses do contain the phrase. This is a constant, even though they differ slightly in their treatment of the surrounding wording, with a variation in the order of words before the phrase (either οὐκ ἔχει χρείαν or οὐ χρείαν ἔχει) and an addition by some of μόνον, 'only', after the phrase. Among the manuscripts containing 'except

are clean, though not every one of you.' (11) For he knew who would betray him; for this reason he said, 'Not every one of you is clean.'

(12) When he had washed their feet and put on his outer garments and taken his place again at supper, he said to them, 'Do you know what I have done to you? (13) You call me Teacher and Lord, and you speak rightly, for I am. (14) So if I, the Lord and Teacher, have washed your feet, you also ought to wash one another's feet. (15) I have given you a model, so that as I have done to you, you also should do. (16) Truly, truly, I say to you, a servant is not greater than his master, nor is one who is sent greater than the one who sent him. (17) If you know these things, blessed are you if you do them. (18) I am not speaking about all of you. I know those whom I have chosen. But in order that the Scripture might be fulfilled, "The one who eats my bread has raised his heel against me." (19) I am speaking to you now before it occurs, so that, when it occurs, you may believe that I am. (20) Truly, truly, I say to you, whoever receives anyone I send receives me, and whoever receives me receives the one who sent me.'

The footwashing episode stands at the start of this new and climactic section of the narrative and in a number of ways foreshadows its major event. At the same time its focus, like that of the rest of the farewell section, is on the impact of that event for Jesus' disciples, those whose faith has brought them to this point still in company with Jesus in contrast to the majority of his people, who have responded in unbelief. The extended farewell discourse that follows functions to prepare these disciples for Jesus' departure and its aftermath, and this opening event introduces that preparation in enacted form. The account proceeds in three main stages. The setting and the initial act of Jesus washing his disciples' feet are

---

for the feet' are p^{66} A B C$\star$ D W Ψ cop^{sa,boh} arm it^{a,b,c,d,e} geo Origen Augustine. This longer reading has the earlier and stronger evidence. But two other factors complicate the question. Normally, the shorter reading is to be preferred in judging these textual matters, and a substantial number of scholars consider that internal considerations rule out the longer reading because its presence would render the footwashing trivial in comparison to a prior bathing. But such reasoning on internal grounds is dependent on one's interpretation of the whole episode and particularly of v. 10 (see comments on this verse). In addition, this particular form of internal argumentation is double-edged, since it makes the longer reading the more difficult reading, which would also normally be preferred, and offers the very reasons why it may have been omitted from the tradition by a scribe or scribes – it was thought not to cohere with its context. There is probably no escaping some form of circularity here, since overall interpretation of the passage is both affected by and affects which text is adopted. It seems best, however, to begin with the better-attested longer reading and to attempt to make sense of the passage in this form.

depicted in vv. 1–5. His dialogue with Peter is related in vv. 6–11. Finally, in vv. 12–20 Jesus provides an explanation of his act that applies it to the disciples' future conduct and develops the earlier assertion of v. 11 that there is one among them to whom what he has said does not apply.

1 The temporal setting for the footwashing and the ensuing discourse material is **Before the festival of the Passover.** Unlike the Synoptic accounts of Jesus' last meal, this one is therefore not a Passover meal. In the light of 19.14, 31, which indicate that Jesus' death takes place on the day of preparation for the Passover, it is apparent that the evangelist has set the meal on the evening that begins that day. There is no indication that Jesus decided to hold his own Passover meal a day earlier, as some hold (cf. also 13.29). There is not space to pursue here at any length the disputed issue of whether, in regard to historical reconstruction, the Synoptic tradition or John is to be followed at this point (but see the discussion in the Introduction). Suffice it to say that our earliest witness, Paul in 1 Corinthians, has both Jesus as the Passover lamb (1 Cor. 5.7–8) and the Passover meal as the background that makes best sense of the eucharistic words (1 Cor. 11.23–5). The Synoptic narratives are in line with the latter emphasis and there is no decisive reason why the Last Supper was not in fact a Passover meal. John pursues the former emphasis in narrative form, making the death of Jesus coincide with the slaughter of the Passover lambs, and that necessitates his altering the timing of Jesus' last meal with his disciples. The theologically more significant temporal indicator in relation to this meal and its footwashing is found in the narrator's characterization of Jesus – **knowing that his hour had come to pass from this world to the Father.** At the end of the public ministry Jesus had announced that the divinely appointed 'hour', to which his mission had been leading, was now upon him (cf. 12.23, 27) and here he is depicted as fully conscious of his imminent death. The hour is described as one of departure from this world to be with the Father (cf. 7.33; 8.21–3) and preparation of the disciples for this departure is a key to the significance of the footwashing episode and will be one of the main themes of the farewell discourse. The concern to prepare them as fully as possible derives from Jesus' love for his followers – **Jesus, . . . having loved his own who were in the world, loved them to the end.** According to the prologue, the Logos' own, meaning Israel as a whole, did not accept him, but there were those who did accept him (1.11–12). The group of followers who are with Jesus on this occasion represent those who have believed and who form a new 'his own', whom he knows (cf. 10.14) and loves. The phrase εἰς τέλος can mean either 'to the end' (of Jesus' life) or 'fully' or 'completely'. The first meaning is likely to be primary here, given the mention of the hour, but, even so, the other connotation may also be in play. Jesus loves his own right up to the end of his mission in

this world and because that mission ends in his death it reveals the full extent of such love (cf. 15.13). Footwashing and farewell teaching are the immediate expressions of that love here.

2 It was supper. The setting is the evening meal or banquet. As has been noted, this was not a Passover celebration and in fact there are some features of the meal that may suggest an adaptation of the customs of a Graeco-Roman symposium for a Jewish setting, particularly the reclining at table (cf. vv. 23, 25) and the conversation prompted by the discourse, some of it enigmatic, of a wise teacher. In order to understand what unfolds at the supper, readers also need to know that Judas has by now determined to betray Jesus to the authorities. The theme of betrayal among this intimate group of followers is an undercurrent throughout this episode before emerging in its own right in the next (cf. 13.21–30). Here Judas' intention is seen as part of the cosmic conflict (cf. the references to 'the ruler of this world' in 13.31; 14.30) that forms the backdrop for Jesus' mission – **the devil had already put it into the heart of Judas, son of Simon Iscariot, to betray him**. The devil, as the personal symbol of evil, has been depicted in 8.44 as a murderer from the beginning and totally opposed to the truth, and, from the first mention of Judas' betrayal, this act leading to Jesus' death is seen as related to the work of the devil (cf. 6.70–1 – 'one of you is a devil'). It features again here in the context of the supper as a further reminder that Jesus' deeds and words are taking place after all that is necessary for Jesus' crucifixion has been set in motion and that they should be interpreted in the light of his coming death on a cross.

3 Before proceeding to the action, the narrator provides another 'inside view' of Jesus that focuses on his knowledge – **knowing that the Father had given all things into his hands and that he had come from God and was going to God**. Jesus knows both the sovereign authority he has been granted by the Father and his own divine origin and destiny. The placing of all things in the Son's hands has been asserted earlier (cf. esp. 3.35), and his origin with God and return to God have been mentioned separately, but this is the first time that his origin and his destiny occur in the same formulation, although earlier language of ascent and descent has the same implications (cf. 3.13; 6.62). Here Jesus' knowledge of his divine power and status serves to highlight what is involved in the act that he now performs. Somebody described in this fashion might have been expected to continue to demonstrate his divine qualities, as he had done in his signs, but certainly not to wash feet.

4–5 Since Jesus **got up from supper**, the footwashing does not take place at the time that it would normally occur – when guests arrived at the house and before they sat down to eat. This footwashing will not be simply the ordinary act of hospitality but will have its own special significance. Each stage of the act is described. Jesus first **took off his outer garments**. The verb used here for removing clothes (τίθημι) and the later one in v. 12 for putting them back on (λαμβάνω) are not the usual ones. The former is employed elsewhere for Jesus laying down his life (cf. 10.11, 15, 17–18; 15.13) and the latter for his taking it up again (cf. 10.17–18). Already there are hints that this act symbolizes Jesus' coming death. **Taking a towel**, he **tied it around himself**. The removal of his outer clothing has left Jesus only in a loincloth, to which he now adds the towel he will need for the job in hand. He is dressed as a slave for the work normally associated with slaves. **He then poured water into a bowl and began to wash the disciples' feet and to wipe them with the towel that was tied around him.** The disciples should probably be envisaged as reclining on couches or mats arranged around the table and, as they faced the table, having their feet behind them, so that Jesus moves around behind them, washing and wiping their feet, without disturbing the whole dining arrangement (cf. Luke 7.38).

Most footwashing in the ancient world was a menial task. It involved washing off not just dust and mud but also the remains of human excrement (which was tipped out of houses into the streets) and animal waste (which was left on country roads and town streets). The task of doing this as an act of hospitality to honour guests was therefore normally assigned to slaves or servants of low status, particularly females, so much so that footwashing was virtually synonymous with slavery. On rare occasions in ancient literature it is depicted as an act of loving service, performed by a daughter or wife for a father or husband. What makes the Fourth Gospel's account so extraordinary is that there is no parallel in extant ancient literature for a person of superior status voluntarily washing the feet of someone of inferior status. Jesus' act therefore represents an assault on the usual notions of social hierarchy, a subversion of the normal categories of honour and shame. But for readers the narrator's opening characterization of Jesus makes it even more than this. It is not just an honoured teacher who is performing a shameful act but a divine figure with sovereignty over the cosmos who has taken on the role of a slave. In this way the footwashing becomes a dramatic enactment of the Christology of the hymn in Phil. 2.6–11, which speaks of one 'who, though he was in the form of God, did not regard equality with God as something to be exploited, but emptied himself, taking the form of a slave'.

6–7 In terms of the story's plausibility it is somewhat surprising that Jesus' action provokes no response until he comes to Peter or that Peter only registers his protest at this point. But for the sake of the story's impact the drawing out of its significance needs to be focused in the particular exchange with Peter as the representative disciple. Peter's questioning of whether Jesus will do this task for him draws attention to the obvious incongruity and scandal of such an act with its juxtaposition of **Lord** and **wash my feet**. Jesus responds to Peter's initial reluctance by acknowledging that what he is doing may be incomprehensible now **but after these things you will understand**. Exactly what Peter will understand is somewhat dependent on the interpretation of vv. 8 and 10. When he will understand emerges in stages in the Gospel's narrative world. There is the possibility of some enlightenment through the explanation that immediately follows, but the appropriateness of Jesus' act and its significance as service that leads to death will only be fully comprehensible after Jesus' hour of death and glorification (cf. also 2.22; 12.16). Its application to Peter himself becomes more pointed after his rehabilitation and the prediction of his death as glorifying God in 21.15–19.

8 But Peter at this point hardens in his resistance to Jesus' servant role and delivers an emphatic negative retort – **You will never wash my feet.** Since the footwashing has already been seen to have links with Jesus' death, Peter's attitude can be viewed as the Johannine equivalent of his rebuking Jesus for teaching about the Son of Man's suffering and death in Mark 8.32. There Jesus issued his own rebuke – 'Get behind me, Satan! For you are setting your mind not on divine things but on human things' (Mark 8.33). Here in reply, Jesus also raises the stakes – **Unless I wash you, you have no participation with me.** Clearly submission to this footwashing is of far more importance than Peter has realized. But what is this importance? The term μέρος, translated here as 'participation', has the force in similar contexts elsewhere of lot, share, inheritance, with particular reference to a person's eschatological destiny (cf. Matt. 24.51; Luke 11.36; Rev. 20.6; 21.8; 22.19; Ignatius, *Pol.* 6.1; *Mart. Pol.* 14.2). Here, then, its reference is to the share in or solidarity with Jesus that enables one to share his destiny. Some scholars, having noted the relation of the footwashing to Jesus' death, conclude that the point is the soteriological one that it is necessary to accept Jesus' death in order to obtain eternal life. But this does not fit either the situation of the disciples in the narrative or the sense of the longer reading of v. 10. If one uses the category of soteriology here, it is important not to define it too narrowly. After all, the disciples have already been described as Jesus' own at the beginning of this episode, and throughout the narrative to this point, in contrast to the response of others, they are said to have believed in Jesus (cf. esp. 6.67–9). Their lack of perception at various stages and the need for the completion of their understanding after Jesus' death and resurrection do not alter the fact that they have already cast their lot with Jesus. The farewell section as a whole is meant to prepare them for continued solidarity with Jesus in their future mission that will lead to being with him in glory (cf. 14.3; 17.24). In this opening episode Jesus is telling Peter that, unless he accepts the footwashing with its transformation of ordinary categories of judgement, there can be no lasting fellowship with Jesus, because both an understanding of Jesus' death and the ability to continue Jesus' cause in a mission of loving service depend on appropriating the new set of values enacted in the footwashing. The requirement to have one's feet washed in order to participate with Jesus is the equivalent to the call to continue in Jesus' word (8.31–2), to keep Jesus' word (8.51) or to abide in him (15.4).

9–11 Peter, now at least recognizing that the washing of his feet by Jesus is important, demands that the other exposed parts of his body – **my hands and my head** – also be washed. But this is again to misunderstand Jesus' action. Jesus explains, **The one who has been bathed has no need to be washed, except for the feet, but is entirely clean. And you are clean, though not every one of you.** This saying has been the source of much confusion and many interpretations. To begin with, there are basic issues of text and translation. Reasons have already been given in the textual note for preferring to work with the more strongly attested longer reading. The chief objection raised against it is that it makes the footwashing, which v. 8 has shown to have such importance, subordinate to and indeed trivial in comparison with a prior bathing. But if the footwashing has the undoubted importance of being necessary for continued fellowship with Jesus, this by no means places it in competition with a bathing that has initiated that fellowship. Both are indispensable for a relationship with Jesus that is to reach eschatological completion. The footwashing points to the death of Jesus but to a particular aspect of that death – its embodiment of the pattern of glory through humiliation. It does not have to represent everything that can be attributed to the significance of Jesus' death. The matter of translation is complicated by two factors. First, should the two verbs λούω ('bathe') and νίπτω ('wash') be treated as synonyms or do they have distinctive force? Those who prefer the shorter reading and who see the footwashing itself as making clean generally opt for the two verbs having the same force, with the former having been introduced for stylistic variation. Yet until this point the verb used for the footwashing has consistently been νίπτω, as it will be also in vv. 12, 14. It would be very strange to introduce another verb here if the same action is in view. More importantly, λούω ('bathe') is not used elsewhere in Greek literature for footwashing, while νίπτω ('wash') always refers to the washing of part of the body. In addition, where the two verbs are found in the same context the distinction is maintained. A complete bath (λούω) is followed by partial washings (νίπτω) (cf. Exod. 29.4 and 30.17–21 LXX; *T. Levi* 9.11). It should be clear, then, that the first verb of washing in Jesus' assertion refers to something different from the second one and this has been signalled by translating it as 'to bathe'. As opposed to the washing of feet, this bathing makes the whole person clean. The second factor relates to the voice of the verbs. They can both be commonly used in the middle voice, where they refer to the subject's action in regard to himself or herself, whether directly or indirectly. This is how most have translated them here – 'the one who has bathed has no need to wash . . .' But the form of the middle is indistinguishable from that of the passive, and it makes more sense here to take these verbs as passive. The dialogue with Peter has not been about what the disciple does for himself but what Jesus does to him. In his response Jesus does not shift the focus to his disciples' own actions. Both the bathing and the washing continue to be actions of which the disciples are the objects and so the translation here opts for the passive.

The distinction between bathing and washing makes sense against the background both of ritual purification and of ordinary life where, in each case, a complete bath would still be supplemented by a partial washing, that of the feet. Jesus reinforces this point by his assertion that the person who has been bathed is entirely clean, a description not appropriate for someone who has only had the feet washed. He makes clear, however, that the description applies to the disciples as a group – 'you [plural] are clean, though not every one of you'. The discussion so far rules out the common interpretation that the footwashing as a symbol of Jesus' death makes the disciples clean. It may be true that elsewhere in early Christian thought the death of Jesus can be said to make believers clean by removing their sin, but if that thought is read into the narrative here, it renders the situation of the disciples, who are already Jesus' 'own', incoherent. What then has made the disciples clean before the footwashing? Some have suggested that their baptism has made them clean. But the Fourth Gospel makes nothing of this as an element in the disciples' belief (despite 3.22; 4.1–2), and in any case the only baptism that it is clear some of them are likely to have undergone earlier is baptism by John. The stress is instead on the disciples' having already believed and the object of their belief to this point is Jesus and his deeds and words. This has made them clean. Jesus' teaching later in the farewell section establishes that this is indeed the case – 'You have already been cleansed by the word that I have spoken to you' (15.3). He immediately goes on to say that, although they have been cleansed, what is now necessary is to abide in him (15.4).

As was made clear in the discussion of v. 8, what is signified by the footwashing is necessary for abiding in Jesus. The questions surrounding the prior cleansing should not be allowed to obscure the fact that Jesus' saying is meant to draw Peter's attention back to the washing of the feet. If Peter wants other parts or the whole body washed, that has already been accomplished. What is required is that, recognizing the scandalous reversal of values it entails, he nevertheless submits to having his feet washed – otherwise he will not be in a position to carry out the form of discipleship Jesus will require in vv. 14–17. All this suggests, and Jesus' subsequent explanation of the act confirms, that, however natural such an interpretation might appear, the main point of the footwashing is not cleansing, whether of sins in general or post-baptismal sins, but lies in the juxtaposition of the identity and status of the one who performs the act and the slave-like nature of the act. Once this main point has been grasped, it remains true on a secondary level, of course, that disciples who falter in accepting and living out the reversal of values Jesus requires will be in need of continuing forgiveness.

With a reminder of his earlier comment in v. 2, the narrator pauses to explain the last words of Jesus' saying – **For he knew who would betray him; for this reason he said, 'Not every one of you is clean.'** Judas' initial belief in Jesus was not the sort of faith adequate for a true relationship with Jesus and so he cannot be considered to be clean, and having his feet washed will not transform the values that lead him to turn away from and betray Jesus.

12–14 After the footwashing has been completed, Jesus offers his own interpretation of his act, introduced by the rhetorical question **Do you know what I have done to you?** Many readers have puzzled over the explanation that follows and have considered that its use of the footwashing as an ethical example simply does not match the more profound soteriological or sacramental significance they have found in the earlier account itself. Some have therefore assigned vv. 6–11 and vv. 12–20 to two different sources as quite different or incompatible interpretations of the same event that have been awkwardly combined by the evangelist. It may well be, however, that the wrong sort of significance has been read into vv. 6–11 and that the account as it stands is not nearly so difficult as some have supposed to interpret as a coherent unit.

Jesus immediately provides an answer to his own question and vv. 13–17 drive home the same answer in a number of ways. The first formulation of the significance of the footwashing is **You call me Teacher and Lord, and you speak rightly, for I am. So if I, the Lord and Teacher, have washed your feet, you also ought to wash one another's feet.** Jesus has been called 'Teacher' (cf. e.g. 1.38; 3.2; 4.31; 6.25; 11.8, 28) and 'Lord' (cf. e.g. 6.68; 9.38; 11.3, 12, 27) several times, and Peter has just addressed him by the latter title (cf. vv. 6, 9). Having acknowledged the appropriateness of such titles, Jesus in his explanation highlights that the point of his action lies in the incongruity between the identity and status to which these titles point and his assumption of the servant's role. What follows from his action is that, since it represents the distinctive nature of his mission and since the disciples have submitted to it, these disciples are now under an obligation to continue this conduct in relation to each other. They can have no objection to washing one another's feet, because, although it means performing the slave's task, the status reversal in their case is nowhere near as massive as in the case of Jesus.

15–17 In other words, Jesus' washing of their feet provides them with a pattern or example to be emulated – **I have given you a model, so that as I have done to you, you also should do.** The formulation of the second part of this saying, with καθώς, 'as', providing a link between what applies to Jesus and what applies to disciples, is a regular feature of the Fourth Gospel. Just as Jesus lives because of the Father, so believers live because of Jesus (6.57). Just as Jesus does not belong to this world, so believers do not belong to this world (17.14, 16). Just as Jesus is one with the Father, so believers are to be one (17.11, 22). Just as the Father has sent the Son, so Jesus sends the disciples into the world (cf. 17.18; 20.21). The principle is repeated here – just as Jesus has washed the disciples' feet, so they are to wash one another's feet. Its point is authorization by analogy. As with all analogy, the concentration is on the similarity in the comparison, while recognizing that there are always significant differences. For disciples there is a mandatory repetition of the pattern of Jesus' life, but this will always be a non-identical repetition, which cannot have precisely the same significance for them as it had for him. The transformation of values enacted by Jesus in the footwashing and in the laying down of his life, to which this act points, is to distinguish the lives of his followers. The symbolic nature of Jesus' act does not mean, however, that his disciples could ignore the actual washing of another's feet. In their culture the repetition of the act continued to be a powerful demonstration of what it symbolized. There is also evidence of its continued practice in various parts of early Christianity. Washing the feet of the saints is one of the qualifications for widows to receive support from the church in 1 Tim. 5.9–10. Later writers who mention or urge the practice, primarily as a form of humble service, include Tertullian (*Cor.* 8), Chrysostom (*Hom. Jo.* 71), Ambrose (*Spir.* 1.15) and Augustine (*Tract. Ev. Jo.* 58.4; *Spir. et litt.* 55.33). But imitation of the reversal of values symbolized in Jesus' act is clearly not limited to washing the feet of another. For his disciples to treat the actual washing of feet as the only thing commanded by Jesus would be to miss the point, but for them to see that the instruction was about the overall pattern of humble service and then to neglect specific demonstrations of this in footwashings would be equally uncomprehending.

A 'double Amen' formulation introduces a saying from the stock of traditional Jesus material and reinforces the point made in v. 14 – **Truly, truly, I say to you, a servant is not greater than his master, nor is one who is sent greater than the one who sent him.** The evangelist appears to have adapted a saying which is found in Matt. 10.24 (cf. also

Luke 6.40), with reference to servant and master and disciple and teacher. The disciples are reminded of the implications of their status in relation to Jesus. If he is the master and Lord and the one who sends and he has washed feet, then those who are his servants and who are sent as his authorized representatives can do no less. But the point is not simply to have understood Jesus' explanation of the footwashing; it is, rather, to demonstrate that understanding in the way they now act toward each other – **If you know these things, blessed are you if you do them.** It is actual deeds of humble service, such as footwashing, that will make disciples the recipients of Jesus' beatitude.

18–19 Again Jesus has to qualify his reference to 'you' (cf. vv. 10b–11). Not all of his followers will be in a position to receive his future blessing. Despite Jesus' choice of his followers – **I know those whom I have chosen** (cf. also 6.70) – he also knows that one of them will betray him. Yet this does not undermine his or his Father's sovereignty. To indicate that even the betrayal can be seen as part of God's purposes, it is said to be a fulfilment of Scripture – **in order that the Scripture might be fulfilled, 'The one who eats my bread has raised his heel against me.'** The reference is to Ps. 41.9, a psalm in which the righteous sufferer describes the actions of his enemies and then asserts that even his bosom friend has betrayed him, describing the treachery in the words quoted here. The more intimate the relationship – breaking bread with someone as a table companion – the crueller the breach of trust. In Mark 14.18 Jesus at the Passover meal speaks of his betrayer as 'the one who eats with me' in language taken from Ps. 41.9 and this may have been the spur for the evangelist here to adapt other language from that verse. Instead of the verb for 'to eat' in Ps. 40.10 LXX and in Mark 14.18, John substitutes the synonym (τρώγω) he consistently used earlier in the bread of life discourse (cf. 6.54, 56–8). Significantly, in that discourse to eat the bread Jesus gives is to eat Jesus, that is, to believe on him, and Judas is mentioned for the first time immediately after this in 6.70–1. It may well be, then, that the reference of 'eats my bread' in this Johannine context is not only to the present supper but to Judas' having initially believed but now turning out to be a defector. The raising of the heel also resonates with the present context of the footwashing. One who has had his feet washed by Jesus in what was meant to be a sign of continued fellowship is now said to raise the heel of his foot against Jesus in contempt of the invitation to fellowship. It is likely that raising and showing the heel in Mediterranean culture was an act of insult and that it was done with one's back turned. To turn one's back on someone was itself an insult but then to raise the heel as well would be to intensify the insult. In this way the scriptural reference serves not only to set Judas' betrayal of Jesus within God's plan but also to depict graphically its heinous nature.

The prediction of the betrayal has a further function: its fulfilment will confirm both the reliability of Jesus' words and his identity – **I am speaking to you now before it occurs, so that, when it occurs, you may believe that I am.** The correspondence between Jesus' predictions and their fulfilment is noted throughout the narrative (cf. e.g. 2.19, 22; 6.70–1; 12.32–3). A similar demonstrable correspondence between Yahweh's predictive word and what had taken place in history was essential to the presentation of Yahweh's claim to be the one true God, the 'I Am', in Isa. 40—55 (cf. esp. Isa. 45.18–22 LXX) and to Israel believing 'that I Am' (cf. Isa. 43.9–10 LXX). Here the fulfilment of Jesus' prediction will be what enables the disciples to believe that he is one with God as 'I Am' (ἐγώ εἰμι). Significantly, at the point at which the fulfilment will take place (18.2–3), Jesus also reveals himself as 'I Am' (18.6, 8) and his audience fall to the ground in the reaction that would be expected to a theophany.

20 Jesus' explanation is rounded off with another double Amen saying, which appears to be loosely attached to what has preceded it – **Truly, truly, I say to you, whoever receives anyone I send receives me, and whoever receives me receives the one who sent me.** Again such a saying has parallels in the tradition. This one appears to be a Johannine adaptation of Matt. 10.40 (cf. also Luke 10.16 and Mark 9.37 parr.). Some have seen its presence here as disrupting the flow of the passage and evidence of awkward redaction. Others have attempted to tie the saying to the previous mention of Judas so that, despite himself, he is to be seen as acting as Jesus' messenger and therefore as playing a role in the divine mission, of which the betrayal is a part. But this is by no means an obvious interpretation, and it is better to see the saying's reference as a return to the notion of the disciples' mission (cf. v. 16). The link is likely to be through the preceding mention of the disciples' belief in Jesus as 'I Am'. Just as this belief about Yahweh had qualified Israel before them to be servant-witnesses (cf. Isa. 43.10–12), so now it qualifies the disciples for their mission as witnesses to Jesus. The saying reflects the notion of the agency of an authorized representative, so that the disciples, on their mission as the accredited agents of Jesus, represent Jesus himself and all that he stands for, just as Jesus fully represents the Father who sent him. The upshot is that a response to the disciples' mission amounts to a response to both Jesus and God. The same principle will underlie the commissioning of the disciples by the risen Jesus in 20.21. What its present context – in the explanation of the footwashing – adds to the saying is that the disciples represent the one who has taken on the role of the slave and so, if their reception is to be a reception of him, their mission will necessarily be characterized by the same humble service.

The footwashing incident is unique to the Fourth Gospel. On the one hand, it is completely compatible with the reversal of values reflected in the kingdom teaching and some of the activities of Jesus for which there is better attestation, yet, on the other, if Jesus actually washed the disciples' feet, it is strange that it is not mentioned elsewhere as a decisive feature in teaching about the nature of discipleship in the midst of discussions about greatness. It is also strange that, if Jesus commanded the disciples to wash one another's feet, this is not mentioned independently elsewhere in early Christianity. As noted earlier, 1 Tim. 5.10 does mention the practice but only as an act of hospitality that widows are to perform if they are to receive assistance from the church. A good case can be made that the account is a further instance of the fourth evangelist's creative use of Synoptic, and especially Lukan, material, in which he has dramatized Jesus' teaching. Mark 10.35–45 (cf. Matt. 20.20–8) has the dispute among the disciples about who would be greatest, provoked by the request of James and John for seats on either side of Jesus in his future glory. Jesus focuses attention instead on their solidarity with him in his sufferings by speaking about their sharing his cup and his baptism. He goes on to say, 'Whoever would be great among you must be your servant, and whoever wishes to be first among you must be slave of all. For the Son of Man came not to be served but to serve, and to give his life a ransom for many.' With the exception of the notion of ransom, all the main themes of this passage are replayed in the footwashing. But what is most interesting is that the Lukan parallel has placed this material in the account of the Last Supper, where it is part of a more extended farewell conversation than in Mark or Matthew, preparing the disciples for the future (cf. Luke 22.14–38). What is more, immediately after Jesus announces that he will be betrayed, Luke explicitly formulates Mark's discussion of greatness in terms of serving at table – 'For who is greater, the one who is at the table or the one who serves? Is it not the one at the table? But I am among you as one who serves' (22.27; cf. also 12.37). John, of course, has an even more expanded farewell section than Luke, but his expansion may well have been on the basis of Luke and have included his own version of Jesus' transformation of values, in which he has Jesus act out this service of those at table and draws again (cf. 12.1–8) on the earlier incident in Luke 7.36–50, where Jesus was the object of a footwashing performed out of love and devotion. Now the roles are reversed, as Jesus out of love for his followers washes their feet, points forward to his death, exemplifies the reversal of traditional values about honour and status, and both shows and teaches that this reversal is necessary for those who are to maintain solidarity with him in his mission.

This description of the account takes its two parts together. There is no need to play off its Christological or soteriological first half against its exemplary second half. Phil. 2.5–11 provides a prime instance of Paul combining the Christological and the ethical, as he employs the pattern of Christ's life in an appeal to those who are in Christ to display the same attitude. The notion of the imitation of the pattern of Christ's life is not foreign to the Fourth Gospel. On numerous occasions the formulation 'just as . . ., so . . .' indicates that what is the case with Jesus is also to be the case with his disciples. In 12.24–5, a saying that has reference to Jesus' death is followed by one about disciples in such a way as to make Jesus the paradigm for what is said about discipleship. Later, in 15.13–14, Jesus himself will be the chief example of the sort of love he asks from his disciples, that which is prepared to lay down one's life for one's friends. The footwashing episode anticipates this passage. Jesus' motivation is love for his own group of followers, and the footwashing and its accompanying stripping down to the garb of a slave foreshadows Jesus' death. The one who has sovereign authority and a divine origin and destiny (v. 3), the one who is presented elsewhere as Israel's king (cf. 1.49; 18.33–7; 19.19–22), in unprecedented fashion performs the task of a slave. The turning upside down of usual assessments of honour and power embodied in this act is precisely what is also entailed in Jesus' acceptance of the shame of the cross being seen as his hour of glory. If Jesus' followers are to continue in their discipleship, the offence taken by Peter at this totally different value system has to be overcome and instead acceptance of it seen as indispensable. Hence acceptance of the footwashing is not identified with the cleansing, forgiveness and receipt of eternal life effected by Jesus' death but is nevertheless said to be absolutely necessary for having a share in Jesus' destiny, which will involve solidarity in his suffering and death. Despite Peter's protest at the scandal of Jesus taking the way of humiliation and the cross, that way is to provide the script for the lives of his followers. Their appropriation of Jesus' alternative set of values will be demonstrated as disciples wash one another's feet, symbolizing the humble service that will also include the readiness to die for the other (cf. 15.13). Thus Jesus' loving service, with its invitation to participation with him, serves as the transformative basis that enables disciples to obey the command to act in the same way toward each other. This will not be a service that perpetuates the structures of domination or subtly manipulates others in meeting their needs but a freely chosen action that genuinely has the interests of others in view. The command for disciples to wash the feet of other believers has been carried out as a rite in various parts of the church and with differing understandings of its meaning. It can still have some symbolic impact. But, given that the washing of another's feet no longer has the same original significance in the daily life of most present cultures, those who engage in the most menial and disparaged acts of service in their own time and place, motivated by the radical love for others that is prepared to risk life, are the ones who have caught the force of the Johannine Jesus' command and are the recipients of his beatitude.

(ii) Jesus' prediction of his betrayal   *13.21–30*

(21) After saying these things, Jesus was troubled in spirit and testified, saying, 'Truly, truly, I say to you, one of you will betray me.' (22) The disciples looked at each other, at a loss about whom he was speaking. (23) One of his disciples, the one whom he loved, was reclining in Jesus' lap. (24) Simon Peter, therefore, signalled to this disciple to enquire who it might be that he was speaking about. (25) So leaning back against Jesus' chest, he said to him, 'Lord, who is it?' (26) Jesus answered, 'It is the one for whom I shall dip the piece of bread in the dish and give it to him.' So having dipped the piece of bread, he took it and gave it to Judas, son of Simon Iscariot. (27) Then, after (he had received) the piece of bread, Satan entered into him. Jesus, therefore, said to him, 'What you are going to do, do quickly.' (28) Now no one reclining at the supper knew why he said this to him. (29) Some were thinking that, since Judas kept the money-box, Jesus said to him, 'Buy what we need for the festival' or that he should give something to the poor. (30) So, having received the piece of bread, he immediately went out. And it was night.

The betrayal of Jesus, which has been a minor motif in the footwashing account, is now given further treatment. Readers have been aware of the identity of the betrayer from as early as 6.71, where the narrator glossed Jesus' comment that one of the twelve was a devil, and have just been reminded that it will be Judas in 13.2 (cf. also 12.4). The disciples, however, have only been given hints that there is a defector in their midst (cf. 6.70; 13.10, 18) but, unlike both Jesus and the readers, do not know who this is. Even after this further explicit announcement of betrayal and the speculation that follows, with the exception of the Beloved Disciple, they remain no wiser. The account serves primarily to give readers greater insight into Jesus' knowledge of and relationship with his betrayer and into Jesus' own role in one of the decisive events leading to his death, and to underline for them the mystery that even one who has been an intimate of Jesus may end up rejecting his offer of love.

21–2 In line with his characterization elsewhere, particularly in the Lazarus story, Jesus is portrayed as fully human in his reactions and yet also as possessing sovereign knowledge of events. Indeed, the same verb (ταράσσω) used to depict his emotional state when affected by the weeping of Mary and 'the Jews' at Lazarus' tomb (cf. also 12.27) occurs here – **Jesus was troubled in spirit**. Despite his knowledge of what will unfold, Jesus is by no means unmoved but rather is extremely agitated at the prospect and at Judas' intended desertion. The solemnity of his announcement is indicated through its introduction both by the verb **testified** and by the double Amen formulation. Again the latter element signals a saying attested in the tradition. **Truly, truly, I say to you, one of you will betray me** is found in exactly the same words (apart from the single Amen introduction) in Mark 14.18 and Matt. 26.21. The verb employed (παραδίδωμι) means 'to hand over or deliver' and also served as a technical term for handing over someone into custody. Whatever its force elsewhere, the Johannine context clearly indicates that this will not be a neutral act but is to be seen as a betrayal on the part of Judas. Again the force is that this event will not catch Jesus unawares, and his prediction of it allows the fulfilment of his witness to take place within the narrative so that its reliability is demonstrated. At this stage, however, the disciples are **at a loss about whom he was speaking**.

23–5 The account would proceed smoothly if taken up again in v. 26b. But the evangelist introduces his own distinctive elements into the tradition with the mention of the Beloved Disciple and his privileged knowledge, and this produces tensions with, if not contradiction of, the later statement in v. 28. This is the first time that one of Jesus' accompanying group of disciples is singled out as **the one whom he loved**. It is true that in 11.3, 5 Lazarus is depicted as one whom Jesus loves, but, apart from other problems with identifying Lazarus with the Beloved Disciple, it would be extremely strange that the narrator goes to great lengths to preserve this disciple's anonymity after he has already been named. Several of the features that will characterize the Beloved Disciple's role in other passages are evident in these verses. His designation as the one whom Jesus loved means that when his authorship role is revealed in 21.24 readers will trust his insight and witness. This privileged relation to Jesus is underlined by the position he occupies at the supper – **reclining in Jesus' lap**. Leaning back on the couch surrounding the table, his head would rest on Jesus' chest (v. 25). The term κόλπος (bosom, chest, lap) is found in only one other place in the narrative – in 1.18, where it is part of the depiction of Jesus' relationship to the Father. This suggests that the intimacy enjoyed by Jesus in relation to God is paralleled by the intimacy the Beloved Disciple has in relation to Jesus. Here, as in a number of future appearances, the Beloved Disciple is shown in another relationship – one with Peter, in which there is usually a suggestion of comparison, if not rivalry, and the Beloved Disciple is consistently depicted as having greater perception than Peter. In this episode Peter has to go through the Beloved Disciple – he **signalled to this disciple** – in his attempt to discover who was intended by Jesus' announcement. But what is strange is that, when the Beloved Disciple is let in on the identity of the betrayer, his knowledge does not affect the action, just as it does not in his depiction in 19.35 and 20.8. He does not tell Peter and does not, of course, do anything to dissuade Judas from his course of action. He is both inside and outside the story line at the same time. The statement of v. 28, that no one knew why Jesus had said what he said to Judas, takes no account of the exchange between Jesus and the Beloved Disciple. His role appears to be for the sake of the reader more than for the sake of the plot. These observations support the view that this figure was likely to have been a real person with a leading role in the evangelist's community (cf. 21.23) but idealized and then read back into the story as a literary device. He represents post-resurrection Johannine insights back among the pre-resurrection disciples and thereby serves to legitimate the evangelist's perspective. Here he serves as key witness to the significance of the first of a number of decisive moments in the last part of Jesus' life (cf. also 19.35; 20.8; 21.7). He provides additional literary confirmation for the view that Jesus knew of and was in control of even his betrayal, the human event necessary for the outworking of his 'hour'.

26–7 The betrayer will be **the one for whom I shall dip the piece of bread in the dish and give it to him**. Dipping a piece of bread in a sauce and handing it to another in the meal would have been a sign of intimacy and friendship. Here the piece of bread is offered to Judas and accepted. Its acceptance without any intention to change his course of action underlines the extent of Judas' disloyalty and in the context of the cosmic battle that is being played out can be seen as the point at which **Satan entered into him**. This is the only place in John's narrative that the power of evil is called Satan. The same language is used about Judas, however, in Luke 22.3, although it refers to the deal he makes with the authorities before the final meal. Here in John readers have been told in 13.2 that the devil was operative in planting the intention to betray. Now that it is clear that the intention has become a settled one, Judas can be depicted as having been taken over by Satan. There are no exorcisms in this Gospel, but there is still a conflict between Jesus and Satan taking place through the responses of people to Jesus. Jesus' words to Judas – **What you are going to do, do quickly** – indicate that he remains in control. He takes the initiative in instructing Judas to proceed rapidly with his liaising with the hostile authorities, to whom he intends to deliver up Jesus (cf. 18.3).

28–9 Despite Jesus' words to Judas, the disciples are oblivious to their import, both in regard to Judas's identity as the betrayer and to the momentous event that has been set in motion: **Now no one reclining at the supper knew why he said this to him**. The narrator's comment, as has been noted, takes no account of the role of the Beloved Disciple. His knowledge of what is happening is ignored, and the disciples are portrayed as hazarding guesses at what Judas has been instructed to do. Both suggestions – buying goods for the festival and donating to the poor – arise from the distinctive Johannine characterization of Judas as in charge of the group's money (cf. 12.6). The former reinforces the observation already made that the narrator does not envisage this meal as the Passover meal. There is no need to dwell on the plausibility of these suggestions for activities at night on the day before Passover. The point of mentioning them is simply to illustrate graphically the gap between Jesus' awareness and his followers' incomprehension of what is taking place.

30 So, having received the piece of bread, he immediately went out. Ironically, even in his act of betrayal, Judas does what Jesus has told him to do. The 'quickly' of the command is matched by the 'immediately' of its execution. **And it was night** serves as a fitting concluding comment on the significance of Judas' action. His walking out into the night is a graphic portrayal of the state of affairs in which 'the light has come into the world, and people loved darkness rather than light because their deeds were evil' (3.19).

The Synoptic Gospels have much briefer accounts of Jesus predicting his betrayal. Mark 14.18–21 and Matt. 26.21–5 are placed before Jesus' eucharistic words at the supper, while Luke 22.21–3 is situated after them. A hypothetical pre-Synoptic source that the Synoptics and John have drawn on independently can be postulated, but it makes just as much sense of the evidence to see John expanding for his own purposes on material that was known to him from the Synoptics themselves. As has been pointed out, the words of the actual announcement in v. 21 are the same as in Mark 14.18 and Matt. 26.21 and the depiction of Satan entering Judas is the same as in earlier material in Luke 22.3. In depicting the responses of the disciples to Jesus' prediction, the Fourth Gospel again has elements from Mark and its parallel in Matthew and from the more distinctive Lukan version. The former has individual disciples asking Jesus whether they are meant, while the latter has them questioning each other. John begins with their focusing on one another (v. 22) before introducing his distinctive Beloved Disciple, who conveys Peter's question to Jesus (vv. 23–5). Jesus' reply to the questioning in Mark 14.20 sheds no further light in stating that the betrayer is one who is dipping with Jesus into the dish. Among the Synoptics only Matthew adds an exchange in which Jesus replies in the affirmative to Judas' direct question, indicating that Jesus himself knows which of the twelve the betrayer is (cf. Matt. 26.25). John creatively combines these features by having Jesus demonstrate his knowledge that the betrayer is Judas through the offer of the piece of bread that he has dipped in the dish.

The Fourth Gospel, then, heightens the apologetic element in its version of the betrayal. How could Jesus have been betrayed by one of his inner circle and how could such an act have been committed by one whom Jesus had chosen? There is no fully satisfactory human explanation, but at least it can be claimed that Jesus not only knew he was going to be betrayed but knew the identity of the betrayer. What is more, even this event was part of the divine plan according to which Jesus was operating. He remains in sovereign control of his destiny because, knowing what has to happen, he takes the initiative and commands Judas to carry out his act. The betrayal can also be depicted in terms of other forces that are at work behind the scenes. In the battle between good and evil, light and darkness, Judas has unwittingly become an instrument of Satan and in going off into the night joins the powers of darkness. In this Gospel, pointing to the cosmic dimension of events, whether to the divine initiative or to Satanic influence, is never a means of diminishing human responsibility. Both the response of faith and that of rejecting Jesus' invitation to discipleship are decisions for which people remain accountable. But this account has a further distinctive feature. Juxtaposed with the defecting disciple is the Beloved Disciple. The latter is the only one who shares Jesus' knowledge in this scene. Just as Jesus' intimate relationship with the Father enables him to make God known (1.18), so this disciple's intimate relationship with Jesus throughout the climactic events of his ministry prepares him to be the witness who makes known the true significance of Jesus (cf. 21.24).

(iii) Jesus' farewell discourse (part one)   *13.31—14.31*

(31) When he had gone out, Jesus said, 'Now the Son of Man has been glorified and God has been glorified in him. (32) If God has been glorified in him,[1] God will also glorify him in himself and will glorify him immediately. (33) Little children, I am with you only a little longer. You will seek me, and, as I said to the Jews, "Where I am going you cannot come," so now I say it to you. (34) I give you a new commandment, that you love one another. As I have loved you, so you also should love one another. (35) By this all will know that you are my disciples, if you have love for one another.'

(36) Simon Peter said to him, 'Lord, where are you going?'

---

[1] This opening subordinate clause is not found in p⁶⁶ ℵ* B C* D L W itᵃ,ᵇ,ᶜ,ᵈ syrˢ,ʰ. Since this makes it both the shorter and the better-attested reading, there would need to be weighty factors for considering the longer reading attested by ℵᶜ A C² K Δ Θ Ψ itᵉ,ᶠ vg syrᵖ,ᵖᵃˡ copˢᵃ goth arm Diatessaron. Two such factors exist. It is extremely difficult to find any reason for the addition of this virtually redundant clause, which is, in any case, characteristic of Johannine style (cf. e.g. 14.3, 7). Accidental dittography is ruled out by the inclusion of εἰ, 'if', at the beginning. On the other hand, there is an obvious explanation for its accidental omission by an early scribe, namely, homoeoteleuton. The repetition of five Greek words would make it easy for the eye to skip from the first αὐτῷ to the καί which follows the second one. The longer reading, therefore, has a good possibility of being the earlier.

Jesus answered, 'Where I am going you cannot follow me now, but you will follow later.' (37) Peter said to him, 'Lord, why can I not follow you now? I will lay down my life for you.' (38) Jesus answered, 'Will you lay down your life for me? Truly, truly, I say to you, the cock will not crow before you deny me three times.

(14.1) 'Do not let your hearts be troubled. You believe in God; believe also in me. (2) In my Father's house there are many dwelling places. If there were not, would I have told you that I go to prepare a place for you? (3) And if I go and prepare a place for you, I will come again and will take you to myself, so that where I am you also may be. (4) And you know the way to where I am going.'[2] (5) Thomas said to him, 'Lord, we do not know where you are going. How can we know the way?' (6) Jesus said to him, 'I am the way and the truth and the life. No one comes to the Father except by me. (7) If you have known me, you will know my Father also. From now on you do know him and have seen him.' (8) Philip said to him, 'Lord, show us the Father and it will suffice us.' (9) Jesus said to him, 'Have I been with you for so long a time and you do not know me, Philip? The one who has seen me has seen the Father. How can you say, "Show us the Father"? (10) Do you not believe that I am in the Father and the Father is in me? The words that I speak to you I do not speak of my own accord. The Father who dwells in me does his works. (11) Believe me that I am in the Father and the Father is in me. If not, believe because of the works themselves. (12) Truly, truly, I say to you, the one who believes in me will also do the works that I do and will do greater ones than these, because I am going to the Father. (13) And whatever you ask in my name I will do, so that the Father may be glorified in the Son. (14) If you ask me[3] for anything in my name, I will do it.

(15) 'If you love me, you will keep my commandments. (16) And I will ask the Father, and he will give you another Advocate to be with you for ever, (17) the Spirit of truth, whom the world

---

[2] This translation represents the shorter reading, lit. 'And where I am going you know the way,' which is found in p⁶⁶ᶜ ℵ B C* L W itᵃ copᵇᵒ eth. The longer variant here – 'And where I am going you know and the way you know' – is syntactically and stylistically smoother, but for that reason less likely to be original. There would be no cause for a scribe to make a change from the longer to the shorter reading.

[3] The best attested reading includes με, 'me', and is found in p⁶⁶ ℵ B W Δ Θ itᶜ·ᶠ vg syrᵖ·ʰ goth. Some witnesses (including A D K L itᵃ·ᵃᵘʳ·ᵈ copˢᵃ·ᵇᵒ) do not have it and two (249 397) have τὸν πατέρα, 'the Father', instead. The evidence is best explained by some copyists wishing to avoid a contradiction with what will be said in 16.23 or to smooth out what is perceived as an awkward syntactical construction containing two forms of the first person pronoun.

cannot receive because it neither sees nor knows him. You know him because he remains with you and will be[4] in you. (18) I will not leave you orphans; I will come to you. (19) In a little while the world will no longer see me, but you will see me, because I live and you will live. (20) On that day you will know that I am in my Father and you are in me and I in you. (21) The one who has my commandments and keeps them is the one who loves me. The one who loves me will be loved by my Father, and I will love and reveal myself to that person.' (22) Judas, not Iscariot, said to him, 'Lord, what has happened, that you will reveal yourself to us and not to the world?' (23) Jesus answered and said to him, 'If anyone loves me, that person will keep my word, and my Father will love him, and we will come to him and make our dwelling with him. (24) The one who does not love me does not keep my words; and the word that you hear is not mine but that of the Father who sent me.

(25) 'I have said these things to you while I remain with you. (26) But the Advocate, the Holy Spirit, whom the Father will send in my name, will teach you all things and remind you of all that I said to you. (27) Peace I leave with you; my peace I give you. I give to you not as the world gives. Do not let your hearts be troubled or afraid. (28) You heard me say to you, "I am going away and I am coming to you." If you loved me, you would rejoice that I am going to the Father, because the Father is greater than I. (29) And I have told you this now before it occurs, so that when it occurs you may believe. (30) I will no longer speak much with you, for the ruler of the world is coming. He has no hold on me, (31) but the world must know that I love the Father and that I do just as the Father has commanded me. Rise, let us go from here.'

In approaching the first part of the more extended farewell discourse material, some preliminary comments, which apply to both parts and to the prayer of chapter 17, are appropriate. With the departure of Judas, Jesus can address the remaining disciples about the future. At this point the evangelist employs the conventional literary device of a farewell speech, by means of

---

[4] Some witnesses have the present tense at this point, including B D★ W it[a,b,c,d] syr[c,p,pal] goth, while others have the future, including p[66,75vid] ℵ A L Δ Θ Π Ψ syr[s,h] cop[bo]. It could be argued that a copyist changed the present to the future to adjust the thought to the perceived time perspective of the disciples in the narrative, for whom the Spirit's indwelling would still be future (cf. also 7.39). Slightly more likely is that the original contained two temporal perspectives – 'remains' (post-resurrection) and 'will be' (pre-resurrection) and that a scribe smoothed out a perceived awkwardness and gave both verbs the same tense.

which a narrative's central character, usually in the face of imminent death, becomes the vehicle for imparting some of its implied author's dominant concerns. Other examples of this form in the Bible include Gen. 49 with Jacob's last words to his sons, Deut. 33 with Moses' final blessing (although the whole of Deuteronomy can be seen as his farewell address), Josh. 23—4 with Joshua's final words, 1 Chron. 28—9 with David's last instructions, Acts 20 with Paul's speech to the Ephesian elders, and 2 Peter, which has the form of Peter's last will and testament. Second temple Jewish literature provides further examples of the genre in 1 Macc. 2.49–70; *2 Bar.* 31–4; 44–7; *2 Enoch* 57–66 and various passages in *Jubilees* and *The Testaments of the Twelve Patriarchs*. Graeco-Roman examples include Plato, *Phaedo* (with Socrates' farewell speech), Xenophon, *Cyropaedia* 8.7.6–28; Dio Chrysostom, *Oration* 30. The content of these farewell addresses is given added force and emotional impact as readers are made to imagine what a particular figure, knowing he was facing death, would have wanted to say most urgently to a later generation who regarded him as an authority and needed continued leadership. Among the typical features of such speeches in ancient literature were the announcement of departure to a gathering of family or friends, words of consolation, predictions or promises about the future, blessings on those who remain, the appointing of a successor, final exhortations and instructions about future conduct, and a prayer. All these, of course, are found in one form or another in John 13.31—17.26.

In John's farewell discourse Jesus instructs about his going away and his coming back and prepares the disciples both for these events and for the time after he has gone away. In the Synoptic Gospels there are two places in which Jesus provides similar teaching before he leaves. The first is in his apocalyptic discourse (Mark 13.1–37 parr.) and the second is at the Last Supper and immediately after the supper on the way out (Mark 14.17–31 parr.). On the latter occasion Jesus talks of the Son of Man going away (cf. Mark 14.21; Matt. 26.24; Luke 22.22) and on the former of the Son of Man coming (cf. Mark 13.26; Matt. 24.30; Luke 21.27). Matthew extends this emphasis on a future coming. He prefaces the whole discourse with the disciples' question, 'What will be the sign of your coming?' (24.3), so that all of it is to be seen as an answer to this question, and adds to the Markan account other references to the coming of the Son of Man or of 'your Lord' (cf. 24.27, 37, 39, 42, 44). John creatively brings together the two issues of Jesus' going and coming, draws traditional material from Jesus' apocalyptic discourse into a farewell speech, and in the process reinterprets what is meant by the coming, so that it is no longer simply an event at the end of history but one which is already being experienced by Jesus' followers in the present.

Also brought into John's farewell material are Jesus' teaching on faith and prayer from Mark 11.22–4 par., taken up in John 14.12–14; 15.7, 16; 16.23–4, and his prediction of his followers' desertion and of Peter's denial from Mark

14.26–31 parr., which appear in John 13.36–8 and 16.32. In the prediction of what will happen to the disciples in their later mission there is a further drawing on Jesus' apocalyptic discourse from Mark 13.9–13 parr., which will form the basis for John's development of the same issues in 15.18—16.4a. In the Synoptic discourse the disciples are told that, because of their allegiance to Jesus, they will find themselves handed over to councils, beaten in synagogues, and standing before governors and kings to bear witness. When they are brought to trial, however, they are not to be concerned about what to say but to utter whatever is given to them at the time, because it will not be they who speak but the Holy Spirit. They will also experience betrayal and death through the opposition of family members and will be hated by all because of Jesus' name. The Johannine Jesus also predicts hatred by the world because of his name, warns about being persecuted, put out of the synagogue and killed, and promises the witness of the Spirit as Paraclete to accompany the witness of the disciples.

Again the fourth evangelist has employed Synoptic material in his own distinctive fashion. There are some signs, however, that different parts of the discourse may reflect different stages of its composition, so that the second half contains greater indications of hostile relations with the synagogue than the first, and the prayer in chapter 17 with its requests for unity may come from the period when there was the danger of false teaching and schism, a situation on which 1 John looks back.

Discussion of the traditions behind the farewell discourse should not make us lose sight of its effectiveness as a literary device which brings to the fore a major characteristic of the Gospel as a whole, namely, its functioning on two levels or its combination of two temporal perspectives. Moses' farewell discourse in Deuteronomy is, of course, set in the time of Moses, but it was written several centuries later and addresses people of that time through its appropriation of the Mosaic law for a new setting. This serves at least two rhetorical purposes. It confers Mosaic authority on the later appropriation and gains imaginative and emotional power by having its readers place themselves back with the Israelites who are on the verge of entering the promised land. Similarly, the Fourth Gospel's farewell address is a creative appropriation of Jesus' teaching for a later situation. Having Jesus himself give this teaching shortly before his death confers his authority on the evangelist's perspective. But, as the content of the discourse indicates, two other factors intensify this claim to authority. Unlike in the case of Moses and other figures who have delivered farewell addresses shortly before their deaths, Jesus is believed by writer and readers to have been raised from the dead and to be present again for his followers, so his farewell words can be heard as the words of the living and exalted Christ. What is more, in this discourse the process of interpreting and updating his teaching is explicitly attributed to the Holy Spirit, who functions as his successor in relation both to his followers and to his mission in the world. The Johannine message is thus endorsed as authoritative by the risen Christ through the Spirit. There is further persuasive force in inviting later readers to place themselves back in the situation of Jesus' disciples before his death, needing both to understand the significance of that event and to be given assurance about their own future. However, both that literary setting and the writer's and readers' own situation – well after the completion of the events still to unfold in the narrative – make their demands on the presentation. For this reason, the language and temporal perspective of Jesus' farewell shifts frequently, sometimes within the same saying, between that appropriate to the pre-resurrection setting of the earthly Jesus' address to his disciples and that appropriate to the post-resurrection situation of the exalted Christ and the readers.

The first part of the discourse as it now stands consists of three sections. (i) 13.31–8 forms its introduction, in which the theme of Jesus' departure is announced (cf. vv. 33, 36). (ii) 14.1–27 is its extended main body, dealing with both Jesus' departure and his return. It is marked off by an *inclusio*, with 'Do not let your hearts be troubled' occurring in v. 1 and again in v. 27. (iii) 14.28–31 provides the conclusion, restating the theme – 'I am going away and I am coming to you' – and the appropriate response to it and supplying the exit line of v. 31c. The main body of the first part of the discourse (14.1–27) itself falls into three subsections. In it vv. 1–3 give a particular statement of the theme of Jesus' departure and return (cf. vv. 2–3), vv. 4–14 then function as an interpretation of the departure (cf. vv. 4–5, 12), while vv. 15–27 function as an interpretation of Jesus' return (cf. vv. 18, 23).

31–2 Judas's exit into the night confirms that Jesus' hour has come. In contrast to Jesus' troubled announcement and the dark mood of the previous scene, a further announcement makes clear yet again that the hour is indeed one of glory: **Now the Son of Man has been glorified and God has been glorified in him. If God has been glorified in him, God will also glorify him in himself and will glorify him immediately.** As has been noted earlier, 'Son of Man' is the title or self-designation for Jesus that has the strongest eschatological associations in this Gospel and it is explicitly linked with descent from and ascent to heaven or God. Characteristically for John, the perspective of this announcement is one of realized eschatology. The Son of Man receives glory from God in the climactic events of his mission. The 'Now' indicates that this glorification does not refer to the past aspects of that mission. Rather, the glorification that takes place through Jesus' death is formulated from two viewpoints. For the implied author that glorification has already taken place and here, as elsewhere, Jesus is made to speak from this post-resurrection vantage point. Yet, from the perspective of the narrative's unfolding plot, Jesus' death is still imminent and so the second formulation employs the future tense. Here the 'immediately' underlines that the reference is to Jesus' death rather than to some event at the end of history. Again, whereas the Synoptics speak of the Son of Man's suffering and death and his coming in glory as two separate events, John's distinctive contribution is to see the Son of Man's glory in the suffering and death.

It is also made plain again in Jesus' announcement that his reputation and honour are inseparable from those of God. God's glory is revealed in the Son of Man's glorification and Jesus in his death gains glory as he is caught up into the glory of God. It is just possible that 'in himself' (v. 32) stresses the distinct, though still inseparable, glory of Jesus in relation to God but more likely that it refers back to the subject of the clause – God. The sense, then, is that God is glorified in Jesus but also enables Jesus to be glorified in God by participating in the divine glory. From the start of the farewell discourse the disciples are being prepared for Jesus' going away by being given a totally different perspective on what his departure in death entails. Far from his crucifixion demonstrating his humiliation and disgrace, it is to be seen as the means by which the God of Israel secures Jesus' honour and in so doing identifies this God's own reputation with that of Jesus.

33 The disciples are addressed as **Little children**. This diminutive term (τεκνία) occurs only here in the narrative, although it is employed seven times in 1 John. The use of this family or kinship language underlines that the prologue's assertion in 1.12, that those who received the Logos were given authority to become children of God, is true of the disciples, and it will occur again in the farewell discourse in the notion of 14.18 that they will not be left orphaned. What follows is the announcement of Jesus' imminent departure – **I am with you only a little longer** – and its consequences for his disciples – **You will seek me, and, as I said to the Jews, 'Where I am going you cannot come,' so now I say it to you.** Jesus has in fact made such an assertion to 'the Jews' twice – in 7.32–6 and 8.21–4. It will become clear, however, that the disciples are only temporarily in the same position as 'the Jews'. After a short period of separation, they will seek him and find him, because he will come to them (cf. 14.18–19; 20.15).

34–5 The promulgation of the love commandment at this point appears to be an abrupt shift of topic, particularly since the announcement of v. 33 will be taken up in the exchange with Peter in vv. 36–8 and the narrative would flow more smoothly without these intervening verses. It may well be that they have been inserted into an earlier form of the discourse. As the text stands now, however, they introduce a theme that will be repeated in 15.12–14, 17 and their position is not totally inappropriate. In the time following Jesus' departure, his disciples may not have his physical presence with them but they have his clear instruction about how to live: **I give you a new commandment, that you love one another. As I have loved you, so you also should love one another.** The commandment is not new because it differs in content from what can be found in the Jewish Scriptures (cf. Lev. 19.18) but because it forms part of the new revelation and the new order that has come with Jesus. It is therefore grounded in his own love for his followers, which entails his death, and it is shaped by and participates in the relationship of love between Jesus and the Father. In particular, Jesus' love for his own (cf. 13.1) serves as the foundation and model for his disciples' love for one another. After Jesus' departure, the carrying out of this command will be the sign of the continuation of his cause and his mission in the world: **By this all will know that you are my disciples, if you have love for one another.** The identifying mark of the community Jesus leaves behind is to be the mutual love of its members.

36–8 In the dialogue between Peter and Jesus that now follows, Peter ignores the challenge of these instructions in order to return to what Jesus has said previously and to press the more immediate question, **Lord, where are you going?** Jesus does not answer this question directly. It will be taken up in the exchange with Thomas in 14.5–6. He focuses instead on Peter's present inability to go with him – **you cannot follow me now, but you will follow later.** Peter's response, though still uncomprehending, does at least recognize that death may be entailed – **Lord, why can I not follow you now? I will lay down my life for you.** It becomes clear at this point that this is a Johannine version of traditional Synoptic material (cf. Mark 14.29–31 parr.). In the Synoptics Peter talks about dying with Jesus and this comes after the prediction of his denials. Here in the Fourth Gospel it comes before the prediction and is formulated in more characteristically Johannine terms, as it takes up the language of laying down one's life for others, already employed by Jesus for the noble shepherd and for himself in 10.11, 17–18 and occurring again in 15.13. Ironically, then, in asserting he will lay down his life for Jesus, Peter is depicted as believing himself capable of the sort of love just depicted in v. 34, the love Jesus has for his followers. He has not understood the crucial distinction between 'now' and 'later' in Jesus' words. Not until Jesus' hour has been completed and his love demonstrated in death will Peter have the resources for living out Jesus' model (cf. 21.18–19). Not only that, but his lack of resources is about to be woefully exposed, as Jesus now tells him: **Truly, truly, I say to you, the cock will not crow before you deny me three times.** Again, the double Amen introduction signals a solemn pronouncement rooted in the tradition. The version of the prediction found in Mark 14.30 and Matt. 26.34 is introduced by a single Amen formula. Whereas Mark's prediction and its later fulfilment have the cock crowing twice, Matthew and Luke (cf. 22.34) have a single crowing in both prediction and fulfilment. John's version follows Matthew or combines Mark and Luke. In the context of the narrative as a whole the prediction and its later fulfilment (cf. 18.17, 25–7) serve to underline further the reliability of Jesus' words.

14.1 The imperatives here set the tone for the body of this first half of the discourse. Its message is to be one of reassurance – **Do not let your hearts be troubled** – but also one that demands full belief – **You believe in God; believe also in me**. The rest of the discussion will elaborate on the relation between Jesus and God in such a way as to show why having faith in God entails having faith in Jesus as the one whom God has sent.

2–4 The reassurance that now follows takes up the traditional language of Jewish and early Christian eschatology: **In my Father's house there are many dwelling places.** Despite 'my Father's house' serving as a reference to the Jerusalem temple in 2.16, there is little warrant for finding here either a reference to rooms in the heavenly temple or to the believing community as a spiritual temple. The imagery is more general and taken from apocalyptic writings about the afterlife, cf. especially *1 Enoch* 39.4–8, which speaks of 'the dwelling-places of the holy, and the resting-places of the righteous' in heaven, which was pictured as God's house. **If there were not, would I have told you that I go to prepare a place for you?** When has Jesus told them this? Some avoid this question by offering a different translation – 'If there were not, I would have told you. For I go to prepare a place for you.' But the first sentence of this rendering reads very strangely after Jesus' announcement, and the logic of the connective 'for', which begins the second sentence, is by no means clear. The first translation is to be preferred syntactically, even if it means accepting there is no clear answer to the question raised by its own question. The closest parallel earlier in the narrative is 12.26, where Jesus says that where he is, there will his servant also be, but this requires a major inference in order to find the notion of a place being prepared. An alternative is to hold that the evangelist intends a reference to a traditional saying known to his readers but not included in the narrative. In any case, this announcement now answers Peter's question from 13.36 about where Jesus is going. He is departing to be with his Father in heaven and this will be beneficial to the disciples because he will prepare places for them there. What is more, he will ensure they take up those places – **And if I go and prepare a place for you, I will come again and will take you to myself, so that where I am you also may be.** The language of Jesus coming again and taking believers to be with him is that of early Christian imminent expectation. Mark's apocalyptic discourse speaks of the Son of Man coming and gathering the elect (13.26; cf. Matt. 24.30–1) and Paul in 1 Thess. 4.15–17 awaits the coming of the Lord, which will result in believers being with the Lord for ever. The Fourth Gospel here follows the pattern of Jewish thought, in which the benefits of the age to come are reserved and guaranteed in heaven for the righteous in the present until the eschaton, and of its Christian adaptation, whereby it is the exaltation of Christ to heaven that secures such benefits until the parousia. Some scholars suggest that the eschatological perspective has already been reinterpreted in these verses so that the reference is to what happens at believers' deaths or to a spiritual relation with Christ after his exaltation. It is more likely, however, that, as with the language of resurrection of the dead and judgement in 5.24–9, traditional future eschatology and a more realized version have been juxtaposed. Here a reference to the parousia and its consequences for believers is maintained (cf. also 21.22–3), but its formulation already contains hints of the reinterpretation of the notions of Christ's coming and of his dwelling together with believers that will be developed later in this chapter. In v. 23, in particular, the same term used here, 'dwelling place' (μονή), refers no longer to a heavenly location but to a presence with believers.

In any case, the statement here serves to develop Jesus' answer to Peter in 13.36. The disciples cannot follow Jesus in his departure to heaven and the Father immediately but they will follow later when Jesus returns for them at the parousia. Not unnaturally, on the basis of what he has said, Jesus adds, **And you know the way to where I am going,** presumably referring to his statement about his coming and taking the disciples with him.

5–6 At this point Thomas, rather than Peter, becomes the representative of the totally uncomprehending disciples with his assertion that they do not know where Jesus is going and so cannot know the way. This is the foil for Jesus' further explanation by means of an 'I Am' saying – **I am the way and the truth and the life. No one comes to the Father except by me.** In a first-century Jewish context this wide-ranging and exclusive claim to embody the avenue to the Father stands over against claims that would have been made for Torah. The Scriptures held that the law provided the way (cf. e.g. Pss. 86.11; 119.30) and the community at Qumran, on the basis of its observance of the law, called itself 'the Way' (cf. 1QS 8.12–16; 9.17–18; CD 1.3). Jesus' statement reiterates in different imagery that of 10.9 – 'I am the gate. Whoever enters though me will be saved . . .' – and the prologue has made a similar claim for him in contrast to the law in 1.17–18. Because of the preceding discussion in 13.36—14.4, Jesus' claim to be the way is the primary one and the claims to be the truth and the life clarify how and why he is the way. He is the way to the Father because he is the truth as the revelation of God. His mission has as its purpose to bear witness to the truth (cf. 18.37), and his life, death, resurrection and exaltation embody that truth. Jesus is the way to the Father because he is the life as the means of participating in the life of God. Again, his mission has as its purpose to bring life (cf. 10.10), and the incarnation of the Logos in whom was life (1.4) is the embodiment of that life (cf. also 11.25). That Jesus alone is the means of access to the Father was a key claim for Johannine Christians in the conflict with the synagogue, but it was one that would also have been upheld over against all rival claims in the Graeco-Roman world to mediate the divine. Its exclusivity is rooted in the claims of Jewish monotheism. In Isa. 43.11, for example, there is no Saviour other than the God who is identified as I Am, and therefore no salvation apart from this God.

7–9 The development of the thought of Jesus' unique mediation of the Father takes up themes from earlier in the narrative. **If you have known me, you will know my Father also. From now on you do know him and have seen him.** On Jesus' mediation of knowledge of the Father, see 8.19; 10.14, 15, 38; and on his mediation of the vision of the Father, see 1.18; 5.37–8; 6.46; 8.38. The first part of the declaration is similar to what has been said to Jesus' opponents; the second part places the disciples in a different and privileged position. 'From now on', from the completion of Jesus' hour, their relation to the Father will be one of authentic knowledge and sight. Philip, with his dull-witted request for what Jesus has explicitly said to be already granted, now becomes the foil for the expansion of this theme. He is rebuked for his lack of recognition of Jesus, despite the time he has spent with him, and Jesus spells out what should have been obvious – **The one who has seen me has seen the Father. How can you say, 'Show us the Father'?** This high estimate of Jesus' identity is related to another major Johannine motif – its Christological elaboration on the Jewish notion of authorized agency, whereby the one who is sent represents completely the one who sends. Since Jesus is the one whom the Father has sent, in seeing him one sees the Father.

10–11 Indeed the relationship between Jesus and the Father is such that Jesus can say, **I am in the Father and the Father is in me**, and assert as a consequence that his words are the Father's words and his works are the Father's works. These are by now familiar themes. On the mutual indwelling of Jesus and the Father, see 10.30, 38; on Jesus speaking the Father's words, see 7.16–17; 8.26–8; 12.49–50; and on Jesus doing the Father's works, see 5.17–20, 36; 9.4; 10.37–8. In fact, the exhortation to the disciples – **Believe me that I am in the Father and the Father is in me. If not, believe because of the works themselves** – is formulated in the same way as the challenge issued to Jesus' opponents in 10.38. As has been observed, in a number of places in the farewell discourse the disciples, despite their insider status, are, because of their lack of understanding, temporarily placed in the same situation as that of outsiders during the public ministry. This is not dissimilar to the depiction of the disciples in Mark, where their failure to understand earns them a rebuke couched in the same terms as were earlier employed for outsiders (Mark 8.17–21; cf. 4.11–12).

12 In the next breath, however, their belief is assumed and they are told that Jesus' departure will put them in the position of being able to continue Jesus' mission by performing the same sort of works as he has done: **Truly, truly, I say to you, the one who believes in me will also do the works that I do and will do greater ones than these, because I am going to the Father.** Both this verse and the following verses about prayer take up Synoptic material. The double Amen formulation again signals a saying from the tradition. In Mark 11.22–3 (cf. also Matt. 21.21) Jesus tells the disciples, as he has just done here, to have faith and promises in an Amen saying that this will enable them to do difficult or seemingly impossible things – 'Have faith in God. Truly I tell you, if you say to this mountain, "Be taken up and thrown into the sea," and if you do not doubt in your heart, but believe what you say will come to pass, it will be done for you.' The works promised in the Johannine version are acts, like those of Jesus, which display the character and power of God. They can be described as greater, presumably not because they are more astounding, but both because they will be done after the events of 'the hour' and are therefore able to reveal the completed story of God's dealings with the world through Jesus, and because they will extend further, making the life and judgement of God known throughout the world. In 5.20 Jesus had earlier talked of his greater works in terms of providing eschatological life and judgement, and the task to which the disciples will be commissioned in 20.23 involves pronouncing a realized judgement of either the forgiveness or the retention of sins.

13–14 Just as the Father's works are done through Jesus, so Jesus' works will be done through the disciples and this will be made possible through their prayers: **And whatever you ask in my name I will do, so that the Father may be glorified in the Son. If you ask me for anything in my name, I will do it.** This is a Johannine elaboration of the verse that follows the Markan passage just cited – 'whatever you ask for in prayer, believe that you have received it, and it will be yours' (Mark 11.24; cf. also Matt. 21.22). Similar teaching is found in Luke 11.9–10 – 'Ask, and it will given you . . . For everyone who asks receives' (cf. also Matt. 7.7–8). In contrast to the Synoptics, in the Fourth Gospel no instruction about prayer is given to the disciples during Jesus' public mission. All the teaching is clustered in the farewell discourse, underlining that this is an activity that will be especially important for disciples in the period after Jesus' departure. The repeated assertion 'I will do. . .' makes clear that it is Jesus who will be at work in the mission of his followers and the repeated phrase 'in my name' indicates that the praying that results in their works will be carried out by the disciples as the authorized representatives of Jesus. For this reason an unconditional response is linked to such prayer. It will be answered because it will represent Jesus, who is completely in line with God's will. The prayer of Jesus that will follow in chapter 17 provides a model for what it is to pray in his name. 'Whatever you ask,' then, in effect means whatever the disciples ask in line with Jesus' prayer, because this represents what he stands for and what his mission in the world entails. The continuity of believers' activity in prayer with the mission of Jesus is further seen in that the purpose of Jesus' response to such praying – 'so that the Father may be glorified in the Son' – is the same as the goal of his mission (cf. 7.18; 11.4; 12.28; 13.31–2; 17.1).

15–17 If the first section of the body of this first part of the discourse has stressed belief as the necessary response of the disciples (cf. vv. 1, 8–10), now the second section emphasizes the response of love (cf. vv. 15, 21, 23–4, 28). To love Jesus is shown to involve keeping his words or commands. Here the focus is on the latter – **If you love me, you will keep my commandments.** A response of love for Jesus will result in obedience to his commands and at the same time that obedience will be an indicator of whether genuine love is present. Talking of Jesus' farewell instructions as his commandments may well be meant to recall the Mosaic law as the summation of the divine commandments and to suggest Jesus' teaching as the new norm for disciples. The commandments immediately in view are to wash one another's feet (13.14–15) and to love one another (13.34), though the command to believe in Jesus (14.1) should not be ignored. In what follows those who love Jesus in this way are made a number of promises. The first is **I will ask the Father, and he will give you another Advocate to be with you for ever, the Spirit of truth.** This constitutes the first occurrence in the narrative of the term παράκλητος as a designation of the Spirit. It will be found again in 14.26, 15.26 and 16.7. Its only other use in the New Testament is in 1 John 2.1, where it refers to Christ. The term has a clear primary meaning in Greek – advocate in a legal context (*advocatus* is the Latin equivalent of the Greek term) – and it was a loan word in Hebrew and Aramaic with precisely this meaning. This need not be taken to imply that 'Paraclete' was the designation for a professional legal office. Instead a person of influence, a patron or sponsor, could be called into a court to speak in favour of a person or their cause, thereby providing advocacy. The most likely background for the term is in the Jewish Scriptures and Second Temple Judaism with their interest in intercessory figures who functioned as advocates, sometimes in the heavenly court, and whose advocacy could sometimes take the form of counter-accusation. Some dismiss the translation 'Advocate' on the grounds that the Paraclete is a prosecuting rather than defending counsel in the Fourth Gospel. But this is to ignore the fact that the Paraclete does have the role of speaking in favour of Jesus and his cause. He witnesses about and glorifies Jesus (15.26; 16.14). The Paraclete also has an advocacy role in relation to the disciples, aiding the disciples in their witness, since his witness takes place through theirs (15.26–7). This role of the Spirit is to be found already in the context of trials in the Synoptic tradition (cf. Mark 13.9–11; Matt. 10.17–20; Luke 12.11–12) and it may well be that precisely such a forensic function in the tradition was the catalyst for the fourth evangelist to adopt the title 'Advocate' for the Spirit. The objection about the Paraclete having a prosecuting function also ignores the fluid and paradoxical characteristics in the presentation of the protagonists in scriptural lawsuits and here in John, in which the witness for the defence can also be the prosecutor and indeed the judge. Those who prefer to interpret the title 'Paraclete' as exhorter, encourager or consoler in terms of the use of παρακαλεῖν and παράκλησις, found elsewhere in the New Testament but not in this Gospel, ignore the fact that it is precisely the appellation παράκλητος and not the verb 'to exhort' or the noun 'exhortation' that is used of the Spirit and his role in this narrative. To be sure, the contexts in the Fourth Gospel qualify and add to this primary meaning of advocate, so that the Spirit's forensic role also encourages and consoles the disciples and helper and teacher can be seen as supplementary roles, but advocate in a trial remains the core referent of the title 'Paraclete'.

The one whom the Father will give to the disciples is *another* Paraclete. This underscores the narrative's presentation of Jesus. His mission also can be seen to involve advocacy. Both his earlier witness in the public ministry and his later witness before Pilate are that of a Paraclete, advocating and prosecuting both God's and his own case in the trial of truth with the world. In the case of the man who was born blind, which has a forensic context, Jesus comes to the aid of the man, both defending him and accusing his judges (cf. 9.35—10.6). At the same time, the description 'another Advocate' means that the Spirit is Jesus' designated successor who will continue the forensic role of Jesus in the ongoing trial after the glorification of Jesus. The gift of this new Advocate is to the advantage of the disciples in the period after Jesus' departure, because he will be with them for ever in a way that Jesus in his physical presence could not be.

The synonym for the Advocate is 'the Spirit of truth' (cf. 15.26; also 16.13). It may well be that the contrast drawn in Second Temple Jewish writings between the spirit of truth and the spirit of deceit or wickedness has contributed to this formulation (cf. *Test. Jud.* 20.1–5; 1QS 3.18–19; 4.23), but frequently in these traditions the two spirits are the equivalent to the good and evil inclinations within humanity, whereas here the Spirit is clearly the Spirit of God, who is not conceived of as already within humans. In the Fourth Gospel truth is the true judgement about God and God's relation to the world that is embodied in Jesus, and it is that which is at stake in the trial, in which Jesus' mission plays the crucial role. Just as Jesus is the witness to this truth (18.37) as he embodies it (14.6), so the Spirit as the successor of Jesus is the revealer of the same truth in the continuing trial.

Just as there has been a difference between the response of the world (humanity in its alienation from and hostility to God) and that of the disciples to Jesus, so there is a difference with respect to the Spirit, **whom the world cannot receive because it neither sees nor knows him**. The world cannot receive the Spirit, otherwise it would cease to be the world in its Johannine sense. It was previously unable to receive (1.11; 3.11; 5.43; 8.43; 12.48), see (9.41; 12.39–40) and know Jesus (1.10; 8.14, 19; 9.29). The disciples, on the other hand, are depicted as those who already **know him because he remains with you and will be in you**.

18–20 Discussion of the plight of followers who are left by their teachers in terms of being orphans can be found elsewhere (cf. Plato, *Phaedo* 116a; Epictetus, *Diss*. 3.24.14–15). Jesus, however, gives his disciples the assurance, **I will not leave you orphans; I will come to you. In a little while the world will no longer see me, but you will see me, because I live and you will live**. The earlier reference to Jesus' coming in 14.3 had in view the parousia, but this return, unlike the public parousia at the end of history, is one not visible to the world, and the events described will take place 'in a little while' and so are associated with Jesus' more immediate departure (cf. 13.33). The most natural reference, therefore, is to Jesus' manifestation of himself to his disciples after the resurrection, the event which demonstrates that he lives and whose consequence for believing followers is that they will live (cf. 11.25–6). The focus of the assurance provided by this return from the dead, however, is not on external appearances but on internal relationships – **On that day** (this phrase has reference to the post-resurrection period in 16.23, 26) **you will know that I am in my Father and you are in me and I in you**. Jesus' exaltation to the Father confirms his relationship with the Father as one of indwelling (cf. v. 10) but his relationship with believers will also be one of mutual indwelling.

21 What is more, this relationship is not confined to the few followers who saw Jesus after his resurrection but involves a self-manifestation of Jesus for all who love him and keep his commandments – **The one who has my commandments and keeps them is the one who loves me. The one who loves me will be loved by my Father, and I will love and reveal myself to that person**. The chain of relationships just expressed in terms of indwelling is now formulated in terms of love. Again keeping

Jesus' commandments indicates one's love for him (cf. v. 15) and one who loves him in this way is in turn loved by both the Father and Jesus.

22–4 A different named disciple now becomes the foil for the development of Jesus' teaching. Taking the place of Peter, Thomas and Philip in the earlier part of the discourse, **Judas, not Iscariot**, who is mentioned elsewhere only in Luke's list of the twelve disciples (cf. Luke 6.16; Acts 1.13), takes up the distinction between the world and the disciples from v. 19 and asks how it is that Jesus will reveal himself to the latter and not the former. This enables Jesus to explain that those who love him and whom the Father loves will experience his manifestation as a joint coming with the Father to set up their home with them – **we will come to him and make our dwelling with him**. This sort of manifestation of love is not for the world, because **The one who does not love me does not keep my words**. The mention of 'words' prompts a reference to 'the word', that is, the teaching of Jesus in this discourse, which, like Jesus' teaching elsewhere, is fully authorized by the Father and therefore to be received as God's word – **and the word that you hear is not mine but that of the Father who sent me**.

As noted earlier with reference to v. 2, the same term (μονή) used there for the heavenly dwelling places awaiting believers is employed here in v. 23 for the dwelling of the Father and Jesus with believers. There the disciples were to be consoled at the prospect of Jesus' departure by the traditional eschatology in which a permanent dwelling with the Father and Jesus was reserved in heaven for them until the parousia. Here they are assured, in a more realized eschatology, that this permanent dwelling can be experienced now as the Father and Jesus take up residence with them. A further dimension is added to the understanding of this present experience when it is observed that the promise about Jesus' coming, which is also a coming of the Father, is surrounded by material about the Paraclete in vv. 16, 17 and 26–7. This suggests that the coming of Jesus and the Father and the sending of the Paraclete are mutually interpretative. Indeed, what has just been said of the former has its equivalent in what was earlier said of the latter in v. 17 – 'he remains with you and will be in you'. The Spirit is the mediator of the presence of Jesus and God to believers. If earlier in the narrative the incarnate Logos, Jesus, was the location of God's presence as the new temple, in the period after Jesus' departure the believing community becomes the temple of God in the Spirit.

25–6 That Jesus' teaching originates with the Father who sent him has just been asserted in v. 24. Now he promises that the teaching he has given while with the disciples will be interpreted in his absence by one who is in full continuity with him because sent by the Father in his name, that is, one who is the authorized representative both of the Father and of him;

the Advocate, the Holy Spirit, whom the Father will send in my name, will teach you all things and remind you of all that I said to you. The Paraclete is none other than the divine power known as the Holy Spirit and part of his work as Advocate for the disciples in their mission to the world is to give them the requisite insight into Jesus' teaching. He will bring to remembrance what Jesus has said, not simply by reproducing his words but by unfolding their significance for the new situation in which the disciples find themselves. It is this sort of remembering, which combines historical tradition and interpretation in the light of later needs, that informs the distinctive Johannine witness to Jesus and shapes its discourses, such as this one, which are built up from reflections on sayings from the tradition. The Spirit not only mediates between the vertical and the horizontal, between the Father and the exalted Christ in heaven and believers on earth, but also between the past and the present, between the pre-resurrection deeds and words of Jesus and the ongoing post-resurrection situation of the believing community. The Advocate's linking of the witness of Jesus with the witness of his followers provides this Gospel's own explanation for its overlapping temporal perspectives and for the way its narrative is frequently played out simultaneously on two levels.

27 In Jesus' physical absence his followers will not only have another Advocate but they are also promised the gift of Jesus' peace: **Peace I leave with you; my peace I give you. I give to you not as the world gives.** This is more than the usual farewell blessing of peace in Jewish and Greek convention. Jesus' departure should not leave the disciples insecure, because the confidence, love and joy that characterized Jesus' life in the midst of opposition and conflict are to be made available to them. The contrast is not primarily between Jesus' peace and the world's peace but between the manner of Jesus' giving and the manner of the world's giving. The world's granting of peace is a conditional, negotiated and contractual matter, whereas that of Jesus is unconditional and incalculable. Like God's giving of the Spirit to the Son without measure (3.34), Jesus' own giving of peace through surrendering his life to violent death is characterized by the excessive generosity of love. Before the risen Jesus commissions the disciples for witness in the world, he will twice say, 'Peace be with you' (20.19, 21). Here on the basis of such a resource, he can exhort, **Do not let your hearts be troubled or afraid.** In the midst of conflict and persecution his followers can know an ultimate security that is an antidote to fear. The exhortation provides an *inclusio* with v. 1a and thus completes the body of this first part of the farewell discourse. The following verses supply its summarizing conclusion.

28–9 The words of farewell have been about Jesus' departure and return – **You heard me say to you, 'I am going away and I am**

coming to you.' They have also been about the need for the disciples' belief and love and these themes are reiterated in reverse order – **If you loved me** and **so that . . . you may believe**. If their response to Jesus' announcement were the right one, they **would rejoice that I am going to the Father, because the Father is greater than I**. The latter clause was the subject of much debate in the Christological controversies of the third and fourth centuries CE, but, though the orthodox view that, within God, the Father is greater as the eternal source of the Son is fully compatible with Johannine thought, a comparison of the nature of Christ with that of the Father does not appear to be the main function of the clause here. Nor is its primary point to make a statement about the incarnate Son's subordinate status in relation to the Father, though this is implied, since Jesus has already said that the one who is sent is not greater than the one who has sent him (13.16), and he is the one whom the Father has sent. Its role, rather, is in being part of the reason why the disciples should rejoice. In this way the sentence as a whole can be seen as a means of reiterating in different form the earlier assertion of v. 12 about Jesus' departure enabling the disciples to do greater works. Because the Father is unlimited in a way that his revelation in the earthly life of the Son has not been, the departure of Jesus and the relation to the Father this establishes for the disciples open up greater possibilities for them and thus should be a cause of rejoicing. In depicting ahead of time in this farewell discourse what the disciples will experience and know to be true in the post-resurrection period, Jesus is again confirmed as the reliable witness, and the authoritative status of his teaching as testimony which is to be believed is underscored (cf. also 13.19).

30–1 Jesus brings his words to a halt with the announcement that **the ruler of the world is coming**. It is made clear in 12.31 and 16.11 that the devil is the ruler of 'this world', that is, the world as the manifestation of this present evil age's hostility to God. Its ruler's imminent coming is a further reference to the cosmic backdrop of the events of Jesus' 'hour' and particularly its evils. Nevertheless, **He has no hold on me** – more literally, 'He has nothing in me', which is a forensic idiom meaning 'he has no valid charge against me' and resembles the modern idiom of the police or the law having nothing on a person. This is a further reminder of the motif of the cosmic trial in which Jesus' death will be a judgement of vindication. He must go to that death because **the world must know that I love the Father and that I do just as the Father has commanded me**. His death will be the expression of his love for and utter obedience to the Father – the relationship with God he has claimed thoughout his mission. God's vindication of his death will turn out to be at the same time the vindication of his cause before the world (cf. also 16.8–11).

All attempts to give the final sentence – **Rise, let us go from here**

– a symbolic or spiritualized sense are contrived. It appears to have functioned as the original ending of the farewell discourse, to which the further material of 15.1—16.33 has now been added. The same words, without 'from here', are found in Mark 14.42 (cf. Matt. 26.46), where they conclude the episode of Jesus' prayer in Gethsemane and move the action on to the encounter with Judas and the arresting party. John, of course, omits the Gethsemane account, and this reinforces the point that at one stage of the Gospel's composition these words had a similar function to the one in Mark; they moved the action on to John's account of the arrest (18.1–11), which followed immediately. What looks like an awkward piece of editing in adding supplementary material after this point may not originally have been thought to be so out of place. Once it is realized, as we have noted, that the narrative is basically following the Markan outline, then Mark 14.43 – 'while he was still speaking' – may have been seen as allowing for Jesus to have spoken further words after his 'Rise, let us go' in 14.42, and these are then supplied in abundance by the fourth evangelist. Whatever may have been the case, in the final version of John's Gospel the exhortation to leave now functions as a pause before the second half of the discourse and Jesus' prayer and as a reminder that Jesus' words in their narrative context still serve as preparation for the hour of death and exaltation to which he is moving.

The aim of the first part of the farewell discourse is to give assurance to Jesus' followers – assurance both about Jesus' future and about their own future. The two aspects of the needed encouragement are inextricably interwoven. What is to happen to Jesus and what this means for his identity make possible what is to happen to his disciples and the consequences for their identity. Jesus' departure in death is to be interpreted as his glorification. It is not the shameful end of one who has attempted to lead the people astray but rather the culmination of his loving obedience to his Father and the very means by which God displays and secures Jesus' and God's own honour and reputation. Further, in terms of the motif of cosmic judgement, Jesus' death is his vindication before the ruler of this world. But, above all, his going away is also a return to the presence of the Father. Unlike other departing leaders who bid farewell before death, quite remarkably Jesus will come again to his followers. The promise of his return to them is interpreted on a variety of levels. In conformity to early Christian eschatological hopes, Jesus will return at the end of history, but he will also return in a little while after his resurrection, and the primary focus of the promise of return is his manifestation to his followers in their experience of his indwelling presence. Because of who Jesus is, this return will also involve the Father and the Spirit. Because he is one with the Father, both the Father and Jesus will take up residence within believers, and because the Paraclete or Advocate is Jesus' successor who comes in his name, this indwelling is also that of the Spirit mediating the continuing presence of Jesus with those who are his own.

Disciples can be assured that by his departure Jesus has gone ahead into the Father's presence to prepare a place for them and will return to take them to be with him. In the meantime full belief in the mutual indwelling of God and Jesus and love for Jesus and for one another are still required. Belief in Jesus as the way to God will mean that to have known and seen Jesus is to know and see God. Love for Jesus will be displayed in obedience and will not be easy, as Peter is warned he is yet to discover. But discipleship after Jesus' departure cannot merely reproduce or continue the relationship with Jesus that obtained before. Jesus' going to the Father introduces a qualitatively new situation with greater potential for his followers. They will not be like orphaned children with no one to love or care for them. They will be loved by God and Jesus and their lives will be shaped by the indwelling presence of both in the Spirit. As a consequence they will have the resources to continue Jesus' mission in the world. In response to believing prayer, Jesus will be at work through the disciples, enabling them to do what he has done and what can be described as even greater deeds. The Spirit as Advocate will continue Jesus' relationship with them but in a more permanent fashion, coming to the aid of their witness by both defending and prosecuting the truth of Jesus' cause and by providing insight into the ongoing significance of Jesus' words. Along with the gift of the Advocate, the disciples will receive the gift of Jesus' peace. In the light of all that has been said about the resources for and the potential of the new situation, instead of leaving them in a state of fear and agitation, Jesus' departure should in fact function as a cause of joy.

This first half of the farewell discourse reflects a setting in which writer and readers are in the process of defining themselves in relation to the larger Jewish community (cf. 13.33, 36) and to the 'world' it represents (cf. 14.17, 22, 30–1). Clearly, belief in Jesus is the all-important marker distinguishing them from the world and so this belief needs to be reinforced. Exposition of the significance and implications of Jesus' departure and return provides the means for the necessary consolidation of the readers' faith and for encouragement for their distinctive mission within the world.

(iv) Jesus' farewell discourse (part two)   15.1—16.33

The much longer second part of the discourse falls into three major sections. 15.1–17 contains the imagery of the vine and the branches, through which the need for remaining in Jesus and in his love is expounded. 15.18—16.4a warns of the world's hatred for the disciples, while 16.4b–33 returns to the themes of Jesus' departure and return and their implications. Because of the length of the overall material, these sections will be translated and discussed separately in this commentary. As it now stands, some of the material in this second part of the discourse repeats themes already set out in the first part and some of it expands on issues only briefly raised previously. But even where themes are repeated they are developed in different directions and with different emphases. The nature of the relationship between the two parts may reflect different stages of composition. The first part constitutes a unit complete in itself and is likely to have formed the earliest stage. The second part is more piecemeal, and the three units we have isolated are likely to have been composed separately as further reflections on the same themes as in the earlier discourse, which meet somewhat different needs and circumstances at later stages, before being added as what is now the second part of the overall discourse.

(a) 15.1–17

(1) 'I am the true vine, and my Father is the vine-grower. (2) Every branch in me that does not bear fruit he takes away, and every branch that bears fruit he prunes clean so that it may bear more fruit. (3) You are already clean because of the word that I have spoken to you. (4) Remain in me, and I in you. Just as the branch cannot bear fruit by itself unless it remains in the vine, so neither can you unless you remain in me. (5) I am the vine, you are the branches. Whoever remains in me and I in him bears much fruit, because without me you can do nothing. (6) If anyone does not remain in me, that one is thrown out like a branch and withers, and people gather them and throw them into the fire and they are burned. (7) If you remain in me and my words remain in you, ask for whatever you want and it will be done for you. (8) By this is my Father glorified, that you bear much fruit and you will become[1] my disciples. (9) As the Father has loved me, so I have loved you. Remain in my love. (10) If you keep my commandments, you will remain in my love, just as I have kept my Father's commandments and remain in his love.

(11) 'I have said these things to you so that my joy might be in you and your joy might be complete. (12) This is my commandment, that you love one another, as I have loved you. (13) No one has greater love than this, to lay down one's life for one's friends. (14) You are my friends if you do what I command

---

[1] It is difficult to decide between the two textual variants here. The subjunctive, γένησθε, is found in p[66vid] B D L Θ it[a,aur,b,c,d] vg cop[sa,bo], while the future indicative, γενησέσθε, is contained in ℵ A K Δ Ψ syr[s,p,h,pal] goth Chrysostom. The latter, however, may well have more claim to originality, since it is syntactically the more difficult reading and a copyist may have altered it to conform to the previous subjunctive verb, thereby providing a smoother link with the preceding clause.

you. **(15) No longer do I call you servants, because a servant does
not know what his master is doing. I have called you friends,
because I have made known to you everything I have heard
from my Father. (16) You did not choose me but I chose you
and appointed you so that you might go and bear fruit and your
fruit might remain, so that whatever you ask the Father in my
name he might give you. (17) I give you these commandments,
so that you may love one another.'**

1 I am the true vine, and my Father is the vine-grower. The
three most familiar trees in the Mediterranean world were the olive, the
fig and the vine. Not surprisingly, all three became images for Israel. In
the Jewish Scriptures, in fact, 'vine' and 'vineyard' could frequently be
used interchangeably to depict the people of God, with 'vine' invoking
'vineyard' by synecdoche, the part standing for the whole. Israel is God's
vineyard (cf. Isa. 5.1–7; 27.2–6; Jer. 12.10), the vine that God has planted
(cf. Ps. 80.8–19; Jer. 2.21; 6.9; 8.13; Hos. 10.1; cf. also *4 Ezra* 5.23). The
only other extended use of a figure of speech by Jesus in this Gospel is in
John 10 in connection with the shepherd and the sheep. The commentary
on that passage noted that, despite the frequent use of this imagery in the
Scriptures, Ezek. 34 provided the chief source for the evangelist. Similarly
here, the main background for the vine imagery may well be the cluster
of passages to be found in Ezek. 15.1–8, 17.1–10 and 19.10–14. In these
passages, as here, there is talk of the vine bearing fruit, a distinction
between the vine and its branches, and mention of branches that are good
for nothing, that wither and that are thrown into the fire to be burned.
As with the shepherds in prophetic passages, where the emphasis is so
often on judgement for their failure, so the vine is frequently indicted for
its fruitlessness. In Jer. 2.21 Israel had been been planted as a 'true vine'
but had become a wild vine. Now in the last pair of 'I Am' sayings with
a predicate (cf. also v. 5), Jesus identifies himself as the true vine. Just as
he has taken up Israel's role as the servant-witness, so now he fulfils that
role as the vine, the true representative of God's people who bears fruit
through the new people of God being formed in him. In its response
to the fall of Jerusalem, the vision of *2 Bar.* 36—40 pins its hopes on
the coming of the Messiah, depicted as the vine who overcomes and
supplants the rule of the tall and wicked cedar tree. Here God's purposes
are to be achieved in a quite different way through the Messiah Jesus as
the vine (cf. also *Did.* 9.2, where thanks is offered for 'the holy vine of
your servant David' made known in Jesus).

Jesus' self-identification is in the context of his relationship with God
as Father. If Jesus is the vine, God remains, as in the Jewish Scriptures,
the owner of the vineyard, the planter and nurturer of the vine. But this
vine-grower is now to be identified as 'my Father'. As the one whom

the Father has sent, Jesus establishes the relationship between God and the people of God. At this point, another earlier reference to the vine should be recalled. In Sir. 24.17, 19 Wisdom is compared to a vine and the invitation is extended to eat of her fruit, and at a number of earlier points in John's narrative, from its prologue on, depictions of the Logos as Wisdom have been employed of Jesus as God's presence in the world. In relation to both Wisdom and Israel, because of his unique relationship to the Father, Jesus is the true vine, just as he is the true light (1.9) and the true bread from heaven (6.32).

2 In the development of the vine imagery, the focus remains initially on God's work as the vine-grower: **Every branch in me that does not bear fruit he takes away, and every branch that bears fruit he prunes clean so that it may bear more fruit.** The passage already assumes what will be made explicit later – that the branches are those who profess belief in Jesus and that fruit-bearing is what should characterize their existence in relation to Jesus. The depiction of God's dealing with unproductive and productive branches involves a play on words. Branches that fail to bear fruit are cut off or taken away (αἴρω), while those that bear fruit are enabled to continue to be fruitful by being cut clean or pruned (καθαίρω). Just as God, as the owner of the vineyard and planter of the vine, is depicted earlier as judging within Israel on the basis of fruitfulness, so Jesus' Father continues this work within the new community centred on Jesus.

3 Now, as the disciples and readers are directly addressed, the emphasis moves to the activity of Jesus in relation to believers – **You are already clean because of the word that I have spoken to you.** The word-play continues, since 'clean' (καθαρός) is a cognate of the earlier verb and evokes both the agricultural imagery (pruned) and the spiritual state of the disciples (clean). Pruning branches was used as a metaphor for training in philosophy, as the instructions of the philosopher were likened to the pruning actions of a farmer (cf. e.g. Plutarch, *Mor.* 4c, 529a). Jesus' word is his teaching as a whole. His words will be referred to in v. 7, and in 6.63 the words that he has spoken were said to be spirit and life. Through such words received in faith the disciples have been made clean (cf. also 13.10) and placed in a relation with Jesus in which they will be able to bear fruit.

4–5 But vital to an appropriately productive life is staying in relation to Jesus as its source – **Remain in me, and I in you. Just as the branch cannot bear fruit by itself unless it remains in the vine, so neither can you unless you remain in me.** The notion of remaining or abiding (μένω) will be to the fore until v. 10 and takes up language already found in the first part of the discourse for the relationships between the Father and Jesus (14.10), the Spirit and believers (14.17), and believers and both the Father and Jesus (14.23). Here there is a mutuality in the remaining, but the emphasis is on the role of believers. The exhortation could be taken in a number of ways – an exhortation for both parties to remain in relationship; a comparison in which remaining in Jesus is paralleled by his remaining in believers (but the absence of καθώς, 'as', counts against this); or a conditional statement with the force of 'Remain in me, and I will remain in you.' The warnings in the surrounding verses about not remaining make the last option the most likely. Remarkably, given the broader context of Jesus' departure from the disciples, the possibility of separation arises not so much from his side of the relationship but from theirs. If the first 'I Am . . .' announcement was in the context of Jesus' relationship with the Father, it is not surprising that its repetition is now in the context of his relationship with the disciples – **I am the vine, you are the branches.** For the branches to bear fruit, they have to remain in the vine. In the same way disciples are totally dependent on their relationship to Jesus, **because without me you can do nothing**.

6 The consequences of failing to abide in Jesus are depicted as severe: **If anyone does not remain in me, that one is thrown out like a branch and withers, and people gather them and throw them into the fire and they are burned.** It is not simply that such branches are useless to the vine, but, as in the passages in Ezek. 15, 17, 19, the withering of the branches and their being thrown into the fire and burned speak of God's judgement on faithlessness. It is significant that earlier in this narrative, those who are said to have believed in Jesus (8.30) are told that, in order to be true disciples, they need to remain in his word (8.31), but then they show that they have failed to do so, since they become the recipients of his strongest condemnation (8.43–7).

7–8 The positive consequences of remaining in Jesus that are now set out take up the emphasis on Jesus' word – **If you remain in me and my words remain in you, ask for whatever you want and it will be done for you.** Remaining in Jesus, then, is synonymous with remaining in Jesus' word (cf. 8.31), just as here Jesus' words remaining in the disciples is synonymous with Jesus remaining in them (cf. v. 5). Promises about answered prayer were made in the first part of the discourse (cf. 14.13–14). There such prayer was to be made in Jesus' name. Here the condition specified is the remaining in Jesus that entails conformity to his words, to his teaching, which, like the earlier qualification of 'in Jesus' name', ensures that the prayer will be in line with what Jesus represents. If without Jesus one can do nothing, with Jesus and through prayer 'whatever you want' can be done.

The thought returns to fruit-bearing: **By this is my Father glorified,** that you bear much fruit and you will become my disciples. The Father's reputation and honour are enhanced not only through the life and death of Jesus but also through the lives of those in union with Jesus. The bearing of much fruit is presumably linked with what has just been said about the answered prayers of those who remain in Jesus and with what will be said about keeping Jesus' commandments, especially the commandment to love one another (vv. 10, 12–14). Prayer, conformity to Jesus' words, and love are the indications of being disciples of Jesus.

9–10 The necessary union between the branches and the vine is now explained in terms of the relationship of love between the disciples and Jesus, which in fact parallels the relationship between Jesus and the Father. In developing the parallelism the language and thought of 14.21, 23–4, 31 are taken up: **As the Father has loved me, so I have loved you. Remain in my love. If you keep my commandments, you will remain in my love, just as I have kept my Father's commandments and remain in his love.** On the one hand, the divine love between the Father and the Son is now the love that the Son extends to disciples, so that all disciples have to do is to remain in the love that embraces them. On the other hand, remaining in love is not automatic and will require the same sort of obedience to Jesus' words as was necessary in the case of the incarnate Son's conformity to his Father's commands. And in both cases, that of disciples and that of Jesus, obedience to commandments is evidenced in lives of love, so that their remaining in love is also a displaying of the love in which they are rooted.

11 I have said these things to you so that my joy might be in you and your joy might be complete. The purpose of Jesus' speaking about the vine and the branches and the necessity of remaining in him and his love has been that his disciples might experience joy. Again, rather than a cause for sorrow, his departure, when seen in the right way, is a reason for rejoicing (cf. 14.28). In the first part of the farewell discourse Jesus had bequeathed his followers his peace (14.27), and now he leaves them his joy. The peace and joy that Paul sees as the fruit of the Spirit, the Fourth Gospel views as gifts of Christ. That it is joy which is to the fore at this point is understandable in the light of the vine imagery. After all, the purpose of the vine is to produce fruit, and the fruit of the vine is wine with all its traditional associations of joy, gladness and conviviality (cf. e.g. Pss. 4.7; 104.15; Eccl. 2.3; 9.7; 10.19; Isa. 16.10; 24.11; Jer. 48.33; Joel 1.12; Zech. 10.7). The joy that Jesus wishes to impart is no temporary drowning of sorrows, however, but a permanent and deep-rooted delight that can be experienced in the midst of troubles by remaining in his love and by loving others. And, in a typically Johannine formulation, this joy is meant to be full or complete (cf. 3.29; 16.24; 17.13; 1 John. 1.4; 2 John 12).

12–13 What follows is less directly connected to the figure of the vine, although the language of fruit-bearing will recur in v. 16. It develops instead one of the applications of the earlier imagery, namely, the notion of remaining in Jesus' love and what this entails. First, the love commandment of 13.34 is restated – **This is my commandment, that you love one another, as I have loved you.** Then the kind of love that is in view is spelled out – **No one has greater love than this, to lay down one's life for one's friends.** Just as Jesus' love for the disciples involves the laying down of his life for them (cf. 10.17–18), so this is to be the extent to which their love for one another has to be prepared to go (cf. also 1 John 3.16). The thought echoes ideals of friendship in the ancient world. Aristotle could say, 'To a noble man there applies the true saying that he does all things for the sake of his friends . . . and, if need be, he gives his life for them' (*Eth. nic.* 1169a; cf. also e.g. Plato, *Symp.* 179b; Diodorus Siculus 10.4.4–6; Seneca, *Ep.* 1.9.10; Epictetus, *Diss.* 2.7.3). Yet what distinguishes disciples' self-sacrificial love for one another is that it is grounded in and reflects Jesus' self-sacrificial love for them.

14–15 That the maxim about the greatest human love refers not only to what disciples are to do for one another but also to what Jesus will do for them is made explicit by Jesus designating them as his friends, and therefore as those for whom his love will involve laying down his life. **You are my friends if you do what I command you.** Those who keep his commandments are those who love Jesus (cf. 14.15, 21, 23), and so loving Jesus and being his friends are synonymous. Despite the notion of obeying Jesus' commandments, being his friend is distinguished from being his servant or slave: **No longer do I call you servants, because a servant does not know what his master is doing. I have called you friends, because I have made known to you everything I have heard from my Father.** Jesus has just spoken of the disciples as servants (13.16) and will almost immediately remind them of this (15.20), so it is not that the master–servant relationship is now entirely superseded. In the Graeco-Roman world too friendship was seen as quite compatible with the patron–client relationship. Here Jesus' followers are no longer the sort of servants who have to obey blindly because they have no idea of their master's intentions or plans. They have a new level of intimacy as friends because they have been made privy, especially in the farewell discourse, to what Jesus himself knows about his and their future, and, what is more, because of Jesus' relation with the Father, this is to be made privy to the Father's own purposes of love for Jesus and his disciples. Part of the ancient ideal of friendship was that friends were open and honest with one another, not withholding secrets or concealing anything (cf. e.g. Cicero, *Amic.* 6.22; Isocrates, *Demon.* 24–5; Seneca, *Dial.* 10.15.2). Here Jesus claims to have concealed nothing his Father has told him from his friends and thereby, implicitly, to have made them also friends of God, a relationship previously attributed in Jewish tradition only to the likes of Abraham (cf. 2 Chron. 20.7; Isa. 41.8) and Moses (cf. Exod. 33.11).

16–17 This friendship with Jesus is a result of his initiative; he has let them into the intimacy of a relationship with himself and with the Father – **You did not choose me but I chose you** (cf. also 6.70; 13.18). Just as Israel's election by God was not only in order to enjoy the privileges of that covenant relationship but also to fulfil a vocation in the world, so Jesus' choice of his followers to be his friends entails not only enjoyment of the relationship's intimacy but also a mission within the world – **so that you might go and bear fruit and your fruit might remain.** The vine imagery is taken up again through the language of bearing fruit. Earlier, disciples had been enjoined to remain in Jesus if they were to bear fruit (vv. 4–5). Now this remaining produces fruit that remains or is lasting, and, as before, the primary reference for such fruit is love, as v. 17 will indicate. Some interpreters hold that the mention of *going* and bearing fruit indicates that mission and its results are involved. The two ideas, of course, are not incompatible, since it has already been suggested that their love for one another will be the disciples' most effective means of witness in the world (cf. 13.34–5). As in vv. 7–8, answered prayer is linked to the notion of bearing fruit – **so that whatever you ask the Father in my name he might give you.** In comparison with the previous reference, it is made explicit that the condition for such prayer is that it be made in Jesus' name (cf. also 14.13–14). In their calling to continue Jesus' mission in the world by embodying his love, his followers are promised that their prayers for the fulfilment of this calling will be answered by the Father. The expansion on the application of the vine imagery in vv. 12–17 ends, as it had begun, with a reiteration of its main purpose as far as the disciples are concerned. Their relationship to Jesus, as branches to a vine, is to enable them to live in love – **I give you these commandments, so that you may love one another.**

When the fourth evangelist made extensive use of shepherd imagery in chapter 10, he not only drew this from the Jewish Scriptures but also gave a more explicitly Christological focus to the Synoptics' use of such imagery. Here too the background is not only vine and vineyard imagery in the Scriptures, especially Ezekiel, but also the Synoptic tradition of Jesus' parabolic teaching about vineyards (cf. Mark 12.1–11 parr.; Matt. 20.1–16; and Luke 13.6–9, where there is no fruit on a fig tree planted in the vineyard) and his saying about the fruit of the vine in the context of his final meal (cf. Mark 14.25 parr.). Immediately after the latter saying in Mark and Matthew Jesus likens himself to the shepherd and his followers to sheep. It would not be surprising if it was this material in particular that provided the catalyst for the fourth evangelist's extended figures of speech. In the Synoptics Jesus has identified his blood with the fruit of the vine and now in the Fourth Gospel he is identified with the vine as a whole.

The narrative setting of Jesus' departure from his followers would appear to necessitate discussion of separation, but the figure of the vine and its branches enables Jesus to continue to speak of connection and union (cf. the theme of mutual indwelling in 14.20, 23). The imagery has both Christological and ecclesiological dimensions. In the Scriptures it had been employed to speak of the people of God. Now Jesus fulfils the role of Israel and his followers are the branches rooted in the vine, so that the imagery refers to the renewed people of God centred in Jesus. Its focus is initially on the relationship of the individual branches to the vine, as his followers are exhorted to remain in Jesus and in his love, but the corporate aspect of their existence is not neglected, since the result of the relationship to Jesus is to be fruit-bearing and that entails his followers' love for one another. In this context his followers are also called his friends, whose greatest deed of love is to lay down their lives for one another, an ideal of friendship in the Graeco-Roman world that Jesus' death on their behalf actually embodies. The union between Jesus and his disciples is to result in a community of love that has its source and model in the love which Jesus demonstrates. The next section of the discourse will stress the world's hostility to Jesus' disciples. The pressures of such a setting and the need for a secure basis for their living make the reminder of their union with Jesus, the call to remain in it, and the command to love one another especially pertinent.

(b) 15.18—16.4a

(18) 'If the world hates you, know that it hated me before you. (19) If you belonged to the world, the world would love its own. Yet because you do not belong to the world but I have chosen you out of the world, for this reason the world hates you. (20) Remember the word that I said to you, 'A servant is not greater than his master.' If they persecuted me, they will also persecute you. If they kept my word, they will also keep yours. (21) But they will do all these things to you on account of my name, because they do not know the one who sent me. (22) If I had not come and spoken to them, they would not have sin; but now they have no excuse for their sin. (23) Whoever hates me hates my Father also. (24) If I had not done among them the works that no one else did, they would not have sin; but now they have seen and hated both me and my Father. (25) But this is in order that the word written in their law might be fulfilled, "They hated me without a cause."

(26) 'When the Advocate comes, whom I will send to you from the Father, the Spirit of truth who proceeds from the Father, he will testify about me. (27) And you also testify because you have been with me from the beginning.

(16.1) 'I have spoken these things to you so that you might not be caused to stumble. (2) They will put you out of the synagogue. Indeed an hour is coming when everyone who kills you will think he is offering worship to God. (3) And they will do these things because they have not known the Father or me. (4a) But I have spoken these things to you so that when their hour comes you may remember that I told you about them.'

Up until this point the focus of the farewell discourse has been on what will happen to Jesus and on the implications for the disciples. The surrounding world has been mentioned (cf. 14.17, 19, 22) but it now becomes the main topic of discussion. The hatred it is said to have for the disciples stands in sharp contrast to the love they are to have for each other (cf. also 1 John 3.13–14). The world's hostility is depicted in general terms in vv. 18–25 and then more specifically in 16.1–4a, while at the centre of the section, in vv. 26–7, the witness of the Paraclete and of the disciples within this world is addressed.

18–19 As has been noted earlier (see on 1.10), the term for 'world', κόσμος, can, in this Gospel, have either the more neutral and broader reference of the totality of creation, including humanity, or the more negative and limited reference of humanity in its alienation from and hostility to its Creator. Here the latter force is clearly in view: **If the world hates you, know that it hated me before you.** Jesus' followers are to expect to encounter the negative response of human society, whose organization and structures reflect its opposition to the divine purposes and to the divine representatives, whether they be Jesus himself or those who continue his cause. Instead of acknowledging them as representatives of its source and of that which sustains it, this world perceives them as a threat to its cohesiveness and reacts in rejection, enmity and hatred. When they experience the world's ill will, Jesus' followers are to recognize that this is a sign of their continuity with Jesus' mission, since this is precisely the reaction Jesus himself experienced. **If you belonged to the world, the world would love its own. Yet because you do not belong to the world but I have chosen you out of the world, for this reason the world hates you.** Like Jesus (cf. 8.23), his followers no longer owe their allegiance to this world, since, in choosing them as his friends (cf. vv. 15–16), Jesus has chosen them out of the world, and the unbelieving world does not take kindly to those who no longer are willing to live by its values and standards. Jesus' disciples will encounter the unremitting antithesis between God and the world in their own lives. To receive the world's love or approval they would in effect have to renounce the choice of them by God's Son to share in his and the Father's love.

20 But those who accept Jesus' call to a mission of love and service should expect to incur the consequences. Jesus reminds them of his earlier saying in 13.16 – **Remember the word that I said to you, 'A servant is not greater than his master.'** In its previous context that saying reinforced the command to the disciples to wash one another's feet. Now it functions as a further warning that the response to their mission will be no different from the response to that of their master. There is a precisely parallel use of the master–servant relationship in Matt. 10.24–5, which is likely to have provided the traditional source here. John develops it in order to indicate that there will be the same divided reception of the disciples' mission as there was for that of Jesus – **If they persecuted me, they will also persecute you. If they kept my word, they will also keep yours.**

21–3 Further reasons for the world's response to Jesus' disciples are now given. **But they will do all these things to you on account of my name.** Jesus' name signifies all that he represents, so that what befalls his followers is because of their continuing identification with his cause. But part of what his name represents is Jesus' relationship with God, and it is the world's culpable ignorance of this that lies behind its hostility – **because they do not know the one who sent me**. The lack of recognition of someone's agent is clear evidence of the absence of a genuine knowledge of his sender. Again it is stressed that, whatever the claims of the opposition to the contrary, rejection of Jesus comes from not knowing God (cf. e.g. 7.28; 8.19, 54–5). A similar point will be made again at the end of this section in 16.3. The mission of Jesus has brought about a radically new situation for humanity's relation to God. Once God's uniquely authorized representative has been encountered, there can be no question of any true knowledge of God without acknowledgement of Jesus. The same holds for the notion of sin. Humanity's alienation from God in unbelief is only truly seen for what it is in the light of the revelation of God that Jesus brings. **If I had not come and spoken to them, they would not have sin; but now they have no excuse for their sin.** This is a similar thought to that expressed earlier in 9.39–41 about the blindness and sin of the Pharisees. The negative consequence of Jesus' mission is to expose the sin of unbelief in such a way that those who fail to believe are now conscious of their response and held accountable for it. Again this makes clear that for the Fourth Gospel the primary expression of sin is failure to believe in Jesus as the one sent by the Father. If, as Jesus has asserted in 13.20b, whoever receives him receives the one who sent him, then the negative counterpart also holds: **Whoever hates**

me hates my Father also. If love for Jesus, as the discourse has already made plain (cf. 14.21, 23; 15.10), means living in conformity to the revelation he has brought, then hatred of Jesus entails an existence shaped by rejection of that revelation and the God it discloses.

24–5 The thought of vv. 22–3 is reiterated in terms of the unique **works** performed by Jesus, and since Jesus' works are also the works of the Father (cf. e.g. 5.17, 19; 10.32, 37–8; 14.10), not to have believed on the basis of them is to **have seen and hated both me and my Father.** The warning about the world's hatred is rounded off with an appeal to Scripture – **But this is in order that the word written in their law might be fulfilled, 'They hated me without a cause.'** The description of Scripture as 'their law' (cf. 'your law' in 8.17; 10.34) is significant. It indicates that the primary group in view as representative of the world's hatred is the Jewish religious authorities in their rejection of Jesus and that the use of this scripture has an apologetic function as it provides accusatory witness against the opposition (cf. also 5.39, 45–7). At the same time it remains important for the evangelist to show that what has happened to Jesus is in fulfilment of Scripture and therefore in accordance with the will of God as revealed there. In this case the words of lament of the righteous sufferer are seen as appropriate, words that appear in two places (Pss. 35.19; 69.4). In both references the LXX wording had the verb in a nominative present participial construction ('those who hate') and so an adjustment to the aorist form ('they hated') in this quotation would have been made in either case. But since Ps. 69 features elsewhere in the narrative (cf. Ps. 69.9 in 2.17 and Ps. 69.21, which lies behind 19.28), it may well be this psalm that provides the scriptural source. Yet, whatever its source, how appropriate is the quotation, given that Jesus has just supplied reasons for the world's hatred of him in terms of its ignorance of God and its rejection of his works? The use of this scripture indicates that the world's hostility to Jesus can be discussed in such terms but they still do not supply any justifiable cause for it. Ultimately, Jesus is the innocent victim of humanity's rejection of its Creator's good purposes for it revealed in him, and this world's evil exposed in that rejection remains irrational and mysterious.

26–7 In the midst of the world's hostility Jesus' cause must still be promoted and this will be done through the twofold testimony of the Advocate and the disciples, thereby fulfilling the Deuteronomic injunction about the need for two witnesses (cf. Deut. 17.6). **When the Advocate comes, whom I will send to you from the Father, the Spirit of truth who proceeds from the Father, he will testify about me.** As in 14.16–17, the Paraclete is depicted as the Spirit of truth, but here, as in 14.26, is more clearly seen as a personal agent, since despite the neuter noun for the Spirit (τὸ πνεῦμα), the pronoun that is the subject of the main clause is nominative masculine (ἐκεῖνος). The Spirit is linked with the two other divine persons in this narrative, the Son and the Father. Just as Jesus as Son has been sent by the Father, so he now sends the Paraclete from the Father. In terms of the motif of agency, later Jewish writings (cf. *b. Kiddushin* 41a) discuss how a person's agent can appoint an agent, and here the Paraclete is seen as the authorized agent of Jesus, who is himself the authorized agent of the Father. At the same time it is made clear that the Paraclete is also more intimately related to God the Father. Jesus sends him from the Father and, as the Spirit of truth, he proceeds from the Father. In both cases the formulation is παρὰ; τοῦ πατρός and this formulation is also used of Jesus' relation to the Father in 16.28. So the Advocate is both the Spirit of Jesus and the Spirit of God, proceeding from the Father through the Son. The particular forensic function of the Advocate highlighted here is that of witnessing about Jesus. Just as Jesus bore witness to the truth before the world, so now the Advocate, as the Spirit of truth, will testify to the truth of Jesus and his cause. Important aspects of the Advocate's testifying will be delineated further in 16.8–11.

Parallel to and linked with the witness of the Paraclete, the disciples also continue the witness of Jesus in and to the world: **And you also testify because you have been with me from the beginning.** Later in the narrative the sending of Jesus functions as the paradigm for the sending of his followers (cf. 17.18; 20.21). Just as witness was at the heart of Jesus' mission, so it defines theirs, and, as the surrounding context makes plain, just as Jesus met persecution and rejection because of his witness, so too will they. The qualification for their role of testifying is their association with Jesus from the beginning of his mission. This puts them in a position to provide witness to the significance of Jesus' mission as a whole. So their first-hand knowledge of that mission will play a foundational part in the disciples' future witness. This is later reinforced by the stress in 20.30 that Jesus' signs were done 'in the presence of his disciples'. Already in v. 26 the disciples have been identified as the recipients of the sending of the Spirit, and the link between their witness and that of the Spirit will become clearer later, when in commissioning them, Jesus breathes on them and says, 'Receive the Holy Spirit' (20.22). The two witnessing roles are not simply distinct. The Spirit's witness is to be primarily in and through that of the disciples, and the witness of the disciples is to receive its impetus and sustaining power from that of the Spirit.

16.1 As will be noted below, Jesus' prophecy of future persecution is also a feature of the Synoptic tradition. Here there is a particular purpose that the portrayal of his prophesying about the hatred of the world is meant to serve: **I have spoken these things to you so that you might not be caused to stumble.** To stumble entails faltering and being tempted to fall away from the faith in the face of persecution and death (cf. also 6.61). The same verb is used in Jesus' warning in Mark 14.27 par. that the disciples will all fall away. This may well be the source for John's terminology at this point, since he has employed the wording of the Markan passage in his account of the prediction of Peter's denials in 13.38 and will do so again in 16.32. Here the thought is that to be forewarned about falling away is to be forearmed and that apostasy is a far greater danger than the extremes of persecution that may need to be faced. When the test actually comes, his disciples by recalling Jesus' words, will be enabled to overcome their fear of possible death and see such an eventuality as a form of the witness they have been asked to bear.

2–3 The predictions about the world's hatred now become more specific in regard to the extreme circumstances Jesus' disciples will face, and an explanation for these threats is provided – **They will put you out of the synagogue. Indeed an hour is coming when everyone who kills you will think he is offering worship to God. And they will do these things because they have not known the Father or me.** Earlier in 9.22 and 12.42 it is the narrator who has mentioned exclusion from the synagogue; now Jesus himself prophesies that his followers will be excommunicated. What the man who was blind experienced (cf. 9.34–5) will become the experience of the disciples. To be driven out from what had been their religious community and cut off from links with those among whom they had previously lived and worshipped would have been extremely traumatic. Indeed such a ban was the social equivalent of a death sentence. But death itself is also predicted as a real possibility. Jesus asserts that for some 'an hour is coming' when witness will become martyrdom. Just as Jesus faces his hour, so his witnesses will face theirs. Those who will carry out the killings are from the same group who will exclude them from the synagogues, namely the Jewish religious authorities. The situation involves the continuing clash of religious commitments and those who carry out the persecution and killing see such activities as part of their devotion to God in rooting out apostasy (cf. the later *Numbers Rabbah* 21 – 'everyone who sheds the blood of the godless is like one who offers a sacrifice' – commenting on the zeal of Phinehas in Num. 25.13). In the mid-second century CE Justin Martyr can still speak of Jewish Christians who have experienced death at the hands of other Jews because of their allegiance to Jesus (cf. 1 *Apol.* 31.6; *Dial.* 95.4; 110.5; 133.6). As in 15.21, this zealous persecution is ascribed to its perpetrators not truly knowing either the one whom they claim to serve or Jesus.

4a The words **I have spoken these things to you so that . . .** provide an *inclusio* for the last part of this section through their parallel with v. 1. This time the purpose of the warnings is that **when their hour comes**

you may remember that I told you about them. The disciples'
remembrance that Jesus had foretold the costly consequences of discipleship will reassure them of the truthfulness of his words and therefore
also of the truth of his cause for which they are suffering. The confirmation of the words of the prophet like Moses and of the divine revealer
will reinforce for them his sovereign control of events, enabling them to
see their unjust treatment from the perspective of the outworking of the
divine purposes in history.

Our introductory discussion of the farewell discourse as a whole had
already mentioned the development of Synoptic tradition in this section.
This can now be shown in a little more detail. The apocalyptic discourses
in the Synoptics provide a functional equivalent to John's farewell
discourse. In Mark 13.9–13 the disciples are told that because of their
allegiance to Jesus they will find themselves handed over to councils,
beaten in synagogues and standing before governors and kings to bear
witness to them. When they are brought to trial, however, they are not to
be concerned about what to say, but to utter whatever is given to them at
the time, because it will not be they who speak but the Holy Spirit. This
will also be a period when they experience betrayal and death through
the opposition of other family members and 'will be hated by all because
of my name'. The Matthean and Lukan parallels (cf. Matt. 24.9–14; Luke
21.12–19) paint similar pictures of this witness in the midst of persecution
and death, though they omit at this point any mention of the Spirit.
Earlier, however, Matthew and Luke do have similar material where they
mention the Spirit. In connection with the mission of the twelve Matt.
10.17–23 speaks of being persecuted within the towns of Israel, being
delivered up to councils and flogged in synagogues, being 'hated by all
because of my name' and 'the Spirit of your Father speaking through
you'. Similarly, Luke 12.11–12 exhorts, 'When they bring you before
the synagogues, the rulers, and the authorities, do not worry about how
you are to defend yourselves or what you are to say; for the Holy Spirit
will teach you at that very hour what you ought to say.' The Synoptic
tradition, then, has already spoken of Jewish Christians experiencing
synagogue discipline, including beatings, and death. But what of the
official excommunication mentioned here in 16.2 (cf. also 9.22; 12.42)?
There is a possible Synoptic equivalent in the Luke 6.22 version of the
beatitude (cf. Matt. 5.11) – 'Blessed are you when people hate you, and
when they exclude you, and revile you, and cast out your name as evil on
account of the Son of Man' – which some take as a reference to excommunication and others as indicating informal ostracism. In any case, it
appears highly likely that the fourth evangelist has reworked this sort of
Synoptic material, much of which has a clear forensic setting, in order to
have Jesus speak about the disciples being hated by the world on account

of his name, about the joint witness of the disciples and the Advocate, and about being persecuted, put out of the synagogue and killed. He has done this under the influence of the more explicitly Christological controversies of his own time, in the light of the experiences of the particular group of Christians with which he is closely familiar, and as part of his overall trial motif.

This passage contributes to that motif the depiction of the Spirit as Advocate, coming to the aid of Jesus' disciples, and of both the Advocate and the disciples continuing Jesus' mission of witness to the truth through their joint testifying. The Spirit not only has this close relationship to the disciples, but in origin is also seen to be intimately related to the Father and the Son in a way that anticipates later trinitarian formulations. The passage also characterizes the opposition in the trial, who are primarily unbelieving Jews and their leaders, as 'the world', and draws a sharp contrast between Jesus' followers and the world. The disciples have been chosen out of the world and so do not belong to it. This is no withdrawal from living fully in the world, where they are to carry out their witness. It means rather that disciples no longer subscribe to the value system of a world that is hostile to its Creator's purposes. Witness to such a world can have the effect of arousing its hatred. This happened in Jesus' mission and it will be no different for his followers. The conflict between disciples and the world is over the issue that is at stake throughout the Gospel – the revelation of the one true God in Jesus – and the world's hatred is seen as a way of life rooted in the failure to recognize this God manifested by its rejection of Jesus. The witness of Jesus and the disciples is perceived by the world as a threat to its values, a threat that needs to be removed by marginalizing it socially and, if necessary, by attempting to eradicate it through violent means. Ironically, the world remains convinced that such attempts to preserve the status quo are actually serving God. In this section of the farewell discourse the disciples are being prepared to embark on their mission to the world in full knowledge of this clash of commitments and its costs, such as excommunication and death, and yet also in unshaken faith that, in the midst of rejection, they are continuing the mission of Jesus, whose control of affairs is displayed in the fulfilment of his prediction of such consequences, and that in their witness to Jesus they are accompanied and empowered by the Spirit.

(c) 16.4b–33

(4b) 'I did not tell you these things from the beginning because I was with you. (5) But now I am going to the one who sent me, yet none of you asks me, "Where are you going?" (6) But because I have spoken these things to you, sorrow has filled your hearts. (7) Yet I tell you the truth: it is to your advantage that I am going

away. For if I do not go away, the Advocate will not come to you; but if I go away, I will send him to you. (8) And when he comes, he will convict the world of sin and righteousness and condemnation: (9) of sin, because they do not believe in me; (10) of righteousness, because I am going to the Father and you will no longer see me; (11) of judgement, because the ruler of this world has been condemned.

(12) 'I still have many things to say to you, but you are not able to bear them now. (13) But when he, the Spirit of truth, comes, he will guide you in all the truth. For he will not speak of his own accord, but he will speak whatever he hears and will declare to you the things that are to come. (14) He will glorify me, because he will take from what is mine and declare it to you. (15) Everything that the Father has is mine. For this reason I said that he will take from what is mine and declare it to you. (16) A little while, and you will no longer see me, and again a little while, and you will see me.' (17) So some of his disciples said to one another, 'What is this that he is saying to us, "A little while, and you will not see me, and again a little while, and you will see me" and "Because I am going to the Father"?' (18) So they said, 'What is this "a little while"? We do not know what he is talking about.' (19) Jesus knew that they wanted to ask him, and said to them, 'Are you discussing with one another what I said, "A little while, and you will not see me, and again a little while and you will see me"? (20) Truly, truly, I say to you, you will weep and mourn, but the world will rejoice. You will grieve, but your sorrow will be turned into joy. (21) When a woman is in labour, she has pain, because her hour has come. But when the child is born, she no longer remembers the pain because of the joy that a person has been born into the world. (22) So you also have sorrow now; but I will see you again, and your hearts will rejoice, and no one takes your joy from you. (23) On that day you will not question me about anything. Truly, truly, I say to you, if you ask the Father anything in my name, he will give it to you.[1] (24) Until now you have not asked anything in my name. Ask and you will receive, so that your joy may be complete.

---

[1] Some textual witnesses place the phrase 'in my name' at the end of the sentence, where it qualifies the verb 'to give' instead of 'to ask'. These include ℵ B C⋆ L D cop^{sa}. Elsewhere, of course, including the next verse, the phrase is connected with asking in prayer (cf. also 14.13–14; 15.16; 16.26). This might mean that it was moved to fall into line with the normal usage. On the other hand, the support for the earlier positioning is widespread – p^{22vid} A D K W Θ Π Ψ it^{a,aur,b,c} vg syr^{s,p,h,pal} cop^{bo} goth arm eth – and the move could have taken place under the influence of the next clause, where the phrase appears at the end.

(25) 'I have said these things to you in figures of speech. An hour is coming when I will no longer speak to you in figures of speech but will tell you plainly about the Father. (26) On that day you will ask in my name, and I do not say to you that I will pray to the Father for you; (27) for the Father himself loves you because you have loved me and have believed that I came from God.[2] (28) I came from the Father and have come into the world; again, I am leaving the world and am going to the Father.' (29) His disciples said to him, 'Now you are speaking plainly and not in any figure of speech. (30) Now we know that you know all things and have no need that anyone question you. Because of this we believe that you came from God.' (31) Jesus answered them, 'Do you now believe? (32) See, the hour is coming, and has come, when you will be scattered, each to his own home, and you will leave me alone. And yet I am not alone, for the Father is with me. (33) I have said these things to you so that in me you might have peace. In the world you will have suffering, but take heart, I have conquered the world.'

This third section of the second part of the farewell discourse returns more explicitly to the major themes of the discourse as a whole – Jesus' departure and the consolation of the disciples – and indeed repeats in a different fashion many of the themes from the first part in 13.31—14.31. While 15.18—16.4a was in the form of an uninterrupted monologue from Jesus, this section takes account of the disciples' reactions and includes further exchanges between Jesus and the disciples. The latter's responses to Jesus' assertions are noted in vv. 5b–6, 17–18 and 29–30 and are followed by further declarations from Jesus. This pattern indicates the section's three main units. In vv. 4b–15 the disciples are told that it is to their advantage that Jesus departs because the Advocate will come, and his work is described in relation both to the world and to the disciples. In vv. 16–24 they are assured that their present sorrow will give way to joy when they see Jesus again imminently. In vv. 25–33 they are reminded of Jesus' destiny upon his departure and of the new relationship they will have with him and with the Father, both of which should be a cause of peace and reassurance for them.

4b–6 I did not tell you these things from the beginning because I was with you. 'These things' have in view the predictions of persecution which have just been made but also the announcement of Jesus' departure

---

[2] Some manuscripts have τοῦ πατρός, 'the Father', after 'God'. But this is likely to represent an assimilation to the language of the following verse. The omission, with or without the definite article before θεοῦ, is widely attested.

that was given earlier and of which persecution by the world will be the consequence. Jesus' personal presence and protection of his followers meant that speaking of such matters was unnecessary until the hour of his departure. He now states again that he is returning to the divine sender: **But now I am going to the one who sent me, yet none of you asks me, 'Where are you going?' But because I have spoken these things to you, sorrow has filled your hearts.** The reference to the disciples' failure to ask about Jesus' destination has frequently been taken to be in sharp contradiction to the earlier material in which Peter had asked precisely this question (13.36) and in which Thomas's further question explicitly presupposed ignorance of the answer to this one (14.5). This interpretation has then been used as part of the evidence that the discourse material is likely to have been composed at different times and as an indication that its final editing was not carried out as efficiently and smoothly as it might have been. This may have been the case, but, as a number of commentators have pointed out, these verses can be read in a way that credits the evangelist with a little more coherence in the final composition of the discourse.

The alternative reading attempts to take account of the characterization of the disciples in the discourse as a whole. It notes that Jesus does not say 'None of you has asked me' but 'None of you is asking me', thus drawing the readers' attention to the difference between the present response of the disciples and their response at the beginning of the discourse. Their earlier superficial questioning had revealed a total lack of comprehension about the implications of Jesus' departure. Since the last question from a disciple, Jesus has given uninterrupted teaching from 14.23 to 16.4. As Jesus' comment in v. 6 makes clear, now at least the disciples' lack of questioning indicates a partial, if still very inadequate, understanding. They have understood enough to be filled with sorrow at the prospect of Jesus leaving them and of what will await them in the world. So drawing attention to their silence at this point is a means of highlighting their profound sadness, with which Jesus will attempt to deal in the rest of the discourse.

7 The antidote for the disciples' sorrow is a reminder of the benefits that will accrue to them as a result of Jesus' departure: **Yet I tell you the truth: it is to your advantage that I am going away** (cf. 14.28). The major advantage results from the coming of the Spirit – **For if I do not go away, the Advocate will not come to you; but if I go away, I will send him to you** (cf. 14.16, 17, 26; 15.26).

8–11 The Advocate will not only be present to help in the disciples' witness to Jesus but will also have a prosecuting role in the continuing trial between God and the world, in which the disciples will be caught up.

In talking of the spirit of truth and the spirit of error, *Test. Jud.* 20.5 could assert, 'the spirit of truth testifies to all things and brings all accusations. He who has sinned is consumed in his heart and cannot raise his head to face the judge.' Just as Jesus' witness has had an accusatory dimension, so will that of the Advocate, who is his successor. His activity will only commence when he comes to the disciples, and the implication must be that the prosecuting will take place primarily through them and their witness. One of the primary contexts for this judicial imagery will have been the trials before synagogue authorities that many will have faced in the process of excommunication, which has just been mentioned (v. 3; cf. also Mark 13.9–11). In the process the Paraclete will make clear the consequences of Jesus' mission, bring accusations, and obtain convictions on three counts. The three issues and the reasons for the world's conviction on these issues are set out cryptically and their interpretation is highly disputed: **And when he comes, he will convict the world of sin and righteousness and condemnation.** The verb 'to convict of' (ἐλέγχειν followed by the preposition περί) has the sense here of exposing the true situation in regard to each issue in such a way as to confront the world with and prove its guilt. This is the force the verb frequently has in the LXX in contexts of judgement (cf. e.g. Ps. 49.8, 21 LXX; Wis. 1.8; 4.20). Whether those in the world are subjectively convinced of their guilt does not appear to be in view here. They may or may not be. Although later in Jesus' prayer the world's coming to believe as a result of the disciples' unity is expressed as a goal (17.21, 23), the dominant characterization of the world here is in terms of not being able to receive the Spirit of truth (14.17) and of hating the disciples and their witness (15.18–22). What is primarily in view is that, whether the world recognizes it or not, the Advocate's role in the cosmic trial is to convict it of its guilt. He will do this in respect to sin, righteousness and judgement. Sin is clearly the world's sin. Righteousness or justice is not the righteousness that belongs to the world but is the rightness of the case of Jesus in the overall cosmic trial, so that in being convicted of the righteousness of Jesus' cause the world is at the same time convicted of its own guilt in his unlawful condemnation. And judgement is not the judgement the world makes but God's judgement on the world, so that it is convicted of the justice and inevitability of its condemnation by the Spirit as the divine judge's agent.

Brief expansions on the three issues are provided – **of sin, because they do not believe in me; of righteousness, because I am going to the Father and you will no longer see me; of judgement, because the ruler of this world has been condemned**. In each case the subordinate clause involved begins with ὅτι and there is debate whether this is explicative, providing the content of sin, righteousness and judgement, or causal, and if causal, whether in the sense of providing reasons why the Paraclete proves the world is wrong or in the sense of providing reasons why the world is convicted. The second causal force makes best sense of the statements here. The clauses state the grounds for the world's conviction. First, the world will be convicted of sin because those who belong to it do not believe in Jesus, and throughout the narrative failure to believe has been the primary characteristic of sin and the grounds for condemnation (cf. e.g. 3.18; 5.45–7; 8.24; 9.41; 12.48; 15.22). Second, righteousness (δικαιοσύνη) here has clear forensic connotations. The noun is not used elsewhere in the Gospel, but the adjective δίκαιος appears twice in the context of right or just judgement (cf. 5.30; 7.24). The Advocate will convict the world of the righteousness of the one it has condemned to death and of the justice of his case. Jesus will have been vindicated by the divine judge, and the Advocate can drive home this verdict because Jesus' departure to a realm where he is no longer visible to his disciples constitutes his glorification, the divine seal of approval on his death. Inseparable from the world's being confronted with the justice of Jesus' cause is its being convicted of the injustice of its own part in his trial and condemnation and therefore of its guilt. Finally, the Advocate convicts the world of its judgement. The negative outcome of the verdict of the trial is in view, and here the grounds for the world's condemnation are that its ruler has been condemned. In line with 12.31–2, Jesus' 'lifting up' in his death and exaltation is seen as the point at which the ruler of the world receives his judgement of being cast out, and this therefore makes certain the condemnatory judgement against the world under his rule. Because its ruler has been judged, the world itself must fall under the same judgement.

The prosecuting work of the Advocate through the witness of the disciples amounts to the establishment of a total reversal of values in the light of the cosmic trial and its divine verdict on the rightness of Jesus' cause. The values of the world, believed by its representatives to express the values of God, will be shown to be mistaken, as they are exposed by the Spirit's witness to Jesus and to the values revealed in his mission and death. In traditional Jewish eschatology these issues of sin, righteousness and judgement were expected to be dealt with at the judgement of the end-times. But by convicting the world on these matters in the present, the Advocate's prosecution anticipates the final judgement. Since this occurs through the witness of the disciples, their proclamation of the divine verdict that has been reached in Jesus' glorification, if it is not accepted by the world, shares in this realized eschatology of condemnation (cf. also 20.23).

12–13 There is a sense in which the revelation imparted by the earthly Jesus to the disciples remains incomplete: **I still have many things to say to you, but you are not able to bear them now.** Yet what the disciples are not able to take in at this point they will receive later from the Spirit – **when he, the Spirit of truth, comes, he will guide you in all the truth**. The verb ὁδηγεῖν, 'to guide, lead', is used of the activity of the divine Spirit in Ps. 142.10 LXX. More generally, the notion recalls the role of Joshua, so that just as he, as Moses' successor, had the task of leading the people of Israel in the land (cf. Deut. 31.7, 23; *Test. Mos.* 2.1–2; 10.15; 11.10–11), so the Spirit, as Jesus' successor, has the task of leading Jesus' followers in the sphere of the truth. If Jesus is the way, because he is the truth (14.6), the Spirit is the guide in the way of truth. He continues where Jesus left off, guiding the disciples into the whole of the revelation embodied in Jesus and its implications. He is able to do this because what was said about Jesus' witness to and revelation of the truth of God is true also of the Spirit – **he will not speak of his own accord, but he will speak whatever he hears** (cf. 5.30; 8.28; 12.49; 14.10). Just as Jesus was in such intimate dependence on his Father that his words were to be considered God's words, so the Spirit has a similar relationship, through which his revelation is also to be seen as deriving from the Father. As part of this revelation, the Spirit **will declare to you the things that are to come**. In the Jewish Scriptures one of the formulations used in connection with Yahweh's predictions of the future, and distinguishing Yahweh from the gods of the nations, is 'declaring the things to come' (cf. e.g. Isa. 41.22–3; 44.7). Employing the formulation here underlines that the Spirit is the divine Spirit who comes from the Father. And just as Jesus has predicted the future, not least in this farewell discourse, so the Spirit will also continue this predictive activity, giving insight into the future the disciples will have to face and into the divine purposes for the world that have already become operative in Jesus.

14–15 He will glorify me, because he will take from what is mine and declare it to you. Through his declarations Jesus has claimed to bring glory to God (cf. 7.18; 17.1, 4). Now, as the Spirit takes the teaching, mission and person of Jesus and declares its significance to the disciples, he speaks for Jesus and brings glory to Jesus. By taking from what belongs to Jesus, the Spirit at the same time gives to Jesus – by promoting his honour and reputation in the world through his believing followers. And since **Everything that the Father has is mine**, in declaring that which belongs to Jesus, the Spirit also declares that which belongs to God. Again this underlines that the Spirit's role is to be seen as a continuation of that begun by Jesus in his declaration of the things of God. In this way also the Spirit's mediation displays what is at issue in the Gospel as a whole, namely, Jesus' oneness with the Father and the divine character of his mission. This is the truth to which the disciples must bear witness and so, in operating in this fashion, the Spirit will enable them to bear such witness.

16–18 Having spoken of the work of his successor after his exaltation, Jesus now returns to the more immediate implications of his departure for the disciples: **A little while, and you will no longer see me, and again a little while, and you will see me.** This echoes the enigmatic language of 14.19, although there seeing and not seeing were employed as part of a contrast between the world and the disciples in regard to Jesus' resurrection appearances. The direct antecedent of talk of the disciples' not seeing is in the assertion of v. 10, giving the grounds of the world's conviction about righteousness by the Spirit – 'and you will no longer see me'. So here the contrast is between the disciples' imminent experience during Jesus' arrest and death, when they will not see him, and their experience, very shortly after, of seeing him because of his resurrection (cf. 20.19–29). But what is clear to implied readers who know the course of events is by no means apparent to the disciples at this point in the narrative, despite Jesus' previous instruction. They are portrayed as not wishing to reveal their bemusement and sorrowful confusion by asking Jesus what he means (cf. v. 5): **So some of his disciples said to one another, 'What is this that he is saying to us, "A little while, and you will not see me, and again a little while, and you will see me" and "Because I am going to the Father"?'** The addition of the query about Jesus' words 'because I am going to the Father' not only points back to the antecedent saying in v. 10 but also reveals that, whatever their limited grasp of the impact of Jesus' departure (cf. v. 6), they have failed to comprehend one of the most basic and repeated themes of the discourse, namely that that departure is a return to the Father. The narrator then has the disciples repeat their questioning about 'a little while' and confess their lack of understanding.

19 As if this were not enough, the motif of Jesus' special knowledge is now drawn upon in order to have him ask the disciples whether they were discussing the saying about 'a little while' and to enable that saying to be repeated yet again. Just as the heavy underscoring of the disciples' inability to understand the metaphor of sleep when applied to Lazarus served to make a point to readers about the resurrection of the dead (cf. 11.11–13), so here it is likely that the labouring of the disciples' confusion about the 'a little while' saying functions to address an issue for the readers. The problem for John's first readers cannot be the same as that for the disciples in the narrative, namely Jesus' resurrection, which has long since occurred. What may well be problematic, however, is the parousia. The Synoptics' apocalyptic discourse, which lies behind John's farewell discourse at several points, speaks of the parousia in terms of seeing the Son of Man (Mark 13.26 parr.; cf. also 14.62 par.). The readers' period of not seeing Jesus is in the present and they need to be assured that this will be of limited duration and will be succeeded by a time when they do see Jesus. Some commentators suggest that the reference to seeing Jesus does refer to the present period of the community's mission and is fulfilled in the coming of the Paraclete, which for the evangelist replaces any further future coming of Jesus. But the disciples' experience of the Spirit is not depicted elsewhere in terms of seeing either Jesus or the Spirit (cf. 14.17) and, though the emphasis on the presence of the Spirit is undoubtedly one of the evangelist's major ways of dealing with the issue of the delay of the parousia, it is by no means the case that the future coming of Jesus and the attendant events of the consummation are simply reduced to the coming of the Spirit with his benefits for believers (see the earlier comments on 14.2–3). For the community represented by the evangelist there are issues about the coming of Jesus associated not with his departure but with the departure of their own leader and teacher, the Beloved Disciple, as 21.21–3 makes clear. It appears most likely then that the extensive discussion of seeing in a little while is working on two levels. For the disciples in the narrative sequence it has in view their encounter with Jesus through his resurrection, while for the first readers it has in view their future seeing of Jesus. Since the resurrection is the decisive anticipation of the consummation, the assurance for the disciples about the resurrection can at the same time function as an assurance for the readers about the parousia.

20–2 Jesus' reply does not address the disciples' questioning directly. It consists of two promises that their sorrow will be turned to joy and, sandwiched between them, an analogy to the experience of a woman in childbirth. The first promise is introduced by the double Amen formula, frequently indicating a traditional source for a saying: **Truly, truly, I say to you, you will weep and mourn, but the world will rejoice. You will grieve, but your sorrow will be turned into joy.** It is likely that this is a reworking of the blessing and woe formulation in Luke 6.21, 25, involving radical reversal between those who weep and mourn and those who laugh (elsewhere in Luke the terminology of joy and rejoicing replaces that of laughter). Here in John Jesus' death will be a cause of rejoicing for his opponents and of weeping and mourning for his followers, and it is again the resurrection that produces a reversal. Mary Magdalene's weeping ceases upon seeing Jesus (20.11–18) and 'the disciples rejoiced when they saw the Lord' (20.20). The sequence of emotions is analogous to that produced by childbirth: **When a woman is in labour, she has pain, because her hour has come. But when the child is born, she no longer remembers the pain because of the joy that a person has been born into the world.** The metaphor of childbirth and the associated idea of birth pangs was used frequently in Jewish writings for the people of God's experience of eschatological salvation. Two references in Isaiah are particularly pertinent because they contain other links to the present passage. Isa. 26.16–21 not only compares the people to a woman giving birth but links this with a time of joy when death gives place to resurrection, while also employing the language of 'a little while' (v. 20). Isa. 66.7–17 depicts Zion as in labour and calls on those who have mourned to rejoice with her when she has delivered her children. They are also told, 'you shall see, and your heart shall rejoice.' The language the evangelist uses for the analogy is adapted for the present context. It is significant that the first term used for the woman's pain is not that usually employed for physical pain but one that connotes emotional pain or sorrow (λύπη) and this relates to the disciples' emotions (cf. vv. 6, 20, 22). The woman's labour pains are described as the coming of her hour, thus evoking the evangelist's terminology for the eschatological timetable – the hour is coming and now is – in which Jesus' hour, shared by the disciples, is climactic. The second term for the woman's labour pain is θλῖψις, which is commonly used in apocalyptic writings and elsewhere in the New Testament for the ordeal, tribulation or suffering that ushers in the end-times. Again Jesus' apocalyptic discourse in the Synoptic tradition is relevant, since this is the term that features in Mark 13.19 par. and 13.24 par. for the end-time sufferings Jesus' followers will need to endure. Here in John the eschatological move from ordeal to joy takes place for the disciples through the coming of Jesus' hour of death and resurrection.

This is spelled out in the application to the disciples in Jesus' second promise: **So you also have sorrow now; but I will see you again, and your hearts will rejoice, and no one takes your joy from you.** This time the disciples' seeing of Jesus becomes his seeing of them in his resurrection appearances (cf. 21.1, 14). Both disciples and readers experience lasting joy as a result of Jesus' resurrection, but since v. 33 will employ the same term as for the woman's labour (θλῖψις) to assert that they are still to experience the ordeal of suffering in the world, there may again be secondary connotation of the metaphor and its application for readers. For them Jesus' death and resurrection serve as the decisive anticipation and guarantee of the end-time reversal when Jesus will appear to them and their joy will be unsullied.

23–4 For the disciples, Jesus has a further promise about their future in the period after his resurrection: **On that day you will not question me about anything.** This could be translated as 'you will ask nothing of me' and be linked with the notion of petitionary prayer that follows, stressing, in line with the next statement, that the Father, and not Jesus, is the one to whom petition will be made. This reading would, however, clash with the earlier assertion in 14.14 which speaks of petitioning Jesus in prayer. The main problem is that the verb ἐρωτάω can mean either 'to ask a question' or 'to make a request' and that both meanings occur almost an equal number of times in this Gospel. In the immediate context the latter will occur in relation to prayer in v. 26, but the former has been employed in vv. 5 and 19 and will again be found in v. 30. Given the way these earlier references have drawn attention to the disciples' confused questioning, it appears best to interpret the promise as referring to a time when their need to ask such questions will have ceased, especially since that time will also be one in which Jesus speaks plainly (cf. v. 25). Their experience of the inauguration of the joy of end-time salvation will obviate the need for uncomprehending questions. The promise of answered prayer is now repeated (cf. 14.13–14; 15.7, 16): **Truly, truly, I say to you, if you ask the Father anything in my name, he will give it to you.** This is the first time, however, that it is introduced by the double Amen formulation, signalling its roots in the tradition. Taken together with the exhortation that follows – **Ask and you will receive** – it becomes clear that the source is the material in Luke 11.9–10 (cf. Matt. 7.7–8) – 'I say to you, "Ask, and it will be given you . . . For every one who asks receives . . ."' Again the fourth evangelist adds that such prayer is to be in Jesus' name. This will constitute a new stage in the disciples' experience of prayer – **Until now you have not asked anything in my name.** As Jesus' authorized representatives who pray in accord with what he himself represents, they will find their requests answered by the Father, who has given to Jesus and will continue to give to them. Such praying is both the way to and part of the joy they have been promised – **so that your joy may be complete** (cf. also 15.11).

25 Jesus now contrasts the way he has been speaking to the disciples in this discourse and how he will communicate with them in the future: **I have said these things to you in figures of speech. An hour is coming when I will no longer speak to you in figures of speech but will tell you plainly about the Father.** On the term for figure of speech (παροιμία), see the comment on 10.6. Here the plural noun certainly refers to the preceding riddling saying about 'a little while' and the analogy about the woman in labour but it may also refer to the dominant mode of the farewell discourse as a whole, which has been enigmatic and cryptic. Earlier in the narrative the notion of speaking plainly was employed to contrast with figurative speech (cf. 10.24; 11.14). In the eschatological hour that is dawning with Jesus' death and exaltation, the disciples are promised direct speaking about the Father. But this announcement remains somewhat enigmatic for readers. When and how is it fulfilled? The disciples believe that Jesus starts to speak plainly almost immediately (cf. v. 29), but even if this response were taken straightforwardly, 'an hour is coming' is not the way one refers to something that will occur in a few moments. There are no post-resurrection speeches of Jesus about the Father placed at the end of this narrative. Jesus does tell Mary Magdalene to pass on the message to the disciples that he is ascending to his Father and their Father, to his God and their God

(20.17), but it seems highly unlikely that this short announcement is the fulfilment of the promise. There is another sense, however, in which most of Jesus' speech in this Gospel has a post-resurrection perspective. This is particularly true, as we shall see, of the prayer in chapter 17. In fact, the prayer begins with the announcement that the hour has come and in its address to the Father, with the disciples as the audience, it does give clear insights into the identity of the Father and his relationship with the Son and into the Father's purposes for Jesus' followers. Or does one need to take the wording of the prediction more loosely and see the events of the hour itself and their interpretation by the Paraclete as Jesus' own future plain revelation of the Father? Jesus' death and exaltation do reveal the Father, and the Advocate who is Jesus' alter ego, his agent who does not speak on his own authority, in declaring to the disciples what belongs to Jesus also declares what belongs to the Father (vv. 13–15). The use of cognate verbs, here ἀπαγγελεῖν for Jesus' speaking, and in vv. 13–15 ἀναγγελεῖν for the Spirit's declaration, reinforces the connection, suggesting that the two descriptions offer alternative perspectives on the same speech act. The primary force of Jesus' words, then, is that the plain speaking will occur when the Spirit interprets for the disciples the significance of the events of Jesus' hour, but readers may also recognize, secondarily, that Jesus' prayer in 17.1–26 represents the clearest expression of this plain speaking about the Father in the narrative after he has made his prediction.

26–7 On that day you will ask in my name, and I do not say to you that I will pray to the Father for you; for the Father himself loves you because you have loved me and have believed that I came from God. The final saying about prayer in the discourse stresses that the disciples will not need Jesus to petition the Father on their behalf. In the light of both 14.16 and 17.1–26, much of whose content reflects the perspective of the exalted Christ, it is unlikely that the force of the saying is a renunciation of any future intercessory role on Jesus' part. Its main point appears to be to assure Jesus' followers that their relationship of love and trust in him puts them in an intimate relationship to the God who loves them, in which they speak to this God as Father and can make claims on this God in prayer. Jesus has mediated the relationship in the first place – it is because he as Son invokes God as Father that disciples can now do the same – and this truth is preserved in the formulation, repeated yet again, that believers' address to God will be in Jesus' name. Jesus' departure is advantageous, since the praying of his followers as representatives of all that he stands for means that there is a sense in which Jesus himself no longer has to ask on their behalf. Their praying will bring them into a new level of intimacy with God as they share in Jesus' loving relationship to the Father.

In that relationship their love for Jesus and their belief in his divine origin will be met by the love of the Father himself for them.

28 Jesus' mention of his origin prompts a further statement of both his origin and destiny, summarizing a major theme of the discourse and of the Christology of the Gospel as a whole: **I came from the Father and have come into the world; again, I am leaving the world and am going to the Father.** To understand Jesus' mission in the world aright, it is necessary to recognize that it is a mission that begins and ends with God the Father. This is why Jesus is the unique Son and why his words and deeds witness to the Father, who is the ultimate source and goal of his mission. In the context of this discourse and Jesus' imminent departure, the formulation makes clear that it is not enough to believe that Jesus has come from God. To appreciate the advantages the new situation will bring, there has to be an understanding that Jesus is departing to the Father (cf. 14.28; 16.5–7).

29–30 On the basis of what Jesus has just said since their questioning, the disciples are confident that they have now at last attained an adequate level of understanding of his instruction – **Now you are speaking plainly and not in any figure of speech. Now we know that you know all things and have no need that anyone question you.** There are already hints here that their confidence is not well founded and this will become even clearer as their conversation with Jesus continues. They take the words of Jesus in vv. 26–8 as the plain teaching to which he has referred and contrast them with the sayings about 'a little while' and the woman in labour that have preceded them, but they have failed to note the eschatological dimension of Jesus' promise about plain speaking ('An hour is coming'). What is more, their correct recognition that Jesus knows all things and does not need their or anyone else's questioning appears to be founded primarily on the exchange in vv. 16–19 and the special knowledge Jesus has displayed about what they were asking among themselves, rather than on any more profound comprehension of what Jesus has said about the new situation that will result from his departure to the Father. The irony becomes obvious through their confession of faith – **Because of this we believe that you came from God.** They are convinced on account of his omniscience that Jesus has come from God, but it is not clear, formally, that this is any advance on Nicodemus' similar confession in 3.2, which was deemed inadequate, or that it takes them as far as Peter's earlier confession in 6.69 or Martha's in 11.27. What it omits is the main thrust of what Jesus has been attempting to teach them in this discourse, namely, that he is also going to God, with all that that implies about his coming death and their future relationship to him.

31–2 That their confession is at best incomplete is underlined first by the question mark Jesus puts against it – **Do you now believe?** – and then by his prediction of their behaviour that will result from the failure to comprehend what he has said about his departure – **See, the hour is coming, and has come, when you will be scattered, each to his own home, and you will leave me alone.** The time of eschatological fulfilment of which Jesus has been speaking (cf. vv. 23, 25–6) has to take in his betrayal, arrest and death and in that decisive hour the disciples will abandon him. The prediction is formulated in terms of the Synoptic tradition's prediction of the shepherd being smitten and the sheep scattered, where Zech. 13.7 is cited (cf. Mark 14.27; Matt. 26.31), a tradition which, as noted earlier, is likely to have influenced the material about the death of the good shepherd in 10.1–18. It is significant for any assessment of the function of the Beloved Disciple in the narrative that the prediction of the scattering of the disciples, resulting in Jesus being left alone, does not appear to have taken into account the episode where this disciple is at the cross with the mother of Jesus in 19.25–7. The disciples' imminent abandonment of Jesus is contrasted with the Father's relationship to Jesus – **And yet I am not alone, for the Father is with me.** There is no room in the Fourth Gospel's perspective for any thought that Jesus will also be abandoned by God (cf. Mark 15.34; Matt. 27.46). The awareness of his intimate relationship with the Father, which has accompanied Jesus in his mission (cf. 8.29), remains throughout its climactic hour.

33 Having exposed the groundlessness of the disciples' confidence about their faith and understanding, Jesus brings the discourse to a conclusion on a strong note of reassurance, pointing again to its main purpose in relation to them – **so that in me you might have peace.** All that he says about his departure and about the situation the disciples will face has been meant to allay anxiety and fear. In a repetition of the promise of the gift of peace from the end of the first half of the discourse (cf. 14.27), Jesus indicates that a security, similar to that which he has because of the relationship to the Father he has just expressed, is available to the disciples because of their relationship to him. This peace is the eschatological peace expected to result from the defeat of every power hostile to God. Indeed Jesus declares that that eschatological victory has already taken place: **In the world you will have suffering, but take heart, I have conquered the world.** Through his death and exaltation Jesus will emerge triumphant and justified from his judgement by the world (cf. vv. 10–11). His followers will still have to endure the ordeal of suffering in the world (θλῖψις; see vv. 21–2), but the decisive victory over the world will have been won and this will make all the difference for them. They will be able to accept the pain and persecution their mission in the world will entail because they are empowered by the confident assurance that the world is now under the control of the one to whom they bear witness.

The main source of this third section of the second part of the farewell discourse is the latter's first part, but, in elaborating on themes in 13.31— 14.31, it also takes up some additional aspects of the Synoptic tradition. The double Amen saying of v. 20 adapts the tradition of Jesus' words in Luke 6.21, 25, the language of ordeal and tribulation in v. 21 echoes that of Mark 13.19, 24, the teaching about prayer reworks Luke 11.9–10, and the prediction about the scattering of the disciples picks up on Mark 14.27.

The Gospel as a whole has been well described as an apocalypse in reverse or inside out. One particular feature of this section of the farewell discourse clearly illustrates such a description. Whereas in an apocalypse the heavenly mystery encountered by the seer is interpreted by an angelic figure and disclosed in the writing, here the revelation supplied by Jesus continues to be mysterious and enigmatic for his disciples and will only be fully disclosed by a divine interpreter, the Paraclete, after Jesus' earthly mission has been completed. As has been noted several times in comments above, the two stages of revelation entail two levels of understanding of the narrative. There is the level of understanding of the disciples within the narrative and the level of understanding of readers, who have benefited from the further stage of revelation supplied by the Paraclete and mediated through the evangelist's perspective.

As in 13.31—14.31, one of the chief means of Jesus' providing consolation for the disciples as he interprets his departure in death and exaltation, and of the evangelist providing reassurance for readers, is to rework the traditional elements of an apocalypse that speak of end-time events and to show their fulfilment in the present. Here not only is the advantageous coming of the Spirit a form of the coming of Jesus but also through this Advocate's work the end-time events of the vindication of the justice of God and the condemnation of sin are already taking place. A future seeing of Jesus and the end-time reversal whereby weeping and mourning become joy will be experienced by the disciples through Jesus' resurrection appearances. They will also be able to know the end-time peace resulting from the defeat of this world and its powers that has become present reality through the death and exaltation of Jesus. All this does not mean, however, that eschatology is swallowed up into present experience without remainder. As in 14.2–3, traditional early Christian eschatological hopes still provide both the framework within which these more realized emphases operate and the horizon for some of the issues still facing the implied readers of Jesus' words. In the wake of the Beloved Disciple's departure through death and the questions this raises about the future coming of Jesus, they can still derive consolation and motivation for their mission from the promises about the Spirit as Advocate and from the gifts of eschatological joy and peace. They can also interpret the promise to the disciples of seeing Jesus through the resurrection appearances as giving assurance for their own future seeing of Jesus at his coming (cf. 1 John 2.28; 3.2).

In regard to their mission in the world in the meantime, it is worth underlining the connection between what is said about the Advocate's activity among the disciples in vv. 12–15 and what is said about his activity in the world in vv. 8–11. If it is through the disciples' witness that the Paraclete carries out his prosecution of the world in regard to the truth of the cause of Jesus, then it is imperative that the disciples have as comprehensive an insight into that truth as possible, and therefore that the Paraclete continually direct them in the whole truth that it is his role to disclose. They too need to be persuaded that their position in the world is not what it appears to be as a result of the world's hostile judgement of them but that the true judge in the cosmic judgement has given a very differerent verdict about Jesus and about their claims for him. Empowered by the Spirit of truth's prosecuting and interpreting activity, their witness to Jesus will play its part in the convicting of an unbelieving world.

What is said about the Spirit also has major implications for understanding how Jesus and his message are presented in this Gospel's narrative discourse. The Spirit's role is to interpret the teaching of Jesus in such a way that it becomes an address to believers in their ever-changing situations – 'he will take from what is mine and declare it to you' (vv. 14–15). This is precisely what the evangelist has done in telling the story of the earthly Jesus and his disciples from the perspective of the exalted Christ and the situation of his later followers. Within its own point of view, this Gospel's creative reworking of and elaboration on the traditions of Jesus' words, which are then placed on his lips, is simply an expression of the Paraclete at work through the evangelist. Jesus' words in this Gospel are the words of the earthly Jesus now interpreted and declared, in the light of the hour of Jesus' death and exaltation, by the Spirit whom he appointed as his authoritative representative and successor.

(v) The prayer of Jesus 17.1–26

(1) After Jesus had spoken these things, he raised his eyes to heaven and said, 'Father, the hour has come; glorify your Son so that the Son[1] may glorify you, (2) since you have given him authority over all flesh, in order that he might give eternal life to all those whom you have given him. (3) Now this is eternal life, that they should know you, the only true God, and Jesus Christ

---

[1] Some translations (e.g. NAB, NJB) follow A and other manuscripts by reading 'your Son' in line with the first part of the petition. But it appears that a scribe was unduly influenced by what had preceded it or added σου for the sake of stylistic consistency, since the shorter reading has the stronger support in p^{60vid} ℵ B C⋆ W.

whom you have sent. (4) I glorified you on earth by completing the work you gave me to do. (5) And now, Father, glorify me in your own presence with the glory I had with you before the world existed. (6) I have made known your name to those whom you have given me out of the world. They were yours and you gave them to me, and they have kept your word. (7) Now they know that all you have given me is from you; (8) for the words you gave me I have given to them, and they have received them and truly know that I came from you, and they have believed that you sent me.

(9) 'I am asking on their behalf; I am not asking on behalf of the world but on behalf of those you have given me, because they are yours, (10) and all that is mine is yours and what is yours is mine, and I have been glorified in them. (11) I am no longer in the world, but they are in the world, and I am coming to you. Holy Father, keep them in your name which you have given me, so that they might be one as we are one. (12) While I was with them, I kept them in the name which you have given me, and guarded them, and not one of them was lost except the one destined to be lost[2], in order that the scripture might be fulfilled. (13) But now I am coming to you, and I speak these words in the world so that they might have in them my complete joy. (14) I have given them your word, and the world hated them, because they are not of the world, just as I am not of the world. (15) I am not asking that you take them out of the world but that you keep them from the evil one. (16) They are not of the world, just as I am not of the world. (17) Sanctify them in the truth; your word is truth. (18) As you have sent me into the world, so I have sent them into the world; (19) and for their sake I sanctify myself, so that they also may be sanctified in the truth.

(20) 'I am asking not only on their behalf but also on behalf of those who believe in me through their word, (21) that they all may be one, just as you, Father, are in me and I am in you, so may they be[3] in us, in order that the world may believe that you have sent me. (22) I have given them the glory that you gave me in order that they may be one, just as we are one, (23) I in them and you in me, that they may be completely one, so that the world may know that you have sent me and have loved them just as you loved me. (24) Father, I desire that those you have

---

[2] Literally, 'the son of perdition'.
[3] This shorter reading is better attested (p^{66vid} B C* D W). Some manuscripts add ἕν, 'one', bringing this clause into line with the first clause in the verse and with that which follows in v. 22.

given me may be with me where I am, so that they may see my glory which you have given me, because you loved me before the foundation of the world. (25) Righteous Father, the world has not known you but I have known you, and these have known that you have sent me. (26) I have made known your name to them and I will make it known, so that the love with which you have loved me may be in them and I in them.'

As has been noted, John 13—17 as a whole takes up the genre of the farewell address familiar from both Jewish and Graeco-Roman literature. Praying for those remaining after the hero's departure or death could feature as part of the genre, as indicated by the biblical examples of Moses in Deut. 33, where some of his blessings of the tribes take the form of prayers (cf. vv. 7–8, 11), and of Paul in his farewell to the Ephesian elders (cf. Acts 20.36). Here in John the prayer element is significantly expanded and becomes the climactic feature at the end of the farewell. So, although the prayer will take up from the prologue and earlier discourses the notions of pre-existence, the relation of love and unity between the Father and Son, and glory, it is most directly related to the discourse material that has immediately preceded it. Just as the latter offered a perspective both on Jesus' departure and on the disciples' future mission in a hostile world, a mission that necessitates love for one another, so does this prayer. It prepares both the disciples in the narrative for what is about to happen and readers for the passion and resurrection accounts that follow, attempting to ensure that the disciples share Jesus' point of view and that readers share the evangelist's point of view on these events.

Although one does not immediately think of the Lord's Prayer (cf. Matt. 6.9–15; Luke 11.1–4) in reading John 17, a good case can be made that this is John's equivalent and is closest to the Matthean version. Its address to God as Father and a reference to heaven are found in v. 1. The notion of the hallowing of God's name is taken up in a variety of ways – the concern with God's name (cf. vv. 6, 11, 26), the address 'Holy Father' (v. 11), and the petition 'glorify your Son' (v. 1), which functions as an equivalent, since, in the Fourth Gospel's discourse, the Father has given the divine name to the Son (v. 11). The Johannine prayer also has two functional equivalents to the notion of the coming of the kingdom in the Lord's Prayer – the coming of Jesus' hour and, more significantly, the concept of eternal life, which is here explicitly linked with the idea of sovereign authority (cf. v. 3). Corresponding to the petition 'Your will be done, on earth as it is in heaven' is the Johannine perspective in which Jesus has done God's will on earth by completing the work God gave him to do (v. 4; cf. also 4.34, where completing this work is synonymous with doing God's will). 'And do not bring us to the time of trial' can be seen as reformulated in 'they are in the world . . . keep them in your name' (v.

11), while 'but rescue us from the evil one' is more precisely reflected in 'keep them from the evil one' (v. 15). John 17 can be viewed, then, as the Lord's Prayer transposed into a Johannine key. Just as the Lord's Prayer functioned for Matthew and Luke as a summary of what Jesus stood for and what his followers need to pray for, so the prayer in John 17 summarizes what the Johannine Jesus stands for and therefore shows what it means to pray in Jesus' name.

The prayer is indeed significant in relation to the preceding instructions to the disciples about praying in Jesus' name. The disciples have been exhorted six times to pray (14.13–14; 15.7–8,16b; 16.23, 24, 26–7). The variety in the form and content of Jesus' teaching about prayer in the Synoptics is missing. Instead there has been a relentless focus on Jesus' promise that whatever the disciples ask in his name they will receive. The narrative is constructed in such a way that, just as the disciples have been told ahead of time about their need to witness and are then able to see Jesus as the paradigm for that witness in his trial and death, so also, having been told about their need to pray in Jesus' name, they are then given a model for such prayer in Jesus' own prayer. He enacts what is entailed in the confident asking of the Father that they are to engage in after his glorification. This is confirmed by the fact that the disciples remain the audience for this prayer, although its words are directed to the Father. There is no indication of Jesus separating himself from the disciples in order to pray.

Jesus here is portrayed like other humans, as one whose relationship to God at a time of crisis, facing impending death, would be expressed in prayer, but the content of that prayer with its divine perspective on the world makes it quite unlike that of any other human. The different facets of the eschatological hour of exaltation, which includes Jesus' death and return to the Father, are also already in play in the temporal perspective that informs the prayer. As elsewhere in the narrative, pre-resurrection and post-resurrection perspectives are combined. On the one hand, Jesus can view his departure and glorification as imminent (vv. 1, 5), see himself as in the process of returning to the Father (vv. 11b, 13a) and consider himself still in the world (v. 13b). On the other hand, Jesus prays as the risen and exalted one, who can speak of himself in the third person as 'the Son' and 'Jesus Christ' (vv. 1, 3), see his work on earth as already completed (vv. 4, 6–8), say that he is no longer in the world (v. 11a), ask that his followers be where he already is (v. 24) and think of himself as in them (vv. 23, 26). But the Jesus who utters this prayer is also the Logos, aware of his pre-existence (vv. 5, 24; cf. 1.1–2) – the Logos who has become flesh but who at the same time is the Son who remains in intimate relation with the Father. The prayer thus constitutes this Gospel's most extensive reflection on what is entailed in the intimate union between the Son and the Father, which was experienced in this world yet transcends its categories of time and space. What is just as striking about this prayer is that the community of Jesus' followers is also envisaged as being able to share in this same intimate union while it carries on its mission in this world.

The prayer's overlapping themes and repetitions mean that the moves in its progression of thought are not always clearly signalled. The treatment here sees the actual petitions as providing the main structural markers and follows those who hold that there are three major units related to the widening scope of the object of the prayer – (i) Jesus' prayer for his own glorification (vv. 1–8); (ii) Jesus' prayer for the disciples (vv. 9–19); and (iii) Jesus' prayer for both present and future believers (vv. 20–6). In line with the evangelist's fondness for structuring episodes in seven parts, the prayer contains seven specific petitions, the first and last sections having two each and the longer middle section three. In the case of each petition the grounds upon which the request is made are also set out. These grounds sometimes precede, sometimes follow and sometimes both precede and follow the request.

1 This verse's introductory transition – **After Jesus had spoken these things, he raised his eyes to heaven** – shows Jesus adopting the stance that signals the beginning of the prayer. Its first part contains two petitions which take up two aspects of Jesus' glorification. Each is introduced by a direct address to the Father, which sets the tone of intimacy for the whole prayer. In the first petition – **Father, the hour has come; glorify your Son so that the Son may glorify you** – the focus is on Jesus' glorification in history, his departure by means of the cross. The hour has been mentioned throughout the narrative and Jesus' mention of its arrival takes up the narrator's reference to its coming in 13.1 at the beginning of the farewell section. Jesus prays that he will be glorified in this hour, and the following purpose clause means that the petition includes the Son glorifying the Father. Throughout the narrative Jesus' cause and God's cause have been intertwined. If Jesus is honoured or glorified, this will mean that God is also honoured and glorified (cf. 13.31–2). Jesus' hour of exaltation through death will be the paradoxical establishment of the reputation of both God and Jesus.

2–3 The petition is backed by the authority to give eternal life that God has delegated to Jesus. Earlier mention of the authority given to Jesus is in terms of his authority to judge (5.27; cf. 5.22). Here the focus of his authority **over all flesh** is on the salvific aspect of his role as judge, the positive verdict he will give – **in order that he might give eternal life to all those whom you have given him** (cf. also 5.21). This gift of life, which goes to all those whom the Father has given to the Son, will, in terms of the narrative's temporal perspective on Jesus' mission, be the result of the divine verdict at the crucifixion. The petition that Jesus be glorified can now be seen to be necessary, because only after Jesus' glorification will eternal life become available, as the rivers of living water flow from him (cf. 7.37–9; 19.34). What is entailed in receiving eternal life is **that they should know you, the only true God, and Jesus Christ whom you have sent.** This summarizing definition of eternal life by the evangelist is in line with the thought of the Johannine epistles (cf. 1 John 5.20). In the Jewish Scriptures knowing God was at the heart of the covenant relationship (cf., e.g., Jer. 24.7; 31.33–4). An intimate knowledge of Israel's God, which was previously primarily gained through Torah, is now available through the words of Jesus which have made this God known (cf. also vv. 6–8). The communion with God entailed in the experience of eternal life requires, however, a proper recognition of Jesus' identity. Because of who he is as the divine agent who is one with God, this saving knowledge is not a double knowledge – first of God and then of Jesus. The formulation also indicates that, for the evangelist, this identification of Jesus does not entail any abrogation of monotheism. Talk of the one true God is reminiscent of the exclusive claims for Yahweh that can be found in the Jewish Scriptures. But if there is one true God, how can this God share the divine glory with Jesus, as this prayer makes clear he does, without Jesus being a second god? The explanation appears to be that, for the evangelist, Jesus in his relationship as Son to the Father is intrinsic to this one God's identity. As the second petition will make clear, Jesus was always included in the identity and glory of the one God, even before the foundation of the world. It is not the case then that in glorifying Jesus God shares the divine glory with some lesser being. Rather the exaltation and glorification of Jesus displays the glory of the one God.

4–5 With the second petition – **And now, Father, glorify me in your own presence with the glory I had with you before the world existed** – the statement of grounds both precedes and follows the request. First, the presupposition for Jesus' return to this glory is underlined – **I glorified you on earth by completing the work you gave me to do.** The perspective is one that views Jesus' death-as-glorification as having already been accomplished and is in line with his final words on the cross – 'It is completed' (19.30). In the second petition itself the reference of the request for glory is the completion of the exaltation via the cross in a return to the presence of God in heaven and it entails the resumption of the experience of glory Jesus enjoyed in the divine presence before the foundation of the world.

6–8 The grounds for the petition are now continued and they elaborate on Jesus' accomplishment of his work: **I have made known your name to those whom you have given me out of the world.** In the ancient world the name stood for who the person was and what the person represented, that person's identity and reputation. Jesus has therefore made known who God is and what is involved in God's reputation. In the process he has employed a particular name of God. One of the distinctive features of his witness in this Gospel is his use of the divine self-identification – 'I Am' (cf., e.g., 8.28, 58; 13.12; 18.5–6).

In Jesus' accomplishment of making God's name known to the disciples both God's sovereign initiative – **They were yours and you gave them to me** – and the disciples' human response – **they have kept your word** – were involved. In the perspective of this prayer disciples are to see themselves as part of the intimate relationship between the Father and the Son, as the gift of the Father to the Son (cf. also 6.37, 39, 44). Jesus' mission has also been successful, since, as a result, these disciples have kept God's word (λόγος). Again from a post-resurrection perspective, the disciples are seen as having received and remained faithful to the divine message spoken and embodied by Jesus, his witness to the truth. In receiving the word, they have also received particular words or sayings (ῥήματα) – **the words you gave me I have given to them, and they have received them.** They know that Jesus' words and Jesus himself are from God. In short, they have believed that God sent Jesus.

9–10 In what follows in the prayer, attention now turns explicitly to those who are the fruit of Jesus' completed work. For those who are his special possession, his own whom he loves (cf. 13.1b), Jesus will make three specific requests – for their being kept in the divine name, protected from the evil one and sanctified in the truth. These requests are preceded by a general statement of intercession – **I am asking on their behalf** – which is grounded by the following statements, which in turn expand on what has already been said about Jesus' mission in v. 6. Jesus is interceding for his disciples and not for the world. κόσμος, 'world', refers here to human society in its hostility to God. The prayer is concerned with mission in such a world (cf. vv. 18, 20–3), but the hope for the world is that it ceases to be the world by receiving the witness of Jesus' followers – hence Jesus' focus on these followers. Again his intercession for them is because they belong to God and Jesus – **they are yours, and all that is mine is yours and what is yours is mine** – and because Jesus has accomplished his work among them – **I have been glorified in them.** Jesus' reputation and honour have been displayed in the response of his disciples.

11–13 The first petition for the disciples – **Holy Father, keep them in your name which you have given me, so that they might be one as we are one** – asks that they be kept or preserved as a community by the revelation of who God is that Jesus has embodied. The purpose clause indicates that in this way they will also be protected against divisions. Since for this Gospel there is a unity between God's name and Jesus' name, it is not surprising that those who are kept in God's name that has been given to Jesus are expected to display this unity. This thought will be developed later in the prayer. The grounds for the petition are stated both before and after it. The disciples had been given to Jesus but now he is no longer in the world and is coming to the Father, so in his absence they need the Father's protection, especially of their unity. The second part of the grounds underlines this – **I kept them in the name which you have given me, and guarded them**. Jesus had been doing what he now asks the Father to do. With the statement that **not one of them was lost or perished** (cf. 6.39), it becomes clear that the keeping or protection that is being requested entails the disciples' salvation. There is a rich scriptural background of 'keeping' language for Yahweh's relation to Israel (cf. e.g., Gen. 28.15; Ps. 121.7–8; Isa. 42.6; 49.8). Yahweh 'will keep Israel, as a shepherd a flock' (Jer. 31.10). There are also echoes here of what was said about Jesus as the good shepherd in 10.28 – 'they will never perish, and no one will snatch them from my hand'. It is immediately made clear that in the case of the obvious exception, Judas, this was not because of Jesus' deficiency in keeping but rather because this was Judas' destiny ('the son of perdition') and in order that Scripture might be fulfilled (cf. 13.18 with its citation of Ps. 41.9). The narrative has in fact already underlined Jesus' sovereignty in regard to Judas by having him predict Judas' destiny ahead of time so that later the disciples would recognize the truth of his word coming to pass in history and, like Israel in relation to Yahweh (cf. Isa. 43.9–13), be able to 'believe that I Am' (13.19). Now here the formulation – **I speak these words in the world** – indicates again that Jesus' prayer is intended to be overheard by the disciples for their encouragement – **so that they might have in them my complete joy**. Just as Jesus' joy stems from his unbroken intimate relationship with God, so the disciples will participate fully in the same joy by being kept in the name that represents that relationship. Both the unity and the joy of the disciples are viewed as dependent on their being kept in God's name.

14–16 In the second petition for the disciples – **I am not asking that you take them out of the world but that you keep them from the evil one** – the reference of the one substantival use of 'evil' in John's Gospel has been taken as most likely to be to the personification of cosmic evil who is portrayed earlier as the ruler of the world (cf. 12.31; 14.30; 16.11). The juxtaposition of the language of being kept in the Father's name and that of being kept from the evil one indicates the two antithetical spheres of power operative in the world. The grounds for this petition are found in its surrounding framework. While they are in the world, the disciples will need protection against the ruler of the world, because, as the recipients of God's word through Jesus, the hatred of the world is against them. Neither the disciples nor Jesus are **of the world**

(vv. 14b, 16; cf. also 15.19). The world in its hostility to God is not the determinative source of their lives. Though they are not of this world, Jesus does not ask that his disciples be taken out of it. They still have a mission within the world, but need protection from its evil ruler while they are engaged in that mission.

17–19 The third petition for the disciples – **Sanctify them in the truth** – is grounded in the following assertions about the continuity between the mission of Jesus and that of the disciples. **As you have sent me into the world, so I have sent them into the world** (cf. also 20.21b). The disciples have been told that their mission in the world is one of witness (15.27), and Jesus will sum up his mission in the world in terms of witness to the truth (18.37). So if his followers are to continue such a mission of witness to the truth, they will need to be set apart in the truth. This too will be in continuity with Jesus, who sanctifies himself for his task. In 10.36, where Jesus is depicted as the fulfilment of the Feast of Hanukkah, which celebrated the rededication of the temple altar, he spoke of himself as 'the one whom the Father has sanctified and sent into the world'. When now Jesus speaks of sanctifying himself, this is in line with the way this Gospel portrays him as sharing what would normally be considered divine prerogatives and also as being in control of his own life and mission (cf. 10.17–18). Both Jesus and the disciples are seen as set apart in the truth. Truth in this Gospel is generally the revelation of God in Jesus. This is confirmed by the explanatory statement – **your word is truth**. The prologue portrayed Jesus as God's word, the Logos (cf. 1.1–2, 14), and earlier in the farewell section Jesus proclaimed himself to be the truth (14.6). More specifically, in terms of the Gospel's dominant trial motif, truth is the issue at stake in the trial – the identity of Jesus in relation to God. The disciples, then, are to be set apart for witnessing to the truth of the trial's verdict, namely that Jesus is the one in whom God displays the divine glory.

20–3 As a result of the disciples' mission in the world others will become believers – **those who believe in me through their word** – and so the scope of the prayer expands to include two further petitions for this whole company of believers. **I am asking . . . that they all may be one.** This request for the unity both of the disciples and of those who come to believe through their witness makes clear that this is a unity that comes from all participating in the foundational unity between Father and Son – **just as you, Father, are in me and I am in you, so may they be in us.** Again the grounds for the petition follow. Jesus states that he has already laid the basis for the sort of unity of which the petition speaks – **I have given them the glory that you gave me in order that they may be one, just as we are one.** God's glory, the honour and reputation of the divine name, has been bestowed on Jesus and Jesus has granted to his community of followers a share in that glory by making known to them the divine name (cf. v. 6) and enabling them to share in his own reputation and honour (cf. v. 10b). Again it is stressed that the complete unity between Father, Son and believers has as its goal the world's coming to know through this the truth about Jesus' mission – that he is the one who has been sent and loved by God – and the truth about believers' relationship to God – that they also are loved by God. It is noticeable that in these verses the world is not seen as in such a permanently hostile state that mission would be futile. Rather the world is expected to be able to receive the witness of Jesus' followers and to be able to believe and know that God has sent Jesus. The community in which believers' witness is embodied is to be a united one and the issues at stake in Jesus' mission hinge on this – **that they may be completely one, so that the world may know that you have sent me and have loved them just as you loved me.** Since the truth established in the cosmic trial is the unity between the one who is sent and the one who has sent him, it is not surprising that the testimony to that truth is displayed by the oneness of the witnesses. It is not simply that the unity of the witnesses mirrors the union between the Father and the Son; their unity actually participates in the unity that defines the relation between Jesus and God (cf. v. 21). In this way in its ongoing mission the life of the community is meant to be an embodied witness to the truth about Jesus. The goal of its mission is not only that the world come to know Jesus' identity as the one sent by God but also that it come to know that his followers are loved by God just as Jesus is loved by God (v. 23c). From the perspective of this prayer, the world comes to know the God of love not only through hearing the witness that Jesus' death is God's loving gift to the world but also through seeing and experiencing the enacted witness of believers united through God's loving acceptance of them and their loving acceptance of one another.

24–6 Whereas vv. 9–23 have had in view the mission of Jesus' followers in the world, the second petition for all believers and the final request of the prayer as a whole turns to their future destiny. **Father, I desire that those you have given me may be with me where I am, so that they may see my glory.** The change of verb from 'ask' to 'desire' (θέλω) serves as a reminder that Jesus' will is one with that of the Father and therefore underscores the efficacy of his prayer. At its beginning Jesus had prayed for his own glorification; now at its end this features in his desire for his followers. Those who have struggled and suffered over the issue of Jesus' glory are to experience it fully for themselves, as they will be with him in the Father's presence and see for themselves the divine glory he has shared from before the foundation of the world. When will this be? The prayer is for Jesus' followers as a whole, giving a vision of their eschatological communal destiny. So the primary referent is probably not what will happen to individual believers at their death. Instead the entire new community that results from Jesus' mission in this world shares at the end in the glory that Jesus enjoyed in the beginning (cf. also 1 John 3.2).

The grounds for this final petition revolve around the difference between believers and the world. Since believers are those who, in distinction from the world, know that God has sent Jesus, since they are those to whom Jesus has made known God's name and will make it known so that God's love for Jesus and Jesus himself are in them, it is appropriate that their destiny is to be with Jesus and see his glory. The address here to God as **Righteous Father** is significant. The adjective 'righteous' and the noun 'righteousness' occur earlier in forensic contexts (cf. 5.30; 7.24; 16.8, 10). The end of the prayer, then, sees the Father as also the righteous judge and sees believers as those who can be confident of God's loving judgement because they have aligned themselves with Jesus' cause and know that God has sent him and revealed through him the divine name and reputation. The final verse takes up the language of v. 6 in summarizing the mission of Jesus – **I have made known your name to them** – and at the same time it points to the ongoing mission – **I will make it known** – that is carried forward through the witness of the Paraclete and the community of Jesus' followers (cf. 15.26–7). This verse also elaborates on v. 23, as again it is stressed that love has everything to do with that ongoing mission – **so that the love with which you have loved me may be in them and I in them**. God's name is made known in the relationship of love between God and Jesus, and it continues to be made known as this relationship of love shapes the life of the community of Jesus' followers and as, through that relationship, Jesus, who embodies God's name, is present in the community.

Jesus' prayer provides a restatement of what the Gospel as a whole and the preceding farewell discourse in particular have said about his mission and the situation of his followers in the world after his departure and return to the Father. The reformulation of earlier themes as a prayer gives them an intensified emotional force. Through this means the readers are also given fuller insight into Jesus' intimate relationship as Son with the Father. As his death approaches, Jesus is depicted as baring his heart to his Father about the future of his cause in the world. He has already given instructions about the future but now he turns that future over to God. Since the Jesus who prays is also the exalted Christ, the prayer has an additional force. It reflects the belief that even after his departure Christ's advocacy in prayer supports the mission of his followers. The knowledge that the risen and exalted Christ prays for his followers should be a major factor in shaping their identity and providing reassurance. The situation in which they find themselves can be seen as both already known by Jesus and part of the outworking of God's purposes for this world. While they have a significant role to play in the ongoing mission of witness, the

ultimate source of their confidence is to be that this remains God's cause
and God can be entrusted with it. Just as God has given Jesus what it took
to accomplish his role, so now Jesus summons God to give what it will
take for his followers to complete theirs. Despite the opposition they face,
believers can be encouraged because they are in an intimate relationship
with the Father and the Son, whose love and protection provide full
support for the mission in the world for which they have been set apart.

2. The Passion   18.1—19.42

The long farewell section has prepared readers, along with the disciples,
to understand the events that now follow. The discourse and prayer in
the extended lull in the action underscore that what is about to happen
is the culminating hour to which Jesus' mission has all the time been
moving and that, despite all contrary appearances, the events of arrest,
interrogation, trial and crucifixion are part of his hour of glory. He
remains in sovereign control throughout these events, aware that they
are essential to his Father's purposes in achieving life for the world. The
various episodes within the passion tradition can now be related and the
distinctive shaping and detail of the Fourth Gospel's narration of these
develop and reinforce the implied author's perspective that has already
been established. In particular, the overall structuring of this section
should be noted. It progresses in five distinct episodes: (i) Jesus' arrest
(18.1–11); (ii) his interrogation by Annas (18.12–27); (iii) his trial before
Pilate (18.28—19.16a); (iv) his crucifixion and death (19.16b–37); and
(v) his burial (19.38–42). The central and most extended scene is Jesus'
Roman trial, and this corresponds to what has emerged as the central,
overarching theme in this Gospel's narrative, that of judgement or cosmic
trial. As will become apparent, the literary artistry and the ironies of
that central episode contribute effectively to the narrative's dominant
perspective, which claims that in Jesus' mission, trial and death it is not he
who is being tried and judged but rather that in him God is trying and
judging the world.

(i) The arrest   18.1–11

**(1) When he had said these things, Jesus went out with his disciples
across the Kidron Valley to where there was a garden, which he
and his disciples entered. (2) Now Judas, who betrayed him, also
knew the place, because Jesus often met there with his disciples.
(3) So Judas, having got a detachment of soldiers and guards
from the chief priests and the Pharisees, came there with lanterns
and torches and weapons. (4) Jesus, knowing everything that was**

going to happen to him, went out and said to them, 'Whom are you seeking?' (5) They answered him, 'Jesus of Nazareth.' He said to them, 'I am[1].' Now Judas, who betrayed him, was also standing with them. (6) When he said to them, 'I am,' they drew back and fell to the ground. (7) So he asked them again, 'Whom are you seeking?' And they said, 'Jesus of Nazareth.' (8) Jesus answered, 'I told you that I am. So if you are seeking me, let these men go.' (9) This was to fulfil the word that he had spoken, 'I have not lost any of those you gave me.' (10) Then Simon Peter, who had a sword, drew it, struck the high priest's slave and cut off his right ear. The slave's name was Malchus. (11) Jesus said to Peter, 'Put your sword into its sheath. Shall I not drink the cup that the Father has given me?'

Although for the sake of convenience this episode has been entitled 'The Arrest', the actual arrest of Jesus is not mentioned until v. 12, where it is simply stated as the necessary prelude to Jesus being taken to Annas. What the episode depicts is the encounter between Jesus and his opponents that leads to his capture. It falls into three parts – (i) a setting of the scene (vv. 1–3); (ii) the exchange between Jesus and the arresting party (vv. 4–9); and (iii) Peter's act of violence and Jesus' rebuke of him (vv. 10–11).

1–2 After the farewell discourse and its final prayer, **Jesus went out with his disciples across the Kidron Valley to where there was a garden.** The Kidron Valley lies to the east of Jerusalem between the city and the Mount of Olives, and the garden would have been at the foot of the Mount of Olives. The entering of the garden, mentioned here, and the exiting from it (v. 4) indicate it was a clearly defined enclosure. The Synoptic accounts of the arrest do not mention the Kidron but specify the place as Gethsemane (Mark 14.62; Matt. 26.36) and the location as the Mount of Olives (Mark 14.26; Matt. 26.30; Luke 22.39). The backdrop for their accounts may well be the incident in 2 Sam. 15.13–31, in which David leaves Jerusalem when he is betrayed by his counsellor, Ahithophel, and, weeping, ascends the Mount of Olives to pray to the Lord. There is the intriguing possibility that John also draws on the same tradition, since his designation of the Kidron Valley is, literally, 'the winter-flowing Kidron', the same phrase that occurs in 2 Sam. 15.23 LXX. The Kidron

---

[1] Some manuscripts supplement 'I am' ('Εγώ εἰμι) with the name ὁ 'Ιησοῦ, either after it (B) or before it (ℵ (without the definite article) A C K L W Δ Θ Π Ψ it^aur,c,f,q vg syr^p,h cop^sa,bo goth arm). The proper name does not occur in p^60 D it^b,e syr^s. It is easy to see why the name might have been added in the light of the arresting party's response in the first part of the verse, and the rest of the episode appears to presuppose that Jesus' initial announcement here was simply 'I am' (cf. vv. 6, 8).

was a brook or watercourse that was dry, except in the winter rainy season (cf. also Josephus, *B. J.* 5.70; *A. J.* 8.17).

Now Judas, who betrayed him, also knew the place, because Jesus often met there with his disciples. Judas' knowledge of the garden both emphasizes that the betrayer was one of Jesus' inner group of trusted followers and makes clear how he would know where to find Jesus (cf. Luke 22.39, which also supplies the information that it was Jesus' custom to go to pray at the Mount of Olives).

3 So Judas, having got a detachment of soldiers and guards from the chief priests and the Pharisees, came there with lanterns and torches and weapons. The Fourth Gospel alone has Judas guiding not only Jewish forces but also Roman soldiers to the garden. A 'detachment of soldiers' (σπεῖρα) is a term that is nearly always used elsewhere for a Roman cohort, which consisted of six hundred soldiers, though it is occasionally used as a translation for the Latin *manipulus* of two hundred troops. On the few occasions the term is employed of Jews, it is with reference to the troops of a local sovereign or a leader of a revolt (cf. 1 Macc. 3.55; 2 Macc. 8.23; Josephus, *B. J.* 2.20.7; *A. J* 17.19.3; Mark 6.21) and never has in view the retinue at the disposal of the Sanhedrin or chief priests, from which it is in any case clearly distinguished here (cf. also v. 12). A number of factors make it historically implausible that Roman soldiers were present at the arrest. These include the size of the detachment (even at the minimal end of the scale), the likelihood that there was only one such Roman cohort in Jerusalem, at the Antonia Fortress (cf. Acts 21.31), and the unlikelihood of Judas having any influence with the Roman tribune or commandant, who is present with his cohort (cf. v. 12). It is also unlikely that the tribune would have made himself and his cohort available to the Jewish authorities at this point and then would agree to take Jesus to the house of Annas, who had been deposed by the Romans, yet fail to arrest the follower of Jesus who had resisted and caused injury. The presence of Roman troops here in the narrative supplies a link between the Jewish authorities and the Romans that is missing from the next section of the passion account because there is no trial before the Sanhedrin and no subsequent resolve to take Jesus to Pilate (see the discussion of the interrogation before Annas). At the same time, it heightens the drama of the arrest and is also in line with the evangelist's extensive treatment of the Roman trial and his concern to show that the hostile 'world' that condemned Jesus included both Roman and Jewish authorities. If there was an increasing trend in early Christian treatments of the death of Jesus to ameliorate the role of the Romans and to give the Jewish authorities the clear primary responsibility for Jesus' fate, then this Gospel does not fit altogether neatly into such a trajectory. It has the Romans included in the proceedings against Jesus from the outset of its passion account.

Typically, the narrator designates the Jewish authorities as 'the chief priests and the Pharisees', the phrase employed earlier for the authorities when they decide to take action against Jesus (cf. 7.32, 45; 11.47, 57). They had already sent out the temple guards or police at their disposal to arrest Jesus earlier in the narrative but had been unsuccessful (cf. 7.32, 45). The mention of the lanterns, torches and weapons reminds readers that the arrest is taking place at night, the night, with its symbolic overtones, into which Judas had gone out in 13.31. It is also ironic, since the lanterns and torches will not be needed to find the one who has claimed to be the light of the world and who will openly announce himself to the forces of darkness (cf. vv. 4–5; 8.12; 9.5), and the weapons will be superfluous in seizing the one whose kingdom is not of this world and therefore not dependent on the use of force (cf. vv. 10–11; 18.36).

4–5 As he has been portrayed in the course of his mission, so here and throughout the passion Jesus has sovereign knowledge and therefore is in control of events. He takes the initiative in confronting the array of forces that have come out to seize him: **Jesus, knowing everything that was going to happen to him, went out and said to them, 'Whom are you seeking?'** It is clear that Jesus is to be no helpless victim but acts in conformity with his earlier claim that no one will take his life from him but he will lay it down of his own accord (10.18). This is reinforced when, in response to the reply that they are seeking Jesus of Nazareth, **He said to them, 'I am.'** This is another Johannine double entendre employing the 'I Am' formula (cf. 4.26; 6.20; 8.28). On the surface it can be read simply as Jesus' self-identification – 'I am he, namely, Jesus of Nazareth, whom you are seeking' – but at the same time it is the divine self-declaration – 'I Am', with its background in Deut. 32.39 LXX and Isa. 40—55. The note that **Judas, who betrayed him, was also standing with them** serves as a prompt for recognizing this latter meaning. The disciples, and therefore readers, have already been prepared for it, because, in predicting Judas' betrayal, Jesus had said, 'I am speaking to you now before it occurs, so that, when it occurs, you may believe that I Am' (13.18–19). Now the reliability of Jesus' word is demonstrated, with both parts of this prediction being fulfilled in the narrative, as Judas' presence with the arresting party shows him as the betrayer and as Jesus utters the divine self-declaration. In this narrative, in contrast to the Synoptics (cf. Mark 14.43–6; Matt. 26.47–50; cf. also Luke 22.47–8), Judas does not take the lead in pointing out Jesus and there is no mention of a kiss, since Jesus has taken the initiative in identifying himself.

6 In order that there be no mistaking the significance of Jesus' self-identification, the narrator now relates that **When he said to them, 'I am,' they drew back and fell to the ground.** This is the typical

human reaction to a theophany (cf. Ezek. 1.28; Dan. 10.9). For a moment
the true status of the characters in the narrative is graphically depicted.
The ultimate powerlessness of the massed representatives of this world's
powers – the Roman forces, the Jewish guards and the disciple turned
betrayer – is revealed, as they have to retreat and prostrate themselves in
the presence of the unique divine agent who is one with God.

7–9 After this brief disclosure in narrative form of the significance of
the central character, he continues to take control of the situation. Jesus'
question and their answer from vv. 4b–5a are repeated, and Jesus underlines his previous response and issues a command – **I told you that I
am. So if you are seeking me, let these men go.** What is to follow
is to be primarily a confrontation between Jesus himself and the Jewish
and Roman authorities and in consequence Jesus orders that his followers
be allowed to go. Both the hostile powers and Jesus' followers are seen to
be under his authority. His followers do not simply flee in confusion, as
in Mark 14.50 and Matt. 26.56; their departure is ordered by him. This,
in turn, underlines the reliability of his earlier teaching about his control
of his followers' destiny, enabling him **to fulfil the word that he had
spoken, 'I have not lost any of those you gave me.'** The saying
quoted does not repeat precisely any previous words of Jesus but clearly
reflects his statement in the bread of life discourse about losing nothing
of all that the Father has given him (6.39) and the assertion of his farewell
prayer that he has guarded those he has been given so that not one of
them has been lost except the one who was destined to be lost (17.12).
The primary connection appears to be with this latter assertion, since
Jesus has just identified himself by means of the divine self-designation,
'I Am', and in the same context Jesus had claimed, 'I kept them in the
name which you have given me, and guarded them' (17.11). But there
is an echo here also of the good shepherd's care for his sheep, of whom
he had said that no one would snatch them from his hand (cf. 10.28).
Though elsewhere in the narrative, and here particularly in relation to vv.
4–5, there has been keen interest in the fulfilment, and therefore trust-
worthiness, of Jesus' predictions, only here and in 18.32 is the fulfilment
formula that is otherwise always used of the words of Scripture applied
to the words of Jesus. This is a further indication that, as in the case of
Scripture's words, Jesus' words can be considered God's words (cf. e.g.
7.16–17; 8.28, 38; 12.48–50).

10–11 The action of Peter that follows momentarily threatens to
undermine this notion of Jesus' control over the disciples: **Then Simon
Peter, who had a sword, drew it, struck the high priest's slave and
cut off his right ear. The slave's name was Malchus.** In the Synoptics
(cf. Mark 14.47 parr.) this incident involves an unnamed bystander or

disciple and an unnamed slave of the high priest. In Mark and Matthew, but not in Luke, the sword is wielded after Jesus' arrest. This Gospel, however, employs the incident as part of its characterization of Peter, reinforcing both the impetuosity of his earlier reactions (as in Luke, the attack with the sword comes before the arrest and appears unprovoked) and the disciples' misunderstanding of the nature of Jesus' mission (cf. 13.9, 36–8). It also supplies a name for the slave, whose severed ear, in line with Luke 22.50, is specified as the right ear, though, unlike Luke's account, here there is no healing of the ear. Instead Jesus immediately restores order with his command to Peter – **Put your sword into its sheath** (cf. Matt. 26.52). Jesus' cause is not furthered by violence. He has chosen a very different route in obedience to the will of his Father – **Shall I not drink the cup that the Father has given me?** Again knowledge of the Synoptic tradition is reflected, this time of the Gethsemane episode, which the fourth evangelist has chosen to omit. There (cf. Mark 14.36 parr.) Jesus had prayed in great distress to the Father that 'this cup' be removed from him, while nevertheless being prepared to accept the Father's will. Here he is firmly resolved to drink the cup of suffering and death that awaits him, so that it can even be depicted as a gift from the Father.

The Synoptic accounts of Jesus' arrest are found in Mark 14.43–52, Matt. 26.47–56 and Luke 22.47–53, where they follow on from Jesus' praying in Gethsemane. John's account has taken care of the Gethsemane episode in its own way through the reference in 12.27–8 and through the extended, but remarkably different, prayer of 17.1–26 that precedes the arrest. Nevertheless, as has been noted, his narrative of the arrest also picks up on the language of the Gethsemane prayer with Jesus' talk of 'the cup' (v. 11). With the possible exception of the distinctive reference to the Kidron Valley, the differences in the Fourth Gospel's depiction of the arrest – Jesus' knowledge of what is about to happen, the presence of Roman troops, Jesus' initiative toward his captors, Judas' diminished role, Jesus' 'I Am' announcement and the response of the arresting party, Jesus' protective control over his disciples' fate, the addition of names to the incident with the sword, and the exchange with Peter – can all be seen, as indicated in the comments above, as the outworking of charac-teristic Johannine themes with the necessary literary elaboration. This suggests not so much independent access to and editing of a supposed pre-Markan passion narrative as the evangelist's creative reworking of the Synoptic traditions. Here, as elsewhere, it should be remembered, this does not entail the evangelist redacting actual copies of the Synoptics but rather knowing these other versions well enough to employ them in developing his own account. This Gospel has already indicated that Jesus' death is to be his hour of glory. In a world in which honour and shame were such pervasive values, the events of Jesus' passion would have been seen as entailing a shameful loss of honour. But in reworking the passion tradition, beginning here with the betrayal and arrest, the fourth evangelist tells the story in such a way as to show that in the apparent shame of these events the divine glory was in fact being displayed.

In the Synoptic accounts, not unnaturally, Judas is a major player in the arrest scene. In this Gospel his role in the arrest is not nearly as prominent. Until this point the focus has been on his act of betrayal of an intimate relationship with Jesus, for which the pervasive explanation offered is that he had come under the influence of the cosmic power of evil (cf. 6.70–1; 13.2, 27). After the arrest Judas will disappear from the narrative. There is no interest in his further fate, as is shown in some of the other narratives (cf. Matt. 27.3–10; Acts 1.16–20). In this final appearance his betrayal is put in perspective and shown not only to have been known by Jesus in advance but also to be under his control, as he, and not Judas, takes the initiative in the actual arrest, and Judas, now aligned with the powers of evil, falls back with them at the declaration of Jesus' divine sovereignty. This self-identification of Jesus as 'I Am' is at the heart of John's retelling of the arrest. Significantly, in the background to this formula of divine self-identification in Deut. 32.39 LXX and Deutero-Isaiah, the claim is made that Israel's God is the one who controls the events of history, can predict what will happen and will bring about Israel's future deliverance. Now here, even at his arrest, as Jesus takes the divine self-identification on his own lips, he is shown to be no mere victim of fate but the one who controls all that takes place, who has predicted this moment (cf. 13.19), and who secures the safety of his disciples, fulfilling another earlier saying connected with the divine name (cf. 17.11–12). His divine sovereignty is displayed both in the temporary recognition of his person and power by his enemies and in the willing acceptance of what he knows to lie before him as the result of the arrest. In this way the final uses in this Gospel of the divine self-predication by Jesus reinforce the point that all that is about to unfold in his suffering and death will be an expression of the unity between Jesus and God. The account strains credibility in terms of historicity but, in doing so, sets out brilliantly at the start of the passion the paradoxes that the one who embraces the consequences of arrest shares the divine identity and that the seemingly degrading events that are now under way constitute his glory.

(ii) Jesus (and Peter) under interrogation   *18.12–27*

(12) So the detachment of soldiers and the tribune and the Jewish guards arrested Jesus and bound him, (13) and brought him first to Annas, for he was the father-in-law of Caiaphas, who was high priest that year. (14) Caiaphas was the one who had advised the Jews that it was advantageous for one man to die for the people.

(15) Simon Peter and another disciple followed Jesus. Now that disciple was known to the high priest, and he entered the courtyard of the high priest with Jesus, (16) but Peter stood outside at the gate. So the other disciple, who was known to the high priest, went out and spoke to the gatekeeper and brought Peter in. (17) Then the female slave who was the gatekeeper said to Peter, 'You are not also one of this man's disciples, are you?' He said to her, 'I am not.' (18) Now the slaves and the guards were standing around, having made a charcoal fire, because it was cold, and they were warming themselves. Peter also was standing with them and warming himself.

(19) Then the high priest questioned Jesus about his disciples and about his teaching. (20) Jesus answered him, 'I have spoken publicly to the world. I have always taught in a synagogue and in the temple, where all the Jews come together, and I said nothing in secret. (21) Why are you asking me? Ask those who heard what I said to them. They know what I said.' (22) When he had said this, one of the guards standing nearby struck Jesus and said, 'Is this how you answer the high priest?' (23) Jesus answered him, 'If I have spoken wrongly, testify to the wrong, but if rightly, why do you strike me?' (24) Then Annas sent him bound to Caiaphas, the high priest.

(25) Now Simon Peter was standing and warming himself. They said to him, 'You are not also one of his disciples, are you?' He denied and said, 'I am not.' (26) One of the slaves of the high priest, a relative of the man whose ear Peter had cut off, said, 'Did I not see you in the garden with him?' (27) Again Peter denied, and immediately the cock crowed.

John's passion narrative simply has this interrogation before Annas rather than a trial or hearing before the Sanhedrin. The account raises a number of questions about the relation of John to the Synoptics and about historicity. The Synoptics have Jesus taken to the house of the high priest, specified in Matthew as Caiaphas, where he is tried by the Sanhedrin (cf. Mark 14.53–65; Matt. 26.57–68; Luke 22.54–71). Why is there no such trial in John? Why is Jesus taken to Annas, who does not appear in the Synoptic passion narratives, rather than Caiaphas, even though John makes clear Caiaphas was the high priest (cf. v. 13)? These issues also impinge on the coherence of John's account of Jesus' interrogation. The questioning of Jesus is said in v. 19 to be conducted by the high priest, whom one would expect to be identified as Caiaphas, but he turns out to be Annas, since, after the exchange, the narrator says in v. 24 that Annas sent Jesus to Caiphas, the high priest.

On the one hand, the fourth evangelist differs obviously from the Synoptic tradition, yet, on the other, he seems clearly aware of it, especially the Markan account. In particular, he follows Mark's intercalation of what is happening to Jesus in the high priest's house with what is happening to Peter outside in the courtyard. This 'sandwich technique' is one of Mark's characteristic redactional features, and while it is possible that the passion story had already taken this form in some earlier tradition to which John had independent access, it is far more likely, as Luke's quite different composition of the material suggests, that John is dependent on Mark for this feature, which he has adapted and developed for his own purposes. Mark sets the scene with Peter warming himself among the servants, then moves to Jesus' faithful witness under trial, and finally returns to Peter to relate his denials under questioning, which were taking place at the same time as Jesus' trial (cf. Mark 14.66). John follows Mark's framing of what happens to Jesus but adds another disciple to the story, most probably his Beloved Disciple, and splits up the denials, placing one before the account of Jesus' interrogation and two after this. He also appears to be aware of the tradition that the Sanhedrin trial took place in the house of the high priest (cf. Mark 14.53; Luke 22.54), who is named as Caiaphas in Matt. 26.57. As noted above, his use of this is rather awkward. Jesus is sent to Caiaphas in v. 24 and then taken from the house of Caiaphas to the praetorium in v. 28, but nothing happens in this halfway house between Annas and Pilate. It is as if, in constructing his own plot, John has left a gap where the Sanhedrin trial originally stood in the tradition. The awkwardness of this arrangement did not escape the eyes of some early copyists. One version of the Palestinian Syriac lectionary and Cyril of Alexandria attempt to ease the problem by placing v. 24 after v. 13 as well as having it in the position it occupies in the majority of texts. Another Syriac witness, Sinaitic Syriac, attempts a more thoroughgoing reconstruction and has the sequence vv. 13, 24, 14–15, 19–23, 16–18, 25–7, which, however, raises its own problems of coherence by making Annas' role superfluous. But these are clearly later attempts to smooth out the more difficult sequence of the original text.

Some scholars hold that, despite the awkwardness of John's account, his difference from the Synoptics is to be explained by his being in possession of an independent and more historical tradition and that the Sanhedrin trial in the Synoptics, with all its illegal procedures according to later Mishnaic tradition, is in any case implausible historically. The historicity of the Synoptics at this point cannot be pursued, though it should be noted that the difficulties are eased considerably if the tradition they represent reflects an informal hearing rather than a formal trial. Yet even if one allows that an interrogation that in some way involved Annas is by no means historically impossible and that John might have had access to such a tradition, it is far more likely that the evangelist has arrived at what might appear to be greater historical plausibility primarily from literary rather than from historical concerns. All of the distinctive or strange features of this passage in comparison with the Synoptics are explained most satisfactorily in terms of literary and compositional factors. They follow logically from two prior decisions the evangelist has made about the shape or plot of his narrative – (i) he has depicted the whole of Jesus' public mission as a trial before Israel and its religious leaders and has included the specific issues of the Sanhedrin trial in his account of the controversy in the temple environs in 10.22–39 and (ii) in particular, he has already had Caiaphas and the Sanhedrin come to a verdict about Jesus' mission and the need to put him to death after the account of the raising of Lazarus in 11.47–53. John knows the sequence of the Markan passion narrative but it now makes no sense at all for him to follow it at this point. He cannot have a Sanhedrin trial and cannot have Caiaphas questioning Jesus and coming to a verdict. Whereas in the Synoptics the trial before the Sanhedrin adds something new to the explicit claims of Jesus in his public mission and provides the Christological climax that leads to his sentencing, in the Fourth Gospel there is nothing further about Jesus' identity to be revealed to the Jewish religious leaders and therefore no need for a further official trial and sentencing. This account of the hearing before Annas explicitly reinforces the point – 'I have spoken publicly to the world. . . . I said nothing in secret' (v. 20). Yet at the same time, in order to remain in touch with the traditional passion narrative and to retain some historical plausibility, John also cannot have Jesus proceed immediately to the Roman trial after his arrest but must in his version have the Jewish authorities deal with Jesus in some way before handing him over to Pilate. The evangelist solves the resulting problem in four main ways. First, he reminds readers of Caiaphas' earlier assertion that had led the Sanhedrin to plan Jesus' death (cf. v. 14). Secondly, he substitutes an interrogation before Annas for the Synoptic Sanhedrin trial in the presence of the high priest, while retaining the juxtaposition with Peter's denials. Thirdly, he takes advantage of the relationship between Annas and Caiaphas, in which both could be called high priest (see the comments below on v. 13), in order to represent this interrogation as one conducted by the highest Jewish religious authority. Among the Synoptic accounts, that of Mark 14.53 allows for this development, since it speaks of Jesus being taken 'to the high priest and all the chief priests'. Finally, he retains a further thread of continuity with the tradition by still having Jesus taken to Caiaphas before being brought to Pilate (cf. vv. 24, 28), although this is superfluous to his own narrative, since he relates absolutely nothing about any actual encounter with Caiaphas.

This last move is the least satisfactory in terms of the coherence of the evangelist's own narrative, but it is forced on him by the tradition. But, in comparison with the Synoptics, this modified, and for the most part plausible, sequence now omits a major part of the logic of the traditional narrative. In the Synoptics, once the Jewish trial has concluded that Jesus deserves to die, there is the further recognition that if the sentence is to be carried out, Pilate will need to be involved and so the Sanhedrin verdict leads on to the Roman trial (cf. Mark 14.64; 15.1; Matt. 26.66; 27.1–2; Luke 22.71; 23.1). But there is no verdict arising from Annas' interrogation of Jesus and therefore no clear link to the Roman trial or explicit explanation for the need for Jesus to appear before Pilate. John's account does, however, compensate for this lack in two major ways, in addition to any reliance it may place on readers' prior knowledge of the tradition. First, as we have seen, it has the Romans involved in the events of the passion through the presence of a cohort under its tribune at the arrest, and therefore by this different means has already secured the link between the Jewish and Roman authorities. Secondly, it waits until the Roman trial itself before explicitly spelling out that if Jesus is to be put to death, as Caiaphas and the Sanhedrin had determined in 11.47–53, then this penalty can only be carried out by the Romans (cf. 18.31).

This resultant reworking of the Synoptic tradition opens with a transitional section in vv. 12–14, narrating Jesus' capture and his being brought to Annas and establishing the identities and relationship of Annas and Caiaphas. The rest of the passage then juxtaposes Peter's denials of discipleship outside in the courtyard with Jesus' defence of his mission inside before Annas. Peter's access to the courtyard, his first denial and the courtyard setting are depicted in vv. 15–18. The scene then shifts to Jesus' interrogation by Annas and his transfer to Caiaphas in vv. 19–24. The focus finally moves back onto Peter and his two further denials in vv. 25–7.

12–13 The combined Roman and Jewish forces now arrest Jesus. That the cohort is a Roman detachment is reinforced by the mention of **the tribune** at this point. Unlike the Synoptic accounts, the narrator then relates that the arresting party **bound him**. Mark and Matthew do not depict Jesus as being bound until after the Sanhedrin trial. Having him bound throughout the proceedings heightens the ironic contrast between the constraints of Jesus' physical situation and the sovereign control he displays. Jesus' captors **brought him first to Annas, for he was the father-in-law of Caiaphas, who was high priest that year.** Annas ruled officially as high priest from 6 to 15 CE before being deposed, but his influence continued because he was succeeded by various members of his family. Of these Caiaphas, his son-in-law, had the longest term of office – from 18 to 36 CE. Annas remained the dominant member of the high priestly family for the first part of the first century (cf. Josephus, *A. J.* 20.198) and retained the title of high priest even though he was no longer in office (cf. Josephus, *A. J.* 18.95). Luke provides further evidence for this by referring to 'the high priesthood of Annas and Caiaphas', as though it were a joint affair (Luke 3.2), and speaking of a later meeting of the

Sanhedrin at which were also present 'Annas the high priest, Caiaphas, John [or Jonathan], and Alexander, and all who were of the high priestly family' (Acts 4.6). It should be no surprise, then, that despite Caiaphas being named as high priest here in v. 13 (on 'that year', see the comment on 11.49), the high priest who questions Jesus in v. 19 turns out to be Annas (cf. v. 24).

14 The narrator now reminds readers that **Caiaphas was the one who had advised the Jews that it was advantageous for one man to die for the people.** The formulation provides yet another instance of this Gospel's distinctive use of the term 'the Jews'. Again it is not simply an ethnic category, since Caiaphas, of course, is himself a Jew, but denotes unbelieving Jews, here especially the religious authorities, who are hostile to Jesus. Evoking the earlier account of 11.47–53 in this way serves to make clear that whatever now happens as Jesus encounters the religious authorities will not affect the fact that their verdict of condemnation to death has already been made and that Caiaphas' formulation of the case for condemnation ironically provides the theological perspective from which Jesus' coming death is to be viewed. That death will indeed benefit the people, not in the way Caiaphas intended, but rather because it contributes to the realization of the divine plan, in which Jesus' vicarious dying brings salvation and life to others.

15–16 This Gospel takes up the Synoptic sequence, where, after Jesus has been led away, Peter follows at a distance and enters the courtyard of the high priest. It introduces, however, a new character, ostensibly to explain how Peter managed to gain access into the courtyard: **Simon Peter and another disciple followed Jesus. Now that disciple was known to the high priest, and he entered the courtyard of the high priest with Jesus, but Peter stood outside at the gate. So the other disciple, who was known to the high priest, went out and spoke to the gatekeeper and brought Peter in.** Some scholars resist the identification of the other disciple with this Gospel's Beloved Disciple, primarily on the grounds that, if the narrator had wished to make this explicit, he could have done so. However, this is scarcely decisive and, as will be observed later in the commentary, the figure who is unidentified when he bears witness in 19.35 is almost certainly meant to be understood as the disciple whom Jesus loved. There are good reasons for making the same identification here. In the other places where the evangelist inserts an additional figure into the Synoptic account of an incident involving Peter, namely 20.10 and 21.1–14 (cf. Luke 5.1–11), that figure is the Beloved Disciple. In 20.2–4, 8, as in the designation here in v. 16, the Beloved Disciple is called 'the other disciple'. Just as here the other disciple provides a link between Peter and Jesus, so does the Beloved

Disciple in 13.23–6 and 21.7. In the passion narrative, the Beloved Disciple is portrayed as the only male disciple not to abandon Jesus, and so is there at the foot of the cross in 19.25–7. Here the other disciple has not left Jesus but is depicted, in line with the Beloved Disciple's characterization as Jesus' closest and most intimate follower, as actually entering the high priest's courtyard with Jesus. This also fits the Beloved Disciple's function as a literary device. As a marginal participant at the various events in the passion story, he serves as a witness who guarantees the Johannine interpretation of these events. Here the mention of his presence with Jesus and his access to the high priest's setting enables him to serve as a narrative source for the knowledge of what takes place at the interrogation. Given that his role at the important events of the passion is a literary device, it is not worth pressing very hard the question whether a prominent follower of Jesus could have been on good terms with the high priest and yet have remained a follower of Jesus. This detail may have been provided simply to give some semblance of plausibility to the Beloved Disciple's being able to remain characteristically close to Jesus throughout the events.

17–18 Then the female slave who was the gatekeeper said to Peter, 'You are not also one of this man's disciples, are you?' He said to her, 'I am not.' As noted earlier, the evangelist has modified the Markan account and heightened its contrast between Jesus and Peter by mentioning Peter's first denial before turning to portray what is happening to Jesus. He also combines his own detail about the gatekeeper, who has been persuaded by the other disciple to give Peter access to the courtyard, with the Synoptics' female slave who first questions Peter (cf. Mark 14.66 parr.), so that here the gatekeeper is a female slave. Whereas in the Synoptic tradition Peter is asked whether he has been with Jesus and responds in Mark and Matthew by claiming not to know what is meant by this, here he is asked, in a question expecting a negative response, whether he is one of Jesus' disciples and he goes along with the expectation in an immediate denial. The narrator then completes his depiction of Peter's courtyard setting: **Now the slaves and the guards were standing around, having made a charcoal fire, because it was cold, and they were warming themselves. Peter also was standing with them and warming himself.** The depiction elaborates on the more basic description of Mark 14.54b, where Peter sits rather than stands with the guards, warming himself at the fire. Here the fire is specifically said to be a charcoal fire and this detail will become significant for evoking the scene of denial when it reappears as part of the setting for Peter's later rehabilitation (cf. 21.9).

19–21 Now the account moves to what is happening to Jesus. In the Sanhedrin trial in Mark and Matthew Jesus is asked about his claim about the temple and whether he is the Christ, the Son of God. This Gospel has already dealt with both topics in its own way. So here instead **the high priest questioned Jesus about his disciples and about his teaching**. These two more general areas for interrogation reflect concerns that have arisen earlier in the narrative. In 11.48 the religious authorities had expressed anxiety about the number of Jesus' followers and the possibility that the size of his following would attract the negative attention of the Romans. Earlier in 7.16 Jesus' teaching is mentioned in the context of accusations that he is a false teacher who is deceiving or leading the people astray (cf. 7.12, 47). Annas' questioning is in reported speech, but Jesus' reply is given in direct speech, making it central to this scene. The issue of the disciples is ignored. Jesus has ensured their safety by dismissing them (cf. 18.8–9). He also does not enter into debate about the content of his teaching. Instead he makes two points. The first is about its public nature – I have spoken publicly to the world. **I have always taught in a synagogue and in the temple, where all the Jews come together, and I said nothing in secret.** This may well be an adaptation of a Synoptic saying that occurs in the arrest scene (cf. Mark 14.49 parr.). But its force here is that Jesus has nothing to add to what he has clearly set out in his public mission and which therefore should already be known. In this context 'to the world' not only reinforces the open and public nature of his teaching but may also carry, along with the use of 'the Jews', the negative connotations of the hostile world, so that Jesus claims to have spoken openly even to those who had responded unbelievingly to his message (cf. also 7.25–6). The references to synagogue (the Greek term is in the singular) and temple reflect accurately the settings for Jesus' teaching in this narrative. The bread of life discourse is said to have been synagogue teaching (cf. 6.59), while the teaching of 2.13–22, 5.1–47, and 7.14—10.39 is depicted as taking place in the precincts of the temple. The second point in Jesus' response is to dispute that he should be asked about his teaching in any case – **Why are you asking me? Ask those who heard what I said to them. They know what I said.** Because of the open nature of Jesus' teaching to all, including the religious authorities, Annas did not need to have Jesus arrested to discover what he was teaching but could have found this out by asking any who had heard. In the context of an interrogation this has further force. If the purpose is to determine whether or not he is a false prophet, the proper procedure would not be simply to question him as the accused but first to produce witnesses who had heard what he said and to question them.

22–3 Jesus' insistence on changing the terms of the interrogation to make it a just one is not appreciated but rather met with further injustice: **When he had said this, one of the guards standing nearby struck Jesus and said, 'Is this how you answer the high priest?'** The account of the Sanhedrin trial in Mark 14.65 also has Jesus being struck by guards. The motivation for the guard's blow here is Jesus' perceived insubordination to the high priest's authority (cf. Exod. 22.28 LXX). But Jesus is not deterred by this act of violence and continues to insist on the justice of his cause – **If I have spoken wrongly, testify to the wrong, but if rightly, why do you strike me?** Jesus' challenge serves as a reminder that, though he is the prisoner, his words serve as the criterion of good and evil, truth and falsehood (cf. also 5.30; 7.18; 8.45–6; 12.48–9), and this challenge ends the hearing.

24 Then Annas sent him bound to Caiaphas, the high priest. As discussed above, it is not in fact surprising that both Annas and Caiaphas could be called high priest, and with the transference to Caiaphas the narrative rejoins the Synoptic sequence, although nothing will be reported of the encounter with Caiaphas (cf. v. 28). There is no need to add to the awkwardness by thinking of the transference being made to some other place. Caiaphas is probably thought of as having his quarters somewhere else within the same high priestly residence.

25 But the narrator now cuts back to the outside courtyard, where Peter is undergoing another type of interrogation. The narration repeats what was said at the end of the previous scene with Peter in v. 18: **Now Simon Peter was standing and warming himself.** Here again the account appears to be following that of Mark, where there is a similar repetition (cf. Mark 14.54, 67). This time a group, presumably the guards who were also warming themselves, ask him the same question posed previously by the female doorkeeper – **You are not also one of his disciples, are you?** The wording of his denial – **I am not** (οὐκ εἰμί) – repeated from v. 16, now invites comparison with Jesus' earlier twofold self-identification as 'I Am' (ἐγώ εἰμί) at his arrest in 18.5, 8 and adds to the contrast being made here between the two. Whereas Jesus had boldly declared who he was, despite the consequences, Peter is unable to identify himself as a follower at all.

26–7 In the Synoptics Peter's third denial follows from the accusation of bystanders that he is 'one of them' because of his Galilean accent. Here the narrator's sense of dramatic irony is seen as he picks up on his own earlier account: **One of the slaves of the high priest, a relative of the man whose ear Peter had cut off, said, 'Did I not see you in the garden with him?'** With reckless boldness Peter had attempted to defend Jesus by using the sword against Malchus in the garden, but now he denies being there and the person before whom he does so is a relative of the same Malchus. **Again Peter denied, and immediately the cock crowed.** With the last clause this account has exactly the same wording as in Matt. 26.74 (Mark 14.72 has the cock crowing for a second time). Unlike the Synoptics, which at this point remind their readers of Jesus' prophecy about this and then describe Peter's weeping, the narrator, despite his interest elsewhere in underlining the truthfulness of Jesus' predictions, simply leaves readers to make their own connection with 13.38. Peter's remorse in reaction to the cock crowing is, of course, presupposed in what follows and reflected in 21.15–17, when Jesus' threefold interrogation of Peter about his love is said to make him sad.

In Jesus' interrogation by Annas his confrontation with official Judaism comes to a culmination. He boldly defends his teaching without entering into further dispute about its content. His mission has been completed and his teaching has been carried out openly. What he has said stands; there is no need to add to it and there is no going back on it. Though bound, the interrogated challenges his interrogator, insisting on a just hearing and on the truthfulness of his words. The account has Jesus' witness at its centre, but it also features another character, Peter, whose portrayal is shaped by both a minor and a major contrast. Peter follows Jesus and, through the agency of another disciple, in all probability the Beloved Disciple, is enabled to be in proximity to Jesus in the courtyard and given the opportunity to be the sort of disciple who goes with Jesus to the cross. He fails the test while the other disciple does indeed go on to be with Jesus at the cross. But it is the framing of Jesus' interrogation by the account of Peter's denials that provides the major contrast. When Peter faces interrogation of a less formal kind, his discipleship falters badly, as he denies three times that he is one of Jesus' followers. For readers who would be familiar with the experience of interrogation before either religious or civil authorities because of their Christian confession, the episode is a graphic reminder that what happens to Jesus happens to his followers (cf. 15.18–20). The question is how they will respond. Will they emulate Jesus by carrying out a courageous witness (note also that of the man born blind in chapter 9) or will they, like Peter, prove under pressure to be faithless followers, despite having made protestations of allegiance in more favourable circumstances?

(iii) Jesus' trial before Pilate　　　　　　　　　　　　　　*18.28—19.16a*

(28) Then they led Jesus from Caiaphas to the praetorium. It was early morning. They themselves did not enter the praetorium in order that they might not become defiled but might eat the Passover. (29) So Pilate went outside to them and said, 'What charge do you bring against this man?' (30) They answered and said to him, 'If this man were not an evildoer, we would not have handed him over to you.' (31) Pilate therefore said to them, 'Take him yourselves and judge him according to your law.' The Jews

said to him, 'We are not permitted to put anyone to death.' (32) This was to fulfil the word Jesus had spoken indicating the kind of death he was to die.

(33) Pilate went back into the praetorium, called Jesus and said to him, 'Are you the King of the Jews?' (34) Jesus answered, 'Are you saying this of your own accord or did others tell you about me?' (35) Pilate answered, 'I am not a Jew, am I? Your nation and the chief priests handed you over to me. What have you done?' (36) Jesus answered, 'My kingdom is not of this world. If my kingdom were of this world, my servants would fight so that I might not be handed over to the Jews. But, as it is, my kingdom is not from here.' (37) Pilate therefore said to him, 'So, then, you are a king?' Jesus replied, 'You say that I am a king. For this I was born and for this I came into the world, to bear witness to the truth. Everyone who is of the truth listens to my voice.' (38) Pilate said to him, 'What is truth?'

Having said this, he again went out to the Jews and said to them, 'I find no case against him. (39) But you have a custom that I release for you one prisoner at Passover. Do you want me therefore to release for you the King of the Jews?' (40) They shouted in reply again, 'Not this man but Barabbas!' Now Barabbas was a bandit.

(19.1) Then Pilate had Jesus taken and flogged. (2) And having plaited a crown out of thorns, the soldiers placed it on his head, and dressed him in a purple cloak, (3) and kept coming up to him and saying, 'Hail! King of the Jews!' and striking him.

(4) Pilate went outside again and said to them, 'See, I am bringing him out to you, so that you may know that I find no case against him.' (5) So Jesus came outside, wearing the crown of thorns and the purple cloak. And he said to them, 'Here is the man!' (6) When the chief priests and the guards saw him, they shouted out, 'Crucify him, crucify him!' Pilate said to them, 'You take him and crucify him, because I find no case against him.' (7) The Jews answered him, 'We have a law, and according to the law he ought to die, because he made himself out to be the Son of God.'

(8) When Pilate heard this, he became more afraid, (9) and went into the praetorium again and said to Jesus, 'Where are you from?' But Jesus gave him no answer. (10) So Pilate said to him, 'Why do you not speak to me? Do you not know that I have authority to release you and I have authority to crucify you?' (11) Jesus answered him, 'You would have no authority over me at all if it had not been given you from above. For this reason the one who handed me over to you has the greater sin.'

(12) From that moment Pilate tried to release him, but the Jews cried out, 'If you release this man, you are not a friend of Caesar. Anyone who makes himself out to be a king is opposing Caesar.' (13) When Pilate heard these words, he led Jesus outside, and seated him[1] on the judge's bench at the place called Stone Pavement or, in Hebrew, Gabbatha. (14) Now it was the day of Preparation for the Passover, and it was about the sixth hour. And he said to the Jews, 'Here is your king!' (15) They cried out, 'Away with him, away with him, crucify him!' Pilate said to them, 'Shall I crucify your king?' The chief priests answered, 'We have no king but Caesar.' (16a) Then he handed him over to them to be crucified.

The dominant trial motif, whose themes of witness, judgement and truth have been noted throughout, reaches its climax in the extended Roman trial of Jesus. The issues in the trial have a Jewish context but also have universal significance, and the trial's taking place before Pilate, the representative of the Roman Empire, underlines this cosmic aspect of this motif. Like the middle panel of a triptych, the Roman trial stands at the centre of the three equally long sections of the passion narrative, with Jesus' arrest and interrogation on one side (18.1–27) and his crucifixion and burial on the other (19.16b—42). It is another of the Gospel's episodes which has seven scenes and these follow the movement of Pilate back and forth between the praetorium and 'the Jews' (18.28–32; 18.33–8a; 18.38b–40; 19.1–3; 19.4–7; 19.8–11; 19.12–16a). 'The Jews' are gathered in the outside court of the praetorium, while Jesus is held in the inside room, and Pilate's constant passing from one setting to the other reflects the pull of two different poles operative in the process of his coming to a judgement. The central scene (19.1–3) indicates the evangelist's perspective on the trial and encapsulates its irony. Here Jesus is presented in the mock insignia of royalty – a crown of thorns and a purple robe. For the evangelist, of course, despite all appearances, the one who is on trial actually is the true King of the Jews.

The trial before Pilate is an episode that all four canonical gospels have in common (cf. Mark 15.1–15; Matt. 27.11–26; Luke 23.1–5,13–25). The basic outline of the Fourth Gospel's account is similar to that of the Synoptics but it is much longer, containing 29 verses as compared to 15 in Mark, 16 in Matthew and 18 in Luke. Some of the main features of the relationship can be noted. The response of 'the Jews' to Pilate in the opening scene of the Johannine account reflects knowledge of Mark

---

[1] The syntax allows the verb to be taken transitively, as here, with Jesus as the object, or intransitively, 'he sat', with Pilate doing the sitting. See the comments on this verse for discussion of these options.

in both its parts. 'If this man were not an evildoer' (v. 30a) picks up on Pilate's question – 'Why, what evil has he done?' – in Mark 15.14, while 'we would not have handed him over to you' (v. 30b) makes use of the notion of the 'handing over' of Jesus by the Jewish leaders in Mark 15.1b. Pilate's question in v. 33, 'Are you the King of the Jews?', is the same as in Mark 15.2 parr., and to the Synoptic reply, 'You say (so)', John adds 'that I am a king' and then the statement of Jesus' mission in terms of witnessing to the truth (v. 37). John's threefold attestation by Pilate of Jesus' innocence in 18.38; 19.4, 6 follows that of Luke in 23.4, 14, 22. John 18.39–40 is the one place where the Synoptic account has been abbreviated. The Fourth Gospel is content with a briefer summary of the Barabbas episode and whereas Mark and Luke portray Barabbas as a murderer, John designates him as a bandit, a term he has employed earlier in 10.1, 8.

The scene of the flogging and mocking of Jesus by the soldiers, which Mark 15.16–20a and Matt. 27.27–31a have after the trial, has been moved up for dramatic effect in John's sequence to become the central of his seven scenes (cf. 19.1–3). The wording 'having plaited a crown out of thorns, they placed' is shared by John and Matthew. Luke had a mockery scene earlier in his narrative with Herod and his soldiers as the mockers (cf. Luke 23.11) and John 19.2 employs the same verb for the dressing up of Jesus as does Luke's account.

Toward the end of John's account of the trial Jesus refuses to give an answer (19.9), just as he had done in Mark 15.5 and Matt. 27.14, and Pilate is depicted as wanting to release Jesus (v. 12), just as in Luke 23.20. Then there is the mention of Pilate's judgement seat, which is found only here in v. 13 and in Matt. 27.19. The issue of Jesus' claim to kingship pitting him against Caesar, which John uses to such effect at the conclusion in vv. 13, 15, had already been introduced by Luke right at the beginning of his account in 23.2, where the accusation was that Jesus was 'forbidding us to pay taxes to Caesar, and saying that he himself is the Messiah, a king'. The final wording of v. 16, 'he handed him over . . . to be crucified', repeats the formulation found in Mark 15.15 and Matt. 27.26. Such similarities and differences among the accounts suggest that John had knowledge in some form of the Synoptics, to which he has made extensive additions to the dialogue and changes to the sequence in order to suit his own distinctive theological and dramatic purposes.

28 The first scene takes place in the outside court of the praetorium, the procurator's or prefect's official residence in Jerusalem. Pilate, with whom readers are expected to be acquainted because he appears in the scene without any introduction, demands to know what the accusation of 'the Jews' (cf. v. 31) against Jesus is, but receives no clear answer. The narrator supplies a reason for 'the Jews' remaining outside – **in order**

that they might not become defiled but might eat the Passover.
It may well be that the ritual defilement to be avoided was contact with
a corpse, which carried a seven-day contamination, and that in view are
laws found later in the Mishnah in which Gentile houses are treated as
unclean because Gentiles sometimes buried corpses in or underneath
them, particularly premature babies or foetuses (cf. *m. Oholoth* 18.7). But
the point in supplying this motivation is both theological and ironic. It
indicates right at the start of the trial what has been apparent throughout
the narrative, namely, that it is their stance toward the law that defines the
opponents of Jesus and that is the source of their determination to see
him sentenced to death (cf. also 19.7). At the same time this enables the
opposition to be depicted as so scrupulously concerned with ceremonial
purity that they will not enter a Gentile house but as lacking any scruples
about making use of its Gentile occupant in order to to do away with
Jesus. They are portrayed as fearing that impurity will prevent them from
eating the Passover lamb, but, from the implied author's perspective, they
are implicated in the death of the true Passover lamb (cf. 19.14, 31, 36).
The temporal reference – **It was early morning** – provides a reminder
that the trial takes place on the day of Preparation for the Passover, 14
Nisan, before the Passover meal would have been eaten on the evening
that began the next day (cf. also 19.14).

29–30 Initially, in response to Pilate's question, 'the Jews' are depicted as
not having a specific charge to bring against Jesus. He is simply presented
in general terms as **an evildoer** (cf. Mark 15.14 parr.), although v. 33 will
soon presuppose that the charge was that Jesus claimed to be King of the
Jews, that he was a political subversive with royal pretensions.

31 The general nature of their charge at this stage allows Pilate to tell 'the
Jews' to **Take him yourselves and judge him according to your
law.** Such a process of judgement is, of course, what the evangelist has
portrayed as already having been taking place in Jesus' public ministry
and as having led to the Sanhedrin's verdict that Jesus should die (cf.
11.47–53). But Pilate's response here serves as a reminder of who has the
political power and the legal ability to execute. His comment provokes
a response from the religious leaders that both expresses their frustration
and exposes their real intention – **We are not permitted to put
anyone to death.** The historical accuracy of this assertion has been
widely debated, but in all probability, even if there are some instances of
the Sanhedrin executing a person by Jewish methods for certain clearly
restricted religious offences, it could not claim the right to do so and
certainly would not have attempted to do so while Pilate was actually
in the city to prevent disturbances. Such a state of affairs also means that
the attempts of Jesus' opponents earlier in the narrative to stone him are

likely to have been viewed as of doubtful legality under Roman jurisdiction. But the evangelist may also well be making a theological point
here about the impotence of the law to do what 'the Jews' want it to do.
From his perspective the law, by which they are judging Jesus, had not
been able itself to lead to his condemnation and death, as they thought it
should. On three occasions in the earlier narrative they had claimed that
the law convicts Jesus of blasphemy and had tried to kill him (cf. 5.18;
8.59; 10.30–1). These earlier attempts to carry out a death sentence on
Jesus on the basis of a religious charge under the law had been thwarted,
and so, as will emerge from the dialogue, his opponents have now been
forced to bring a political charge and involve the Romans in order to
convict Jesus of a capital offence.

32 The narrator's comment is that all this only brings about the
fulfilment of Jesus' own words **indicating the kind of death he was
to die**. Earlier Jesus had talked of the Son of Man being lifted up (3.14;
8.28; 12.32), and in connection with the third use of this 'lifting up'
terminology the narrator had already intimated that the nature of Jesus'
death was in view (12.33). Jesus, as master over his own life and death (cf.
10.17–18), had already determined that being lifted up on a Roman cross
was the way he would die. So, in this light, 'the Jews' transference of his
case to Pilate is simply the means of enabling his words to be fulfilled.

33–4 The second scene moves inside – **Pilate went back into the
praetorium** – and provides dialogue between Pilate and Jesus about
the fact and nature of Jesus' kingship. To Pilate's question, **Are you the
King of the Jews?** (cf. also Mark 15.2 parr.), Jesus responds with his
own question, asking about the origin of Pilate's question. The exchange
presupposes that Pilate has been apprised of Jesus' mission and of the
politically subversive interpretation that could be put on it. Jesus' counter-
question clearly hints at this. These first words of Jesus also serve to put
Pilate on the defensive. They belong to a pattern by now familiar whereby
Jesus, the accused, becomes the accuser, and the one on trial can be seen
as the judge.

35 At one level Pilate's response, **I am not a Jew, am I?**, is simply
meant to distance him from any personal interest in his earlier question,
but at another level this later question epitomizes one of the major
issues in the narrative. The distinctive use of the term 'the Jews' in this
Gospel's narrative is underlined by the play on its ethnic and symbolic
senses here and in the following verse. It has become clear that 'the Jews'
refers not just to an ethnic group but represents the unbelieving world,
hostile to God's authorized agent and witness. So the question can be
understood as 'I do not belong to the world that rejects you, do I?' As

with the discourse's other ironic questions, this one grammatically expects a negative answer but the reader is meant to supply a positive one. The development of the trial soon confirms that positive answer. Pilate will not be allowed to distance himself from the issues in some neutral role but is himself judged, as he ultimately places himself at the disposal of 'the Jews' and fails to recognize Jesus' witness to the truth. Pilate intends to dissociate himself ethnically from 'the Jews' but ironically is aligned with them symbolically because they represent the world in the dispute between God and the world. The former dissociation is furthered by his telling Jesus that it is **Your nation and the chief priests** who handed him over and raised the disputed issue of his kingship.

36 Jesus now defines that kingship and at first does so negatively – **My kingdom is not of this world.** As Jesus had declared about himself in 8.23, the origin of his kingdom does not lie in this world, and, as in that earlier declaration, this means that it is from above, i.e. from God. It is for this reason that Jesus would have nothing to do with those who wanted to make him king earlier in 6.15; his kingship can only be established by God, not by human means. And so Jesus makes clear to Pilate, who is used to thinking in terms of political power, that he is not planning an uprising to bring about his kingdom by this-worldly means: **If my kingdom were of this world, my servants would fight so that I might not be handed over to the Jews.** In this formulation Jesus the Jew now also dissociates himself from 'the Jews' symbolically. Unbelieving Jews are the hostile opposition who have had him arrested. In the earlier narrative Peter, the one follower who did use the sword in an attempt to prevent the arrest, was severely rebuked (cf. 18.10–11). The negative definition does not mean that Jesus' kingdom is totally other-worldly. Its origin is not from this world but it manifests itself in this world wherever people listen to his voice, as v. 37 will make clear. And though it will not be achieved by political means, it will have political implications, as this trial itself reveals. Religious and political dimensions of the kingdom are inextricably interwoven, since for both 'the Jews' and Pilate acknowledgement of Jesus' kingship is shown to clash with loyalty to Caesar's rule.

37 When Pilate asks again, **So, then, you are a king?**, Jesus does not give unequivocal confirmation. Presumably this would still be open to misunderstanding despite his explanation of the nature of his kingdom, and it is by no means clear that Pilate has appreciated the all-important definition Jesus has provided. Jesus therefore puts some distance between himself and the title – **You say that I am a king.** He does not categorically refuse to be known as king, but this time, and most significantly, redefines the nature of such kingship positively in the light of his mission to be a witness to the truth: **For this I was born and for this I came into the**

world, to bear witness to the truth. The twofold introduction gives
this statement of Jesus' mission special weight. Its distinctiveness is shown
in that no other mission statement in the narrative is given such emphasis
(cf. e.g. 6.38; 10.10; 12.46). Jesus' mission in this world can be summed
up in terms of witness and truth. His kingship is subsumed under and
reinterpreted by his witness to the truth. The issue of Jesus' kingship will
continue to play a dominant part in the trial and crucifixion, because it
provides the political dimension that enables 'the Jews' to present Jesus as
a threat to Rome (cf. 19.12), but kingship is not Jesus' own characterization of his role. Instead, by subordinating kingship to his role as witness,
he also subordinates the issue of power to that of truth: **Everyone who
is of the truth listens to my voice.** So Jesus does not so much have
subjects over whom he rules as followers who accept his witness and
who hear his voice as truth. As earlier in the narrative, this witness to
truth is at the same time a judgement that exposes people's basic loyalty
and commitment, their attitude to the truth. 'The Jews' were accused of
not hearing the word of Jesus when he spoke the truth and the reason
given for their failure to hear was that they were not 'from God' (8.45–7).
In contrast, Jesus had also spoken of sheep who do hear the shepherd's
voice – 'you do not believe because you do not belong to my sheep. My
sheep hear my voice' (10.26–27a; cf. also 10.3, 4, 16). Jesus' assertion to
Pilate then puts his judge on trial in regard to the truth. It can be seen as
amounting to a challenge in response to which Pilate will show himself
to belong either to 'the Jews' or to Jesus' sheep.

38a Pilate's response with the famous question – **What is truth?** – is
best taken neither as sneeringly sarcastic nor as profoundly philosophical
but simply as an attempt to evade Jesus' witness and a sign of his failure
to listen. Of course, the irony of the question derives from the reader's
knowledge that the one to whom he asks it has earlier announced, 'I am
. . . the truth' (14.6). As if to demonstrate the superficial nature of his
question, Pilate apparently does not stay for an answer. His question and
subsequent action have, however, clearly aligned him with those who do
not hear Jesus' witness to the truth and in this way answered his earlier
rhetorical question in v. 35 – 'I am not a Jew, am I?'

38b–9 In the third scene, Pilate, having retreated outside immediately
after his dialogue with Jesus, announces that he finds Jesus not guilty and
appeals to the custom of releasing a prisoner at Passover. No reference
to this custom or any real analogies to it have been found outside the
canonical Gospels. As noted earlier, John's account of this episode is much
briefer than that of the Synoptics. It also differs in that Pilate refers to the
custom as a Jewish one – **you have a custom** – whereas Mark (15.6),
followed by Matthew (27.15), more plausibly understands the custom

to be one instituted by the Romans. Again more plausibly, all three Synoptics have the crowd call for the custom to be practised, while here it is Pilate who first mentions it. The changes may well be part of John's characterization of Pilate as mockingly toying with the Jewish religious authorities. Pilate's declaration of Jesus' innocence – **I find no case against him** – means that from this point the trial is being carried out with the judge explicitly aware that the accused is innocent and so constitutes a travesty of justice. But here the declaration is made subordinate to the offer to release Jesus. However, since it has already been made plain to Pilate what 'the Jews' wish to do with Jesus (v. 31), it is difficult for the reader to give him credit for making a genuine offer. He knows that the Jews do not want Jesus released and calling him 'King of the Jews' is not calculated to achieve that release. The sincerity of his pronouncement of Jesus' innocence will also be undermined by Pilate's action at the beginning of the next scene in having Jesus scourged, which suggests that Jesus' innocence is not a matter of much consequence for Pilate. He again appears to be more interested in toying with Jewish nationalistic and messianic hopes. But, whatever his motives, his failure to act decisively on his own announcement of Jesus' innocence, like his attempt to evade the issue of the truth, is itself a decision.

40 They shouted in reply again, 'Not this man but Barabbas!' This is in fact the first time in the account that 'the Jews' have shouted out and so the 'again' here suggests that the evangelist is drawing on and expects his readers to be aware of a longer account of this incident, such as that in Mark, where already the crowd had been stirred up by the chief priests to call for Barabbas to be released. To increase the dramatic effect and heighten the irony, the narrator's comment about the identity of Barabbas is left to the end of the scene – **Now Barabbas was a bandit.** The term employed – λῃστής – was used by Josephus for bandits and insurrectionists (cf. e.g. *B. J.* 2.253–4, 585) and by the time of the evangelist would also have been associated with the revolutionaries who participated in the revolt against Rome. Pilate's declaration of Jesus' innocence can now be seen to have served as a foil for exposing the hypocrisy of 'the Jews'. They had presented Jesus to Pilate as a political subversive who deserved death. But even though Jesus has been declared innocent, they prefer to have released to them someone who is undeniably an insurrectionist. There is further irony in the narrator's comment. In rejecting 'the King of the Jews' for a robber-bandit, 'the Jews' show again that they do not belong to the flock of the good shepherd and are unable to hear his voice, because in the only other uses of λῃστής in the narrative, in 10.1, 8, bandits are contrasted to the good shepherd. What is more, although the narrator does not exploit this, early readers could well have been aware that Barabbas' name (literally, son of the father) contains its own irony. In this narrative, where the claim of Jesus to be the Son of the Father has brought about his trial, 'the Jews' now choose instead of Jesus not only an insurrectionist but one whose name reflects Jesus' claim. Unlike the Synoptics (cf. Mark 15.15; Matt. 27.26; Luke 23.24–5), this account does not make explicit the outcome of this episode and assumes that its readers will know that Barabbas was in fact released instead of Jesus.

19.1–3 Pilate's move inside the praetorium for this central fourth scene is also assumed. He has Jesus scourged and the Roman soldiers mock Jesus by investing him with the insignia of royalty. In distinction from the accounts in Mark (15.17–20) and Matthew (27.28–31), John's has no mention of a reed as part of the mockery or the soldiers spitting at Jesus. The **crown** plaited out of thorns and the **purple cloak** comprise the two mock insignia, and the theme of royalty is at the heart of the physical abuse endured by Jesus. The soldiers come up to him as if to swear allegiance with the words, **Hail, King of the Jews!** but then suddenly hit him in the face instead. Luke has moved the mocking scene to an earlier place in his narrative. It is recounted briefly in Jesus' appearance before Herod (23.11). John too changes the location of the incident from that of the Markan and Matthean accounts by placing it earlier in the trial. In this Gospel's narrative the scourging and mocking occur *before* Pilate has given Jesus over to be crucified. In terms of historical plausibility, the other two Gospels are, of course, to be preferred. Any flogging of the prisoner would have come after the sentence of condemnation and crucifixion, when Roman soldiers would have been more able to do what they wished with him. The different sequence in John has the effect of displaying at the centre of its account the blatant dramatic irony of the one who is on trial being robed as king and of this then colouring the rest of the proceedings.

4–5 Pilate went outside again, this time in order to announce that he finds Jesus not guilty and to employ his mockery of Jesus to mock the crowd. This fifth scene has no parallels in the Synoptics and has clearly been composed by the evangelist on the basis of his changing the sequence in the tradition. Its sense of theatre is striking. Pilate emerges from the praetorium to announce that he is about to bring out Jesus and confirm his innocence. But then, as all eyes are fastened on the portico, Jesus emerges dressed as the king 'the Jews' have accused him of wanting to be. And, as Pilate and the chief priests go on to discuss who has the authority to crucify him, it will now be in the presence of the one who stands there in the trappings of royal power. Pilate adds to the theatricality and underlines his mockery both of Jesus and of the whole business of Jewish royalty. He gestures toward the parodied king and taunts 'the Jews' with the words **Here is the man!**

The force of this short mock acclamation has been much discussed. Some have claimed that 'the man' (ὁ ἄνθρωπος) is to be seen as the equivalent of the Son of Man (ὁ υἱός τοῦ ἀνθρώπου). But although 'Son' and 'Son of Man' are virtually synonymous in a number of places, nowhere else is 'man' used as an abbreviation or equivalent for 'Son of Man'. Others have attempted to argue that 'man' was an eschatological title, but the evidence for this, based on interpretation of Greek versions of Num. 24.17 which have the term ἄνθρωπος in them, is meagre and the correspondence with the wording here is by no means obvious. Zech. 6.12 is sometimes held to be a candidate for an allusion with its command to crown Joshua the high priest as king and to make the declaration, which employs a messianic title, 'Behold, the man whose name is the Branch.' But the LXX wording has ἀνήρ not ἄνθρωπος. By far the most plausible suggestion for a secondary and ironic connotation to the straightforward 'Here is the man [whom you have accused of claiming to be king]' is the one that points to 1 Sam. 9.17 LXX as the background. The correspondence in wording is precise. God is said to have told Samuel concerning Saul, 'Here is the man [ἰδοὺ ὁ ἄνθρωπος] .... He it is who shall rule over my people.' The irony is appropriate. John's formulation of Pilate's mockery of both Jesus and Jewish notions of kingship employs the words used of Israel's very first king and thereby reinforces Jesus' true identity as 'King of the Jews'. In this way 'Here is the man' anticipates Pilate's explicit 'Here is your king' in v. 14.

6–7 But instead of acclamation, the Jewish opposition, which is now specified as the **chief priests and the guards,** i.e. the temple police, yells out, **Crucify him, crucify him!** This provokes Pilate's reply – **You take him and crucify him, because I find no case against him.** With this third declaration of Jesus' innocence (cf. also 18.38b; 19.4), Pilate again indicates both that he finds Jesus to pose no real threat to Roman power and that he is contemptuous of the Jewish religious authorities, because he knows very well that they have no legal power to do what he says, and they have reminded him explicitly of this in 18.31. He is simply rubbing salt in the wound of their sense of lack of sovereignty as a nation. His response is enough, however, to force them to come clean about their real reason for wanting Jesus' death and to express the religious accusation behind the political charge: **We have a law, and according to the law he ought to die, because he made himself out to be the Son of God.** The law in view is presumably Lev. 24.16 – 'One who blasphemes the name of the Lord shall be put to death.' This statement of 'the Jews', of course, encapsulates the main issue in the clash between the synagogue with its Torah and Johannine Christians with their Christology that is reflected in the Gospel's narrative. It is a charge already known to readers from earlier in the story (cf. esp. 5.18 and 10.33–5). Such readers also know by now that, from the evangelist's point of view, Jesus has indeed claimed to be Son of God, but he has not made himself Son of God. On the contrary, his claim has always been that he says and does nothing on his own and that his identity and functions as the Son have been granted him by the Father (cf. e.g. 5.19, 20, 26).

So by this stage the two titles and the charges concerning them that feature in the trial before the Sanhedrin in the Synoptics and were taken up in 10.22–39, namely, Messiah and Son of God, have also emerged in this trial before Pilate. King of the Jews has been the equivalent of Messiah, focusing on the Messiah as a royal figure, and Son of God has now occurred here in v. 7. For John's Gospel Jesus is the sort of royal Messiah who is Son of God, and this is reflected in its statement of purpose in 20.31 – 'that you may believe that Jesus is the Christ, the Son of God'.

8–9 After the charge about Jesus being the Son of God is laid before Pilate, **he became more afraid**. Mark (15.5) speaks of Pilate being amazed and Matthew (27.14) of him being greatly amazed, but John speaks of his fear. Since there has been no previous indication that Pilate is afraid, the comparative term μᾶλλον should probably be understood intensively, as it can be on occasion, signalling Pilate's great fear. It is the accusation about Jesus being Son of God that has reduced the representative of Roman power to fear before the man accused on a capital charge, who would normally be expected to fear him. This fear causes him to move back into the praetorium in this sixth scene so that he can question Jesus about his origins. Despite his earlier arrogance, Pilate is now depicted as realizing that he may have become embroiled in an issue that goes beyond the political, one in which having to make a decision might well have greater consequences than he had previously imagined. The mention of the title 'Son of God' prompts Pilate to ask the question that has been raised about Jesus throughout his ministry – **Where are you from?** This has been one of the ironically ambiguous themes in the narrative (cf. the use of πόθεν in 7.27–8; 8.14; 9.29–30) and readers know by now that the appropriate answer is 'from heaven, from above, from God'. If they required help with the answer, the use of the term ἄνωθεν, 'from above', in the ensuing dialogue in v. 11 would jog their memory. The answer needs to be supplied, however, because Jesus does not give one. His silence under questioning at the trial was also part of the tradition (cf. Mark 15.5; Matt. 27.14). Here in John Jesus had already suggested an answer when he told Pilate that his kingdom was 'not of this world'. But the time when Pilate could have appreciated the answer and listened to Jesus' witness to the truth has passed, as has been seen from 18.38.

10–11 When Pilate receives no reply, he resorts to reminding Jesus of his plight as the accused and of his own power over him: **Do you not**

know that I have authority to release you and I have authority to crucify you? When Jesus does respond, his point about power is a different one – **You would have no authority over me at all if it had not been given you from above.** Pilate's authority over Jesus comes from the same place as Jesus himself. It does not derive from Pilate or from the emperor; it comes from above, from God. The Roman trial is here put in cosmic perspective. Pilate has power as judge in this trial only because God has assigned him this role. That role and its responsibility are then qualified in a further way – **For this reason the one who handed me over to you has the greater sin.** So Pilate is culpable or 'has sin' in this situation, but there is an agent with greater culpability. To whom does this refer? Given the force of the preceding clause, one might have thought of God, but assigning ultimate causality to God is one thing, imputing sin to God is quite another, and so this possibility must be ruled out. The verb 'to hand over' is used to characterize Judas' role in a number of earlier references (cf. 6.64, 71; 12.4; 13.2, 11, 21; 18.2, 5). The consistency of this characterization makes it conceivable that he is in view. On the other hand, once Judas' act of betrayal is over, the narrative depicts the chief priests and 'the Jews' as responsible for the actual handing over to Pilate (cf. 18.30, 35). The formulation in the singular is capable of having a general referent and so it may be best to see 'the greater sin' as lying with 'the Jews', as represented particularly by the chief priests, who should have known better. So Jesus as the witness who has been put on trial not only points to the one with ultimate authority in the cosmic trial but also again becomes judge himself as he hands down his own verdict of guilty on the earthly judge and on those who have brought him to trial.

12 From that moment Pilate tried to release him. Jesus' statement about the limits of Pilate's power prompts Pilate's first really serious attempt to achieve his release in this final scene of the trial. But 'the Jews' now drop the religious charge and revert to the political issue in forceful terms – **If you release this man, you are not a friend of Caesar.** There are questions about the historical referent here – whether 'friend of Caesar' has in view the particular title *amicus Caesaris*, which belonged to all senators but was also granted to other exceptional citizens, or whether it is simply a general reference to someone in the emperor's favour. If the former is meant, it has been suggested that Pilate may have gained this distinction because he was a favourite of Sejanus, who had great influence with Tiberius. In any case, 'the Jews' are depicted as playing on Pilate's political relationship with a suspicious Tiberius, who was known to act swiftly and brutally in response to any hint of treason. They present Jesus' kingship as a rival to Caesar's power – **Anyone who makes himself out to be a king is opposing Caesar.** On this interpretation of the situation, of course, for Pilate to release Jesus would be tantamount to taking sides against Caesar. Pilate's dilemma now becomes even clearer. He is faced not simply with a decision between Jesus and 'the Jews' but also with a decision between Jesus and Caesar.

13–14 Pilate is, however, determined to attempt to humiliate 'the Jews' a little more. In a repetition of the action of the central scene he leads out Jesus, who is, of course, still attired in the crown of thorns and the purple robe, and this time makes his mockery of 'the Jews' more explicit by declaring not 'Here is the man!' but **Here is your king!** There is, however, a further difference in this scene that has been the cause of interpretative debate. Does Pilate sit or does he seat Jesus on the judgement seat? As the note on the translation of this verse indicates, the question arises because the verb ἐκάθισεν can be taken as transitive or intransitive in force. The syntactical considerations are inconclusive. On the one hand, it can be pointed out that the only other use of the verb in this Gospel is intransitive (cf. 12.14). But on the other, the object does not need to be repeated after ἐκάθισεν if it is already there with a previous verb, and elsewhere, when 'Jesus' is the object of two verbs, the object is positioned between the two (cf. e.g. vv. 1, 6 earlier in this account). This point is clear also from Eph. 1.20, where ἐκάθισεν is used transitively with 'Christ' as the object without the pronoun being repeated. Some have suggested that the narrator is being deliberately ambiguous and allowing for both interpretative possibilities. But this is the least satisfactory solution, since, although the narrative is characterized by various double meanings, nowhere else do these depend on a grammatical ambiguity. There are parallels in other narratives for both interpretations. In Matt. 27.19 mention is made of Pilate sitting on the judgement seat during the exchange about Barabbas, but in Justin, *Apol.* 1.35 and in *Gos. Pet.* 5.7 Jesus is mocked by Jews setting him on the judgement seat and calling on him to judge ('Give righteous judgement, O King of Israel' – *Gos. Pet.*). If Pilate is the one on the judgement seat here in John, then he only takes this position at the end of the trial, and it is somewhat strange that, having done so, he makes no formal pronouncement of a verdict, as occurs in Matt. 27.24. But if Jesus is seated on the judgement seat, this reads more naturally as a further aspect of Pilate's humiliation of Jesus, which he also employs to mock 'the Jews'. Jesus has already been dressed up as king; now the judge's bench serves as his throne in this mock coronation. On either interpretation there is the irony of the one on trial being the real judge, while the judge is himself put on trial. Since the irony in terms of kingship is blatant and since the judgement seat is mentioned in the context of the mocking of Jesus as king, this tilts the balance towards taking the irony of judging as also blatant and therefore taking the verb as transitive. To dismiss this interpretation on the ground that Jesus functions exclusively as king and not as judge in the Roman trial is to ignore that 'king' as a title has already been subordinated to 'witness' in 18.37 and that earlier in this Gospel Jesus the witness has also been seen to function as judge. It is also to forget that in Jewish scriptural tradition there is frequent identification of king and judge (cf. e.g. Ps. 10.16–18; Isa. 11.1–4; Dan. 4.37).

A specific location is given for the judgement seat – **the place called Stone Pavement or, in Hebrew, Gabbatha.** While the Greek term has been translated as 'Stone Pavement', the Aramaic term means a hill or high place. Neither is of decisive help in determining the site. The matter of the location of the prefect's praetorium has been disputed by scholars, with some holding that, when he was in residence in Jerusalem, this would have been at the Antonia Fortress at the north-west corner of the temple area on the eastern hill of Jerusalem, and others that it would have been at Herod's Palace on a hill on the west of the city. At one time the discovery of a pavement of huge stone slabs in the Antonia area was thought to be the one mentioned here, but more recent archaeology dates it to the second century CE and so this particular pavement would not have existed at the time of Jesus. The weight of the evidence from a variety of references in Josephus and Philo to the prefect's visits to Jerusalem favours the more luxurious quarters of Herod's Palace as his residential choice.

In the midst of this scene of mockery the narrator also inserts a chronological note – **Now it was the day of Preparation for the Passover, and it was about the sixth hour.** It fills out the hint already given in the explanation of the behaviour of 'the Jews' in the first scene (cf. 18.28b) and will be exploited more fully in the narrative of the crucifixion (cf. 19.31, 36). Here in the final trial scene it prepares for what can be taken as the faithlessness of 'the Jews' in their renunciation of their Passover confession in the next verse, a renunciation that takes place at the very time they would be about to commemorate God's faithfulness to them in the exodus event.

15–16a Pilate's second attempt to humiliate 'the Jews' by presenting Jesus as their king is followed by a similar response to that of v. 6. This time, however, those who cry out are simply designated as 'the Jews' and the response is more vehement. There are three imperatives instead of the two in 19.6, with **Away with him** being repeated before **crucify him!** Pilate does not give up on his sarcastic jest and what he says next is a further provocation – **Shall I crucify your king?** This produces the final and shocking words of the chief priests – **We have no king but Caesar.** The irony is immense. Not only is Jesus rejected as messianic king but so also apparently are all expectations of a royal Messiah who would deliver Israel from foreign oppression. Instead there is a profession of allegiance to the oppressor. What is more, this assertion demonstrates one of the themes of the narrative – that to reject Jesus is to reject God. By proclaiming their loyalty to Caesar as a way of securing Jesus' death, the chief priests end up renouncing their God. Israel had always claimed Yahweh as its king (cf. e.g. Judg. 8.23; 1 Sam. 8.7). Indeed 'We have no king but Caesar' turns out to be a parody of Israel's profession to have no king but God. The eleventh of the Eighteen Benedictions contains the prayer 'May you be our King, you alone!', and certainly by the second century CE the Passover liturgy included the Nishmat hymn with the lines,

> From everlasting to everlasting you are God;
> Beside you we have no king, redeemer or saviour,
> No liberator, deliverer, provider,
> None who takes pity in every time of distress and trouble.
> We have no king but you.

With the chief priests' words this narrative portrays 'the Jews' as judging and condemning themselves. They have accused Jesus of blasphemy but now they are shown to be guilty of apostasy by accepting Caesar's exclusive claim to kingship instead of God's.

Then he handed him over to them to be crucified. If, from the evangelist's perspective, the Jewish religious leaders have just completed their self-condemnation, Pilate now completes his. Having gained from the chief priests a declaration of their loyal subjection to Rome, he now hands Jesus over to be crucified, despite his threefold avowal of Jesus' innocence. But to whom does he hand Jesus over? The natural referent given the antecedents in vv. 14–15 would be 'the Jews', represented by the chief priests. This would certainly complete the account neatly. The Jews have brought Jesus to Pilate at the beginning and now he hands Jesus back to them at the end, underlining that the major responsibility for the death of Jesus lies with them (cf. v. 11). Yet the 'they' who crucify Jesus (cf. vv. 18, 23) are the Roman soldiers, and these are surely also then the referents in v. 16b – 'So they took Jesus' – and thus also those to whom Jesus is handed over in the first place in v. 16a. In Mark 15.14, followed by Matt. 27.27, it is clearly the Roman soldiers to whom Jesus is delivered and it is then that the mocking by the soldiers takes place. It may well be, then, that moving the mocking scene forward in John's account has produced the ambiguity at this point in his handling of the tradition.

Whatever traditions lie behind this narrative, they have been elaborated and woven into an account in which, by his witness to the truth, Jesus becomes the judge, and both 'the Jews' and Pilate are judged through their response to Jesus. In this way the Roman trial becomes the vehicle for the irony of the apparent judge and the apparent accusers being in fact judged by the apparent accused. In rejecting the one who claims to be the authorized representative of their God, 'the Jews' also end up abjectly rejecting this God's exclusive claim. In effect, the chief priests' final words mean that they see themselves as just one of the nations subject to Caesar rather than the special people of God. The portrayal of Caesar's representative, Pilate, also makes the point that, despite his mockery of this Jewish issue, he too is faced with a decision about the truth embodied in Jesus and his witness that cannot be avoided. His failure to decide in favour of Jesus means that he ends up aligned with 'the Jews' as part of the unbelieving hostile world in this trial with cosmic dimensions. A further aspect of the account's intricate irony is that Pilate as the judge who is judged also acts, despite himself, as a witness to Jesus through his threefold declaration of Jesus' innocence and his announcement, 'Here is your king!'

(iv) Jesus' crucifixion and death   *19.16b–37*

(16b) So they took Jesus; (17) and carrying the cross by himself, he went out to what is called the Place of the Skull, which in Hebrew is called Golgotha. (18) There they crucified him, and with him two others, one on either side, with Jesus in the middle. (19) Pilate also had an inscription written and placed on the cross. It read, 'Jesus the Nazorean, the King of the Jews.' (20) Many of the Jews read this inscription, because the place where Jesus was crucified was near the city; and it was written in Hebrew, Latin and Greek. (21) The chief priests of the Jews therefore said to Pilate, 'Do not write, "The King of the Jews" but "This man said, I am King of the Jews." ' (22) Pilate replied, 'What I have written, I have written.'

(23) When the soldiers had crucified Jesus, they took his clothes and divided them into four parts, with one part for each soldier. They also took his tunic. Now the tunic was seamless, woven in one piece from the top. (24) So they said to one another, 'Let us not tear it, but let us cast lots for it to see whose it shall be.' This was to fulfil what the scripture says, 'They divided my clothes among themselves, and for my clothing they cast lots.' So that is what the soldiers did. (25) Near Jesus' cross were standing his mother and his mother's sister, Mary the wife of Clopas, and Mary Magdalene. (26) When Jesus saw his mother and the disciple whom he loved standing near her, he said to his mother, 'Woman, look, your son.' (27) Then he said to the disciple, 'Look, your mother.' And from that hour the disciple took her into his home.

(28) After this, knowing that everything was now completed, in order that the scripture might be fulfilled, Jesus said, 'I am thirsty.' (29) A jar full of sour wine was standing there. So they put a sponge full of sour wine on a hyssop and held it up to

his mouth. (30) When he had received the wine, Jesus said, 'It is completed.' Then, bowing his head, he gave up the spirit.

(31) Since it was the day of Preparation, and in order that the bodies should not remain on the cross on the sabbath, for that sabbath was a special one, the Jews asked Pilate to have the legs broken and the bodies removed. (32) So the soldiers came and broke the legs of the first and of the other who was crucified with him. (33) But when they came to Jesus, they saw that he was already dead, and did not break his legs. (34) But one of the soldiers pierced his side with a spear, and at once blood and water came out. (35) And he who saw this has testified, and his witness is true, and he knows that he speaks the truth, in order that you also may believe. (36) For these things happened in order that the scripture might be fulfilled, 'None of his bones will be broken.' (37) And again another scripture says, 'They will look on the one they have pierced.'

It is worth sketching briefly and in broad strokes the ways in which John's account of Jesus' crucifixion and death is distinctive in comparison with the other canonical Gospels. There is no Simon of Cyrene to help carry the cross (cf. Mark 15.21; Matt. 27.32; Luke 25.26), no mockery from bystanders or from the two others crucified with Jesus (cf. Mark 15.29–32; Matt. 27.39–44; Luke 23.35–9), no cry of abandonment (cf. Mark 15.34; Matt. 27.46), no portents, whether darkness at noon, the tearing of the temple curtain or an earthquake (cf. Mark 15.33, 38; Matt. 27.45, 51–3; Luke 23.44–5), and no centurion who responds positively to what he has seen (cf. Mark 15.39; Matt. 27.54; Luke 23.47). If the evangelist knew either a passion tradition that lies behind the Synoptics or, more likely, one or more of the Synoptic accounts, he has embellished his source in five main ways that are distinctive to him. He has added the dispute between Pilate and 'the Jews' about the *titulus* or inscription on the cross (vv. 19–22); he employs different Scripture texts to indicate that everything that happens to Jesus is in accord with the divine plan and purpose (vv. 24, 28, 36, 37); he inserts material about the relation between the Beloved Disciple and Jesus' mother (vv. 26–7); he stresses the notion of accomplishment (vv. 28, 30); and he provides the witness of the Beloved Disciple to the flow of blood and water resulting from the piercing of Jesus' side (vv. 34–5). The significance of these distinctive aspects for the evangelist's portrayal of the death of Jesus will emerge in the commentary and in the summing up that follows.

16b–18 As we have noted, whatever the ambiguity of the referent of those to whom Pilate handed Jesus over in v. 16a, the subject of **they took Jesus** has to be the Roman soldiers (cf. vv. 18, 23). Jesus' sovereignty in going to his own death is immediately underlined by the depiction of him as **carrying the cross by himself**. In this Gospel he needs no help of a Simon of Cyrene. The topographical note about Golgotha, **the Place of the Skull**, as the site of the crucifixion is taken from the tradition (cf. Mark 15.22; Matt. 27.33; Luke 23.33), and indicates the shape of the piece of ground outside the city that resembled the top of a skull. The Church of the Holy Sepulchre in today's Jerusalem claims plausibly that this area is now part of its site. The **two others** crucified with Jesus are mentioned in all the accounts with differing degrees of elaboration (cf. Mark 15.27, 32b; Matt. 27.38, 44; Luke 22.32, 39–43). The fourth evangelist does not embellish this aspect of the tradition at all at this point, though he will use the two as contrasting foils to Jesus for the point he wishes to make about the breaking of the legs in v. 32.

19–22 Pilate also had an inscription written and placed on the cross. The translation has taken the verbs in this sentence to be causal in force. Pilate did not undertake these activities himself but had them carried out on his behalf. It is usually held that the basic tradition about the inscription can lay excellent claim to historicity. The title, **the King of the Jews**, was not one derived from Jewish messianic expectation. Josephus (*A.J.* 14.34–6; 16.311) can use it of Alexander and of Herod, but there is no evidence for a royal Messiah being described in such terminology. 'King of the Jews' was also not an early Christian title for Jesus. Outside the passion narratives it occurs only in Matt. 2.2 and there almost certainly it is employed under the influence of the passion narrative title. The title, then, appears to have been forced on early Christian tradition from the wording of the cross inscription rather than having been created by it. The weight of the tradition is such that John makes no alteration to this basic title, despite the fact that the predominant reference of 'the Jews' in the narrative is the negative one of the unbelieving opposition to Jesus and that his preference is likely to have been 'the King of Israel'. The charge would originally have signified that Jesus of Nazareth was worthy of death because he set himself up against Roman rule as 'King of the Jews'. John has added the personal identification of the King of the Jews as **Jesus the Nazorean**, which also gives the inscription a more formal and memorable ring. He underlines the irony of the ambiguity in the charge by having **The chief priests of the Jews** protest against its wording. The mention of the languages in which the inscription was written – **Hebrew, Latin and Greek** – is another instance of elaboration of the tradition (cf. Mark 15.26; Matt. 27.37; Luke 23.38). Some tomb inscriptions and edicts with all three languages have been found, but it is improbable that the Romans would have taken this trouble in the case of someone sentenced to crucifixion. This detail about the kingship of Jesus being proclaimed in the vernacular, in the language of the Roman government, and in the language of trade and commerce, is making the point that his is a universal reign over the whole civilized world. In the face of requests for the modification of the inscription, Pilate ironically insists on its irrevocability – **What I have written, I have written.** This assertion functions both as part of Pilate's continuing attempt to humiliate the religious authorities and, for those who understand, as underlining that the title for Jesus is true and unalterable. For the evangelist, the divine king reigns from the cross, despite his rejection by his subjects and their attempt to eradicate his claim.

23–5a It appears that for the early followers of Jesus there was a two-way process operative in the interpretative relationship between the historical traditions about his death and the psalms about the suffering righteous one, especially Ps. 22. There was one particular element in the earliest layer of the tradition that linked it to Ps. 22 – the cry of abandonment recorded in Mark and Matthew – and perhaps other elements in the original tradition, such as the distribution of Jesus' garments, were then seen also to correspond to Ps. 22. The other side of the process was that Ps. 22 was then ransacked for further possible parallels to the circumstances of Jesus' death and such details began to shape the way in which the tradition itself related and passed on the passion story.

These verses reflect both sides of such a process. The incident of dividing up Jesus' clothing is mentioned briefly and in passing in the tradition with which the evangelist is familiar (cf. Mark 15.24; Matt. 27.25; Luke 23.34). Although the mention of casting lots could already be an elaboration based on the psalm, there is no strong reason for doubting the historicity of such an incident. An execution squad was entitled to what its victim was wearing. John, however, embellishes the incident with further details in order to draw attention to the fulfilment of the divine plan in Jesus' death – **This was to fulfil what the scripture says.** He quotes both lines of the parallelism in the LXX version of Ps. 22.18 – **They divided my clothes among themselves, and for my clothing they cast lots.** In the original Hebrew 'clothes' and 'clothing' were simply two ways of saying the same thing, but the LXX translation allows for a distinction between clothes (τὰ ἱμάτια) and one particular item of clothing (ὁ ἱματισμός), and it is the latter that is connected with the casting of lots. The evangelist, therefore, shapes his narrative and builds in a conversation among the soldiers in order to explain how, in line with Scripture, they cast lots for one particular garment – the tunic. Jesus' tunic, a long undergarment worn next to the body, he informs the readers, was seamless, woven in one piece from the top. The soldiers did not want to tear it, and so they preferred to cast lots for this piece of clothing. Commentators have frequently looked for a symbolic explanation of the emphasis on the seamlessness of the garment. Some have suggested an allusion to the high priest's robe. Although the description of the high priest's robe in Josephus (*A. J.* 3.161) employs the same term as John does for the tunic (ὁ χιτών) and speaks of it as 'woven from a single thread', the high priest's garment was a long, flowing outer robe fastened with a gold-embroidered belt. It is doubtful whether by this detail the evangelist meant Jesus to be understood as priest as well as king, especially since a high-priest Christology plays no role elsewhere in his narrative. Others, including Cyprian, have, more fancifully, seen a link between the seamless unity of Jesus' tunic and the unity between Jesus and his followers. There does appear to be community symbolism in the next incident, involving the Beloved Disciple and Jesus' mother, but attempts to find a symbolic reference are superfluous, because the evangelist's concern to find an exact fulfilment of Scripture quite adequately accounts for the inclusion of this description of the tunic. The intent was to show that those who put Jesus to death were all the time, though unwittingly, enacting the divine saving will, with which Jesus was in perfect harmony.

25b–7 The tradition on which John built contained a mention of women at the crucifixion, though at a distance, but placed after Jesus' death (cf. Mark 15.40–1; Matt. 27.55–6; Luke 23.49). John moves the episode up and moves the women near the cross to allow for the conversation between Jesus and his mother, who is not specifically listed among the women in the Synoptic accounts, unless, as a few hold, Mark's readers are meant to identify Mary, the mother of James the younger and of Joses, with the Mary in Mark 6.3, who has among her sons James and Joses as well as Jesus. John specifies the women as **his mother and his mother's sister, Mary the wife of Clopas, and Mary Magdalene**. Among the named women in Mark, Matthew and John, Mary Magdalene is the only one they clearly have in common. The fourth evangelist appears to have inserted this unique material about the mother of Jesus and the Beloved Disciple in order to make a theological point. From the cross Jesus utters his last will and testament, in which the two are entrusted to each other. The announcements **Woman, look, your son** and **Look, your mother** both establish the Beloved Disciple as Jesus' successor and bring about a new fictive kinship, which comes into effect **from that hour**. In the farewell discourse Jesus had designated the Paraclete as his successor. Now the Beloved Disciple is to be his human successor, taking over Jesus' responsibility as son toward his mother but doing so in a metaphorical sense. A partial parallel is provided by 1 Macc. 2.65, where, as Mattathias is on the point of death, he makes provision for his children by announcing, 'Look, your brother Simeon who, I know, is wise in counsel; always listen to him; he shall be your father.' He passes over his first-born son and makes Simeon, the second son, his successor as a metaphorical father, who in the role of wise teacher is to secure his descendants' allegiance to the covenant. While Simeon succeeds Mattathias as father, the Beloved Disciple succeeds Jesus as son, yet is to have a similar role as successor by instructing Jesus' future followers about authentic allegiance to Jesus. In the only previous mention of the mother of Jesus in the narrative, at the wedding in Cana (2.1–11), when she expected him to do something about the lack of wine, she was also addressed by Jesus as 'woman' and told that his 'hour' had not yet come. Despite the rebuff, she remained expectant and told the servants to do whatever Jesus ordered them to do. Now that Jesus' hour of death and glorification has arrived, she is featured again as she is handed over to the care of the Beloved Disciple. It appears that she represents all who are receptive to salvation from Jesus, perhaps believing Jews in particular, who are now referred to the disciple who is the witness par excellence, the founding figure of the evangelist's community. By taking care of the future through bringing the Beloved Disciple, as his successor, and his mother together as the new family of his followers, Jesus is seen as providing for the welfare of believers by entrusting them to the one whose witness will ensure the true interpretation of the revelation he has proclaimed and embodied.

28–30 Having secured the future of his cause, Jesus knew **that everything was now completed** (τετέλεσται). This is the same term that Jesus will employ as his final word (cf. v. 30) and here forms part of yet another of the narrator's inside views that stress Jesus' special sovereign knowledge (cf. e.g. 2.24–5; 6.6, 64; 13.1; 18.4). It is in this knowledge that he also utters the words **I am thirsty.**

The offering of a drink of the cheap sour wine that quenches thirst quickly is part of the tradition. In Mark (15.23, 36) and Matthew (27.34, 48) two such drinks are offered, and Jesus refuses the first, in which wine had been mixed with a pain-killing drug. In Luke 23.36 the offering of the wine is part of the mockery of the soldiers. John employs this piece of tradition differently. Whereas in the Synoptics the offering of the wine is initiated by others, only here, in the Fourth Gospel, is it Jesus himself who, by saying he is thirsty, prompts the gesture in order deliberately to ensure **that the scripture might be fulfilled.** This is the only place where the evangelist uses τελειόω, 'to complete', rather than πληρόω, 'to fulfil', for this notion of the fulfilment of Scripture. The particular scripture in view is Ps. 69.21 – 'and for my thirst they gave me vinegar to drink'. The LXX employs the term ὄξος for vinegar and this is the same noun used here for the common wine. In John's presentation, then, Jesus completes his work by consciously choosing to bring the divine plan revealed in Scripture to complete fulfilment.

The account contains the strange detail that **they put a sponge full of sour wine on a hyssop and held it up to his mouth.** One would have expected the sponge to have been attached to a reed, as in Mark, because the hyssop is a small plant that does not have a large stem. It has, therefore been suggested that the reading ὑσώππῳ/ is a very early error in the text and that the original would have been ὑσσιῷ/, the term for a javelin. But the latter reading is found only in two minuscule manuscripts (476* 1242) and the external evidence is overwhelmingly in favour of the more difficult reading. It could be, then, that the reference to hyssop is meant to provide an allusion to the Passover lamb theme, mentioned earlier in 19.14 and recurring in the material immediately following in vv. 31, 36, because in Exod. 12.22 it was specified that hyssop was to be used to sprinkle the blood of the Passover lamb on the doorposts of the Israelites' houses.

After receiving the sour wine and bringing Scripture to completion, the note of accomplishment is sounded yet again in Jesus' last word, **It is completed** (τετέλεσται). In keeping with the evangelist's presentation of Jesus' death as his glorification, as his coronation as king, Jesus' last word is not the cry of abandonment but the cry of achievement, signifying the completion of his work. The reader has been prepared for this perspective not only by the previous references to the decisive 'hour' but also by earlier mentions of the necessity of Jesus completing the work he had been given to do (cf., e.g., 4.34; 9.4; 17.4). After the announcement of the triumphant accomplishment of his work, Jesus can bow his head and die peacefully. **He gave up the spirit** underscores that to the last Jesus is in control, taking the initiative, and recalls the earlier assertion of 10.17–18 – 'I lay down my life . . . No one has taken it from me, but I lay it down of my own accord. I have authority to lay it down, and I have authority to take it up again.' It may well be that the formulation about giving up or handing over the spirit, in which there is no possessive pronoun, allows a reference to and prepares for the giving of the Spirit, which, according to 7.39, would occur when Jesus was glorified. This possibility is strengthened by the fact that 7.38–9 lie behind the reference to the water emerging from Jesus' side in the passage which follows.

31–3 There is again a reminder of the timing of the crucifixion through the mention of **the day of Preparation** and the note that **that sabbath was a special one** (literally, a great one). This contributes to the interpretation of Jesus' death in terms of Passover imagery (cf. v. 36). The approaching Passover sabbath also heightens the concern of 'the Jews' that the bodies not be left on their crosses (cf. the legislation in Deut. 21.22–3 about the bodies of hanged criminals not being left overnight because of the threat of their defiling the land). Such concern with purity for Passover and with details of ritual practice parallels that of the Jewish leaders at the start of the Roman trial narrative in 18.28. Breaking the legs of those crucified would hasten death and enable the timely removal of the corpses. So the legs of the two others crucified with Jesus are broken by the Roman soldiers. **But when they came to Jesus, they saw that he was already dead, and did not break his legs.** That the breaking of the legs was not necessary in Jesus' case serves two major functions in the telling of the story. It confirms that he had already died and makes possible the reference to his death as the unblemished Passover lamb, which will be exploited in v. 36.

34 But one of the soldiers pierced his side with a spear. No motivation is supplied for this action. After all, the soldiers have already concluded that Jesus was dead. Instead, the evangelist's focus is on the result of the action – **at once blood and water came out.** That this is of major significance is underlined by the testimony that follows in v. 35. Within the frame of reference of the Gospel itself the significance of the blood and water is not hard to discover. The significance of the blood is set out in 6.52–9, where there are clear eucharistic overtones, but the basic level of reference is to the necessity of believing in the effectiveness of Jesus' death in order to have life – 'unless you eat the flesh of the Son of Man and drink his blood, you have no life in you. Whoever eats my flesh and drinks my blood has eternal life' (6.53–4). In regard to the water, 7.38, with its talk of rivers of living water flowing from Christ's belly, provides the key. The water that comes from Jesus' side signifies the life of the Spirit that comes from Jesus' glorification. The formulation in 7.38 had taken up the Exodus tradition about water from the rock in the desert. So now the account of the significance of Jesus' death in all likelihood incorporates not only that Exodus tradition but also the strand of its interpretation in which Moses struck the rock twice, and the first time it gushed blood and the second time water flowed out (cf. *Tg. Ps.-J.* on Num. 20.11; *Exod. Rab.* 122a on Exod. 17). Both the blood and the water, then, point unmistakably to the theme of life, seen here as God's salvific verdict on the death of the one who has been presented as the divine agent in his mission of witnessing and judging.

35 The importance of this positive verdict that overturns humans' condemnation of Jesus to death is emphasized in three ways. First, a witness is supplied – **he who saw this has testified.** Secondly, the narrator quite unusually stops and addresses the readers, telling them that this witness is given **in order that you also may believe.** Thirdly, there is a double underlining of the truth of this witness – **and his witness is true, and he** (literally, that one – best understood as the witness himself) **knows that he speaks the truth.**

The material in vv. 31–7 is the evangelist's own or that of his tradition, but it may well be that he inserted this verse into it at a late stage. The narrative flows smoothly without it, so that 'these things' that are said to be the fulfilment of Scripture in vv. 36–7 are a reference to the two events of vv. 31–4 – the legs not being broken and the piercing – and the Scripture citations could well have followed straight on from the relating of the events. The NRSV attempts to deal with this phenomenon by placing v. 35 within brackets.

But who is the witness about whom the narrator speaks in the third person? He is usually identified with the Beloved Disciple. There is, however, one other plausible candidate for this character – the soldier who pierced Jesus' side. This soldier is the direct antecedent in the narrative for the clause 'he who saw this has testified', and such an identification could then be said to be John's equivalent to the confession of the centurion in the Synoptic accounts. It can also be argued that the scripture cited by the narrator in v. 37 points in this direction, since in that text it is the same group which has done the piercing that looks on the one it has pierced. On this interpretation, the clause 'in order that you also may believe' is then taken as indicating that the testimony of the soldier has been passed on by the narrator to produce or enhance the readers' faith. In support of this reading it is also claimed that the reader would expect from v. 27b – 'And from that hour the disciple took her into his home' – that the Beloved Disciple had left the scene.

Despite these claims, the best candidate for this role of witness remains the Beloved Disciple. It is in keeping with his function of being a key witness to significant moments in the last part of Jesus' ministry – the announcement of the identity of the betrayer (13.23–6), the meaning of the death here, the significance of the empty tomb (20.8) and the recognition of the risen Lord (21.7). 'From that hour' in 19.27b cannot be held to rule this out as a possibility. The use of the term 'hour' is not only highly significant but also very elastic in this narrative discourse. The hour of glorification is depicted as having already arrived as early as 12.27 (cf. also 13.1). It is possible that 'hour' here is coloured by the broader connotations of its earlier use, and in fact the glorification that characterizes the hour of death is only explicitly displayed at this point, when the blood and water comes from Jesus' side, recalling the prediction of 8.38 and the narrator's comment that this awaited fulfilment until Jesus' glorification (8.39). So 'from that hour' can plausibly be taken as 'after Jesus' death as glorification'. Two other factors support the identification of the witness with the Beloved Disciple. In the same way that the narrative's ending in 21.24–5 will endorse the truth of the Beloved Disciple's witness, so also the truth of the witness here is endorsed. And 20.31 states the purpose of the witness, which constitutes the Gospel and will be attributed at the end to the Beloved Disciple, in terms of an address to the readers – 'so that you may believe' – while here also is the only other place that readers are addressed directly and again the witness's testimony is 'in order that you also may believe'.

Witness terminology in this verse, unlike its predominant usage earlier in the Gospel, is linked to a reference to what could be seen with one's eyes. There is no explicit object of the seeing mentioned, but it is most likely that this is given in the antecedent clause – 'at once blood and water came out'. The Beloved Disciple is therefore portrayed as an eyewitness of the blood and water, yet clearly his witness is not given simply to enable readers to believe that blood and water flowed from Jesus' side but to believe in the significance of this phenomenon, namely, that Jesus' death was a sacrifice that brought life, a judgement that produced a positive verdict. This bearing witness takes place not within the story line itself but in the addressing of the readers ('you') that constitutes the writing of the Gospel.

This suggests that the Beloved Disciple's role in the narrative constitutes a particular literary device (see Introduction). He enables the narrator's retrospective knowledge and insights to be communicated to the readers within the story line while giving it the authority of a character who was present at the time being narrated. If this is the case, what are the implications for the emphasis on the truth of this character's witness? At the historical level there is nothing intrinsically impossible about blood and water coming from Jesus' corpse and yet these details are completely unknown to any other tradition about Jesus' death. But the truth claim must be seen as related first of all to what is implied by this verse's assertions within the narrative's universe of discourse. In this narrative, where the language of seeing and testifying is equivalent to believing and confessing, what is claimed as true is the witness's belief about the significance of Jesus' death, in which the judgement Jesus experienced results in the positive verdict of life. The flow of blood and water is the narrative means for conveying this significance.

36–7 The narrator indicates that the events that follow Jesus' death are the fulfilment of not just one but two scriptures. The soldiers' not breaking Jesus' legs is seen as the fulfilment of **None of his bones will be broken.** One likely source for such a citation is the regulation about the Passover sacrifice in Exod. 12.46 and Num. 9.12. In absorbing the sentence of death and thereby bringing about life, Jesus is at the same time, in the words of John the Baptist's testimony, the lamb of God who takes away the sin of the world (cf. 1.29). Yet, as with a number of this Gospel's scriptural citations, the wording serves to recall more than one tradition. The other tradition involved here, as in the 'lamb of God' reference in 1.29, is that of the suffering righteous one. In Ps. 34.19–22 the sign that the Lord rescues the righteous and redeems their life so that none of them will be condemned is 'He keeps all their bones; not one of them will be broken.' The combination of Passover and righteous sufferer traditions is also found in *Jub.* 49.13, where not breaking the bones of the lamb is linked with no bone of the children of Israel being broken. Here in John the failure to break Jesus' legs is seen as itself a sign of God's verdict.

Against all appearances Jesus has not been condemned but approved as righteous. The source of the second citation is clear. **They will look on the one they have pierced** is taken from Zech. 12.10, which occurs in a passage about the death of the good shepherd that goes on to speak of mourning for him as for an only child, a first-born, and to say that 'on that day a fountain shall be opened for the house of David and the inhabitants of Jerusalem, to cleanse them from sin and impurity' (13.1). In this way the Zechariah quotation not only highlights the piercing but its context also enables a connection to be made between the piercing and what the evangelist has said results from this action, namely, the flow of water, which provides new life through its cleansing from sin.

The discussion about the inscription on the cross early on in the account means that the theme of Jesus as king colours this crucifixion story. It can then be seen as treating the crucifixion as Jesus' enthronement with the cross as his mock throne. Despite the elements of Jesus' pain and degradation, the account is pervaded by a strange sense of calm, with the protagonist, Jesus, clearly in control of what is happening, sovereign even on the cross. From the cross he addresses his mother and the Beloved Disciple, establishing a new community with new relationships. His death is the completion of the task his Father has given him to do. This is significant for all the major earlier depictions of that task in this Gospel, whether in terms of witnessing to the truth, judging, making God known, glorifying God or bringing life. The truth about God and humanity is most clearly witnessed in Jesus' martyr's death. The task of judging is accomplished as the judge becomes the one who is judged. God is supremely made known in this death that appears to be so ungodlike. God's glory is most clearly displayed in the shame and humiliation of Jesus' cross. Jesus brings life in undergoing the sentence of death. In this way Jesus' death is both the world's judgement on him and God's judgement on both him and the world. This divine verdict is established after Jesus' death. By absorbing the negative verdict of death, Jesus is shown to be the source of the positive verdict of life, as blood and water flow from his side. His death is not only the completion of his mission but also completes God's plan revealed in Scripture. At point after point, the events that take place are to be seen as bringing the Scriptures to fulfilment, not least in the way that they confirm Jesus' death as that of the true Passover lamb.

(v) The burial   19.38–42

(38) After these things Joseph of Arimathea, a disciple of Jesus, but a secret one for fear of the Jews, asked Pilate if he could remove the body of Jesus. And Pilate gave permission. So he went and removed the body. (39) Nicodemus, the one who had first

come to him at night, also came, bringing a mixture of myrrh and aloes, weighing about a hundred pounds. (40) So they took the body of Jesus and bound it in burial cloths with the spices, according to the Jews' custom for burial preparation. (41) Now in the place where he had been crucified there was a garden, and in the garden a new tomb in which no one had yet been laid. (42) So there, on account of the Jewish day of Preparation, and because the tomb was nearby, they laid Jesus.

The Synoptic accounts of the burial of Jesus are found in Mark 15.42–7, Matt. 27.57–61 and Luke 23.50–6. All three accounts feature Joseph of Arimathea, who asks for Jesus' body, wraps it in a linen shroud and places it in a tomb, and women followers of Jesus who see where the body has been laid – and, in Mark (cf. 16.1) and Luke, prepare to take spices to anoint the body. John's account has Joseph of Arimathea performing the same function as he does in the Synoptics. It omits any mention of the women followers, however, and instead replaces them with a character from earlier in the narrative, Nicodemus, who joins Joseph in taking and burying the body and brings the spices with which it is wrapped in linen cloths. Mark 15.43 and Luke 23.50–1 depict Joseph as a member of the council or Sanhedrin who was looking for the kingdom of God. The fourth evangelist ignores these descriptions. His additional character, Nicodemus, has already been shown to be part of the ruling council (cf. 7.50; also 3.1, 10) and the kingdom of God is not one of his major themes. Instead, in line with Matt. 27.57, Joseph is presented as a disciple, but then, with reference to one of this Gospel's own motifs, a secret one for fear of 'the Jews' (cf. 12.42–3). In Mark 15.44–5, after Joseph has asked for the body, Pilate ascertains from the centurion whether Jesus is already dead before handing over his body. John omits this, since he has already treated the same matter in his own fashion in 19.31–3. But he has further links with the Synoptics in regard to the place and time of burial. Mark 15.46 describes the tomb as having been hewn out of rock, but Matt. 27.60 adds that it was Joseph's own new tomb and Luke 23.53 that no one had yet been laid in it. John adds that the tomb is located in a garden, omitting any mention of it as rock-hewn, but taking up part of both Matthew's and Luke's descriptions – it is new and no one has ever been laid in it. Finally, in regard to the temporal setting, Mark mentions at the beginning of his account that it was the day of Preparation, that is, the day before the sabbath (Mark 15.42), while Luke places the two time references after the burial (Luke 23.54). John follows the Lukan sequence with a reference to 'the Jewish day of Preparation' at the end of his account.

38 Appropriate burial of a body was an important duty in Judaism. The body of Jesus, however, was that of someone crucified by the Romans. To the best of our knowledge, the normal fate of such Roman victims would have been to be left to decompose on the cross and therefore frequently to become carrion for the vultures. Jews, however, would have been concerned about the law of Deut. 21.23 that someone who is executed and hanged should have his corpse removed the same day lest the land be defiled (cf. 19.31). Josephus records that on various occasions, therefore, Jews were given permission to remove the bodies of those crucified (cf. *B. J.* 4.5.2). The Mishnah later speaks of the corpses of condemned criminals being put in a mass grave rather than being handed back to families for a decent burial, but even then the bones were expected to be gathered a year later for families to place them in an ossuary, indicating that, though in a common grave, bodies and bones were not scattered indiscriminately (cf. m. *Sanh.* 6.5–6). On some occasions, however, bodies were handed over to families or individual Jews for a more dignified burial (cf. e.g. Philo, *Flacc.* 10.83–4). In the case of Jesus, **Joseph of Arimathea, a disciple of Jesus, but a secret one for fear of the Jews, asked Pilate if he could remove the body of Jesus. And Pilate gave permission.** Mark and Luke provide some explanation for why Joseph might have prevailed with Pilate, because they describe him as a respected member of the council. This account may suggest a similar status for Joseph but by more indirect means. By describing him as a secret disciple for fear of 'the Jews', the narrator harks back to the portrayal of a particular group of followers in 12.42, those who belonged to the authorities but who did not confess their belief openly 'because of the Pharisees' and for fear that they would be put out of the synagogue. Presumably Pilate acceded to the request of this particular member of the religious authorities because he believed that any Jesus movement had been quashed as a result of the death of its leader and had no reason to think people would make a martyr of Jesus.

The description of Joseph of Arimathea is also formulated, of course, in the light of the later circumstances of Johannine Christians and their conflict with the synagogue authorities, where fear of 'the Jews' and of expulsion from the synagogue was a major factor (cf. 9.22; 16.2; also 7.13; 20.19) and produced the temptation to remain within the synagogue as a secret disciple. Joseph's courageous public action in going to Pilate and securing Jesus' body for burial is therefore exemplary and indicates that he has moved out of the category of covert follower and is willing to put devotion to Jesus before consideration of human honour or prestige (cf. 12.43).

39 After removing the body, Joseph is joined by **Nicodemus, the one who had first come to him at night**. This formulation invites readers to recall the earlier appearances of Nicodemus in the narrative, particularly the initial one. The reminder that he had come to Jesus at night highlights the secretive nature of his interest in Jesus and the account in 3.1–21 indicates rather clearly that he had remained in the dark as far as any true understanding of Jesus was concerned. Though in 7.50–2 he again shows his sympathy for Jesus by asking for proper procedure in judging him, he is still described simply as 'one of them', i.e. one of the religious authorities, and there is no suggestion that he has become a believer in Jesus. How far does this third and final reference to Nicodemus change the picture? The majority of scholars think that his actions in this episode show that he has at last become someone who is willing to acknowledge Jesus publicly, but a sizeable minority interpret the nature of his actions less favourably. The main issue is how to evaluate what he brings with him to the burial. He **came, bringing a mixture of myrrh and aloes, weighing about a hundred pounds**. The myrrh and aloes are probably meant to be thought of as in powdered rather than oil or ointment form, but what is clear is that this is a quite extraordinary amount of spices. The lavish and extravagant nature of Mary's act of devotion in 12.3 has been noted earlier. She had used a pound of nard, worth a year's wages for a labourer. What Nicodemus brings is one hundred times heavier and more expensive! What, then, does this gift of spices symbolize? Josephus records that it took five hundred servants to carry the spices for Herod's burial (cf. *B. J.* 1.173; *A. J.* 17.199). It appears then that the burial is being depicted as one fit for a king. That would also be in line with the portrayal of Jesus in both his trial and his death as the true King of the Jews. But are readers meant to assume that Nicodemus was aware of what he was doing and so now has come to an authentic recognition of Jesus' status? Some interpreters take a very different view and argue, in the light of the previous characterization of Nicodemus, that the ludicrous amount of spices is intended to suggest that, though attracted to Jesus, he is still evaluating Jesus on a merely human level, is unable to move beyond an extravagant display of grief, and sees no prospect for this prophet's future beyond the finality of this burial. It may be wiser to take a mediating position and to hold that the story line about Nicodemus himself does not have a clear progression or conclusion. Although, on the one hand, his association with Joseph in the burial episode lends a certain positive light to his portrayal, on the other, he is only associated with Joseph after the latter's courageous public act of going to Pilate and so does not himself acknowledge any allegiance to Jesus as openly. While Joseph is characterized as a disciple, albeit a secret one, Nicodemus, despite his two previous appearances, has not attained that status but is only a sympathizer who stills needs his categories for evaluating Jesus to be radically changed. Further, although his action contributes to the portrayal of Jesus as king not only in his trial and death but also in his burial, there is no explicit indication that this is actually the intention of Nicodemus himself. If there remains some ambiguity about Nicodemus' stance, it may reflect the evangelist's awareness of the tensions faced by those who are secret admirers of Jesus and whom he is inviting to take the further step of making a full confession of faith.

40 Nicodemus helps Joseph to move the body and the two **bound it in burial cloths with the spices**, which, the narrator makes clear for any Gentile readers, was **according to the Jews' custom for burial preparation**. Jesus received a proper Jewish burial. The body was wrapped in linen grave-cloths (cf. also 20.5–7) and packed or sprinkled with spices. There is no mention of anointing and, given that the spices were most likely in powdered form, the burial preparation is not intended to be interpreted as an anointing. This had already been carried out proleptically by Mary in 12.1–8. The fragrant spices were meant to deal with the odour caused by decomposition, and this was a major problem to be overcome because the tombs would have been used for more than one body and people would have returned to place other bodies on the various shelves. In addition, it was the custom to return after about a year to an individual body to see whether it had completely decomposed and to take the bones of the skeleton and place them in an ossuary, which would be stored in the tomb or elsewhere, ready for the resurrection of the end-time. That this second stage in the burial process was not to happen to Jesus' body is, of course, the feature of this narrative that will make Jesus' burial distinct from other Jewish burials.

41–2 As yet, however, there were no other bodies in the tomb where Jesus was placed, because it was **a new tomb in which no one had yet been laid** (cf. Matt. 27.60; Luke 23.53). This account locates the tomb in a **garden**. So John's passion narrative begins with Jesus and the disciples in a garden before the arrest and ends with the burial in a garden. It also prepares for the detail in the resurrection account of Mary Magdalene mistaking the risen Jesus for the gardener. Having presented Jesus' burial as a proper and dignified one, the narrator now makes clear that it was in fact carried out in some haste. Burials took place preferably on the day of the person's death or, if not, then on the following day. The narrator underlines for Gentile readers that this day was **the Jewish day of Preparation** (cf. 19.14) and he has already related that the following day was an especially important sabbath, given that it was also Passover, so that the Jewish authorities wanted the bodies removed before then (cf. 19.31). Since Joseph had only asked Pilate's permission after Jesus' death had been established, the removal of Jesus' body would now require particular haste if the Passover sabbath was not to be infringed. The narrator has already stated that the garden was **in the place where he had been crucified**, so, **because the tomb was nearby**, this conveniently enabled the body to be taken and the burial to be done quickly. The account can now conclude simply and tersely with **there . . . they laid Jesus**.

That Jesus was buried was an essential part of early Christian tradition (cf. 1 Cor. 15.4). In John's narrative, the account of the burial of Jesus, though relatively brief, is, of course, important as the necessary link between the account of the crucifixion and that of the resurrection. Its symbolic features indicate that the one who is buried is in fact Israel's king. There is, however, nothing docetic about the main aspect of this episode in the story of the Logos who became flesh. The one in whom was life chose to give up his temporal human life and, in so doing, experienced the reality of death and its aftermath in burial, yet he does not abandon that life but will take it up again (cf. 10.17–18), and so the ensuing narrative of resurrection will be one that also involves a body and an empty tomb. In their different ways the portrayals of the two characters who carry out the burial contribute to the Gospel's call for genuine belief. In the case of Joseph, the invitation is to move from secret to open and courageous discipleship and in the case of Nicodemus, from sympathy for Jesus' cause to authentic faith.

3. The Resurrection   20.1–31

(i) Discovery of the empty tomb and appearance to Mary Magdalene   20.1–18

(1) On the first day of the week Mary Magdalene came to the tomb early while it was still dark and saw that the stone had been taken away from the tomb. (2) So she ran and went to Simon Peter and the other disciple, whom Jesus loved, and said to them, 'They have taken away the Lord from the tomb and we do not know where they have laid him.' (3) Peter and the other disciple therefore set out and were going to the tomb. (4) The two were running together, but the other disciple ran faster than Peter and came to the tomb first. (5) Bending down to peer in, he saw the linen wrappings lying there, but he did not enter. (6) Then Simon Peter also arrived, following him, and he entered the tomb and saw the linen wrappings lying there (7) and the cloth which had been round his head, lying not with the linen wrappings but rolled up in a place by itself. (8) Then the other disciple, who had come first to the tomb, also entered, and he saw and believed; (9) for as yet they did not understand the scripture that he must rise from the dead. (10) The disciples then went back to their homes.

(11) But Mary was standing near the tomb, weeping outside. As she wept, she bent down to peer into the tomb, (12) and she saw two angels in white, sitting where the body of Jesus had been lying, one at the head and one at the feet. (13) And they said to her, 'Woman, why are you weeping?' She said to them, 'They

have taken away my Lord, and I do not know where they have
laid him.' (14) When she had said this, she turned around and saw
Jesus standing there, but she did not know it was Jesus. (15) Jesus
said to her, 'Why are you weeping? For whom are you looking?'
Thinking that he was the gardener, she said to him, 'Sir, if you
have carried him away, tell me where you have laid him, and
I will take him away.' (16) Jesus said to her, 'Mary.' She turned
and said to him in Hebrew, 'Rabbouni' (which means Teacher).
(17) Jesus said to her, 'Do not hold on to me, for I have not yet
ascended to the Father.[1] But go to my brothers and tell them, "I
am ascending to my Father and your Father and my God and
your God."' (18) Mary Magdalene went and announced to the
disciples, 'I have seen the Lord,' and these words he had said to
her.

This version of the empty tomb story falls into three scenes in which
Mary Magdalene provides the link. In vv. 1–2 she discovers the tomb
empty and reports back to Peter and the Beloved Disciple. In vv. 3–10
they then visit the tomb, and in vv. 11–18 Jesus appears to Mary, who is
again at the tomb. All the way through the account until v. 16 the focal
point is the tomb, and the reader is faced with the question of why it
is empty. In vv. 1–2 Mary comes 'to the tomb', sees that the stone has
been removed 'from the tomb', and tells Peter and the Beloved Disciple
that the Lord has been taken 'from the tomb'. In vv. 3–10 Peter and the
Beloved Disciple head 'to the tomb'. The Beloved Disciple 'came to
the tomb first', and looked in. Then Peter 'entered the tomb' and was
followed by the Beloved Disciple. After the two disciples have left, the
reader is still at the tomb in vv. 11–15 but this time again with Mary,
who at first 'was standing near the tomb, weeping outside', but then 'bent
to peer into the tomb' and her responses to the angels and to Jesus in vv.
12–15 are concerned with where Jesus' body now is.

1–2 As in the Synoptic accounts of the discovery of the empty tomb,
the action takes place **On the first day of the week** and is in line
with the early Christian tradition associating three days with the period
encompassing Jesus' death and resurrection (cf. 2.19). No motivation is
supplied for Mary Magdalene's visit. It is not in order either to anoint
or to prepare the body, as with the women in Mark 16.1, because in this
narrative the preparation has already been done by Joseph of Arimathea
and Nicodemus (cf. 19.38–42). In Mark the earliness of the women's

---

[1] Some early manuscripts (p⁶⁶ A K L X) have 'my Father', but the shorter reading of ℵ
B D W is to be preferred, since the addition is likely to have been influenced by what
follows in this verse.

visit is elaborated as after sunrise, while here in contrast the earliness of Mary's visit is described as **while it was still dark**. As in other places in the narrative, the darkness may well be intended to symbolize the realm of doubt and unbelief, from which the weeping Mary is yet to emerge. Not until v. 11 is there any mention of Mary looking into the tomb. Apparently at this stage the sight of the stone having been removed from the tomb's entrance is enough to convince her that the body must no longer be there. Since this Gospel's account of the burial has not mentioned a stone being rolled in front of the tomb and indeed has not mentioned women followers being there or seeing this, Mary's observation about the stone's removal presupposes the Synoptic tradition at this point (cf. Mark 15.46–7; Matt. 27.60–1; cf. also Luke 23.51).

Although Mary has come to the tomb alone, when she reports to Peter and the Beloved Disciple, she does so in the plural – **we do not know where they have laid him**. Of the various explanations offered for the plural, two seem more likely than others. (i) Despite John's narrative being set up in terms of this one representative woman – Mary Magdalene – the plural still reflects the use of Synoptic tradition, where she was one among a number of women; cf. also the four women at the cross earlier in John 19.25. (ii) As elsewhere in the narrative (cf. 1.14; 3.11), 'we' can be seen as representative, reflecting the position of Johannine Christians over against Jewish opposition. As such, it would continue the response to the charge that the disciples of Jesus stole the body (cf. Matt. 28.13–15) with its stress that these earliest disciples did not know where the body was.

3–4 Through the introduction of the Beloved Disciple, the Fourth Gospel elaborates on the tradition of Peter running to the tomb, found in Luke 24.12. The emphasis that **the other disciple ran faster than Peter and came to the tomb first** reflects this Gospel's concern with the relationship between the two disciples. In 13.24–6 Peter has to ask the Beloved Disciple to find out from Jesus about the betrayer and it is only the Beloved Disciple who has this insight at the time of the supper. In 21.7–8 the Beloved Disciple recognizes the risen Jesus before Peter, enabling Peter then to act on the recognition. It is plausible to see the evangelist's perspective on the relation of Johannine Christians to the wider church as the issue lying behind such episodes, with the Beloved Disciple representing the Johannine community and Peter symbolizing the great church. On this view the episodes indicate that the community is at one with the wider church but stress the superior insight and unique contribution of Johannine Christians and their Christology. Here the early arrival of the Beloved Disciple reinforces his status as the ideal disciple and is a sign of his greater love for Jesus. He will also demonstrate his superior insight by believing on the basis of what he sees in contrast to Peter. The delay in entering the tomb is in order to make his response the climax of the episode.

The introduction of the two male disciples into the story may also have a secondary function in supplying the witness of two men to the empty tomb, fulfilling the Jewish requirement for valid testimony laid down in Deut. 19.15, which this Gospel stresses elsewhere (cf. 5.31; 8.17–18), and supplementing what would have been considered the dubious witness of a woman.

5–7 The Beloved Disciple **saw the linen wrappings lying there, but he did not enter.** When Peter arrived and entered, he also **saw the linen wrappings lying there and the cloth which had been round his head, lying not with the linen wrappings but rolled up in a place by itself.** The repeated mention of the grave-clothes makes two major points. (i) A contrast with the earlier resurrection of Lazarus is intended. The term σουδάριον for head cloth had been employed previously in 11.44. In the case of Lazarus, at Jesus' command he had come out of the tomb still bound, with his hands and feet in bandages and his head still wrapped in a cloth. Now the linen wrappings from around the body are lying in one place and the cloth from around the head is rolled up and in a place by itself. Lazarus had had to be freed in order to take up life again in this world. But Jesus' own sovereignty over death is shown in the way he has left behind the wrappings associated with death. (ii) There is also an apologetic significance. The tomb had not been robbed and the body stolen, otherwise why would the clothes have been carefully removed? With its claim that others have not taken Jesus away but he himself has demonstrated that death could not hold him, the description of the grave-clothes suggests a narrative fulfilment of the saying about Jesus' bodily life in 10.18 – 'No one has taken it from me, but I lay it down of my own accord. I have authority to lay it down, and I have authority to take it up again.'

8–9 In response to the situation in the tomb the Beloved Disciple **saw and believed.** There is some debate about the content of his belief. The debate turns in part on how the following explanation – **for as yet they did not understand the scripture that he must rise from the dead** – is to be interpreted. Is it meant to exclude Jesus' resurrection from whatever the Beloved Disciple believed or to serve as a backdrop against which the Beloved Disciple's faith in the resurrection is somehow highlighted? On the former reading, some have suggested that the Beloved Disciple merely believes Mary's report that the tomb was empty. But this would appear to be too banal an object of belief for the evangelist to emphasize in this way. Others have suggested that the object of his belief is Jesus' glorification in his return to the Father through the event of crucifixion rather than the resurrection as such. Yet this is surely too fine a distinction. What is a bodily glorification and return to the Father if not a resurrection of some sort? It is far more likely that the reader is meant to assume that the Beloved Disciple is the first to believe that Jesus has been raised and that he demonstrates immediate and exemplary faith in contrast to Peter. This is in line with his depiction as the ideal witness who has insight into the key moments of Jesus' passion. That the following statement appears to ignore what has just been said about this insight is also in line with earlier awkwardnesses in the narrative caused by insertion of material about the Beloved Disciple. His response here contrasts with that of Mary Magdalene earlier at the tomb and with that of Thomas later in his demand for visible proof of the bodily reality of the risen Lord. The Beloved Disciple believes on the basis of the empty tomb and without resurrection appearances. The relation of his faith to what is said about that of later believers in 20.29 – 'Blessed are those who have not seen and yet have come to believe' – is slightly more ambiguous. Given the contrast with Thomas, who demands to see the risen Jesus, the Beloved Disciple's faith is similar to that of later believers in that he believes without seeing Jesus. On the other hand, he does see the empty tomb and his faith in the resurrected Jesus retains a uniqueness in that it does not rest on the testimony of others.

It is the emphasis on Scripture that provides the key to the narrator's explanatory comment. As has been noted, the running to the tomb has been taken from Luke 24.12 and there the incident is followed by the resurrected Jesus' exposition to the two on the Emmaus road and to the other disciples of how the Scriptures must be fulfilled (cf. Luke 24.26–7, 44–5). The uniqueness of the Beloved Disciple's belief in Jesus' resurrection is highlighted, therefore, because it occurs before and is independent of any such understanding of Scripture on the part of the disciples as a whole. Only later would they see that the resurrection was necessary for the fulfilment of Scripture (cf. also 2.22; 12.16 on the need for post-resurrection insight into Scripture). In Luke 24 all the Scriptures are seen as containing the pattern of suffering and then glory for the Messiah. Here a particular scripture appears to be in view and, if so, the most likely candidate is Ps. 16.10 (cf. Acts 2.27).

10 This scene's closing comment that **the disciples then went back to their homes** underlines that, as earlier in the narrative, the Beloved Disciple's insight does not affect any other character or have an impact on the action. It is depicted for the sake of the reader and not passed on to those in the story. The comment also leaves open the question of whether and how Peter will also come to believe and allows the narrator to focus again on the figure of Mary Magdalene.

11–12 Mary Magdalene has not been mentioned since her running to speak to Peter and the Beloved Disciple in v. 2. Now she is depicted as

standing near the tomb, weeping outside. In terms of the narrative's composition this may reflect the insertion of the incident with the Beloved Disciple and Peter into an earlier tradition, in which originally v. 11 followed on from v. 1. As it now stands, the reader is meant to assume that Mary has followed the two male disciples back to the tomb. Her weeping, a distinctive feature of the Johannine version of the tradition about women at the tomb, signals her grief at Jesus' departure and is underscored by both the angels and Jesus asking her why she is weeping (cf. vv. 13, 15). The farewell discourse contained material designed to prepare the disciples for dealing with Jesus' departure (cf. 14.19–20, 27–8) and 16.19–22 explicitly predicted a period of weeping and mourning that would give way to joy on seeing Jesus.

When, like the two male disciples, Mary **bent down to peer into the tomb, . . . she saw two angels in white, sitting where the body of Jesus had been lying, one at the head and one at the feet**. The presence of angels is a sign that God has been at work. Their position is a reminder to the reader of the testimony of the grave-clothes, which the Beloved Disciple had believed, and underscores even more clearly that God, not robbers, has been involved in the removal of Jesus' body. Some have suggested that the two angels are meant to recall the two cherubim positioned to face each other at the two ends of the mercy seat on the ark of the covenant (cf. Exod. 25.17–22). This would mean that the divine presence had been between the two angels in the resurrected body and would fit with the evangelist's stress elsewhere on Jesus as the embodiment of the divine presence. But it is hard to prove that the reader was meant to pick up this allusion. If any intertextual allusion is at work, it is more likely to be within the narrative itself to the passage at the beginning about angels ascending and descending on the Son of Man (cf. 1.51). Since this is the only other passage that links angels with Jesus, it may suggest that one particular aspect of the fulfilment of Jesus' saying is to be found in what happened at his resurrection.

13–15 In contrast to the Synoptic accounts, there is no mention of any amazement or fear at the presence of the angels. Mary's response to their question – **They have taken away my Lord, and I do not know where they have laid him** – shows her to be strangely oblivious to the significance of their presence. She is completely absorbed in her grief at the body having been removed and gives this as the explanation for her weeping. She does, however, become aware of the presence of someone else near the tomb, yet in her absorption with the question of the location of Jesus' corpse, she fails to recognize the risen Lord – **she did not know it was Jesus**. The pattern here of initial dialogue and non-recognition will appear again in the scene in 21.4–14. There is still the need for the giving of recognition. Jesus initiates this process with his questions – **Why**

are you weeping? For whom are you looking? The second question recalls the similar one that had been Jesus' first words in this Gospel's narrative – 'For what are you seeking?' (1.38). This Gospel's characteristic device of ironic misunderstanding is employed to double effect in Mary's response. Not only does she think Jesus is the gardener but she also asks him about the location of his own body.

16 The revelation to Mary of Jesus' identity then takes place through the personal address with its utterance of her name, **Mary**, in contrast to **Woman**, which had introduced the previous questions. As the good shepherd, Jesus calls his own sheep by name, and Mary turns to face him directly because now she knows his voice (cf. 10.3–4). This is the moment that breaks her absorption with the realm of the dead, as she hears the voice of the Son of God (cf. 5.24–5). She answers Jesus in the way she used to address him – **Rabbouni** – indicating her respect and deference for the Teacher. The first disciples had responded to Jesus' question in 1.38 by calling him Rabbi, and Rabbouni is an extended form of this address, and there also the narrator had provided an explanation of the title for non-Jewish readers.

17 Jesus' words, **Do not hold on to me, for I have not yet ascended to the Father,** indicate that a new form of encounter with him is about to begin. Presumably Mary has acted like the women in Matt. 28.9 and has attempted to hold Jesus' feet, but from this Gospel's viewpoint that would entail not having understood Jesus' promise in the farewell discourse to return to his disciples and thinking that it involved a continuing physical presence rather than a presence through the Spirit. It is a reminder that the proper relationship with Jesus after his glorification will be a mutual indwelling (cf. esp. 14.19–20).

The mention of Jesus' ascent to the Father reflects the Johannine understanding of Jesus' hour of crucifixion and glorification as his return to his Father. For the evangelist, Jesus' death, resurrection, ascent, and glorification can all be grasped as one event. Jesus' words about his ascent are part of the evangelist's attempt to bring this perspective to expression within the constraints of the traditional resurrection accounts. Jesus' brief resurrection appearance to Mary is a temporary stop in the one movement of ascent (cf. 3.13; 6.62). The later resurrection appearances to the disciples will, therefore, be appearances of the already ascended Jesus. Ascent as return to the sender, the Father, was introduced earlier in the narrative discourse in 7.33; 13.1, 3; 14.28; 16.17, 28; 17.11, 13. Jesus' departure as ascent and return to the Father introduces a new and 'greater' situation for the disciples (cf. 14.12) and is necessary if the Spirit is to be bestowed on them (cf. 15.26; 16.7). So the desire to hold on to the bodily form of the risen Lord must be restrained. It impedes the realization of the new universal and abiding relationship with this Lord. Mary's desire to cling to Jesus can therefore be distinguished from Thomas' later wish to touch him. Once the new relationship with Jesus has been established through his return to the Father, he can offer his hands and side to Thomas (cf. 20.27) in order to demonstrate that as the ascended and glorified one he is also none other than the one who was crucified.

The message Mary is to take is for Jesus' brothers and is that **I am ascending to my Father and your Father and my God and your God.** These powerful phrases retain Jesus' distinctive relationship to the Father but also stress his solidarity with his disciples as his brothers and sisters in the new family relationship. The intimacy of Jesus' relationship to God is now made available to believers. As the farewell discourse promised, the mutuality between Jesus and the Father is opened up to embrace believers and in particular the promise of 14.18–21 – that the disciples will not be orphaned but will be loved by the Father – is fulfilled. They are part of the new family of believers (cf. 19.26–7; also 1.12–13), and the community of Johannine Christians will be explicitly described in this way in 21.23 – 'the rumour spread among the brothers and sisters [ἀδελφοί]'. So this announcement does not promise resurrection appearances to the disciples, as in the Synoptics, but states that Jesus' glorification is now being completed. The Fourth Gospel's version of the empty tomb tradition focuses primarily not on the disciples' faith, though the belief of the Beloved Disciple and Mary's recognition of Jesus play their part, but on the completion of Jesus' glorification and return to the Father, from whom he came.

18 Mary has a distinctive role as the one who takes the resurrection message to the disciples – **Mary Magdalene went and announced to the disciples.** What she reports is given in a mixture of direct and indirect speech, the latter – **these words he had said to her** – avoiding the need for the repetition of Jesus' actual statement. Along with the announcement with which she has been entrusted, she tells them, **I have seen the Lord.** The two designations she uses for Jesus in this account – Rabbouni and Lord – reflect Jesus' earlier affirmation to the disciples in 13.13: 'You call me Teacher and Lord, and you speak rightly, for I am.' Her announcement will also later be that of the disciples – 'We have seen the Lord' (20.25) – and has links with Thomas' climactic confession – 'My Lord and my God' (20.28). Mary Magdalene, then, has a remarkable role in the narrative. She is near the cross at Jesus' death (19.25), discovers the opened tomb, receives the first resurrection appearance, and, as part of this, is given the commission to make the key announcement to the disciples. It is not surprising that she has been called 'the apostle to the apostles'. If an apostle is one who has received a resurrection appearance and a commission, then clearly Mary's testimony deserves to be called apostolic. Within this account Mary moves from weeping and panic to recognition and commissioning, from not knowing where Jesus' body is to knowing the destination of his ascension. While the Beloved Disciple has primacy when it comes to belief based on the empty tomb, Mary Magdalene has primacy when it comes to belief in connection with resurrection appearances.

In composing this account the evangelist appears to have interwoven two traditions, both of which he has altered and elaborated, that of an appearance to women at the tomb and that of a visit by Peter to the tomb. There is a slight awkwardness in his linking of them, because in this telling it is as if Mary had simply remained at the tomb. The reader is not told when or how she returned after going off to report to Peter and the Beloved Disciple. The evangelist builds on the tradition of women at the tomb from Mark 16.1–2, in which Mary Magdalene is mentioned first, but now focuses simply on her. This is in line with his tendency to deal with representative figures rather than groups in his narrative. He has also introduced the Beloved Disciple into the tradition about Peter derived from Luke 24.12, where Peter alone runs to the tomb, stoops and looks in, sees the linen cloths by themselves, and returns home amazed (cf. also Luke 24.24 with its report that 'some of those who were with us went to the tomb and found it just as the women had said, but they did not see him'). The theme of resurrection as the fulfilment of Scripture, which follows in Luke 24.26–7, 44–5, is also reworked in 20.9. The slightly awkward insertion of the material about the Beloved Disciple (20.8) into the rewritten Lukan story has caused difficulties for later interpreters. The evangelist takes up the reference to two men in dazzling clothes seen by the women in the tomb in Luke 24.4 (cf. Luke 24.23, where this is described as a 'vision of angels'), as Mary now sees two angels in white in the tomb in 20.12. Their question, 'Why do you look for the living among the dead?' (Luke 24.5), becomes 'Why are you weeping?' (20.13). Finally, Matt. 28.9–10 has also been taken up and reworked. There two women, one of whom is Mary Magdalene, take hold of Jesus' feet and are then instructed, 'Go and tell my brothers . . .' Here in John the command 'Do not hold on to me' assumes a similar action on the part of Mary Magdalene and the message to her for Jesus' brothers is given a distinctive Johannine content.

The focus on one woman at the empty tomb, together with a number of its other emphases, means that this account is reminiscent of conventions in ancient Greek romances (cf. especially Chariton's *Chaereas and Callirhoe*), where a lover distractedly seeks the body of the beloved at a tomb, finds the tomb empty, believes it has been robbed, later meets the beloved, who was not dead after all, but fails to recognize him or her until the beloved's voice triggers recognition, and they finally embrace each other before falling to the ground together. Mary's weeping and absorption in her grief, her obsession with finding the body, her initial supposition that Jesus is the gardener, her ensuing recognition of his voice and her attempt to embrace might well remind readers of such conventions and encourage them to perceive her in the role of the lover, betrothed or spouse in search of the body of her beloved. If so, this would be in line with earlier portrayals in this Gospel of Jesus as the bridegroom and other representative figures as his bride (e.g. the Samaritan woman). As elsewhere, however, significant features of this Gospel's symbolic account make its distinctiveness clear. Jesus has really died and been resurrected and not simply appeared to have done so, and the expected ending is subverted, as Mary's attempted embrace is refused and it is made clear that the nature of Jesus' relationship to his bride will be dependent on his return to the Father, which enables that relationship to be a new and abiding spiritual one.

It is highly significant that in the Fourth Gospel's account the resurrection is treated as entailing ascension back to the Father and as thereby completing Jesus' hour of glorification from the cross. The announcement that Mary is given to pass on is not that Jesus is risen but that he is ascending. This puts the empty tomb and appearance traditions squarely within the Johannine framework. The climax of this story is not the resurrection itself or the appearances but the return of Jesus to the Father. His resurrection becomes part of the overall theological point the evangelist makes about Jesus – he is the unique revelation of God, the one who has come from God and is going to God (cf. e.g. 16.28). In this way the resurrection is not an addendum but an integral part of the story of the Logos. Just as Jesus' origin is as the Logos who was with God, so his destiny is to return to this same God.

(ii) Jesus' appearance to the disciples 20.19–23

(19) When it was evening on that day, the first day of the week, and the doors were locked, where the disciples were, for fear of the Jews, Jesus came and stood in the midst and said to them, 'Peace be with you.' (20) And having said this, he showed them his hands and his side. The disciples therefore rejoiced when they saw the Lord. (21) He said to them again, 'Peace be with you. As the Father has sent me, so I send you.' (22) And when he had said this, he breathed on them and said to them, 'Receive the Holy Spirit. (23) If you forgive the sins of any, they are forgiven[1] them; if you retain those of any, they are retained.'

---

[1] This is a translation of the perfect passive form of ἀφίημι. There are variants which have the present and future passive forms and may have been attempts to ease the sense of an original perfect passive, but the latter, though it conforms to the tense of the following main clause, has the slightly stronger manuscript evidence, including ℵ^c A D L and possibly B★.

19 Later on the same day as the resurrection the disciples are gathered. Their number is not specified, unlike Luke 24.33, which indicates that they are only the eleven. But in any case the narrator will later explain that Thomas was absent. The setting is a place where **the doors were locked . . . for fear of the Jews**. Despite having heard Mary Magdalene's message from the risen Lord, their fear of possible consequences from the religious authorities, who had had Jesus condemned and killed, remains. The phrase 'for fear of the Jews' is associated with an unwillingness to make a public confession about Jesus in 7.13 and 19.38 (cf. also 9.22), and here also the disciples are not yet ready to proclaim the risen Lord openly. The scene may also reflect the later situation when Johannine Christians were expelled from the synagogue for their confession of Jesus as Son of God and some were tempted to meet secretly for fear of possible repercussions (cf. 9.22; 12.42; 16.1–2). The locked doors provide no obstacle to the risen Jesus being able to manifest himself and stand in their midst. It is not surprising that his first words to the frightened disciples are **Peace be with you**. This is, of course, a conventional greeting but it also functions as a reminder and fulfilment of Jesus' earlier promises of peace in the farewell discourse in 14.27 and 16.33. In the latter reference the peace the disciples can experience in Jesus was contrasted with the persecution they face in the world. The reception of this gift of peace provides a sense of ultimate security that no locked doors can assure.

20 Jesus then **showed them his hands and his side**. Rather than demonstrating that Jesus was not some form of ghost, as in Luke 24.37, or serving as an anti-docetic polemic, this display simply underscores the identity of the risen Lord with the crucified Jesus, whose hands had been nailed to the cross and his side pierced with a spear. It is usually held that crucifixions involved nailing through the wrists rather than through the hands as such, since the palms would not have borne the weight of a body for any length of time at all, unless ropes were employed in addition. The Greek term for 'hand' can also include the sense of 'lower arm' on some occasions, so it is probably best to see 'hands' here also as actually meaning wrists. The disciples are said to respond with joy at seeing the one whom the narrator designates as the Lord. Despite Mary's earlier announcement that she had seen the Lord, it takes this appearance to them before the narrator can speak of their rejoicing instead of their fear. They too have now seen the Lord. Again Jesus' earlier words in the farewell discourse come to realization – 'In a little while the world will no longer see me, but you will see me' (14.19) and 'A little while, and you will no longer see me, and again a little while, and you will see me' (16.16). In explanation of this latter statement Jesus had also said, 'So you also have sorrow now; but I will see you again, and your hearts will rejoice, and no one takes your joy from you' (16.22). Now this resurrection appearance brings the fulfilment, as their sorrow and fear are transformed into joy on seeing the Lord.

21 The risen Jesus, whose mission has now been vindicated, tells his followers that that mission is by no means over yet; they are to carry on where he has left off: **Peace be with you. As the Father has sent me, so I send you.** These words echo those in the prayer of Jesus in 17.18, which view the disciples' mission in retrospect as already under way – 'As you have sent me into the world, so I have sent them into the world.' The repetition of the pronouncement of peace underlines its significance for the commissioning that follows. This peace that comes from knowing the authority of the vindicated Jesus will free his followers to fulfil their commission, because it removes any need to fear others' opinions, hostile attitudes or persecuting actions.

As noted in the comments on 17.18, the most striking and emphatic description of Jesus' mission in the narrative is in the words of 18.37 – 'For this I was born and for this I came into the world, to bear witness to the truth.' For the disciples to continue his mission will, therefore, entail their own bearing witness, and this was made explicit earlier in 15.26–7, where the double witness that was always necessary under the law is now to be carried out by the Spirit acting as Advocate and by Jesus' followers. Now the risen Jesus formally commissions these followers, making them his authorized agents in the overall cosmic trial, just as he has been the Father's uniquely authorized agent. And just as Jesus' mission entailed loving service to the point of giving his life, so the manner of his mission will be the pattern for his witnessing representatives, since those who are sent are not greater than the one who sends them (cf. 13.15–16). The display of Jesus' wounded hands and side, which has preceded the commissioning, reinforces this point.

22 The resources for the disciples' mission of witness are to be found in the risen Jesus' impartation to them of his own Spirit: **And when he had said this, he breathed on them and said to them, 'Receive the Holy Spirit.'** The one who sends them will not leave them alone in their mission; his presence and power will be with them in the person of the Holy Spirit. This gift of the Spirit is the fulfilment of predictions about Jesus and the Spirit from earlier in the narrative. John the Baptist had been told that 'he on whom you see the Spirit descend and remain is the one who baptizes with the Holy Spirit' (1.33) and now Jesus confirms the Baptist's identification by endowing the disciples with the Spirit. In connection with Jesus' Scripture citation – 'Out of his belly shall flow rivers of living water' – the narrator had observed, 'Now he said this about the Spirit, which believers in him were to receive; for as yet there was no Spirit, because Jesus was not yet glorified' (7.38–9). Now the disciples' reception of the Spirit indicates that Jesus has indeed been glorified. At his death water flowed from his side, showing the Spirit was now available, and here after his resurrection Jesus specifically confers this Spirit on the disciples. In the farewell discourse the presence and activity of the Paraclete with the disciples had been promised (cf. 14.16–17, 26; 15.26; 16.7–15). Now, with the risen Jesus' bestowal of the Spirit on the disciples, the work of this Advocate, who will take Jesus' place, can begin.

The manner in which Jesus is said to confer the Spirit – breathing on the disciples – recalls the creation narrative of Gen. 2.7 (the same verbal form, ἐνεφύσησεν, is used in the LXX), where God breathes into the man and he becomes a living being, and also the formulation of Wis. 15.11 that the One who formed humans 'breathed a living spirit into them'. In addition, it is reminiscent of Ezekiel's vision of Israel's end-time renewal, which involved a resurrection in which new life was breathed into dry bones – 'Thus says the Lord God to these bones: I will cause breath to enter you, and you shall live' (37.5; cf. also 37.9–10). In this light this resurrection appearance to the disciples can also be viewed as entailing an eschatological new creation. The God who endowed humanity with life is now endowing it with new life through Christ's gift to the disciples. Their reception of this life through the Spirit is therefore also their birth from above by the Spirit (cf. 3.3–8). 'Because I live, you also will live,' had been Jesus' promise to his followers in 14.19, and here they are depicted as experiencing this connection through Jesus' breath of life.

23 What is entailed in the disciples' mission is now elaborated: **If you forgive the sins of any, they are forgiven them; if you retain those of any, they are retained.** In this Gospel's discourse sin is primarily failing to acknowledge the revelation of God in Jesus (cf. 8.24; 9.39–41; 15.22, 24). Jesus' words and works have been depicted as bringing about a judgement which the recipients make on themselves, as they either respond in belief or expose their sinful state of unbelief. The same holds for the future work of the Spirit, about whom Jesus has said that 'when he comes, he will convict the world of sin . . . because they do not believe in me' (16.8–9). Similarly, as the disciples, accompanied by the Spirit, witness to God's verdict accomplished in Jesus, the lamb of God who takes away the sin of the world (cf. 1.29), and press home its implications, they will be pronouncing forgiveness for those who receive their witness but will be retaining the sins of those who reject it. It is true that the notion of sin in this Gospel cannot be reduced completely to unbelief (cf. e.g. 5.29) and that here the plural term 'sins' is employed, which might indicate a broader reference. But in the two other instances of the use of the plural in the narrative it is more or less synonymous with the singular (cf. 8.24 with 8.21, and 9.34 with 9.2), and in Luke 24.47–8 the risen Christ commissions his disciples to a witness that involves the proclamation of 'repentance and the forgiveness of sins'. While post-baptismal sins cannot be excluded from the remit of the disciples' commission (cf. 1 John 1.9–10; 5.16–17), the primary emphasis here also appears to be on the disciples' witness to the world.

The response of the recipients of the message is decisive for whether their sins are forgiven or retained, but the formulation of the two subordinate clauses makes this an active effect of the disciples' witness. At the same time, the two main clauses with their passive forms of the verbs are to be taken as involving divine passives. God stands behind the disciples' witness, so that forgiveness or retention of sins by them is forgiveness or retention by God. Just as Jesus' mission constituted a realized judgement of either salvation or condemnation, so the disciples' witness to that mission will entail a realized judgement of either forgiveness or retention of sins.

Jesus' appearance to the disciples on the evening of the first day of the week has its parallel in the longer, and most probably original, text of Luke 24.36–43. There also Jesus is said to have 'stood among them and said to them, "Peace be with you!"' (Luke 24.36). Luke also has Jesus showing the disciples his hands and feet (Luke 24.39–40). The fourth evangelist has taken up these traditions and elaborated on them, changing the showing of hands and feet to that of hands and side in order to reflect the distinctive interest of his crucifixion narrative in the spear thrust into Jesus' side.

The saying about forgiving or retaining sins in 20.23 has some similarities with the authorization of the disciples to bind or loose in Matt. 18.18 (cf. also 16.19), but the Fourth Gospel broadens the notion from teaching authority in the church to mission in general, and the commissioning of the disciples thereby has its closest conceptual links with Luke 24.46–9. There, before his ascension, Jesus speaks of repentance and forgiveness of sins being preached in his name to all nations, of the disciples being witnesses, which, as has been noted, is implicit in John 20.21, and of the promise of the Father being sent on them, which will entail being clothed with power. In Luke's writings witness under the power of the Spirit is promised again in Acts 1.8 and realized in the Pentecost account of Acts 2.1–42. Not surprisingly, therefore, the giving of the Spirit to the disciples here in John has been called the 'Johannine Pentecost'. Whereas Luke spreads out the events chronologically and distinguishes between the episodes of resurrection, ascension, and giving of the Spirit, John brings them all together on one day.

The account of this resurrection appearance establishes the identity of the crucified with the risen one. The same person who completed his task at the cross now ensures that God's continuing dealings with the world on the basis of that completed task are carried on through the agency of his followers. The links with the preceding narrative that have been pointed out show that Jesus' resurrection is essential to his keeping his word about himself and, particularly through the numerous connections with the farewell discourse, keeping his word to the disciples about their seeing him and about his gifts of the Spirit and of joy and peace to accompany them in their mission in the world. In fact, this resurrection account also takes readers back to the prologue, which confessed that through the Logos all things came into being and that in the Logos was life (1.3–4). Now the incarnate Logos has demonstrated through the resurrection that the life in him overcomes death and he bestows this life through his Spirit on the disciples. For the evangelist the gift of the Spirit is inseparable not only from the death of Jesus but also from his resurrection, and in this account Easter and Pentecost come together. For the disciples, to experience the risen Christ is to be commissioned to continue his task, and clearly this episode is vital for their story line within the Gospel's narrative world. Their continued distinctive mode of being in the world as a witnessing community and agency of forgiveness receives its impetus from their experience of the risen Christ and his imparting of the Spirit.

(iii) Jesus' appearance to Thomas   *20.24–9*

(24) But Thomas, called Didymus, one of the twelve, was not with them when Jesus came. (25) So the other disciples told him, 'We have seen the Lord.' But he said to them, 'Unless I see in his hands the mark of the nails and put my finger in the mark of the nails and put my hand in his side, I will not believe.' (26) Now a week later his disciples were again inside and Thomas was with them. Jesus came, though the doors were locked, and stood in the midst and said, 'Peace be with you.' (27) Then he said to Thomas, 'Put your finger here and see my hands, and reach out your hand and put it in my side; do not be disbelieving but believing.' (28) Thomas answered and said to him, 'My Lord and my God.' (29) Jesus said to him, 'Have you believed because you have seen me? Blessed are those who have not seen and have believed.'

24–5 Only now does the narrator mention that there had been a conspicuous absentee from the previous scene, namely Thomas. He is described not only by the Greek name, **Didymus** (twin), which supplies the meaning of the Semitic name Thomas, but also by the phrase **one of the twelve**. It is not clear whether the 'them' in **was not with them** is to be taken as simply a loose reference to the disciples or as a narrower reference to the antecedent 'the twelve'. If the latter is the case, this might suggest that Judas was at the previous occasion. But it may well be that, although this Gospel does not narrate what happened to Judas after the crucifixion, the implied reader is meant to assume (perhaps on the basis of Matthew's story) that Judas would not have been present. This would add to the probability that the depiction of Thomas as one of the twelve is not necessarily meant to indicate which disciples were present at the earlier appearance.

At that appearance in 20.19–23 there had been no explicit confessional response to Jesus' presence. But now the disciples can repeat Mary's testimony to them in their testimony to Thomas – **We have seen the Lord.** Thomas' response – **Unless I see in his hands the mark of the nails and put my finger in the mark of the nails and put my hand in his side, I will not believe** – involves an adamant refusal to believe the account of the other disciples and their testimony. They had needed to see the risen Jesus before they echoed Mary's testimony, but, unlike them, Thomas sets his own conditions for accepting testimony.

26–7 A week after the first appearance to the disciples, the setting is the same again. The disciples are behind locked doors; despite this, Jesus comes and stands in their midst; he pronounces peace (cf. v. 19). There is one difference. This time **Thomas was with them**. It is as if the earlier scene has been restaged for Thomas' benefit. The focus is immediately on him as Jesus, showing knowledge of what Thomas had said to the other disciples, invites him to fulfil the conditions he had made – to see and finger Jesus' hands and to handle his side. The invitation is accompanied by an exhortation – **do not be disbelieving but believing**.

The traditional designation of this disciple as 'doubting Thomas' and a number of translations (cf. e.g. NRSV and NIV) tend to mislead. The verb 'to doubt' (or some cognate form) does not occur in the passage. Instead, Jesus asks Thomas to change from being disbelieving or unbelieving (ἄπιστος) to believing (πιστός). The account is concerned with the need and grounds for faith. What exactly prompts Jesus' exhortation? On the basis of v. 29 it is often suggested that Thomas' problem was the wish to see Jesus rather than simply to believe and that he is employed as a means of showing that it should not be necessary to see Jesus in order to believe in him. But while containing truth, this is not a sufficiently nuanced explanation of his role. After all, by asking to see Jesus' hands and side, he is requesting no more than was given to the other disciples in v. 20. The Beloved Disciple (with the object being the empty tomb) and Mary Magdalene and the other disciples (with the object being the risen Lord) all saw and believed. Thomas' fault, therefore, cannot merely lie in his wish to see the risen Lord. Nor does it lie in his adding to the wish to see the wish to touch. This simply makes his desire more graphic. More to the point is his disbelief of the other disciples' testimony. Even here it should be noted that the testimony of Mary did not appear to be enough for the other disciples. It took an actual appearance to them before their fear turned to joy. The difference seems to be that the others are not said to have actively disbelieved Mary's testimony. Thomas comes to faith not because he actually touches Jesus' hands and side – there is no indication that he takes up Jesus' invitation – but because Jesus graciously offers himself for Thomas to do so. Jesus' words of invitation take up and accommodate the words Thomas had used in v. 25 in setting his conditions for believing. In this way, he is in fact granted what is necessary for him to move from unbelief to belief.

28 Despite his initial disbelief, Thomas is not only granted faith but now given the climactic Christological confession of the narrative – **My Lord and my God.** Mary Magdalene and the other disciples have acclaimed Jesus as Lord, but this is the first time that a character in the story actually calls Jesus God. Significantly, it was in reply to Thomas and his earlier question about the way that Jesus had answered, 'No one comes to the Father except through me. If you know me, you will know my Father also. From now on you do know him and have seen him' (14.6–7). Now Thomas is able to make explicit the implications of Jesus' words. For readers, of course, this unique status of Jesus has been made clear from the beginning of the narrative. The prologue had already stated that the Logos was God (1.1) and that it is the only God who has made the Father known (1.18). But readers have then had to watch from this position of superior knowledge to see whether the various characters in the ensuing narrative are able to recognize Jesus' identity. The confession of some that Jesus is Son of God and Lord has amounted to much the same thing because of the connotations of these titles within the narrative discourse. However, it takes the resurrection of Jesus before a character spells out the full force of the evangelist's characterization of Jesus' relationship to the Father. The linking of Lord and God in address goes back to the Jewish Scriptures (cf. Ps. 35.23 – 'my God and my Lord'), but it is also worth noting that Thomas' confession would have been recognized by readers as the counterpart to the titles ascribed to the emperor in the imperial cult. It was under Domitian, who claimed the title *dominus et deus noster,* 'our Lord and God', that the cult had grown in popularity.

29 Have you believed because you have seen me? Blessed are those who have not seen and have believed. In the light of the discussion above, the force of Jesus' final words to Thomas can be seen as, 'Have you believed their testimony because you have seen me? Blessed are those who have not seen and have believed their testimony.' This underscores the authority and reliability of the disciples' witness. Those who will later come to believe will do so because they have the testimony both of the one who saw the grave-clothes in the empty tomb and of those who saw the risen Lord himself. On the basis of such testimony contained in this narrative they too will be able to echo Thomas' confession of faith.

The Synoptic Gospels contain traditions about lingering unbelief among the disciples after the resurrection. In Matt. 28.17, at an appearance of the risen Jesus to the eleven in Galilee, 'when they saw him, they worshipped him; but some doubted'. The fourth evangelist has already taken over the tradition of the risen Jesus showing his wounds from the account in Luke 24.36–43, which also says of the disciples that 'in their joy they were disbelieving and still wondering' (v. 41). The language of the Fourth Gospel is closest to that of Luke, who uses the participle ἀπιστοῦντες, while Jesus' rebuke of Thomas here in v. 27 is μὴ γίνου ἄπιστος. This Gospel also sets the appearance in Jerusalem, makes one figure the representative of the disbelievers, in line with its tendency elsewhere, and exploits the concepts of seeing and believing for its own theological purposes.

The depiction of a separate appearance for the sake of Thomas becomes the vehicle for an explanation about the nature and grounds of the belief available to readers. Despite his initial refusal to believe the witness of the other disciples, Thomas is given the opportunity to believe. The wounds in the body of Jesus serve for him as a sign, pointing to the revelation of God in Jesus as the crucified and risen one and eliciting from him the appropriate response of belief in Jesus as Lord and God. But it is made clear that a relationship with the risen Jesus is not limited to his immediate followers. Authentic faith is based on testimony and the Gospel narrative itself, with its witness to Jesus' signs, including his resurrection, makes such faith available to later readers.

(iv) The purpose of the narrative   20.30–1

(30) Now Jesus also did many other signs in the presence of his disciples, which are not written in this book. (31) These are written in order that you may continue to believe[1] that Jesus is the Christ, the Son of God, and that by believing you may have life in his name.

---

[1] This translation takes the present subjunctive, πιστεύητε, as the original text. It has the slightly stronger external support of p[66vid] ℵ* B Θ, while the alternative reading with πιστεύσητε, an aorist subjunctive, is found in ℵ[c] A C D K L. The former can have the force of continuation in belief, while the latter indicates an initial coming to belief. For further discussion, see the comments on this verse.

This statement of the narrative's purpose follows on directly from the dialogue in the preceding episode. The witness of the disciples to the signs that were done in their midst and that have now been written down precisely as the record of that witness enables 'you', the readers who have not seen Jesus but are now directly addressed by the narrator, to believe.

30 But the narrator first informs the readers that **Jesus also did many other signs in the presence of his disciples, which are not written in this book**. This is not the first time that it has been indicated that Jesus performed other signs than those the narrator has chosen to include (cf. 2.23; 3.2; 6.2, 26; 7.31; 9.16; 11.47; 12.37). A reference to the selectivity necessary for an author in producing a written record was a familiar phenomenon (cf. esp. Lucian, *Demon*. 67, where it concludes the account). This motif, the reference to 'this book' and the following statement of purpose are indicators that an early version of the Gospel ended at 20.30–1 (see further discussion below).

31 Despite the selectivity, what has been included is sufficient for readers to have faith. But what is the scope of **These are written . . .**? The contrast between those signs which have been recorded and the many others occurs here in the context of the accounts of the resurrected Jesus' appearances to his disciples, and Jesus' final response to Thomas could well suggest that the signs that have been written to produce belief have as their primary referent the empty tomb story and the resurrection appearances from earlier in this chapter that brought about the belief of the Beloved Disciple, Mary Magdalene, the disciples and Thomas. Yet the 'in this book' formulation of v. 30 indicates that by extension these signs that have been written would naturally also include the signs from the public ministry in the earlier part of the narrative – the last mention of signs occurred in 12.37 in a summary of that mission. So is it simply the miraculous events that have been recorded in the book that are designed to produce belief? That would be difficult to maintain, since clearly Jesus' words are also meant to be believed and to result in life (cf. e.g. 5.24; 6.63, 68). It is more likely that, in this summary statement of purpose about the book as a whole, the term 'signs' has the further connotation of being able to represent Jesus' mission as a whole. That mission is depicted in terms of words and deeds, discourse or disputes and signs, and either of the two is able to stand for the whole. This interpretation gains support from the fact that in 12.37–8 Jesus' performance of signs that did not result in belief is explained in terms of the Isaiah citation (Isa. 53.1) that speaks of believing our report or message. Further, both ways of viewing Jesus' mission can be linked to the one term 'works' (ἔργα). The signs are seen as 'works' in 5.36; 7.3; 9.3–4; 10.25, 32, 37–8; 14.10–11; 15.24, while the words of Jesus are closely associated with such works in 10.25–7; 14.10;

15.22–4. In two places – 4.34 and 17.4 – the whole of Jesus' mission, both his signs and discourses, can be categorized under the one term 'work'. There are good reasons, then, for thinking that, here in this statement of the book's purpose, 'signs' too can draw in the whole revelatory aspect of Jesus' mission.

What has been written in this book about the revelatory activity of Jesus is meant to produce belief. But is this belief initial belief, and so the purpose evangelistic? Or is it meant to produce continuance in belief, so that the implied readers are already Christians? Our translation – **in order that you may continue to believe that Jesus is the Christ, the Son of God** – has opted for the present subjunctive as the original text and supported the second view. But the matter of tense alone is probably insufficient to decide the purpose of the Gospel and the other questions of interpretation about this verse bear on the issue of the intended readership.

Some scholars have proposed that what readers are meant to believe is not that 'Jesus is the Christ, the Son of God' but that 'the Christ, the Son of God is Jesus'. On this view, where Jesus is the predicate rather than the subject of the clause, the question the Gospel would be answering is not 'Who is Jesus?' but 'Who is the Messiah?', and such a question would be asked by unconverted Jews, proselytes and God-fearers, for whom the category 'Messiah' would be of interest and importance. While such a reading is obviously syntactically possible, it is much more likely and in line with the pattern elsewhere in the Gospel that Jesus is the subject of the clause. Certainly the Gospel as a whole does not read as if it addresses those who already know what the titles 'Christ' and 'Son of God' entail and simply need to be persuaded that Jesus is a worthy candidate for such titles. Rather, again and again, what appears to be at issue is the identity of Jesus, and the narrative attempts to make clear what is involved in claiming that Jesus is the sort of Messiah who is Son of God. The narrator records that the mission of Jesus has provoked different judgements about who exactly he is and attempts to reinforce his own point of view about Jesus' identity, which is made explicit from the start in the prologue. Implied readers are expected to share this point of view in order to appreciate the unfolding story and to have it confirmed by the time the narrative reaches its conclusion. If implied readers were envisaged primarily as those who needed to be converted, one could easily think of quite different rhetorical strategies that would have taken into account their initial unbelieving stance and therefore would have been more likely to be effective. The amount of space given in the narrative in chapters 13—17 to addressing explicitly the concerns of Jesus' followers reinforces the view that the implied readers are far more likely to be those who know of the outcome of Jesus' mission but need to be given a perspective on this that will support a belief about him that is at odds with the verdict of official Judaism. The purpose of this Gospel's written record, then, is to enable believers to continue in their faith. It sets out its convictions about Jesus in the prologue and then illustrates, confirms and reinforces these convictions in the narrative in the midst of their being contested. Implied readers are invited to make the same journey and to have belief strengthened in the process.

Simply believing Jesus was the Messiah would not have resulted in excommunication from the synagogue for Johannine Christians. The narrative is intended to confirm the belief both that Jesus is the Messiah of Jewish expectations and that he is the sort of Messiah who is Son of God, with all the connotations of a unique divine identity that the latter title has in this Gospel's discourse. It was this aspect of their belief about Jesus' identity as divine Son that had caused Jewish Christians to experience opposition and persecution from their Jewish religious leaders. For the evangelist it is essential to have the right belief about Jesus' identity in order to experience eternal life – **that by believing you may have life in his name**. As elsewhere in the narrative, Jesus' name represents his identity and reputation, all that he stands for in relation to God. It has been made clear in 17.3 that life, the positive outcome of Jesus' mission for humanity, is dependent on recognition of his identity – 'this is eternal life, that they should know you, the only true God, and Jesus Christ whom you have sent'. And this life can be enjoyed both in the present and after physical death because it entails sharing in the life of the Father and the Son (cf. e.g. 3.15–16; 5.25–9; 11.25–7). In this way the statement of purpose reflects both the Christological focus and the accompanying soteriological emphasis of the preceding narrative.

For a long time the consensus view has been that 20.30–1 constituted the ending of the original Gospel. Some also claimed this passage was the ending of an earlier signs source which then was transposed as a suitable ending for the first edition of the Gospel. There are, however, too many aspects of the evangelist's own characteristic style and vocabulary in these verses for the latter view to be persuasive. More recently, particularly under the influence of literary approaches that attempt to read documents as a whole in their final form, others have attempted to argue that there is no need to see vv. 30–1 as ending an earlier edition of the Gospel. But, although making sense of the Gospel as we have it in its canonical form is entirely appropriate, this need not mean ignoring signs of its compositional history. Recent arguments are unconvincing at two main interrelated points. While the clause, 'these are written...' most probably includes the empty tomb and the resurrection appearances, which have just been recounted, as among these signs, it is difficult to think, as argued above, that they are the exclusive reference. Since the previous verse has ended by talking of the signs not written *in this book*, the most natural reading of what follows is that it refers to the signs that are written in the book as a whole. And reference to the book at this point surely suggests that what follows is the author's summing up of the purpose of this book, not simply of the resurrection accounts. If this is so, it remains probable that an earlier edition of the Gospel ended at this point. As will be discussed in what follows, study of chapter 21, with its elements of discontinuity alongside those of continuity, supports this position.

D. THE EPILOGUE   21.1–25

All known textual traditions of the Fourth Gospel contain chapter 21. Whatever the stages in the composition of the Gospel, therefore, it should be seen as an integral part of the final form, as the Gospel's epilogue, and not simply as material that was attached to it much later. It does, however, contain features that suggest it may have been composed by the final editor of the Gospel after there had been an earlier version that concluded at 20.31. It is by no means impossible that the Gospel was originally designed to end in two stages, but, as has been noted, 20.30–1 with its statement of purpose and reference to the book as a whole, reads very much like a decisive ending rather than one that was meant to point beyond itself. Despite the links with the preceding narrative that a final editor would obviously wish to make, there are also gaps and awkwardnesses that indicate an addition which is not all of a piece with the earlier story. After a blessing has been pronounced on those who believe without seeing, it comes as somewhat of a surprise to find that there will be further narrative involving actual seeing of the risen Lord. In addition, there is no explanation of why, after their commissioning, the disciples go from Jerusalem back to Galilee and to their former profession of fishing, which has not been mentioned at all in this Gospel's account of their call. After the joy and the gift of the Spirit that accompanied the first appearance and its commissioning, the disciples' behaviour and their response to Jesus in Galilee is not the most natural sequel. In particular, while the failure to recognize the risen Jesus makes sense in accounts of his first appearances to his followers, it is strange that, after having encountered the risen Jesus twice, the disciples fail to recognize him at a third appearance to them. In addition, the account of Peter's rehabilitation might well be thought to belong more naturally before the disciples as a group are given the Spirit and commissioned. There are also a number of distinctive stylistic traits in this chapter which cannot simply be explained by a different choice of subject matter and the accompanying special vocabulary. Finally, although the earlier story has one eye on the situation of the later church, the focus here on matters of structure and authority, in the discussions of the commissioning of Peter as shepherd of the sheep and his death and of the role of the Beloved Disciple and his death, suggest later reflection on specific issues that have arisen at a late stage in the Gospel's composition.

The content of the epilogue falls into four parts. It opens with the miracle of the catch of fish (vv. 1–14), moves to Peter's rehabilitation and recommissioning (vv. 15–19) and the discussion of the Beloved Disciple's role (vv. 20–3), and ends with a statement about the writing of the Gospel (vv. 24–5). In the Gospel's final form the epilogue fits appropriately and balances the prologue. There is an *inclusio* on the theme of witness, with the mention of John's witness in 1.7, 8, 15 and the Beloved Disciple's witness in 21.24. The prologue takes readers back to Jesus' role at the beginning of history and beyond that to his origins in the life of God, while the epilogue points them forward through the time of the church and its mission and the deaths of prominent disciples to the parousia, signalled by Jesus' final words, 'until I come' (21.23). It may well be, therefore, that whoever was responsible for the placing of the prologue was also responsible for the epilogue.

1. THE MIRACULOUS CATCH OF FISH   21.1–14

(1) After these things Jesus again revealed himself to the disciples at the Sea of Tiberias; he revealed himself in this way. (2) Simon Peter, Thomas, who was called Didymus, Nathanael from Cana in Galilee, the sons of Zebedee and two others of his disciples were together. (3) Simon Peter said to them, 'I am going fishing.' They said to him, 'We will also go with you.' They went out and got into the boat, and that night they caught nothing. (4) When it was already dawn, Jesus stood on the shore; but the disciples did not know that it was Jesus. (5) Jesus said to them, 'Children, you have caught nothing to eat, have you?' They answered him, 'No.' (6) He said to them, 'Cast the net to the right side of the boat and you will find something[1].' So they cast it, and they were no longer able to haul it in because of the huge number of fish. (7) So that disciple whom Jesus loved said to Peter, 'It is the Lord.' Thereupon Simon Peter, hearing that it was the Lord, wrapped his outer garment around himself, for he was naked, and plunged into the sea. (8) But the other disciples came in the boat, dragging the net with the fish, for they were not far from land, about a hundred yards[2] away. (9) When they came ashore, they saw a charcoal fire there, with fish placed on it, and some

---

[1] An object, absent in Greek, has been supplied in the English translation.
[2] The Greek text has 'two hundred cubits' here.

bread. (10) Jesus said to them, 'Bring some of the fish you have just caught.' (11) So Simon Peter went on board and hauled the net to land, full of large fish, one hundred and fifty three; and although there were so many, the net was not torn. (12) Jesus said to them, 'Come and have breakfast.' Now none of the disciples dared to ask him, 'Who are you?' because they knew it was the Lord. (13) Jesus came and took the bread and gave it to them, and in the same way the fish. (14) This was now the third time Jesus was revealed to the disciples after being raised from the dead.

This episode is framed by an *inclusio*, which mentions a revealing or manifesting of Jesus (vv. 1, 14), and incorporates a miracle story and a recognition motif. Verses 1–3 establish the setting for the miracle, vv. 4–6 recount the miracle itself and vv. 7–14 relate the response to and attestation of the miracle. The recognition elements are twofold and occur in the last section. First there is the recognition of Jesus by the Beloved Disciple, which is acted upon by Peter (v. 7), and then there is the recognition of Jesus by all the disciples at the breakfast (v. 12).

1–2 With a loose chronological link to what has preceded – **after these things** – the narrator recounts that **Jesus again revealed himself to the disciples**. This appearance in Galilee **at the Sea of Tiberias** (cf. 6.1) is designated twice here as a self-revelation of Jesus, an epiphany (cf. also v. 14). It is made to a group of seven disciples. That there are seven, with that number's connotation of completeness, may suggest that this group is meant to be seen as representative of the entire community of Jesus' followers. Heading the list is **Simon Peter**, who was last singled out at the empty tomb. **Thomas** is mentioned next and again, as in the previous reference to him in 20.24, designated **Didymus** or 'the Twin'. **Nathanael from Cana in Galilee** has not been referred to since 1.49–50, where he was told, 'You will see greater things than these,' and now this further manifestation of Jesus may be regarded as part of the fulfilment of such a promise. **The sons of Zebedee** are singled out for the first time in the Gospel. Readers would need to be familiar with the Synoptic Gospels or tradition to know that there are two of them and that they are named James and John. Finally **two others of his disciples** are mentioned and left unnamed. The most likely inference is that one of these is the Beloved Disciple, who features in v. 7, since he is also unnamed in the rest of the narrative.

3 Peter's decision – **I am going fishing** – initiates the action, in which the others join. It seems strange that after their commissioning in Jerusalem, the disciples are now back in Galilee fishing. This may well be one of the indications that chapter 21 is a later addition whose links with what precedes it are not entirely smooth. Nevertheless, once it is recognized that the miracle of the fish is symbolic of the disciples' mission, a continuity with the theme of mission from 20.21–3 can be seen. Again readers would probably need to be familiar with the Synoptic call narratives to make the connection, although this story itself gives broad hints of its symbolic nature. They would also not realize apart from knowledge of the Synoptics that fishing was Peter's original occupation. The call stories in John 1 do not mention the previous occupations of the disciples. But with such knowledge from elsewhere, the appearance to Peter and the others while they are fishing functions as a second call to mission. As so often in the Fourth Gospel, the story works on two levels. There is the straightforward reading of it as an episode in the lives of the disciples where they go fishing and, at least in part, need the fish for sustenance. But there is also the reading that sees the fishing continually pointing beyond itself to the disciples' mission. The fishing metaphor is not only to be interpreted in the light of the Synoptic Jesus' words about making the disciples those who fish for people (cf. Mark 1.17; Matt. 4.19; Luke 5.10), but behind those words lie also the tradition from the Jewish Scriptures that pictures God's eschatological judgement in terms of fishing or catching people in nets (cf. Jer. 16.16; Ezek. 29.4–5; Amos 4.2; Hab. 1.14–17; cf. also 1QH 5.7–8). A saving function now attaches to God's eschatological mission, of which Jesus and the disciples are agents. Just as here the disciples will be involved in the harvesting of fish, so earlier in the narrative their mission was depicted as involvement in agricultural harvesting (4.38). At this second level of reading, the comment that **that night they caught nothing** suggests the failures and frustrations of mission. Readers are reminded of Jesus' words in the farewell discourse, that where fruitfulness is concerned, 'apart from me you can do nothing' (15.5).

4–6 In Jesus' absence the disciples' fishing has met with no success. Yet when he becomes present on the shore **When it was already dawn** (the contrast between day and night can be seen as part of this Gospel's darkness/light symbolism), the disciples fail to recognize him. His words reinforce their plight and force them to make it explicit: **Children, you have caught nothing to eat, have you?** The only answer to this question is **No.** Jesus' sovereignty and supernatural knowledge, which have been seen frequently in the earlier narrative, reappear in his command to them to **Cast the net to the right side of the boat.** Their compliance brings about the miracle of the haul of a **huge number of fish.** This may well be meant to recall scriptural prophecy. When the life-giving waters flow from the eschatological temple in Jerusalem, according to Ezek. 47.10 LXX, one of the consequences is that the fish will be like the fish of the Great Sea; there will be an exceedingly great number. Now in this account, when the disciples obey the word of the risen Jesus, who has earlier been depicted as the new temple, they are unable to haul in the net because of the great number of fish.

7–8 In the response to the miracle it is again **that disciple whom Jesus loved** who, consistent with his earlier depiction, shows superior insight and tells Peter, **It is the Lord**. The relation between these two disciples has been in view at earlier points (cf. 13.23–6; 18.15–16; 20.2–10) and will be resolved later in 21.20–3. Here, unlike the depiction in the earlier narrative, the Beloved Disciple's insight does affect the action, as Peter reacts to the Beloved Disciple's recognition. Peter **plunged into the sea** while the boat was only one hundred yards from shore, suggesting his eagerness and impatience to get to Jesus. He may have been outrun to the tomb, but he is determined to be the first to get to shore. The narrator's comments, however, are intriguing, because he describes how before jumping into the water, Peter **wrapped his outer garment around himself, for he was naked**. Some have suggested that the verb can also refer to tucking up and tying in a garment, and that the passage should therefore be translated, 'he tucked in his outer garment (for he was otherwise naked)'. It was, however, common to to be naked while fishing, and readers were probably intended to infer that Peter thought it more appropriate to be attired in some fashion in order to meet Jesus. The other disciples follow behind him in the boat, bringing the haul of fish.

9 They discover that Jesus has already prepared breakfast. There is **a charcoal fire there, with fish placed on it, and some bread**. The charcoal fire recalls the scene of Peter's denial in the high priest's courtyard, where he had stood warming himself at a charcoal fire (18.18, 25). Peter's threefold avowal of love and recommissioning in the scene that follows in 21.15–19 will have the same stage prop as his earlier threefold denial. The provision of fish and bread recalls the feeding of the five thousand in 6.1–14.

10–11 Jesus now invites the disciples to bring some of the fish he has supplied for them, presumably to add them to the breakfast. Peter again is the one who responds: **So Simon Peter went on board and hauled the net to land, full of large fish, one hundred and fifty three; and although there were so many, the net was not torn**. The details about the size of the catch and the untorn net not only attest to the miracle but may also at the other level of the narrative suggest the completeness and unity of those drawn in by the disciples' mission. In fact, the verb 'to haul' (ἕλκω) is the same verb translated as 'to draw' earlier in the Gospel when Jesus says, 'No one can come to me unless drawn by the

Father who sent me' (6.44) and 'I, when I am lifted up from the earth, will draw all people to myself' (12.32). Peter's action, then, can be read as the disciples' involvement in the mission of God and Jesus in drawing people to Jesus. If the untorn net has symbolic significance, it points to the unity that is effected by Jesus' mission and should characterize the resultant believing community. The specificity given to the number of the fish does suggest that symbolism is likely to be involved and has attracted a great variety of proposals about its meaning. Of these, two in particular remain worthy of note. Since at least Augustine's time it has been observed that 153 is the sum of the numbers from 1 to 17 and is a triangular number because 153 dots can be arranged in an equilateral triangle which has 17 dots on the base line. The number 153 would therefore represent the full sum, completeness. Attention was drawn to Ezek. 47.10 as the background for the huge number of fish mentioned in v. 6. A second explanation draws on the same text, which speaks of people fishing beside the sea from En-gedi to En-eglaim. Employing the notion of *gematria*, where each letter has a numerical value, it points out that the consonants of Gedi and Eglaim in Hebrew add up to 17 and 153 respectively and that, as has been noted, these two figures have a special mathematical relationship. One objection to this explanation is that it would require readers to know Hebrew but the final form of the Gospel was meant to include Gentiles among its readers, who needed to have elementary Hebrew terms, such as Rabbi, interpreted for them. This is not a fatal objection, since the tradition could well have originated among Jewish Christians who knew Hebrew and then have been retained in a narrative, which has other aspects that would not have been fully fathomed by those without a thorough knowledge of its Jewish and scriptural background. Whether originally involving *gematria* or simply the choice of a number with special mathematical characteristics, the 153 fish most likely suggest the full amount of those who will be drawn in through the mission of Jesus' disciples.

12–13 The focus returns to the meal with the risen Jesus as its host. He first invites the disciples to **Come and have breakfast** (the verb ἀριστάω can refer specifically to eating breakfast or more generally to eating any meal). Significantly, it is after Jesus gives this invitation to the meal that the narrator inserts the mention of the recognition of the risen Jesus by the whole group of disciples – **Now none of the disciples dared to ask him, 'Who are you?' because they knew it was the Lord.** As in the recognition scene in Luke 24.30–1, it is Jesus' hosting of the meal that opens disciples' eyes to his identity. The reference to their not questioning him about his identity because they knew it can be seen as a fulfilment of Jesus' words in the farewell discourse – 'On that day you will not question me about anything' (16.23). As the host, who is now recognized for who he is, Jesus has supplied and now distributes the bread and then the fish. The language echoes that of the earlier feeding. In 6.11 'Jesus took the loaves, and . . . distributed them . . .; so also the fish' and here **Jesus . . . took the bread and gave it to them, and in the same way the fish**. Both scenes carry overtones of the church's eucharistic meal. Jesus has empowered the disciples for their mission of fishing, enabling them to make their catch, and he now provides nourishment for them in their task.

14 The last verse of this unit returns to the initial theme of Jesus' revelation (cf. v. 1). It indicates that this has been the third post-resurrection appearance, in which **Jesus was revealed to the disciples**. The reference is to the appearances to the group and does not include the appearance to the individual woman, Mary Magdalene.

In relation to the Synoptics, this account of an appearance of Jesus to the disciples in Galilee means that the final version of the Fourth Gospel combines a Lukan emphasis on appearances in Jerusalem (cf. John 20) with Markan and Matthean traditions about an appearance in Galilee. But what is the relation of this account to Luke 5.1–11, which also contains a miracle involving a great haul of fish? The basic structural elements of the miracle are the same. The disciples spend all night fishing and catch nothing (v. 3; cf. Luke 5.5). Jesus commands them to let down their nets (v. 6; Luke 5.4). On following his instructions, they obtain a huge catch of fish (vv. 6, 8, 11; cf. Luke 5.6–7, 9). In both accounts the chief character among the disciples is Simon Peter (vv. 2–3, 7, 11; cf. Luke 5.3–5, 8–10) and the sons of Zebedee are present (v. 2; cf. Luke 5.10). But the verbal agreements within these parallels are minimal (boat, net, night, nothing, great number of fish), and the framework (post-resurrection in John and initial call narrative in Luke) and the rest of the details are significantly different. It is noteworthy that, while Luke's account reports that the nets were tearing apart (5.6), John explicitly states that the net was not torn (v. 11).

The main options are that (i) both know of and use differently a tradition of a post-resurrection appearance that involved a miraculous catch of fish, and this source may already have combined a tradition of a miracle from the ministry with a tradition of an appearance in Galilee or (ii) Luke knew John's account or (iii) the fourth evangelist knew of Luke's account and this provided the starting point for his own reworking of the story. There is little to be said for the second option. None of the distinctive emphases of John's account appear in Luke and the latter's incorporation of the miracle into a call story derived from Mark is best explained on the basis of his knowledge of a post-resurrection tradition which he includes here because his exclusively Jerusalem-oriented ending does not allow for it later and it provides a plausible explanation for why the first disciples were willing to leave all to follow Jesus. Such a tradition would also make sense of Peter's words, 'Go away from me, Lord, for I am a sinful man!' (Luke 5.8), if they were originally set after his denials. There is more to be said, however, for knowledge of Luke's version of this tradition on the part of the fourth evangelist and his readers, particularly since a recognition scene at a meal with Jesus, reminiscent of that in Luke 24.28–35, is included in the story of the miraculous catch of fish in this Gospel. As has been noted, for the Fourth Gospel's story to be appreciated, there needs to be an awareness of the call of the disciples in the Synoptics, with its link between the original occupation of fishing and the mission of fishing for or catching people. Luke's placing of the tradition in the setting of the call supplies all this; cf. especially Luke 5.10 – 'Do not be afraid; from now on you will be catching people.' The evangelist's knowledge of Luke's account enables him to develop the failure to catch anything at night into an explicit contrast with what happens in the day and to change the detail of nets being torn into that of an untorn net, which suits his emphasis on completeness and unity. Luke's highlighting of Peter's sinfulness can be seen as a further implicit backdrop for the need for his rehabilitation, which follows in John.

This sign points beyond itself to the continuation of Jesus' mission through that of the disciples. After the completion of his own work in his glorification, the risen Jesus graciously supplies the needs of his followers in their mission through his continuing empowering presence and through his nourishment of them. Even though this chapter was probably added later, its concerns mesh with earlier emphases in the narrative about the disciples' future mission and their need for dependence on Jesus. There are also links between this last sign and the first sign in the Gospel. At Cana in Galilee Jesus manifested (ἐφανέρωσεν) his glory and his disciples believed in him (2.11). Here also in Galilee Jesus manifested (ἐφανέρωσεν) himself (vv. 1, 14) and the disciples are said to have known it was the Lord (v. 12). In the first case there was the abundant supply of wine; in the last case there is an abundant supply of fish, so that just as Jesus' mission began with a miracle displaying abundance, so also does that of his followers. There is a further connection with the feeding miracle in 6.1–14, which also took place at the Sea of Tiberias in Galilee. There Jesus supplied fish and especially an excess of bread. Here Jesus supplies bread and especially an excess of fish.

2. THE REHABILITATION OF PETER   21.15–19

(15) So when they had eaten breakfast, Jesus said to Simon Peter, 'Simon, son of John, do you love me more than these?' He said to him, 'Yes, Lord, you know that I love you.' Jesus said to him, 'Feed my lambs.' (16) He said to him again for a second time, 'Simon, son of John, do you love me?' He said to him, 'Yes, Lord, you know that I love you.' Jesus said to him, 'Tend my sheep.' (17) He said to him the third time, 'Simon, son of John, do you love me?' Peter was saddened that he said to him the third time, 'Do you love me?' And he said to him, 'Lord, you know all things, you know that I love you.' Jesus said to him, 'Feed my sheep. (18) Truly, truly, I say to you, when you were younger, you would fasten your belt and go wherever you wanted. But when you grow old, you will stretch out your hands and someone else[1] will fasten your belt and take you where you do not want.' (19) He said this to indicate by what kind of death he would glorify God. And having said this, he said to him, 'Follow me.'

The previous episode with the great catch of fish is complete in itself, yet it also serves as a preparation for the extensive dialogue between Jesus and Peter that now follows. After Peter has been singled out in the passion narrative for his denials of Jesus, readers are left with questions about his future story line. Is he to be remembered primarily for these denials? Or will he be singled out again in a way that suggests some closure for his particular relationship to Jesus? The Synoptic accounts all provide a positive answer to the second question in their varying ways. Mark 16.7, in the announcement of the young man at the tomb, gives special recognition to Peter despite his previous denials – 'But go, tell his disciples and Peter . . .' Matthew handles Peter's place in the post-resurrection situation differently. He omits any mention of Peter in the announcements by the tomb but has already informed his readers ahead of time that Peter will be the rock on which Jesus builds his church, the one who has the keys of the kingdom (cf. 16.16–19). Luke mentions a special appearance of the risen Lord to Peter in his Gospel (cf. 24.34) and then is able to continue Peter's rehabilitation by giving him the leading role at Pentecost and in the outreach of the earliest days of the Christian movement in his second volume. The Fourth Gospel moves toward its positive answer slowly,

---

[1] The translation reflects the formulation in the singular in most of the early textual witnesses. Those variants which employ the plural and D it^d, which change the second verb to ἀπάγουσιν, 'lead away', appear to be attempts to make the text slightly less vague and conform it to what was thought to have actually happened to Peter – his seizure by a number of people and his being led away as a criminal to his death.

building expectation. So far, Peter has been present at the empty tomb but did not share the Beloved Disciple's immediate belief. Presumably, however, he was present at the first two appearances of the risen Lord to the group of disciples when they all believed, but he was not singled out for any special notice. In the third appearance, which has just been portrayed, he played an increasingly leading role, but readers have still been left to guess at the dynamics of his relation to Jesus. But now that Peter has been brought face to face with Jesus through swimming ashore to meet him and through bringing the miraculous catch of fish to the meal, there is a sense of anticipation that there will be a fuller resolution of his situation, and it is not disappointed.

15–17 It is after breakfast has been eaten that Jesus singles out Peter with a question: **Simon, son of John, do you love me more than these?** Jesus reverts to the disciple's original name rather than the new name he had given him (cf. 1.42 – 'You are Simon, son of John. You are to be called Cephas'). This may well signal that in what follows the nature of their relationship needs to be re-established. Peter is asked whether he loves Jesus more than the other disciples do, not whether he loves Jesus more than he loves the other disciples. The comparison of Peter's love for Jesus with that of the other disciples, while opening up the way for the comparison with the Beloved Disciple in vv. 20–3, may also have in view two earlier scenes involving Peter. The first is Peter's avowal in 13.37 that he would lay down his life for Jesus. The second is the immediately preceding scene, where Peter has apparently again been eager to demonstrate his love by jumping into the sea to meet Jesus and by being the one to haul in the net full of fish from the boat (cf. 21.7, 11).

Peter's response does not pick up on the comparative aspect of the question but assures Jesus of his love and appeals to Jesus' knowledge of that love – **Yes, Lord, you know that I love you.** His appeal to Jesus' sovereign knowledge throughout the conversation is poignant, since Peter now has experienced for himself that knowledge. His threefold denial had been predicted by the Jesus who knows all things (cf. 13.38; 18.15–18, 25–7). No particular significance is to be read into the fact that in this dialogue two different verbs for 'to love' are used. In the first exchange, as in the following one, Jesus employs the verb ἀγαπάω in his question, while Peter employs φιλέω in his responses, and then Jesus himself switches to φιλέω for the third question. The two verbs can be used interchangeably and have been earlier in this Gospel (cf. 11.3 with 11.5 for Jesus' love for Lazarus; 5.20 with 3.35 and 10.17 for the Father's love for the Son; 14.21 with 16.27 for the Father's love for disciples and their love for Jesus; 13.23 with 20.2 for the disciple whom Jesus loved). The different choice of words in the threefold exchange is stylistic. What is most important is the threefold pattern itself and it is understandable that the narrator would feel the need to introduce some variation into the repetition. The pattern, of course, matches the earlier threefold denial, and the presence of the charcoal fire as backdrop on both occasions (cf. 18.18; 21.9) underscores the parallel. Within the narrative it is suggested that Peter himself feels the force of the parallel, because the narrator comments that **Peter was saddened that he said to him the third time, 'Do you love me?'** Again it would appear that readers are expected to know the Markan account. If so, they will recall that there Peter was similarly grieved after his third denial and 'broke down and wept' (Mark 14.72).

After each protestation of love on the part of Peter, Jesus directs his attention to his responsibility toward other believers – **Feed my lambs; Tend my sheep; Feed my sheep**. The force is that Peter will demonstrate the genuineness of his love by caring for those who belong to Jesus, the good shepherd. Jesus has already described what it means to shepherd the flock in 10.1–18, 26–8 and has proved his identity as the good shepherd in laying down his life for the sheep before taking it up again (cf. 10.15b, 17–18). Now Peter is charged with the privilege and responsibility of being the undershepherd who will protect, nourish and tend the flock of the good shepherd himself. This task is in continuity with the charge to all the disciples in the farewell discourse to love, serve and lay down their lives for another (cf. 13.14–15, 34; 15.12–14, 17). Indeed, Peter is being reminded of Jesus' teaching about what it really means to love him, since in 14.23 Jesus had already said, 'Those who love me will keep my word, and my Father will love them, and we will come to them and make our home with them.' So Peter's love will show itself as he keeps Jesus' word about loving others in the particular form of shepherding the flock.

18–19 Not only that, but in a saying introduced by the double Amen formula, Jesus predicts that Peter will later follow in the footsteps of the good shepherd himself by laying down his life. The content of the actual prediction is vague. Adapting a saying comparing the vigour of youth with the dependence of old age, it contrasts the voluntary actions of a younger Peter – **you would fasten your belt and go wherever you wanted** – with the movements forced on an older Peter – **you will stretch out your hands and someone else will fasten your belt and take you where you do not want**. The depiction of the younger Peter can be seen as including a reference to the action he has recently taken in fastening his garment before jumping into the sea to meet Jesus. The emphasis on stretching out the hands by the older Peter need signify no more than stretching out the hands to be bound as part of being girded and taken away to death. On the other hand, the stretching out of the hands was often viewed by early Christian writers as a reference to crucifixion, so that, for example, both *Barnabas* 12 and Justin, *Dial.* 90–1 see Moses' stretching out his hands in Exod. 17.12 as a type of Christ on the cross. The fact that stretching out the hands is mentioned before having the belt fastened and being led away need not be thought of as an insuperable problem, since the victim of crucifixion would have had outstretched hands secured to the crossbeam or *patibulum* that he then carried as he was led away to death. Whatever the precise manner of his death, the narrator's comment makes explicit that the reference is to Peter's martyrdom – **He said this to indicate by what kind of death he would glorify God.** The earliest evidence about Peter's death outside the canonical writings is in *1 Clement* 5. There, in a warning about the sin of jealousy, Peter and Paul are adduced as examples of those who suffered because of jealousy and envy. Of the former it is simply said that 'it was by sinful jealousy that Peter was subjected to tribulation, not once or twice but many times; it was in that way that he bore his witness, 'ere he left us for his well-earned place in glory' (5.4). The tradition that Peter was martyred in Rome is probably first evidenced in the *Acts of Peter* 36—41 from around the end of the second century CE, where a dramatic depiction of the apostle's death situates this during the persecution under Nero and has Peter crucified upside down. Tertullian, at the beginning of the third century, also refers to Peter being crucified upside down (*Scorp.* 15.3). Eusebius too records this tradition (cf. *Hist. eccl.* 2.25.8; 3.1.2), citing a letter of Dionysius of Corinth, written around 170 CE, for the death occurring under Nero in Rome. The consistency of the basic tradition about crucifixion in Rome makes it likely that the readers of John 21 would also have understood Peter's martyrdom to have taken place in that city during the Neronian persecution. The language used about Peter's death takes up that of the earlier narratorial comments in 12.33 and 18.32 about the kind of death Jesus was to die. The comment that Peter's death was the means by which he would glorify God also links his fate with that of Jesus, since again and again the evangelist has made clear that Jesus' death was his means of glorifying God (cf. e.g. 12.23, 28; 13.31–2; 17.1, 4–5).

The rehabilitation of Peter is rounded off by Jesus' command – **Follow me.** This constituted Peter's initial call to discipleship, according to Mark's account (cf. Mark 1.17), and was the call issued to Philip in John 1.43. So Peter's charge to feed the sheep is also a recommissioning to discipleship, a reminder that shepherding Jesus' sheep will also mean being one of those sheep and following the good shepherd himself (cf. 10.4, 27). Further, the call to follow Jesus picks up on Peter's earlier question and claim in 13.37 – 'Lord, why can I not follow you now? I will lay down my life for you.' It was immediately following this that Jesus had predicted Peter's denial of his discipleship, and Peter went on to demonstrate his failure to follow and to be ready to lay down his life. But now the situation has changed.

In the light of the preceding prediction it is clear that Jesus deems Peter ready to be the sort of follower who is now able to follow even to the extent of laying down his life.

3. THE ROLE OF THE BELOVED DISCIPLE   21.20–3

(20) Peter turned and saw the disciple whom Jesus loved following – the one who had leant back on his chest at the supper and had said, 'Lord, who is the one who will betray you?' (21) So when Peter saw him, he said to Jesus, 'Lord, what about this man?' (22) Jesus said to him, 'If I want him to remain until I come, what is that to you? You follow me.' (23) So the word spread among the brothers and sisters that that disciple would not die. But Jesus did not say to him that he would not die, but rather, 'If I want him to remain until I come, [what is that to you?]'[1]

20 When the relationship between the Beloved Disciple and Peter was introduced in 13.23–5, it was the Beloved Disciple who was close to Jesus and whom Peter asked to obtain information from Jesus about the betrayer. The earlier scene at the supper is explicitly recalled in the description of the Beloved Disciple here – **the one who had leant back on his chest at the supper and had said, 'Lord, who is the one who will betray you?'** But now it is the rehabilitated Peter who in this scene is in the immediate company of Jesus, and he asks Jesus about the Beloved Disciple who is following behind them.

21–22 Peter's question, **Lord, what about this man?**, is presumably aimed at ascertaining the comparative fate of the Beloved Disciple and whether he too will die a martyr's death. But Jesus does not have a particular prediction to make about the Beloved Disciple, over whose role Peter has no control, and instead he attempts to refocus Peter's attention away from concern with the task of others and back to his own discipleship – **If I want him to remain until I come, what is that to you? You follow me.** The exhortation to discipleship in v. 19 is now repeated in more emphatic form. The resolution of any tension

---

[1] It is uncertain whether the clause in square brackets should be included as part of the original text. It is omitted by ℵ* C² f¹ 565 it^{a,c} syr^s arm. The shorter reading is generally to be preferred and this one would avoid an unnecessary lengthy repetition, as elsewhere the evangelist often attempts to do, placing the emphasis on the part of Jesus' previous saying that had been misinterpreted. On the other hand, it is possible that later copyists wanted to make absolutely clear that Jesus had not made a false prediction and so omitted the final words in order to underscore those that should not in fact have led to the misunderstanding.

or sense of rivalry between the two leading disciples in this narrative will lie in their having different but equally significant roles to play. What is important is that both roles are to be seen as in line with Jesus' sovereign will and as appropriate to discipleship.

The notion of a final coming of Jesus is, of course, part of traditional early Christian eschatology. The reference here to that coming should not be seen as an alien reference within the more realized eschatology of the rest of the Fourth Gospel. There are other references to Jesus' role in judgement and giving life at the last day (cf. e.g. 5.28–9; 6.39–40), and earlier, in the farewell discourse, Jesus had also promised, 'if I go and prepare a place for you, I will come again and will take you to myself, so that where I am you also may be' (14.3). Jesus' last words in the Gospel contain a reference to the parousia, while the Gospel's first words had echoed the opening of Genesis with its reference to the creation. In this way the Gospel's story world encompasses the whole of history, from its beginning to its consummation.

23 But the saying of Jesus preserved in the tradition had triggered off a further issue, one that concerned the Beloved Disciple's death. It had been interpreted as a prediction that he would not die – **the word spread among the brothers and sisters that that disciple would not die.** The fact that the evangelist devotes a lengthy verse to scotching the rumour suggests a number of factors at work. (i) In order for the rumour to have had the troubling effect it did, it must have been deeply rooted in the tradition. Its origin could well have been the saying of Jesus in Mark 9.1 that some of his followers would remain alive until the coming of the kingdom in power. Over time this would have become linked with the Beloved Disciple, a veteran leader in Johannine circles and held by many to be the longest-surviving follower of Jesus from the first generation. (ii) It indicates that, however idealized his portrayal in the narrative, the Beloved Disciple is a real figure who has played a founding role in the Johannine community, the brothers and sisters mentioned here. It would be very strange and highly contrived to attempt to expose a rumour about a purely fictional character. (iii) It is most likely that the Beloved Disciple's death has already occurred and was not a martyr's death. Hence the rumour would have been damaging to his reputation and the need would have arisen to compare his fate with that of Peter. (iv) A major emphasis in the Gospel's narrative has been the reliability of Jesus' word and the fulfilment of his predictions. The existence of a rumour about this prediction of Jesus that had now proved false would be a major concern. If Jesus has proved unreliable on this point, this would undermine the rest of the sayings tradition. So this comment strives to make clear that there has been no mismatch between what Jesus actually said and the fate of the Beloved Disciple – **But Jesus did not say to him that he would not die, but rather, 'If I want him to remain until I come . . .'**

An account such as this, written down in its final form around the end of the first century CE, clearly reflects the ecclesial concerns of its writer and readers. Johannine Christians recognize the leadership role of Peter in the wider church and his martyr's death. Some may have questioned the status of their own leading figure, the Beloved Disciple, since he did not die a martyr's death like his Lord. The saying of Jesus here and the narrator's statement that will follow in v. 24 provide assurance that the importance of the Beloved Disciple's contribution is not diminished either by the fact or the manner of his death. It is not only the status of the Beloved Disciple that has been at issue but also, and more importantly, the credibility of Jesus. This passage deals in its own way with the problems created by the tradition that Jesus had predicted the survival of some original followers until the parousia. In the form that that tradition took in attaching itself to the Beloved Disciple, any potential damage could be contained by emphasizing its first clause, which gave the prediction a conditional element, making it dependent on Jesus' will.

The roles of Peter and the Beloved Disciple can be seen as two models for the continuation of Jesus' mission through the lives of his followers. While the witness of Peter is characterized by his shepherding and his following of Jesus to death, the witness of the Beloved Disciple will be characterized by his foundational role in the passing on of authentic interpretation of the tradition about Jesus in this narrative. Martyrdom has always been a crucial model and in the global context of the church remains so. But other forms of witness and discipleship that do not lead to the ultimate sacrifice of one's life are not therefore devalued in comparison. Disciples are to be faithful followers in whatever role the risen Lord assigns them.

4. CONCLUSION   21.24–5

(24) This is the disciple who is testifying about these things and has written them, and we know that his witness is true. (25) There are also many other things that Jesus did, which I suppose, if written down individually, the world itself would not have room for the books that would be written.

24 The concluding words of the whole Gospel spell out what has been the significance of the Beloved Disciple's role: **This is the disciple who is testifying about these things and has written them.** His role has been that of the ideal witness who has been responsible for the written testimony constituted by the narrative. Some scholars have taken 'these things' as a reference only to what has been related in vv. 21–3 or only to the content of chapter 21. But the following verse's contrast with all the things that were not written down makes it much more likely that the reference is to the narrative as a whole. The last clause – **and we know that his witness is true** – distinguishes between the Beloved Disciple and the narratorial 'we' who are confirming his witness as true. The narrator, who again invokes the community of faith with which he is aligned (cf. the 'we' in 1.14, 16; cf. also 3.11), is not himself the Beloved Disciple. This also indicates that γράψας, 'has written', is best taken loosely in the sense of having instigated or been responsible for the writing of the bulk of the narrative rather than actually having penned it. In 19.19, 22 the verb is also employed in this looser way to describe Pilate's role in writing the inscription on the cross. The mention of the writing of an account and, in the following verse, of books also connects this ending with 20.30–1, which, as has been noted, may well have constituted an earlier ending. Now the purpose of the book can also be linked with the Beloved Disciple. His written testimony has been intended to produce the right sort of belief among the readers (cf. also 19.35), the belief that Jesus is the Christ, the Son of God, which results in the experience of the positive judgement of eternal life. The Beloved Disciple is being claimed as the authority for the distinctive perspective that has shaped and pervaded the witness of the narrative.

The narrator also claims that the Beloved Disciple's witness is true, just as he had done earlier in 19.35. Only in regard to three characters is there an underlining of the truth of their witness – God the Father in 5.32 (cf. also 8.17), Jesus in 8.13–18 and now also the Beloved Disciple. Just as in the prologue in 1.14 the endorsement of the narrator and his community was added to that of John the Baptist, so here it is added to that of the Beloved Disciple in what constitutes another form of the dual witness required by Scripture (cf. 8.17; Deut. 19.15).

There is a final irony attached to the witness of the Beloved Disciple. Even though the readers have now been told that Jesus did not predict that this disciple would remain until he came, the writing down of his witness provides for that witness to remain until the coming of Christ. Despite his death, his witness will have a continuing role in the further playing out within history of the narrative's motif of a cosmic trial.

25 His written witness can play this role, even though it is not a final or exhaustive witness. The narrator, now employing the first person singular – **I suppose** – indicates that not only did Jesus do **many other things** (cf. 20.30 – 'many other signs . . . which are not written in this book'), but also, **if written down individually, the world itself would not have room for the books that would be written**. This ending follows typical extravagant rhetorical conventions. It combines the *topos* of selecting a few items out of many possible (cf. commentary on 20.31) with that of there being too many things to tell (cf. Plutarch, *Mor.* 115e).

Similar sentiments occur in four places at the end of a narrative or report – Philo, *Spec.* 4.238; Lucian, *Demon.* 67; Aelius Aristides 2.362; 1 Macc. 9.22.

These verses provide an appropriate closure to the narrative. Not only do they link back with 20.30–1, which has described the purpose of the writing of the book, but they also provide an *inclusio* with the prologue in terms of the notion of witness that was introduced in 1.7, 8, 15. They reinforce the importance of the motif of the cosmic judgement, in which the truth of God's revelation in Jesus is on trial, as a major framework for discerning the coherence of the narrative as a whole. Now the writing down of the narrative itself and the Beloved Disciple's witness that it represents play an integral role in the continuation of Jesus' mission within history. And just as it has been claimed that the witness of Jesus was true and self-authenticating, so a similar claim is made for this written witness.

APPENDIX: THE CONTROVERSY ABOUT THE WOMAN TAKEN IN ADULTERY 7.53—8.11

(7.53) Then each of them went home, (8.1) while Jesus went to the Mount of Olives. (2) Early in the morning he appeared again in the temple, and all the people came to him, and, having sat down, he was teaching them. (3) The scribes and the Pharisees brought a woman, who had been caught in adultery, and having made her stand in the middle, (4) they said to him, 'Teacher, this woman was caught in the very act of committing adultery. (5) Now in the law Moses commanded us to stone such women. So what do you say?' (6) They said this to test him, so that they could bring a charge against him. But Jesus bent down and wrote on the ground with his finger. (7) When they persisted in asking him, he straightened up and said to them, 'Let the one among you who is without sin be the first to throw a stone at her.' (8) And again he bent down and wrote on the ground. (9) Those who heard went away, one by one, beginning with the elders, and he was left alone with the woman who was in the middle. (10) Jesus straightened up and said to her, 'Woman, where are they? Has no one condemned you?' (11) She said, 'No one, sir.' Then Jesus said, 'Neither do I condemn you. Go, and from now on sin no more.'

Despite occasional attempts to argue for the originality of this pericope in its placement between John 7.52 and 8.12, the overwhelming consensus of scholarship is that the earliest and best manuscript witnesses did not contain it and that it was inserted at a later stage in the transmission of the Gospel. It is lacking in numerous and diverse witnesses, such as p[66,75] ℵ B L N T W Y Δ Θ Ψ 0141 0211 22 33, and was almost certainly absent from A and C, which, although defective at this point in the Gospel, did not have enough space to have included it. It is also missing from the oldest forms of the Syriac and Coptic texts, from the Gothic version, and from many Old Georgian, Armenian and Old Latin manuscripts. Early Greek patristic writers do not include it in their commentaries on the Gospel of John. The one major exception in the midst of this external evidence is D (from the fifth or sixth century): other Western texts also contain it (G H K), as does the Vulgate, and it is known to the Latin fathers Ambrose, Jerome and Augustine. Some other later manuscripts which include the story provide markings around it to indicate that the copyists were aware of its dubious originality. Finally, although most texts containing the story have it as 7.53—8.11, it is also placed at other points – after 7.36 (225), after 7.44 (some Georgian manuscripts), after 21.25 (some Armenian manuscripts, 1 156 1976 *f*[1]) and after Luke 21.38 (*f*[13], from *c.* twelfth century).

The external evidence in itself is not absolutely decisive on the question of originality. It could in theory be possible that the story was original but that a number of early witnesses independently decided to omit it for some reason. The usual reason suggested is that the copyists found the story objectionable because it depicted Jesus as taking too lenient a view toward adultery. Augustine, who used the passage to challenge the values of his society by urging husbands to accept back adulterous wives without condemning them, asserted, 'Some of little faith, or rather enemies of the true faith, I suppose from a fear lest their wives should gain impunity in sin, removed from their manuscripts the Lord's act of indulgence to the adulteress' (*Con. Adult.* 2.6). It is true that there was extremely strict discipline about sexual sin in the first two centuries of the church's life and that when forgiveness of a sin such as adultery was considered possible, it was expected that it would always be accompanied by clear signs of repentance. The story could therefore have appeared dangerous because it appears to forgive adultery without demanding repentance. But, on the other hand, there is, of course, no suggestion in the story of Jesus condoning adultery and he tells the woman to sin no more; there are no other instances of whole passages being omitted because they were found morally offensive; and it is unlikely that such diverse witnesses would have done this for the same reason and that they would all have also cut out the transitional material of 7.53—8.2 before the story proper. When the major stylistic differences between this passage and the rest of John's Gospel (see the comments on individual verses below) and the disruption to the sequence and flow of argument in chapters 7 and 8 are considered, it is virtually certain that this story was not part of the original Gospel.

What then is its origin? Two different aspects of this question need initially to be disentangled – the origin of the story and the origin of the piece of written text that found its way into the Fourth Gospel at a later stage. Evidence about both is sparse and therefore it will not be surprising if discussion does not lead to firm conclusions. Separate from the textual discussion of John, Eusebius (*Hist. eccl.* 3.39.16) records that Papias knew a story, contained in the *Gospel according to the Hebrews*, of 'a woman, accused in the Lord's presence of many sins'. It is not at all obvious, however, that this is the same story as one about a woman accused of the particular sin of adultery. In fact, the story of the woman in Luke 7.36–50 corresponds better with this description. Simon the Pharisee calls her a sinner and Jesus speaks of 'her sins, which were many'. The first clear evidence for the existence of the story is to be found in the third-century Syriac *Didascalia* 7, which is reproduced in the fourth-century *Apostolic Constitutions* 2.24. The latter version says: 'The elders set before him another woman who had sinned, handed over the judgement to him, and went out. But the Lord, who knows men's hearts, enquired of her whether the elders had condemned her. When she said, "No," he said to her, "Go then; neither do I condemn you."' There is no mention of adultery and Jesus' final words do not include the exhortation to sin no more, but this certainly looks like a briefer version of the same story as in John 7.53—8.11. It is significant that this first written version was immediately preceded by an address to a bishop, warning him not to be too severe with those who repent of their sins. The story that follows does not fit the warning precisely, because there is no mention in it of the woman's repentance, but this rehearsal of it suggests the story may have circulated, probably orally, in Syria in the second century before it was co-opted for this specific use in the first extant written version in the *Didascalia*.

Another version of the story is found in the writings of the fourth-century Alexandrian exegete Didymus the Blind. He uses it to illustrate a point in his commentary on Ecclesiastes (*Com. Eccl.* 223.6b–13a) when exhorting his readers not to judge others inappropriately. The story he rehearses involves a woman who has been condemned by the Jews for a sin and is on her way to be stoned. Jesus sees this and intervenes by saying, 'He who has not sinned, let him take a stone and cast it.' At this her accusers 'perceived that they were guilty in some matters' and did not dare to carry out the punishment. Tantalizingly, Didymus claims to find this story 'in certain Gospels'. This could mean that he knew of Alexandrian manuscripts of John that contained it and/or, as has been conjectured, that it was in the *Gospel according to the Hebrews*.

These two references to the story confirm that it circulated and was known in different parts of the church well before the first extant text that includes John 7.53—8.11. It is far more difficult to ascertain whether these two references indicate distinct versions of the story, one containing the entrapment motif in relation to interpretation of the law and the other dealing with Jesus' acquittal of a sinful woman. If so, then it would appear that John 7.53—8.11 is a conflation and embellishment of the two earlier traditions. But since *Didascalia* and Didymus both use the story to make pastoral points, it is equally possible that they have selected those elements from a longer version which contained both sets of features and have done so in order to illustrate the points they wished to make. If so, this longer version of the tradition would be similar to the story now found in John. The dramatic integrity of this story and its balanced treatment of Jesus' relationship to the scribes and Pharisees, on the one hand, and his relationship to the woman, on the other, with a pronouncement addressed to each, does not make it an obvious candidate for a tradition-historical analysis that breaks it down into discrete earlier units.

Whatever decision is reached about the relation of John 7.53—8.11 to these earlier accounts, its immediate antecedent is neither a longer form nor two shorter forms of the story from the oral tradition. The first two or three verses appear to be the ending of another story, which forms a transition into this one, and indicate that the text was taken from a longer written source. Other stories about Jesus still in circulation were often read in the liturgy alongside canonical Gospels, were sometimes written down for lectionary purposes, and then on occasion found their way via copyists into the canonical texts. This appears to have happened with the story of Jesus' encounter with the man working on the sabbath found at Luke 6.5 in D, which is also the earliest extant text containing John 7.53—8.11. In the case of the latter, however, the first three verses are very close in wording to Luke 21.37–8 and the best guess may be that the actual story involving the woman first got added to a version of Luke after these verses. When later it was seen that the story might be even more appropriate in the middle of John 7 and 8, it was removed and placed there but with a form of the Lukan material that now served as its introduction still attached. If this is the case, it is interesting that in one still later textual tradition (f^{13}) the whole text in this form is found at the end of Luke 21.

Although this story disrupts the sequence in John 7 and 8, there is a certain logic in its having been placed at the point at which it occurs in the majority of manuscripts that include it. Its setting is Jesus' teaching in the temple, the same setting as in John 7 and 8. It is a story of controversy and conflict between Jesus and the religious authorities, which is the context that now surrounds it, and it deals with the issue of judgement, which is the major motif in the context. It further illustrates both the faulty judgement of the authorities based on the law (cf. 7.47–52) and the attitude of Jesus that will be set out in what follows – 'You judge by human standards; I judge no one' (cf. 8.15).

Some modern scholars choose to interpret the story within this Johannine narrative context and can thereby achieve illuminating readings. Such an interpretive choice should not, however, be confused with a 'canonical reading'. To do so raises the question of what is canonical. Some Christian churches are influenced by the presence of this passage as part of John in the Vulgate. But if one takes the view that the process of canonization established an authoritative list of authoritative books, then the issue of the precise extent of any of those books was not in view. For present-day readers that question remains to be decided by the usual textual and historical-critical means. For these reasons the passage will be discussed here as an isolated piece of valuable early non-canonical tradition whose immediate textual context is unknown.

Although the story's two decisive sayings of Jesus mean that it has some similarities with pronouncement stories in the Synoptic Gospels, it most closely resembles the Synoptic controversy stories, particularly those where the religious leaders raise issues in order to test or trap Jesus (cf. Mark 10.2–12 par.; Mark 12.13–17 parr.; Mark 12.18–27 parr.; Mark 12.28–34 parr.). In this case, however, the testing is not merely verbal, but Jesus' opponents employ what appears to be actual incident in which a woman's life is at stake. The structure of the pericope is as follows: (i) introductory transitional material, providing a setting (7.53—8.2), (ii) presentation of the issue in the controversy (vv. 3–6a), and (iii) Jesus' response to the issue (vv. 6b–11).

7.53—8.2 The text begins with what appears to be the ending of a previous episode, which refers to the dispersal of Jesus' audience, presumably a crowd – **Then each of them went home.** Jesus himself, however, **went to the Mount of Olives.** The Mount of Olives does not feature in John's Gospel but is frequently mentioned in the Synoptics as part of Jesus' itinerary during the last period of his ministry (cf. Mark 11.1 parr.; Mark 13.3 par.; Mark 14.26 par.). Luke 22.39 speaks of it being Jesus' custom to go to the Mount of Olives, referring back to Luke 21.37, which recounts that, after teaching in the temple every day, 'at night he would go out and spend the night on the Mount of Olives, as it was called'. As has been noted, this introductory material for the controversy story appears in fact to be dependent on Luke 21.37–8, which continues 'and all the people would get up early in the morning to listen to him in the temple'. While there the subject is the people, here it is Jesus, but a cognate form of **Early in the morning**, and then **the temple, all the people** and **teaching** are common to both passages. There are other features of the text that are more characteristic of Luke's writings than of any other part of the New Testament. The actual term ὄρθρος, 'early in the morning', is found elsewhere in the New Testament only in Luke 24.1 and Acts 5.21; παραγίνεσθαι, 'to appear again', occurs only once in John but eight times in Luke and twenty times in Acts; λαός, 'people', occurs twice in John but 37 times in Luke and 48 times in Acts; and, while elsewhere in John Jesus stands to teach, he sits down to teach in Luke 4.20 and 5.3 (cf. also Mark 4.1 par.; Matt. 5.1). Here, then, Jesus' teaching of large numbers in the temple becomes the setting for the incident that follows.

3–4 The scribes and the Pharisees brought a woman, who had been caught in adultery. Some modern readings, which focus on the woman's plight, suggest that, in the light of the irregularities which appear to surround her being seized, she may not have actually been guilty of adultery and that this is simply the false witness of those who have brought her to Jesus. But this is not to take seriously either the beginning, the middle or the end of the incident. Here at the outset, the narrator, whom readers have to take as a reliable one, makes it his own presupposition that the woman has been caught in adultery. Readers do not learn this only from the religious leaders in v. 4. Jesus' acceptance of the dilemma which has been posed for him, rather than attempting to deny or refute one of its aspects, and his final exhortation to the woman to sin no more leave little doubt that he too believes that legally she is guilty of adultery.

The religious authorities are described as scribes and Pharisees. 'Scribes' are not mentioned in John's Gospel but the combination of scribes and Pharisees is found once in Mark, seven times in Matthew and five times in Luke. This particular combination of religious groupings makes the woman **stand in the middle**, as the accused might be made to do in a court setting. Addressing Jesus as **Teacher**, they state their accusation – **this woman was caught in the very act of committing adultery**. The Greek term for 'teacher' is frequently used in address to Jesus in the Synoptics, but not in John, despite Jesus' words in 13.13–14. Here it prepares for the attempt to catch Jesus out in his teaching about the law. If a charge of adultery was to be upheld, it was necessary for the offender to have been caught in the act, with two witnesses to the act required because a conviction involved the death penalty (cf. Deut. 17.6; 19.15). These conditions would not have been easy to fulfil and would presumably have entailed prior suspicion on the part of the woman's husband which then led to some form of entrapment.

5–6a The entrapment that concerns the narrator, however, is not that of the woman but that of Jesus. The scribes and Pharisees remind him, **Now in the law Moses commanded us to stone such women. So what do you say? They said this to test him, so that they could**

bring a charge against him. Their formulation of the law, however, is not strictly accurate. Moses commanded not only the women caught in adultery but also their male sexual partners to be put to death. This highlights a major irregularity in the way the accusers in this case have acted. There should have been two accused. Where is the man, why has he apparently not also been seized, and why have the accusers singled out the woman for punishment? This looks like a patriarchal abuse of what was already a patriarchal legal system in its treatment of adultery.

The main Mosaic legislation about adultery is found in Deut. 22.13–29 and Num. 5.11–31 (cf. also Lev. 20.10). Adultery for a man was always against another man, not against the woman involved. A man's extramarital sexual activity was therefore only considered adultery if the woman was betrothed or married. The extramarital sexual activity of a woman who belonged to a man through betrothal or marriage, however, was an offence against that man's honour. It flouted the man's authoritative claim to his wife's sexuality, threatened the purity of his blood-line, and implied that he was incapable of protecting her or gaining her submissive obedience. No proper provision was made for any involuntary sexual participation on the part of the woman, such as through assault or rape. If she was married, the penalty was death, however the illicit sexual act came about. If she was betrothed, it depended on whether the act took place in the city or the countryside. In the former case, the woman had an insoluble dilemma. In theory, if she cried out, this would be a sign that she had been assaulted. Yet, if she cried out and her cry were to be heard by two people, then they would be witnesses to her being with another man and she would be liable to condemnation anyway. This is precisely the double-bind to which Susanna gives anguished expression in Sus. 22–3. Given the compressed nature of the story in John 7.53—8.11, it is just possible that the woman taken in adultery had participated involuntarily. The narrator, however, shows no interest in the preceding circumstances and, as has been pointed out, both he and his protagonist, Jesus, assume at least that the woman is guilty of the legal definition of adultery.

The scribes and Pharisees claim that Moses commanded stoning. In fact, stoning is the mode of execution prescribed for both parties only in the case of a man's intercourse with a betrothed woman (Deut. 22.23–4). No particular mode of execution is set out when one of the adulterous parties is a married woman, and in later regulations (*m. Sanh.* 7.4) such a case is differentiated from that of a betrothed woman by being punished by strangulation. This has led some interpreters to propose that the woman here must have been betrothed. But it is by no means clear that such a distinction in modes of punishment existed in the first century and more likely it was held that the means of execution laid down in Deuteronomy applied to both types of adultery (cf. also Ezek. 16.38–40; 23.45–8) and that the woman in this case was married.

In the Synoptic tradition there are frequently attempts to test or trap Jesus by posing some difficult question in the hope that his answer would get him into trouble (cf. Mark 3.2 parr.; Mark 8.11 par.; Mark 10.2 par.; Mark 12.13, 15 parr.; Matt. 22.35; cf. Luke 10.25; 11.16). In this case the test clearly has to do with whether Jesus will endorse the Mosaic law and its judgement on adultery. Presumably the religious leaders know of Jesus' reputation as a friend of tax collectors and 'sinners', who practises table fellowship with those, like this woman, who would be under the law's condemnation. The dilemma for Jesus, then, is whether to go back on his mission of extending forgiveness to those whom society rejects or to risk explicit repudiation of the Torah on the issue of sanctions for adultery and thus finding himself charged with teaching against Moses. Since Jews did not have the right to carry out capital sentences (see comments on 18.31), some suggest a further aspect of the dilemma, namely, that if Jesus endorses the law and the punishment it requires, he would be encouraging the flouting of Roman authority and find himself in trouble with the occupying forces. But where Jesus' attitude to Roman authority is at stake elsewhere, this is made explicit in the account (cf. Mark 12.13–17 parr.). Here the focus is simply on Jesus' attitude to the Jewish law. As it turns out, he will, in practice, end up repudiating the law's requirement for punishment, but he manages to do so without explicitly saying so and without doing so in the presence of those who want to test him and catch him out.

6b–8 Jesus first meets this public challenge to his teaching and honour through an action that constitutes a counter-challenge – he **bent down and wrote on the ground with his finger**. This has the effect of disengaging him from the immediacy of the challenge and diverting attention away from the opponents, who are temporarily caught off their guard and disadvantaged, as their then having to persist in asking their question indicates. Jesus' action has provoked from later interpreters a variety of interesting speculations about why he wrote and what he might have written. Many have claimed that it is a symbolic action, evoking Jer. 17.13, which speaks of those who have turned away from God being written on the earth, because they have forsaken the fountain of living water. But, at best, this might be an illuminating intertextual allusion for an informed reader; it seems unlikely that the actual audience would immediately have recognized this significance. Others pick up on the mention of Jesus' finger, see an allusion to Exod. 31.18 and 'the tablets of stone, written with the finger of God', and suggest that Jesus wrote down the commandments which convicted his opponents. Still others suggest Jesus wrote down the accusers' sins. Yet another proposal is that Jesus wrote down Exod. 23.1b the first time and Exod. 23.7 the second time, thereby accusing his accusers of having borne false witness. All such suggestions overlook the fact that there is no indication in the story that the opponents read what Jesus was writing and fail to recognize that if the narrator had considered its content at all important he would have provided it.

When Jesus does give a verbal response, it too diverts attention from the original question and turns the challenge back on the challengers – **he straightened up and said to them, 'Let the one among you who is without sin be the first to throw a stone at her.'** At this point the woman's plight appears to be forgotten. She is still a pawn in a situation of challenge and riposte between male teachers of the law, and, since Jesus does not question the woman's guilt, he risks the possibility that she might yet be stoned. Readers sympathetic to Jesus and wishing to preserve his concern for the woman's life have to assume that he is confident about the outcome of his counter-challenge. It takes up the ruling about death by stoning in Deut. 17.7, which stated that 'the hands of the witnesses shall be the first raised against the person to execute the death penalty' and thereby to some extent ensured the integrity of their witness, since, if it were discovered that this had been false, they were liable to the same punishment. It is not clear whether the witnesses to the woman's act are present with the scribes and Pharisees, but in any case Jesus alters the ruling to specify that the one without sin should cast the first stone. Is Jesus requiring sinlessness before anyone can carry out the sanctions demanded by the law? Some suggest that the force of 'without sin' is restricted to the case in point and the sin refers either to being complicit in a false or at least irregular accusation or to having committed a similar sexual sin. The latter need not be excluded but there is nothing in the story itself, except the silence about the man involved, that would demand taking 'without sin' as meaning guiltless in prosecuting this particular case. It seems best to take 'without sin' as meaning not having engaged in specific breaches of the law. If this is the case, Jesus' challenge about sin is broad in scope and has radical implications, similar to those entailed by his saying in Matt. 7.1 about condemning others – 'Do not judge, so that you may not be judged.' The withdrawal of the scribes and Pharisees will implicitly amount to a recognition of the truth of such a saying about life in the kingdom of God. As in the same sermon in Matthew, Jesus here also in effect ultimately collapses the distinction between different sorts of sin, whereby adultery and murder are seen as deserving the law's full sanctions, while lust and anger are treated lightly.

And again he bent down and wrote on the ground. The repetition of this non-verbal response again enables Jesus to dissociate himself from his opponents' challenge and puts them on the defensive. It also provides a dramatic pause in which his words are allowed to sink in and have their effect.

9 The effect is the desired one: **Those who heard went away, one by one, beginning with the elders**. Once the leading older men are prepared to acknowledge that in passing judgement on the woman in accordance with the law, they are, by the same criterion of the law, condemning themselves, the others follow suit and leave the scene. It is not often noted, but Jesus' strategy here, with its intended positive ending for the woman, depends on there being some virtue in the scribes and Pharisees. They are not depicted as beyond the pale but as having enough conscience and contrition to admit their own lack of innocence before the law. Some manuscripts in fact add 'being convicted by their conscience' to v. 9, which spells out what is implicit. There is no repentance or remorse demanded of the woman but the opponents of Jesus do show signs of at least conviction of their sin. Again there is no clear indication that such sin was limited to the injustice of requiring the woman to take the punishment alone for what had been the act of two parties.

Jesus is now **left alone with the woman who was in the middle**. There is no reason to think that the temple crowd has also disappeared. It is those who tested Jesus and whom he addressed directly in v. 7 who have departed the scene.

10–11 For the first time the woman is addressed as a person in her own right. Preparing her for his own verdict, Jesus' questions allow her to interpret the situation for herself and elicit from her what he already knows – her accusers have left without condemning her. When the only one who was without sin in this situation and who could have carried out the law's requirement faces her, he refuses to pronounce a negative judgement – **Neither do I condemn you. Go, and from now on sin no more.** Jesus' final words to the woman are those of acquittal. Again, there is no suggestion that she is not guilty of that of which she has been accused. Rather she is not to be condemned to punishment for such an act. Pardon is granted by Jesus and along with this the possibility of a new life is offered. Her response to the pronouncement of mercy is to be a life free from her previous sins, especially that which has brought her to this situation. Since the story was recounted earlier without the last clause about sinning no more (cf. *Didascalia* 7 and the version Didymus gives), it may be the formulation of whoever placed the passage in John, because the same words are found in 5.14, where they also include reference to a previous sin (see comments on 5.14). The clause is now, however, an original part of the text to be interpreted and integral to this particular narrative, whatever decision is made about its tradition history. Jesus is presented through his words to the woman as bypassing the sanctions of the Mosaic law, mediating God's forgiveness and calling for a different kind of life in response.

Somewhat ironically, this passage, which has virtually no claim to textual originality, may have greater claim to essential historicity than some of the material in the original text of the Gospel. It relates the sort of event and the sort of behaviour on the part of Jesus that seem to be characteristic of Jesus' ministry from what is known from other sources. But can more be said about its actual historicity? The issue with which it deals fits the time and setting of Jesus' mission in first-century Palestine. Jesus' response to it meets the criterion of dissimilarity in that it differs from the standard Jewish attitudes to the punishment for adultery and also differs from the strict discipline imposed in relation to adultery in the first two centuries of the early church. The existence of different, more compressed versions of the story in *Didascalia* 7 and Didymus raises the possibility of it having multiple attestation. The first extant version of the story is comparatively late (early third century) but the lateness of a tradition does not necessarily rule out its basic historicity. While the story as found in John 7.53—8.11 has undoubtedly been redacted and shaped in the process of transmission, there are no decisive arguments that tell against the likelihood that its essential features reflect an incident in the life of Jesus.

Despite the uncertainties surrounding its origins, this story has captured the imaginations of later readers. Part of the reason for this is the significant number of gaps in the narrative which leave room for those imaginations to work. When an episode is part of a longer narrative, certain contextual constraints are operative on the way in which readers supply what is missing. But with this free-floating story such constraints are largely absent. Among the unanswered questions it raises, some of which have already been discussed, are the following. What is the status of the woman involved – is she betrothed or married? Who is the man who was her sexual partner, and, if they were caught in the act, why does he not appear in the story? Is the woman being taken to or from her trial and was this a formal trial or is mob justice at work? Are the original witnesses to the act present in the story? What, if anything, did Jesus write on the ground? What were the sins of which the scribes and Pharisees were convicted? Interesting as it is to pursue such questions, many of them cannot be answered with any certainty. But since the narrator did not think it necessary to supply further details, most of them are also ultimately irrelevant to the main point of his story. It portrays Jesus as the authoritative and skilful interpreter of the Mosaic law, who challenges those who insist on its sanctions for others while they themselves are by no means guiltless, and who offers forgiveness for past sin and the possibility of a different future to a woman who, because of her adultery, had faced death by stoning and been treated as mere bait in a trap to ensnare Jesus.

In the absence of any immediate literary context for this story, a brief comparison with the story of Susanna (Dan. 13 LXX) may prove worthwhile. In that story a married woman, Susanna, becomes the object of desire for two Jewish elders who had been made judges. They surprise her in her garden and tell her that if she resists their advances, they will claim to have witnessed her committing adultery with a young man. When she refuses to do what they want, they go through with their plan, and she is taken to court and condemned to death. On her way to execution, there is a divine intervention as a young Daniel is inspired to recognize the woman is innocent. He then exposes the false witness of the elders, who receive the death penalty that the court had passed on the woman. This is an entertaining moral tale, which at the same time reinforces the point that loyalty to God in adverse circumstances will be rewarded and contributes to the portrayal of Daniel as a man endowed by God with wisdom.

As noted above in relation to vv. 5–6a, the story found in John illustrates in passing the law's lack of protection in practice for a woman who is falsely accused of adultery by witnesses. Susanna's trial has in common with the interrogation by the scribes and Pharisees the absence of any male partner who should also have been seized and punished. In Susanna the witnesses claim that he overpowered them and got away. Apart from God, the main characters in the Susanna story are Susanna herself, the elders, and Daniel and they correspond to the woman, the scribes and Pharisees, and Jesus. In the former all are portrayed as ideal types. Susanna is the perfect woman, beautiful, refined, fearing the Lord and trained according to the law of Moses. She is married to a wealthy man, has children and their home serves as a centre for the Jewish community in Babylon. The two elders are portrayed, despite their position, as entirely perverted through lust, as having abused other women and as having passed unjust judgements. Daniel is depicted in such a way as to boost his reputation – he is a wise young man, inspired by God, and a courtroom hero who cleverly exposes contradictions in the false testimony. The realism and ambiguities of John 7.53—8.11 form a striking contrast. Though the missing male suggests some injustice in the treatment of this married woman, she is not depicted as innocent but as being given a fresh chance to live a righteous life. Susanna, while vindicated, is never directly addressed or given her own voice in the process, yet in the presence of Jesus the woman both speaks to him and is spoken to by him. The scribes and Pharisees are out to trap Jesus, keen to rush to judgement on the woman and prepared to use her life as part of their plotting, yet when they are put to the test they show enough integrity to acknowledge their own shortcomings and to realize that these undermine their pursuit of the woman's condemnation. While Daniel and Jesus both display wisdom, their situations are very different. Daniel acts skilfully to right what has been revealed to him as a clear injustice and can appeal to the Mosaic law in so doing. Jesus has to deal with a far more complex dilemma in which the woman's accusers can with some legitimacy appeal to Moses in their own support. He also does not have the possibility of being able to expose false and contradictory witness. He finds himself having to rely on the accusers' own consciousness of sin and thus risking that the woman might indeed be stoned. While Daniel is a clear agent of God's intervention from outside, Jesus is far more embroiled in the exigencies of the situation. Yet at the same time Jesus ends up doing what is simply not envisaged for Daniel, namely, setting aside the sanctions of the law, bringing the scribes and Pharisees to a conviction of their sin and offering forgiveness to the woman. In short, in negotiating the test to which he has been put, Jesus as God's agent exercises divine prerogatives in the midst of human ambiguities in such a way as to give both the accusers and the accused the chance to break from their past ways. It is not surprising that, despite its disputed status, this intriguing story has continued to function as a compelling witness to Jesus.

SELECT BIBLIOGRAPHY OF
WORKS IN ENGLISH

COMMENTARIES

Barrett, C. K., *The Gospel according to St. John*, 2nd edn (London: SPCK, 1978).

Beasley-Murray, G. R., *John* (Waco, Tex.: Word, 1987).

Brodie, T. L., *The Gospel according to John: A Literary and Theological Commentary* (Oxford: Oxford University Press, 1993).

Brown, R. E., *The Gospel according to John*, 2 vols (New York: Doubleday, 1966, 1970).

Bultmann, R., *The Gospel of John* (ET Oxford: Blackwell, 1971).

Carson, D. A., *The Gospel according to John* (Grand Rapids: Eerdmans, 1991).

Culpepper, R. A., *The Gospel and Letters of John* (Nashville: Abingdon, 1998).

Grayston, K., *The Gospel of John* (London: Epworth, 1990).

Haenchen, E., *John*, 2 vols (ET Philadelphia: Fortress, 1984).

Hoskyns, E. C., *The Fourth Gospel*, ed. F. N. Davey (London: Faber & Faber, 1954).

Howard-Brook, W., *Becoming the Children of God: John's Gospel and Radical Discipleship* (New York: Orbis, 1994).

Keener, C. S., *The Gospel of John*, 2 vols (Peabody, Mass.: Hendrickson, 2003).

Kysar, R., *John* (Minneapolis: Augsburg, 1986).

Lightfoot, R. H., *St. John's Gospel: A Commentary*, ed. C. F. Evans (Oxford: Oxford University Press, 1956).

Lindars, B., *The Gospel of John* (London: Oliphants, 1972).

Malina, B. J., and Rohrbaugh, R., *Social-Science Commentary on the Gospel of John* (Minneapolis: Fortress, 1998).

Marsh, J., *Saint John* (Harmondsworth: Penguin, 1968).

Michaels, J. R., *John* (Peabody, Mass.: Hendrickson, 1989).

Moloney, F. J., *The Gospel of John* (Collegeville, Minn.: Liturgical Press, 1999).

Morris, L., *The Gospel according to John* (Grand Rapids: Eerdmans, 1995).

Newbigin, L., *The Light Has Come* (Grand Rapids: Eerdmans, 1982).

O'Day, G. R., 'The Gospel of John', in *The New Interpreter's Bible*, vol. 9 (Nashville: Abingdon, 1995), 493–865.

Ridderbos, H., *The Gospel of John: A Theological Commentary* (ET Grand Rapids: Eerdmans, 1997).

Sanders, J. N., *The Gospel according to St. John*, ed. B. A. Mastin (London: A. & C. Black, 1968).

Schnackenburg, R., *The Gospel according to St. John*, 3 vols (ET vols 1–2 New York: Seabury, 1980; vol. 3 New York: Crossroad, 1982).

Smith, D. M., *John* (Nashville: Abingdon, 1999).

Stibbe, M. W. G., *John* (Sheffield: JSOT Press, 1993).

Talbert, C. H., *Reading John: A Literary and Theological Commentary on the Fourth Gospel and Johannine Epistles* (New York: Crossroad, 1992).

Westcott, B. F., *The Gospel according to St. John*, 2 vols (London: John Murray, 1908).

Whitacre, R. A., *John* (Leicester: Inter-Varsity Press, 1999).

Witherington, B., III, *John's Wisdom* (Louisville: Westminster/John Knox, 1995).

OTHER LITERATURE

Alexander, L. C. A., 'Ancient Book Production and the Circulation of the Gospels', in R. Bauckham (ed.), *The Gospels for All Christians* (Grand Rapids: Eerdmans, 1998), 71–111.

Anderson, P. N., *The Christology of the Fourth Gospel: Its Unity and Disunity in the Light of John 6* (Tübingen: Mohr, 1996).

Appold, M., *The Oneness Motif in the Fourth Gospel* (Tübingen: Mohr, 1976).

Ashton, J., *Understanding the Fourth Gospel* (Oxford: Clarendon, 1991).

—— *Studying John: Approaches to the Fourth Gospel* (Oxford: Clarendon, 1994).

—— (ed.), *The Interpretation of John* (London: SPCK, 1986).

Asiedu-Peprah, M., *Johannine Sabbath Conflicts as Juridical Controversy* (Tübingen: Mohr, 2001).

Ball, D. M., *'I Am' in John's Gospel: Literary Background, Function and Theological Implications* (Sheffield: Sheffield Academic Press, 1996).

Barrett, C. K., *Essays on John* (London: SPCK, 1982).

Bassler, J. M., 'Mixed Signals: Nicodemus in the Fourth Gospel', *JBL* 108 (1989), 635–46.

Bauckham, R., 'The Beloved Disciple as Ideal Author', *JSNT* 49 (1993), 21–44.

—— 'Papias and Polycrates on the Origin of the Fourth Gospel', *JTS* 44 (1993), 24–69.

—— *God Crucified: Monotheism and Christology in the New Testament* (Carlisle: Paternoster, 1998).

Beck, D. R., *The Discipleship Paradigm: Readers and Anonymous Characters in the Fourth Gospel* (Leiden: Brill, 1997).

Belle, G. van, *The Signs Source in the Fourth Gospel: Historical Survey and Critical Evaluation of the Semeia Hypothesis* (Leuven: Leuven University Press, 1994).

Beutler, J., and Fortna, R. T. (eds), *The Shepherd Discourse of John 10 and its Context* (Cambridge: Cambridge University Press, 1991).

Bieringer, R., Pollefyt, D., and Vandercasteele-Vanneuville, F. (eds), *Anti-Judaism and the Fourth Gospel* (Assen: Royal van Gorcum, 2001).

Blomberg, C. L., *The Historical Reliability of John's Gospel* (Leicester: Inter-Varsity Press, 2001).

Boer, M. C. de, 'Narrative Criticism, Historical Criticism, and the Gospel of John', *JSNT* 47 (1992), 35–48.

—— *Johannine Perspectives on the Death of Jesus* (Kampen: Kok Pharos, 1996).

Boers, H., *Neither on This Mountain nor in Jerusalem: A Study of John 4* (Atlanta: Scholars, 1988).

Bond, H. K., *Pontius Pilate in history and interpretation* (Cambridge: Cambridge University Press, 1998).

Bonney, W., *Caused to Believe: The Doubting Thomas Story as the Climax of John's Christological Narrative* (Leiden: Brill, 2002).

Borgen, P., *Bread from Heaven: An Exegetical Study of the Concept of Manna in the Gospel of John and the Writings of Philo* (Leiden: Brill, 1965).

—— 'God's Agent in the Fourth Gospel', in J. Neusner (ed.), *Religions in Antiquity* (Leiden: Brill, 1968), 137–48.

—— 'John 6: Tradition, Interpretation and Composition', in R. A. Culpepper (ed.), *Critical Readings of John 6* (Leiden: Brill, 1997), 95–114.

Brodie, T. L., *The Quest for the Origin of John's Gospel* (Oxford: Oxford University Press, 1993).

Brown, R. E., *The Community of the Beloved Disciple* (New York: Paulist, 1979).

—— *The Epistles of John* (New York: Doubleday, 1982).

—— *The Death of the Messiah*, 2 vols (New York: Doubleday, 1994).

—— *An Introduction to the Gospel of John*, ed. F. J. Moloney (New York: Doubleday, 2003).

Bultmann, R., *Theology of the New Testament*, vol. 2 (London: SCM Press, 1955).

Burge, G. M., *The Anointed Community: The Holy Spirit in the Johannine Tradition* (Grand Rapids: Eerdmans, 1987).

Burkett, D., *The Son of Man in the Gospel of John* (Sheffield: JSOT Press, 1991).

Burridge, R. A., *What Are the Gospels? A Comparison with Graeco-Roman Biography* (Cambridge: Cambridge University Press, 1992).

Byrskog, S., *Story as History – History as Story* (Leiden: Brill, 2002).

Carroll, J. T., 'Present and Future in Fourth Gospel "Eschatology"', *BTB* 19 (1989), 63–8.

Carson, D. A., 'The Function of the Paraclete in John 16:7–11', *JBL* 98 (1979), 547–66.

—— 'The Purpose of the Fourth Gospel: John 20:31 Reconsidered', *JBL* 106 (1987), 639–51.

Casey, M., *Is John's Gospel True?* (London: Routledge, 1996).

Cassidy, R. J., *John's Gospel in New Perspective* (New York: Orbis, 1992).

Catchpole, D., *Resurrection People: Studies in the Resurrection Narratives of the Gospels* (London: Darton, Longman and Todd, 2000).

Charlesworth, J. H., *The Beloved Disciple* (Valley Forge, Pa.: Trinity Press International, 1995).

Collins, R. F., *These Things Have Been Written: Studies on the Fourth Gospel* (Louvain: Peeters, 1990).

Coloe, M. L., *God Dwells With Us: Temple Symbolism in the Fourth Gospel* (Collegeville, Minn.: Liturgical Press, 2001).

Conway, C. M., *Men and Women in the Fourth Gospel: Gender and Johannine Characterization* (Atlanta: SBL, 1999).

Culpepper, R. A., *Anatomy of the Fourth Gospel* (Philadelphia: Fortress, 1983).

—— 'The Plot of John's Story of Jesus', *Interpretation* 49 (1995), 347–58.

Culpepper, R. A., and Black, C. C. (eds), *Exploring the Gospel of John* (Louisville: Westminster/John Knox, 1996).

——*John, The Son of Zebedee: The Life of a Legend* (Minneapolis: Fortress, 2000).

—— (ed.), *Critical Readings of John 6* (Leiden: Brill, 1997).

Daly-Denton, M., *David in the Fourth Gospel: The Johannine Reception of the Psalms* (Leiden: Brill, 2000).

Davies, M., *Rhetoric and Reference in the Fourth Gospel* (Sheffield: JSOT Press, 1992).

Denaux, A. (ed.), *John and the Synoptics* (Louvain: Louvain University Press, 1992).

Dewey, J., 'Paroimiai in the Gospel of John', *Semeia* 17 (1980), 81–100.

Dodd, C. H., *The Interpretation of the Fourth Gospel* (Cambridge: Cambridge University Press, 1953).

—— *Historical Tradition in the Fourth Gospel* (Cambridge: Cambridge University Press, 1963).

—— 'A Hidden Parable in the Fourth Gospel', in *More New Testament Studies* (Manchester: Manchester University Press, 1968), 30–40.

Duke, P., *Irony in the Fourth Gospel* (Atlanta: John Knox, 1985).

Dunderberg, I., 'Thomas' I-Sayings and the Gospel of John', in R. Uro (ed.), Thomas at the Crossroads (Edinburgh: T&T Clark, 1998), 33–64.

—— 'Thomas and the Beloved Disciple', in R. Uro (ed.), Thomas at the Crossroads (Edinburgh: T&T Clark, 1998), 65–88.

Dunn, J. D. G., 'Let John Be John: A Gospel for its Time', in P. Stuhlmacher (ed.), Das Evangelium und die Evangelien (Tübingen: Mohr, 1983), 309–39.

Edwards, R. B., 'ΧΑΡΙΝ ΑΝΤΙ ΧΑΡΙΤΟΣ (John 1.16): Grace and Law in the Johannine Prologue', JSNT 32 (1988), 3–15.

—— 'The Christological Basis of the Johannine Footwashing', in J. B. Green and M. M. B. Turner (eds), Jesus of Nazareth: Lord and Christ (Grand Rapids: Eerdmans, 1994), 367–83.

—— Discovering John (London: SPCK, 2003).

Ensor, P. W., Jesus and His 'Works': The Johannine Sayings in Historical Perspective (Tübingen: Mohr, 1996).

Evans, C. A., Word and Glory: On the Exegetical and Theological Background of John's Prologue (Sheffield: JSOT Press, 1993).

Fee, G. D., 'On the Text and Meaning of Jn 20, 30–31', in F. van Segbroeck (ed.), The Four Gospels 1992: Festschrift Franz Neirynck (Louvain: Louvain University Press, 1992), 193–205.

Fehribach, A., The Women in the Life of the Bridegroom (Collegeville, Minn.: Liturgical Press, 1998).

Ferreira, J., Johannine Ecclesiology (Sheffield: Sheffield Academic Press, 1998).

Fiorenza, E. S., 'The Quest for the Johannine School: The Apocalypse and the Fourth Gospel', NTS 23 (1977), 402–27.

Forestell, J. T., The Word of the Cross: Salvation as Revelation in the Fourth Gospel (Rome: Biblical Institute, 1974).

Fortna, R. T., The Gospel of Signs (Cambridge: Cambridge University Press, 1970).

—— The Fourth Gospel and its Predecessor (Philadelphia: Fortress, 1988).

—— and Thatcher, T. (eds), Jesus in Johannine Tradition (Louisville: Westminster/John Knox, 2001).

Franck, E., Revelation Taught: The Paraclete in the Gospel of John (Lund: Gleerup, 1985).

Freed, E. D., Old Testament Quotations in the Gospel of John (Leiden: Brill, 1965).

Gardner-Smith, P., St. John and the Synoptic Gospels (Cambridge: Cambridge University Press, 1938).

Gaventa, B. R., 'The Archive of Excess: John 21 and the Problem of Narrative Closure', in R. A. Culpepper and C. C. Black (eds), Exploring the Gospel of John (Louisville: Westminster/John Knox, 1996), 240–52.

Giblin, C. H. 'Confrontations in John 18, 1–27', Biblica 65 (1984), 210–32.

—— 'John's Narration of the Hearing Before Pilate (John 18,28–19,16a)', *Biblica* 67 (1986), 221–39.

Glasson, T. F., *Moses in the Fourth Gospel* (London: SCM Press, 1963).

Hanson, A. T., *The Prophetic Gospel: A Study of John and the Old Testament* (Edinburgh: T&T Clark, 1991).

Harris, E., *Prologue and Gospel: The Theology of the Fourth Evangelist* (Sheffield: JSOT Press, 1994).

Hartman, L., and Olsson, B. (eds), *Aspects on the Johannine Literature* (Stockholm: Almqvist & Wiksell, 1987).

Harvey, A. E., *Jesus on Trial* (London: SPCK, 1976).

Hengel, M., 'The Interpretation of the Wine Miracle at Cana: John 2:1–11', in L. D. Hurst and N. T. Wright (eds), *The Glory of Christ in the New Testament* (Oxford: Clarendon, 1987), 83–112.

—— *The Johannine Question* (London: SCM Press, 1989).

—— 'The Old Testament in the Fourth Gospel', *HBT* 12 (1990), 19–41.

Horbury, W., 'The Benediction of the *Minim* and Early Jewish-Christian Controversy', *JTS* 33 (1982), 19–61.

Horst, P. W. van der, 'The Birkat ha-minim in Recent Research', *ExpTim* 105 (1994), 363–8.

Johnson, L. T., 'The New Testament's Anti-Jewish Slander and the Conventions of Ancient Polemic', *JBL* 108 (1989), 419–41.

Jones, L. P., *The Symbol of Water in the Gospel of John* (Sheffield: Sheffield Academic Press, 1997).

Jonge, M. de, *Jesus: Stranger from Heaven and Son of God* (Missoula, Mont.: Scholars, 1977).

Käsemann, E., *The Testament of Jesus* (London: SCM Press, 1968).

Kerr, A. R., *The Temple of Jesus' Body: The Temple Theme in the Gospel of John* (Sheffield: Sheffield Academic Press, 2002).

Kimelman, R., 'The *Birkat Ha-Minim* and the Lack of Evidence for an Anti-Christian Jewish Prayer in Late Antiquity', in E. P. Sanders *et al.* (eds), *Jewish and Christian Self-Definition*, vol. 2 (Philadelphia: Fortress, 1981), 226–44.

Koester, C., *Symbolism in the Fourth Gospel: Meaning, Mystery, Community* (Minneapolis: Fortress, 1995).

—— 'The Spectrum of Johannine Readers', in F. F. Segovia (ed.), *'What Is John?': Readers and Readings of the Fourth Gospel* (Atlanta: Scholars, 1996), 5–19.

Köstenberger, A. J., *The Missions of Jesus and the Disciples according to the Fourth Gospel* (Grand Rapids: Eerdmans, 1998).

Kreitzer, L. J., and Rooke, D. W. (eds), *Ciphers in the Sand: Interpretations of the Woman Taken in Adultery (John 7.53–8.11)* (Sheffield: Sheffield Academic Press, 2000).

Kurz, W., 'The Beloved Disciple and Implied Readers', *BTB* 19 (1989), 100–7.

Kysar, R., *John: The Maverick Gospel*, revd. edn (Louisville: Westminster/John Knox, 1993).

Lee, D. A., *The Symbolic Narratives of the Fourth Gospel* (Sheffield: JSOT Press, 1994).

—— *Flesh and Glory: Symbolism, Gender and Theology in the Gospel of John* (New York: Crossroad, 2002).

Lieu, J., 'Temple and Synagogue in John', *NTS* 45 (1999), 51–69.

Lincoln, A. T., ' "I Am the Resurrection and the Life": The Resurrection Message of the Fourth Gospel', in R. N. Longenecker (ed.), *Life in the Face of Death: The Resurrection Message of the New Testament* (Grand Rapids: Eerdmans, 1998), 122–44.

—— *Truth on Trial: The Lawsuit Motif in John's Gospel* (Peabody, Mass.: Hendrickson, 2000).

—— 'The Beloved Disciple as Eyewitness and the Fourth Gospel as Witness', *JSNT* 85 (2002), 3–26.

Lindars, B., *Behind the Fourth Gospel* (London: SPCK, 1971).

—— *John* (Sheffield: JSOT Press, 1990).

Loader, W., *The Christology of the Fourth Gospel*, 2nd edn (Frankfurt: Peter Lang, 1992).

Maccini, R. G., *Her Testimony is True: Women as Witnesses according to John* (Sheffield: Sheffield Academic Press, 1996).

McGrath, J. F., *John's Apologetic Christology: Legitimation and Development in Johannine Christianity* (Cambridge: Cambridge University Press, 2001).

Martyn, J. L., *History and Theology in the Fourth Gospel* (New York: Harper & Row, 1968; 2nd edn Nashville: Abingdon, 1979).

—— *The Gospel of John in Christian History* (New York: Paulist, 1978).

Matera, F. J., 'Jesus Before Annas: John 18,13–14, 19–24', *ETL* 66 (1990), 38–55.

Matson, M. A., *In Dialogue with Another Gospel? The Influence of the Fourth Gospel on the Passion Narrative of the Gospel of Luke* (Atlanta: SBL, 2001).

Meeks, W. A., *The Prophet-King: Moses Traditions and the Johannine Christology* (Leiden: Brill, 1967).

—— 'The Man from Heaven in Johannine Sectarianism', *JBL* 91 (1972), 44–72; repr. in J. Ashton (ed.), *The Interpretation of John* (London: SPCK, 1986), 141–73.

Meier, J. P., *A Marginal Jew*, vol. 2 (New York: Doubleday, 1994).

Menken, M. J. J., *Old Testament Quotations in the Fourth Gospel: Studies in Textual Form* (Kampen: Kok Pharos, 1996).

Metzger, B. M., *A Textual Commentary on the Greek New Testament* (London: United Bible Societies, 1971).

Minear, P., *John: The Martyr's Gospel* (New York: Pilgrim, 1984).

Moloney, F. J., *The Johannine Son of Man*, 2nd edn (Rome: Libreria Ateneo Salesiano, 1978).

—— *Belief in the Word: Reading John 1–4* (Minneapolis: Fortress, 1993).

—— *Signs and Shadows: Reading John 5–12* (Minneapolis: Fortress, 1996).

—— *Glory Not Dishonor: Reading John 13–21* (Minneapolis: Fortress, 1998).

Momigliano, A., *The Development of Greek Biography* (Cambridge, Mass.: Harvard University Press, 1971).

Motyer, S., *Your Father the Devil? A New Approach to John and 'the Jews'* (Carlisle: Paternoster, 1997).

Mussner, F., *The Historical Jesus in the Gospel of St. John*, tr. W. J. O'Hara (London: Burns and Oates, 1967).

Neirynck, F., 'John and the Synoptics', in M. de Jonge (ed.), *L'Evangile de Jean* (Louvain: Louvain University Press, 1977), 73–106.

—— *Evangelica: Collected Essays by Franz Neirynck*, ed. F. Van Segbroeck (Louvain: Louvain University Press, 1982).

—— 'John 4.46–54. Signs Source and/or Synoptic Gospels?', *ETL* 60 (1984), 367–75.

—— *Evangelica II: 1982–1991. Collected Essays by Franz Neirynck*, ed. F. Van Segbroeck (Louvain: Louvain University Press, 1991).

Neyrey, J. H., 'John III – A Debate over Johannine Epistemology and Christology', *NovT* 23 (1981), 115–27.

—— 'Jesus the Judge: Forensic Process in John 8,21–59', *Biblica* 68 (1987), 509–42.

—— *An Ideology of Revolt: John's Christology in Social-Science Perspective* (Philadelphia: Fortress, 1988).

—— ' "Despising the Shame of the Cross": Honor and Shame in the Johannine Passion Narrative', *Semeia* 68 (1994), 113–37.

—— 'The "Noble Shepherd" in John 10: Cultural and Rhetorical Background', *JBL* 120 (2001), 267–91.

Ng, W.-Y., *Water Symbolism in John* (New York: Peter Lang, 2001).

Nicholson, G. C., *Death as Departure: The Johannine Descent-Ascent Schema* (Chico, Calif.: Scholars, 1983).

Nicol, W., *The Semeia in the Fourth Gospel: Tradition and Redaction* (Leiden: Brill, 1970).

Nissen, J., and Pedersen, S. (eds), *New Readings in John* (Sheffield: Sheffield Academic Press, 1999).

North, W. E. S., 'Monotheism and the Gospel of John: Jesus, Moses, and the Law', in L. T. Stuckenbruck and W. E. S. North (eds), *Early Jewish and Christian Monotheism* (London: T&T Clark International, 2004), 155–66.

O'Day, G. R., *Revelation in the Fourth Gospel: Narrative Mode and Theological Claim* (Philadelphia: Fortress, 1986).

Okure, T., *The Johannine Approach to Mission: A Contextual Study of John 4.1–42* (Tübingen: Mohr, 1988).

Olsson, B., *Structure and Meaning in the Fourth Gospel: A Text-Linguistic Analysis of John 2.1–11 and 4.1–42* (Lund: Gleerup, 1974).

Painter, J., *John: Witness and Theologian* (London: SPCK, 1975).

—— 'John 9 and the Interpretation of the Fourth Gospel', *JSNT* 28 (1986), 31–61.

—— *The Quest for the Messiah: The History, Literature and Theology of the Johannine Community* (Edinburgh: T&T Clark, 1993).

Pancaro, S., *The Law in the Fourth Gospel* (Leiden: Brill, 1975).

Pelling, C. B. R., 'Truth and Fiction in Plutarch's *Lives*', in D. A. Russell (ed.), *Antonine Literature* (Oxford: Clarendon, 1990), 19–52.

Petersen, N. R., *The Gospel of John and the Sociology of Light* (Valley Forge, Pa.: Trinity Press International, 1993).

Pollard, T. E., *Johannine Christology and the Early Church* (Cambridge: Cambridge University Press, 1970).

Pryor, J., *John: Evangelist of the Covenant People* (London: Darton, Longman and Todd, 1992).

Quast, K., *Peter and the Beloved Disciple* (Sheffield: JSOT Press, 1989).

Reinhartz, A., *The Word in the World: The Cosmological Tale in the Fourth Gospel* (Atlanta: Scholars, 1992).

—— *Befriending the Beloved Disciple: A Jewish Reading of the Gospel of John* (New York: Continuum, 2001).

Rensberger, D., *Overcoming the World: Politics and Community in the Gospel of John* (London: SPCK, 1989).

Resseguie, J. L., 'John 9: A Literary-Critical Analysis', in K. R. Gross Louis (ed.), *Literary Interpretations of Biblical Narratives*, vol. 2 (Nashville: Abingdon, 1982).

Rhea, R., *The Johannine Son of Man* (Zurich: Theologischer Verlag, 1990).

Ringe, S. H., *Wisdom's Friends: Community and Christology in the Fourth Gospel* (Louisville: Westminster/John Knox, 1999).

Sabbe, M., 'The Footwashing in Jn 13 and its Relation to the Synoptic Gospels', *EThL* 58 (1982), 279–308.

—— *Studia Neotestamentica: Collected Essays* (Louvain: Louvain University Press, 1991).

—— 'The Trial of Jesus before Pilate in John and its Relation to the Synoptic Gospels', in A. Denaux (ed.), *John and the Synoptics* (Louvain: Louvain University Press, 1992), 341–85.

—— 'The Johannine Account of the Death of Jesus and its Synoptic Parallels (Jn 19,16b–42)', *ETL* 70 (1994), 34–64.

—— 'The Denial of Peter in the Gospel of John', *Louvain Studies* 20 (1995), 219–40.

Salier, W. H., *The Rhetorical Impact of the Semeia in the Gospel of John* (Tübingen: Mohr, 2004).

Schneiders, S. M., *Written That You May Believe* (New York: Crossroad, 1999).

Schnelle, U., *Antidocetic Christology in the Gospel of John* (Minneapolis: Fortress, 1992).

Scott, M., *Sophia and the Johannine Jesus* (Sheffield: Sheffield Academic Press, 1992).

Segovia, F. F., *The Farewell of the Word: The Johannine Call to Abide* (Minneapolis: Fortress, 1991).

—— 'The Journey(s) of the Word of God: A Reading of the Plot of the Fourth Gospel', *Semeia* 53 (1991), 23–54.

—— 'The Final Farewell of Jesus: A Reading of John 20:30–21:25', *Semeia* 53 (1991), 167–90.

—— 'Inclusion and Exclusion in John 17: An Intercultural Reading', in F. F. Segovia (ed.), *What Is John?*, vol. 2 (Atlanta: Scholars, 1998), 183–210.

Senior, D., *The Passion of Jesus in the Gospel of John* (Leominster: Gracewing, 1991).

Smalley, S. S., *Thunder and Love: John's Revelation and John's Community* (Milton Keynes: Nelson Word, 1994).

—— *John: Evangelist and Interpreter*, 2nd edn (Carlisle: Paternoster, 1998).

Smith, D. M., *John among the Gospels: The Relationship in Twentieth-Century Research* (Minneapolis: Fortress, 1992).

—— *The Theology of the Gospel of John* (Cambridge: Cambridge University Press, 1995).

Sproston North, W. E., *The Lazarus Story within the Johannine Tradition* (Sheffield: Sheffield Academic Press, 2001).

Staley, J. L., *The Print's First Kiss: A Rhetorical Investigation of the Implied Reader in the Fourth Gospel* (Atlanta: Scholars, 1988).

—— 'Stumbling in the Dark, Reaching for the Light: Reading Character in John 5 and 9', *Semeia* 53 (1991), 55–80.

—— *Reading with a Passion: Rhetoric, Autobiography, and the American West in the Gospel of John* (New York: Continuum, 1995).

Stibbe, M. W. G., 'The Elusive Christ: A New Reading of the Fourth Gospel', *JSNT* 44 (1991), 20–39.

—— *John as Storyteller* (Cambridge: Cambridge University Press, 1992).

—— '"Return to Sender": A Structuralist Approach to John's Gospel', *Biblical Interpretation* 1 (1993), 189–206.

—— *John's Gospel* (London: Routledge, 1994).

—— 'A Tomb with a View: John 11.1–44 in Narrative-Critical Perspective', *NTS* 40 (1994), 38–54.

Streeter, B. H., *The Four Gospels: A Study of Origins* (London: Macmillan, 1924).

Thomas, J. C., *Footwashing in John 13 and the Johannine Community* (Sheffield: JSOT Press, 1991).

—— ' "Stop sinning lest something worse come upon you": The Man at the Pool in John 5', *JSNT* 59 (1995), 3–20.

Thompson, M. B., 'The Holy Internet: Communication between Churches in the First Christian Generation', in R. Bauckham (ed.), *The Gospels for All Christians* (Grand Rapids: Eerdmans, 1998), 49–70.

Thompson, M. M., *The Humanity of Jesus in the Fourth Gospel* (Philadelphia: Fortress, 1988).

—— *The God of the Gospel of John* (Grand Rapids: Eerdmans, 2001).

Tilborg, S. van, *Imaginative Love in John* (Leiden: Brill, 1993).

—— *Reading John in Ephesus* (Leiden: Brill, 1996).

Tolmie, D. F., *Jesus' Farewell to the Disciples: John 13:1–17:26 in Narratological Perspective* (Leiden: Brill, 1995).

Tovey, D., *Narrative Art and Act in the Fourth Gospel* (Sheffield: Sheffield Academic Press, 1997).

Wahlde, U. C. von, *The Earliest Version of John's Gospel: Recovering the Gospel of Signs* (Wilmington, Del.: Michael Glazier, 1989).

Walker, W. O., 'The Lord's Prayer in Matthew and John', *NTS* 28 (1982), 237–56.

Warner, M., 'The Fourth Gospel's Art of Rational Persuasion', in M. Warner (ed.), *The Bible as Rhetoric* (London: Routledge, 1990), 153–77.

Watt, J. G. van der, *Family of the King: Dynamics of Metaphor in the Gospel according to John* (Leiden: Brill, 2000).

Whitacre, R. A., *The Johannine Polemic* (Chico, Calif.: Scholars, 1982).

Wiles, M., *The Spiritual Gospel: The Interpretation of the Fourth Gospel in the Early Church* (Cambridge: Cambridge University Press, 1960).

Williams, C. H., *I am He: The Interpretation of 'Anî Hû' in Jewish and Early Christian Literature* (Tübingen: Mohr, 2000).

Yee, G. A., *Jewish Feasts and the Gospel of John* (Wilmington, Del.: Michael Glazier, 1989).

INDEX OF SCRIPTURAL
REFERENCES

INDEX OF MODERN AUTHORS

This index covers authors cited in the Introduction; further information is listed in the Bibliography. After a page number, 'bib.' indicates a bibliographic reference.

INDEX OF SUBJECTS